THE
BATTLE
of
BRITAIN

THE BATTLE of BRITAIN

Richard Townshend Bickers

Foreword by Air Marshal Sir Denis Crowley-Milling, KCB. CBE. DSO. DFC. AE.

a Salamander book

Published by Salamander Books Limited
LONDON • NEW YORK

A SALAMANDER BOOK

Published by Salamander Books Ltd.,
129-137 York Way, London N7 9LG, United Kingdom.

©Salamander Books Ltd. 1990

ISBN 0 86101 477 4

Distributed in the UK by Hodder & Stoughton Services,
P.O. Box 6, Mill Road, Dunton Green, Sevenoaks, Kent TN3 2XX.

All correspondence concerning the content of this volume should be addressed to Salamander Books Ltd.

CREDITS

Editors: Ray Bonds, Graham Smith.
Designers: Mark Holt, Paul Johnson, Nigel Duffield, Phil Gorton.
Colour Artworks: Derek Bunce. ©Salamander Books Ltd
Line Artworks: Geoff Denney Associates. ©Salamander Books Ltd
Cutaways and Colour Profiles: ©Pilot Press.
Colour Photography: Michael Dyer Associates. ©Salamander Books Ltd
Filmsetting: The Old Mill. **Colour Reproduction:** Scantrans. Pte. Singapore.
Printed in Italy.

THE AUTHORS

Air Marshal Sir Denis Crowley-Milling, KCB. CBE. DSO. DFC. AE. flew with Douglas Bader's 242 Squadron during the Battle, and served in the RAF for many years after the war. He is the Chairman of the Douglas Bader Foundation, a charity which encourages limbless people to lead a full and active life.

Richard Towshend Bickers served in the RAF during and after the war, seeing service in the UK, North Africa and Italy. He has published many books, including a biography of the late Sqn Ldr J.H. (Ginger) Lacey.

Gordon Swanborough has spent most of his working life as an aviation writer and journalist, and has contributed to many Salamander books including ''Flying Colours'' and ''An Anatomy of Fighters''.

William Green entered aviation journalism in World War II and has gained an international reputation for many works of aviation reference. He has contributed to many Salamander books with Gordon Swanborough.

Bill Gunston is a former RAF pilot and flying instructor and has become one of the most respected aviation writers and broadcasters. He has produced numerous aviation books for Salamander.

Air Vice-Marshal J.E. (Johnnie) Johnson, CB. CBE. DSO. DFC. DL. ended the war as the RAF's top scoring fighter pilot, and served in the RAF for many years after. He is a trustee of the Douglas Bader Foundation.

Mike Spick was born in London less than three weeks before the maiden flight of the Spitfire, and is an aviation author and consultant specialising in air combat tactics and operations.

Group Captain Sir Hugh Dundas, CBE. DSO. DFC. DL. flew with 616 Squadron during the Battle of Britain and after, and became the RAF's youngest Group Captain at the age of 23.

OTHER CONTRIBUTORS

The late Sqn Ldr J.H. (Ginger) Lacey, DFM. Wg Cdr P. (Paddy) Barthropp, DFC. AFC. The late Gp Capt Bobby Oxspring, DFC. AFC. Air Cdre Alan Deere, CBE. DSO. DFC. Air Cdre Peter Brothers, CBE. DSO. DFC. Lt Gen Adolph Galland, Knights Cross.

NEVER IN THE FIELD OF HUMAN CONFLICT WAS SO MUCH OWED BY SO MANY TO SO FEW — CHURCHILL

CONTENTS

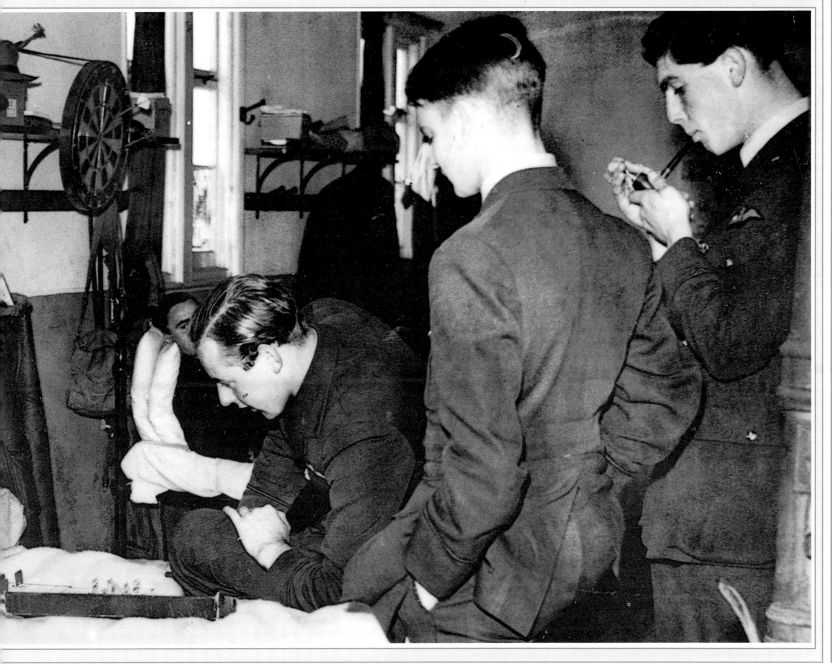

I AM delighted that Salamander have taken on the task of producing this special book to mark the 50th anniversary of a famous victory when Britain stood alone. Some people may think that, over the years, more than enough books have been written on the subject and there can be little new ground to cover. I believe, however, that this volume comes as a timely reminder of what was at stake in those dark hours of 1940. So let us consider for a moment, fifty years on, how different history would have been had the German air force gained that vital air superiority over Britain — so necessary before there could be any thought of the invasion that Goering had boasted could be launched within a matter of weeks, with forces moving across the Channel unmolested by air attack to achieve final occupation.

First, there would have been no American intervention and support in arms or men, no massive bombing offensive against Germany, and no base from which to launch a second front. Hitler's war machine would have been largely committed to the defeat of Russia and under these circumstances it could well have been successful. Also, having no disruption in their nuclear research and development work, it is conceivable that

Below: Denis Crowley-Milling flew with 242 Hurricane Squadron during the Battle of Britain. He is posing here with the windscreen of his aircraft after it was hit by defensive fire from a Ju 88.

FOREWORD

Air Marshal Sir Denis Crowley-Milling, KCB, CBE, DSO, DFC, AE. Chairman, The Douglas Bader Foundation

Germany would have had the atomic bomb within a few years, thus further strengthening her position as the master of Europe. Britain could well have been an occupied country to this day.

So I believe it is right that we, as a nation, should once again be invited to look back to a time in history, now half a century ago, which proved to be the turning point leading to the eventual defeat of Hitler's Nazi Germany.

1940 was the year that air power truly came of age. The success of all campaigns that followed depended heavily upon gaining and sustaining air superiority. When General Montgomery (as he then was) returned home in triumph after the battle of Alamein I was present at a talk he gave at Camberley. He told us in his forthright manner that he had rewritten the 'principles of war' and his first new principle was, as he put it, "to win my air battle." He never moved his forces without being sure of his air cover from then on.

This new publication also brings to mind some of the vital factors affecting the outcome, some happening well before, and others during, the Battle. For instance, the British public to some extent still look down on Neville Chamberlain for deceiving the country in September 1938 with "peace in our time" and with the Munich agreement and appeasement of Hitler, but it is clear that Chamberlain was not deceived by Hitler, and in fact, on his return, accelerated the rearmament programme.

Admittedly, the situation in 1938, had we gone to war, would have been different in many ways. But had events then led to the Germans reaching the Channel, it is worth recording that we would have had only 70 Hurricanes and 9 Spitfires in the front line. Also, the radar detection and fighter control systems, the

Below: While the Hurricane provided the bulk of the RAF's fighter strength, the Spitfire has come to symbolise the Battle in the popular mind. These are two Mk Is serving with 616 fighter Squadron.

Above: By July 1940, German fighter pilots had triumphed over Poland, Norway, France, Holland and Belgium. They had no reason to believe that they would not meet with similar success over Britain.

Below: Hurricane LE-H was used by 242 Squadron and often flown by Denis Crowley-Milling. Structurally less advanced than the Spitfire, the Hurricane was a tough and manoeuvrable dogfighter.

creation of which Air Chief Marshal Dowding had played a major role in, were still incomplete. It is of interest that the German air force, in their written appreciation covering Operation 'Sea Lion' (their invasion plan), acknowledged the existence of our radar stations, but showed no knowledge of the use of that information for controlling the fighter force which had been developed to such great effect. In fact, it came as a great surprise to them to find the extent to which their formations were being intercepted.

When the Battle of France showed all the signs of

being lost, it was Dowding who first faced up to Churchill's Cabinet and flatly refused to allow any more Fighter Command squadrons to be sacrificed in that contest. Even so, with all the squadrons available in late August 1940, at the height of the Battle of Britain, and with the enemy's continued attacks on our radar installations and airfields, the outcome hung in the balance. At that point, some bombs fell in central London and it was then decided to bomb Berlin in retaliation and to serve as a morale booster at home. Fortuitously, this caused Goering, who had boasted that Berlin would never be attacked, to switch, with Hitler's agreement, the main weight of attack to London. This crucial misjudgement allowed our fighter stations to recover. Within weeks, the tide in the air battle had been turned and Hitler decided to postpone the invasion indefinitely. By early the next year he finally resolved to turn against Russia regardless of his failure to overcome the United Kingdom.

The Battle of Britain was an attempt to defeat the will of the British people, and the whole country played a part in defeating the German plan.

While the RAF fighter pilots were the tip of the sword, we must also acknowledge the contributions of many others, whether serving in the RAF or elsewhere. The nation has much to 'owe' to those bomber crews who battled all the way to Berlin in their comparatively slow aircraft, and who also played a vital part with their attacks on the invasion ports and enemy shipping. I cannot praise them too highly. Nor must

we forget other services — Anti-Aircraft Command, the Observer Corps and Civil Defence as well as Coastal Command and the Royal Navy, with its flotilla of light vessels which were ever vigilant in eastern and southern ports, ready to counter the threat of invasion ships and barges. But, in all, the key was 'command of the air'. We were short of pilots from the start, but fortunately, we were never short of aircraft thanks not only to the aircraft factories but also to the Civil Repair Organisation and RAF Repair Depots, the latter, between them, turning out 60 aircraft per week. It was not just the 'Few', it was the 'Many'.

As to the conduct of the Battle, day to day operations were in the hands of the 11 Group Commander with the other Groups playing a supporting role as

Below: The Battle of Britain was a people's war with civilians also in the front line. Spitfire Funds boosted public morale by allowing ordinary people to contribute to the purchase of individual aircraft.

necessary. Dowding at Fighter Command provided the means and the strategy, while the A.O.C. 11 Group, Air Vice Marshal Keith Park fought and won the tactical battle. For this he deserves the highest praise. However, it must be admitted that this subordination of other Groups to 11 Group was the cause of some bad feeling and friction between 11 and 12 Groups, particularly over tactics.

Much has been written over the years about 'Big Wing' tactics, leading in some cases to harsh criticism of the parts played by Air Vice Marshal Leigh-Mallory and in particular Douglas Bader. However, we have had available for some time the relevant Air Ministry and Fighter Command files of September/October 1940 covering operations during the battle, and also the reports submitted to Dowding by both Park and Leigh-Mallory. These subsequently were passed to the Air Ministry, and here I find that some authors have not only been selective in their material, but also biased in their interpretations. For example Leigh-Mallory's first report in September 1940 on Wing Operations was

forwarded by Fighter Command to the Air Ministry with the final comment ''AOC 12 Group is working on the right lines in organising his operations in strength''. While in Park's report it is clear that 11 Group squadrons operated in a 'Wing' of three squadrons on a number of occasions when conditions and warning time were favourable, and in fact he issued at least two instructions to his units covering the methods and tactics of 'Wing' operations.

Clearly Park was unhappy, to say the least, with the use the Air Ministry made of the various reports, and he had good reason to be, but there is no evidence that Fighter Command were critical of the way Leigh-Mallory was operating his squadrons, if anything the reverse is true.

Below: Douglas Bader and Lord Dowding at a victory celebration in 1945. 50 years after the Battle, controversy still rages about the supposed disagreements over tactics and the way it was fought.

It was as a result of these Group Commanders reports that Air Vice Marshal Sholto Douglas (Deputy Chief of Air Staff) began to take an interest, and set up the now famous meeting in October to ''Discuss future Fighter Tactics''. Douglas Bader only spoke once at that meeting, when invited by the Chairman; but Leigh-Mallory, in bringing him along had put him in

a mighty privileged position for a Squadron Leader. Frankly he had no business to do it, as it was bound to invite comment as to his motives and, of course, upset Park, whose Squadron Commanders in 11 Group had borne the brunt of the battle. Even so, when the minutes of the meeting were circulated, Dowding and Leigh-Mallory had relatively minor amendments. Keith Park submitted a copy of the notes he used at the meeting and requested that they be attached to the minutes, Douglas refused. Here I must add that I know from many conversations I had with Douglas Bader in his lifetime that he had the highest regard for both Keith Park and Dowding. Indeed, he gave the address at the Service of Thanksgiving for the life of Park and he wrote the following tribute to Dowding:— ''To the fighter pilots of 1940 Dowding was the father figure. Seldom seen, many pilots did not know even how he looked. Nevertheless we knew he was there in Fighter Command minding our affairs, so all was well. We held him in esteem which after the war became affection. We read about him; how he had fought the Treasury to get hard runways built on grass airfields, waterlogged and unusable in winter; how he had insisted on bullet-

Above: This famous photograph shows some of the pilots of 242 Hurricane Squadron. The Commanding Officer, Douglas Bader, is fourth from the right and Denis Crowley-Milling is at the far left.

proof windscreens in our Hurricanes and Spitfires. After the war at Battle of Britain dinners we actually saw him and spoke with him. We were proud that he had chosen to be known as Lord Dowding of Bentley Priory — our home from home — Headquarters, Fighter Command. At last we felt this gruff, withdrawn, inarticulate 'Stuffy' Dowding really had become one of us. We thought it a bad show that he had not been made a Marshal of the Royal Air Force.''

As I look back now to those days as a young, very junior officer flying daily alongside Douglas Bader, I realise how fortunate I was. It was a never-to-be-forgotten experience which materially shaped my subsequent career. I believe this book will appeal to most. It covers every aspect — pilots, aircraft and equipment — in great detail, and will contribute to our understanding of this key period in our nation's history.

AT 0445HRS ON September 1, 1939, the first shots in World War II were fired when the Luftwaffe attacked Poland. An hour later German ground forces crossed the Polish frontier. A new style of warfare devised by Germany had been unleashed: *der Blitzkrieg,* the lightning war, synchronising simultaneous massive assaults by dive bombers and tanks.

Why was the German invasion of Poland of consequence to France and Britain? Because on April 1, 1939, Britain and France had guaranteed to defend Poland against any threat by Germany.

On August 24, 1939, Germany had signed a non-aggression pact with Russia. The British General Staff was sceptical about this, knowing that Nazism was the avowed enemy of Communism and expecting Hitler to turn on his new ally as soon as he felt strong enough. The British made two appreciations of the situation. One was that, as Hitler had no strategic need to enter Poland, he would, faced with the certainty of British and French intervention, attack the Ukraine as a first step towards the conquest of Russia. The other was that Hitler would take on Poland, France and Britain, that the first two would quickly succumb, that Britain was his main objective and he would immediately order the Luftwaffe to obliterate London and its docks, then send his Army to invade England.

In fact, Hitler did not expect to have to fight the British at all. Joachim von Ribbentrop, who had been Ambassador in London before becoming Foreign Minister in 1938, had constantly assured him that the British were éffete and would not go to war. Hitler himself thought that Neville Chamberlain, the Prime Minister, had made an empty promise to Poland merely to frighten Germany. The British Government had been pusillanimous and appeasing throughout Hitler's time as Chancellor and dictator. He had easily deceived Chamberlain at their meetings in Munich in September 1938. All this made him certain that once again the British Cabinet would prove too cowardly to face war with Germany.

Immediately on the invasion of Poland, the British and French Governments demanded German withdrawal. Hitler ignored them. The next day there were frantic talks in Paris and London. As usual, Chamberlain and his Ministers took a passive line. The French Government showed no more courage or sense of honour than the British. But the British Parliament felt differently and prevailed on the Government to give Germany an ultimatum. France followed suit. At 1100hrs on September 3, 1939, Britain declared war, and France did so at 1700hrs. Thus, while the Germans were conquering Poland, a British Expeditionary Force and units of the RAF were establishing themselves in France.

The defeat of Poland

In anticipating the German conquest of Poland, Field Marshal Walter von Brauchitsch, Commander-in-Chief of the German Army, to whom Hitler had given responsibility for the campaign, summarised his objective as, "To anticipate an orderly mobilisation and concentration of the Polish Army and to destroy the main bulk of it west of the Vistula-Narev line by concentric at-

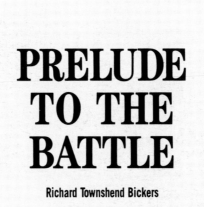

PRELUDE TO THE BATTLE

Richard Townshend Bickers

tacks from Silesia, Pomerania and East Prussia.'' The plan was intended to squeeze most of the defending Army in a pincer-grip and prevent it from escaping over the Vistula. This meant that the Luftwaffe must first establish air superiority. On a vast scale, never attempted before, bombers would disrupt road and rail traffic deep in Poland; and, the more significant tactic, bombers and fighters would maintain constant bombing and strafing of ground troops.

The latter is invariably described as a total innovation. It was nothing of the sort. Britain's Royal Flying Corps introduced it on the Somme in 1916 with terrifying effect described by a German infantryman, who wrote home: "One can hardly calculate how much additional loss of life and strain on the nerves this cost us." By 1918 it was standard practice on both sides, for which purpose-designed aircraft were built. What

the Germans did do, with their traditional thoroughness, was to develop air-to-ground attack to its ultimate potential.

The resolution of these and all the other associated problems, by preliminary theory and by practical experience in Poland, was the rehearsal for what was to follow eight months later in Belgium, Holland and France; and would have been inflicted on the British if RAF Fighter Command had not won the Battle of Britain. The first purpose, to destroy the Polish Air Force, if possible on the ground, also foreshadowed Goering's design in July, August, September and October 1940.

The Polish General Staff was old-fashioned, the Army was inadequately equipped and poorly deployed to defend the 1,750 miles (2,815km) of frontier adjoining East Prussia and Nazi-occupied Czechoslovakia. No defences had been built, the armoured force was small, and the cavalry was the Army's pride. The Poles, with their traditional dash, relied on the efficacy of counter-attacks. When the German tanks rolled across the Polish plains they were met by cavalry charges.

The Germans sent in two Army Groups: one comprising the Third and Fourth Armies, the other the Eighth, Tenth and Fourteenth.

The Luftwaffe Order of Battle for this campaign numbered 648 bombers, 219 dive bombers, 210 single- and twin-engine fighters, 30 ground attack aircraft and 474 reconnaissance and transport types.

The Polish Air Force was organised in regiments, wings and squadrons. The strength on September 1, 1939, was 159 PZL P7 and PZL P11 single-seat fighters, all three to seven years old, 154 PZL 37 and PZL 23B bombers and light bomber/recce aircraft capable of offensive operations, and 84 observation aircraft.

German intelligence mistakenly estimated the Polish Air Force front-line strength as more than 900, including 150 bombers, 315 fighters, 325 reconnaissance, 100 liaison and 50 naval aircraft.

The Polish combat aircraft were nowhere near as capable as those of the Luftwaffe. From the Luftwaffe strength given above and the specifications of its aircraft given in a later chapter, it is clear that the Polish Air Force was at a huge disadvantage in numbers and in aircraft performance and armament.

The Polish War Plan and General Directive for Air Operations, issued on July 28, 1939, laid down that fighter squadrons were to be used as an integral part of the Armies, with the exception of the Pursuit Brigade, consisting of five squadrons, which was to be under the control of the Supreme Commander of the Polish Forces. The tasks for the Army fighter squadrons (known as the Army Air Force) were; interception of enemy aircraft over the Army sector, Air cover of Polish aircraft operating over the Army sector, and in critical situations, air attacks on enemy ground forces. The task of the Pursuit Brigade was air defence of the country.

Left: One of the first events to convince Hitler that the rest of Europe would never seriously oppose German expansion was when his army reclaimed the de-militarised Rhineland in March 1936.

The eight squadrons operating with the four Armies covered large sectors but had no radio, and therefore no co-operation with, or information from, the ground when airborne. Enemy activity was so intense, however, that most take-offs were followed by combat. The rapid advance of the German Army and the Luftwaffe's attacks on airfields necessitated frequent changes of base. Heavy losses of aircrew and aircraft were suffered on the ground and in the air.

After 12 days the Army Air Force ceased to operate effectively and was withdrawn to join the remnants of the Pursuit Brigade. There was one exception: the Poznan Army Wing, commanded by Major M. Mumler, fought until September 16, 1939. It shot down 31 enemy aircraft, lost two pilots killed, four wounded and six missing, and lost all but one of its aircraft. This last, flown by the commanding officer, landed in Romania on September 18 — all that remained of an initial strength of 22.

The Pursuit Brigade was based on airfields near Warsaw to defend the capital and its environs. Eight radio stations provided a means of communication and control, although the radio range was only 9 to 12 miles (15 to 20km). The Warsaw surveillance centre provided information on the enemy. On September 7 the Brigade, with 16 serviceable aircraft, was moved to the Lublin area, to be joined later by the surviving pilots and aircraft of the Army squadrons. The combined fighter force, short of fuel and deprived of adequate communication, shot down only five enemy aircraft bet-

Below: The Junkers Ju 87 Stuka gained early laurels in Poland and France in the close air support role. Events were to show that it could only be successful in conditions of local air superiority.

ween September 7 and 17, after which the Polish Air Force ceased to operate. The Polish Army fought on until October 3.

It is customary to dismiss the performance of the Polish Air Force with the statement that it was wiped out on the ground before it could put up a fight. As the foregoing proves, this is wildly inaccurate and a calumny on brave men who died disproving it, and on those who survived to fight on in the RAF.

The Luftwaffe suffered 285 aircraft destroyed and 279 severely damaged; 189 Luftwaffe aircrew were killed, 224 missing and 126 wounded.

Out of 435 aircraft engaged, the Polish Air Force lost 327 from all causes, of which 264 were by direct enemy action, destroyed in combat or on the ground; at least 33 were shot down by their own anti-aircraft gun fire and 116 escaped to Romania. Aircrew killed and missing numbered at least 234.

The experience of 18 days' hard air fighting contributed nothing to help the RAF in the Battle of Britain. The German aircraft destroyed and aircrew killed or disabled were more than replaced by then. The disparity between the quality and quantity of the Polish and British fighters was obvious: the Polish PZL P7s and P11s had been at a crippling disadvantage, but if Germany had attacked Britain then, Hurricanes and Spitfires would have mauled the Luftwaffe.

Although scores of Polish fighter pilots managed to reach France and Britain and were interrogated by French and British intelligence officers, no conclusions were drawn from the fact that the Luftwaffe fighter formation based on loose pairs was obviously more effective than the conventional threes of the Polish and French Air Forces, and the RAF. Nothing was deduced about how defending fighters should deal with formations of 50 to a 100 bombers accompanied by an equally large fighter escort, or the best technique for shooting down dive bombers.

The Lutwaffe, on the contrary, benefited from a

Above: Luftwaffe equipment and tactics had been thoroughly tested during the Spanish Civil War, including the infamous bombing of Guernica. Here a Heinkel He 111E of the Legion Kondor unloads over a Spanish target.

Below: German groundcrew toil with the inertia starter of the Junkers Ju 87 during the Polish campaign. The handle turned a flywheel which, when enough momentum had been built up, was used to start the engine.

tremendous boost to its morale, the satisfaction of knowing that it had made devastatingly effective use of what it had learned in the Spanish Civil War, and the combat knowledge gained by its pilots and crews.

The Battle of France

At the time of France's declaration of war against Germany, her air force was poorly equipped to conduct either a defensive or an offensive campaign. Despite the warnings of General Vuillemin, the Air Force Chief of Staff, and Captain Stehlin, the Air Attaché in Berlin, the French High Command had refused in the 1930s to recognise Germany's aerial rearmament. No pressure was put on indigenous aircraft manufacturers to design and build fighters or bombers that would meet realistic modern requirements. Little air-to-air firing was done; gunnery training was almost totally limited to camera gun practice. Fighter pilots were trained to make beam attacks ending with a full deflection firing pass at 820ft (250m). These were to prove mostly abortive against the Luftwaffe because the French aircraft lacked sufficient performance.

The total fighter strength of aircraft considered to have a performance capable of taking on the Messerschmitt 109 was 250 Morane 405/406 and 120 Curtiss H75 (US-supplied Curtiss P-36). The bomber and reconnaissance strength consisted of 120 Bloch 151/152, 85 Potez 630 and 205 Potez 631.

Regular officer pilots were trained at l'Ecole de l'Air and NCOs at l'Ecole d'Istres. Pilots and observers on the Reserve were trained during their compulsory military service. Pilot candidates aged 18 could, on passing an examination, be trained initially as civilians at a civil flying school. They would then sign on for three years and complete their training at Istres, after which they joined a squadron. At the end of the contract period they were put on the Reserve, in which there were two classes. Class A reservists were assigned to a squadron, with which they did about 10 hours' flying a year. Class B did no continuation flying and were sent on a refresher course in the event of mobilisation.

The organisation of France's Air Force, l'Armée de l'Air, in 1939 was: groupements comprising several groupes; escadres comprising two groupes (until May 1939, when some were increased to three); groupes comprising two escadrilles (squadrons); escadrilles comprising three patronilles (patrols) of three aircraft in each.

In addition, there was one unit similar to a British Auxiliary Air Force squadron: l'Escadrille de Paris, based at Villacoublay.

The normal aircraft establishment for a groupe was 25, but for those flying the Curtiss it was 30. The pilot establishment for all groupes was 30.

On August 28, 1939, fighters were based as follows: at Etampes: 1st Escadre, comprising two groupes of obsolescent Dewoitine 510; Escadrille 1/13, night fighter, equipped with Potez 631. At Chartres: 2nd Escadre, three groupes of Morane 406; 6th Escadre, two groupes of Morane 406. At Dijon: 3rd Escadre, three groupes of Morane 406; 7th Escadre, two groupes of Morane 406. At Rheims: 4th Escadre, two groupes of Curtiss H75; 5th Escadre, two groupes of Curtiss

H75; Escadrille 2/13, night fighter equipped with Potez 631. At Marignane: 8th Escadre, comprising two groupes, one with Dewoitine 510, the other with Potez 631.

By August 1939, there were dispersed on active service aerodromes that were mostly bare fields among woods or forests, far from a town. The aircraft were kept in the open air. The pilots were often billeted with civilians if a village were near enough. The ground troops lived in barns and slept on straw.

The standard fighter formation was three aircraft, with the leader in the centre and his wing men laterally separated by 220 yards (200m) from him, one 55 yards (50m) below him, the up-sun aircraft taking the higher position.

The control and reporting system was, by British standards, ramshackle. Warning of hostile aircraft was based on the *System de Guet*, the Look-Out System, similar to the Observer Corps in Britain but less reliably served by the telephone lines on which it depended. This was weakly supported by a radio method of detection, *détection électromagnétique* or D.E.M., consisting of a chain of alternate transmitters and receivers. These gave a rough plan position of aircraft by observations on the bearing produced between the direct wave from the transmitter to the receiver and the reflected wave from the aircraft. It had a range of approximately 50km and did not give satisfactory results on more than one aircraft.

Fighter control was handicapped by poor radio equipment. Aircraft sets needed frequent returning in the air. Their air-to-ground range was 93 miles (150km)

Below: Allies. A French Morane Saulnier MS 406 is seen with a Fairey Battle light bomber of the British Advanced Air Striking Force. Neither proved very successful in the Battle for France that followed and suffered heavy casualties from flak and fighters.

at heights above 3,280ft (1000m), and air-to-air 31 miles (50km).

This small Regular air force and inchoate Reserve, with its scanty supply of modern fighters and enduring hard living conditions, nevertheless entered the war with high morale.

The entire nation felt secure behind the Maginot Line, the most impressive fortification ever built, consisting of three lines of reinforced concrete outposts, block houses and forts with underground arsenals, living quarters and hospitals. Defended by enormous artillery pieces and tens of thousands of infantry, it stretched along the German frontier from Belgium to Switzerland. The French believed it was impregnable.

The British Expeditionary Force

The first units of the British Expeditionary Force (BEF), under the command of Field Marshal Lord Gort, began to land in France on September 10, 1939. Two RAF formations had preceded them. The Advanced Air Striking Force (AASF) was commanded by Air Vice Marshal P.H.L. Playfair, CB, CVO, MC, who had joined the Royal Flying Corps in 1912 from the royal Artillery and won his Military Cross in France during World War I. His headquarters was near Reims, around which his squadrons were based. Their task was to work with the French Army along the German frontier. The Air Component of the BEF, under Air Vice Marshal C.H.B. Blount, CB, OBE, MC, with his headquarters near Arras, was based in the Pas de Calais. Its function was to operate with the BEF, which went into the line along the Belgian frontier, and to patrol Channel convoys. Blount, who transferred from the Royal West Surreys to the RFC in 1913, had also won his gallantry decoration in the Great War, when commanding No 34 Squadron in France and Italy.

The Advanced Air Striking Force consisted of 10 bomber squadrons and two fighter squadrons. Nos 12, 15, 40, 88, 103, 105, 142, 150, 218 and 226 flew the

Fairey Battle. This was an obsolescent three-seater type with a single 1,030hp Rolls-Royce Merlin engine and armed with one fixed .303in Browning gun forward and one .303in Vickers K aft. Its maximum speed was 241mph (388km/h) at 13,000ft (3,960m) and its ceiling 23,500ft (7,160m). The bombload was 1,000lb (453kg). Nos 85 and 87 had Hurricanes, whose specification is given elsewhere. The Battles landed in France on September 1 and the Hurricanes on the 7th.

The Air Component, whose records were almost totally destroyed during the hasty retreat of the British forces in June 1940, comprised the following: *Four corps squadrons*, whose function was army co-operation: Nos 2, 4, 13 and 26, flying Lysanders. These were two-seater, single-engined, high-wing monoplanes with 890hp Bristol Mercury XII engines and armed with two fixed .303in Brownings firing forward and one .303in Vickers or Lewis in the rear cockpit firing aft; maximum speed 219mph (352km/h) at 10,000ft (3,050m); ceiling 26,000ft (7,925m).

Four army squadrons, Nos 18, 53, 57, 59, flying Blenheims, whose specification is given elsewhere.

Six fighter squadrons. Those equipped with Hurricanes were Nos 1, 17, 85 and 87. Those with Gladiators were 607 (County of Durham) and 615 (County of Surrey), both of the Auxiliary Air Force.

None of the 12 airfields designated for the Air Component was in the area allotted to the British Army, which was supposed to supply them with rations, tents, fuel, pay, works, postal service, furniture, billets, etc. The French Army proved helpful and supplied rations, wine and petrol. All these airfields were covered in clover, not grass, and would become soggy and non-operational in wet weather. None had hangars or had been provided with any other resources. The RAF did not know this beforehand, because Britain had made a gentlemen's agreement with France not to do any intelligence studies there.

Above: Officers of No.1 Sqn at Neuville, France. L to R. Drake, Clisby, Lorrimer, Hanks, Mould, Halahan, Demozay (French liason officer), Walker, Medical Officer, Richey, Kilmartin, Stratton, Palmer.

The British Army came to the rescue of the Air Component in the person of an officer on Gort's staff. He was Brigadier Appleyard of the Territorial Army, who was Chief Engineer of a major road-construction company and undertook to provide 20 proper airfields by the spring. He returned to England and visited the managing directors of his own employers and four other leading road contractors. With their wholehearted co-operation he raised five companies for the Royal Engineers, each bearing the name of the firm that it represented and by which it was provided with all the necessary equipment needed for earth moving, road construction and the building of accommodation. Having been vested with virtual omnipotence in achieving his objective, he obtained commissions in the rank of major for company directors and captain for managers. Foremen became instant sergeants and charge hands were enlisted as corporals. Uniforms were supplied immediately. Swiftly they were in France, putting up huts for themselves and sowing grass seed on the ploughland that had been selected for conversion it is appropriate to confirm here that by the spring they had indeed rolled the new grass and laid down concrete runways on nearly all their 20 sites.)

The war began with a period of comparative inactivity that was, in comparison with the eventual Blitzkrieg that came in 1940, retrospectively known as the Sitzkrieg. The French refer to it as *La Drôle de Guerre* — The Joke War. The Allied land and air forces stagnated. Their armies patrolled in front of the Maginot Line and fought occasional skirmishes. Their air forces were forbidden to bomb Germany for fear of reprisals. The Luftwaffe was under the same restriction over Britain and France. The BEF's artillery did gunnery practice, for which the Air Component's Lysanders spotted as they used to on Salisbury Plain. They also did some close reconnaissance and photography. The Blenheims were more interestingly employed on photographic reconnaissance over Germany.

The only sector of the Franco-German frontier across which the Allies or the Germans could attack, was the 90 miles (145km) between the Rhine and the Moselle. Well within her own territory, Germany had built strong defences, the Siegfried Line or West Wall. The Blenheims photographed the whole of it, as well as more distant objectives. Nos 1 and 73 Squadrons filled their time with convoy patrols and the normal practice flying.

The RAF squadrons based at home had meanwhile been more active than those in France. On the night of September 3, Whitley bombers flew the first of many leaflet raids — codenamed Nickel — and dropped six million copies of an exhortation to Germany to abandon the war. Not only was the penalty for reading them severe, which ensured that few would be picked up, but also this was psychologically an absurd time at which to spread propaganda, German morale was at its height with the invasion of Poland going so much in Germany's favour. The time to spread propaganda is when one has the upper hand and the enemy's resolve is wilting. Casualties among the crews who flew these sorties were, like those of the crews who carried bombs across the North Sea or made daylight sorties in Battles and Blenheims from France, particularly sad in their wastefulness. All three activities were futile. At Air Ministry and in Bomber Command HQ was a theory that casualties on leaflet raids could have been heavier, because the enemy hesitated to betray the siting of his flak and searchlights when he knew that neither bombing nor photography was their purpose. This was not shared by the men who actually did the job. What was true was that the elementary radar was of scant help in controlling night fighters, which were therefore less lethal than they might have been.

On September 1, President Roosevelt of the USA had appealed to the German and Polish Governments to limit bombing to legitimate military objectives. On the same date Hitler said in the Reichstag: "I will not war against women and children. I have ordered my air force to restrict itself to attacks on military objectives." On that very day, the Luftwaffe bombed 60 towns and villages in Poland. On September 3 Hitler replied to Roosevelt: "It is a precept of humanity in all circumstances to avoid bombing non-military objectives, which corresponds entirely with my own attitude and has always been advocated by me." On September 13 he attempted to justify his savage bombing of Polish civilians by claiming that it was legitimate because the Polish Government had incited its citizens to fight the Germans as *franc-tireurs*.

Although bombing the German mainland was forbidden and German bombers were under orders not to attack mainland Britain or France, shipping in port was a permitted target. Flying Officer A. MacPherson of

No 139 (Blenheim) Squadron flew a reconnaissance off Wilhelmshaven on September 3 but his wireless report was too distorted by atmospherics to read. On September 4 he took off again at 0835hrs to repeat the sortie. Despite cloud and rain squalls he obtained photographs of ships in Brunsbüttel, Wilhelmshaven and Schillig Roads, including the pocket battleship *Admiral Scheer* and training cruiser *Emden*. Once more his message was unreadable. After he reported verbally on landing, 15 Blenheims of Nos. 109, 110 and 139 Squadrons set out to bomb Wilhelmshaven and 14 Wellingtons from No. 9 and 149 Squadrons to bomb two battleships in Brunsbüttel.

With cloud base at 500ft (150m), only three Blenheims of 110 were able to attack. One hit the *Admiral Scheer* but the 500lb (227kg) bombs were too light for the task and the 11-second fuse did not detonate it until after the bomb had bounced off the warship's deck. Another Blenheim crashed on the *Emden*, fatally for the crew. Only one Blenheim of No. 107 Squadron returned and there is no record of any hits. No 139 Squadron could not find its target in the adverse weather and returned unscathed without having bombed anything. None of the Wellingtons claimed hits. Most failed to find the target or turned back early because of bad weather. Two did not return. All aircraft met accurate and heavy flak and the Wellingtons were attacked by Bf 109s.

On September 29, 12 Hampdens of Nos. 61 and 144 Squadrons took off for Heligoland and the Frisian Islands. One turned back. Six saw two destroyers, which three attacked unsuccessfully and three could not get in position to attack. Five were attacked by Bf 109s and all were shot down.

These heavy losses did not shake the sacred Bomber Command axiom that a section of three bombers in close formation in broad daylight had the combined defensive fire power to drive off any number of heavily armed attacking fighters.

In France, by mid-September two Blenheim squadrons, Nos 114 and 139, had joined the AASF. From the outset both the Allies and Germany had been making several daily photographic reconnaissance sorties. While the Germans evaded anti-aircraft fire and fighters, the Battles and Blenheims constantly suffered casualties from both. Flak over Germany was heavy and accurate. The information gained was not worth the loss of one or two Blenheims day by day, so daylight sorties stopped and night reconnaissance began. Take-offs by the light of six blue glim lamps at 200-yard (183m) intervals was inherently hazardous. Over Germany, not only were German searchlight crews highly efficient but, in order to take photographs, flares were used which attracted flak and night fighters. Heavy losses continued.

Above: The outbreak of war and his first active operation warranted an entry in red ink for Hampden observer/gunner Flying Officer Chesters of No.44 Squadron, as this extract from his logbook shows.

It was No 1 Squadron that scored the first British success, on October 30, a sunny day with no low cloud. Flying Officer P.W. ''Boy'' Mould, who had joined as a Halton apprentice in 1934 and been selected for Cranwell in 1937, had barely refuelled after a patrol when a Dornier 17 flew high over the airfield. He took off without awaiting orders, caught up with the Dornier at 18,000ft (5,485m) and attacked it from astern. It caught fire and spun vertically until it crashed into the ground.

On October 31 a member of 73 Squadron who was destined to become the best-known pilot in the Battle of France destroyed his first enemy aircraft, Flying Officer Edgar James Kain, known as Cobber, was a New Zealander who had come to England in 1936 to join the RAF. He gave an aerobatic display at the Empire Air Day show in 1938.

On patrol in a Hurricane he saw anti-aircraft shells bursting and headed towards them. At 27,000ft (8,230m) he intercepted a Do 17 and fired at it. Its port engine began to smoke and its rear gunner returned his fire while its pilot took evasive action. Kain gave the Dornier a long burst with the remainder of his 14.8

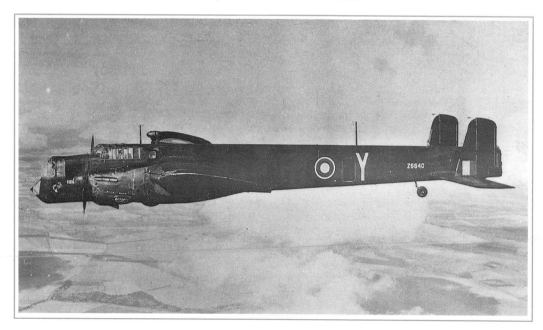

Left: A Whitley V of No.78 Sqn. One of the three British heavy bombers of the period, it was too slow to be risked over Germany in daylight but dropped ''bombphlets'' over the Reich during the Phoney War period.

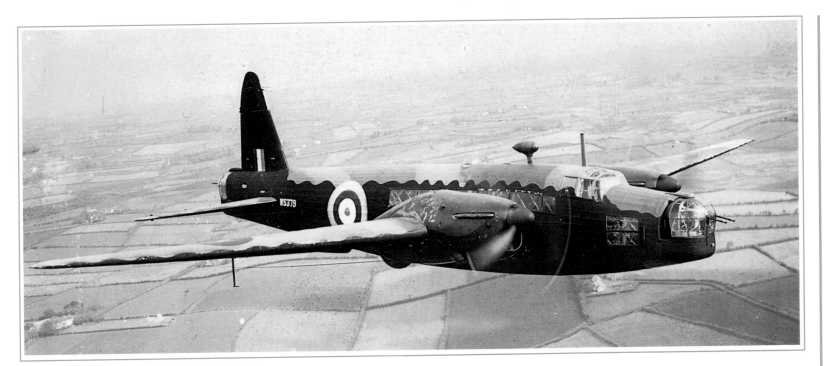

Above: The Wellington was the best of the British bombers of the early war period; its geodetic construction making it very damage resistant. This is the Merlin-engined Mk II which entered service in 1941.

Below: RAF air crew pose self consciously with their tin hats ''somewhere in France''. The white flying overalls are a legacy of prewar days. Conditions at the French airfields were primitive to say the least.

seconds'-worth of ammunition and it fell into a vertical dive. His Hurricane could not keep up with it and he pulled out at 400 mph (643km/h). The Dornier crashed in a village street. This combat set an altitude record for air fighting. On November 23 Kain shot down another Do 17.

On November 7 Germany's assault on the Low Countries was postponed on account of the weather. It was put off 13 times more and the last definite date Hitler chose was January 16, 1940.

The best day of 1939 for the RAF fighters was November 23, when several enemy aircraft were plotted on the map in the Operations Rooms of Nos 1 and 73 Squadrons, and Hurricanes were scrambled. Sqn Ldr ''Bull'' Halahan and Flying Officer ''Hilly'' Brown, a Canadian, intercepted a Do 17 and shot it down in flames. A section led by Flt Lt ''Johnny'' Walker caught an He 111, which they set on fire. While it was going down out of control a formation of Moranes came dashing in, one of which collided with Sgt. ''Darky'' Clowes's Hurricane and tore off an elevator and half the rudder. The French pilot's aeroplane was even more badly damaged and he baled out. Clowes landed at 120mph (193km/h), overshot and nosed in, but was unhurt. Another section of No.1 Squadron, led by Flt Lt ''Pussy'' Palmer, attacked a Do 17, set it alight and saw the rear gunner and navigator bale out. Palmer flew alongside to ensure that the pilot was dead. He found out that the German was not when the bomber swerved onto his tail and riddled his Hurricane with 43 bullets. His engine stopped with coolant smoke issuing from it but he made a forced landing, while FO Kilmartin and Soper resumed shooting at the Dornier, which in turn forced landed with both engines on fire. The German pilot waved at them as they circled the wreckage. No 73 Squadron destroyed three Do 17s, one of which fell to Cobber Kain.

The first Czech pilots arrived in France after long circuitous journeys and were distributed among the Morane groupes. They were soon followed by Poles,

Above: **Hurricane pilot Cobber Kain of No.73 Squadron. It was official policy to preserve anonymity among their top scorers while publicising their exploits, but the identity of the New Zealand ace leaked out.**

who were given their own groupe, No 1/45, under the command of Major Kepinski and equipped with Moranes.

By the end of the month an exceptionally severe winter had the Continent in its grip. On December 10 the temperature fell to minus 26 degrees Fahrenheit ($-32°C$) and on the 12th to minus 29. Air activity by both sides greatly diminished. It would be March before the Luftwaffe resumed large-scale operations.

Throughout the four months from the outbreak of war to the end of 1939, Coastal Command, which attracted the least attention from the press, had been going about its business over the Atlantic and the North Sea, achieving successes that indirectly contributed to the RAF's victory in the Battle of Britain. Oil, petrol and raw materials of every kind were as necessary to maintain Fighter Command's operational strength as were aircraft and pilots. Coastal Command constantly made reconnaissance sorties in search of enemy

warships and, with the Royal Navy, protected merchant shipping bound for Britain and limited the depradations of the U-boats. In the first fortnight of the war the enemy sunk 21 British merchant ships with a total tonnage of 122,843. During the two weeks ending October 9, 1939, only 5,809 tons of shipping were lost, and on November 14 it was announced that 3,070 ships had been convoyed with a loss of only seven.

''We faced the freezing winter of 39/40. Since this was part of the phoney war, the Luftwaffe generated very little action. We spent most of the time in cold unheated dispersals at Watton and Horsham interrupted by twice daily convoy patrols over the North Sea. For some reason ops always wanted these patrols flown at heights between 25,000 and 30,000 feet. We seemed to spend the entire winter in fleece-lined jackets, trousers and flying boots and never getting warm. As we clambered up to high altitudes the unpressurized cockpit sucked in icy draughts from the intensely cold atmosphere. Hands and feet, already cold before take-off, got steadily more numb. Once at altitude, we settled down to an hour's freezing patrol up and down a twenty-mile-long beat over the east coast convoys. Everything went Arctic. Mist formed on the glass of the instruments and hoar frost covered the inside of the canopy, which got worse as the moisture from our breath froze on oxygen masks. Occasionally we suffered from the dreaded 'bends'. The reduced atmospheric pressure caused the muscles to swell inducing lactic acid particularly in the elbow, knee and ankle joints. It caused a painful and persistent ache, and once smitten the pain could only be abated by a descent to lower altitude. If the ops controller refused requests to reduce height when the bends set in, we'd have to sweat it out for the remainder of the patrol.

On the let-down at the end of the patrol, we would point our aircraft out to sea and press the firing button just to see how many guns were so frozen up they wouldn't fire. Usually a couple would not.''

**Group Captain Bobby Oxspring
DFC, AFC.**

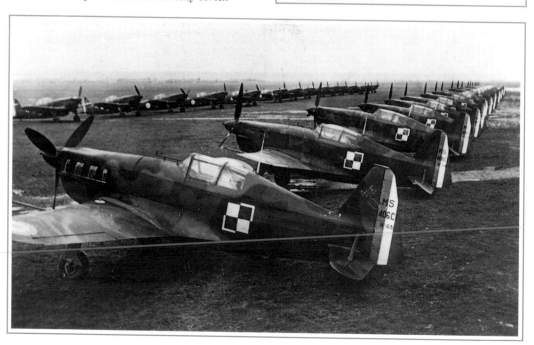

Right: **These Morane Saulnier MS 406s carry French rudder markings with Polish insignia on the fuselages as they line up to make a perfect target for strafing Germans. This is believed to be the Polish manned unit 1/45.**

General Gamelin, the French Commander-in-Chief, had been insisting that there should be an RAF chief responsible for both the AASF and the Air Component of the BEF. Accordingly, on January 9, 1940, Air Marshal Sir Arthur Barratt was appointed Air Officer Commanding-in-Chief, British Air Forces in France. He made his HQ at Coulommiers, where the French Air Force C-in-C had his. Barratt, known as "Ugly", had adequate credentials. He served in France during the Great War and immediately before his new appointment was Principal RAF Liaison Officer with the French forces.

On January 16, Hitler postponed his advance through the Low Countries until the spring.

The scale of air fighting over France began to increase in March 1940. Most combats developed to the same pattern: British and French fighters patrolling above 20,000ft (6,010m), seeking German bombers escorted by fighters, the opposing fighters each striving to have the height advantage at the moment of interception.

Kain made his third kill, a Bf 109, on March 3, but his Hurricane was hit and he had to bale out. He got his fourth, another 109, on March 26, but his aircraft was set on fire. Despite this he destroyed one more 109 before baling out. His score of five qualified him as

Below: Shooting down a German aircraft was a rare event in 1939 and as such a cause for celebration. RAF fighter pilots and their ground crews cluster round their latest trophy cut from a recent victim.

Above: Fairey Battles of No.88 Squadron. Despite its fighter-like appearance the Battle was a turkey in air combat and a sitter for light flak. Casualties in France were catastrophic.

an "Ace", the first Allied pilot of this war to achieve this, and he was awarded the Distinguished Flying Cross. He was now the most famous pilot in the RAF, as well-known to the public as "Sailor" Malan, Douglas Bader and Bob Stanford Tuck were destined to become.

Another Commonwealth pilot who had spectacular success in France was an Australian, Flying Officer Leslie Clisby of No 1 Squadron. He opened his score with a Bf 110 on March 31. Flying Officer Newell "Fanny" Orton, who had been in No.73 Squadron since 1937, also shot down a lot of Germans, starting with two Bf 109s on March 26.

In April the pace, like the weather, became warmer in patches interspersed with rain that hampered flying. Clisby bagged a Bf 109 on April 1 and another next day. Peter "Johnny" Walker, commanding A Flight of No.1 Squadron, had joined the Service in 1935 and performed in the squadron aerobatic team at the Hendon Air Pageant in 1937. Having shot down a Bf 110 on March 29 he added a Bf 109 on April 20. Orton got a Ju 88 on April 8 and on the 21st a 109 and a 110. "Boy" Mould had accounted for a 110 on March 31, and on April 1 he shot down another. Sergeant Harold "Ginger" Paul of No.743 Squadron made his

first kill on April 21, a Bf 109. Flt Lt Peter Prosser Hanks, known by his second forename, commander of B Flight, No.1 Squadron, another member of the aerobatic team, had sent a 110 down on March 31 and got an He 111 on April 20.

The Invasion of Scandinavia

While the Allies awaited Hitler's spring offensive in Western Europe, Germany carried out a lightning invasion of Denmark and Norway on April 9. Two Divisions under General Kaupitsch and an air force of some 500 combat aircraft, and nearly 600 transports, made the assault on both countries simultaneously. Both victims of the Nazis' latest aggression had only token air forces that were given no time to make even a gesture in defence of their countries. The Danish Army numbered only 15,000. Resistance was pointless.

At 0530hrs the Ju 52 transports carrying paratroops took off, but the approaches to both Oslo and Stavanger were obscured by fog from sea level to 2,000ft (610m). Low-level flight was impossible, and from above cloud the aerodromes on which the paratroops were to drop and the aircraft to land could not be seen. The first objectives of the paratroops were the airfields at Aalborg East and Aalborg West in Denmark, and Oslo-Fornebu and Stavanger-Sola in Norway. The first two were attacked at 0700hrs. Twelve hours later Copenhagen had been taken and the conquest of Denmark completed.

As with the Polish invasion, writers about this operation habitually state that the Norwegian Air Force, which comprised about 100 aeroplanes, nearly all fighters and reconnaissance types, was obliterated on the ground before it could put up a fight. That is not true either. While the Ju 52s were trying to land at Fornebu, Oberleutant Hansen, commanding I/ZG76 (Bf 110s), was giving them fighter cover. At 0838hrs his

Above: Pilots of No.87 Squadron run to their Hurricanes at Vassincourt during the Battle of France. Seven of the ten aircraft still have the two-bladed fixed pitch wooden propeller, giving inferior performance.

eight 110s were attacked out of the sun by nine Norwegian Gloster Gladiators, which shot down two of them.

The German landings by air and sea went ahead despite delays caused by weather, in the face of a brave defence by the Norwegian Army, Navy and what was left of the Air Force after the swift capture of the airfields. The Luftwaffe occupied the airfields and provided all the forms of air support essential for success in modern warfare. The fighting spread throughout the country.

Both Britain and France sent expeditionary forces but, to quote the archives, "With regard to air forces it was decided that none should accompany the expedition in the first instance." Critics have always deplored this as indicative of the backwardness of military thinking in Britain and France. Admittedly, the General Staffs in both countries were still imbued with out-dated notions about the use of air power, but one wonders where their critics suppose the aircraft could have come from? Neither the RAF nor l'Armée de l'Air could spare an adequate number of fighters from home defence. The French bombers were too poor in performance, bombload and armament to be effective or to protect themselves. From the first day of this campaign RAF Bomber and Coastal Commands were doing the best they could by sparing aircraft from other tasks to reconnoitre the Norwegian coast, to sow mines and to bomb. Even long-range Blenheim fighters were sent all the way to hunt enemy aircraft in the region of Stavanger and Bergen. Bombing raids were carried

out against the two German-occupied airfields at Aalborg, Denmark.

On April 15, Britain's 24th Guards Brigade arrived at Harstad. Next day, 146 Brigade landed at Namsos. On the 18th, 148 Brigade landed at AAndalsnes and part of the 5th Demi-Brigade Chasseurs Alpins landed at Namsos.

On April 21, No.263 (Gladiator) Squadron sailed for Norway in the aircraft carrier HMS *Glorious*. None of its 18 pilots had ever done a deck landing or take-off, so Fleet Air Arm pilots flew the 18 Gladiators on board for them. At 1700hrs on April 24, 50 miles (80km) to seaward of Trondheim, the RAF pilots flew them off, each flight of nine led by a naval Skua two-seater, which carried a navigator, to guide them in the threatening weather. By 1900hrs all the fighters had landed on the frozen Lake Lesjaskog. During the night the carburettors and controls of the aircraft froze. The only way to warm an engine was to run it, which was done with some aircraft in readiness for dawn. The ground crews were not at full strength, so pilots had to share in guarding the aircraft.

At 0445hrs on the 25th two Gladiators took off on patrol and shot down an He 115. At 0745hrs the Luftwaffe began dive-bombing and strafing the lake. By 1230hrs bombs had destroyed eight Gladiators, four of which had not even flown. At 1305hrs bombs destroyed four aircraft and wounded three pilots. All day, aircraft took off whenever they could, harrassed by bombers. There were several combats and two He 111s were destroyed. By the evening, 11 Gladiators had been burned out and two, beyond repair, were set

Below: The Gloster Gladiator was the last of the British biplane fighters. They were used in Norway, flying from a frozen lake, but their performance was insufficient when opposed by much faster modern aircraft.

alight. The squadron moved to Setnesmoen. On the 26th only three Gladiators were left. Next day there was none. The squadron had flown 49 sorties and made 37 attacks against enemy aircraft. Six victories were confirmed by the finding of wreckage, and eight claims remained unconfirmed. On April 28 the squadron personnel embarked in a cargo vessel and arrived in England on May 1.

On May 20 the re-formed No.263 Squadron flew their new Gladiators off the aircraft carrier HMS *Furious*, 100 miles (160km) from Bardufoss, led by two Fleet Air Arm torpedo/reconnaissance Swordfish. In low cloud and mist, two fighters crashed, killing one pilot and severely injuring the other. On the 21st the squadron flew 40 standing patrols. On the 22nd it flew 54 sorties. One pilot was killed in action against He 111s. An airfield had been prepared at Bodø, with shelters and underground accommodation. On May 26 three Gladiators began operating from there.

No 46 (Hurricane) Squadron had been sent to join No.263. On May 26 the new arrivals took off in their Hurricanes from HMS *Glorious*, to attempt a landing on the Skånland airstrip where a wire mesh runway had been laid. Ten landed but sank four inches (10cm) through the soft ground, and two pitched onto their noses. The remaining eight were diverted to Bardufoss. Next day another Hurricane stood on its nose at Skånland, so the remaining seven also moved to Bardufoss.

In bad weather and under heavy bombing, the two squadrons slogged on until June 7. By then 263 had flown 389 sorties over 12 days, been in combat 69 times and claimed 26 successes. No 46 had also operated on 12 days to take part in 26 fights and claim 11 kills and eight probables. No 263 landed their remaining eight Gladiators on *Glorious* during June 7. No 46, none of whom had yet attempted a deck landing, followed with their 10 Hurricanes.

Left: Reconnaissance is one of the most important functions in all warfare. German groundcrew remove a long focal length camera from a Dornier Do 17P following a successful mission over France.

On June 8 the German battle cruiser *Scharnhorst* sank *Glorious* with 1,474 of her ship's company and 41 officers and men of the RAF. Only two of the pilots who had fought so bravely and endured so much hardship in Norway survived.

This brief campaign contributed nothing directly that was of any help to Fighter Command in the Battle of Britain. On the contrary, it deprived the RAF of over 30 experienced fighter pilots and 36 aircraft. The operating conditions bore no resemblance to those in the coming Battle. Altogether, it was an entirely wasteful venture except for one significant indirect influence it had on the Battle of Britain, in Britain's favour. Luftwaffe losses were 79 bombers and 68 Ju 52 transport aircraft. Among the Luftwaffe crews lost were several that were experts at blind bombing by radio beam. Training replacements greatly delayed the introduction of this highly effective technique to night bombing against British industry and seaports, and cities such as London, Coventry and Liverpool, where the prime target, though denied by Germany, was the civilian population.

The Blitzkrieg

While this brief and hopeless campaign was being waged, the Blitzkrieg had burst upon Holland and Belgium as the first move in Germany's long-awaited attack on France. The most important weeks of the whole prelude to the Battle of Britain were imminent. L'Armée de l'Air has always maintained that the Battle of Britain really began in May 1940,

Above: A sad scene as a member of the Luftwaffe examines the remains of this Potez 63 on an airfield in Northern France. In the background can be seen the Messerschmitt Bf 109Es belonging to the new occupants.

and that it has never been given due credit for the part it played in Fighter Command's victory six months later by the damage the French inflicted on Luftwaffe aircraft and air crews in May and June.

The delay in making the assault had not been caused by the weather alone. On January 10 a Luftwaffe major flying from Münster to Bonn with the detailed operational plan for the attack was blown off course in bad weather and forced landed in Belgium. The Belgians handed the documents to the Allies and Germany had to make a new plan.

At dawn on May 10 the Luftwaffe struck. Ignoring the Maginot Line, the Germans simply went around its northern end. In addition to the brilliant use of aircraft and armour in cooperation they exploited their other new technique, the spearhead of paratroops and airborne infantry, both carried in Ju 52s. The first targets in Holland were its capital, The Hague, its main port, Rotterdam, the military airfields, and the bridges across the Rhine at Dordrecht and Moerdijk, which had to be kept intact for the advancing ground forces. In Belgium, the objectives were the two Albert Canal bridges, and Fort Eben Emael on the frontier. Paratroop engineers landed on the fort and blew up the anti-aircraft guns and artillery emplacements, with a new high explosive and equipment carried in another innovation, towed gliders. The garrison held out for 24 hours.

With 136 divisions, the Germans were outnumbered by the 149 divisions of the BEF, the French, Belgians and Dutch. But their air force was bigger than the four opposing ones combined, their tactics were dazzling and their High Command was cleverer than those of Britain and France. They also had the supreme advantage of unity, whereas communication in every respect between the British and French ground and air commands was poor. The German tanks were concentrated in armoured divisions, which gave them maximum effectiveness. The British were similarly organised, but had not sent any armour to France. The powerful French tank force was mostly fragmented in support of the infantry.

The Luftwaffe had at its disposal 860 Bf 109s, 350 Bf 110s, 380 dive bombers, 1,300 long-range bombers, 300 long-range recce aircraft, 340 short-range recce aircraft, 475 Ju 52 transports and 45 gliders.

The British Air Forces in France had seen little change since their arrival. In the Air Component, Nos.607 and 615 Squadrons were converting from Gladiators to Hurricanes. The AASF had gained two Blenheim squadrons in place of two Battle squadrons and on the afternoon of May 10 was joined by No.501 (Hurricane) Squadron of the Auxiliary Air Force, with which Sergeant J.H. ''Ginger'' Lacey was serving.

The air forces of the Low Countries were rapidly swamped and their airfields captured. The Dutch Air Force, *De Luftvaartafdeling*, numbered 124 aeroplanes. The 1st Regiment had one reconnaissance squadron, one medium bomber squadron, and four fighter squadrons with a strength of 20 Fokker D31s and 23 Fokker G1As. The 2nd Regiment had four reconnaissance squadrons, and two fighter squadrons flying Fokker D31s and Douglas DB8s.

L'Aéronautique Belge mustered 157 aeroplanes. The 1st Regiment consisted of 59 reconnaissance types. The 2nd Regiment comprised 78 fighters: 11 Hurricanes, 13 Gladiators, 30 Fairey Foxs and 24 Fiat CR423. The 3rd Regiment had 40 reconnaissance and light bomber types.

There had been little growth in the French Air Force; indigenous manufacture was slow and deliveries were awaited from the United States. The first Bloch 151 and 152 single-seater fighters had been delivered. These had a 1,080 hp Gnome-Rhône engine, two 20mm cannon and two 7.5mm machine guns. Their top speed was 323mph (520km/h) and ceiling 32,810ft (10,000m). From February the Potez 631 had six additional 7.5mm machine guns, under the wings.

On May 10, 1940, which is when the French insist that the Battle of Britain began, l'Armée de l'Air fighter groupements and groupes had available to them 828 combat aircraft, of which 584 were serviceable. Of these serviceable aircraft, 293 were Morane Saulnier MS 406s, and 121 were Bloch 151s and 152; the others were Curtiss 75s, Dewoitine 520s and Potez 630s and 631s.

Operationally, l'Armée de l'Air basic organisation was territorial, with four *Zones d'Opérations Aérienne:* Nord (ZOAN), Est (ZOAE), Sud (ZOAS) and Alpe (ZOAA).

While the Dutch and Belgian Air Forces were being knocked out and the vagaries of the rudimentary control and reporting system were starving the British Air Forces in France of information, both the AASF and Air Component were hectically embroiled in the air

Above: Spread out to present a diffuse target against air attack, the 25th Panzer Regiment takes a break before crossing the Somme. In the foreground is a PzKpfw Mk IV while behind are Czech-built PzKpfw 38(t)s.

Below: An eight-wheel SdKfz 232 armoured command car advances through a smoke screen in Luxembourg in May 1940. The Wehrmacht blitzkreig concept was highly successful in France.

battle. Nos 85, 87, 607 and 615 Squadrons had seen little action hitherto. No 1 Squadron had shot down 26 enemy aircraft, and No.73 Squadron 30 during their first eight months in France. From May 10 onwards all the fighter squadrons were fully stretched from dawn to sunset.

On the first day of the Blitz, Kain bagged a Do 17. On the following day he shot down another and an Bf 109. On the 12th, an HS 126. Orton, who by now also had a DFC, was shot down on the 10th but got his own back next day by destroying a Ju 88 and a Do 17. Clisby, the fiery and aggressive Australian, made two kills on the 10th, both Do 17s, before being hit by French anti-aircraft fire. On the 11th he brought three Bf 109s down, followed on his last sortie that day with an He 111. This landed in a field and Clisby lobbed in beside it to make sure none of the crew got away. One of them did run for it, but Clisby sprinted after him and brought him down with a rugby football tackle.

Three more Hurricane squadrons arrived to join the Air Component: No.504 on the 10th, Nos 3 and 70 on the 11th. By then No.501 had settled in and Flying Officer Pickup had recorded its first kill, a Do 17. ''Ginger'' Lacey flew two sorties that day but did not encounter the enemy. Six of his comrades were luckier: Pilot Officer C.L. Hulse and Sgt P. Morfill each got a Bf 110; Flying Officer C.E. Malfroy, a New Zealand Davis Cup player, and F/Sgt A.D. Payne each shot down an He 111 and Flt Lt E.S. Williams and Sgt R.C. Dafforn destroyed Do 17s. The day after that, Lacey flew patrols totalling 3 hours and 45 minutes without result. Others on the squadron destroyed 12 of the enemy.

The first hours of the Germans' surprise attack had brought disaster to the Fairey Battle squadrons. Nos 12, 103, 105, 142, 150, 218 and 226 were all ordered to make a low-level attack on a German column in Luxembourg strongly protected by 20mm and 37mm Flak. Thirty-two bombers went in at 250ft (75m) and 13 were shot down. All the others were damaged. On May 11, Do 17s bombed Condé-Vraux airfield, where they destroyed six of No.114 Squadron's Blenheims and left all the remainder unserviceable. Enemy troops on the move in Luxembourg were again a target for eight Battles, of which only one, severely damaged, returned.

May 12, incongruously Whit Sunday, witnessed one of the most tragic and bravest ventures of the war, as well as one of the most crass. This unholy day began with the loss of seven out of nine Blenheims from No.139 Squadron during an attack against one of the ubiquitous German columns, this time near Maastricht. It was succeeded by an attack that 24 Blenheims based in England carried out on Maastricht town, where they lost 10.

The second sacrificial slaughter by the AASF occurred over the two Albert Canal bridges, for which six volunteer crews of 112 Squadron were required. Every crew stepped forward, so the first six captains' names on the squadron's daily battle order were called. The

Left: The main attribute of the Stuka was its ability to make precision attacks on small targets. The steep diving attack made aiming easy; after bomb release an automatic pull-out system operated for recovery.

wireless in one aircraft was found to be unserviceable and when the crew transferred to another its hydraulic system was proved faulty. Of the five that took off, two were shot down and their crews taken prisoner. Another crash-landed at base, full of holes. Two were destroyed, but one damaged the bridge at Weldwezelt with bombs. The leader of the formation, Flying Officer ''Judy'' Garland and his observer, Sgt T. Gray both won the Victoria Cross. With callous injustice, the air gunner, Leading Aircraftman L.R. Reynolds, was ignored.

On May 11 two of the AASF's Blenheim squadrons had been obliterated by bombs, and now, on this darkest of days yet, No.139 Squadron lost seven more Blenheims out of nine that made an attack on German troop concentrations near Maastricht.

Lacey had his first success on the 13th. Detailed for dawn patrol with two other sergeants, he could not start his engine and took off after they were out of sight. No thought of the folly of flying alone on an offensive patrol occurred to him: he was too inexperienced. At 20,000ft (6,096m), enjoying a BBC programme of dance music that was all his radio would pick up, he saw ''. . . a big, fat Heinkel all on its own''. A moment later a Bf 109 came in sight 5,000ft (1,525m) below and between him and the Heinkel. Lacey dived, shot it down at 50 yards (45m) range, then gave the He 111 the same treatment. Hardly had he landed when he was ordered on another patrol and destroyed a Bf 110.

Below: Bristol Blenheims of the Advanced Air Striking Force set out on a mission. Faster and better protected than the Battle, they were still hacked from the skies of France by the Messerschmitts and flak.

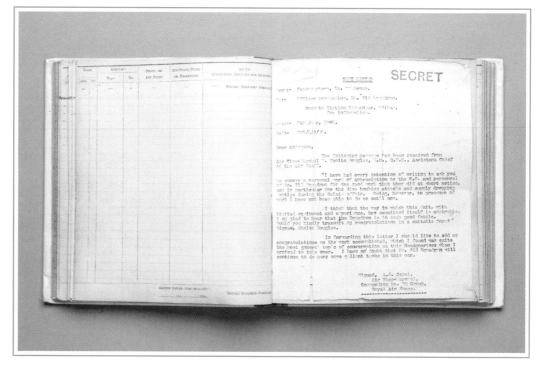

On the 14th, 35 Battles out of 63 that took off, and 10 Blenheims out of 15, were destroyed. The Air Component lost 11 Hurricanes and the AASF lost five. Against this, 12 enemy aircraft were brought down.

A momentous change in Britain's outlook on the war had coincided with the German onslaught: the dynamic and optimistic Winston Churchill had replaced the torpid and doleful Chamberlain as Prime Minister. At a meeting of the War Cabinet that morning two cardinal decisions were taken: to bomb the oil refineries and marshalling yards in the Ruhr; and

Above: A letter preserved in the logbook of Paddy Barthropp congratulates No.613 Sqn, whose Hector biplanes divebombed German troops in Calais on May 26, and dropped supplies to the British garrison.

''On May 17 1940 I flew to France from Biggin Hill, and refuelled at a base in France. It was chaos there. No food. We were carrying out day fighting missions without instructions. I went on patrol and saw the enemy for the first time: an Me 109 flew so close overhead that I could see the scratches on its fuselage. It turned to get on my tail, and I had to turn sharply toward him and got into a couple of whirls. I managed to out-turn him and got onto his tail and shot him down. I remember being frightened, and that Taffy (Higginson) had said I would be, but the enemy would be more frightened. There were times when we were terrified, but were in a state of such surprise during action that we didn't get much time to think. We would get down, then analyse the action and the tactics.

I remember tips from old-timers — like turning into the enemy's tracer when fired at from behind, since the enemy pilot would probably have re-aligned his aim and wouldn't expect you to react in the opposite direction.

One Belgian pilot who had flown Me 109s in Spain gave us some tips, and we sat goggle-eyed, listening. But, in fact, he was one of the first to be shot down in the war.''

**Air Commodore Peter Brothers
CBE, DSO, DFC.**

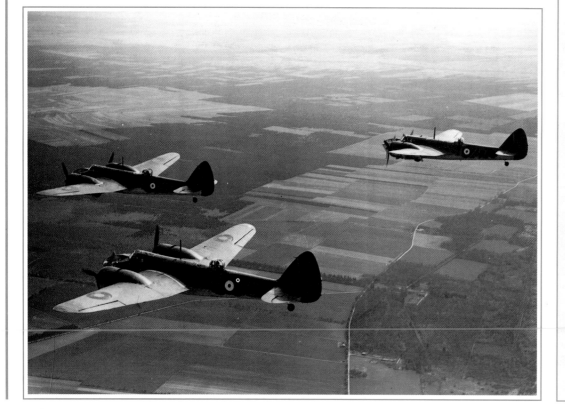

not to post any more valuable and irreplaceable fighter squadrons to France.

Fighter reinforcements were, however, being provided. Each morning one flight from each of six Hurricane squadrons flew to a French base, where it joined a flight from another squadron to make up a composite unit of 12, and operated from there throughout the day. Air Commodore P.M. Brothers, CBE, DSO, DFC, then a flight lieutenant on No.32 Squadron, recalled the fatigue this imposed. It meant being woken at 0230hrs and landing back at Biggin Hill as late as 2230hrs. But he was a flight commander and that wasn't the end of his day. The ground crews were as much a part of the squadron as the pilots, so he would visit them, probably taking a crate of beer, and tell them how the flight had fared. He made his first kill on May 19 over Dunkirk: a Bf 109.

Flights from eight other squadrons were sent for periods of a few days. Wing Commander F.W. "Taffy" Higginson OBE, DFC, DFM, was a flight sergeant on No.56 Squadron when he landed at Vitry-en-Artois on the 17th for what turned out to be a brief but turbulent spell. On the first day he shot down a Do 17 and an He 111; on the next a Bf 110. On the 19th what was left of the flight moved westwards before the rapid enemy advance, to a temporary landing ground. He was ordered to return by road to Vitry and destroy any Hurricanes and petrol that remained. He drove there through a tide of refugees, to find the Germans so close that small arms fire was audible. His only means of destroying the three or four abandoned Hurricanes was to shoot holes in the petrol tanks with his revolver and throw a match at the vapour. It was not as easy as it sounded and as soon as he had the fires raging he dashed back to his own aeroplane, the only one left at the other field. He arrived in time to see a strange pilot clambering into the cockpit. His reaction was instantaneous, irrespective of the other's rank. Taffy, a trifle under middle height, but a boxing champion and a tough rugger player, ". . . grabbed him by the collar and dragged him off the wing", he remembers, and asked, "Where d'you think you're going?"

"To England," was the reply. "Not in my ———— aeroplane, you're not!" said Taffy. Of the six pilots of No.56 Squadron who had come to France, only two returned: Taffy Higginson and one other.

The fighter pilots who achieved high scores during the Battle of France and the Battle of Britain modestly attribute the RAF's victory to their comrades who grafted away day after day exactly as they themselves had done, repeatedly met the enemy and engaged in many combats, but had only two or three confirmed victories to show for it; some claimed none at all. In their hundreds, they contributed modest scores that in aggregate far exceeded that of the star performers.

Like the Poles, Norwegians, Dutch and Belgians before them, the British and French armies had been reeling back under the weight of the German avalanche of tanks and dive bombers, supplemented by a horde of conventional bombers and swarms of fighters. With the Allied soldiery, perforce, went their air forces, stumbling in the direction of the Channel coast.

The German General Staff had remembered, while the British and French had forgotten, the basic tactical lesson of the Great War: that air power is not merely a matter of numbers of aircraft; it is the power to establish air superiority applied to conquest. The nation unable to establish air superiority over the vital area must fail to frustrate the enemy's major plans and cannot hope to influence decisively the course of the land battle to gain and hold territory. The British had proved in 1918 that they understood this, when the Royal Air Force was created as an entity independent of the Army, instead of a mere branch of it as the Royal Flying Corps had been. Trenchard, who had commanded the RFC in France, and Lloyd George, the Prime Minister, had learned that while one army can overcome another by attrition, the modern way must be first to blind the enemy by eliminating his aerial reconnaissance and then to defeat his bombers and fighters.

The Germans had blasted their way across Belgium and France along five parallel routes. From north to south, the 39th Panzer Korps under Schmidt, the 16th under Höppner, the 15th under Hoth, the 41st under Reinhardt and the 19th under Guderian had surged ahead at such speed that the British and French forces that had advanced into Belgium began retreating on May 16. On the 18th St Quentin and Cambrai were taken; Amiens and Abbeville fell on the 20th and German advanced units reached the Channel coast at Noyelles. From there the whole of Guderian's attack turned northwards towards Boulogne, Calais and Dunkirk.

Kain still figured in the headlines. On May 19 he accounted for a Ju 88, a Do 17 and a Bf 110; on the 20th an Hs 126 and, his 17th victory, a Do 17. By now he was one of the last two original pilots still with No.73 Squadron, and was kept on to train new pilots before being sent to England on leave in early June. Taking off, he did a farewell slow roll over the airfield, crashed and was killed.

Clisby took his score to 16 by May 15, before being killed in action. Orton, who in one action fought 27 Bf 109s and took out two of them, had been credited with 15 confirmed kills and three strong probables before being shot down, burned on the face and returned to England by the end of the month. No 87 Squadron, which had been marking time until May 10, soon produced some outstanding performers, one of who was Flying Officer R.M.S. "Roddy" Rayner. He opened his score with a Bf 109, an He 111 and a Do 17 on May 19 and went on to shoot down two more before being wounded in the leg and repatriated. He fought again in the Battle of Britain.

One of the least-known episodes of the air fighting over France occurred on June 5. At 1700hrs eight

Below: The most successful Defiant team, Flt Sgts Thorn (pilot) and Barker (gunner), of No.264 Squadron, who shot down seven enemy aircraft plus one shared over France, and a further five in the Battle of Britain.

Above: Dunkirk has passed into British legend; a triumph for the Royal Navy and a victory for the RAF, but for the British Expeditionary Force this picture of those who remained says it all.

Dewoitines of Groupe 2/7 took off to patrol the d'Athis-Péronne area. Within 15 minutes 15 Bf 109s bounced them out of sun. A bigger formation of 109s was covering the attackers. Warrant officer Ponteins was shot down in flames. Sergeant Bret broke away from an attack so violently that he suffered a severe heart lesion and barely managed to land. Second Lieutenant Louis was the next to go down in flames. Three others got away unharmed. Second Lieutenant Pommier Layrargues set his sights on a 109 and gave it a burst from 45 degrees off head-on. Bits flew off it and its pilot parachuted out and hid in a corn field but was seen by some infantry who caught him and took him to be interrogated.

He was the great Werner Mölders, who already had 25 confirmed victories and was destined to precede Galland as Commander of the Luftwaffe fighter arm. (The French Air Force records claim that he had 34 victories then, eight in France and the rest in the Spanish Civil War.) He asked to meet the pilot who had vanquished him, but Pommier Layrargues never knew how eminent was his adversary: he was killed in a fight with three Bf 109s a few minutes after having taken Mölders out. He was 24 years of age and considered to have a brilliant career in prospect. Mölders was in captivity for less than three weeks: France surrendered on June 22.

Some leading exponents of fighter combat and leadership who won fame in the Battle of Britain emerged from obscurity at this period. Douglas Bader, a flight commander on No.222 Squadron, shot down his first Hun on June 1: a Bf 109 over Dunkirk. Also over Dunkirk, Robert Stanford Tuck, a flight commander on 92 Squadron, drew blood for the first time when he destroyed a 109 on May 23. A day later he added two Bf 110s to his score and on the next two Do 17s. He had a third share in a Do 17 on the 25th and destroyed an He 111 and a Bf 109 on June 2. A.G. "Sailor" Malan, whom his comrades of the time regard as the outstanding leader in the Battle of Britain, shot down a Ju 88 and an He 111 on May 21, and a Ju 88, an He 111 and a Bf 109 during the next six days.

Unsung Heroes
It is fitting at this point to pay tribute to the least-known fighter pilots and their air gunners who took a massive toll of the enemy over a period of a few weeks during the spring of 1940: the air crews of 264 Squadron, who flew two-seater Defiant fighters, that are always eclipsed by the Hurricanes and Spitfires. The first Defiant squadron, No 264 commanded by Sqn Ldr Philip Hunter, a greatly liked and admired leader, had made a discouraging début on May 12 on a patrol near The Hague. A Ju 88 was seen over the sea, bombing two British ships. Hunter and two others went after it and Hunter's air gunner, Leading Aircraftman F.H. King, shot it down. On May 20, 264 Squadron shot down 17 Bf 109s without loss and 11 Ju 87s and 88s, which established an unbroken record for the number of aircraft destroyed by any squadron in one day.

The reason for this success, it appears, was that the enemy mistook the Defiant for a Hurricane. Bf 109 pilots thought they could attack it from astern with impunity but were disabused when the four guns in its rotating turret, blasted them to oblivion. Bomber crews were unperturbed when a Defiant flew in front of them for the same reason and were equally astonished to find themselves under fire. The ideal attack by a Defiant was to cross ahead of its target at 90 degrees, so that the air gunner could swing his guns to point over the beam. The guns could not fire forward, so a Defiant was defenceless against a head-on attack.

On May 27 over Dunkirk 264 Squadron met Bf 109s for the first time. Seeing eight of these, Hunter ordered the squadron to form line astern. LAC King sent a 109 down in flames. Two other Defiants shared another 109 destroyed. The squadron landed, refuelled and returned to the Dunkirk area. This time they saw 12 He 111s of which they bagged three. By May 31 the squadron's total victories stood at 65.

The Evacuation at Dunkirk
The evacuation of the British Expeditionary Force, and Allies, is one of the epic and best-recorded accomplishments of the war, and needs no full and detailed account here. The evacuation, mainly through Dunkirk, began on May 26 and continued under extreme pressure until June 4. Altogether 338,226 men were taken off the Dunkirk beaches to safety in Britain, among them 112,000 Frenchmen who wanted to keep on fighting. Remnants of the British and French armies fought on in France until the last were rescued from St Malo, Brest, St Nazaire, Nantes, Bayonne and St. Jean-de-Luz by June 19.

No 501 Squadron was the last of the RAF units to depart. It continued patrolling until June 18, first from Le Mans, then Caen and finally Dinard. On June 18 Ginger Lacey left France with five victories to his name.

The Effect on the Battle of Britain
What of the effect of those nine months of prelude to the Battle of Britain? At the outset the RAF had less knowledge of air fighting than the Luftwaffe, which had learned much in the Spanish Civil War. It returned from France enriched by new knowledge: the fighters' guns were now harmonised at 250 yards (228m) instead of 400 (365m); the tight V formation was being abandoned in favour of the flexible pairs of the Luftwaffe; the set pattern attacks had been discarded and pilots had adapted themselves to the realities of action, in which the formations of attackers and defenders split into individual combats.

Dowding, who had resisted constant demands from the French and pressure from Churchill to base more fighter squadrons in France during May and June, had proved himself right and a Commander-in-Chief of genius. Park, from whose Group the majority of the fighters that were detached to France for one or a few days belonged, demonstrated his unequalled worth as a tactical commander, and the harmony between these two men, essential to Britain's survival in the coming months, was made clear. The Battle of France was, in fact, a perfect rehearsal for the Battle of Britain.

Fighter Command, however, was weakened by the loss of many pilots and aircraft, but so was the Luftwaffe. The consequence of pilot casualties was that many British fighter squadrons were under-strength during the coming months, but the same applied to

Above: April 1940, and British fighter pilots lumber into action. It was soon standard practice to leave parachutes in the cockpit or on the wing, and hang helmets on the control column or the gunsight.

Below: We will fight them on the beaches; German style, as sappers and anti-tank troops of the Wehrmacht practice for the invasion, code-named Operation Sealion, in the summer of 1940.

the Germans. Britain had the better of it in that her aircraft production under Lord Beaverbrook exceeded Germany's, and losses of Spitfires and Hurricanes were made good more quickly than Messerschmitts were replaced.

The RAFs morale had always been high and was even higher after its success against an air force that greatly outnumbered it. The morale of the Luftwaffe after Poland, Norway, Holland and Belgium had been hugely inflated by complacency, conceit and arrogance. Its experience in France left it severely shaken.

One final question remains: why didn't Hitler invade Britain immediately he had sent the BEF and its accompanying RAF formations packing?

The answer seems to lie partly in the fact that he could not resist halting his advance at the coast in order to focus world attention on the signing of the French instrument of surrender. Another is his admitted reluctance to smash Britain because it would lead to the disintegration of the British Empire, to the benefit of the USA and Japan at the cost of German blood.

A third and highly convincing reason is that the Luftwaffe had never been properly equipped for such an operation and neither it not the Army had been suitably trained. The Luftwaffe and Army generals were experts in Blitzkrieg warfare. They were tactical geniuses and brilliant exponents of land warfare conducted by the Army and Luftwaffe in cooperation. But an assault on the British Isles would have entailed strategic planning that was entirely strange to them: they were simply not up to the task. It is true that Holland and Belgium had been taken at devastating speed by the use of paratroops. But at that time Germany possessed only 4,500 of these, and by June 1940 this force had scarcely increased in size. It was far too small to take and hold an adequate area of southern England, let alone cope with the difficulty of transporting an invading army across the Channel, when the Royal Navy dominated the seas and would have seen the German Navy off in quick time. Anyway, barges towed at an average of four knots against a current that runs at times at five knots would have been at a ludicrous disadvantage even without a determined opposition.

The most convincing reason of all is clear to anyone who has read Hitler's autobiography, *Mein Kampf*. In it he declares that his mystical intuition always warned him that any war waged against Britain must end in disaster for Germany.

AT 1100HRS ON September 3, 1939, Britain declared war on Germany. One hour and three minutes later a Royal Air Force Bomber Command Blenheim of 139 Squadron took off from Wyton on the first operational sortie of World War II. Its task was reconnaissance of German naval ports, and to ensure accurate identification of vessels a Royal Navy officer was aboard. From a height of 24,000 ft (7,270 m), in perfect visibility, he noted three battleships, four cruisers and seven destroyers in Schilling Roads, off Wilhelmshaven.

The weather was deteriorating. Thundery atmospheric conditions and the long distance from base distorted the signal reporting the sighting and delayed further action until the Blenheim landed. At 1815hrs, nine Wellingtons of 37 and 149 Squadrons from Feltwell and Mildenhall, respectively, with 18 Hampdens of 49 and 83 Squadrons from Scampton and 44 and 50 Squadrons from Waddington, were airborne on what would have been the first British bombing raid of the war. Bad weather and nightfall frustrated them and they returned without having seen their targets. By 2240hrs the Wellingtons had touched down, and the Hampdens by two minutes after midnight.

The combined firepower of the battleships or the cruisers alone would have ensured that a force of 27 contemporary medium bombers was inadequate to sink or even damage severely one quarter of the 14 ships it was intended to attack. But these two formations were a generous provision out of Bomber Command's modest total of up-to-date aircraft.

The RAF's Order of Battle at home at that date was:

Bombers: 529 Battles, 338 Blenheims, 169 Hampdens, 160 Wellingtons and 140 Whitleys. The Battles were obsolescent and only the Blenheims and Wellingtons met contemporary performance requirements.

THE RAF

Richard Townshend Bickers

Fighters: 347 Hurricanes, 187 Spitfires, 111 Blenheims, 76 Gladiators and 26 Gauntlets. The biplane Gauntlets and Gladiators were obsolescent and the three-seater Blenheims, designed as bombers, were a makeshift as nightfighters.

Coastal General Reconnaissance (GR) aircraft: 301 Ansons, 53 Hudsons, 30 Vildebeests, 27 Sunderlands, 17 Londons and 9 Stranraers.

Army Co-operation aircraft: 95 Lysanders, 46 Hinds and 9 Hectors.

There were also Oxfords, Harvards, Harts, Tiger Moths and Blackburn D2s at training schools; Magisters, Mentors and Vega Gulls for communication; Henrys and Wallaces to tow targets for gunnery practice and to exercise anti-aircraft batteries.

The total of operational types was paltry compared with Germany's. In particular the fighter strength was smaller than the Luftwaffe's and even more heavily outnumbered by the huge enemy bomber force against which it was to defend the United Kingdom. But, although Fighter Command was still at a numerical disadvantage when the Battle of Britain began ten months later, its numbers had grown and only one squadron of the obsolescent Gladiator fighters remained.

In Britain, flying by the armed forces began in 1912 with the formation of the Royal Flying Corps. It comprised two Wings: Military, under War Office control, and Naval, answerable to the Admiralty. In 1914 they separated and the Naval Wing became the Royal Naval Air Service. On April 1, 1918, both were combined to form the world's first independent air arm, the Royal Air Force, with its own Air Ministry. (In 1924 the Admiralty created the Fleet Air Arm.)

The development of British military aviation was precipitated in August 1914, when Germany, ambitious to rule Europe, invaded Britain's allies France and Belgium. The total aircraft strength of the Service was 179. When the war ended in November 1918 the RAF had 397 operational and training squadrons, at home and in France, Italy, the Middle East, India and Canada, with some 3,300 aircraft.

After the armistice the RAF quickly diminished as squadrons were disbanded, but its campaigning continued. No 221 Squadron had been sent to Russia in 1918 to help the White Russians, who were fighting the Bolsheviks, followed by 47 Squadron in June 1919. In August, No 221 returned home, then went to Somaliland in 1920 to put down a rising. No 47 stayed in Russia until April 1920.

Britain had an empire to protect. The RAF maintained a higher level of training and a sharper state of operational preparedness than any other air force

Left: At the outbreak of war, the Handley Page Hampden was numerically the most important British medium bomber. This example, from No.49 Sqn, is seen here with its standard load of 250lb bombs.

Below: Two Hurricanes of No.615 Squadron are seen taking off from Kenley early in the battle. An Auxiliary Air Force squadron, No.615 were credited with a total of 36½ confirmed victories.

Above: Spitfire Is of No.19 Sqn meet the press for the first time at Duxford on May 4, 1939. Propellors were still two-bladed and fixed pitch, while squadron codes had only recently been introduced.

Below: ''The Duster'', as the ensign of the Royal Air Force is irreverently known, carries the cockade adopted for aircraft identification during the First World War by the Royal Flying Corps.

ween India and Afghanistan, across which Pathan tribes constantly made armed forays into India.

By January 1925 the RAF, most of whose aircraft were types that had seen service in World War I, consisted of 43 squadrons and four flying training schools, stationed in Britain, Malta, Iraq, Palestine, Egypt, Aden, Sudan and India.

It was organised in geographical commands: at home, Inland Area and Coastal Area (the RAF College at Cranwell and School of Technical Training at Halton also had Area status); overseas, Middle East (headquarters in Cairo), Iraq (HQ Baghdad), India (HQ Ambala) and Mediterranean (HQ Malta).

Of its squadrons, 10 were fighter, flying the wartime Snipe or Bristol Fighter and the 1924 Grebe or Siskin; 19 were bomber, operating the wartime DH9A or Vimy, and 1924 Fawn or Virginia; two were bomber-transport, equipped with the 1922 Vernon; and 10 were Army co-operation, with the Bristol Fighter. In 1927 the Air Ministry posted squadrons to Hong Kong and Shanghai; and to Singapore in 1928.

The service was also pioneering in the wider practice of aviation. It carried mail between Britain and its army on the Rhine and between Cairo and Baghdad. It made long-distance proving flights, such as from the Cape to Cairo in 1925 and from England to Australia in 1927. Between December 1928 and February 1929 it carried out the world's first large-scale airlift when 318 British and other European women and children, followed by 268 men from the British Legation and other diplomatic missions, were evacuated from Kabul.

Later in 1929 a specially built Fairey monoplane made the first non-stop England to India flight, in under 51 hours. In 1931, flying the Supermarine S6B from which the Spitfire was developed, the RAF set the world's speed record at 407.5mph (652km/h) and

in the world and was gaining operational experience that was denied to anyone else. In 1923 the aircraft carrier *Ark Royal* took three squadrons to the Dardanelles to prevent a threatened attack by Turkey against Greece, which would destabilise the Levant. These were joined by a squadron from Egypt, another from Malta and one from Scotland. Throughout the 1920s and 1930s the Service was responsible for keeping the peace in the Middle East, where aeroplanes were the only means of patrolling the vast desert areas, and in the mountains of the North-West Frontier bet-

won the Schneider Trophy outright for three successive victories in the biennial race. In 1933 it achieved the world long-distance record of 5,309 miles (8,494km), in 57 hours 25 minutes, non-stop between Cranwell and Walvis Bay, South Africa, again in a Fairey monoplane built to Air Ministry specification. In 1937, it broke the world altitude record with a climb to 53,937ft (16,344m) in a Bristol 138A. The RAF was experienced and a world-beater in aviation matters, with excellent equipment and highly trained personnel, but was unprepared for the tremendous conflict that was to come.

A minority of officer pilots, those who had graduated at the Royal Air Force College, Cranwell, were granted Permanent Commissions. The majority entered on Short Service Commissions that gave them four or five years with the regular force and four years on the Reserve. To ensure a civilian back-up on which to draw in an emergency, the Auxiliary Air Force was formed in 1925, to train air and ground crews at weekends and annual camps. By 1939 the AAF comprised 21 squadrons. Also in 1925, the Oxford and Cambridge University Air Squadrons were raised and in 1935 one at London University.

Nazi Germany's depredations in Europe and Fascist Italy's aspirations in Africa were a warning of imminent war that would involve Britain. In 1934 the RAF Expansion Scheme was announced. The Service now numbered 52 squadrons. These would be increased to 75. In 1935, when Italy went to war with Abyssinia, Britain moved three flying boat, four fighter and five bomber squadrons from their home bases to Middle East airfields from which they could protect Egypt, East Africa and Sudan. In 1936, with Germany and Italy even more aggressively on the rampage and threatening to provoke a conflict that would engulf the whole of Europe and spill over into the rest of the world, the Air Ministry took steps to increase the strength of regular squadrons to 136. In addition, it introduced

a new stand-by pool, the RAF Volunteer Reserve, which aimed to train 800 pilots a year.

In May 1936, the RAF was restructured into four Commands: Fighter, Bomber, Coastal and Training. Geographical Commands, embracing the whole gamut of air operations, were retained overseas.

Fighter Command, with Air Chief Marshal Sir Hugh Dowding as Commander-in-Chief, had its Headquarters in Stanmore, a North London suburb. His immediately previous appointment had been on the Air Council as Member for Research and Development, so he was well acquainted with radar, an indispensable asset in his new post. Dowding had, as a captain, commanded No 9 Squadron — formerly the Wireless Squadron — in 1915, on the Western Front. In 1916, as a major, he commanded No 16, a scout — as fighters were called — squadron. Later that year, as a lieutenant-colonel, he took over 9th Wing. After the war he was successively Director of Training at the Air Ministry, and Air Officer Commanding-in-Chief, Transjordan and Palestine, before rising to the Air Council.

The Commands were sub-divided into Groups. In Fighter Command, these were on a geographical basis, further divided into Sectors, each named after its main airfield.

By the time the Battle of Britain was fought, Winston Churchill was Prime Minister of the Coalition Govern-

Above: It happened like this; just prior to the outbreak of war, the RAF Auxiliary and Reserve forces were called up. This form calls future Spitfire pilot Sandy Johnstone to No. 602 City of Glasgow Squadron.

Left: A Hawker Hart of No.6 Sqn. The standard light bomber of the RAF during the early 1930s, many Battle of Britain pilots gained their wings on the trainer variant between 1935 and 1939.

Below: The shape of things to come. Pilots of No.3 Elementary Flying Training School run to their aircraft, the ubiquitous Tiger Moth. They quickly learned that one cannot run with a parachute clipped on.

ment. Sir Archibald Sinclair, leader of the Liberals, who had been Second-in-Command of Churchill's battalion of the Royal Scots Fusiliers in World War I, was Secretary of State for Air. Air Chief Marshal Sir Cyril Newall, who, as a lieutenant-colonel, had commanded 9th Wing of the Royal Flying Corps, was Chief of Air Staff. During his three years and two months in the post, ending on 24 October 1940, he presided over the Service during the period of its most vigorous peacetime expansion. Marshal of the RAF Sir John Slessor described him as ''the prime architect of the wartime Air Force''.

Dowding was the only one of the Command C-in-Cs appointed in 1936 who was still in office. His Groups were: No.10, which began forming in January 1940 and was operational by the end of July, Headquarters at Box, Wiltshire; No.11, Commanded by Air Vice Marshal (AVM.) Keith Park, HQ Uxbridge, a London suburb; No.12, Commanded by AVM. Trafford Leigh-Mallory, HQ Watnall, Notts; No.13, Commanded by AVM. Richard E. Saul, HQ Newcastle-on-Tyne.

Bomber Command, under Air Chief Marshal (ACM.) Sir Charles Portal, with Headquarters near High Wycombe, Bucks, was divided into Groups according to the type of aircraft they flew. The operational Groups were: No.1, equipped with Battles, Headquarters at Hucknall, Notts; No.2, Blenheims, HQ Huntingdon; No.3, Wellingtons, HQ Exning, near Newmarket; No.4, Whitleys, HQ York; No.5, Hampdens, HQ Grantham, Lincolnshire. The Operational Training Groups were No.5, HQ Abingdon, and No.7, HQ Brampton, Huntingdon. For convenience, the stations in each Group were situated in as close proximity as possible. Portal had joined No.8 Squadron as an observer in 1915 before converting to pilot. From C-in-C Bomber Command he went to Air Ministry as Chief of Air Staff until the armistice. A wise and competent commander, he exercised much influence over Churchill.

Coastal Command was under ACM. Sir Frederick Bowhill, who had joined the Navy in 1904, obtained his pilot's licence in 1913 and entered the Royal Naval Air Service. With his understanding of naval needs, he was ideally fitted for his new post. His Command, which operated closely with the Navy, consisted of No.15 Group, HQ Plymouth; No.16, HQ Chatham; No.17, HQ Gosport; No.18, Pitreavie Castle, Scotland. None of these was related to any particular type of aircraft. Only No.18 Group had any geographical connotation: its squadrons were all based in the north, mostly in Scotland and the Shetlands, with one in Iceland and two in Yorkshire.

Training Command had been split, in May 1940, into Technical Training and Flying Training Commands.

Left: The uniform of Air Chief Marshal Sir Hugh Caswall Tremenheere Dowding, later Lord Dowding of Bentley Priory, as displayed in the RAF Museum at Hendon. A flyer from the very early days, Dowding commanded No.16 Squadron RFC on the banks of the river Lys in 1915 before going on to greater things. Appointed to be Commander in Chief of Fighter Command in 1936, his tenure of high office was far longer than average.

Left: The Chain Home radar stations were marked by these extremely lofty towers. Although easy to see, they proved difficult targets. Those carrying receiving equipment were of wooden construction.

Right: The last of the biplane fighters in RAF service was the Gloster Gladiator, which saw peripheral service during the battle, operating from airfields too small to accommodate the new monoplane fighters.

Below: RAF Volunteer Reserve squadrons, like the Auxiliaries, composed of weekend flyers, gave sterling service in the battle. Here future top-scoring fighter ace Johnnie Johnson undergoes instruction.

While Britain designed and built a wide variety of fighters and bombers in the two decades between the world wars, armament received scant attention. Most aircraft carried the rifle-calibre (.303 inch) Vickers gun of 1914-1918. The other RAF weapon, dating from 1916, was the American 0.3 inch Browning adapted for rimmed .303 ammunition. Fighters usually had two Vickers machine guns. The Gladiator, which entered squadron service in February 1937 and was the RAF's last biplane fighter, was the first to be armed with a battery of four machineguns: they were Brownings. Its immediate successor, the Mk 1 Hurricane, entered service in December 1937 with eight Brownings, as did the Mk 1 Spitfire when delivered to its first squadron in June 1938.

These measures were not accompanied by an equally rational training programme for fighter pilots. The individual combat techniques developed in World War I were discarded. Combat practice was reduced to six set attacks made in section, flight or squadron strength. Air-to-air firing exercises were carried out on a drogue towed behind a comparatively slow aeroplane flying straight and level.

At the outbreak of World War II the RAF, was highly efficient technically in both flying and maintaining its aircraft. It was experienced in the swift movement of squadrons from one country or continent to another. Among those who had served in World War I there reposed a substantial fund of expertise in full-scale war. In the Spitfire it had the world's best fighter and in the Hurricane another that was in many other respects better than the enemy's. But its numbers were comparatively small and its fighter combat training had been dangerously inflexible.

Numerical weakness was compensated for by possession of a unique adjunct to the country's defence: a chain of radar stations that gave early warning of air raids. The word "radar", standing for "radio direction and ranging", was coined by the Americans and adopted by the RAF in 1943. Originally, it was called "RDF", meaning "range and direction finding", which was also good security; the process was thought to be concerned solely with radio direction finding as an aircraft navigation aid, which attracted little curiosity.

Development was carried out during the 1930s and exceeded the expectation of the Air Defence Sub-Committee of the Committee for Imperial Defence. On September 16, 1935, these bodies agreed that a chain of radio detection stations should be established bet-

ween the Tyne and Southampton, to the number of about 20. These were to constitute "Chain Home", referred to as "CH".

The expected ranges at which these would detect aircraft were:

83 miles at 13,000ft (132km at 3,939m).
50 miles at 5,000ft (80km at 1,515m).
35 miles at 2,000ft (56km at 606m).
25 miles at 1,000ft (40km at 303m).

The original scheme envisaged a transmitting station every 20 miles (32km), alternate ones to have a receiver also. Each mast was to be not less than 200ft (60.6m) high, on land not less than 50ft (15m) above sea level and not more than two miles (3.2km) from the coast.

Range measurement by a transmitter-receiver station would fix an aircraft as lying in a certain circle. Measuring the time interval between the pulse transmitted by a neighbouring station would put the aircraft in a certain ellipse. Thus a transmitter-receiver with its two flanking transmitters could get a fix. Height finding was not to be introduced at first, although the height of an aircraft at 7,000ft (2,121m) altitude and 15 miles (24km) range had been measured to within one degree's error in elevation (1,200ft

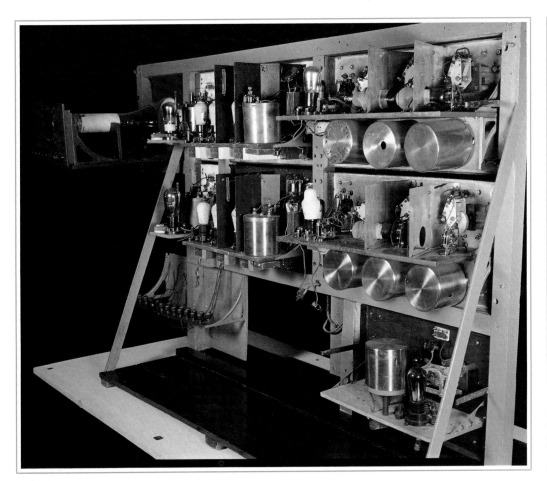

Above: British radar equipment of the period looked very cumbersome by modern standards, as shown in this RAF Museum reproduction. WAAFs proved to be excellent radar operators and more patient with inactivity than men.

Above: Rear view of Robert Watson-Watt's original radar receiver, now preserved in the Science Museum. The Germans also had radar, but the primary British advantage lay in practical application rather than having a technological lead.

/363m) by comparing signals received by two vertical aerials. In February 1936 the main experimental work was moved to Bawdsey, south of Orfordness, where a CH station was built. There, on March 13, a Hawker Hart was seen at a range of 75 miles (120km) at a height of 15,000ft (4,545m).

Trials in 1937 showed that most aircraft appearing in the observed area were reported with good accuracy up to 80 miles (128km); bearing was less reliable than range; height was good above 8,000ft (2,425m), unreliable below 5,000ft (1,515m). Estimates of the size of formations were not reliable. By the time the annual Home Defence Exercise was held in the summer of 1939, C-in-C Fighter Command Air Chief Marshal Sir Hugh Dowding reported: ''The system worked extremely well, and although doubtless capable of improvements as a result of experience, may now be said to have settled down to an acceptable standard.''

At Easter 1939, with the outbreak of war expected at any moment, the radar chain had begun continuous watch-keeping. The Germans were curious about the tall towers that had sprung up on the English coast. In May General Wolfgang Martini, Chief of Luftwaffe Signals, flew up the east coast in the airship *Graf Zeppelin*, which radar picked up and, by the size and slow

speed of the response on the cathode ray tube, identified. In August the airship, without Martini aboard, made a second sortie that radar did not detect, but which was seen by people in Scotland and intercepted outside the three-mile (5km) limit by a section of Auxiliary Air Force fighters. Both espionage ventures were abortive, as the Germans' receivers picked up only a miscellany of confused noises that betrayed nothing about the existence of radar. Generalleutnant Adolf Galland has since revealed that right up to the Battle of Britain the Luftwaffe thought that the main purpose of the towers was the detection of shipping.

Chain Home operated on a wavelength of 10 to 13.5 metres, on frequencies of 22 to 30 MHz, with 200 kW peak power output. Its range was 120 miles (192km) and it could read height. The aerials were stationary, the transmitter was on a 350ft (106m) steel tower and the receiver on a 240ft (73m) wooden one. The coverage was described as ''floodlight'', i.e., it was diffused in a wide arc or complete circle, which both inhibited the obtaining of accuracy in azimuth and allowed low-flying aircraft to go undetected. A shorter wavelength was needed to pick up at low altitude, and a rotating aerial to enable a narrow ''searchlight'' beam to sweep from side to side or be pointed in any required direction.

Such equipment was devised and formed the Chain Home Low, or CHL. Its wavelength was 1.5m, frequency 200MHz, and power output 150kW. Range was 50 miles (80km) and it could not read height. The aerial, adapted from 200MHz gun-laying radar that had also been designed at Bawdsey, was a gantry 20ft (6m) high, mounted on a 185ft (56m) tower.

The first CHL station began operating in November 1939. Mobile units were also being built. The vehicles on and in which they were installed became known as a ''convoy''. The wavelength was 5.4 to 10m, frequency 30-56MHz, power output 40kW, range 90 miles (144km) and it indicated target height. The combined CH and CHL system gave the RAF an excellent probability of detecting virtually any intruders.

At the time of the 1936 reorganisation, the main question for Fighter Command was how to make the best use of radar. A control and reporting system (in RAF parlance ''C & R'') had to be devised, to report the presence of enemy aircraft and control the movements of the fighters sent up to intercept them. Overall tactical control would be vested in Headquarters Fighter Command. Tactical control within each Group area would be delegated to Group Headquarters. Once fighters were airborne they would be controlled directly by their Sector. This meant that each Group and Sector, as well as HQ Fighter Command, had to have an Operations Room, in which the air activity within its area of responsibility could be shown. The general situation map (commonly referred to as the plotting table) in a Sector Ops Room needed to show the whole sector area and a large part of the adjacent sector or sectors. In a Group Ops Room, the whole Group area and part of the adjacent Group or Groups had to be displayed. In the Fighter Command Ops Room, a picture of the whole of the British Isles was necessary.

In addition to the CH stations, another source of information had to be integrated: the Observer Corps.

BRITISH RADAR

The Luftwaffe were never to fully appreciate the value to Fighter Command of the workings of the British detection and reporting system during the Battle. Its overall effect was to allow the outnumbered British fighters to turn up in the right place and the right time, even if not often in adequate numbers, to intercept the majority of Luftwaffe raids. It gave a flexibility to the defenders which was entirely lacking in the attackers. Had the Germans known how the system operated, they would have been able to employ anyone of three tactics; or a combination of them all. To continue attacks on the radar stations and put them out of action; to concentrate on the Sector stations from where the RAF fighters were controlled; to degrade control by swamping the system with multiple raids. In the event, the Luftwaffe followed no coherent strategy, which gave the British a defensive advantage. Some idea of the flexibility of the British system can be gained when one considers that the boundaries between Sectors were not hard and fast lines as they appear to be on a map, but really quite fluid demarcations. Squadrons from one sector could roam freely into other Sectors under their own controllers, as happened frequently during the Battle.

RAF Fighter Command
- ● High-level radar station
- ○ Low-level radar station
- ● Fighter base
- ○ Sector station
- ■ Group Headquarters
- □ Command Headquarters

Luftwaffe
- ● Bf 109 base
- ○ Bf 110 base
- ■ Bomber base
- □ Dive bomber base

LOCATION OF AIRCRAFT IN RAF FIGHTER COMMAND JULY 31, 1940

AIRFIELDS	SQUADRONS	AIRFIELDS	SQUADRONS
No. 10 GROUP		**No. 12 GROUP**	
Middle Wallop	238 Hurricane	Debden	85 Hurricane
	609 Spitfire		17 Hurricane
Filton	8 AACU, Various	Martlesham	25 Blenheim
Exeter	213 Hurricane	Duxford	19 Spitfire
	87 Hurricane		264 Defiant
Pembrey	92 Spitfire	Wittering	266 Spitfire
St. Eval (Coastal Command station)	234 Spitfire		23 Blenheim
AstonDown	5 OTU, Spitfires		229 Hurricane
	and Blenheims	Digby	611 Spitfire
Sutton Bridge	6 OTU Hurricane		46 Hurricane
Hawarden	7 OTU Hurricane		29 Blenheim
	and Spitfire	Kirton-in-Lindsey	222 Spitfire
No. 11 GROUP			253 Hurricane
Northolt	1 Hurricane	Coltishall	66 Spitfire
Kenley	64 Spitfire		242 Hurricane
	615 Spitfire	**No. 13 GROUP**	
Hawkinge	79 Hurricane	Catterick	41 Spitfire
Biggin Hill	32 Hurricane		219 Blenheim
	610 Spitfire	Church Fenton	73 Hurricane
Gravesend	604 Blenheim	Leconfield	616 Spitfire
North Weald	56 Hurricane		249 Hurricane
	151 Hurricane	Usworth	607 Hurricane
Hornchurch	54 Spitfire	Turnhouse	141 Defiant
	65 Spitfire		245 Hurricane
Tangmere	43 Hurricane	Drem	602 Spitfire
	145 Hurricane		605 Hurricane
	601 Hurricane	Grangemouth (22 Group station)	263 Hurricane
	FIU Blenheim	Wick (Coastal Command station)	3 Hurricane
Southend	74 Spitfire	Castletown	504 Hurricane
Manston	600 Blenheim	Dyce (Coastal Command station)	603 (1 flight) Spitfire
Croydon	1 (Canadian) Hurricane	Montrose (Flying Training Command station)	603 (1 flight) Spitfire
	501 Hurricane		
	111 Hurricane	Acklington	152 Spitfire
Hendon	257 Hurricane		72 Spitfire
	24 Various		

This organisation originated in 1914 on the outbreak of World War I. The Royal Naval Air Service being responsible for home defence, the Police were instructed to report to the Admiralty by telephone when enemy aircraft were seen or heard. In 1916, the Army, of which the Royal Flying Corps was an arm, took over from the Admiralty. Cordons of civilian observers were now positioned at a radius of 30 miles (48km) around vulnerable areas, to inform the War Office when they saw or heard enemy aircraft and, if possible, to give an estimate of course and height. In 1921 the Observer Corps was restructured into observation posts that reported to observation centres reporting in turn to Fighting Area HQ, which was responsible for the defence of Great Britain.

By the time the RAF was restructured in 1936, the Observer Corps had grown in numbers. It took over from radar the tracking by sound and sight, and reporting, of aircraft when they crossed inland over the coast. The Observer Corps was a body of mostly part-time civilian members. At the end of the war the accuracy of their estimations was assessed most commendably. Height: visual, average error 10 per cent up to 20,000ft (6,060m); sound, 20 per cent. Strength: visual, exact; sound, good.

With three systems (Chain Home, Chain Home Low and the Observer Corps) reporting aircraft movements, a means of resolving disparities and duplication had to be found. Filtering was the name given to this process. At Bawdsey, an experimental filter room was set up in July 1937, to sort out the plots passed by the three CH stations then operating — Bawdsey itself, Dover and Canewdon (Essex) — and telling the filtered plots through to the Ops Room at Fighter Command during the annual exercise in August. On November 8, 1938, this was closed and the Filter Room opened at HQ Fighter Command.

A report from Bawdsey on August 30, after the annual exercise, noted:

''Information is to be told to Groups and thence broadcast simultaneously to Sectors:

''Experience with Biggin Hill has shown that Sectors require information accurately and speedily at a rate of one plot per minute per raid.

''Information required by the three Groups will be obtained by at least 15 RDF stations, the observers (NB: the people who read the display on the cathode ray tube) at which, in time of high raid density, will tell plots at a high rate. This information is to be filtered and passed accurately and speedily to Groups and Sectors simultaneously. This means that on the average, when stations are all bringing in raids, the Group teller will have to tell information received from 5 RDF stations and will therefore have to tell information at five times the rate of the RDF observers.

''A Sector requires information accurately and speedily at the rate of one plot per minute per raid.

Left: Pilots of No.64 Squadron run to their Spitfires during a practice scramble in April 1940. This unit was to be in the front line for most of the Battle, and by the end of the Summer of 1940 was credited with a total of 43 combat victories.

If each Sector can handle even four simultaneous raids, plots must be received at the rate of four per minute."

No. 11 Gp had six sectors; Nos. 12 and 13 had three each. Hence the Filter Room had to pass plots at the rate of 12 per minute to Nos. 12 and 13 Gps, and 24 per minute to No. 11 if all Sectors were to be able to work to capacity. These were only the plots required by Sectors for interception, but there would also be information on distant approaching raids to tell.

In July 1940 Nos. 12 and 13 Gps each had six Sectors and No. 11 had 8. By the following month, with No. 10 Gp operational, three more Sectors were added. No. 10 in fact had four Sectors, but one of these had formerly been in No. 11, which now was reduced to 7. With four Groups totalling 27 Sectors, it is clear why careful selection of radar operators, plotters and filterers was essential.

When the war began, the control and reporting system, the most sophisticated in the world, was functioning smoothly. By the time the first sorties in the Battle of Britain were flown, it had reached a degree of efficiency far higher than that of the equivalent German organisation.

The Women's Auxiliary Air Force provided an increasingly large proportion of the personnel employed within it, at radar stations and Filter and Operations Rooms. This body, formed on June 28, 1939, was the successor to the Women's Royal Flying Corps of World War I, which had become the Women's Royal Air Force in 1918 and been disbanded in 1920. When three typists in the early days at Bawdsey had been trained to read and tell the responses on a cathode ray tube, it became apparent that women adapted better in many ways than men to this type of work.

The young women selected to be "Clerks, Special Duties", their camouflaged job description, and known less pompously as "plotters", had to have a higher than average educational standard. Predominantly, they belonged to the class that their comrades described as "boarding school girls". To the pilots, who were

Above: A view of the operations room at 11 Group Headquarters, showing some of the "beauty chorus". Filter staff occupy the raised position, with the "croupiers" at table level with their rakes at the ready.

Below: Three WAAFs from Biggin Hill were decorated during the Battle. Seen here in October 1940 are, from left to right, Sgt Joan Mortimer MM; Flying Officer Elspeth Henderson MM; and Sgt Helen Turner MM.

Above: A WAAF recruiting poster from 1940. The girls filled many important roles, freeing men for other duties. At first regarded as suspect under fire, they were to prove themselves solid as rocks.

supposed to visit the Ops Room frequently, in order to understand the difficulties of the Controllers' job, they were ''the beauty chorus'' and it was more the sight of a group of attractive girls than duty that drew the young men there.

The Observer Corps was organised in posts and groups. The system was fully tested during the exercise in August 1939. Secrecy about radar was so strict that, although the Corps was under the Air Ministry and received information from the radar chain, only a few officers were allowed to know the details of how this was obtained.

Posts were sited at any convenient place that allowed a good field of view: rooftops were good vantage points. They were not comfortable places in which to spend several hours at a time. In a small sandbagged enclosure with scant weather protection, equipped with an instrument for estimating height and position of aircraft, binoculars and a telephone, these dedicated men kept watch. Every group HQ had a centre where 12 plotters seated around a map table each received information from two or three posts, thus co-ordinating the efforts of about 30 posts.

Here again, the problem of duplication had to be resolved. A teller passed the plots to a maximum of six Fighter Sectors. An Observer Corps Liaison Officer was on duty at each Fighter Group. At the period with which we are concerned, there were some 30,000 observers, manning more than 1,000 posts radiating from 32 centres.

It was in the Sector Operations Rooms, ''the sharp end'', that direct action against the enemy resulted from this nationwide and complicated network of interlocking data, which converged on the general situation map, the GSM.

An Ops Room had a thick concrete roof and surrounding blast walls. The main floor was some five feet (1.5m) below ground level. The GSM, with plotters wearing head-and-breast sets sitting or standing around it receiving filtered plots, occupied most of the space. With a long rod like a croupier's rake, the plotters moved arrows representing a single aircraft or a formation. A wall clock was divided into five-minute segments successively coloured red, yellow and blue. The arrows forming a track corresponded in colour with the current segment. Thus the Controller could see whether it was fresh or stale. Beside the track was a small block with an identification letter and track number. ''F'' in red on a white ground stood for ''friendly''. ''X'' in black on a yellow ground meant ''unidentified''. A black ''H'' on yellow was ''hostile''. A plot was known as a ''raid'', whether identified as friendly or hostile.

On the first tier of positions overlooking the GSM, running along one side of the large room, sat two NCO deputy controllers. On the next level, stepped slightly back, sat the Controller, a squadron leader in rank: in the early days of the war, this would be a pilot or observer, probably one who had flown in World War I. Gradually, to meet the growing need, non-flying officers were trained in the work. The controller had two assistants: Ops B, a junior RAF or WAAF officer, and Ops A, usually an airwoman.

There was also a Royal Artillery anti-aircraft liaison officer, who warned anti-aircraft sites when friendly aircraft were near their area and ordered them to cease fire when any entered it and also tried to prevent friendly aircraft being illuminated to the benefit of the enemy.

On the wall facing the Controller's dais were the clock, and the aircraft state boards on which the

number of aircraft available in each squadron was shown, with the various states of availability to which the Group Controller had ordered them.

''Stand-by'' meant that the engine had been warmed up and the pilot was strapped into his cockpit, ready to be airborne in two minutes. ''Readiness'' called for pilots to run to their aircraft and take off within five minutes. The average time for a whole squadron to be off the ground was three minutes. The usual states of availability were 30 minutes or an hour, which meant that pilots had to be at their dispersal point on the airfield perimeter, either in the rest hut or, in fine weather, sitting outside it. Sometimes the Group Controller would order 10 or 15 minutes availability, or two hours, when pilots were allowed to be anywhere on the station (in their messes, if they wished). The final state was ''Released''.

Ops A took instructions from Group — such as ''One flight of 222 Squadron come to readiness''; ''64 Squadron to 30 minutes''; ''56 Squadron released''. He wrote this on a pink form and gave that to the Controller who, having read it, handed it to Ops B, who took action. For example, this might have involved calling the squadron concerned on the telephone and passing on the order.

Behind the Controller's dais were four radio-telephony (R/T) cabins with WAAF, or airmen on listening watch. The transmitter was situated elsewhere within the station, on open ground. The HF receiver was in the cabin and the operator had the often difficult job of tuning it. When, late in the Battle, VHF began to be installed, the receiver was also remote from the cabin and kept tuned on site.

When one of the station's squadrons was ordered to take off — singly, or as one section, or a flight, or the whole 12 — the Controller would speak to the leader on the R/T and tell him what course and height to fly and the enemy's position, height, course, and numbers, and all other essential information. He would try to direct the fighter(s) to the best position — up-sun — but usually the individual pilot or leader preferred to make his own tactical decisions. The Controller would continue informing and directing until contact with the enemy was made.

Mention has been made of Biggin Hill in connection with exercises carried out at Bawdsey. In 1936, No.32 Squadron, stationed at Biggin Hill and flying Gauntlets, carried out the first exercises with the first embryo Sector Operations Room. It was as a result of these exercises that, with the pilots having the major say, the R/T code was drawn up.

All exchanges on the R/T were logged, so the operators had to write fast and use abbreviations: ''V''

Left: The 11 Group Operations Room at Uxbridge was the nerve centre of the Battle; the place where momentous decisions were made. The ''tote board'' on the far wall shows the exact states of readiness of the British fighter squadrons sector by sector, while below them is the famous colour coded clock used to determine old plots, which are then cleared from the table. Note that the controller's view is from the German angle!

R/T CODES

CODEWORD	MEANING
Scramble	Take off
Saunter	Minimum cruising speed
Liner	Economical cruising speed
Buster	Maximum cruising speed
Gate	Maximum speed. Limited to 5 minutes
Vector	Course to steer
Angels	Height in thousands of feet
Orbit	Circle a given point or present position
Pancake	Land, refuel and rearm
Bogey	Unidentified aircraft
Bandit	Enemy aircraft
Tallyho	Am about to attack. It was also commonly used by pilots to announce that they had sighted the enemy: who might be many miles away, and too far to attack at once.

Right: The Ops Room at Fighter Command HQ, Bentley Priory, appears very much an ad hoc affair compared with that of 11 Group. As is obvious, the whole country had to be covered rather than just Southern England, and everything is thus to a much smaller scale.

for vector, ''A'' for ''Angels'', ''T/H'' for ''Tallyho'', a circle with a dot in the centre for ''Orbit'', ''RULC'' for ''Receiving you loud and clear''. ''R'' stood for ''Strength''. If a message said, ''Receiving you strength five'', it was logged as ''RUR5''. ''Target'' was ''tgt''. ''Are you receiving me?'' became ''RURM''. ''Listening out'' was ''L/O'', and ''Over'' was ''O''.

The method of stating figures was also laid down. To avoid confusion, some were given in whole numbers and others in separate digits: Vector in separate digits (eg, Vector one-five-zero); Angels in whole numbers (eg ten, fifteen, twenty-two) *never* in separate digits.

To avoid mishearing through heavy atmospherics or other interference on the R/T, a set pattern was used

by controllers. In this way, pilots knew what the first, second, third, etc, parts of a faintly heard message must be about. First, the pilot had to be told his course and height: ''Vector two-three-five, Angels twenty-one.'' Next, where to look. The enemy's relative position was given in clock code, taking 12-o'clock as dead ahead of the pilot: ''Bandit(s) three-o'clock''. Then, how far away the enemy was: ''Ten miles''. Then enemy height; ''Bandit's angels thirteen''.

At the end of a message that required no answer, the caller, whether Controller or pilot, said ''Listening out'' or ''Out''. If an answer were required, the ending was ''Over to you'' or ''Over''. The ludicrous ''Over and out'' much used in fiction would have been

a contradition. (The acknowledgments ''Roger'', meaning ''Received'', and ''Wilco'' for ''I will comply'', also misused in fiction, were US Air Corps terms adopted by the RAF in 1943 and unknown in the Battle of Britain.)

The TR9D HF transmitter-receivers in aircraft were of poor quality. Their range was rated 35 to 40 miles (56 to 64km) at 15,000ft (4,545m), although in ideal

Below: RAF headgear, clockwise from top left: ORs and NCOs; officers; officers ''operational hat''; Group Captain; field rank officer's cap badge; officer's then ORs and NCOs glengarry; chaplain's cap badge.

conditions this could be more. The set was vulnerable to all manner of interference, including BBC radio programmes. It had two channels, of which only one was available for voice. Each squadron operated on a different frequency. The second channel was common to all and used for the transmission of a 1,000-cycle note, a shrill whistle, codenamed ''Pipsqueak'', which sounded for 14 seconds. One aircraft in each formation was allocated a quadrant of each minute during which its pipsqueak would come on. While it was transmitting, the voice channel was cut off. The purpose of the device was to fix the position of a single fighter or a formation every minute. With VHF, voice transmissions were used and a good, experienced operator could take an accurate bearing in five seconds.

A sector had three direction-finding (D/F) stations sited at the corners of a triangle about 30 miles (50km) apart, each of which was tied by landline to a position at the fixer table, a much smaller version of the GSM and placed in the Fixer Room, off the main plotting hall. The site of each D/F station on this map table was surrounded by a compass rose marked in 360 degrees. A length of string was anchored at the site. As each station took a bearing on a pipsqueak, it passed it to a plotter who laid off the string along the given bearing. The point at which they intercepted was the fix, the position of the aircraft. A fourth plotter told this through to the GSM, where the fighter's track was duly shown by a fresh arrow. If the cut was precise, it was a first class fix. If the strings formed a small triangle, it was second class and the centre of it was taken as the fix. If they formed a big one, it was known as a ''cocked hat''.

This was the most useful way of showing the position of friendly fighters because the fix was obtained and plotted within seconds. One of a Controller's most acute problems was that plots that had been through the filtering system were a couple of minutes late by the time he saw them on the GSM. During the interval between being picked up by radar or Observer Corps and plotted at Sector, aircraft had moved several miles and their relative positions might have altered drastically, making interception of a Hostile lengthy or impossible.

Pilots had individual two-figure callsigns, starting at 14 for the squadron commander, which were always given in separate digits. Sectors and squadrons also had callsigns, mostly of two syllables, which were changed from time to time for security. A typical call from the Controller to a single aircraft would be ''Hello Tomcat One-Four. This is Locust calling. How do you read me?'' This would soon be abbreviated to ''Tomcat One-Four from Locust. D'you read?''

When VHF became general and reception much clearer, with ranges of over 100 miles (160km) at 20,000ft (6,060m) in good conditions, messages became briefer. VHF aircraft sets had four channels with push-button selection. Two were guard frequen-

Right: A handful of Americans flew with Fighter Command during the Battle. The ''Three Musketeers'' shown here are Andy Mamedoff, Red Tobin, and Shorty Keough, of No.609 Squadron.

cies on which a 24-hour listening watch was maintained for aircraft in trouble. Command Guard was common to all Fighter Command aircraft and Group Guard common to all those in that Group.

The four sections of three aircraft in a squadron were identified by a colour. This had no physical significance such as aircraft markings. ''A'' Flight's sections were Red and Yellow; ''B'' Flight's Blue and Green. When operating in section, flight or squadron strength, pilots' callsigns would be their section colour followed by the number of their position in it. The Leader was ''One'' (eg, ''Red One''), his right wing man ''Two'', and left winger ''Three''.

Radio had also become a valuable source of in-

Above: A post-sortie discussion, March 1940 as the pilots gather around the CO. On the extreme left is Gp Capt. Kenneth Brian Cross, DSO, DFC, who is wearing the old fashioned Sidcot suit for this mission.

telligence before the war. The organisation that provided it was the Y Service, which listened to German broadcasts and provided clues to the *Luftwaffe*'s strength, movement and intentions, helping the Intelligence Branch to compile the *Luftwaffe*'s Order of Battle. Coded messages were broken down at the Government Code and Cypher School, Bletchley Park.

At first the Y service was confined to Morse transmit-

POLISH PILOTS WITH THE RAF

The total number of Polish fighter pilots who took part in the Battle of Britain was 145. There were 85 pilots flying with the RAF Squadrons and 60 pilots flying with two Polish Squadrons: 302 and 303. The combat record of these pilots is shown in the table of enemy aircraft destroyed or damaged.

	Destroyed	Probably destroyed	Damaged
302 Polish Squadron	17	11	2
303 Polish Squadron	125	14	9
Polish pilots in the RAF squadrons	77½	16	29
Total	219½	41	40

Included within this total number are enemy aircraft shot down by two commanding officers and four flight commanders in the two Polish squadrons who were British RAF officers. (One flight commander was F/Lt John Kent, a Canadian.)

302 Polish Squadron	3	3	0
303 Polish Squadron	15	5	3
Total	18	8	3

302 and 303 Sqns were all-Polish, but when first formed they had British squadron and flight commanders. Later, Poles took over these posts.

Above: Volunteer pilots from nations in occupied Europe, such as Poland and Czechoslovakia, established an enviable record whilst serving in the RAF, whether as individuals or in complete squadrons.

ted by wireless telegraphy (W/T). In December 1939 steps were taken to begin listening to R/T on the 40 megacycle band. No suitable sets were made in England, so some Hallicrafter 510s, manufactured in the USA and popular among radio "hams", were bought and set up in a hut at Hawkinge by March 1940. Two months later the first message was picked up. Only then did anyone realise that none of the operators knew German. A German-speaking soldier on an anti-aircraft site at the airfield was found and rushed to the R/T receiver, and willy-nilly transferred to the RAF within days.

What was really needed were not people who had studied German academically but those who had lived in Germany and acquired a command of idiom. Recruiting from within the WAAF began immediately and by June 15 six airwomen had been posted to a new listening site at Fairlight, near Hastings, equipped with two Hallicrafters.

Left: Typical flying clothing of an RAF fighter pilot is shown in this RAF Museum presentation. A fleece-lined leather flying jacket is worn over the standard uniform to protect the wearer from cold at high altitude and similar leather flying boots protect the feet. A 'Mae West' life jacket, flying helmet with face mask and goggles, silk scarf and a seat parachute harness complete the ensemble.

Above: Two of the many Polish pilots who flew with Fighter Command during the Battle are Sgt F. Kozlowski (left) and Fg Off. S. Witorzenc of No.501 Squadron, pictured on August 16, 1940, having scored on the 15th.

Right: Naval uniforms added a touch of colour; on the left is Sub. Lt Dicky Cork, later to fly with No.242 Sqn as Douglas Bader's wingman, and Sub. Lt A. G. Blake who flew Spitfires with No.19 Sqn.

Experienced RAF wireless operators searched the air for traffic and as soon as a transmission was picked up a WAAF interpreter would take over and log it. Anything of immediate tactical significance was passed at once to No.11 Group.

Much of the traffic was from E-boats (*Schnellboote*, or fast boats, known logically to the Germans as S-boats and bizarrely to the British as above), and this was forwarded to the Admiralty via Air Ministry. Less urgent material was sent to Air Ministry for analysis.

The girls quickly learned the *Luftwaffe* R/T code and became familiar with individual enemy fighter pilots by their callsigns, accents and personalities. They recorded exchanges between fighters and bombers attacking airfields and convoys, and reports from reconnaissance aircraft when convoys were sighted. These last were passed to the naval authorities at Dover as well as to No.11 Group.

Increasing knowledge of the callsigns and frequencies used by the *Luftwaffe* enabled the listeners to warn No.11 Group of the *Geschwader* and the type of aircraft involved in an imminent attack. Some of the intercepted messages even gave the time, height and place for a rendezvous between fighters and bombers, and their target. Y intelligence was also a useful means of cross-checking reports of enemy casualties, when, in the speed and confusion of a fight, more than one pilot claimed the same victory.

Among the less salubrious events recorded were the occasions when British pilots commented on comrades

Above: Czech pilots also played a part in the Battle; this is No.310 Squadron which formed at Duxford on July 10, 1940, and which became operational as part of the Duxford ''Big Wing''.

being shot at by the enemy's gallant fighter pilots while parachuting out of aircraft they had been forced to abandon. Added to the use for reconnaissance of supposedly ambulance aircraft, allegedly on air-sea rescue missions, and the strafing of civilian refugees on French roads, which was also frequently reported, the RAF was inclined to be cynical about the *Luftwaffe*'s boast that it was fighting a clean and chivalrous war.

To provide accommodation for more sets, six more WAAF and additional RAF wireless operators, the unit was moved to Hawkinge in July. Towards the end of that month it was they who intercepted messages indicating that the enemy was using aircraft marked with

the red cross on reconnaissance over the Channel. Air Ministry duly warned the German High Command that such aircraft would no longer have immunity; as related elsewhere, Ginger Lacey was among the pilots who shot one down.

By August, the unit moved again, to a small house and adjacent toy factory at West Kingsdown on the Kentish Downs, the highest point in the county, which increased the range of the R/T receivers. The other Fighter Groups soon asked for the same information as No.11 Group was getting. The listening posts were given the name ''Home Defence Units'' (HDU) and by the time the Battle of Britain was coming to an end new ones had been set up at Street, Devon, for No.10 Group; Gorleston, Norfolk, for No.12; and Scarborough, Yorkshire, for No.13. An HDU was also placed on Beachy Head as a back-up to Kingsdown — which had become the HQ of the Y Service — to concentrate on raids against convoys and southern airfields and ports.

The examination of enemy aircraft that crashed in Britain, the interrogation of captured aircrew, and agents in Germany were other sources of intelligence, but the most prolific and versatile was photographic reconnaissance. This was one of the earliest uses to which aeroplanes had been put in World War I, yet Britain allowed it to languish in the inter-war years. It was indispensable in the planning of both strategy and tactics. In 1938 General Werner von Fritsch, Commander-in-Chief of the German Army, said, ''The military organisation that has the best photographic intelligence will win the next war.'' The RAF School of Photography at Farnborough was formed in 1912, but in the 1920s and 1930s its skills were turned mainly to the photographing of British colonial territories for map-making. The system was cumbersome. All three of the armed Services required aerial intelligence: the RAF took the photographs, but only the Army had photographic interpreters. It took a week for the results of a sortie to be delivered.

When, in 1936, information about German industry was sought, a squadron leader was sent to Germany to collect photographs and maps. It was only when Wing Commander F.W. Winterbotham, Chief of Air Intelligence in the Special Intelligence Service, wanted specific information about the *Luftwaffe's* air defence of the German frontier that aerial ''photo recce'' or ''PR'', as it was called, began to be used. In co-operation with the French intelligence organisation, the *Deuxième Bureau*, the right man was found to take on the work.

F. Sidney Cotton was an Australian pilot who had done pioneering work in Canada and Greenland and over the Atlantic. In 1938 the colour film business he owned failed. He accepted the task of spying on Germany and a company named Aeronautical Research and Sales Corporation was formed as a cover. The aircraft had to be one that could fly on ostensibly legitimate civil business. Cotton chose a Lockheed 12A, which could carry six passengers, and one was delivered in January 1939. He asked for a first-class engineer who was also a pilot, and a Canadian in the RAF, Flying Officer R.H. Niven, was selected. The *Deuxième Bureau* provided a photographer and on March 25 the operation was based at a pretty little airfield 15 miles (24km) south-west of Paris, Toussus-le-Noble.

Cotton and his crew made their first flight on March 30, over Krefeld, Hamm, Münster and the Dutch frontier to photograph the road and rail systems. More flights were made on April 1, 7 and 9, covering the Black Forest, armament factories and new aerodromes in the Mannheim area and the Siegfried Line. There was no intercommunication between cockpit and passenger cabin. Monsieur Blois, the photographer, tied a long string to each of Cotton's elbows and tugged the appropriate one to indicate the direction in which to turn! They also made flights over Italy and the North African coast.

One man who knew that special equipment and training were needed for first class PR was Air Chief Marshal Sir Edgar Ludlow-Hewitt, who had joined the RFC in August 1914 and served at the Western Front throughout World War I. When appointed C-in-C Bomber Command in September 1937 he had stated the need for a special long-range reconnaissance aircraft. But the Service showed little interest and, anyway, the Defence Budget could not afford it. He had to compromise by fitting cameras to the Blenheim bombers of Nos.21, 82, 107, 114 and 139 Squadrons. In 1938 the Air Ministry did, under pressure from him, set up the Air Intelligence Department to co-ordinate PR. In 1939 an Air Intelligence Section was introduced at HQ Bomber Command and Station Intelligence Officers were made responsible for a preliminary interpretation of photographs.

In the summer of 1939 Cotton and Niven flew to Germany allegedly to sell colour film. His camera was installed under the cabin floor in a dummy fuel tank. This ruse enabled him to fly all over the country, sometimes with German passengers, taking photographs of enormous value. Two weeks after the outbreak of war, when Blenheims on photographic sorties had suffered casualties without achieving adequate results, Sir Cyril Newall, Chief of Air Staff, authorised Cotton — who was in due course commissioned in

Above: RAF bomber flying gear shown here consisted of a 1930 pattern Sidcot suit, oxygen gear with an emergency bottle; heavy gloves and boots, all to guard against the extremes of cold found at altitude.

Below: A Hurricane of No.310 (Czech) Squadron being re-armed. Each of the eight Browning machine guns needed a belt containing three hundred rounds, which gave roughly 15 seconds of firing time.

the RAF and rose to be a wing commander — to form and command a specialised unit, for which he would select his own personnel, aircraft and equipment. Based at Heston, it was named Photographic Development Unit (PDU).

Dowding had been greatly impressed by Cotton's achievements and, in October, agreed to lend him two Spitfires so that undetected reconnaissances could be made at a height above the limit of heavy *flak* (25,000ft/7,575m), at a speed greater than the Bf 109. These Spitfires had to be stripped of guns and ammunition to reduce weight and allow adequate range and height. From take-off the aircraft could attain 30,000ft (9,090m), and as they consumed fuel their ceiling rose to 35,000ft (10,600m). They were camouflaged duck egg blue to merge with the sky and relied on speed and stealth for survival.

The first Spitfire PR sortie was flown on November 18, 1939, and revolutionised the whole concept of this means of intelligence. The Spitfires flew only 15 flights but achieved twice as much, in half the time, as seven Blenheim squadrons. Between September 3 and December 31, 1939, the Blenheims had flown 89 sorties over 2,500 square miles (6,475km²), obtained photographs on only 45 sorties and lost 16 aircraft. In just 15 sorties, the Spitfires came back with photographs on 10 and covered 5,000 square miles (12,950km²) without loss. By the end of February 1939 Cotton had three Spitfires, one of which was for training.

In bad weather, the recce Spitfire's solitary pilot was handicapped by lack of navigation instruments: of 19 sorties flown in the first quarter of 1940, weather made 13 ineffective. The PDU acquired three Hudsons in February, to reconnoitre above cloud the weather along a Spitfire's intended route and report by radio. If conditions were unsuitable for a Spitfire, the Hudson would descend below cloud and take the photographs.

On July 8, 1940, as the Battle of Britain was about to be fought, the PDU became the Photographic Unit of the RAF and command was given to Wing Commander Geoffrey Tuttle.

Among the most valuable items of intelligence

garnered by the RAF was one that was delivered from the enemy side. In the early hours of November 5, 1939, a parcel was left outside the British Consulate in Oslo with a letter signed, "A German scientist who wishes you well." In it were a proximity fuse for anti-aircraft shells, details of the new Junkers 88 and its intended use as a high-speed dive bomber, an account of German rocket development and a description of the device known as Y-Gerät that enabled German bombers to find their targets by following a beam.

A final gift to Britain's benefit was possession of a machine that could decypher German codes. It was invented in Holland and the patent was bought by a German manufacturer in 1923. It was discovered by Polish Intelligence when Customs examined one that had been sent to the German Legation in Warsaw. In 1934 the RAF began development of this machine, known as the Typex, which the Government Code and Cypher School had bought in 1928 and neglected. In August 1939 the Poles gave the British the result of their work in breaking the latest German codes.

The Germans had called their first encyphering machine "Enigma" and the British gave this name to all German cyphers. "Ultra" was the British codename for intelligence derived from Enigma and other machine cyphers. The only two commanders in the RAF who knew of Enigma and Ultra were Dowding and No.11 Group's Air Vice Marshal Keith Park. A specific instance of its importance in the Battle of Britain was that the heavy air raids on August 15, 1940 did not take these two senior officers by surprise. The information given to them was precise: *Luftflotten 2, 3* and *5* would make the attacks, which were timed to keep the defenders at full stretch throughout the day. F.W. Winterbotham, who, as a group captain, was responsible for Ultra, recorded that Dowding told him that it was of the greatest help to him to know what Goering's policy was and enabled him to use his fighter squadrons with the greatest possible economy.

Fighter Command entered the Battle of Britain with an infrastructure that provided increasingly skilled and detailed intelligence and a Ministry of Aircraft Production that achieved an output of fighters much in excess of the scheduled number. It was closely integrated with Anti-Aircraft Command, which comprised seven Divisions with an establishment of 2,232 heavy and 1,860 light guns, and 4,128 searchlights, under Lieutenant General Sir Frederick Pile.

The third weapon of defence was the barrage balloon. On November 1, 1938, Balloon Command had been formed and expanded with Auxiliary Air Force balloon squadrons. It operated in three Groups. No.31 Group consisted of Nos.901 to 910 Squadrons, numbering 450 balloons. No.31 Gp squadrons were Nos.911 to 926, with 456 balloons. No.32 Gp squadrons were Nos.927 to 935, totalling 224 balloons. No.33 Gp squadrons were 936 to 947 squadrons, with 320 balloons. As would be expected, the RAF's Order of Battle changed many times during the Battle of Britain, as shown in a later chapter. A secret document, "State of Aircraft in Operational Commands", was issued every week. In the week beginning July 5, 1940, the state of Fighter Command aircraft was as shown in the table.

RAF FIGHTER COMMAND AIRCRAFT, JULY 5, 1940

	SPITFIRE	HURRICANE	DEFIANT	BLENHEIM
No of Sqns available	19	24	2	6
Sqn Establishment	16	16	16	16
Total Establishment	304	384	32	96
Serviceable Reserve:				
In Sqns	10	112	1	0
In Air Storage Units	107	229	34	33
Total Serviceable Res.	117	341	35	53
RADAR CHAIN				
31 CH and 25 CHL stations operational.				

Above: The squadron Intelligence Officer, or "spy" was responsible for debriefing pilots after combat and making sure they submitted written reports. In real life, the pilots would take their helmets off first!

Below: No.601 was generally known as the "millionaire's squadron", and when petrol rationing was introduced early in the war, pilots kept their cars running by buying their own filling station.

FIGHTER Command's Order of Battle for August 8, 1940 shows 30 squadrons equipped with the Hawker Hurricane I, 19 squadrons of Supermarine Spitfire Is, two flying the two-seat Boulton Paul Defiant turret fighter and six squadrons of twin-engined Bristol Blenheim IFs. One squadron was equipped with ancient Gloster Gladiator biplanes, but saw no action during the period of the Battle of Britain. In the hectic weeks of the Battle itself, there was little time to re-equip the squadrons in the front line and, other than the early withdrawal of the Defiants, the disposition of the RAF's fighters remained substantially unchanged up to the end of the Battle. Thus, it was the Hurricane that bore the brunt of the fighting in the air, and was responsible for the major share of losses inflicted on the Luftwaffe, although the Spitfire was to capture the public imagination as the fighter *par excellence*.

Both Spitfire and Hurricane had been conceived at a time when ''fighter'' meant, to the RAF, a single-seat, fixed undercarriage biplane with an armament of four 0.303in machine guns and no greater concession to fighting efficiency than an enclosed cockpit for the pilot. Advances in aerodynamics, aeronautical engineering and power plant development in the mid

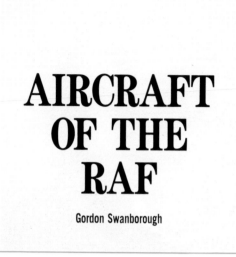

AIRCRAFT OF THE RAF

Gordon Swanborough

Below: Having borne the brunt of the air fighting over Britain during the Battle, the Hawker Hurricane went on to serve the RAF and Royal Navy in numerous other rôles for the remainder of the war. Here, a Sea Hurricane IB keeps company with two Seafire IICs.

'thirties, however, opened up the possibility of major improvements in performance and combat ability — improvements that were quickly seized upon by Reginald Mitchell and Sydney Camm in their positions as chief designers, respectively, of Supermarine and Hawker Aircraft.

Often going beyond the Air Ministry's ''official'' requirements as set out in a succession of Specification documents in the early 'thirties, Mitchell and Camm both produced low-wing monoplanes with enclosed cockpits, retractable undercarriages and eight-gun armament, powered by the then new Rolls-Royce Merlin liquid-cooled in-line engine. In design terms, the Hurricane was a little older than the Spitfire, and later in the war it would prove less amenable to development. What mattered in 1940, though, was the fact that it was available in useful numbers, was easy to fly, rugged and able to sustain considerable damage and still return to base. Slower in the climb and in level speed than the nimble Spitfire, the Hurricane was well suited to the task of intercepting the relatively slow bomber formations, leaving the Spitfires to deal with the escorting fighters. This division of roles also helped to account for the greater success of the Hurricane in kill-to-loss ratio during the Battle.

Hawker Hurricane

Design of the Hurricane had begun in 1934, and its first flight had been made, from Hawker's establishment within the confines of the historic Brooklands motor racing circuit at Weybridge in Surrey, on November 6, 1935. Sydney Camm's design team at nearby Kingston upon Thames already had long experience of fighter design for the RAF, and drew heavily upon this experience to produce what was at first seen as a ''Monoplane Fury'' — the Fury being the elegant biplane that still epitomised the equipment of Fighter Command upon its formation within the RAF in July 1936. Such advanced features as an enclosed cockpit and retractable undercarriage were combined with traditional methods of construction using a tubular metal structure and fabric covering, that meant that the Hurricane could be easily and rapidly produced in existing facilities — an advantage not enjoyed by the Spitfire with its advanced stressed-skin construction and complex shapes.

In February 1936, the prototype Hurricane (as yet unnamed), powered by an early Merlin C producing 990hp and driving a Watts fixed-pitch two-bladed wooden propeller, was tested at the Aircraft and Armament Experimental Establishment (A & AEE) at

Above: Sydney Camm became chief designer for the Hawker company at Kingston in 1925, becoming responsible for a long series of successful biplanes for the RAF and export. With the Hurricane, he combined monoplane design with an in-line engine.

Martlesham Heath, giving Service pilots their first opportunity to experience the improvements in performance and handling that were to become available. At a weight of 5,672lb (2,572kg), the prototype demonstrated a speed of 315mph (506km/h) at the Merlin's rated altitude of 16,200ft (4,937m) with 6lb/sq in boost. After taking off into a 5mph (8km/h) wind with a run of 795ft (242m) to reach the 81mph (130km/h) lift-off speed, the Hurricane climbed to 15,000ft (4,570m) in 5.7 minutes and to 20,000ft (6,100m) in 8.4 min. Service ceiling was 34,500ft (10,515m) and the estimated absolute ceiling was 35,400ft (10,800m).

Convinced that the RAF would buy the new fighter in the prevailing mood of rearmament, the Hawker company decided, in March 1936, to proceed with the production drawings and to make plans for large scale production. Three months later, that action was vin-

Below: First flown at Brooklands on 6 November 1935, the Hurricane prototype K5083 is seen here early in 1936, by which time the cockpit canopy had been stiffened to meet the early reservations of the Company's chief test pilot.

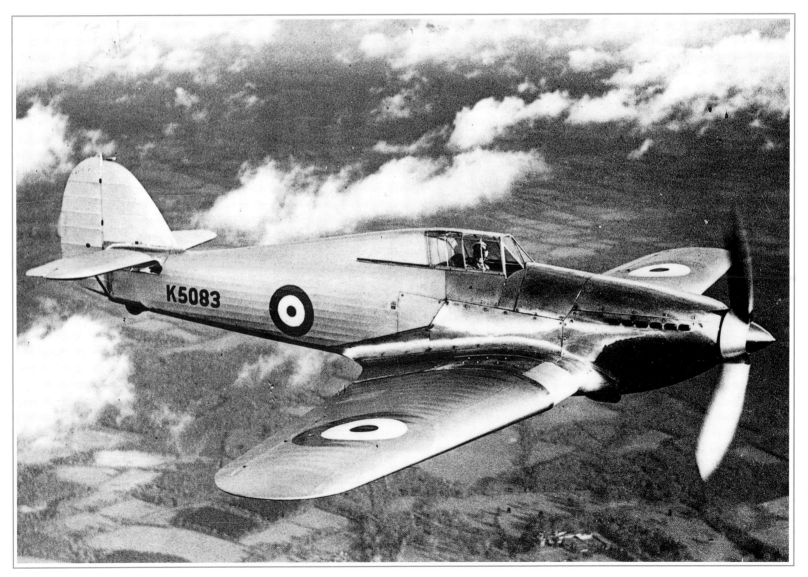

HAWKER HURRICANE Mk I
Cutaway Drawing Key

1 Starboard navigation light
2 Wing tip fairing
3 Fabric covered aileron
4 Aluminium alloy wing skin panelling
5 Aileron hinge control
6 Starboard outer wing panel
7 Inboard torsion box heavy-guage skin panel
8 Starboard landing lamp
9 Rotol three-bladed propeller
10 Spinner
11 Propeller hub pitch change mechanism
12 Spinner back plate
13 Propeller reduction gearbox
14 Cowling fairing
15 Starboard machine gun muzzles
16 Upper engine cowling
17 Coolant pipes
18 Rolls-Royce Merlin III twelve-cylinder liquid-cooled Vee engine
19 Exhaust stubs
20 Engine drive generator
21 Forward engine mounting
22 Ignition control units
23 Engine bearer struts
24 Lower engine cowlings
25 Starboard mainwheel
26 Manual-type inertia starter
27 Hydraulic pumps
28 Carburettor air intake
29 Cooling air scoop
30 Rear engine mounting
31 Single stage supercharger
32 Port magneto
33 Coolant system header tank
34 External bead sight
35 Coolant filler cap
36 Starboard wing gun bay
37 Ammunition magazines
38 Starboard Browning 0.303-in (7.7-mm) machine guns (4)
39 Fuel filler cap
40 Engine bay canted bulkhead
41 Rear engine mounting struts
42 Pneumatic system air bottle (gun firing)
43 Wing spar centre-section carry-through
44 Lower longeron/wing spar joint
45 Rudder pedals
46 Pilot's foot boards
47 Control column linkage
48 Fuselage (reserve) fuel tank, capacity 28 Imp gal (127 l)
49 Fuel tank bulkhead
50 Control column hand grip
51 Instrument panel
52 Reflector gunsight
53 Starboard split trailing-edge flap
54 Bullet proof windscreen panel
55 Canopy internal handle
56 Rear view mirror
57 Sliding cockpit canopy cover
58 Plexiglass canopy panels
59 Canopy framework
60 Canopy external handle
61 Starboard side 'break-out' emergency exit panel
62 Safety harness
63 Seat height adjustment lever
64 Oxygen supply cock
65 Engine throttle lever
66 Elevator trim tab control handwheel
67 Oil pipes to radiator
68 Radiator flap control lever
69 Cockpit section tubular fuselage framework
70 Coolant system piping
71 Pilot's oxygen cylinder
72 Boarding step
73 Seat back armour
74 Pilot's seat
75 Armoured headrest
76 Turn-over crash pylon struts
77 Canopy rear fairing construction
78 Sliding canopy rail
79 Battery
80 TR 9D radio transmitter/receiver
81 Radio shelf
82 Downward identification light
83 Flare launch tube
84 Handgrip
85 Plywood skin panel
86 Dorsal fairing stringers
87 Upper identification light
88 Aerial mast
89 Aerial lead-in
90 Wooden dorsal section formers
91 Fuselage upper longeron
92 Rear fuselage fabric covering
93 Aluminium alloy tailplane leading edge
94 Starboard fabric covered tailplane
95 Fabric covered elevator
96 Aluminium alloy fin leading edge
97 Forward fin mounting post
98 Tailplane spar attachment joint
99 Elevator hinge control
100 Fin rib construction
101 Tailfin fabric covering
102 Diagonal bracing strut
103 Stern post
104 Rudder mass balance weight
105 Aileron cable
106 Rear aerial mast
107 Fabric covered rudder
108 Aluminium alloy rudder framework
109 Tail navigation light
110 Rudder tab
111 Elevator trim tab
112 Port elevator rib construction
113 Elevator horn balance
114 Port tailplane rib construction
115 Diagonal spar bracing struts
116 Rudder control horn
117 Tail control access panel
118 Ventral tailwheel fairing
119 Fixed, castoring tailwheel
120 Dowty shock absorber tailwheel strut
121 Ventral fin framework
122 Lifting bar socket
123 Aluminium alloy lateral formers
124 Tail control cables

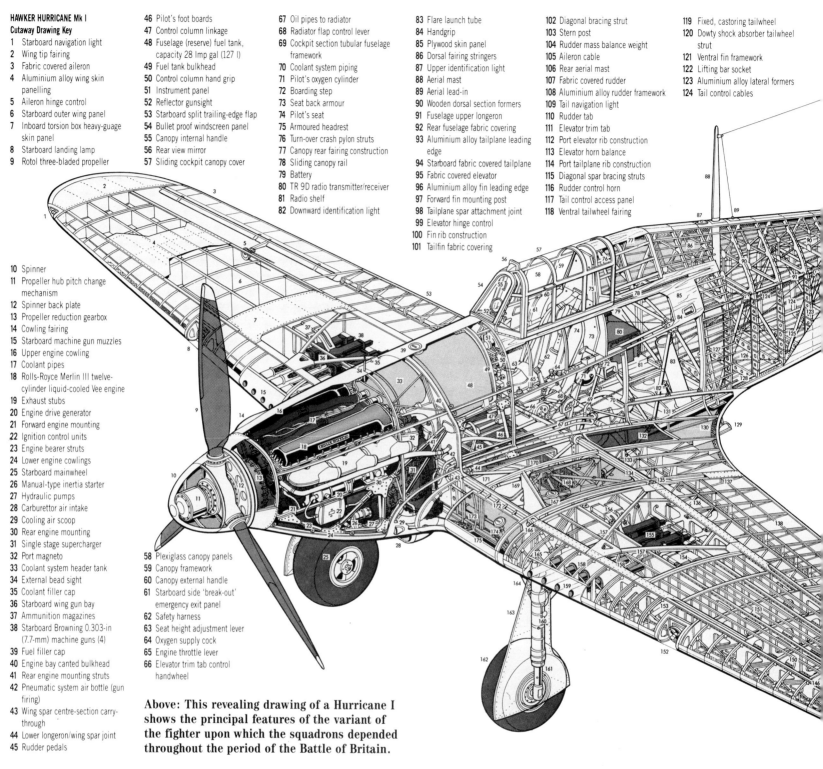

Above: This revealing drawing of a Hurricane I shows the principal features of the variant of the fighter upon which the squadrons depended throughout the period of the Battle of Britain.

dicated when the Air Ministry confirmed that 600 Hurricanes were to be included in its expansion Plan F (which also provided for 300 Spitfires). By the time the Battle of Britain began, every single fighter in the hands of the RAF counted, and the early launch of Hurricane production had helped to ensure that just enough machines were in fact available to Fighter Command.

Even so, meeting the RAF's rapidly expanding needs proved to be no simple matter and the Plan F target of 600 Hurricanes to be delivered by March 1939 was missed by some six months. There had been a succes-

sion of relatively minor but time-consuming problems with prototype development, especially related to the Merlin, and the early intention to fit the Merlin F (Mk I) in the production Hurricane was changed to make use of the improved Merlin G (Mk II) — which required a redesign of the installation and the front fuselage profile before production could begin. The cockpit canopy also produced its share of problems, with five failures recorded on the prototype before a satisfactory design was evolved.

The first production Hurricane I flew at Brooklands on October 12, 1937, fitted with an early example of

the Merlin II and at a weight of 5,459lb (2,476kg). The second aircraft was in the air six days later, and production deliveries then built up rapidly. Meanwhile, during 1936, the prototype had been fitted with the planned armament of eight Browning machine guns and first firing trials had been made. Design of a metal-covered wing was in hand, but to avoid production delays the Hurricane I retained the fabric-covered wing, in which the guns were grouped in two quartets, positioned to fire just outside the propeller disc and therefore requiring no complicated synchronisation gear. Each gun was provided with 300 rounds, and the

125 Rear fuselage tubular framework
126 Diagonal wire bracing
127 Lateral stringers
128 Fuselage lower longeron
129 Pull-out boarding step
130 Wing root trailing edge fillet
131 Ventral access hatch
132 Walkway
133 Flap hydraulic jack
134 Inner wing panel rear spar
135 Outer wing panel spar attachment joint
136 Gun heater air duct
137 Wing panel joint cover strip
138 Flap shroud ribs
139 Port split trailing edge flap
140 Aluminium alloy aileron rib construction
141 Port fabric covered aileron
142 Aileron hinges
143 Wing tip fairing construction
144 Port navigation light
145 Leading edge nose ribs

146 Front spar
147 Intermediate spars
148 Ventral pitot head
149 Rear spar
150 Aluminium alloy wing rib construction
151 Wing stringers
152 Port landing lamp
153 Inboard double-web strengthened spar section
154 Outboard ammunition magazines, 338 rounds each
155 Port Browning 0.303-in (7.7-mm) machine guns (4)
156 Inboard ammunition magazines, 324 and 338 rounds
157 Diagonal gun bay ribs
158 Gun barrel blast tubes
159 Machine gun muzzles
160 Main undercarriage leg strut
161 Oleo-pneumatic shock absorber strut
162 Port mainwheel
163 Mainwheel leg fairing
164 Side locking strut
165 Main undercarriage leg pivot fixing
166 Outer wing panel front spar bolted joint
167 Fuel filler cap
168 Port wing main fuel tank, capacity 34.5 Imp gal (157 l)
169 Centre section strut framework
170 Ventral oil and coolant radiator
171 Main undercarriage wheel bay
172 Oil tank attachments
173 Mainwheel hydraulic retraction jack
174 Oil filler cap
175 Leading edge oil tank, capacity 9 Imp gal (41 l), port side only

Above: The second Polish fighter squadron to form in the RAF, Northolt-based No.303 (''Kościuszko'') flew Hurricane Is in intensive actions throughout September 1940 to become the top-scoring squadron in No.11 Group.

Below: Squadrons of the Auxiliary Air Force were flying Hurricane Is alongside the Regular air force units throughout the Battle. The photo shows a pair of Hurricanes of 501 Squadron scrambling from Gravesend on 15 August 1940.

two batteries of guns were harmonised to converge at 650 yards (594m) — although with experience this distance was to be reduced eventually to 200 yards (183m).

Service use of the Hurricane began with No 111 Squadron at Northolt, which was fully equipped by February 1938. By July 1939, 12 regular squadrons were flying the Hurricane I, to be followed by six Auxiliary Air Force squadrons, converting to the fighter role from bomber or army co-operation in which the AAF had previously operated. Powered by the Merlin II and still using the two-bladed fixed-pitch wooden propeller, the standard Hurricane I in 1938 had a tare weight of 4,732lb (2,146kg) and a normal loaded weight of 6,056lb (2,747kg) when carrying full ammunition and 77.5 Imp gal (352 l) of fuel. This gave a range of 340 miles (547km) at 275mph (442km/h) at 15,000ft (4,575m), but with full tankage of 97 Imp gal (441 l), the max take-off weight was 6,202lb (2,813kg) and the range increased to 680 miles (1,094km), with an endurance of 4.2 hrs, at the economical cruising speed of 162mph (261km/h). Max speed was 312mph (502km/h), the time to 15,000ft (4,575m) was 7 min and service ceiling was 33,000ft (10,058m). The take-off distance to clear 50ft (15.2m) was 1,800ft (549m) at normal weight and 1,890ft (576m) at max weight.

A second major version of the Hurricane would make its first flight on June 11, 1940 and, as the Hurricane IIA, would begin to reach the squadrons on September 4, 1940, just too late to figure effectively in the Battle of Britain itself. Thus, those squadrons engaged throughout August and most of September were still mounted on the Hurricane I, albeit somewhat improved by comparison with the 1938 delivery standard. An armoured bulkhead had been introduced forward of the cockpit and, when Hawker Aircraft's second production batch began leaving the assembly line in September 1939, a bullet-proof windscreen had been standardised. This batch also adopted the Merlin III engine which featured a shaft capable of taking either Rotol or de Havilland three-bladed constant-speed propeller. While some Hurricanes were produced during 1939 with the DH two-position propeller, a major conversion programme was started on June 24, 1940 to fit the Rotol constant-speed unit which allowed the pilot to select optimum engine power for the various stages of flight. Significantly improving the Hurricane I's climb performance, Rotol propellers had been fitted to all Hurricanes by mid-August 1940. With the 81st Hurricane of the second batch, the fabric-covered wing finally gave place to an all-metal stressed-skin wing and, on February 2, 1940 the first Hurricane with rear armour protection for the pilot was flown.

Before battle was joined, the fact that the Hurricane was inferior in most performance respects to its principal German opponent, the Messerschmitt Bf 109E, had been accepted. The Bf 109E was faster at all altitudes, and could out-climb and out-dive the Hurricane with ease. Thus, if the German pilot elected to break off the engagement, the pilot of the Hurricane was powerless to pursue his erstwhile opponent. But in low-altitude manoeuvrability and turning circle at all altitudes the Hurricane had the upper hand and, provided the Bf 109E did not join combat with an altitude advantage, the Hurricane was its match. Apart from its performance inferiority, the Hawker fighter was not found wanting, and its sturdier structure enabled it to withstand battle damage that would have rendered its antagonist *hors de combat*.

The Hurricane's admitted shortcomings in performance compared with that of the Bf 109E led to it being allocated the primary task of dealing with the Luftwaffe bomber formations — which seldom operated much above 16,000-17,000ft (4,877-5,181m) — leaving the faster-climbing Spitfires to keep the escorting Bf 109Es occupied. In the heat of battle it rarely proved possible to co-ordinate the attacks of both Hurricane and Spitfire formations in such an optimum fashion, however, and all too frequently Hurricanes intercepting a bomber formation were attacked from above by escorting Bf 109Es.

Above: The work of ground crews made an essential contribution to the RAF's success. This photograph shows mechanics at work on a Polish squadron Hurricane

By the end of 1939, the RAF had received more than 600 Hurricane Is and production was at the rate of 100 a month — a figure that had been more than doubled by the middle of 1940. Losses had been suffered in France, totalling almost 300 machines and many of the RAF's most experienced pilots, but the massive production effort — in which Gloster joined with Hawker, flying its first Hurricane I at Hucclecote on October 20, 1939 — and the herculean task of repairing those aircraft damaged during the Battle of Britain itself ensured that "the Few" did not run out of fighters in 1940. By the end of the Battle, some 1,700 Hurricanes had served with Fighter Command, and

''As a Hurricane pilot, I had a certain fear and respect for the Me 109. For one thing, it could dive faster. If an Me 109 pilot saw you, it would drop down taking a shot at you, go past, pull the stick back and start climbing very fast. You just couldn't keep up with him. The only way to overcome this was to roll over inverted and dive after him in positive g. When the 109 pulled up to level out or climb, we'd aileron-turn to right-way-up and see his plan view and get in a perfect shot.

The Hurricane's visibility was pretty good, except above and below to the rear. The mirror was useful, but not as effective as it might have been. I replaced mine with a curved rear-view mirror, and actually felt it gave me a touch extra speed besides giving a better view.

I once looked in my mirror and saw the biggest, fattest Me 109 ever, or so it seemed. All at once his front lit up as he fired at me. The 109 went over the top, to be followed by my No 2, who was firing at me! When we got down I put him on gun practice for two days and told him: 'Don't shoot at your friends . . . and if you shoot at anything, make sure you hit it!'

Air Commodore Peter Brothers
CBE, DSO, DFC

696 had been lost to the service, either permanently or temporarily, in the two months of fighting.

Had the Battle continued longer, the Hurricane IIA would have been able to reduce substantially the margin of performance superiority enjoyed by the Bf 109E. With a 1,260hp Merlin XX engine, this mark could reach 20,000ft (6,095m) in 8.2 minutes and had a maximum speed of 342mph (550km/h) at 22,000ft (6,705m). Soon to have the benefit of heavier firepower — either 12 machine guns or four cannon — the Hurricane IIs would continue to do battle with the Luftwaffe, by night as well as day, in the months that followed the Battle of Britain itself.

Below: No.85 Squadron, flying Hurricane Is at Debden, acquired the code letters VY in September 1939. Day fighter finish in 1940 is shown here on V6611, with dark green and dark earth camouflage and duck-egg blue on the undersides.

Supermarine Spitfire

Like the Hawker team, the design staff of the Supermarine Aviation subsidiary of Vickers (Aviation) Ltd had become interested in the early 'thirties in the RAF's need for a new fighter, and by 1934 was actively engaged in the design of an "experimental high-speed single-seat fighter". Known as Design 300, this was conceived by the team led by R.J. Mitchell and based more on experience of high-speed flight obtained through the design of the Schneider Trophy-winning seaplanes than upon familiarity with fighter design. Ordered by the Air Ministry as a single prototype in December 1934, the Supermarine 300 — forerunner of the Spitfire — owed more to the instinctive creativity of a brilliant designer than to the intelligent application of experience, as exemplified by the Hurricane.

Be that as it may, the result was an aircraft that was of similar configuration to the Hurricane, similarly powered and armed and first flown some six months after the Hawker prototype, on March 5, 1936, at Eastleigh near Southampton. If the Hurricane was a reliable workhorse — albeit a thoroughbred — the Spitfire was a ballerina, an impression fostered by the powder-blue finish adopted for the prototype and enhanced by the frail, narrow-track undercarriage. Outnumbered by the Hawker fighter in the Battle of Britain, the Spitfire was destined to outproduce, outfly and outlast the Hurricane. But it was in 1940 that (in the words of test pilot Jeffrey Quill) "the little Spitfire somehow captured the imagination of the British people at a time of near despair, becoming a symbol of defiance and of victory in what seemed a desparate and almost hopeless situation".

The Spitfire prototype went to the A & AEE in July 1936, at which time it had a Merlin C driving a de Havilland fixed-pitch two-bladed wooden propeller. It was tested at a weight of 5,322lb (2,418kg), and was found to have a speed of 349mph (561km/h) at 16,800ft (5,120m) and 324mph (521km/h) at 30,000ft (9,145m). It took 17 minutes to reach the latter altitude and 5 min 42 sec to get to 18,000ft (5,485m), and had a service ceiling of 35,000ft (10,670m). The performance edge over the Hurricane was thus already evident, and handling was good, too, the Service pilots at the A & AEE reporting that the prototype was "simple and easy to fly and [had] no vices". It had well-harmonised controls, which appeared to give an excellent compromise between manoeuvrability and steadiness for shooting. The report concluded that the Spitfire (as the Supermarine 300 was to be named before it entered service) could be "flown without risk by the average fully trained service fighter pilot".

One of its most endearing qualities, evident from the prototype onwards, was its extremely docile behaviour at the stall, particularly under conditions of high g. On the debit side, longitudinal stability was a matter of some concern from the start, and called for a constant development effort as later marks were introduc-

Right: As chief designer of the Supermarine company, Reginald Mitchell gained valuable experience in the design of high-speed seaplanes for the Schneider Trophy contests before embarking on design of the Spitfire.

Above: The (unpainted) Spitfire prototype K5054, shortly before its first flight in March 1936, in the hands of chief test pilot, Captain J "Mutt" Summers.

ed. Of more concern during the period of the Battle of Britain were the high lateral stick forces encountered at the upper end of the speed range, and not overcome until modified ailerons were introduced in 1941.

In accordance with the provision of Expansion Plan F, the Air Ministry ordered 310 Spitfire Is on June 3, 1936 defining a standard of aircraft that was generally similar to the prototype. Powered, like the contemporary version of the Hurricane, by a 1,030hp Merlin II, the first production aircraft flew on May 14, 1938,

"On August 21, volunteers were called for to fly Spitfires. Having flown biplanes and Lysanders over the past year, I was pleased to have a go in something with a little more glamour and power attached to it. The Spitfire has been described as the best fighter aircraft of World War II and I wouldn't disagree except to say that the narrow undercarriage and the early hydraulic system took some getting used to. The latter necessitated pumping the hydraulics manually and, during a hasty take off, gave rise to some hairy moments.

Having flown Spits from Mk1s to (later) Mk 24s I can say that the Spitfire was the most beautiful machine ever invented. I used to talk to mine all the time . . . "Keep going . . ." and so on, and it almost talked back to me."

Wing Commander Paddy Barthropp
DFC, AFC

SUPERMARINE SPITFIRE 1
Cutaway Drawing Key
1 Starboard navigation light
2 Wing tip fairing
3 Starboard fabric covered aileron
4 Aileron mass balance weights
5 Outboard Browning 0.303-in
(7.7-mm) machine gun
6 Outboard ammunition tanks
(350-rounds per gun)
7 Aileron bellcrank hinge control
8 Central pair of Browning 0.303-in
(7.7-mm) machine guns
9 Aileron control cables
10 Starboard split trailing-edge flap
11 Flap hydraulic jack
12 Starboard mainwheel bay

24 Ejector exhaust stubs (paired)
25 Forward engine mounting
26 Cowling integral oil tank, capacity
5.6 Imp gal (25 l)
27 Engine mounting struts
28 Generator
29 Main engine mounting sub-frame
30 Starboard wheel fairing door
31 Starboard mainwheel
32 Carburettor air intake
33 Suppressor
34 Single stage supercharger
35 Engine control linkages
36 Main engine bearer attachment
joint
37 Engine accessory equipment
38 Hydraulic reservoir

45 Lower fuel tank, capacity 37 Imp
gal (168 l)
46 Rudder pedal bar
47 Sloping fuel tank bay bulkhead
48 Rudder pedals
49 Engine throttle, mixture control
and propeller pitch control levers
50 Control column handgrip
51 Back of instrument panel
52 Radio controller
53 Reflector gunsight
54 Externally armoured windscreen
panel
55 Pilot's rear view mirror
56 Canopy framing
57 Windscreen side panels
58 Sliding cockpit canopy cover
59 Headrest
60 Canopy direct vision panel
61 Pilot's seat

62 Safety harness
63 Folding side entry hatch
64 Crow bar stowage
65 Elevator trim handwheel
66 Rudder trim handwheel
67 Chart case
68 Windscreen de-icing fluid
reservoir
69 Gun heater air ducting
70 Adjustable seat mounting
71 Pilot's back armour
72 Battery
73 Pilot's head armour
74 Canopy aft glazing
75 Voltage regulator
76 Starboard side oxygen bottle
77 Sliding canopy rail
78 Pneumatic system air bottles
79 Fuselage main longeron
80 Flare launch tube

81 Radio Compartment access hatch
82 HF radio transmitter/receiver
83 Aerial mast
84 Aerial lead-in
85 Upper identification light
86 Harness cable anchorage and
release unit
87 Rear fuselage frame and stringer
construction
88 Fuselage skin panelling
89 Starboard tailplane

90 Starboard fabric covered elevator
91 Fin front spar (fuselage frame
extension)
92 Fin rib construction
93 HF aerial cable
94 Rudder horn balance
95 Fabric-covered rudder
construction
96 Sternpost
97 Trim control jack
98 Rudder trim tab

13 Inboard Browning 0.303-in
(7.7-mm) machine gun
14 Inboard ammunition tanks (350
rounds per gun)
15 Machine gun barrels
16 Machine gun ports (patched)
17 De Havilland three-bladed
variable pitch propeller
18 Spinner
19 Propeller hub pitch change
mechanism
20 Armoured spinner backplate
21 Coolant header tank
22 Coolant filler cap
23 Rolls-Royce Merlin II, liquid-
cooled 12-cylinder Vee engine

39 Detachable engine cowling panels
40 Engine bay firewall/fuel tank bay
bulkhead
41 Fuel filler cap
42 Upper main fuel tank, capacity 48
Imp gal (218 l)
43 Compass mounting
44 Fuel tank/longeron attachments

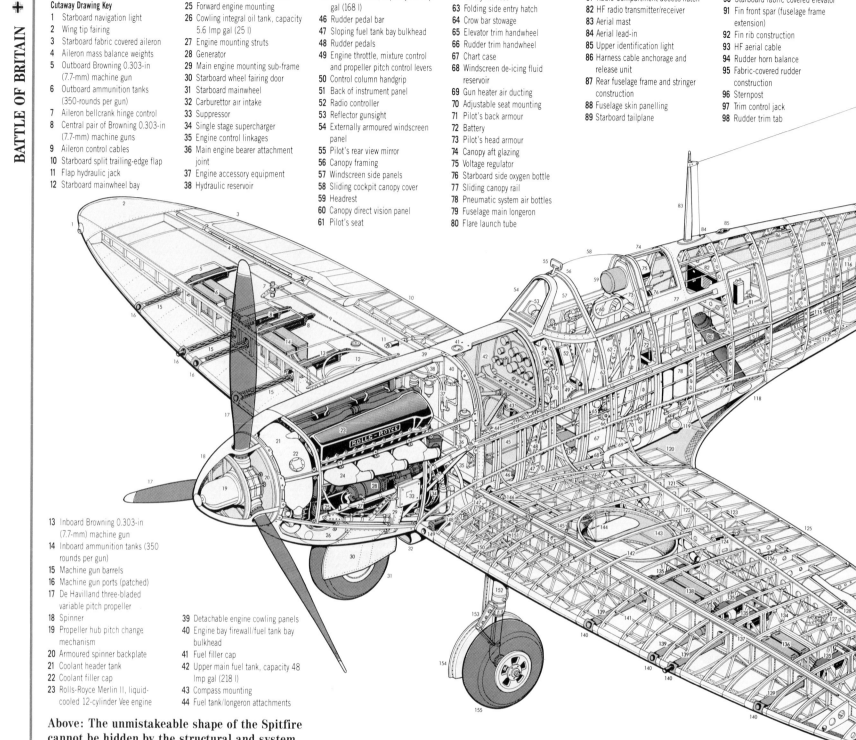

**Above: The unmistakeable shape of the Spitfire
cannot be hidden by the structural and system
detail shown in this drawing. The eight-gun
Spitfire I was used during the Battle.**

at Eastleigh, where the final assembly line was fed
by the manufacturing centres at Woolston and Itchen,
near Southampton.

Like Hawker, Supermarine failed by some six months
to meet the Plan F target of delivery completion by
March 1939. The problem was that the Spitfire, which
was of all-metal, stressed-skin construction, was not
a simple aeroplane to build, the wing leading-edge being especially difficult. As time went by, and in par-

ticular after the Supermarine works in Southampton
had been heavily bombed in September 1940, Spitfire
production would be dispersed widely over southern
England and would bring 65 different manufacturing
units into play.

That development was still well in the future in
August 1938, however, when No 19 Squadron at RAF
Duxford received two early production Spitfires and
began a 400-hour intensive flying trial. Two more

squadrons received Spitfires in 1938 and, by September
1939, another four Regular units were flying the Supermarine fighter, and four AAF squadrons were equipped or equipping.

Like the early Hurricanes, the first Spitfires off the
assembly line had the Merlin II engine driving a two-
bladed fixed-pitch wooden airscrew. They attained
352mph (566km/h) at 19,000ft (5,790m) a maximum
climb rate of 2,420ft/min (737m/min), and an altitude

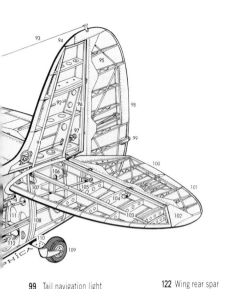

99 Tail navigation light
100 Elevator tab
101 Port elevator rib construction
102 Elevator mass balance
103 Tailplane rib construction
104 Elevator trim control jack
105 Rudder control rod
106 Elevator hinge control
107 Tailplane spar/fuselage frame
attachment joint
108 Fuselage double frame
109 Non-retracting castoring tailwheel
110 Tailwheel strut
111 Tailplane control cable quadrants
112 Control access panel
113 Sloping tail assembly attachment
main frame
114 Tailwheel shock absorber strut
115 Tailplane control cables
116 Rear fuselage starboard side
access hatch
117 Fuselage bottom longeron
118 Wing root trailing edge fillet
119 Radio and electrical systems
ground socket
120 Inboard auxiliary flap segment
121 Trailing edge flap shroud ribs

122 Wing rear spar
123 Flap torque shaft
124 Flap hydraulic jack
125 Port split trailing-edge flap
126 Flap synchronising jack
127 Aileron control bellcrank
128 Aileron hinge control rod
129 Port fabric covered aileron
130 Aileron rib construction
131 Wing tip construction
132 Port navigation light
133 Ventral pitot tube
134 Wing lattice rib construction
135 Browning 0.303-in (7.7-mm)
machine guns
136 Outboard ammunition tanks (350
rounds per gun)
137 Front spar
138 Inboard ammunition tanks (350
rounds per gun)
139 Machine gun muzzle blast tubes
140 Machine gun ports (patched)
141 Leading-edge rib construction
142 Wheel bay external skin stiffeners
143 Port main undercarriage wheel bay
144 Ventral oil cooler (coolant radiator
on starboard side)
145 Undercarriage position indicator
146 Hydraulic retraction jack
147 Wing spar/fuselage attachment
joint
148 Gun camera
149 Camera port
150 Inboard leading-edge lattice ribs
151 Main undercarriage pivot fixing
152 Mainwheel leg shock absorber
strut
153 Torque scissors links
154 Mainwheel fairing door
155 Port mainwheel

Above: The Rollys-Royce Merlin (developed as the P.V.12) was vital to the success of both the Hurricane and the Spitfire. The Merlin III, shown here, was used in later Spitfire Is, with either DH or Rotol propellers.

Below: The first production Spitfire I, K9787, flown by Jeffrey Quill, who was responsible for most of the development testing of successive marks throughout the period of the war. The photograph was taken in May 1938.

of 20,000ft (6,100m) in 9.4 minutes. With the 78th production aircraft, the wooden two-blader gave place to a de Havilland Hamilton two-pitch three-bladed metal propeller which, although incurring a weight penalty and having only a marginal effect on level speed, bestowed a significant improvement in the climb. No bullet-proof windscreen or armour was initially fitted, and although standard armament was envisaged as eight wing-mounted 0.303in Browning guns each with 300 rounds of ammunition, a shortage of these weapons led to the installation of only four guns each in early machines. Later, the introduction of a bullet-proof external windscreen was to be followed by provision of a 6mm armour plate behind the pilot's head. After pilots on the first squadron had complained that they banged their heads on the flat roof of the cockpit canopy, a ''humped'' canopy was introduced, giving the Spitfire its characteristic profile.

With the DH two-position propeller, the Spitfire I had a tare weight of 4,517lb (2,049kg) and operated at a normal loaded weight of 5,844lb (2,651kg). It had a maximum speed of 346mph (557km/h) and cruised at 304mph (489km/h) at 15,000ft (4,570m). The time to that altitude was 6.85 min and service ceiling was 30,500ft (9,300m). From a standing start, it reached 50ft (15m) above the ground in a distance of 1,605ft (489m), but required almost 300ft (91m) more than this distance to come to a stop, from the same altitude. The normal range of 415 miles (668km) included a 15-min allowance for take-off and climb, and could be extended to more than 600 miles (965km) by reducing the cruising speed to 175mph (282km/h).

Like the Hurricane, the Spitfire I benefited considerably from the installation of a variable-pitch constant speed propeller, to permit which a switch was made to the Merlin III with effect from the 175th aircraft. A massive effort between June and August 1940 ensured that all the Spitfire Is then in service were fitted with the DH constant speed unit and this became standard on the later production Spitfire Is.

Evaluation of a Bf 109E-3 captured in France had already revealed that the German fighter was superior in a number of respects to the Spitfire I when originally fitted with the two-position propeller. The Messerschmitt fighter was marginally faster than its British contemporary at most altitudes, and it could out-climb the Spitfire up to 20,000ft (6,070m), above which height the British fighter enjoyed an edge. Both fighters suffered some aileron heaviness at the upper end of their speed scale. While the Spitfire possessed superior manoeuvrability at all altitudes as a result of its lower wing loading, its turning circle being appreciably smaller, the Bf 109E could always elude the Spitfire in a dive, the float carburettor of the British fighter's Merlin engine placing it at a distinct disadvantage in this situation.

Above: The first mark of Rolls Royce Merlin used to power the Spitfire was the Mk II which had a maximum output of 1,030 brake hp at 16,250 ft (5,000m), at 3000 rpm and 6¼-lb boost. Originally with a two-bladed wooden propeller, the Merlin could also turn a three-blade metal propeller.

During 1939, single examples of the Spitfire I and the Hurricane I had each been fitted with a pair of 20mm cannon, with 60 rounds per gun. The Hurricane, with Oerlikon guns, was credited with destruction of a Dornier 17 on August 13, 1940, while undergoing evaluation with No.151 Squadron, but the large-scale application of cannon armament to the Hawker fighter had to await the production of the Mk IIC, with four of the 20mm weapons apiece. The Hispano guns fitted in the Spitfire proved prone to stoppages but, after

trails with the prototype installation, a batch of 30 Mk Is was similarly fitted and — with four 0.303in Brownings later added to the wing armament — were delivered from June 1940 for use by No 19 Squadron. They were the only cannon-armed fighters operated by the RAF during the Battle of Britain. These Spitfires were designated Mk IBs, and those with the original eight-gun armament then became, retrospectively, Mk IA.

Also paralleling Hurricane development, a Mk II version of the Spitfire emerged during the course of the Battle, but reached the squadrons too late to have a decisive effect. The Spitfire IIA retained the eight-gun armament of its predecessor but introduced a 1,175hp Merlin XII engine which drove a Rotol constant-speed airscrew. Whereas the Spitfire IA had its armour added in service, the IIA left the factory with armour installed. The Spitfire IIA attained a maximum speed

Below: The Spitfire IIA P7666 reached No.41 Squadron at Hornchurch in late 1940, and is shown here in the day fighter finish of the Battle of Britain period, and the markings of the squadron's commanding officer, Sqn Ldr D O Finlay, DFC.

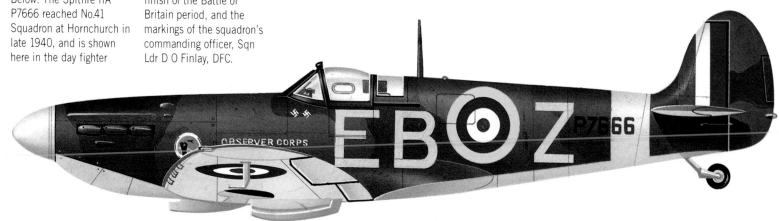

of 357mph (574km/h) at 17,000ft (5,180m), could reach an altitude of 20,000ft (6,070m) within seven minutes of unstick and had a maximum climb rate of 2,620ft/min (798m/min). The first two squadrons converted to fly Spitfire IIs in September 1940.

Once RAF Fighter Command had discarded its outdated tactics, of which the Luftwaffe's Bf 109E fighters took full advantage during the opening phases of the Battle, the Spitfire and its German opposite number proved remarkably evenly matched. Each possessed some characteristics superior to those of its opponent and, all things being equal, the outcome of a combat depended largely on the prowess of the pilots involved.

The production difficulties with early Spitfires were shown by comparative figures for mid-1940, when the rate was still averaging only 80 a month compared with 236 a month for the Hurricane. It would be early 1942 before the monthly output of Spitfires exceeded that

of Hurricanes, and the slow build-up of production in 1938/39, combined with losses suffered by Fighter Command during the fighting over France (despite Dowding's insistence that the precious Spitfires should not be deployed with either the AASF or the Air Component of the BEF) meant that the line was drawn exceedingly thin in August 1940.

Although outnumbered by Hurricanes in the ratio of three to two throughout the summer of 1940, the Spitfires of Fighter Command inflicted more than half the total losses suffered by the Luftwaffe in the assault on Britain — a statistic that underlines the Supermarine fighter's particular merit in air-to-air fighting. By the very nature of the conflict, the Luftwaffe's losses in single-seat fighters were appreciably lower than those of the RAF, however, and the Spitfire squadrons alone lost 118 fighters in combat during August, a further 55 being damaged. Adding to those lost or

Above: Producing the Spitfire proved to be a more exacting process than for the Hurricane, so the build-up of the Supermarine fighters in the RAF inventory was at first slow. Production accelerated after the establishment of the Castle Bromwich Aircraft Factory, where this Mk IIA was built.

damaged in accidents or by enemy bombing, 237 Spitfires were deleted from the inventory during that month alone, and total output of the factories engaged in Spitfire production amounted to only 163 machines. Attrition in September was even more serious, 156 being manufactured and 281 being lost to strength, of which 130 were destroyed and 80 damaged in combat. In the week ending September 13, the reserves reached their lowest ebb, with only 47 Spitfires ready for delivery in storage units.

Below: In the revised camouflage colours that were in use in 1942, with dark green and ocean grey for the upper surfaces and light grey undersides, this Spitfire VB bears the markings of No.306, the third Polish squadron formed in 1940.

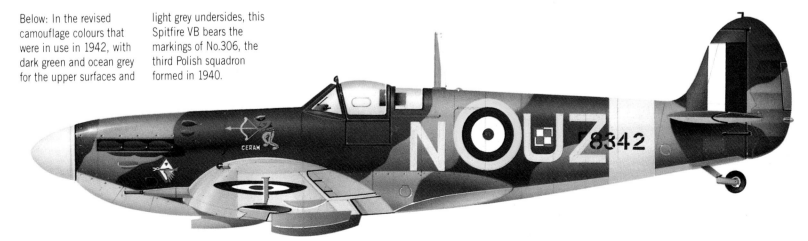

Boulton Paul Defiant

What the outcome of the Battle of Britain would have been had the Spitfire not been available is now purely of academic interest, but what is certain is the fact that no combat aircraft ever gave better service to the country of its birth. Sadly, the same cannot be said of the Boulton Paul Defiant, the operational record of which as a day fighter can only be described as disastrous.

The concept of a two-seat single-engined fighter with all of its armament concentrated in a massive power-operated turret was based in the belief that a gunner with no responsibility for flying the aircraft and able to traverse his battery of guns through 360 degrees had more chance of hitting the enemy than a pilot who had to point his aircraft in the direction in which he wished to fire. Not properly appreciated by those who fostered this concept was the way that it divided responsibility between pilot and gunner, and required the pilot not only to fly the aircraft, but also to think in abstract terms of his gunner's line of sight. All too easily, it would transpire, enemy fighters could creep in under cover of the blind spot beneath the tail and deliver a *coup de grace*.

Designed to an Air Ministry Specification under the direction of J.D. North, the P.82, as the Defiant was at first designated, was an aircraft generally similar in overall size to the Hurricane. Its all-metal structure was conventional in most respects, its only unusual feature being the method of attaching the light alloy skinning to the stringers and ribs and then attaching these to the fuselage frames and wing spars. This obviated the need to preform the skins and, by riveting

BOULTON PAUL DEFIANT II
Cutaway Drawing Key
1 Three-bladed Rotol propeller, diameter 11ft 9in (3.58-m)
2 Spinner
3 Propeller hub
4 Coolant header tank
5 Rolls-Royce Merlin XX 12-cyl Vee engine
6 Exhaust manifold
7 Engine accessories
8 Engine bearer support
9 Oil cooler intake
10 Intake duct
11 Oil cooler fairing
12 Starboard mainwheel

13 Engine bearer/bulkhead lower attachment
14 Coolant pipe
15 Engine bearer
16 Oil filter
17 Engine control linkage
18 Forward firewall/bulkhead
19 Engine bearer/bulkhead upper attachment
20 Hydraulic reservoir
21 Starboard landing lamp
22 AI Mk VI radar transmitter aerial
23 Wing front spar
24 Starboard navigation light

25 Wing undersurface (load-bearing)
26 Wing rear spar
27 Aileron control linkage
28 Starboard aileron
29 Oil tank, capacity 10 Imp gal (45 l)
30 Oil tank filler cap
31 Tank attachment
32 AI Mk VI radar azimuth aerials, both sides of fuselage
33 Control column
34 Compass
35 Wingroot fairing
36 Seat support frame
37 Pilot's seat
38 Throttle quadrant

39 Instrument panel
40 Windscreen
41 Cockpit canopy
42 Cockpit coaming
43 Fuselage/rear spar frame (No 7)
44 Seat adjustment
45 Aileron control linkage assembly (accumulator and power unit frame deleted for clarity)
46 Pilot's safety harness attachment
47 Compressed air cylinder (brakes/dorsal fairings)
48 De-icing tank
49 W/T crate mounting frame

50 Transmitter/receiver, TR.113A or TR.9D
51 Fairing actuating ram
52 Dorsal forward fairing (retractable)
53 Four-gun power-operated turret, Type A Mk IID
54 Four 0.303-in (7.7-mm) Browning machine guns
55 Turret entry hatch
56 Reflector gunsight bracket
57 Gunner's armour plate
58 Gun-firing button
59 Turret ring
60 Turret ring/fuselage fillet
61 Turret electric motor
62 Gunner's (folding) seat

63 Radiator flap control and distributor access
64 Turret frame support
65 Oxygen cylinder
66 Ammunition containers
67 Forward/aft fuselage construction break (frame No 11)

68 Equipment/stores
69 Fairing actuating ram
70 Dorsal aft fairing (retractable)
71 Corrugated decking
72 Ballast weight hatch
73 Dorsal navigation/identification light
74 Fin root fillet
75 Fin/tailplane spar attachments
76 Starboard tailplane
77 Starboard elevator
78 Fin structure
79 Fin leading-edge
80 Rudder mass balance
81 Rudder upper hinge
82 Rudder structure

83 Rudder trimming/balance tab
84 Trim tab control linkage
85 Tear-off patches (trim tab control access)
86 Rear navigation light
87 Elevator tab
88 Port elevator

89 Elevator mass balance
90 Port tailplane
91 Rudder hinge
92 Stern post
93 Fuselage rear wedge
94 Non-retractable tailwheel
95 Articulated tailwheel strut
96 Rudder control chain linkage
97 Elevator control lever assembly
98 Retractable aerial mast
99 Aerial mast guide pulleys
100 Ventral aerial
101 Elevator control rods
102 Fuselage brace struts

103 Fuselage frames
104 Rudder control rods
105 Service/escape hatch
106 Wingroot fillet
107 Radiator flap control linkage
108 Radiator flap gearbox
109 Radiator flap fairing

110 Radiator bath
111 Coolant thermostat control
112 Wing rear spar
113 Radiator
114 Auxiliary spar (inboard only)
115 Split flaps
116 Inboard/outboard section wing joint
117 Attachment fittings
118 Split flaps (outboard)
119 Bellcrank levers
120 Flap rod
121 Rear spar (outboard)
122 Port aileron

123 Port wingtip assembly
124 Port navigation light
125 Wing stringers
126 Outboard ribs
127 Front spar
128 AI Mk VI radar elevation aerials (above and below port wing)

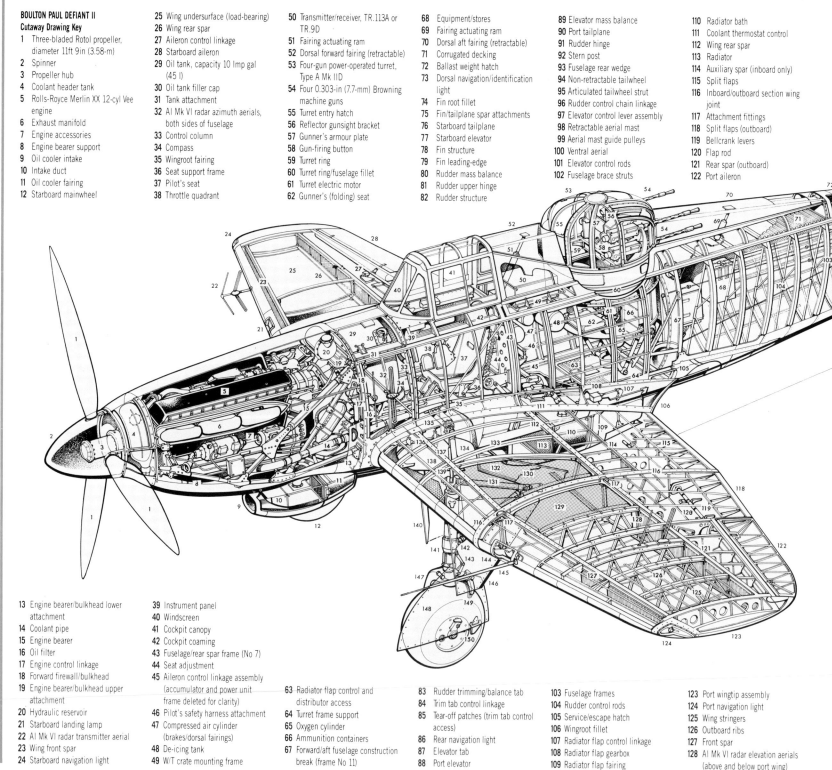

them while flat and countersinking the rivets, an exceptional surface finish was obtained, helping to obviate the adverse effect on performance of the drag of the bulky dorsal turret.

The first prototype made its inaugural flight at Wolverhampton on August 11, 1937, and attained 302mph (486km/h) on the power of its Merlin I engine. Its flying characteristics were pronounced excellent. It displayed very few vices, stability was highly satisfactory, and there was practically no change of trim when the undercarriage and flaps were lowered.

An initial contract for 87 Defiant Is was placed in March 1937, and 363 more were ordered in 1938. Production was delayed, as for the Hurricane also, by the decision to use the Merlin II rather than the Merlin I, and by the time the first production Defiant flew on July 30, 1939, it was powered, in fact, by a Merlin III, the version with a standardised shaft for DH or Rotol constant-speed propellers.

In its production form, the Defiant I had an empty weight of 6,078lb (2,757kg) and a normal loaded weight of 8,318lb (3,773kg). At that weight, the maximum speed was 250mph (402km/h) at sea level and 304mph (489km/h) at 17,000ft (5,180m), the cruising speed being 259mph (417km/h) at 15,000ft (4,572m). Initial rate of climb was 1,900ft/min (579m/min), the time to 15,750ft (4,800m) was 8.5 min and the service ceiling was 30,350ft (9,250m). A range of 465 miles (748km) was achieved at the quoted cruising speed.

Installed in the Defiant I as a removable, self-contained unit, the Boulton Paul A Mk IID turret mounted four 0.303in belt-fed Brownings each with 600 rounds, and its hydraulic system formed an integral part of the turret itself. The bare turret weighed 361lb (164kg), to which was added the 88lb (40kg) of the four guns, 106lb (48kg) for ammunition, and some 35lb (16kg) for the gunner's oxygen equipment, sights, etc. Normal loaded weight at 8,318lb (3,773kg) was some 1,700lb (771kg) more than that of the similarly-powered Hurricane, yet the gross wing area of the two-seater was less than that of the single-seater. It was hardly to be expected, therefore, that the Defiant would be able to compete on the score of level speed, climb rate of manoeuvrability.

This was soon borne out by comparative trials between a Defiant and a Hurricane conducted by No 111 Squadron in October 1939, but the RAF now had a desperate need for fighters, the Defiant was just coming ''on stream'' and there could be no going back. That same month, No 264 Squadron formed at Sutton Bridge to be the first to fly the Defiant, with which it became operational from Martlesham Heath in 1940. Early operational results were, at best, mixed, although there were claims of remarkable successes in the last weeks of May 1940, during patrols over Dunkirk, when

the Defiants were probably mistaken for Hurricanes by Luftwaffe fighter pilots who tried to attack from above and behind — a fatal error.

Even so, the operations over France took a heavy toll of No 264 Squadron and it was back to strength only just in time for the Battle of Britain, alongside No 141, which had formed in June as the second squadron to fly Defiants. The latter had a disastrous first engagement with Bf 109Es south of Folkestone on July 19, losing two aircraft in the first firing pass by the Luftwaffe fighters and four more when the enemy made a second attack from below and dead astern — revealing that the Defiant's fatal weakness had been taken to heart. Thrown into battle at the end of August, No 264 Squadron suffered a similar fate, being left with only three serviceable Defiants within a week. Both squadrons were then withdrawn from further action in the Battle, leaving the Defiant to find its *forte* in nocturnal operations, which it would soon be called upon to fulfil.

Below: Dividing the responsibility for 'flying' and 'fighting' between two crew members in the Boulton Paul Defiant seemed like a good idead on paper, but when theory was put to practice, the Defiant was quickly found wanting in the day fighter rôle.

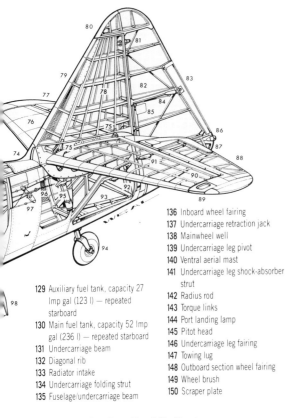

129 Auxiliary fuel tank, capacity 27 Imp gal (123 l) — repeated starboard
130 Main fuel tank, capacity 52 Imp gal (236 l) — repeated starboard
131 Undercarriage beam
132 Diagonal rib
133 Radiator intake
134 Undercarriage folding strut
135 Fuselage/undercarriage beam
136 Inboard wheel fairing
137 Undercarriage retraction jack
138 Mainwheel well
139 Undercarriage leg pivot
140 Ventral aerial mast
141 Undercarriage leg shock-absorber strut
142 Radius rod
143 Torque links
144 Port landing lamp
145 Pitot head
146 Undercarriage leg fairing
147 Towing lug
148 Outboard section wheel fairing
149 Wheel brush
150 Scraper plate

Left: The Boulton Paul Defiant was conventional in its structural design, as this cutaway drawing reveals. Its unconventionality lay in the use of a dorsal turret.

Below: No.264 Squadron, in whose markings this Defiant I is depicted, participated in the Battle for only a few days at the end of August 1940, suffering losses that reduced its effective strength to only three aircraft in a week.

PS•A N1535

Bristol Blenheim

Night operations were also to prove to be the most suitable for the Bristol Blenheim IFs that equipped six squadrons of Fighter Command in mid-1940. The Blenheim had been designed, under the direction of Frank Barnwell, to provide the RAF with a high-speed light bomber, and a version had then been produced to provide the RAF with a replacement for the Hawker Demon turret fighter. The concept of a twin-engined multi-seat long-range fighter was to prove as flawed as that which produced the Defiant.

The first all-metal cantilever monoplane of stressed-skin construction to enter production for the RAF, the Blenheim marked the beginning of a new era in the equipment of the service after several years of acute uneasiness concerning the obsolescence of the RAF's operational aircraft inventory. It was a cornerstone of the expansion programme, and its conversion from three-seat light bomber to heavy fighter in 1938 was prompted by what was considered, by the standards of the day, a fully adequate performance coupled with sturdiness and excellent handling characteristics.

Credited, at the time of its service introduction, with a performance that would allow it to outpace most contemporary service aircraft in all categories, the Blenheim was to be revealed wanting early in the conflict. As a bomber it proved woefully vulnerable to fighter attack, being deficient in both defensive armament and armour, and it lacked the performance necessary for a fully effective strategic fighter.

For the fighter role, the Blenheim was simply adapted from the standard Mk I bomber by the addition of a ventral pack manufactured by the Southern Railway's Ashford workshops, containing four 0.303in Browning guns plus 500 rounds of ammunition for each weapon. This supplemented the normal armament of a single wing-mounted Browning and a Vickers ''K'' gun of similar calibre in a B.I. Mk III semi-retractable hydraulically-operated dorsal turret. Some 200 Blenheims were modified to fighters, the first examples entering service with No 600 AAF Squadron at Hendon in September 1938.

Powered by two 840hp Bristol Mercury VIII air-cooled radial engines, the Blenheim IF, as the fighter was designated, weighed in at 8,840lb (4,100kg) and had

a loaded weight of 12,200lb (5,534kg). At that weight, the max speed was 237mph (381km/h) at sea level and 278mph (447km/h) at 15,000ft (4,572m), and the aircraft cruised at 215mph (346km/h) at 15,000ft. Initial rate of climb was 1,480ft/min (451m/min), the time to 5,000ft (1,524m) was 3.9 min, and to 10,000ft (3,048m) was 8.1 min. Service ceiling was 24,600ft (7,498m), and the aircraft had a reasonably high maxi-

mum range of 1,050 miles (1,690km).

Early operational experience with the Blenheim IF dictated the provision of a reflector sight, self-sealing tanks and some armour. No 23 Squadron undertook the first night intruder sortie of the war on December 21-22, 1939. The fact that the operation of the Blenheim fighter by day was suicidal in areas where enemy single-seat fighters were likely to be en-

Below: Flying Bristol Blenheim Is during 1940, No.25 Squadron at North Weald was engaged in radar trials and was committed to regular work as a night fighter unit by November of that year, in this compromise partial night fighter finish.

Left: This April 1940 photograph depicts the Blenheim Is of No.604 Squadron, at Northolt. Learning to operate with radar through the period of the Battle, this unit soon progressed onto the Beaufighter.

Above: This 1938 photograph shows the standard bomber variant of the Blenheim I being flown by No.44 Squadron. This was before the wartime squadron code letters system was applied to RAF aircraft.

Left: There were other variants of the Blenheim as well as the standard bomber and night fighter. This 1940 experimental reconnaissance variant was lightened and unarmed to boost flight performance. By 1940, however, the Blenheim was outclassed by the new generation of fighters.

countered in strength quickly became obvious in the course of fighting over the Continent during May and June 1940, and subsequently the Blenheim IF was restricted largely to nocturnal activities. On June 5, the Luftwaffe made its first night attack on London, and Blenheim IFs instituted a system of nocturnal patrols which, on June 18, resulted in the destruction of five bombers in conditions of moonlight.

Meanwhile, the Blenheim IF had been closely involved in the development of airborne intercept radar. A flight of three aircraft of No 600 Squadron operating from Manston had performed operational trials with AI Mk III radar, and on the night of July 2-3 a Blenheim IF from the Fighter Interception Unit at Ford gained the first ''kill'' by means of this equipment. Subsequently the Blenheim IF was to provide the backbone of RAF Fighter Command's night interception force, soldiering on through the Luftwaffe's nocturnal Blitz of 1940-41 until finally supplanted by the Beaufighter.

AT THE outbreak of war the Luftwaffe had 1,180 bombers, 366 dive bombers, 771 single-engine fighters and 408 twin-engine fighters, 40 ground attack aircraft and 887 for reconnaissance. With 552 transport aeroplanes, its operational force totalled 4,204 machines.

Considering the greatly increased complexity of airframe and engine design and manufacture since 1918, this was an impressive strength for an arm that the peace treaty at the end of World War I had reduced from some 20,000 aircraft to fewer than 5,000, for defence only. Moreover, until Hitler became Chancellor in 1933, this reconstruction had to be done in secret. The armistice terms were impracticable to enforce on a nation that had been one of the leaders in the development of military flying. Germany was free to develop a civilian aircraft industry and airlines, so took advantage of this obvious opportunity to train a new air force under cover.

At the Ministry of Defence General Hans von Seeckt, Chief of the Army Command, appointed former Luftstreitkräfte officers — future Luftwaffe Field Marshals, Albert Kesselring and Hugo Sperrle, and General Hans-Juergen Stumpf among them — to deal with aviation matters. The Director of Civil Aviation at the Ministry of Transport was a wartime pilot and the two Ministries set about forming the nucleus of a reborn Luftwaffe. Manufacturers of civil aircraft and aero engines began to design and build also for military purposes. In 1920 State-financed gliding clubs began the instruction of new pilots and by 1929 had 50,000 members. Crews flying for Deutsche Lufthansa, the national airline formed in 1926 under the chairmanship of Erhard Milch, who had commanded a fighter Geschwader in World War I, were training for future service in the air force.

Russia allowed Germany to set up a flying school at Lipesk, 200 miles (322km) southeast of Moscow, where, from 1924 to 1933, hundreds of air and ground

THE LUFTWAFFE

Richard Townshend Bickers

crews were trained. Germany also did development work on aircraft and equipment in Russia.

In 1933, Adolf Galland, at the age of 19, was typical of the young glider pilots who were selected for conversion to powered flight in Lufthansa and then went to Lipesk to train as fighter pilots. Next they went to Italy for further experience with the Italian Air Force. By now his course of 20 had each logged some 300 hours in aeroplanes and were keen to practice air fighting.

"Instead", he says, "the Italians, ignoring that we were already trained fighter pilots, concentrated on aerobatics." Young Galland and his comrades convinced their instructors that there was more to air combat than performing elegant arabesques in the sky. "But

there was little the Italians could teach us about actually fighting." The time spent in Italy was nonetheless considered to be of great value. Galland says, "We had the all-important opportunity to fly modern types of Italian aeroplanes. In addition to aerobatics and general training, we did target practice with live ammunition, which we weren't able to do in Germany."

They returned to Lufthansa to fly multi-engine types, perfect their instrument flying and navigation and travel the international air routes.

Hermann Goering, who had joined the Nazi Party in 1922, was appointed Air Minister in 1933 with Erhard Milch, another wartime Geschwader commander, as his Deputy. Goering had shot down 22 Allied aircraft in World War I and, in 1918 as a Hauptmann, commanded Jagdgeschwader I, whose first leader was Manfred von Richthofen. In 1923 he was wounded in the groin during the Munich Putsch, suffered excruciatingly for years, took heroin to ease the pain and became a lifelong addict. The habit sapped his concentration, unbalanced his mind and distorted his judgment, much to the detriment of his air force.

In 1935 the Luftwaffe, now comprising 1,888 aircraft and 20,000 officers and men, came out of concealment. Milch became Secretary of State for Air and set about a vigorous expansion of the Service. The production of military aircraft accelerated and by late 1935 averaged 300 a month. Among the new types were the Bf 109 and 110, the Ju 87 and 88, the Do 17 and He 111, all of which would be unleashed against Britain five years later. The anti-aircraft artillery — Flak — and the balloon defence units had always formed part

Below: The German national battle ensign, used by all their armed forces, is seen here. Individual Geschwader would also have their own standard, often flown at their base airfield.

Below: Erhard Milch was promoted to the rank of Generalfeldmarshall during the Battle, on July 19, 1940. A superb organiser, his influence on the growth of the Luftwaffe was profound and long-lasting.

of the German Air Force and were now incorporated in the new expansion. A Signals Service was formed and the Air Force Staff College was founded.

The man who is regarded as the father of strategic air power was an Italian, General Giulio Douhet (1869-1930), first Commander of the Italian Air Force. One of his theories was that decisions about air strategy must be made before decisions about land strategy. Many of his principles, expounded in his best-known work, ''The Command of the Air'', were adopted before and during World War II by the major powers. Germany and Britain were among those that shared the belief that the bomber would always get through, however numerous the opposing fighter force and anti-aircraft guns. Despite this, the Luftwaffe was deprived of a long-range heavy bomber capable of 12 hours' endurance and carrying a 13,000 to 22,000lb (5,897 to 9,980kg) bombload.

In 1936 General Wever, a pilot and a man of outstanding talent, was appointed the first Chief of Air Staff. Among his plans was the manufacture of a large number of four-engine bombers. Milch also became a general in the Luftwaffe. His exceptional ability as an administrator, organiser and planner had always rankled with Goering, whose jealousy drove him to open hostility. In consequence, another figure of seminal importance in the supply of equipment to the German Air Force came to prominence. This was Generalleutnant Ernst Udet, who had scored 62 victories as a young fighter pilot in 1917-18 and was the most popular man in German aviation circles. Goering promoted him to replace Milch as chief of the Technical Department. Although the two men were close friends, Milch said of Udet, ''Hitler recognised in him one of our greatest pilots, and he was right. But he also saw him as one of the greatest technical experts, and here he was mistaken.'' This was true: Udet was far out of his depth. He floundered about at the head of an enormous bureaucracy, while exercising inadequate control over aircraft production. He indulged his enthusiasm for the Bf 109 and dive bombers by equipping the Luftwaffe as a tactical rather than a strategic air force. This, linked to Goering's irrational appraisal of every changing facet of Germany's air campaign against Britain, and Hitler's insanity that led

Above: (Top row, left to right): OR's cap; OR's summer cap; officer's cap; officer's summer cap. (Bottom row, left to right): Aircrew officers rank badges, Lt, 1st Lt, Capt, Maj, Lt.Col and Col.

to wild decisions and the issue of orders based on ''intuition'', was a major factor in the Luftwaffe's defeat.

An equally disastrous flaw was that the only four-engine bombers were the Focke-Wulf Kondors: converted airliners, used only for maritime reconnaissance and attacking ships on the Atlantic; they carried a mere 4,600lb (2,086kg) bombload (RAF twin-engine bombers carried from 4,000 to 7,000lb (3,175kg). General Wever's foresight had come to nothing (he had been killed in an air crash in June 1936). Two four-engined prototypes, a Dornier and a Junkers, were test flown soon after. Wever's successor, Kesselring, told Goering that two four-engine purpose-designed bombers could be built for the same cost and factory

Below: Luftwaffe tunics (left to right): Senior Engineer, Engineer Corps; Oberfeldwebel, Aircrew and Telephonist Private, Signal Corps. The third tunic is of superior pre-war quality.

Above: Hermann Goering, the titular head of the Luftwaffe, talks to pilots in France in 1940. His rank of Reichmarschall was unique, as were his fancy uniforms. His Blue Max is almost hidden by other medals.

Left: This greatcoat and breeches were worn by a Luftwaffe Generalfeldmarschall (Field Marshal) as normal field dress. Now at the Luftwaffenmuseum, it is not known who these specific items belonged to.

Right: In the Luftwaffe, command was often more to do with prowess than rank. Adolf Galland, seen here with Herman Goering, became Kommodore of JG 26 while still a Major, although promotion followed.

Below: They also serve, who only stand and talk. Luftwaffe officers confer on the ''Holy Mountain'', Cap Blanc Nez. Second from the left is Generalfeldmarshall Albert Kesselring, Commander of Luftflotte 2.

space as three twin-engine bombers. Goering retorted that Hitler would ask how many bombers there were, not how big they were, and decided to limit the Luftwaffe to fast medium bombers and dive bombers.

July 1936 presented Hitler and Goering with a welcome chance to display the aggressiveness of the resurgent Luftwaffe. Civil war broke out in Spain between the Nationalists, an apology for Fascists, led by General Franco, and the Republican Party, which was a euphemism for Communists. Within a month, 85 German air and ground crew volunteers, 20 Ju 52/3m transport aircraft and six He 51A-1 biplane fighters arrived to support Franco. During October and November, 30 more fighters of the same type, with 400 volunteers who travelled by sea under the guise of ''strength through joy'' tourists, joined them to form the Legion Kondor under the command of General Hugo Sperrle. They included pilots from III/JG134 and JG234,132 (''Richthofen'', later JG2) and 26. Sperrle returned home the next year on promotion to General of Aviators and was replaced by General Wolfram von Richthofen.

Among those who had their first experience of air operations in the Legion Kondor and profited greatly by it in enhancing their skill, were future fighter aces Wilhelm Balthasar (47 victories, 7 in Spain), Herbert Ihlefeld (130 victories, 7 in Spain), Walter Oesau (125 victories, 8 in Spain), Werner Mölders (115 victories, 14 in Spain), and Adolf Galland (104 victories, none in Spain; but a thorough education in air co-operation with infantry and armour). Mölders was destined to become General of Fighters in November 1940, with the rank of Generalmajor, at the age of 28. When he was killed a few months later, Galland, aged 29 then, replaced him.

The Spanish Civil War was immensely useful to the Luftwaffe in gaining expertise at fighter-to-fighter combat and perfecting the technique of close support

for ground troops, which culminated in 1939 and 1940 with the Blitzkrieg. It was in this rôle that Hauptmann Galland (who, like all officers posted to Spain, had been temporarily promoted one rank) had his baptism of fire, as commander of Jagdstaffel 3 in November 1936. The enemy was equipping with American Curtiss and Russian Polikarpov monoplane fighters, which compelled the antiquated He 51s to be relegated to ground attack. They flew in formations of nine, each carrying six 22lb (10kg) bombs that they released from a

height of 49ft (150m) before strafing with their twin 7.92 Rheinmetall machine guns.

Ju 87 and Hs 123 dive bombers arrived in the closing months of 1937, to practise the terrorist tactics that would defeat Poland, the Low Countries, Norway and France, and fail against Britain.

In April 1938 Werner Mölders took over from Galland and two months later the Staffel re-equipped with the new Bf 109B. Now, it could cover the low-flying He 51s from attacking fighters. Mölders soon found that

Above: Oberleutnant Boxhammer, who as a Leutnant flew with the experimental trials unit Erprobungsgruppe 210 on raids against England. Like so many German flyers, he was later killed on the Russian front.

the classic formation based on close Vs of three aircraft was unwieldy. When opposing fighters met, they broke formation and fought singly. But a pilot on his own had no one to watch his tail and warn him of an attack from astern. So he devised a new formation of which the basis was a loose pair, called a Rotte. Two Rotten operating together became a Schwarm and tactical freedom of manoeuvre was paramount.

As fighter pilots returned home on completing a tour in Spain, they became instructors in the new fighter tactics. Mock combat was not limited to dogfights between single aircraft. Rotte would fight Rotte, Schwarm would fight Schwarm, and even a whole Staffel would take on another. This typically Teutonic thoroughness was of inestimable value: no other air force in the world practised in this manner. Attacks in Staffel strength were made against bomber formations, and the escorting of bombers was also practised. These exercises again were generally neglected by other nations.

While the RAF was accumulating a varied experience in the 1920s and '30s, Lufthansa's 120 aeroplanes were

Left: Like their RAF equivalents, Luftwaffe pilots wore various official and unofficial forms of flying dress. This picture shows the lightweight canvas summer flying suit, fleece-lined leather flying boots, leather flying gloves, light canvas flying helmet (without earphones or microphone) and large flying goggles. This example has no rank badges, although these were often worn on the sleeve.

LUFTWAFFE FIGHTER CODEWORDS

Kirchturm	(Church tower) Own height in hundreds of metres
Hanny	(Johnny or ''bloke'') Enemy height
Caruso	Course
Zirkus über	(Circus over) Assemble at
Gartenraum	(Garden room) Airfield
Horrido	I have shot down enemy aircraft
Ente	(Duck) Range from enemy aircraft
Bodo	Unit Headquarters or own base
Orkan	Enemy's speed
Tuba	Bearing
Pauke-Pauke	Attack!
Viktor	Understood
Ich berühre	(I touch) I have seen the target
Otto-Otto	Target in searchlight
Normaluhr in	(Usual time) Wait at
Ich habe Durst	(I am thirsty) I am short of petrol
Radfahrer	(Cyclist) Own single-engine aircraft
Möbelwagen	(Furniture van) Own twin-engine aircraft
Dicke Möbelwagen	(Bulky ditto) Own 3-engine aircraft
Feindlich Jäger	Enemy fighters
Autos (Cars)	Enemy twin-engine aircraft
Dicke Autos	(Bulky cars) Enemy three-engine aircraft
Freie Bahn	(Free road) Enemy fighters breaking formation
Donnerkeil	(Thunderbolt) Night attack
Stacheldraht	(Barbed wire) Flying within certain height limits forbidden
Objekt	(Object) Designated object being defended e.g. town, port, ship
Mauerblume	(Wallflower) Contact with the enemy
Spielbeginn	(Start of the game) Enemy formation recognised at (followed by place name)
Halbzeit	(Half time) Abandoning engagement
Ich suche	(I am looking) I haven't seen, or have lost, the target
Gehen Sie ins Vorzimmer	(Go into the anteroom) . . . Wait
Konkurrenz	(Competition) Danger warning
Weiss	(White) Fighter operating with searchlights
Schwartz	(Black) fighter operating without searchlights

Above: Pre-war German fighter affiliation exercises as three Heinkel He 51A-0 fighters in the tight vic formation used by all air services at this time, sweep in behind a flight of Dornier Do 23 bombers.

Below: These items were all taken from aircraft downed in the UK, and include (top left) OR's peaked cap, (top right) officer's peaked cap, officer's dagger and scabbard, officer's side cap and signet ring.

flying up to four million miles (6,437,200km) a year, operating by night as well as by day: an excellent training for future night-bomber pilots and navigators. From 1935 all Lufthansa crews became Luftwaffe reservists.

When Hitler came to power on 1 January 1933, the German aviation industry's output of aircraft averaged 31 a month. One year later Milch presented his production schedule for the next 24 months: 4,021 aircraft with which to lay the foundation for six fighter, six bomber and six reconnaissance Geschwader. These in turn would complete the operational training of newly fledged aircrew and ground staff. Although 25 types of aircraft were involved, by the end of 1934, 164 a month were coming out of the factories, to a total of

Above: Unteroffizier Leo Zaunbrecher (left) poses in front of his Messerschmitt Bf 109E shortly before being shot down and taken prisoner. His Staffel, 2/JG 52, lost a total of three aircraft on this day.

840 operational types; and by December 1935, 265 a month were being produced, of which 1,923 were for the Luftwaffe. In 1937 the monthly average reached 467. In 1938 it fell to 436. For the war that Hitler intended to provoke, a minimum of 700 a month was necessary. Under Udet's incompetent direction, German aircraft production struggled to attain a monthly 691 in 1939.

Another of Douhet's precepts, that Germany did not fulfil and Britain did, was "Modern war is an industrial war, in the sense that the troops are no more than the workers in an immense factory for the destruction of men and objects. The value of any army depends on the worth, the perfection and the number of machines it possesses . . . war is a game of economics . . . it is necessary to have means suitable to the end that one wishes to attain."

In electronics, Germany was in some ways ahead of Britain. For Lufthansa's benefit — and that of the future bomber crews it was training — night flying and blind flying aids had received more attention than in any other country. As early as 1926 there were 13 radio stations and a chain of beacons. In the 1930s airports

Left: This figure represents a navigator or observer from a bomber crew. Shown are the so-called 'channel trousers' with their multiple large pockets for essential survival items, the dark blue fleece-lined flying jacket with 1st Lieutenant sleeve badges, summer net flying helmet and throat microphone assembly, shatterproof goggles and oxygen mask. Note the large leather map and document case.

Left: Standard Luftwaffe fleece-lined flying boots. Sartorial standards among the German officers were such that they often preferred to fly in their topboots, while at least one pilot wore carpet slippers over England.

Above: Leo Zaunbrecher is second from the left in this picture of pilots of Jagdgeschwader 52's second Staffel. JG 52 was the only Bf 109 unit to fail to produce an *experte* of note during the Battle.

Below: Some very temporary war art is applied to the fin of this 500lb/250kg German bomb by two enthusiastic Luftwaffe armourers. Did Winston Churchill really wear a top hat like this?

began to install the Lorenz beam approach system. Although radar had been invented in Germany in 1904 and neglected until development was resumed 30 years later, General Wolfgang Martini, Director of Luftwaffe Signals, was ignorant of the superiority of British equipment until it was too late, during the Battle of Britain.

The first demand for radar, in 1934, was not made by the Luftwaffe but by the German Navy for gun ranging, target search and air surveillance. In 1936 the Luftwaffe began to examine radar as a means of aircraft detection and ordered a dozen 240cm, 125 MHz sets that could read range and azimuth. They were codenamed Freya, after the Norse Venus who sacrificed her honour for a magic necklace guarded by Heimdall, the watchman of the gods who could see a hundred miles by day or night. In fact, the Freya's range was 75 miles (120km). The first experimental site was being set up on the North Sea coast when war broke out. In July 1939, 200 more were ordered. At the same time work began on a 53cm, 566 MHz type, the Würzburg, of which 800 were eventually ordered for the Flak arm and began to be delivered during the Battle of Britain. Their range was only 30 miles (48km) but they could estimate height. Although German scientists were competent, there was no central coordination of their work and no liaison between the flying and anti-aircraft branches of the Luftwaffe.

The German listening service was comparable with Britain's and as effective. Lacking a control and reporting system as ingenious and mature as the RAF's, the Luftwaffe had to resort to passing information to fighters by radio from listening posts.

For the guidance of bombers a beam system had been developed from the Lorenz blind landing equipment, codenamed Knickebein — Crooked Leg. The bomber received signals from Germany on its 30 MHz Lorenz beam-approach landing sets. A continuous note indicated to the pilot that he was following the beam accurately towards his target. If he drifted to the left he heard dots; to the right, dashes. An additional note — accurate only to within 1,640ft (500m) — warned that he was over the target and should bomb. For a nation that did not care how many civilians it killed as long as its bombs were somewhere near the target, it served well enough.

The Luftwaffe intelligence organisation, Abteilung (Department) Five, was formed on January 1938 under Major Josef Schmidt, who was neither a pilot nor a linguist. His equivalent in the RAF was Air Commodore Goddard — a pilot who knew German and French — a disparity in rank which indicates the relative importance that the opposing Services placed on intelligence. Schmidt relied heavily on information from Air Attachés, particularly Oberst Wenniger in London, with whom Goddard was on most friendly terms although always guarded. Schmidt used occasions such as the annual air display at Hendon and Empire Air Day for a sight of British aircraft and military airfields, and counted on the press for general information. He had the benefit of further airfield and target intelligence obtained from photographic reconnaissance by Heinkel 111Cs with civil markings, based near Berlin and ostensibly carrying out proving flights

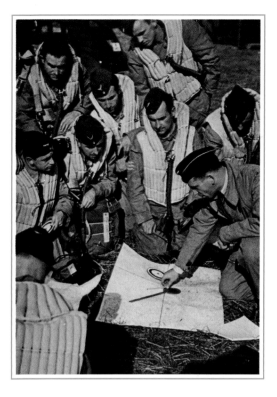

Above German bomber crewmen cluster around wearing their kapok-filled life jackets as an officer strikes a pose with the map, in this rather artificial scene constructed for the magazine *Signal*.

on potential new European civil air routes.

Before and during the Battle of Britain little could be learned from interrogating prisoners of war, as viritually all British aircrew who were shot down landed in England or behind the Allied lines in France. Once the RAF abandoned France, the Luftwaffe also lost the ability to glean new technical intelligence from the wreckage of downed enemy aircraft. The basic business of espionage was also most ineptly performed: the majority of spies who landed in Britain by sea or parachute were quickly caught.

Schmidt's first summary of comparative effectiveness, in early 1939, was ill-informed. He described the RAF as "much out of date" and Britain's defence as "still weak". German aircraft he claimed, were superior, with their advantage in armament, armoured fuel tanks and flying instruments. He calculated that the RAF had 200 first-line fighters. The actual strength was 608. He made a better guess about bombers: 500, only 36 short of the real number.

In November he delivered a plan for the attack on

Left: Like all of Hitler's armed forces, the Luftwaffe believed in smart dress uniforms. This shows the dress tunic, riding breeches and side cap of a 1st Lieutenant; the yellow background to his collar tabs indicate that he is aircrew. Some units were given honorific titles and the band on the right sleeve of this tunic shows that the wearer belonged to the Geschwader named after General Wever.

Britain, in which he gave as priority targets ports and supply lines. He named London, Liverpool, Bristol, Glasgow and Hull as the most important objectives: not only to destroy shipping but also dockyards, food warehouses and oil storage tanks.

On July 16, 1940 he submitted a comparative survey of Luftwaffe and RAF striking power, in which he assessed the British bomber force as 400 Hampdens, 350 Wellingtons, 300 Whitleys and 100 Hudsons. The air Ministry's weekly ''State of Aircraft'' dated July 14 shows 96 Hampdens and 55 in reserve; 128 Wellingtons and 28 in reserve; 96 Whitleys and 56 in reserve; 105

Left: Aero engines often require to be warmed up before they can be started. The Luftwaffe developed numerous ingenious heater systems for this task as shown in this early colour view of a Heinkel He 111.

Below: German equipment. In the back row is a mask taken from a Heinkel He 111 shot down over Sheffield at night, while in the front two helmets flank a high altitude oxygen mask from a Junkers Ju 86P.

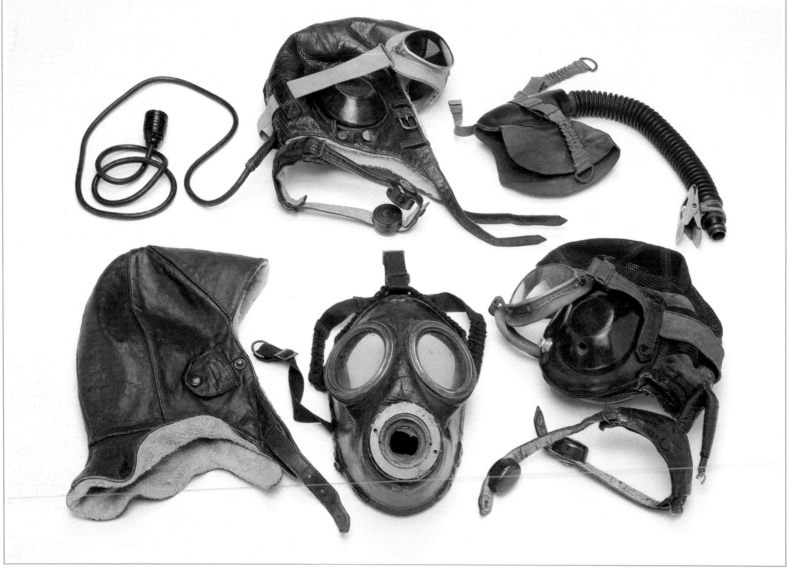

LUFTWAFFE AIR FLEETS, SEPTEMBER 7, 1940 ORDER OF BATTLE

LUFTFLOTTE 2 (Holland, Belgium, France)		LUFTFLOTTE 3 (France)	
Commanded by Generalfeldmarschall Albert Kesselring		Commanded by Generalfeldmarschall Hugo Sperrle	
Aufkl GR 122 Stab		Stab,1,2,3Aufkl Gr 123	Ju88, Do17
1(F)22	Do17 & Bf110	**Fliegerkorps IV**	
2(F)122	Ju88	3 (F)121	Ju88, He111
4(F)122	Ju88, He111, Bf110	Stab,1,2,4,Reserve Staffel LG1	Ju88
Fliegerkorps 1		Stab,1,2StG3	Ju87
Commanded by Generaloberst Ulrich Grauert		StG2	Ju87
5(F)122	Ju88, He111	KGr806	Ju88
Stab,1,2 KG1	He111	Stab,1,2,3,Reserve Staffel KG27	He111
3KG1	Ju88	KGr100	He111
Stab,1,2 KG30	Ju88	KGr606	Do17
Stab,1,3 KG76	Do17	3(F)31	Bf110, Do17
2 KG76	Ju88	1KG40	FW200 (Naval co-op)
Stab,1,2,3 KG77	Ju88	Stab,1,2,3ZG76	Bf110
Fliegerkorps II		Stab,1,2,3JG53	Bf109
Commanded by General Bruno Lörzer		5LG1	Bf110
1(F)122	Ju88	**Fliegerkorps V**	
7(F)LG2	Bf110	4(F)121	Ju88, Do17
Stab,1,2,3 KG2	Do17	4(F)14	Bf110, Do17
Stab,1,2,3 KG3	Do17	Stab,1,2,3,Reserve Staffel KG51	Ju88
Stab,1,2,3 KG53	He111	Stab,1,2,Reserve Staffel KG54	Ju88
IV(St)LG1	Ju87	Stab,1,2,3,Reserve Staffel JG2	
IILG2 (Schlacht)	Bf109	(Operating with both	
Epr Gr210	Bf109, 110	Luftflotten 2 & 3)	Bf109
Stab StG1	Do17, Ju87	Staab,1,2,3JG27	Bf109
2StG1	Ju87	**Fliegerkorps VIII**	
1,2StG26	Ju87	Stab StG1	Do17, Ju87
Fliegerdivision XI		1,2StG1	Ju87
Commanded by Generalmajor Joachim Cöler		Stab StG2	Do17, Ju87
3(F)122	Ju88, He111	1,2StG2	Ju87
Stab,1,2KG4	He111	Stab StG77	Do17, Ju87
3KG4	Ju88, He111	1,2,3StG 77	Ju87
KGr126	He111 (minelaying)	II LG2	Do17
Stab KG40	Ju88 (minelaying)	2(F)11	Do17
Kü F1 Gr106	He115, Do18	2(F)123	Ju88
Jagdfliegerführer 1		5(Z)LG1	Bf110
Stab,2JG76	Bf109	**LUFTFLOTTE 5** (Norway)	
5ZLG1	Bf110	Commanded by Generaloberst Hans-Jurgen Stumpf	
Luftgaukommando VI		**Fliegerkorps X**	
One Schwarm of 1JG52	Bf109	Commanded by Generalleutnant Hans Geisler	
One Schwarm of 3JG3	Bf109	Stab Aufk1 GR(F)	He111, Ju88
Luftgaukommando XI		1(F)22	Do17
One Schwarm each of 1,2,3JG54	Bf109	1(F)120	He111, Ju88
One Schwarm of 2JG51	Bf109	1(F)121	Do17, Ju88
Luftgaukommando Holland		3(F)122	Do17, Ju88
One Schwarm each of 1,2,3JG54	Bf109	One Kette Aufk1 Gr 506	He115
One Schwarm 2JG51	Bf109	1,2,3 Aufk1 Gr506	He115
Luftgaukommando Belgium		2JG77	Bf109
Army co-operation only			

Above: The quick-fire marksmanship of Helmut Wick saw him rapidly promoted to Kommodore of JG 2. The Luftwaffe's ranking ace with 56 victories, he fell to the guns of Flt Lt John Dundas of No.609 Sqn.

Hudsons with a further 11 in reserve.

About the quality of senior RAF officers, he was as fatuous. They were, he alleged, badly out of touch with modern conditions of air warfare and no longer in flying practice. The truth was that RAF Wing Commanders and Group Captains commanding stations flew often. When war came many of them took part in operations. Air Vice Marshal Park went up in his Hurricane to see the air battle over France for himself.

The Luftwaffe's leadership at all levels was inferior to the RAF's. The outbreak of war found Goering as Commander-in-Chief, with General Hans Jeschonnek as Chief of Air Staff.

Instead of functional Commands, the Luftwaffe was organised in Air Fleets, each of which comprised fighter, bomber and reconnaissance functions. The biggest tactical formation was a Geschwader (G), consisting of three Gruppen. Within a Gruppe (Gr) there were three or four Staffeln. The Staffel, the equivelent of an RAF squadron, numbered 12 to 16 aircraft and 20 to 25 pilots. The smallest element in a fighter Staffel was a pair, or Rotte; the smallest element in a bomber squadron, was three aircraft, a Kette.

Other formations, which had no fixed establishment were: Fliegerkorps (Flying corps); Fliegerdivision (Flying Division); Luftgaukommando (Air District Command).

The system for identifying Staffeln, Geschwader and Gruppen was somewhat convoluted. A Gruppe's number was shown in Roman numerals, a Geschwader's and Staffel's in Arabic numerals.

Kampfgeschwader (bomber), was abbreviated to KG; Jagdgeschwader (fighter) to JG; Stukageschwader (dive

bomber) to StG; Zerstörergeschwader (destroyer, i.e. heavy fighter) to ZG; Nachtjagdgeschwader (night fighter) to NJG; Aufklärungsgruppe (Fern), (reconnaissance long range) to Aufkl Gr (F); Küstenfliegergruppe (coastal) to Kü Fl Gr; Lehrgeschwader (operational training) to LG; Erprobungs (proving or test) to Epr. A ground attack or close support formation was suffixed Schlacht (battle).

II JG 26 meant No.2 Gruppe of Jagdgeschwader 26. 2 JG 26 meant Staffel No 2 of Jagdgeschwader 26.

A Gruppe Kommandeur's staff (Stab) was the Gruppe's Headquarters unit (Gruppenstab) and included an HQ Flight (Stabsschwarm) of four aircraft, which he led on operations. A Geschwader Kommodore had a similar HQ unit and flight.

During the period that saw the first heavy daylight air raid on London on September 7, 1940 and the RAF's decisive victory on the 15th, which finally won the Battle of Britain, the Order of Battle of the three Air Fleets involved was as shown in the table.

FIFTY YEARS ago, Adler Tag, the "Day of Eagles", found Hermann Goering supremely confident in the outcome of the immense assault on the United Kingdom that was about to be launched by his Luftwaffe. On that fateful thirteenth day of August, which was to mark the commencement of the aerial offensive proper, the Reichsmarschall was convinced, and not without some justification, that the warplanes that he, as Oberbefehlshaber der Luftwaffe, was committing to the attack had no peers. They were manned by the best-trained and most experienced crews available to any air arm in the world.

The aircraft of the Luftwaffe had been proven in combat; their crews had been blooded over Spain, Poland, France and the Low Countries. How could Adler Tag signify anything *but* commencement of an operation that would end in yet another victory for the Third Reich? Goering saw every reason to assure his Führer that what opposition could be expected from the Royal Air Force would be despatched, probably within days; that his Kinder ("children") would soon be roaming British skies without let or hindrance.

Unfortunately for the loquacious Reichsmarschall, whose technical knowledge fell far short of that which his position warranted, his single-seat fighters, even then taking-off from their bases in the Pas de Calais and elsewhere, lacked sufficient endurance for the type

Below: The starboard rudder of a Do 17 claimed by the 408th Coastal Battery and LX 58th Heavy Regiment of the Royal Artillery at North Foreland, Kent, on August 28, 1940. This aircraft had been overpainted black for nocturnal operations.

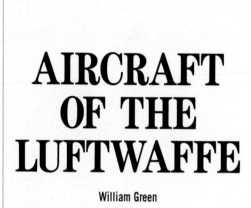

AIRCRAFT OF THE LUFTWAFFE

William Green

of campaign on which they were about to embark. The conceptual limitations of his long-range heavy fighters had still to be understood and his bombers possessed defensive armament that presupposed a measure of Luftwaffe air superiority.

Furthermore, he and his staff had been deluded by the so-called "Studie Blau", the vital, yet fundamentally inaccurate, intelligence appraisal of RAF capabilities prepared by the Operations Staff of the Oberkommando der Luftwaffe. Thus, unknowingly, the Luftwaffe was being committed on that day to a gruelling battle of attrition for which it was ill equipped; a battle from which it was eventually to withdraw battered and exhausted — the aerial drama of all time: the "Battle of Britain".

Of the *dramatis personnae* of the epic aerial conflict that was to unfold over Southern England in the weeks that followed, it was to be the pilots of the single-seat fighters of the opposing sides that, contemporaneously at least, were to receive the most acclaim. This was understandable in view of the more emotive part that they played in the drama. Indeed, today, a half-century later, military aviation's annals devote more attention to their activities than to those of the crews manning other participating warplanes.

In so far as the Royal Air Force was concerned, its role of defender entirely justified the emphasis placed on the exploits of its fighter pilots. For the Luftwaffe, the aggressor, the situation was different, however, for its single-seat fighters had a supporting task, their primary mission being protection of the bomber forces engaged. How well they fulfilled this role during the historic encounter remains to this day a matter for contention. Nonetheless, of the personnel operating the six basic types of warplane employed by the Luftwaffe during the Battle, it was the pilots of the Bf 109E single-seat fighter that were then and remain to this day the *prima donnas* of the German effort; those responsible for the major share of the combat losses sustained by their opponent. Their Messerschmitt mount was to become virtually synonymous with this episode of World War II.

Below: Luftwaffe machine guns including those used in the "Battle of Britain". These Rheinmetall-Borsig weapons are: (top to bottom) the 7,92-mm MG 17, the 13-mm MG 131; the 7,9-mm MG 15 and the MG 81Z "Zwilling" or "Twin".

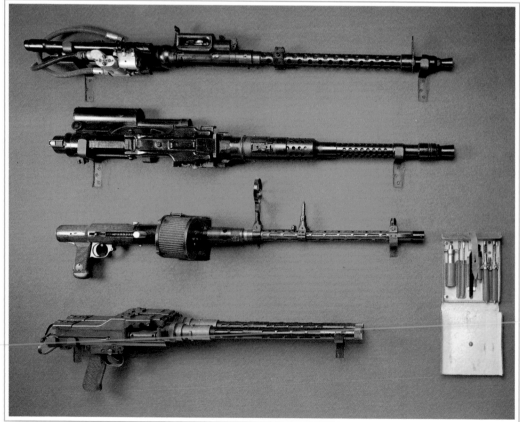

The Messerschmitt Bf 109E

There can be no doubt that the Bf 109E flown by all elements of the Jagdflieger involved in the Battle was a highly competent warplane; as outstanding a fighting machine as either of its principal opponents, Hurricane or Spitfire, and a highly dangerous adversary. By the time that this Messerschmitt fighter appeared in force in British skies, it was the object of carefully fostered mystique; a myth of invincibility assiduously created by the Propaganda Ministry in Berlin. In some respects, the Luftwaffe itself was to fall victim to this myth as a result of the comparative ease with which the Bf 109E had conquered all pre-Battle adversaries.

There was nothing mysterious about the Bf 109E, however. It was a well-conceived, soundly-designed fighter that, like its opponents, possessed its share of shortcomings. It offered excellent handling characteristics and response at low and medium speeds; it was extremely stable, could be pulled round in high-g turns, and its climb and dive performances were second to none. On the debit side, its controls tended to heavy up as speed increased. demanding more physical effort from its pilot than did its British contemporaries; the absence of a trimmer necessitated continuous application of rudder in order to fly straight at high speeds, and it suffered an incipient swing during take-off and landing. A big advantage was its direct fuel injection which was much superior to the carburettor feed of its British opponents, but there was little to choose between Bf 109E and Spitfire between 12,000 and 17,000ft (3,660 and 5,180m), the German fighter being undeniably superior above 20,000ft (6,100m).

Designed by Dipl-Ing Willy Messerschmitt and Dipl-Ing Robert Lusser, the Bf 109 flew some months before the Hurricane or Spitfire, on May 28, 1935, with Hans-Dietrich ''Bubi'' Knoetzsch at the controls. For this event, which took place at the small factory airfield between Augsburg and Haunstetten, the first prototype had been fitted with a Rolls-Royce Kestrel V liquid-cooled inline engine affording 695hp for take-off, its intended Junkers Jumo 210 engine being unavailable. When first arriving at the Erprobungsstelle, or Proving Centre, of the Luftwaffe, the E-Stelle test and evaluation pilots looked askance at this then radical and highly innovative fighting machine. Its steep ground angle, with poor view for taxying in consequence, its cramped cockpit with sideways-hinging canopy, its narrow-track undercarriage and its automatic wing leading-edge slots aroused extreme scepticism among the conventionalists.

Second and third prototypes were meanwhile completed with the intended Jumo 210A inverted-vee engine rated at 680hp for take-off; the Messerschmitt fighter gained the approbation of the Luftwaffen-führungsstab, the Operations Staff, and, in March 1936, the decision was taken to build the Bf 109 as the next service fighter of the Luftwaffe. This *production* decision virtually coincided with the first flight of the Spitfire prototype, the German fighter's future principal antagonist.

The initial example of the first production model, the Bf 109B, left the Augsburg-Haunstetten assembly line in February 1937, the impetus behind the Messerschmitt fighter enabling conversion to the new

warplane of the premier Luftwaffe fighter Geschwader, JG 132 Richthofen, to begin almost immediately at Jüterbog-Damm. Indeed, the programme tempo was such that, in the following month, March, 16 Bf 109Bs were shipped direct from the factory to the Tablada airfield, Seville, for use by the Condor Legion committed to the Nationalist cause in the ongoing Spanish Civil War. Personnel of III Gruppe of JG 132 were hurriedly assigned to 2 Staffel of Jagdgruppe 88, which relinquished its He 51 biplanes, and operational status with the new fighter was achieved by late April 1937, less than three months from the first production Bf 109B rolling from the asembly line!

The early career of the Messerschmitt fighter seemed shrouded in mystery, but on November 11, 1937, a pre-series airframe, the Bf 109 V13, fitted with a specially-boosted Daimler-Benz DB 601 engine, raised the world airspeed record for landplanes to no less that 379.38mph (610.53km/h). While being blooded in action in Spanish skies, the fighter was the subject of extraordinarily rapid development. Series manufacture of the Bf 109B gave place successively to the improved Bf 109C and D, but these retained the comparatively low-powered Jumo engine. Design emphasis was now being placed on the perfection of a very much more powerful model, the Bf 109E employing the new inverted-vee Daimler-Benz engine.

The first series Bf 109E fighters began to leave the assembly lines at the beginning of 1939, all production of the fighter by the parent company having meanwhile been transferred to Regensburg. The Erla Maschinenwerk at Leipzig and the Gerhard Fieseler Werke at Kassel had become the principal suppliers of the Bf 109, however, and the Wiener-Neustädter-Flugzeugwerke in Austria was preparing for large-scale manufacture of the fighter. The DB 601A engine of

Above: A Bf 109B of the initial production batch delivered to the Luftwaffe in the spring of 1937. A precursor of the Bf 109E that participated in the ''Battle'', the Bf 109B had been phased out of first line service by then.

Below: A Bf 109E-3 of an unidentified Jagdgeschwader's II Gruppe photographed over the Channel during operations in September 1940. Note the pilot's personal emblem on the nose.

MESSERSCHMITT Bf 109E-4
Cutaway Drawing Key

1 Hollow airscrew hub
2 Spinner
3 Three-blade VDM variable-pitch propeller
4 Propeller pitch-change mechanism
5 Spinner back plate
6 Glycol coolant header tank
7 Glycol filler cap
8 Cowling fastener
9 Chin intake
10 Coolant pipe fairing
11 Exhaust forward fairing
12 Additional (long-range) oil tank
13 Daimler-Benz DB 601A engine
14 Supplementary intakes
15 Fuselage machine gun troughs
16 Anti-vibration engine mounting pads
17 Exhaust ejector stubs
18 Coolant pipes (to underwing radiators)
19 Oil cooler intake
20 Coolant radiator
21 Radiator outlet flap
22 Cowling frame
23 Engine mounting support strut
24 Spent cartridge collector compartment
25 Ammunition boxes (starboard loading)
26 Engine supercharger
27 Supercharger air intake fairing
28 Forged magnesium alloy cantilever engine mounting
29 Engine mounting/forward bulkhead attachment
30 Ammunition feed chutes
31 Engine accessories
32 Two fuselage-mounted MG 17 machine guns
33 Blast tube muzzles
34 Wing skinning
35 Starboard cannon access
36 20-mm MG FF wing cannon
37 Leading-edge automatic slot
38 Slot tracks
39 Slot actuating linkage
40 Wing main spar
41 Intermediate rib station
42 Wing end rib
43 Starboard navigation light
44 Aileron outer hinge
45 Aileron metal trim tab
46 Starboard aileron
47 Aileron/flap link connection

48 Combined control linkage
49 Starboard flap frame
50 Cannon ammunition drum access
51 Fuselage machine gun cooling slots
52 Gun mounting frame
53 Firewall/bulkhead
54 Instrument panel rear face (fabric covered)
55 Oil dipstick cover
56 Control column
57 Oil filler cap (tank omitted for clarity)
58 Rudder pedal assembly
59 Aircraft identity data plate (external)
60 Main spar centre-section carry-through

61 Underfloor control linkage
62 Oxygen regulator
63 Harness adjustment lever
64 Engine priming pump
65 Circuit breaker panel
66 Hood catch
67 Starboard-hinged cockpit canopy
68 Revi gunsight (offset to starboard)
69 Windscreen panel frame
70 Canopy section frame
71 Pilot's head armour
72 Pilot's back armour
73 Seat harness
74 Pilot's seat
75 Seat adjustment lever
76 Tailplane incidence handwheel
77 Cockpit floor diaphragm
78 Landing flaps control handwheel

79 Seat support frame
80 Contoured ('L'-shape) fuel tank
81 Tailplane incidence cables
82 Fuselage frame
83 Rudder cable
84 Oxygen cylinders (2)
85 Fuel filler/overspill pipes
86 Baggage compartment
87 Entry handhold (spring loaded)
88 Canopy fixed aft section
89 Aerial mast
90 Aerial
91 Fuel filler cap
92 Fuel vent line
93 Radio pack support brackets
94 Anti-vibration bungee supports
95 FuG 7 transmitter/receiver radio package

96 Aerial lead-in
97 Tailplane incidence cable pulley
98 Rudder control cable
99 Monocoque fuselage structure
100 Radio access/first-aid kit panel
101 Elevator control cables
102 Fuselage frame
103 Lifting tube
104 Tailfin root fillet
105 Tailplane incidence gauge (external)
106 Tailplane support strut
107 Starboard tailplane
108 Elevator outer hinge
109 Elevator balance
110 Starboard elevator
111 Tailfin structure
112 Aerial stub

113 Rudder balance
114 Rudder upper hinge
115 Rudder frame
116 Rudder trim tab
117 Tail navigation light
118 Port elevator frame
119 Elevator balance
120 Rudder control quadrant
121 Tailplane structure
122 Elevator torque tube sleeve
123 Tailplane end rib attachment
124 Fuselage end post
125 Elevator control rod
126 Port tailplane support strut

the Bf 109E had received final clearance for service use late in 1938 and, in addition to being built by the Daimler-Benz plants at Genshagen and Marienfelde, this was being produced by the Henschel Flugmotorenbau at Altenbauna and the Niedersächsische subsidiary of the Büssing-Werke of Braunschweig.

Installation of the DB 601A engine in the Bf 109 airframe transformed the performance of the Messerschmitt fighter from good to excellent. It was a remarkable engine by international standards and its use of direct fuel injection was to endow the Bf 109E with a considerable advantage. Negative *g*, such as occurred in sudden transition from level to diving flight and interrupted the fuel supply to engines possessing normal float carburettors, no longer presented a pro-

blem, enabling the Messerschmitt fighter to out-dive its opponents. Furthermore, fuel injection reduced fuel consumption and afforded better results from relatively low octane petrol. The DB 601A was rated at 1,175hp for take-off and was thus more powerful than the Merlin then being installed in contemporary production versions of the Hurricane and Spitfire.

The Bf 109E retained the 40-mile (65km) range FuG 7 R/T equipment of earlier versions of the fighter, together with the Carl Zeiss C/12C reflector sight, armament of the initial model, the Bf 109E-1, comprising four 7.9mm Rheinmetall Borsig MG 17 machine guns. However, the Luftwaffenführungsstab by now generally favoured the more lethal if slower-firing 20mm MG FF cannon as a wing-mounted weapon and

it had been decided to standardise on these as soon as the supply situation permitted. Thus, the cannon-armed sub-type, the Bf 109E-3, was to follow closely on the heels of the initial production Bf 109E-1, this retaining the twin fuselage-mounted synchronised MG 17 machine guns with 1,000 rounds per gun and mating them with a pair of MG FF cannon, each with 60 rounds, to provide a combined weight of fire of 290lb/min (131kg/min). At this juncture, no armour protection was provided for either pilot or fuel tank; these, as was also a bullet-proof windscreen, were features to be introduced in the light of operational experience.

In general, the handling characteristics of the DB 601A-engined Bf 109 were essentially similar to those

127 Non-retractable tailwheel
128 Tailwheel leg
129 Elevator control cable/rod link
130 Tailwheel leg shock-absorber
131 Rudder control cable
132 Fuselage stringer
133 Accumulator
134 Fuselage half ventral join
135 Electrical leads
136 Fuselage panels

157 Control access panel
158 Main spar/fuselage attachment fairing
159 Wing control surface cable pulleys
160 Port mainwheel well
161 Wheel well (zipped) fabric shield
162 20-mm MG FF wing cannon
163 Wing front spar
164 Undercarriage leg tunnel rib cut-outs

137 Radio pack lower support frames
138 Entry foothold (spring loaded)
139 Wingroot fillet
140 Flap profile
141 Port flap frame
142 Port aileron frame
143 Aileron metal trim tab
144 Rear spar
145 Port wingtip
146 Port navigation light
147 Wing main spar outer section
148 Solid ribs
149 Leading-edge automatic slot
150 Rib cut-outs
151 Control link access plate
152 Wing rib stations
153 Port wing 20-mm MG FF cannon installation
154 Ammunition drum access panel
155 Inboard rib cut-outs
156 Flap visual position indicator

165 Undercarriage lock mechanism
166 Wing/fuselage end rib
167 Undercarriage actuating cylinder
168 Mainwheel leg/fuselage attachment bracket
169 Leg pivot point
170 Mainwheel oleo leg
171 Mainwheel leg door
172 Brake lines
173 Torque links
174 Mainwheel hub
175 Axle
176 Port mainwheel
177 Mainwheel half-door
178 Ventral ETC centre-line stores pylon, possible loads inc:
179 Early-type (wooden) drop tank
180 66 Imp gal (300 l) (Junkers) metal drop tank
181 551-lb (250 kg) HE bomb, or
182 551-lb (250 kg) SAP bomb

Above: The Bf 109E-4, represented by this cutaway drawing, had MG FF cannon of improved fire rate and was replacing the E-3 in the summer of 1940.

Below: A Bf 109E-3 of I Gruppe of Lehrgeschwader 2 at Calais-Marck in August 1940. Sporting a non-standard camouflage

finish, this aircraft displays the emblem of 3 Staffel, but inappropriately a red aircraft numeral over the green mottle finish.

of its Jumo 210A-engined predecessors, marked increases in loadings notwithstanding. Admittedly, turning circle suffered somewhat and control was noticeably heavier at the upper end of the speed range. In other respects, the Bf 109E handled well. Take-off with flaps at 20 degrees was remarkably short and initial climb was excellent. Although the fighter stalled at quite high speeds, this phenomenon was gentle even under g, with no tendency to spin, and aileron vibration and buffeting afforded ample warning of the approach of the stall. At a normal take-off weight of 5,875lb (2,665kg), the Bf 109E achieved maximum speeds ranging from 290mph (466km/h) at sea level, through 322mph (518km/h) at 6,560ft (2,000m) to 348mph (560km/h) at 14,560ft (4,440m). A fuselage tank following the contours of the pilot's seat housed 88 Imp gal (400 litres) of fuel, but this was sufficient for only a 1.1-hour endurance at maximum continuous power at 19,685ft (6,000m), but at range cruise of 233mph (375km/h) at 22,965ft (7,000m) maximum range was 410 miles (660km). With weight reduced to 5,400lb (2,450kg), initial climb rate was 3,280ft/min (1,000m/min), and an altitude of 9,840ft (3,000m) could be attained in 3.6 min.

Whereas total Bf 109 production had barely exceeded 400 machines in 1938, no fewer than 1,091 examples of the E-model, were to leave the assembly lines between January 1 and September 1, 1939, representing an average monthly production tempo of 136.4 aircraft, and the spring and summer months saw the Jagd-

Above: A Schwarm — four-fighter section — of Bf 109E-3s seen on the ''Channel Front'' in the late summer of 1940. These display the most widely-used of the Luftwaffe fighter finishes of the period.

staffeln feverishly engaged in conversion to the Bf 109E. When the code word Ostmarkflug launched the assault on Poland, the Quartermaster-General's strength return to the Oberbefehlshaber listed 1,056 Bf 109s on Luftwaffe strength, of which 946 were serviceable.

Prior to Adler Tag, the lessons taught by the French campaign had hastily been incorporated in the Bf 109E. These included a cockpit canopy of revised design and embodying heavier framing, together with some protection for the pilot. This took the form of 8mm seat armour weighing 53lb (24kg) and a curved plate attached to the hinged canopy weighing a further 28.6lb (13kg). The fire rate of the MG FF cannon was being improved and the enhanced weapon was to be introduced by the Bf 109E-4 which rapidly replaced the E-3 during the summer and autumn of 1940.

By August 10, three days before Adler Tag, 934 Bf 109Es (against an establishment of 1,011) were available to Luftflotte 2 based in the Netherlands, Belgium and northern France, and Luftflotte 3 based in France, and of these 805 were serviceable. On Adler Tag, the Bf 109E-equipped element of the former Luftflotte was provided by the Stab and three Gruppen of

Below: A Bf 109E-3 of III Gruppe of Jagdgeschwader 26 "Schlageter" operating from Caffiers during August 1940. Note the "Schlageter" Gruppe emblem forward of the windscreen and the emblem of 9. Staffel beneath the cockpit.

each of Jagdgeschwadern 3, 26, 51 and 52, and the Stab and I Gruppe of JG 54, plus the Bf 109E-1/B and E-4/B fighter-bombers of 3/Erprobungsgruppe 210. Luftflotte 3 included the Stab and three Gruppen of each of Jagdgeschwadern 2, 27 and 53.

The Jagdflieger were aware that their Bf 109Es possessed sufficient endurance for a mere 20 minutes actual combat over Britain and that London represented the effective limit of their tactical radius. This embarrassing limitation had been foreseen and a jettisonable 66 Imp gal (300 litre) fuel tank had been developed, and, in fact, manufactured in some numbers. However, produced from moulded plywood, it was found to leak seriously after comparatively short exposure to the elements and its incendiary proclivity resulted in its rejection by Bf 109E units.

Influenced by the "Studie Blau", Hermann Goering and his staff seriously underrated the effectiveness of the British fighter opposition to be encountered. At the outset, the Bf 109Es were assigned the task of engaging the British fighters in open combat, a role for which the German fighters were ideally suited, but when the vulnerability of the twin-engined Bf 110 became obvious to the Luftwaffenführungsstab, it became necessary for the single-seaters also to provide close escort for the bombers. The fewer than 700 serviceable Bf 109Es available to Luftflotten 2 and 3 were to be found inadequate for the dual task.

Initially, the Bf 109E-equipped Jagdruppen were able to take full advantage of the superior climbing and diving capabilities of their mounts, and the excellent tactics that had been evolved during the Spanish Civil War enabled them to play havoc with the outmoded tactics retained by RAF Fighter Command. During the first

Below: Luftwaffe ground personnel servicing a Bf 109E-3 of III Gruppe of Jagdgeschwader 54 "Grünherz" between sorties at Guines airfield, near Calais. Note the Staffel pennant attached to the radio mast.

weeks of the Battle, the compact, but totally impracticable formations flown by the Hurricanes and Spitfires were frequently bounced by Bf 109Es with frightening results for the defending forces. The inflexible RAF fighter tactics were disastrous and, eventually, the defending fighters were forced to imitate their opponents.

There can be no doubt that the Bf 109E was highly effective and the master of both the Spitfire and the Hurricane in several performance respects, although it lacked certain qualities inherent in the British warplanes. The combination of cannon and machine guns provided the Messerschmitt fighter with a formidable armament and, although the MG FF cannon had a very much lower rate of fire than the Browning machine guns of the British fighters, their explosive shells could do infinitely more damage. Insofar as the Jagdsruppen were concerned, however, by September they had largely lost their freedom of action, being assigned to the close escort of bombers, and were severely handicapped in being no longer permitted to pursue the tactics best suited to the Bf 109E.

Unable by this time to use its speed to advantage, the fact that the Bf 109E could be out-turned by both Hurricane and Spitfire took on an importance that it had not previously possessed, the operational attrition of the Jagdgruppen steadily escalating. Infuriated by the losses sustained by his bombers, Reichsmarschall Goering made matters worse by insisting that the Bf 109Es stay still closer to their charges. The Bf 109E-equipped Jagdgruppen were thus emasculated, continuing the struggle until October 31, when, the Luftwaffe having achieved little of strategic significance, the fighters were withdrawn from the assault.

Throughout the Battle, the RAF fighter pilots had treated their Bf 109E-mounted opponents with the *greatest* respect. Indeed, most of the 1,172 aircraft lost by RAF Fighter Command during July-October 1940 had fallen to the guns of the Messerschmitt single-seater. In that period, 610 Bf 109Es had been lost on operations. During the course of the epic conflict, the Jagdflieger, who had considered themselves the *hunters* at the outset, had begun to see themselves as the *hunted*, not as the result of overwhelming qualities displayed by their opponents, but because of the strict limitations imposed on their tactics by their own Oberbefehlshaber. The Reichsmarschall had scored an "own goal", but for which the outcome of the Battle might have been different.

The Messerschmitt Bf 110

When committed to the Battle of Britain, the Messerschmitt Bf 110 enjoyed an awe-inspiring reputation, albeit one that owed more to German propagandists than to operational feats. Referred to as a Zerstörer, or ''destroyer'', a term borrowed from naval parlance, the Bf 110 was a product of the strategic fighter concept; a high-performance, twin-engined, multi-seat aircraft, the primary task of which was that of clearing a path through an enemy's defensive fighter screen for bombers following in its wake. Secondary roles included close escort of bomber formations and the free-ranging intruder mission within enemy airspace. The concept was particularly favoured by Goering, who saw his Bf 110-equipped Zerstörergruppen as the élite of the Luftwaffe.

Development of the Bf 110 had virtually paralleled that of the single-seat Bf 109, following the structural formula established by its stablemate and displaying much the same independence of spirit. Neither Dipl-Ing Willy Messerschmitt nor his Chief Engineer, Dipl-Ing Robert Lusser, had subscribed to the view that the requirement that the Bf 110 was intended to meet was practicable in the form envisaged by the Luftwaffenführungsstab. Accordingly, they had elected to ignore some parameters of the *official* specification and, as with the Bf 109, place accent uncompromisingly on ultimate performance.

The result was an elegant and competent, indeed, outstanding combat aircraft. It was to be found supremely tractable, its basic design proving amenable to power plant changes and to accommodation of armament, avionics and other equipment far beyond anything envisaged at the time of its creation. But its designers never anticipated its deployment other than in conditions of local Luftwaffe superiority if not supremacy; a situation such as that in which the Bf 110 was to find itself over Southern England during the Battle was *totally* unforeseen.

No aircraft designer, however talented, had at that point in time come up with a formula enabling a large and heavy twin-engined long-range fighter to compete in terms of agility with a relatively lightly loaded short-range single-seater. Thus, the Bf 110 was to fall lamentably short of the expectations generated by the reĉlame of the Ministry of Propaganda in Berlin. This was to lead to a widespread belief that the Messerschmitt twin-engined fighter was an *indifferent* warplane. On the contrary, its lack of success in that summer of 1940 stemmed from an inadequate understanding of the intrinsic limitations of its concept rather than inherent weaknesses in the aircraft itself.

The first prototype, the Bf 110 V1 powered by two Daimler-Benz DB 600A engines each affording 910hp at rated altitude, was flown for the first time on May 25, 1936 at Augsburg-Haunstetten by Dr-Ing Hermann Wurster. During an early test phase a speed of 314mph (505km/h) was clocked in level flight at 10,830ft (3,300m) at a loaded weight of 11,025lb (5,000kg). For a relatively large, twin-engined aircraft it proved very agile and, in mock combat with a pre-series single-seat Bf 109B flown by Ernst Udet, the newly-appointed Inspector of Fighter Pilots repeatedly failed to keep his larger opponent in his gun sight for sufficient time

Above: The Messerschmitt Bf 110 V1, the first prototype of this elegant strategic fighter, which, in Bf 1100 form, proved such an abysmal failure during the ''Battle'' owing to inaccurate appreciation of its capabilities.

Below: Messerschmitt Bf 110D-3, seen here during a shipping escort mission, had provision for larger drop tanks with a supplementary oil tank beneath the fuselage for extended-range tasks.

to render a hit likely, and experienced some difficulty in staying with the twin-engined fighter in steep turns.

In January 1937, as a result of evaluation of a second prototype, the Bf 110 V2, at the Rechlin Erprobungsstelle, instructions were given that Messerschmitt should commence preparations for a pre-production series of aircraft. The proposed series model, the Bf 110A, was to be powered by a pair of DB 600Aa carburettor-equipped engines affording 986hp for take-off. By the time that the pre-series Bf 110A airframes had attained an advanced stage in construction, however, the DB 600 engine was considered basically unsuited for fighter installation and was

already being phased out of production in favour of the direct-fuel-injection DB 601. The Reichsluftfahrt-ministerium confidently expected that the DB 601 would be available by the spring of 1938, when deliveries of the Bf 110 to the schweren (heavy) Jagdgruppen were expected to commence. Accordingly, instructions were issued to curtail the Bf 110A series, adapting the four airframes that had reached an advanced stage in assembly to take Junkers Jumo 210Da engines of 680hp for take-off.

As it became increasingly obvious that the more sanguine predictions for DB 601A engine delivery could not be met, the decision was taken to build an interim model, the Bf 110B with direct-fuel-injection two-stage supercharged Jumo 210Ga engines. While it was considered that the Bf 110B would possess an inadequate performance for combat purposes, it was seen as an ideal tool for equipment and armament evaluation, and the development of operational techniques. It was accordingly issued during late 1938 to I (Schweren Jagdgruppe)/LG 1 of the so-called Luftwaffe Lehrdivision, or Instructional Division, whose task was that of formulating tactics and techniques. In January 1939, this Gruppe was to become I(Z)/LG 1 when the title schwere Jagd was abandoned in favour of that of Zerstörer.

With the DB 601A engine, the Messerschmitt Zerstörer became the Bf 110C, a pre-series of 10 being delivered to the Luftwaffe early in January 1939, and acceptances of the initial production Bf 110C-1 by I(Z)/LG 1 began before the end of that month. Production of the Bf 110C-1 gathered momentum rapidly owing to the high priority that it enjoyed, and by the early summer of 1939, Focke-Wulf and the Gothaer Waggonfabrik had tooled up to supplement the output of Messerschmitt's Augsburg-Haunstetten factory, and MIAG at Braunschweig was preparing to phase into the programme.

By August 31, 1939, a total of 159 Bf 110C fighters had been accepted, although the Quartermaster-General's strength returns for that date indicated that only 68 of these, plus 27 Bf 110Bs, had actually been taken into the inventory. Two Zerstörergruppen, I/ZG 1 and I/ZG 76, had meanwhile been working up on the new warplane, and these, together with I(Z)/LG 1, were to be included in the Order of Battle against Poland.

Output of the Bf 110C had risen to more than 30 per month, and a further 156 were to be delivered during the first four months of hostilities when tempo was progressively rising — the average monthly production during 1940 was to be 102.6 aircraft — and the Zerstörer element of the Luftwaffe expanding commensurately. Powered by two DB 601A-1 12-cylinder inverted-vee engines each rated at 1,050hp for take-off, the Bf 110C-1 carried an armament of two 20mm MG FF cannon each with 180 rounds, four fixed forward-firing 7.9mm MG 17 machine guns each with 1,000 rounds and a flexibly-mounted aft-firing MG 15 with 750 rounds. With maximum speeds ranging from 295mph (475km/h) at sea level to 336mph

(540km/h) at 19,685ft (6,000m), and a high-speed cruise of 262mph (422km/h) at sea level and 304mph (490km/h) at 16,400ft (5,000m), performance compared favourably in these respects with the best single-seat fighters extant.

Normal maximum range at economic cruise of 217mph (350km/h) at 13,780ft (4,200m) was 680 miles (1,095km), but the introduction of auxiliary tanks in the wing outboard of the engine nacelles raised internal fuel capacity by a further 121 Imp gal (550 litres) to increase maximum range to 876 miles (1,410km).

Early operational experience had resulted in the successive introduction of the Bf 110C-2, differing solely in having FuG 10 HF radio in place of the original FuG 3aU R/T and the Bf 110C-3 which differed in having improved MG FF cannon. These now gave place to the Bf 110C-4 in which, for the first time, some attempt was made to provide at least nominal armour protection for pilot and gunner, normal loaded weight rising some 490lb (222kg) over that of the Bf 110C-1 to 13,779lb (6,250kg). Further escalation in weight

resulted from a demand for adaptation of the aircraft for the Jagd-bomber (Jabo) mission, two ETC 250 racks being introduced beneath the fuselage centre section for a pair of 551lb (250kg) bombs.

The substantially increased overload weight necessitated more power for take-off and emergency use, and thus the Jabo model, the Bf 110C-4/B, was fitted with DB 601N engines which, with increased compression and 96 Octane fuel, had a maximum take-off output of 1,200hp with full boost for one minute. Issued to the Erprobungsgruppe 210, the Bf 110C-4/B fighter-bombers of two staffeln of this unit were to operate throughout the ensuing Battle singly and in small groups, and taking maximum advantage of the element of surprise by using terrain-following tactics.

Below: The Bf 110D-0, the pre-series model of the Dackelbauch (Dachshund-belly) equipped version which suffered disastrously on August 15 when flown by I/ZG 76. One-third of 21 participating aircraft were lost!

Below: A Messerschmitt Bf 110C-2 of the Stab (Staff) of I Gruppe of Zerstörer-geschwader 2 based at Darmstadt-Griesheim in April 1940, immmediately prior to the assault on France. I/ZG 2 subsequently participated in the Battle.

Below: A Messerschmitt Bf 110C-2 of I Gruppe of Zerstörergeschwader 52 which was operating from Charleville, in June 1940. This differed from the C-1 solely in rear gun position and radio type.

A parallel development was the Bf 110C-5 which had a single Rb 50/30 reconnaissance camera in the cockpit floor, forward-firing armament being restricted to the quartet of machine guns. This sub-type was to reach the Aufklärungstaffeln, or reconnaissance squadrons, in time to participate in the Battle, initially in mixed units with the Do 17P and Do 17Z.

On July 20, 1940, a total of 278 Bf 110s was available to Luftflotten 2, 3 and 5, and of these 200 were serviceable. Overall strength of the Zerstörergruppen that were to participate in the assault on the United Kingdom was virtually unchanged on August 13, Adler Tag, comprising 289 aircraft of which 224 were serviceable. Apart from the langstrecken Zerstörergruppen I/ZG 76 and V(Z)/LG 1 with Bf 110C-4s and D-1s*, and 1. and 2. Staffeln of E.Gr.210 with Bf 110C-4/Bs, the principal Bf 110-equipped units committed to the Battle were the Stab and I and II/ZG 2, the Stab and I, II and III/ZG 26, and II and III/ZG 76.

Theoretically, with their superior endurance, the Bf 110s were to entice the RAF fighter squadrons into combat. The bomber squadrons would then follow at a suitable distance, arriving when the defending fighters had exhausted their fuel and were thus powerless to intervene. Furthermore, it was anticipated that the RAF fighters, sitting on their bases rearming and refuelling, would be extremely vulnerable and would afford excellent targets for the bombers and the additional Bf 110s escorting them.

This theory was to prove fallacious from the outset. To the chagrin of the Zerstörergruppen, the capabilities of their mounts fell far short of their expectations. The flying characteristics of the Bf 110 were very pleasant; its controls were fairly light, well harmonised and very effective up to 250mph (402km/h), although they began to heavy up above this speed. Stability was good fore and aft and directionally, but neutral laterally, and manoeuvrability was very good for so large an aeroplane. It was sluggish by comparison with the manoeuvrability of the Hurricane and Spitfire, however, and a serious fault was provided by the wing leading-edge slots which kept popping open unevenly in tight turns, gun sighting being ruined by the resultant lateral wobble.

While the forward-firing armament was undeniably lethal, it was difficult to bring to bear on the Bf 110's more agile opponents, and the single 7.9mm MG 15 wielded by the radio operator/gunner in the rear cockpit afforded little protection against attack from astern. The acceleration and speed of the Bf 110 were insufficient to enable its pilot to avoid combat when opposed by superior numbers of interceptors, and as soon as RAF Fighter Command had taken the measure of the Messerschmitt Zerstörer, the Bf 110-equipped Gruppen began to suffer frightful operational attrition. During August alone a total of 120 Bf 110s was lost on operations, the preponderance of them after Adler Tag. Thus, within less than three weeks, the Zerstörergruppen lost some 40 per cent of the aircraft on strength when the assault began.

Below: A Bf 110C-4 reconnaissance-fighter formerly of 4.(F)/14 that was forced down at Goodwood on July 21, 1940, and subsequently repaired with parts salvaged from another crashed example.

It was patently obvious that the Bf 110 should have been withdrawn from the aerial offensive, but an overall shortage of Bf 109Es, coupled with their inadequate range, necessitated retention of the Messerschmitt Zerstörer. Incapable of defending the bombers that it was intended to escort, the Bf 110 was hard put to defend itself and its losses were out of all proportion to its achievements. Despite a substantial reduction in sorties and changes in tactics, the Zerstörergruppen had lost a further 83 aircraft by the end of September, their presence in the area providing a defensive liability for the overstretched Bf 109E units.

The catastrophic losses had already dictated the disbandment of some Gruppen, including I and II/ZG 2, and the folly of pitting the Bf 110 against a determined force of single-seat fighters was finally accepted by the Oberkommando der Luftwaffe, which, throughout the final weeks of the Battle confined the Messerschmitt twin to the fighter-bomber and reconnaissance tasks. Reichsmarschall Goering's boastful claims for his élite Zerstörergruppen had been proven singularly hollow.

*The Bf 110D-1 was a so-called langstrecken, or long-distance, Zerstörer with a 264 Imp gal (1,200 litre) auxiliary fuel tank made of plywood and dubbed a "Dackelbauch" (Dachshund-belly). This was found to "hang up" under extremely low temperatures after its fuel had been exhausted, the highly incendiary fumes remaining in the "empty" tank tending to explode.

The Junkers Ju 87B

No warplane possessed greater réclame in the opening months of World War II than the Junkers Ju 87 two-seat dive bomber, its notoriety assiduously propagated by German publicity. Indeed, the Polish and French campaigns in which it had participated had endowed the Ju 87 with a fearsome reputation as an outstandingly effective precision bombing instrument and a supremely effective ground strafer. With its banshee-like wail emitted as it hurtled vertically earthwards, it had a devastating psychological effect on the recipients of its attention. Synonymous with the sobriquet of Stuka — a derivation of *Sturzkampfflugzeug*, a term embracing *all* dive bombers — the Ju 87 was seen by the German High Command as a successor to long-range artillery, and first and foremost a tool for the direct support of ground forces.

Lacking all aesthetic pretentions, the Junkers dive bomber was an angularly ugly creation, but it was an extremely sturdy aircraft, offering its pilot light controls, pleasant flying characteristics and, for an aircraft of its size, a comparatively high standard of manoeuvrability. Its crew members enjoyed good visibility and it was reputed to be capable of hitting its target with an accuracy of less than 100ft (30m). All very desirable though these characteristics were, successful operation of the Ju 87 presupposed a considerable measure of control in the air without which it became an anachronism the natural prey of the fighter. Once the Ju 87 encountered determined fighter opposition, such as was to be found over the United Kingdom, its career dramatically entered its eclipse.

Like many German prototypes of the period, the Ju 87 began flight test with a *British* engine, a fully supercharged Rolls-Royce Kestrel V rated at 640hp at 14,000ft (4,267m). Flown at Dessau in the late spring

of 1935, this, the Ju 87 V1, was to enjoy only a brief test career. During diving trials in the following summer, the entire tail assembly began to oscillate, the starboard element of its twin vertical tail surface breaking away when the pilot attempted to recover from his dive. This necessitated Dipl-Ing Herman Pohlmann and his design team, who had initiated work on the Ju 87 in 1933, undertaking hurried redesign of the tail surfaces, a new single fin-and-rudder assembly being applied to the second prototype, the Ju 87 V2, with which the flight test programme was resumed in the late autumn of 1935.

Unlike the first prototype, the Ju 87 V2 was powered by the intended Junkers Jumo 210Aa inverted-vee 12-cylinder engine for which the dive bomber had been designed, this being rated at 610hp at 8,530ft (2,600m). This aircraft was fitted with dive brakes prior to its delivery to the Rechlin test centre for official evaluation in March 1936. Attached beneath the wings just aft of the leading edges and outboard of the main undercarriage, these took the form of slats turning through 90deg. Prior to commencing the dive, the pilot had to throttle back the engine in order to close the cooling gills, switch over to the sea-level supercharger and turn the propeller to coarse pitch, a series of lines of inclination marked on the starboard front side screen of the cockpit enabling the pilot to estimate the dive angle by aligning the lines with the horizon.

Two more prototypes, the V3 and V4, offered various refinements, the latter introducing a single

Below: Junkers Ju 87A-1 dive bombers of Stukageschwader 163 ''Immelmann'' photographed late in 1937. The Ju 87A was the progenitor of the Ju 87B which played a largely unsuccesful role in the Battle.

JUNKERS Ju 87B-2
Cutaway Drawing Key
1 Rudder trim tab
2 Trim-tab actuating linkage
3 Rudder frame
4 Rudder hinges
5 Rudder post
6 Rudder tab control rod
7 Tailfin structure
8 Rudder balance
9 Aerial attachment
10 Aerial
11 Elevator trim tab
12 Port elevator

13 Elevator balance
14 Port tailplane
15 Tailplane bracing struts
16 Tailfin/fuselage fillet section
17 Fuselage aft frame/tailfin front spar
18 Tailwheel leg shock-absorber
19 Tailplane attachment points
20 Inspection panel
21 Rudder control
22 Elevator trim tab
23 Tailplane structure
24 Starboard elevator
25 Elevator balance
26 Tailplane leading edge
27 Tailplane bracing struts
28 Fixed tailwheel
29 Lifting point
30 Rudder control cables
31 Elevator control cables
32 Fuselage stringers
33 Fuselage skin panels
34 First-aid kit (access port side)
35 Fuselage frame
36 Radio installation
37 Crew entry step
38 Gunner's seat
39 Spare ammunition drum stowage
40 Entry hand/footholds
41 Aft-canopy additional side armour
42 Aft-section canopy track
43 Hand-held 7.9-mm MG 15 machine gun
44 Ring-and-bead sight
45 Machine gun flexible mounting
46 Canopy aft sliding section
47 Aerial mast
48 Canopy fixed centre-section
49 Electrical leads

50 Cross-brace
51 Canopy track
52 Crash turnover structure
53 Pilot's sliding canopy section
54 Pilot's seat and harness
55 Centre-section bulkhead
56 Fuselage main frame
57 Control column
58 Rudder pedals
59 Instrument panel
60 Dive-bombing sight (Stuvi)
61 Windscreen
62 Oil tank
63 Wing ribs
64 Aileron centre-section
65 Aileron control linkage
66 Aileron control rods
67 Hinge fairing

68 Fixed tab
69 Aileron outer section
70 Aileron outer-section mass balances
71 Port wing tip
72 Wing skinning
73 Wing leading edge
74 Underwing weapon racks (2)
75 Two 110-lb (50 kg) bombs

7.9mm MG 17 machine gun in the starboard wing and a crutch on swing links which, attached immediately aft of the radiator bath, lowered and swung the bomb — either of 551lb or 1,102lb (250 or 500kg) — forward on release to ensure clearance of the propeller arc.

The first pre-series Ju 87A-0 dive bombers came off the Dessau assembly line before the end of 1936, 10 of these being followed by the series Ju 87A-1 early in the following year. Late in 1937, three aircraft were detached from the I Gruppe of Stuka Geschwader 162 Immelmann and sent to Spain to evaluate dive bombing techniques under operational conditions. The Ju 87A-1 gave place to the A-2 with a Jumo 210Da engine

82 Fixed forward-firing 7.9 mm MG 17 machine gun
83 Ammunition tank
84 Engine bearer/bulkhead ball-and-socket fixing
85 Firewall/bulkhead
86 Engine-bearer fixing fairing
87 Cooling hose
88 Oil cooler outlet cowl
89 Oil cooler
90 Oil cooler intake
91 Junkers Jumo 211 Da engine
92 Anti-vibration engine mounting pad
93 Engine main bearer forging
94 Main bearer support fixing
95 Supercharger intake duct
96 Engine supercharger air intake
97 Engine exhaust stubs
98 Spinner backplate
99 Three-bladed Junkers VS-5 propeller
100 Propeller hub
101 Spinner
102 Radiator intake
103 Radiator
104 Radiator gill mechanism
105 Adjustable radiator cooling gills
106 Bomb crutch pivot
107 Engine main bearer lower support strut
108 Ventral bomb shackle
109 Vent
110 Bomb crutch (extended)
111 Port mainwheel
112 Alternative main bomb load inc 1,102-lb (500 kg) SC-type fragmentation bomb
113 1,102-lb (500 kg) SC-type semi-armour-piercing bomb
114 1,102-lb (500 kg) PC-type Pauline armour-piercing bomb
115 Starboard mainwheel
116 Mainwheel spat
117 Axle fork/spat fixing lugs
118 Axle fork
119 Aerodynamic siren fairing (capped)
120 Undercarriage leg
121 Torque link
122 Machine gun muzzle fairing
123 Undercarriage leg/wing front spar fixing
124 Inboard leading edge
125 Main spar centre-section carry-through
126 Wing-root entry/maintenance walkway
127 Wing tank fuel filler cap
128 Starboard wing fuel tank
129 Wing ribs
130 Starboard aileron inboard section
131 Outboard wing section attachment rib
132 Wing join capping strip
133 Ball-and-socket spar fixings
134 Starboard wing MG 17 machine gun
135 Leading-edge panels
136 Nose ribs
137 Outer wing fuel tank position (Ju 87R)
138 Wing front spar
139 Wing ribs
140 Aileron control rods
141 Starboard aileron centre-section
142 Wing rear spar
143 Fixed tab
144 Starboard aileron outboard section
145 Wing skinning panels
146 Pitot head
147 Starboard navigation light

76 Alternative underwing stores inc drop tank (Ju 87R)
77 Anti-personnel bomb container
78 110-lb (50 kg) bombs with percussion rod fuzes and fin 'screamers'
79 Landing light
80 Port underwing divebreak
81 Machine gun muzzle fairing

Below: This outaway drawing depicts the Ju 87B-2 which succeeded the original B-1 late in 1939, embodying a number of refinements including ejector exhausts.

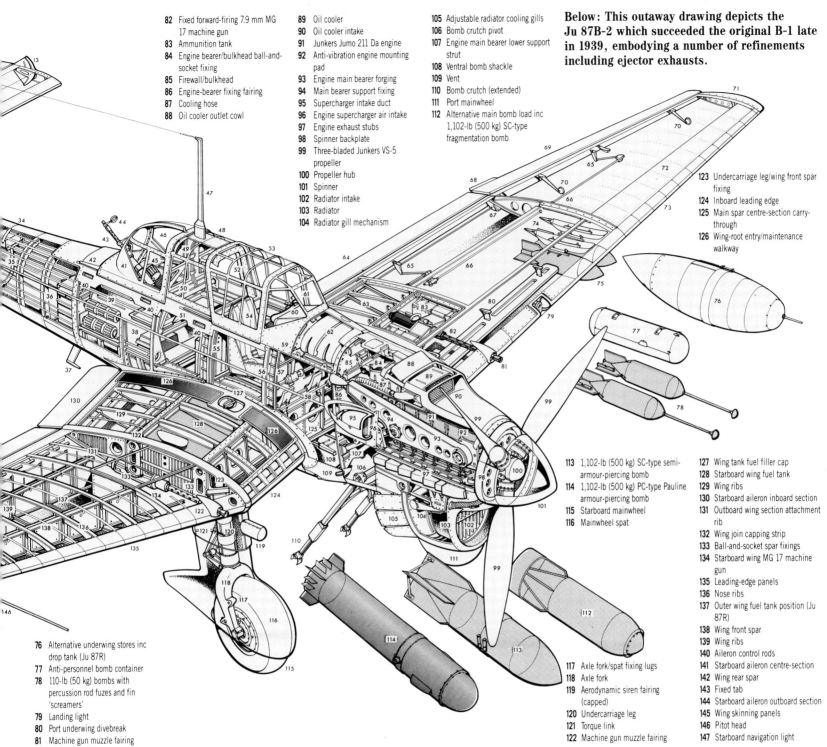

affording 680hp for take-off late in 1937, but by that time a major redesign of the aircraft was in train to accommodate the Jumo 211A engine which offered 1,000hp for take-off.

The more powerful engine was installed in the pre-series Ju 87B-0, the Jumo 211A giving place in the series model, the Ju 87B-1, to the Jumo 211Da with direct fuel injection and an emergency take-off rating of 1,200hp. The substantial boost in power enabled the Ju 87B-1 to lift a 1,102lb (500kg) bomb with both crew members *in situ* whereas the Ju 87A had only been able to carry this weapon when flown as a single-seater. An alternative warload consisted of a 551lb (250kg) bomb on the fuselage crutch and four 110lb (50kg) bombs on underwing racks. Forward-firing armament was increased to two 7.9mm MG 17s with 500rpg, and a single MG 15 machine gun of similar calibre was attached to a flexible mounting in the rear cockpit with 900 rounds.

Five of the first Ju 87B-1s were despatched to Spain in October 1938, these emulating the success enjoyed by the Ju 87As that had preceded them, and with the transfer of the assembly line from Dessau to the ''Weser'' Flugzeugbau at Berlin-Tempelhof, production tempo of the Junkers dive bomber increased dramatically, exceeding 60 aircraft monthly by mid-1939, in which year 557 were to be delivered. Nine Ju 87B-1-equipped Stukagruppen were to be included in the Luftwaffe Order of Battle on September 1, 1939, these possessing 336 aircraft of which 288 were serviceable.

Operating under ideal conditions, with negligible aerial opposition, the Stukagruppen had a devastating effect during the Polish campaign, serving primarily as a weapon for back-area bombing and exploiting to the full the accuracy of bomb aiming inherent in the steep diving attack. Only 31 Ju 87Bs were lost during Polish operations, or less than 10 per cent of the total Stuka force engaged; the legendary reputation that had been in the making in Spanish skies had now been firmly established in Polish skies and was to be consolidated seven months later over France.

The Ju 87B-2 had succeeded the B-1 on the "Weser" assembly line late in 1939, this incorporating several refinements, such as a broad-bladed propeller, hydraulically-operated radiator cooling gills and ejector exhausts. Manufactured in parallel was a longer-range version, the Ju 87R — the suffix letter indicating "Reichweite", or Range — which, for extended-range missions such as anti-shipping operations, made provision for substantial additional quantities of fuel and oil. Although there were some factions in the Luftwaffe that, because of the relative low speed and the vulnerability of the Ju 87, now considered this warplane to be approaching obsolescence, its successes in the Polish campaign boosted the influence of the pro-Stuka element and, far from phasing out, production was boosted, and a total of 769 was to be built during the course of 1940.

Prior to the Battle of Britain, some dive bombing attacks against British coastal shipping took place in July, but these were no more than a prelude to the main assault. By July 20, Luftflotten 2 and 3 had available 316 Ju 87Bs and Ju 87Rs for the assault on the United Kingdom, 248 of these being immediately serviceable. The bulk of the dive bombes were included in the VIII Fliegerkorps of Generalleutnant Wolfram Freiherr von Richthofen with seven Stukagruppen comprising the Stab, I and III/StG.1, the Stab, I and II/StG.2, and the Stab, I, II and III/StG.77. The newly-formed I/StG.3 was assigned to the IV Fliegerkorps, while II Fliegerkorps embodied II/StG.1 and IV(St)/LG 1.

The first Ju 87 sorties in strength actually took place on August 8, five days before Adler Tag, suffering severe losses despite Bf 109Es providing top cover. On Adler Tag itself, Ju 87s *en route* for Middle Wallop airfield were bounced by Spitfires of No 609 Sqn, nine of the dive bombers being promptly despatched. But this was only a foretaste of what was in store for the Stukagruppen. Within six days, 41 Ju 87s had been lost; it was

Above: Junkers Ju 87B-1 dive bombers of II Gruppe of Stukageschwader 77 which was included in the VIII Fliegerkorps of Generalleutnant Wolfram Freiherr von Richthofen. On August 18, StG.77 was to lose no fewer than 16 aircraft after attacking Ford and Thorney Island.

patently obvious that this was no replay of the Polish and French campaigns, and the Stuka had been revealed for what it was — an inadequately armed and highly vulnerable warplane. To prevent the Stukagruppen

from being decimated, the Oberkommando der Luftwaffe had no recourse but to withdraw the Ju 87 from the Cherbourg area to the Pas de Calais where it was to sit out the closing phases of the Battle. The last Stuka sorties in force against British targets took place on August 16, when I and III/StG.2 lost nine aircraft in an attack on Tangmere, and on August 18, when StG.77 lost 16 aircraft after attacking Ford and Thorney Island. The shock administered by the combat attrition of the Battle was sufficient to disenchant some of the most ardent of the Ju 87's protagonists within the Luftwaffe.

Above: A Junkers Ju 87B-2 of 3 Staffel of Stukageschwader 2 "Immelmann" which crashed at Selsey on 16 August 1940, after a raid on Tangmere. The Staffel emblem (coat of arms of the city of Breslau) appeared beneath the windscreen.

The Heinkel He 111

With the creation of the Third Reich in 1933, elaborate measures were taken to conceal the extent of the rearmament that was taking place in Germany. Later it was to be alleged that the appearance in the mid-'thirties of what were presented as high-speed commercial transports but were, in reality, the prototypes of bombers provided as but one glaring example of this subterfuge. In fact, these airliners were *not* the progenitors of future bombers, their basic designs having been conceived from the outset of fulfil both civil and military roles, commercial transport and bomber versions evolving in parallel.

One of these dimorphic aircraft was the Heinkel He 111, an elegant, well-conceived and efficient design created by the brothers Siegfried and Walter Günter. It was a classic aeroplane coupling exceptional handling characteristics with a performance which, in the early days of its career at least, enabled it to show a clean pair of heels to most contemporary single-seat fighters. Fully representative of the then latest aerodynamic refinements and structural techniques, it was one of the most outstanding aircraft of the mid-'thirties by any standard.

In bomber form, the He 111 temporarily placed Germany in the forefront of development of this category of warplane but, while still a formidable weapon, it had lost some of its potency by the time it was to be committed to the Battle of Britain.

The first bomber prototype, the He 111a, flew on February 24, 1935; a state-of-the-art all-metal stressed-skin monoplane powered by two 690hp BMW VI 6,0Z glycol-cooled 12-cylinder engines and knowing few if any peers on the score of elegance. A commercial airliner prototype, the He 111 V4, garnered considerable publicity on January 10, 1936, when demonstrated to the international press at Berlin-Tempelhof as ''The fastest aircraft on the world's air routes.''

It was, of course, the potential of the He 111 as a bomber for the future Luftwaffe that was the primary reason for the intense official interest in this aircraft, and construction of a pre-series batch of 10 He 111A-0 bombers had begun at Rostock-Marienehe some months before the commercial He 111 V4 prototype had been demonstrated to the press with such verve by Heinkel's test pilot Gerhard Nitschke. From this point in time, the He 111 was to undergo incremental redesign that was to result in two distinct generations of the Heinkel bomber.

The first generation of which the first production representative was the He 111B, was to achieve a measure of fame as a result of its participation in the Spanish Civil War, initially with Kampfgruppe 88 of the Legion Kondor and subsequently with the Spanish Nationalist Air Force as well. By the beginning of World War II, however, the He 111-equipped Kampfgeschwader had virtually completed conversion to the second generation bomber which comprised the vast bulk of the equipment of 21 Gruppen and one Staffel with a total strength of 789 aircraft.

The second generation He 111 bomber mated the entirely new wing introduced by the first generation He 111F and J with a completely revised forward

Above: A Heinkel He 111P-6, the last of the P-series bomber which was phased out of production early in 1940. Both the DB 601-engined P-series and Jumo 211-engined H-series of the He 111 saw extensive use.

fuselage. Whereas the original wing had been of aesthetically attractive and aerodynamically desirable elliptical form, its somewhat complex structure undoubtedly inhibited large-scale production. Thus, early in 1936, Siegried Günter had begun redesign of the wing, eliminating the elegant ellipses in favour of a straight-tapered planform, a modest reduction in gross wing area resulting in the process. Comparatively small numbers of bombers were completed with the new wing before, in the summer of 1938, an equally radical change was introduced on the assembly lines; this was an entirely new forward fuselage, resulting in what was considered to be the second generation bomber.

Intended to improve both aerodynamics and crew visibility, the new forward fuselage was innovative in that it eliminated the pilot's windscreen that had previously broken the upper fuselage contour in conventional fashion. In place of the stepped windscreen the entire nose section was broadened and deepened, being largely formed by transparent panelling and resulting in forward fuselage contours unbroken by any projection. The pilot was seated to port and all flight and engine instruments were mounted on a panel suspended from the roof. The nose terminated in an Ikaria universal mounting for a 7.9mm MG 15 machine gun.

In order to overcome the problems that would be presented in adverse weather by the surfeit of transparent panels, provision was made for elevating the pilot's seat and controls for landing and taxying, his head projecting through a sliding panel and being protected from the slipstream by a small retractable windscreen. Although the new cockpit glazing was to receive some criticism owing to the mirror effect when the sun was aft of the aircraft, the new forward fuselage was standardised for subsequent production aircraft, these beginning to leave the assembly lines in the winter of 1938-39.

Below: A navigator consulting his charts in the extreme nose of an He 111 bomber. The nose, which terminated in a revolving Ikaria gun mounting, was largely formed of transparent panelling and had no stepped windscreen.

From the outset, the second generation bomber had been planned to take either Daimler-Benz DB 601A or Junkers Jumo 211 engines with equal facility, the bomber being assigned the designation He 111P with the former power plant and He 111H with the latter, priority being given to the DB 601A-engined version owing to the supply situation.

Deliveries of the initial production model, the He 111P-1, began during the early spring of 1939, the first He 111H-1s following some six weeks later. The P-1 gave place to the P-2, which differed solely in the type of radio installed, the H-1 being equipped to a similar standard with deliveries commencing in the same month (May).

One shortcoming of the second generation He 111 was its inflexibility concerning bomb loading arrangements. The bombs were loaded into individual vertical cells, four on each side of a gangway, and this meant that the largest bomb that could be accommodated internally was a 551-pounder (250kg). Perhaps the most surprising fact in view of experience

HEINKEL HE 111H-3
Cutaway Drawing Key
1 Starboard navigation light
2 Starboard aileron
3 Lattice ribs
4 Front spar
5 Rear spar
6 Aileron tab
7 Starboard flap
8 Outboard fuel tank (220 gal/ 1,000 litres capacity)

21 Starboard mainwheel
22 Rudder pedals
23 Bomb aimer's prone pad
24 Additional 7.9mm MG 15 machine gun (fitted by forward maintenance units)
25 Repeater compass
26 Bomb aimer's folding seat
27 Control wheel
28 Throttles
29 Pilot's seat

30 Retractable auxiliary windscreen (for use when pilot's seat in elevated position)
31 Sliding roof hatch
32 Forward fuselage bulkhead
33 Double-frame station
34 Port ESAC bomb bay (vertical stowage)
35 Fuselage windows (blanked)
36 Central gangway between bomb bays

37 Double-frame station
38 Direction finder
39 Dorsal gunner's (forward) sliding canopy
40 Dorsal 7.9mm MG 15 machine gun
41 Dorsal gunner's cradle seat
42 FuG 10 radio equipment
43 Fuselage window
44 Armoured bulkhead (8mm)
45 Aerial mast
46 Bomb flares
47 Unarmoured bulkhead

48 Rear fuselage access cut-out
49 Port 7.9mm beam MG 15 machine gun
50 Dinghy-stowage
51 Fuselage frames
52 Stringers
53 Starboard tailplane
54 Aerial
55 Starboard elevator
56 Fin front spar
57 Fin structure
58 Rudder balance
59 Fin rear spar/rudder post

60 Rudder construction
61 Rudder tab
62 Tab actuator
63 Remotely-controlled 7.9mm MG 17 machine gun in tailcone (fitted to some aircraft only)
64 Rear navigation light
65 Elevator tab
66 Elevator structure

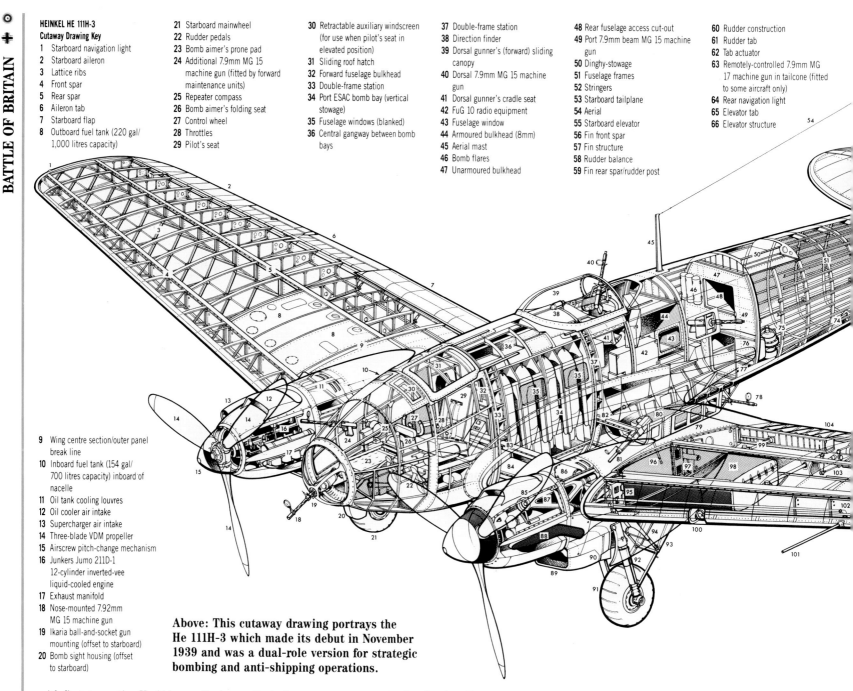

9 Wing centre section/outer panel break line
10 Inboard fuel tank (154 gal/ 700 litres capacity) inboard of nacelle
11 Oil tank cooling louvres
12 Oil cooler air intake
13 Supercharger air intake
14 Three-blade VDM propeller
15 Airscrew pitch-change mechanism
16 Junkers Jumo 211D-1 12-cylinder inverted-vee liquid-cooled engine
17 Exhaust manifold
18 Nose-mounted 7.92mm MG 15 machine gun
19 Ikaria ball-and-socket gun mounting (offset to starboard)
20 Bomb sight housing (offset to starboard)

Above: This cutaway drawing portrays the He 111H-3 which made its debut in November 1939 and was a dual-role version for strategic bombing and anti-shipping operations.

with first generation He 111s over Spain was the lack of any attempt to increase defensive armament which remained three 7.9mm MG 15 machine guns. The crew comprised pilot, navigator/bombardier, radio operator and ventral gunner. The DB 601A-1 engines of the He 111P were each rated at 1,175hp for take-off and the Jumo 211A-1 engines of the He 111H each offered 1,075hp for take-off.

Such was the importance of the Heinkel bomber that the He 111P was built by Heinkel's Rostock-Marienehe and the NDW factories, these being joined by Arado at Warnemünde, while the He 111H was built in parallel by Heinkel's Oranienburg facility, the Junkers plant at Dessau and the new ATG factory at Leipzig. The decision had been taken to standardise on the Jumo 211-engined version as soon as the power plant supply situation permitted, and, in the meantime, sub-types began to proliferate. The He 111P-4 introduced

some armour protection for the pilot and dorsal and ventral gunners, and heavier defensive armament, this being raised to six 7.9mm MG 15s. Furthermore, the port bomb bay was blanked off and occupied by a supplementary fuel tank, bomb racks being introduced beneath the blanked-off bay.

Production of the P-series was to be finally phased out early in 1940 with the He 111P-6, this reverting to the standard internal bomb stowage arrangement but having 1,275hp DB 601N engines. The He 111H-2 embodied similar armament changes to those introduced on the P-4, the He 111H-3, which made it début in November 1939, being a dual-role version, which, adding anti-shipping operations to its repertoire, was fitted with a single forward-firing 20mm MG FF cannon in its ventral gondola. The H-3 sub-type also benefited from installation of Jumo 211D-1 engines each rated at 1,200hp for take-off. These engines were

retained initially by the He 111H-4 which began to come off the lines early in 1940, but were eventually to be supplanted by the Jumo 211F-1 offering 1,400hp for take-off.

When World War II commenced, the Luftwaffe inventory of He 111 bombers was fairly evenly divided between P-series and H-series, with 389 of the fomer and 400 of the latter on strength, all having been taken on charge over a period of less than six months, such was the impetus placed behind the production of the Heinkel bomber. Committed to the Polish Campaign, the He 111 achieved generally favourable results, but attrition was higher than anticipated, a total of 78 bombers being lost. For the onslaught on France and the Low Countries on May 10, 1940, Luftflotten 2 and 3 possessed a total of 1,120 twin-engined bombers of which approximately half were He 111s, but the numerical heyday of the Heinkel bomber was already

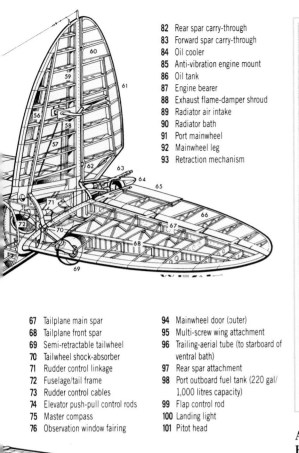

82 Rear spar carry-through
83 Forward spar carry-through
84 Oil cooler
85 Anti-vibration engine mount
86 Oil tank
87 Engine bearer
88 Exhaust flame-damper shroud
89 Radiator air intake
90 Radiator bath
91 Port mainwheel
92 Mainwheel leg
93 Retraction mechanism

67 Tailplane main spar
68 Tailplane front spar
69 Semi-retractable tailwheel
70 Tailwheel shock-absorber
71 Rudder control linkage
72 Fuselage/tail frame
73 Rudder control cables
74 Elevator push-pull control rods
75 Master compass
76 Observation window fairing

94 Mainwheel door (outer)
95 Multi-screw wing attachment
96 Trailing-aerial tube (to starboard of ventral bath)
97 Rear spar attachment
98 Port outboard fuel tank (220 gal/ 1,000 litres capacity)
99 Flap control rod
100 Landing light
101 Pitot head

77 Glazed observation window in floor
78 Ventral aft-firing 7.9mm MG 15 machine gun in tail of 'Sterbebett' ('Death-bed') bath
79 Ventral bath entry hatch
80 Ventral gunner's prone pad
81 Forward-firing 20mm Oerlikon MG FF cannon (for anti-shipping operations)

102 Pitot head heater/wing leading-edge de-icer
103 Flap and aileron coupling
104 Flap structure
105 Aileron tab
106 Tab actuator
107 Rear spar
108 Forward spar
109 Port aileron
110 Port navigation light

Below: An He 111H-3 of II Gruppe of Kampfge-schwader I "Hindenburg" operating from Montdidier, France, in August 1940.

Note the temporary formation marking on the rudder which was repeated on the wing surfaces on this aircraft.

Above: The second generation, definitive Heinkel He 111 Bomber as used in the Battle in its H- and P-series versions featured an extraordinary glazed nose, as seen above. The surfeit of transparent panels resulted in a mirror effect when the sun was aft.

passing as Kampfgruppen converted to the Junkers Ju 88A. Thus, by Adler Tag, only four Kampfgeschwader remained completely equipped with He 111s, these being KG 26 based in Norway, KG 27 operating from Tours, Dinard and Rennes, KG 53 at Lille-Nord and KG 55 at Chartres, Dreux and Villacoublay.

After initial strikes across the Straits of Dover, the first sorties in force by He 111s took place on August 15 when 72 He 111H-4s of I and III Gruppen of KG 26 flew from Stavanger with the intention of attack-ing RAF bases at Dishforth, Ulsworth and Linton-upon-Ouse. The bomber force was escorted by Bf 110 fighters of I/ZG 76, but owing to a navigational error none was to find its target. Only 63 of the He 111s actually cross-ed the coast and eight of these fell victim to RAF fighters. Despite heavy operational attrition, daylight attacks by He 111 formations against targets in the United Kingdom continued for a month.

The provision of stronger escorts of Bf 109E fighters barely alleviated the situation in which the Kampfgrup-pen found themselves, and, on occasions, when the hard-pressed Jagdgruppen failed to rendezvous with their He 111 charges, the casualties among the bombers were unacceptable. Thus, by mid-September, a change of tactics had become imperative and, from the 16th of that month, the He 111 was to be largely confined to nocturnal sorties.

The Dornier Do 17Z

To become known throughout the aeronautical world by the sobriquet of ''Flying Pencil'' as a result of its immoderately slim side profile, the Dornier Do 17 was, at the time of its début, one of the most elegant and beautiful shapes ever to have taken to the skies. This slimness was seen to be illusory in planform as the near-cylindrical cross section of the fuselage of this aircraft changed rapidly to what can only be described as an inverted triangle to produce an abnormally broad centre fuselage, the section then transforming once more to an ellipse. By the time of the Battle, even the pencil-like side contours had been impaired, for operational experience gained in Spanish skies had dictated fundamental redesign of the forward fuselage of the bomber, and the variant that participated in the fighting over southern England, the Do 17Z, scarcely warranted the popular epithet.

The origins of the Do 17 pre-dated the birth of Germany's Third Reich, stemming from an outline specification drawn up in July 1932 which euphemistically referred to a ''high-speed passenger transport and mailplane''. From the outset the Do 17 was, in fact, a dedicated medium bomber and reconnaissance aircraft, the pacific roles that, at the time, it was allegedly designed to fulfil being pure fiction. The first prototype, the Do 17c — shortly afterwards to be redesignated Do 17 V1 — was flown on November 23, 1934, this having a single fin-and-rudder tail assembly whereas the second prototype, the Do 17 V2 (formerly Do 17a), was fitted with a twin fin-and-rudder assembly for comparison purposes, this latter flying on May 18, 1935.

The Do 17, like its contemporary, the He 111, took full advantage of state-of-the-art aerodynamic developments and structural concepts, and was a highly advanced design for the early 'thirties. It initiated the German predilection for grouping all crew members in the forward fuselage and it was faster than virtually any single-seat fighter then extant. Preparations for the large-scale production of the Do 17 at Dornier's Manzell, Allmansweiller and Löwenthal factories were in train by early 1936, when plans were also being formulated for additional production by Henschel at Berlin-Schönefeld, Siebel at Halle and by the Hamburger Flugzeugbau.

The initial models were the Do 17E bomber and the Do 17F reconnaissance aircraft, and during the early months of 1937 these began to enter Luftwaffe service, the first examples of the former being commit-

Above: A Dornier Do 17Z releasing its load of bombs in level flight rather than in a shallow diving attack that was favoured by Kampfgruppen operating this type during the Battle. The Do 17Z-equipped units specialised in low-level, terrain-following attack.

ted to operations over Spain with Kampfgruppe 88 of the Legion Kondor in March of that year. Powered by the BMW VI 7,3 12-cylinder vee engines, the Do 17E and F were, in fact, phased out of production during the course of 1937 after delivery of 536 aircraft, being succeeded on the assembly lines by the Do 17M and P, respectively bomber and reconnaissance aircraft, the former with BMW-Bramo 323D nine-cylinder radial engines of 900hp and the latter with BMW 132N nine-cylinder radials of 865hp.

The principal shortcomings of the Do 17 revealed over Spain were its limited warload and its poor defence against attack from below and to the rear, and the Do 17M did little to remedy these defects. General re-equipment of the Do 17E-mounted Kampfgruppen was therefore held in abeyance pending availability of the

much improved second generation Do 17Z which was following the Do 17M by less than a year and utilised most of the jigs and tools employed by the earlier model. The same considerations did not apply to its reconnaissance equivalent, the Do 17P, however. Production of this model was launched in 1938 by Henschel, Hamburger Flugzeugbau and Siebel, a total of 330 being built for the Aufklärungsgruppen.

The Do 17Z, the design of which began early in 1938, featured an entirely new forward fuselage owing everything to the dictates of operational efficiency and little to aerodynamic refinement. The downward-firing MG 15 machine which was poked through a hatch in the floor of preceding Do 17 versions had too limited a field of fire to provide anything approaching satisfactory protection from below and to the rear. Furthermore, crew accommodation had always been somewhat cramped for maximum operational efficiency. Thus, for the Do 17Z, the cockpit roof was raised and fully glazed. The nose containing the bombardier's station was also extensively glazed with a series of small, flat panels, or ''facets'', and the lower part was bulged and extended aft to a point just forward of the wing leading

Below: A Dornier Do 17Z of 4 Staffel of Kampfge-schwader 2 as operated from Arras in August 1940. KG 2 bombed Eastchurch on Adler Tag as the sole KG failing to receive the postponement.

Below: A Dornier Do 17Z of 9 Staffel of Kampfgeschwader 76 at Cormeilles-en-Vexin in July 1940. After the Battle the entire Geschwader converted from the Do 17Z to the more effective Ju 88A, completing conversion by the end of 1940.

edge, terminating in a position for an aft-firing MG 15 machine gun.

The pre-series Do 17Z-0, which appeared late in 1938, was a four-seat bomber, defensive armament comprising three 7.9mm MG 15 guns — one on a pillar-type mounting at the rear of the flight deck, a second protruding through the starboard panels of the windscreen and the third on a hemispherical mounting firing below the fuselage. This armament was augmented on the production Do 17Z-1 by a fourth MG 15 protruding through the nose cone. Appearing before the end of 1938, the Do 17Z-1 was somewhat underpowered by its two 900hp BMW-Bramo 323A-1 radial engines when carrying its full 2,205lb (1,000kg) bomb load. Accordingly, bomb load was reduced to 1,100lb (500kg), but was restored to the full load early in 1939 with the appearance of the Do 17Z-2 with 1,000hp Bramo 323P engine with two-speed superchargers. Restoration of the full bomb load dictated some reduction in fuel load, however, reducing depth of penetration in maximum loaded condition to a mere 205 miles (330km).

The Do 17Z rapidly proved popular with its air and ground crews, establishing a reputation as the most reliable Luftwaffe bomber, but it lacked the load-carrying capability of the He 111 and the speed of the Ju 88, and production was already tapering off by the end of 1939, and was finally to terminate during the early summer of 1940 with some 500 delivered. These shortcomings notwithstanding, the Do 17Z-2 was to perform the first operational sortie of World War II when aircraft of III/KG 2 took-off from Heiligenbeil, East Prussia, 45 minutes after the official outbreak of war, to bomb the approaches to the railway bridge at Dirschau, a major link across the Polish Corridor.

Equipping nine Kampfgruppen of KG 2, KG 3, KG 76 and KG 77, the Do 17Z-2 was in the forefront when the first attacks on channel convoys took place in July 1940, and the Kommodore of KG 2, Oberst Fink, was, in fact, assigned the title of Kanalkampfführer with the task of clearing the channel of British shipping, his Do 17Z-2s providing the principal component of the battle group entrusted with this mission. On Adler Tag the Do 17Z-2s of KG 2 bombed Eastchurch as the sole Kampfgeschwader failing to receive Goering's postponement order, losing four aircraft in the process.

The Do 17Z-2s of KG 3 bombed Eastchurch and Rochester two days later, and on the 16th those of KG 76 attacked West Malling, following up this mission with attacks on Biggin Hill and Kenley on the 18th.

The incursions over Britain of the Do 17Z rapidly revealed the deficiencies of its defensive armament, forward maintenance units first adding two MG 15 machine guns which could be fired laterally from the radio operator's position and then yet another pair to

Below: Despite its designation, the Do 17Z (seen below in its Z-2 version), bore limited resemblance to the original Do 17 which had been dubbed the ''Flying Pencil''. The Do 17Z introduced an entirely redesigned nose which owed little to aerodynamic refinement.

Above: The station in the Do 17Z for the bombardier was fully glazed with a series of small flat panels, or facets, and, unlike earlier Do 17s, was bulged below to provide more spacious accommodation.

provide a total defensive armament of eight machine guns. The Dornier bomber possessed good manoeuvrability and its structural integrity enabled it to undertake shallow diving attacks at speeds in excess of 370mph (590km/h), but it carried no armour protection for its crew. The element of surprise was employed by the Do 17Z formations whenever possible by recourse to low-level, terrain-following attacks, but attrition remained high, and, by mid-September, the numerical importance of the Dornier bomber in the first-line operational strength of the Luftwaffe had begun to dwindle.

The Junkers Ju 88A

Created to fulfil a 1935 demand for a so-called *Schnellbomber*, or high-speed bomber, the Junkers Ju 88A was the newest aircraft in the inventory of the Luftwaffe to participate in the Battle of Britain. Although conceived as a bomber in the design of which there was no need to compromise performance by considering potential in other roles, the Ju 88 was to prove itself extraordinarily amenable to adaptation and modification for a variety of tasks unforeseen at its conception. Even though at the time it participated in the Battle it had barely crossed the threshold of its operational career, it was tacitly recognised by the RAF as the most formidable warplane in its category extant.

First flown on December 21, 1936, the first prototype, the Ju 88 V1, was a low-wing cantilever monoplane powered by two 1,000hp Daimler-Benz DB 600Aa 12-cylinder inverted-vee engines with annular radiators. The Junkers-Werke at Schönebeck began the manufacture of production tools and jigs early in 1938, by which time contracts had been placed for 20 pre-series Ju 88A-0 and 50 series Ju 88A-1 bombers, these shortly being followed by a further contract for 100 of the latter. Manufacture was highly dispersed and such was the scale of the programme that, by the late spring of 1938, contracts had been placed for a total of 1,060 Ju 88As and by October 1 of that year 53 per cent of the total German airframe industry workforce was committed to the programme.

With the third prototype, the engines had been changed from DB 600s to Junkers Jumo 211s which were standardised for the series model, the Ju 88A-1 having Jumo 211B-1 engines each rated at 1,200hp for take-off. Its four crew members were closely grouped in the fuselage nose forward of the front wing spar; two internal bomb bays were provided, these being capable of accommodating a maximum of 28 110lb (50kg) bombs, and two external carriers were fitted beneath each wing, each capable of lifting a 1,102lb (500kg) bomb, but normally carrying a 220lb(100kg) bomb when maximum internal load was being lifted. Initially, defensive armament comprised a single forward-firing 7.9mm MG 15 machine gun in the starboard side of the cockpit windscreen and two similar weapons firing aft, one from the rear of the cockpit and the other from the rear of the offset ventral cupola. This armament was hurriedly augmented, a second aft-firing MG 15 being added while forward maintenance units improvised mountings for a pair of lateral-firing MG 15s. As these weapons had each to be operated independently, no great weight of fire could be brought to bear.

The first production Ju 88A-1s were delivered in August 1939 to the I Gruppe of Kampfgeschwader 25, this unit being redesignated as I Gruppe of Kampfgeschwader 30 on September 22. Like most new combat aircraft, the Junkers bomber suffered its share of teething troubles. For example, the slatted dive brakes

Right: Although the Junkers Ju 88A-4, illustrated by this cutaway drawing, appeared in service too late to participate in the Battle, it was similar, apart from engine sub-type, to the Ju 88A-5 which did take part.

JUNKERS Ju 88A-4
Cutaway Drawing Key
1 Starboard navigation light
2 Starboard wing tip
3 Aileron actuating hinges
4 Starboard aileron
5 Internal mass balance
6 Front spar
7 Aileron damper hydraulic line
8 Wing-section construction break
9 Rear spar
10 Starboard flap profile
11 Flap actuating rod
12 Starboard outer wing fuel tank
13 Aerial mast
14 Starboard inner wing fuel tank
15 Nacelle aft fairing
16 Starboard underwing dive-brake (extended)
17 Engine bearers
18 Three-blade propeller
19 Propeller boss
20 Oil cooler intake section
21 Annular radiator
22 Radiator gills
23 Exhaust manifold
24 Undercarriage hydraulic tank
25 Wing leading-edge hot-air de-icing trunk
26 Cockpit canopy roof section
27 Anti-glare/dazzle curtain
28 Windscreen-mounted fixed MG 81 machine gun
29 Ring sight sunshield
30 Machine gun forward mounting
31 Nose glazing flat panels
32 Bomb selector control
33 Nose frames
34 Nose-mounted hand-held MG 81 machine gun
35 Camera mounting
36 Nose lower panels (heated)
37 Bombsight (BZG II) installation
38 Sidewall window
39 Control linkage
40 Aileron damper foot pedal control
41 Rudder pedals
42 Oxygen supply regulator
43 Pilot's control column
44 Instrument panel (arched)
45 Pilot's dive-bombing sight (Stuvi)
46 Engine fuel gauge panel
47 Pilot's contoured/armoured seat (Bomb-aimer/front gunner's folding seat in well to starboard)
48 Sliding side-panel
49 Trim handwheel
50 Flap/undercarriage levers
51 Throttle levers
52 De-icing control
53 Electrical wiring conduits
54 Control runs
55 Ammunition box
56 Wireless-Operator/Gunner's seat (Second gunner's folding seat in well to starboard)
57 Radio transmitters (3)
58 Radio receivers (short-range to starboard/long-range to port)
59 Bulged canopy roof panel sections
60 Remote control unit (FBG 3)
61 Dorsal gun armoured mounting ring
62 Dorsal MG 81 machine guns
63 Fuselage main frame/front spar attachment
64 Fuselage main fuel tank
65 Filler cap/fuel air vent
66 Dump vent pipe
67 Fuselage aft main frame/rear spar attachment
68 Fuselage bomb-bay (optional additional internal fuel bay)
69 Bomb-bay/aft fuselage access
70 Upper longeron
71 Dorsal access hatch
72 Stringers
73 Aft fuselage walkway
74 Frames
75 Electrical looms
76 4-man dinghy pack
77 Master compass installation
78 Control runs
79 Fuselage aft structure
80 Oxygen bottles
81 Tailwheel retraction strut
82 Fuel dump vent
83 Starboard tailplane
84 Aerial
85 Starboard elevator mass balance
86 Starboard elevator
87 Elevator trim tab
88 Tailfin
89 Ball and socket attachment
90 Fin front spar
91 Rudder main hinge
92 Tailfin structure
93 Rudder mass balance
94 Rudder frame

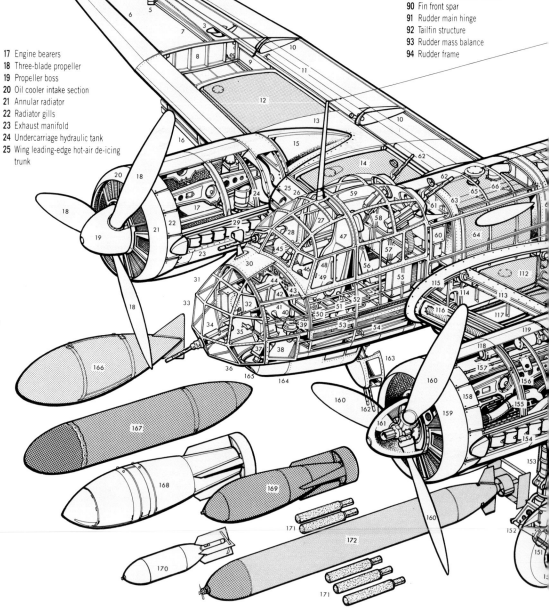

Below: A Ju 88A-1 of I Gruppe of Kampfgeschwader 51 "Edelweiss' operating from Melun-Villaroche in the Autumn of 1940 with temporary black undersurfaces for nocturnal operations. All three KG 51 Gruppen had Ju 88As by Adler Tag.

95 Sternpost
96 Rudder trim tab
97 Tab hinge fairing
98 Rear navigation light
99 Fuel dump vent outlet fairing
100 Port elevator tab
101 Port elevator
102 Port tailplane
103 Tailplane ball and socket attachment
104 Tailwheel well
105 Retractable tailwheel
106 Tailwheel leg attachment mounting
107 Ventral skinning
108 Ventral antenna
109 Fixed aerial
110 Fuselage bomb-bay door
111 Rear spar attachment (ball and socket)
112 Port inner wing fuel tank
113 Front spar
114 Front spar attachment (ball and socket)
115 Centre-section carry-through structure
116 Leading-edge de-icing trunk
117 Underwing inner-section ETC bomb racks/stores carriers
118 Oil cooler
119 Generator
120 Engine accessories
121 Nacelle aft fairing
122 Port wing flap actuating rod
123 Port wing flap
124 Wing structure
125 Nacelle aft section mainwheel well
126 Port outer wing fuel tank
127 Front spar/undercarriage retraction gear attachment
128 Undercarriage retraction yoke
129 Front spar/underwing dive-brake attachment
130 Landing light
131 Wing ribs
132 Wing-section construction break
133 Rear spar inner section
134 Outer wing structure
135 Front spar
136 Rear spar outer section
137 Internal mass balance
138 Port aileron tab
139 Port aileron
140 Wing skinning
141 Port wingtip
142 Port navigation light
143 Wing leading-edge (heated)
144 Pitot head
145 Port underwing slatted dive-brake (extended)
146 Port mainwheel door
147 Undercarriage retraction mechanism
148 Mainwheel leg sleeve
149 Brake line
150 Port mainwheel
151 Wheel hub
152 Torque link
153 Oleo leg
154 Exhaust manifold
155 Engine air trunking
156 Engine bearer
157 Junkers Jumo 211 engine
158 Radiator gills
159 Annular radiator assembly
160 Three-blade propeller
161 Propeller hub
162 Ventral twin MG 81Z machine guns
163 Crew entry hatch (ventral fairing hinged aft section)
164 Ventral fairing (Bola)
165 Bomb-aimer's optically flat panel
Underwing stores (see 117) capability includes:
166 Jettisonable auxiliary fuel tanks
167 2,205-lb (1,000-kg) (SC 1000) HE bomb
168 2,205-lb (1000-kg) aerial mine (parachute in jettisonable cap)
169 1,100-lb (500-kg) (SC 500) bombs (2)
170 550-lb (250-kg) (SC 250) bombs (4)
171 Incendiaries (in containers)
172 LTF5b aerial torpedo (Ju88A-17)

hinged beneath the front spar presented serious problems when extended. The fuselage was already highly stressed and limitations had to be imposed on high-speed manoeuvres. The undercarriage, too, was beset by problems, and the first 10 Ju 88A-1s delivered by Arado's Brandenburg factory were all damaged during landings as a result of one or other oleo leg failing. Most of these shortcomings had been ironed out, however, by the time that the Ju 88A was committed to the Battle of Britain.

On Adler Tag, all three Gruppen of KG 30 were fully equipped with the Ju 88A, as were the three Gruppen of KG 51 and both Gruppen of Lehrgeschwader 1. The I and II Gruppen of KG 54 had converted, with the III Gruppe still in process of conversion, and the III Gruppe of KG 1 had also converted to the Ju 88A. The Luftflotte 2 included the Ju 88As of III/KG 1 under I Fliegerkorps, III/KG 4 under IX Fliegerdivision, the Gruppen of LG 1 under IV Fliegerkorps, and KG 51 and KG 54 under V Fliegerkorps.

Ju 88A highlights during the Battle included the mass attack by 63 aircraft from KG 51 and KG 54 on Portsmouth on the day preceding Adler Tag, with 15 aircraft detached to bomb radar installations at Ventnor, and, on August 15, an unescorted attack by 50 Ju 88As of KG 30 on Driffield in which seven aircraft were lost to British fighters. On the same day, LG 1 despatched from Orléans-Bricy 12 aircraft from I Gruppe against Middle Wallop and 15 from II Gruppe against Worthy Down. The Ju 88As of I/LG 1 took Middle Wallop entirely by surprise, a number of Spitfires suffering damage on the ground, but only three aircraft of II/LG 1 found Worthy Down, and of the seven aircraft of this Gruppe's 4 Staffel participating all but two were shot down.

Although the Ju 88A faired better than other Luftwaffe bombers participating in the Battle, its high diving speed enabling it to evade even the Spitfire, combat attrition was by no means inconsiderable. Manoeuvrable for its size, the Ju 88A was a very efficient warplane and its innate sturdiness enabled it to withstand considerable battle damage and remain airborne. But it was deficient in both defensive armament and armour protection, and although some effort was expended during the Battle to rectify these deficiencies, the Junkers bomber was still considered by RAF fighter pilots to be comparatively "easy" prey when the epic aerial conflict drew to its close.

TODAY, every front-line combatant who goes into battle against the enemy is supported by people who stand behind him. The further back you look, the greater the number of supporters. Even 50 years ago every pilot of RAF Fighter Command was probably immediately backed up by about 100 people, with many times more in other places.

When a nation is totally at war almost everyone can be said to have a supporting role, but in the Battle of Britain this stage had not yet been reached. Despite grave reverses, the British nation had sky-high morale and not much else. Even the Army was still largely shocked and lacking weapons left behind at Dunkirk. So the effective support to ''The Few'' was provided by organisations that had been set up years beforehand. Politicians love to think that one can ignore war and then make good the deficiency by a few days of intense effort. Even in 1940 that was nonsense. Had crucial decisions not been taken years beforehand the battle would unquestionably have been lost.

To some degree Britain enjoyed many giant strokes of good luck. The dying R.J. Mitchell at Supermarine (Aviation) designed the Type 300, later named Spitfire, as a purely private venture (PV). Indeed, his boss, Sir Robert McClean, wrote to the Air Ministry, ''After unfruitful discussions with the Air Ministry, my opposite number in Rolls-Royce, the late A.F. Sidgreaves, and I decided that the two companies together should themselves finance the building of such an aircraft. The Air Ministry was informed of this decision, and were told that in no circumstances would any technical member of the Air Ministry be consulted or allowed to interfere with the designer.''

Hawker's chief designer, Sydney Camm, would never have dreamed of writing such a letter, but the fact remains that Britain's most important Battle of Britain fighter, the Hurricane, was likewise a PV design. Though he kept the Air Ministry informed, Camm's design was entirely his own and, like the Spitfire, the Hurricane had an Air Ministry specification written around it after it had been completely drawn by Camm's ''young gentlemen'' at Canbury Park Road. Had the two firms merely built to the official specification — the uninspired F.7/30, using a 680hp Goshawk engine — there would have been no chance of Fighter Command winning in 1940.

In the case of the Hurricane a further factor was that, showing unprecedented nerve in an industry not yet used to massive financial risk, the Board of the newly formed Hawker Siddeley Group decided in March 1936 to produce all the drawings, factory plans and everything else needed for production of 1,000 Hurricanes. Land was found at Langley, near Slough, Buckinghamshire, and a large new factory built specifically for the Hurricane. This unprecedented act, long before the Air Ministry had drawn up any contract, was later estimated to have resulted in Fighter Command receiving between 400 and 600 essential extra Hurricanes by August 1940.

What about the Merlin engine, which powered both the Hurricane and Spitfire, as well as the Defiant and many other RAF aircraft? Without it RAF Fighter Command could hardly have existed, yet it too owed nothing to any Air Ministry requirement. Whereas in 1925 Air

THE SUPPORT TEAMS

Bill Gunston

Above: All three single engined British fighter types used the same power plant; the Rolls Royce Merlin, which eased maintenance problems. Removal of a few panels gave easy access for servicing.

Marshal Trenchard had almost forced Rolls-Royce to get back into aviation with a new engine for the RAF, in the early 1930s the official view was that the Goshawk, a steam-cooled version of the old Kestrel, would be the preferred engine for the next generation of fighters. With a capacity of 21 litres (1,292 cu in), the Goshawk was unlikely to get much beyond 700hp. Sir Henry Royce could see that more power would be needed, and authorised the go-ahead on a bigger and newer engine, the P.V.12 (private venture, 12 cylinder). Royce died on the day the last P.V.12 drawing was issued (April 22, 1933). The first engine ran on October 15, 1933. Only at this point did the Ministry offer to finance detailed development, the P.V.12 thereupon becoming the Merlin.

The company extended the factories at Derby several times, and in 1938 began building an enormous new works at Crewe just in time for Crewe-built Merlins to fly in the Battle of Britain. Other Merlin factories got into action later.

One vital factor often overlooked in accounts of the Battle of Britain was the power increase RAF aircraft gained from using 100 octane fuel. To get to an octane rating of 100 demanded a very complicated process which, done on a commercial scale, called for large and expensive refinery plant. Though Dr S.F. Birch, of Anglo-Iranian's laboratory at Sunbury-on-Thames, was the pioneer of this ''alkylation'' process, it was the US Army Air Corps that pioneered 100-octane aviation fuel. Probably nothing would have happened in Britain had it not been for a great engine man, Air Commodore Rod Banks, who in January 1937 urged that RAF engines should be able to use 100-octane ''even if the supply of such fuel were limited, because the use of high-duty equipment might prove decisive in the air in the early stages of a war''.

Below: The new breed of eight gun fighters took a lot of rearming, as cleaning eight guns, fitting eight 300 round belts of ammunition, and checking compressed air, caused much duplication of effort.

Accordingly, two British engines, one of them the Merlin, were tested and developed to run on 100 octane, which was available only from abroad. Eventually an outstanding fuel called BAM.100 (British Air Ministry 100) was developed, and the first cargo was shipped to Britain from the Esso refinery at Aruba in June 1939. The Air Ministry stockpiled the valuable fuel, which was dyed a distinctive green: this fact remained unknown to German intelligence. This stockpiling went on throughout the war, but in May 1940, when the chips were down and everything counted, the RAF began to use the special fuel, in Merlins of Fighter Command. At a stroke the maximum boost was doubled, from 6lb (1.36ata) to 12lb (1.82ata), increasing maximum power from 1,030hp to 1,310hp. This significant increase made a major difference to the Hurricane and Spitfire. It brought the former pretty much up to the level of the Bf 109E, when it would otherwise have had a distinctly lower performance. As for the Spitfire, it gave that aircraft a vital edge, despite the fact that its rival was smaller yet had a bigger engine. This again was long-distance foresight.

A further factor was that, whereas both the Hurricane and Spitfire had gone into service with crude fixed-pitch two-blade wooden propellers, by mid-1940 almost all had three-blade constant-speed propellers giving better takeoff, faster climb and better high-speed performance. One of the first re-propellered Hurricanes was used by F/O ''Cobber'' Kain in France to shoot down a Do 17 from 27,000ft (8,230m), and it was officially stated that the enemy bomber could never have been intercepted without the improved propeller. Fitting controllable-pitch propellers, followed by constant-speed propellers, was a crash programme involving round-the-clock work by the two manufacturers, de Havilland and Rotol.

It is difficult to explain the apparent lack of interest shown by the Air Ministry between the World Wars in aircraft armament. To some degree it can be explained by lack of money, but at the eleventh hour available foreign guns were evaluated and the choice fell on the rifle-calibre Browning and 20mm Hispano-Suiza. Both dated from World War I, but in the absence of anything newer preparations were urgently made to have both guns manufactured under licence in Britain. Because of their ancient design, neither gun was really competitive in the context of World War II, but they were at least eventually made reliable. The Hispano cannon was made by British MARC (Manufacturing and Research Co.) at Grantham, but it played only a very minor role in the Battle of Britain (though Hawker Aircraft had proposed a four-20mm Hurricane in January 1936). Most of the cannon-armed aircraft in the Battle were Spitfires, but very few pilots at that time thought the bigger gun an advantage. The Browning, modified to fire British rimmed 0.303in ammunition, was virtually the standard gun of the RAF fighters, and it was made under Colt Automatic Weapon Corporation licence by BSA (Birmingham Small Arms).

Of course, both the new monoplane fighters had their guns mounted well outboard inside the wings, whereas almost all previous RAF fighters had had them in the fuselage. In the traditional installation the pilot could clear stoppages (he often carried a mallet for this pur-

RAF FIGHTER COMMAND WEEKLY AIRCRAFT STATE

OPERATIONAL SQUADRONS AVAILABLE		TOTAL ESTABLISHMENT OF AIRCRAFT	ACTUAL STRENGTH	TOTAL SERVICEABLE RESERVE	OPERATIONAL SQUADRONS AVAILABLE		TOTAL ESTABLISHMENT OF AIRCRAFT	ACTUAL STRENGTH	TOTAL SERVICEABLE RESERVE
JULY 5, 1940					**SEPTEMBER 6, 1940**				
Spitfire	19	304	304	117	Spitfire	19	304	304	41
Hurricane	24	384	384	341	Hurricane	32	512	512	183
Defiant	2	32	32	35	Defiant	2	32	32	70
Blenheim	6	96	96	33	Blenheim	6	96	96	18
JULY 12, 1940					**SEPTEMBER 13, 1940**				
Spitfire	19	304	304	107	Spitfire	19	304	304	54
Hurricane	27	432	432	222	Hurricane	33	528	528	120
Defiant	2	32	32	48	Defiant	2	16	32	82
Blenheim	6	96	96	33	Blenheim	6	96	96	17
JULY 19, 1940					**SEPTEMBER 20, 1940**				
Spitfire	19	328	328	105	Spitfire	19	304	304	45
Hurricane	27	540	540	232	Hurricane	33	528	528	121
Defiant	2	32	32	50	Defiant	2	32	32	87
Blenheim	6	96	96	35	Blenheim	6	96	96	11
JULY 26, 1940					**SEPTEMBER 27, 1940**				
Spitfire	19	328	328	96	Spitfire	19	304	304	53
Hurricane	27	540	540	249	Hurricane	33	528	528	154
Defiant	2	32	32	65	Defiant	2	32	32	93
Blenheim	6	96	96	40	Blenheim	6	96	96	6
AUGUST 2, 1940					**OCTOBER 4, 1940**				
Spitfire	19	328	328	92	Spitfire	19	304	304	55
Hurricane	28	560	560	212	Hurricane	33	528	528	149
Defiant	2	32	32	72	Defiant	2	32	32	92
Blenheim	6	96	96	41	Blenheim	6	96	96	6
AUGUST 9, 1940					**OCTOBER 11, 1940**				
Spitfire	19	328	328	129	Spitfire	19	304	304	47
Hurricane	28½	568	568	224	Hurricane	33½	536	536	144
Defiant	2	32	32	74	Defiant	2	32	32	94
Blenheim	6	96	96	40	Blenheim	6	96	96	6
AUGUST 16, 1940					**OCTOBER 18, 1940**				
Spitfire	19	328	328	150	Spitfire	19	304	304	67
Hurricane	28½	568	568	181	Hurricane	33½	536	536	192
Defiant	2	32	32	81	Defiant	2	32	32	98
Blenheim	6	96	96	40	Blenheim	6	96	96	0
AUGUST 23, 1940					**OCTOBER 25, 1940**				
Spitfire	19	328	328	113	Spitfire	19	304	304	62
Hurricane	31	634	634	120	Hurricane	34	544	544	212
Defiant	2	32	32	81	Defiant	2	32	32	120
Blenheim	6	96	96	13	Blenheim	6	96	96	0
AUGUST 30, 1940					**NOVEMBER 1, 1940**				
Spitfire	19	328	328	74	Spitfire	19	304	304	46
Hurricane	32	638	638	98	Hurricane	34	544	544	184
Defiant	2	32	32	70	Defiant	2	32	32	127
Blenheim	6	96	96	17	Blenheim	6	96	96	1

pose) and recock the weapon to continue firing. He could no longer do this with the Hurricane and Spitfire, and moreover the Dunlop company had to devise and supply electrically controlled pneumatic cocking and firing systems. Other companies provided hot air ducts to prevent the gun lubricant from freezing at the unprecedented heights at which combats could now take place.

Of course, guns are useless unless they can be aimed accurately. Unless a fighter is directly astern of its target the pilot has to ''aim off''. He has to aim at a point ahead of the enemy so that the bullets and the enemy aircraft (EA) arrive at the same place at the

same time. In extreme cases the lead angle — the angular distance between the sightline to the target and the direction of aim — can be as great as 11 degrees. Few pilots survived long enough in combat to master this, so from the mid-1930s the Royal Aircraft Establishment at Farnborough tried to devise a sight that would do this automatically. In 1937 it finalised the design of the gyro gunsight (GGS), in which a rapidly spinning mirror is mounted on a Hooke's (universal) joint connecting it to a hemisphere of thin copper rotating between the poles of powerful magnets. This sight, for the first time, enabled the pilot to fly his fighter so that an illuminated ring was centred on the target, the lead angle, and even the gravity drop of the bullets, being automatically allowed for.

Many prototypes of the GGS were used to great effect in the Battle of Britain, but they were still the exception. The sight was licensed to Ferranti, whose new factory at Edinburgh was built to make the GGS and began deliveries in 1942. The standard sight in 1940 was the newly introduced reflector sight, which projected an illuminated ring, usually with a central cross, on to an oval glass behind the armoured windscreen. The only adjustment the pilot could make was to vary the size of the ring, and if he knew the span of the target he could obtain a range indication (most pilots in the Battle tended to open fire at far too long a range). The Hurricanes and Spitfires almost always had a traditional ring-and-bead sight as well. Some pilots in 1940 actually used this, as being simple and foolproof, but it was really provided as a standby aiming system in case of failure of the electrical system.

Unquestionably, the greatest aid to accurate aiming was looking at the results of practice combats on cine film. The need to carry a "camera gun" was agreed only immediately before the war, and it proved its worth from the first day. Apart from being a marvellous training aid it was a reliable witness to actual combat, and could confirm or refute a pilot's claims made in his Combat Report. All the cameras used by Fighter Command in the battle were standard 16mm products from Williamson Manufacturing Co., of London (Willesden) and Reading.

In the Battle of Britain radio assumed a totally new importance. During the 1930s it had been standard practice for defending fighters to mount a standing patrol across the expected line of approach of enemy bombers and at what was considered a likely altitude. In actual war this would have been far too costly in

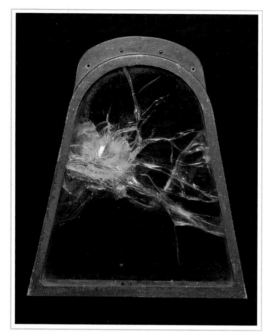

Above: British windscreens could stop bullets from behind as well as from in front. On September 9, Arthur Blake of No.19 Sqn was hit from behind by fire from a Heinkel. The bullet pierced his canopy, tore his flying helmet, and came to rest embedded in his windscreen without penetrating it.

Below: The greatest difference between WWI and WWII air combat lay in the use of air-to-air and air-to-ground radio. Mechanics of No.601 Squadron check that everything is working as advertised between sorties.

terms of engine hours, fuel, pilot fatigue and on many other counts, and with the Luftwaffe able to attack from an arc ranging from Norway to Spain the whole idea would have been impractical. Radio had been introduced by the British to enable ground controllers to transmit details of enemy attacks to squadrons on standing patrol, the source of the intelligence being the Observer Corps. Radio also enabled squadron and flight commanders to issue commands to their pilots, and of course in actual combat it was needed almost constantly by everyone involved, both to shout warnings and instructions and to listen for others.

The ubiquitous TR.9D was a high frequency (HF) set. It was connected to a wire antenna (aerial) loosely slung between a rigid mast projecting vertically above the rear fuselage and the top of the rudder. Despite careful screening of the engine ignition system, interference (static) was invariably obtrusive and often deafening. Probably more than half "The Few" were seldom able to understand the clipped bursts of noise that assailed their ears, and "say again" became one of the most common transmissions.

In 1939 Hawker's civil trial installation Hurricane, G-AFKX, was fitted with among other things, the first very high frequency (VHF) radio, TR.1133. This worked with marvellous clarity, and it also needed only a simple "whip antenna" offering hardly any drag, but it was fitted to only a few aircraft in the Battle of Britain. The first aircraft in service with VHF was Spitfire R6833 of No 19 Sqn on August 20, 1940. It was to be 1942 before all the old HF sets had been replaced in Fighter Command.

Two completely new radio functions were introduced just in time for the battle. One was IFF (identification friend or foe), a semi-automatic method in which a friendly radio station, especially in a fighter, would

"We had tremendous support from all services, including the controllers and ground artillery, but there were problems. One of these concerned the German 'spoof' raids. The controllers often held squadrons back in case these raids were followed by later, bigger raids which would get you on the ground during refuelling. But this meant that you couldn't sometimes get the height you needed to attack the enemy formations.

And in night/darkness fighting, you had to be very lucky to be positioned by a controller behind an enemy aircraft and see its exhaust. The Army would put up a single searchlight, but in the pitch darkness the Hurricane's own exhausts gave off a nasty glare and interfered with your vision.

During attacks on daylight raiders, one often had to fly through one's own anti-aircraft fire. It seemed that the AA was always behind the enemy, about a mile; didn't seem to allow enough deflection."

Air Commodore Peter Brothers
CBE. DSO. DFC

precisely at the bomber. No way of doing this existed, but Watson Watt suggested that, though this had not been mentioned, it should be possible to use radio methods to detect and locate hostile aircraft. The committee studied the idea on January 28, 1935. On February 26, Rowe and two assistants parked an ancient van in a field about ten miles from the powerful BBC transmitting station at Daventry. They set up a receiving antenna and connected it to a cathode-ray tube (CRT). Soon they heard the drone of Kestrel engines. It was a biplane Heyford bomber, flying a prearranged track overhead. As expected, the bright green line across the face of the CRT grew a small spike or "blip". As the bomber passed overhead the blip moved along the display and grew until it was big and impressive. Then it shrank, as it moved to the other side of the tube. Rowe could not only follow the bomber's track but he could have told the pilot that he was a few hundred feet off to one side of the prescribed route!

This triggered off a gigantic programme of thinking, planning, designing, building, manning and testing the first air-defence radar chain in the world. It started on July 24, 1935 when an historic set of photographs was taken of the CRT display at the pioneer RAF radar station at Orfordness in Suffolk. Clearly visible, in eight pictures of the display from 1126hrs to nearly 1216hrs, were the blips (echoes) from a Westland Wallace, two Hawker Harts, a single Hart and an unknown aircraft. By the outbreak of war the Chain Home (CH) stations sprouted their huge 350ft (107m) steel towers all round the coast from the Isle of Wight to the tip of Scotland.

The CH stations could clearly see aircraft at a height of 15,000ft (4,572m) for a distance of at least 40 miles (64km). In some cases the range was greater, and during the Battle of Britian the vital stations from Ventnor (Isle of Wight) round to Kent could actually watch the Luftwaffe formations forming up over France and Belgium before starting to cross the Channel. These big stations operated on a wavelength of 33ft (10m). They could not detect aircraft flying at low levels, and so from September 1939 a second row of stations was

Above: WAAF billets were spartan, to say the least, as is evident in this RAF Museum reconstruction. Sticky paper crosses on the windows guarded against splinters in the event of blast from nearby explosions.

Below: The 350ft (107m) high Chain Home (left) and their attendant 185ft (56m) high Chain Home Low (right) towers provided radar coverage around the south and east coasts, but they were unable to look inland.

"interrogate" all aircraft in the vicinity. Friendly aircraft would instantly and automatically respond with a very short coded signal, which would be changed frequently to prevent it from being copied by the enemy. Absence of such a response would brand the aircraft as "not friendly", and in wartime this tended to be equated with "hostile". The other new asset was radio D/F. Direction finding by radio was not new, but it had never before been available to enable a ground controller to keep track of the position of fighter formations. Each Sector Commander had two or three specially built D/F stations which received signals automatically transmitted at regular intervals by particular fighters, giving an almost immediate indication of bearing.

In 1934 the Air Ministry, in the person of scientist Percival Rowe, became concerned that the file on how science could help air defence contained only a few more or less useless pieces of paper. A special committee was formed, and in January 1935 the Director of Scientific Research, Dr H.E. Wimperis, sought the opinion of the top radio expert, Dr Robert Watson Watt, on whether it would be theoretically possible to build a "death ray", an idea much in vogue in the popular press and works of fiction. The eminent physicist replied that, for practical purposes, the answer was "No". Almost all civil servants would have left it at that, but "Wattie" added a little comment that had not been asked for, and by so doing he changed history and almost certainly changed the outcome of the Battle of Britain and of World War II.

He casually pointed out that, to destroy an enemy bomber with a "death ray" you had to aim the ray

from the direct telephone lines to the Fighter Command stations.

The radar observers who, like the plotters, were mainly members of the Womens' Auxiliary Air Force (WAAF) soon became extremely skilled not only at estimating target ranges, which were relatively easy, but also target bearings, heights and numbers, which were more difficult. The existence of this nationwide radar barrier meant that if an RAF squadron was scrambled it was almost bound to meet the enemy and engage in combat. Detailed instructions on the enemy's movements could be radioed by the Controllers right up to joining battle, with the hoped-for added advantage of getting into a favorable (eg, up-sun) position beforehand.

In 1940 the CH and CHL radars looked out to sea, but had very limited performance in the other direction, over land. Therefore, enormous responsibility continued to be placed on the Observer Corps, which expanded in numbers to 32,000, refined its methods and manned 1,400 posts during the Battle of Britian. The Corps received the prefix "Royal" in 1941. Among their many duties was immediate and accurate reporting of the location of every crashed aircraft and every

Above: Once inland, enemy formations could only be tracked by the Observer Corps, a body of volunteers who manned a network of posts across England, everyone of which was connected to Fighter Command by landline.

Right: The sextant-like gadget seen in this RAF Museum presentation was used by the Observer Corps to obtain approximations of the course, altitude and speed of enemy formations in conditions of good visibility.

added to plug the gap. Called Chain Home Low (CHL), these stations operated on only 5ft (1.5m) wavelength, with rotating antenna arrays on top of 185ft (56m) and 20ft (6m) towers. They could see a fighter speeding in at only just above sea level, out to a distance of up to 30 miles (48km). By August 1940 the CHL stations stretched right round South and East England and up to the Shetlands.

Thus, throughout the Battle of Britain, every raid by the Luftwaffe was detected as soon as it took off and kept under continuous radar surveillance as it approached the English coast. In the crucial years 1937-39 the entire RAF defence network was perfected, the information from all the radar stations being collected and sifted at Filter Centres and the overall battle control from Sector, Group and finally Fighter Command plotting rooms, the command room being at Bentley Priory, Stanmore. The central feature of the Operations Room at Fighter Command was a giant map of Great Britain, arranged horizontally at table height. The land area was divided into about 130 Warning Districts, in each of which, depending on the threat situation, a Warning or an All Clear would be sounded, the first by a distinctive rising and falling note on powerful sirens and the latter by a steady note. There were many subsidiary arrangements, all concerned with the population at large and quite separate

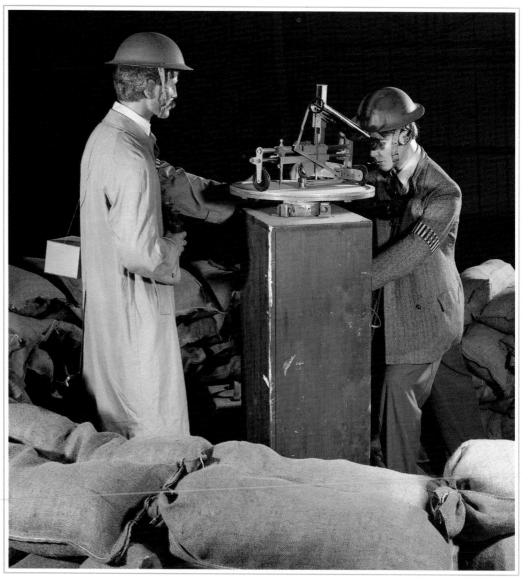

parachuted pilot or crew-member, both over land and off the coast. In the latter case the RAF's ever-alert air/sea rescue service would swing into action, using fast power boats and Supermarine Walrus amphibians to fish friend and foe alike out of the Channel.

Unfortunately, parachutists over England were almost automatically judged to be German, and many RAF fighter pilots were shot at or in other ways attacked by the Army and newly formed Local Defence Volunteers (later named Home Guard). The most famous example was Fighter Command's F/Lt J.B. Nicolson VC, who was almost burned to death in the air and did not really need sustained rifle fire (fortunately inaccurate) as he descended. Another task of "the Brown Jobs" was to guard crashed aircraft, though when convenient this was also done by armed RAF personnel. Every recognisable Luftwaffe wreck was carefully examined by Intelligence Officers. Indeed, it was a single scrap of paper examined by British Intelligence which alerted the RAF to the fact that the Luftwaffe bombers were using radio beams for precision guidance.

Intelligence plays a central and crucial role in any modern war. Through abysmal intelligence in the late

Above: This Messerschmitt Bf 110C-4 of I/ZF 2 came down at Rye Hill, Essex, on the morning of September 3 following a mid-air collision with another 110 during a combat with Hurricanes of Nos.17 and 46 Squadrons.

1930s the aircraft of the Luftwaffe were largely unknown in Britain. Even their designations were often invented, such as "Me 109" and "He 111K Mk Va". Quite suddenly, from the summer of 1940 southern England became littered with the aircraft themselves, and there was no ignorance any more. In particular, each type was found to have weaknesses, which the RAF quickly learned to exploit. But at an even higher level, British intelligence surpassed itself, in a way that perhaps can never be repeated. Thanks in part to the Poles and French, the ultra-secret Enigma machines, used by the German armed forces to encode all radio messages, were "broken" by a combination of brilliant thinking, fantastic electro-mechanical devices and, at Bletchley Park, Buckinghamshire, the ceaseless labours of large teams of cryptoanalysts. In his book "The Ultra Secret" former RAF intelligence officer F.W. Winterbotham explained how glad Lord Dowding was to avail himself of the content of Luftwaffe operational messages, which in effect gave him, on a daily basis, the policy of Goering himself.

In the 1930s the RAF controlled all repairs to aircraft, and did a great deal itself in 43 Group. On May 14, 1940 the Ministry of Aircraft Production (MAP) was established under the dynamic Lord Beaverbrook, who personally masterminded the expansion of a gigantic Civilian Repair Organization (CRO) which was dispersed even more widely than the parent aircraft factories. MAP also created order out of chaos and by the time of the Battle of Britain had more or less solved countless problems and shortages and got airframes, engines and accessories not only made at maximum rate but also — and this was vitally important during the Battle — repaired at maximum rate. It is on record that one Hurricane was shot down three times during the battle, while a Spitfire got through the Battle with five different propellers.

With such a massive programme of aircraft production and repair it was recognised in 1939 that tremen-

Below: A Spitfire on the assembly line. The Ministry of Aircraft Production, headed by Lord Beaverbrook, who was also the father of Max Aitken, ensured by an adequate supply of fighter aircraft during the battle.

BRITISH MONTHLY AIRCRAFT PRODUCTION, 1940

	PLANNED ALL TYPES	ACTUAL	PLANNED FIGHTERS	ACTUAL
February	1,001	719	171	141
March	1,137	860	203	177
April	1,256	1,081	231	256
May	1,244	1,279	261	325
June	1,320	1,591	292	446
July	1,481	1,665	329	496
August	1,310	1,601	282	476

NOTE: These are the only figures extant. Records were kept by the Ministry of Aircraft Production and the relevant files have disappeared, apparently destroyed, among many others.

AMMUNITION EXPENDITURE AND ENEMY DESTROYED THROUGHOUT ANTI-AIRCRAFT COMMAND FOR JULY, AUGUST AND SEPTEMBER 1940.	
July 1940—	
Day*	344 rds. per aircraft.
Night	(26 a/c=8,935 rds.)
August 1940—	
Day*	232 rds. per aircraft.
Night	(167 a/c=38,764 rds.)
September 1940—	
Day†	1,798 rds. per aircraft.
Night	(144 a/c=258,808 rds.)

*Mainly by day, little night activity.
†Including considerable night activity and large expenditure of amunition by night.

Above: The British 3.7in Mk IIIA quick firing anti-aircraft gun threw a 28lb (12.7kg) shell to an effective engagement ceiling of 25,000ft (7,600m) with a practical rate of fire of 10 rounds per minute.

dous manpower would be needed merely to ferry aircraft from one place to another and to deliver them to Britain's Service units. The answer was the Air Transport Auxiliary (ATA). It was formed on September 1, 1939 by G. (later Sir Gerard) d'Erlanger, and made use of amateur and quasi-professional pilots, men and women, and mostly aged 30 to 50. Naturally the authorities were horrified at such a novel idea, and poured the ATA candidates into the front seats of Harvards and Blenheims in the hope that they would fail. Nearly all made the grade, and indeed on January 1, 1940 an all-female Ferry Pool was opened at Hatfield. The ATA eventually numbered 650 pilots who, though civilian, wore distinctive dark blue uniform. During the war they made over 300,000 deliveries of every kind of RAF and RN aircraft, in every kind of weather, with no armament and no radio. In summer 1940 the ATA was really getting into its stride, and it played an important part.

Of course, other important roles were played by ground-based defensive systems, notably anti-aircraft (AA) guns and the balloon barrage. At this time the RAF Regiment had yet to be formed, and all AA units were part of the Army. AA Command covered the whole country, large sub-areas being allocated to particular divisions. heavy AA (HA) guns, notably the 3.7in (94mm) and 4.5in (114mm), could engage Luftwaffe aircraft of 1940 up to their practical ceiling, but even when targets were visible it was difficult to aim accurately, and actual expenditure of ammunition per kill was higher than the figures recorded at the time. Firing on unseen targets (above cloud or at night) had essentially no more than a morale-boosting effect. In the same way, searchlights served a useful purpose at night in giving a general indication of where targets were to be found, to night fighters, but because they were linked with sound locators they had little hope of illuminating targets (it was a very different story later when individual lights had their own target-tracking radar).

Engagements during the Battle took place at all heights from 35,000ft (10,670m) down to sea level. At lower levels what was later to be called "light flak" was very important, but Britain suffered from lack of weapons. Had it not been for belated adoption in 1938 of the Swedish 2pdr (40mm) Bofors the situation might have been called ridiculous. As it was, Bofors guns were available in pitifully small numbers, and — hand-loaded with clips of four — could get off only a few rounds against a fast low-flying target. Britain had no equivalent of the deadly light flak that travelled with

Below: A British ack-ack battery fires at night. On the night of 15/16 October, 235 German bombers raided London. The guns fired 8,326 shells to destroy two and damage two. Night firing was generally ineffectual.

Above: 90cm searchlight, with a carbon projector giving 210 million candlepower, was an integral part of the night defences. While not intended that way, its greatest effect was to blind the bomber crews.

Below: WAAFs handle a barrage balloon in Central London. The function of the balloon barrage was to prevent enemy bombers from attacking at low level, where they were likely to do the most damage.

the German armies, notably twin-37mm and quad (flak-vierling) 20mm guns, available in thousands.

The balloon barrage was deployed in increasing numbers from 1938 onwards. The primary purpose of the barrage, formed by kite balloons moored by strong steel cables, was to prevent hostile aircraft from attacking at low level. The balloons seldom rode above 5,000ft (1,524m), and were disposed around London and such cities as Southampton, Portsmouth, Dover and the Medway towns, and from coastal convoys. Later in the war they were responsible for the loss of numerous Allied aircraft and almost none of the Luftwaffe, but in the autumn of 1940 their presence did exert a significant extra demoralising effect on Luftwaffe aircrew. The balloons were organised into RAF squadrons, numbered from 900 upwards, each subdivided into flights and with balloon spacing a compromise between the ideal, on the one hand, and the available and accessible sites on the other.

This matter of sites was crucial, yet at no time did any branch of the armed forces use high-handed tactics and commandeer sites. Thanks to the years between Munich and the war, sufficient sites had been obtained through the laborious legal processes to satisfy almost every need of the defence forces throughout the Battle. This was especially important in the case of airfields, which of course (even in 1940) were much larger than sites for AA guns or balloon vehicles. Time and again it was demonstrated that the best way to allow aircraft to survive on the ground was dispersal. In 1940 repeated and prolonged attacks on airfields destroyed remarkably few aircraft, and the large numbers of satellite fields enabled operations to be maintained even after heavy damage to the main airfields. Fortunately the Battle took place at a time of year when personnel could live under canvas and work on aircraft in the open without discomfort.

The RAF had just begun to construct paved (invariably tarmac) runways at the start of the war. Fighter Command's aircraft did not need runways, and almost all takeoffs during the battle (on both sides, in fact) were from grass. Bomb craters in grass are relatively easy to fill in, but large craters in the paved areas around the hangars — which is where most bombs were aimed — were another matter. Despite stockpiling of hardcore months beforehand, during the most crucial phases of the Battle, when the Luftwaffe was concentrating its attacks on the fighter airfields, craters were being made faster than they could be filled and resurfaced. Modern earthmoving machinery did not exist, and the first bulldozers arrived with US forces in 1942.

Damage to houses and other civilian property did not begin in earnest until near the end of the Battle, and repairing such damage was not then a serious drain on resources. Thus, until late September almost all efforts could be directed towards repairing, or at least rendering usable, such vital structures as radars, hangars and telephone lines (which formed the links between all parts of the air defence system).

The Battle of Britain was the first time the RAF had been called upon to attend to injuries to its personnel on a large scale. Casualties now included not only aircrew but also personnel on the ground. From the formation of the Service it had possessed a Medical Branch, under an Air Vice Marshal, and in 1919 an RAF hospital was opened at Halton, greatly enlarged and improved in 1928 as part of the Princess Mary's RAF Nursing Service (PMRAFNS). Suddenly in 1940 it was overloaded, and in particular, it was inundated with serious burn cases. A special burns unit was opened at Halton during the battle, and it grew rapidly in size and skill, soon becoming a world leader alongside the civilian unit at East Grinstead under Sir Archibald McIndoe. Another major PMRAFNS hospital was open-

and the fighters of Jagdfliegerführer 2) and Luftflotte 3 (FlKps IV, V and VIII and the fighters of Jagdfliegerführer 3). Either of these ought to have been a match for RAF Fighter Command. By mid-July their 50 main bases and approximately the same number of satellite airfields had been made fully operational and stocked with preliminary supplies of fuel and ordnance. Supplies continued to be built up, using trains and Ju 52/3Ms, until the main assault began on 8 August. For the longer term, a modest programme of airfield improvements began, concerned chiefly with providing paved runways and taxiways and luxurious living quarters, but the West was not expected to be more than a garrison theatre. All the long-term campaign plans continued to be directed towards the East.

The propaganda ministry of Josef Goebbels incessantly stated that the war in the West had already been won, and their view was actually reflected in German decisions and planning. Aircraft production was increased in early 1940 in readiness for the attrition of the campaign in Scandinavia and especially, in the West. Monthly output after the battles in Poland was 495 aircraft in February 1940, with single-shift work-

ed near RAF Wroughton, Swindon. The RAF also became famous for its Institute of Aviation Medicine at Farnborough, but this is concerned primarily with physiological research rather than treatment.

With hindsight we know that Hitler had not expected to find Germany at war with Britain (at least, not yet) and genuinely wanted to find an ''out'' — some kind of negotiated settlement which would leave him in undisputed control of the European countinent. The summer of 1940 found Germany's armed forces totally victorious throughout mainland Europe; the untried philosophy of Blitzkrieg — lightning war, ironically invented and described in detail by British officers who were ignored in their own country — had proved itself unstoppable. Hitler's real ambitions lay to the East, but quite unexpectedly he found he had a foe separated by 21 miles (34km) of water. On June 25, 1940 his troops were exhausted, but their morale was sky-high. There seemed to be just about time to invade and subdue this unexpected enemy before the bad weather of the winter set in.

With his eyes fixed on the Soviet Union it was also a surprise to Hitler to find his forces in command of the whole of northern France, the Low Countries, Denmark and Norway. This was especially gratifying to the Luftwaffe, which was thus placed in a perfect position to carry out the orders of Goering, its bombastic leader, to eliminate the RAF as a fighting force. Strategically, the situation was ideal. The Luftwaffe had at its disposal over 120 airfields within Bf 109E range of southern England, and after surveying all of them more than 50 were selected as main airfields for Luftflotte 3, in the west, and Luftflotte 2, in eastern France and the Low Countries. Many other good airfields in Denmark and Norway became home to Luftflotte 5, and this forced the RAF to maintain substantial fighter forces in northern England and Scotland.

Virtually the whole strength of the Luftwaffe ranged against the RAF No 11 and No 10 Groups comprised units of Luftflotte 2 (Fliegerkorps I, II and IX,

Above: First into the devastated areas were the firemen and the heavy rescue squads. They risked fire, falling buildings, gas, explosion, and unexploded bombs in their efforts to minimise the damage.

Right: Delayed action bombs hampered remedial works, while many simply failed to go off on impact. Many brave men gave their lives in attempts to defuze weapons such as this German 1,200 pound (500kg) bomb.

Below: A Dornier Do 17Z refuels before a sortie over England in August. Some non-standard machine guns have appeared in an attempt to give all-round defensive cover against the eager British fighters.

ing and a 40 hour week. Without altering the working week, output was boosted in April to 990, and to a peak of 1,205 in September. This peak resulted from the inevitable lag between issuing orders and getting results; it had nothing to do with the Battle of Britain. In fact, orders had gone out to reduce production in early July, just after the fall of France, and output fell to 930 in October 1940 and a mere 693 in November. It stayed around the 700 mark until the forthcoming campaign in the East forced it to rise to over 1,000 once more. Subsequently, gigantic fighter production was to push the figure beyond 4,300 in 1944. Thus, there was never any expectation of any real problem in subduing the RAF, and the 1,653 frontline combat aircraft actually shot down in the Battle of Britain took a long time to replace. All of this took place at a time long before the political frictions and traumatic upheavals that were to afflict German production later in the war.

From the start, the *Luftwaffe* was to some extent an élite force. It concentrated upon war in the air, a mission which it saw as including training of most of its personnel. This broad mission also included the provision of *flak* (AA artillery). Nearly all secondary functions were assigned to a secondary force, the *Luftdienst* (air service). This was essentially a civilian organization, though it came to include large numbers of personnel from the *Luftwaffe* and other forces who were wounded or in any other way medically unfit for combat duty. The *Luftdienst's* aircraft were often indistinguishable from those of the *Luftwaffe*, and could be seen wearing theatre bands. The *Luftdienst* grew in strength throughout the war, carrying out such tasks as transport and liaison, front-line supply, aircraft ferrying, target towing, rescue and casualty evacuation, photography and surveying (not over enemy territory) and increasing duties brought on by RAF bombing, such as dispersal of industry.

In such matters as intelligence, command and control, raid warning and medical services the *Luftwaffe* generally paralleled the RAF. The main difference was that in 1940 the *Luftwaffe* was doing the attacking and the fighting was over England and the Channel. There was not much need for intelligence or raid warning, and the chain of command could hardly have been simpler. Policy was decided by Goering (or, on 4 September, Hitler himself in the case of opening the *Blitz* on London) and orders sent by Enigma to Albert Kesselring *(Luftflotte* 2) and Hugo Sperrle *(Luftflotte* 3). Though almost all the crews were experienced in battle, a great deal had to be learned by experience; but the *Luftwaffe* never expected to fail to subdue the Royal Air Force.

Right: Like the RAF, the Luftwaffe made extensive use of women in various support roles. This Luftwaffenmuseum presentation shows the uniform of a female Obergefreiter (Corporal) in normal working dress. The badge on her sleeve is that of the air-raid warning branch of the service. The colour variation between tunic and skirt seem to show that this example combines elements from two different uniforms.

BEFORE we can study the air fighting tactics of both sides during the Battle of Britain, we need to look at the state of the art during the high summer of 1940. One of the most important lessons from the air fighting of the Kaiser's War was that the best formation for combat was the open abreast style, with a spacing of 50 or 60 yards (45-55m) between each scout, so that pilots could keep station with each other, fly near their leader without the risk of collision, search the surrounding sky against the possibility of surprise attack, and turn inside each other to face an astern attack. This formula was learned by both British and German pilots under the constant and unforgiving hammer of battle, was recorded in a thousand memoirs and memoranda, and seemingly lost with the cease fire. For in 1939 when the Messerschmitts began to fight in Spain they flew in close wing-tip to wing-tip formation totally unsuited for combat because of the lack of manoeuvering space and the absence of cross-cover.

However, German fighter pilots like Werner Mölders and Adolph Galland soon realised that their close formations were vulnerable and they adopted a far better style of air fighting. This perfect formation — for it is still flown today — was based on the Rotte, the element of two fighters. Some 200 yards (180m) separated a pair of fighters, and the chief responsibility of number two, or wingman, was to guard his leader

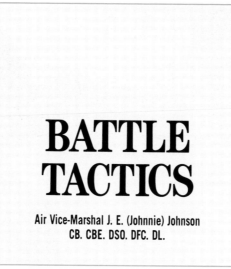

BATTLE TACTICS

Air Vice-Marshal J. E. (Johnnie) Johnson
CB. CBE. DSO. DFC. DL.

from attack; meanwhile the leader navigated and covered his wingman. The Schwarm, of four fighters, simply consisted of two pairs and was exactly the same abreast pattern as that devised by Oswald Boelcke, the leading tactician of air fighting in World War I, except that the spacing between aeroplanes had increased from about 60 yards (55in), the turning radius of Boelcke's Albatross, to some 300 yards (275m), the turning radius of a Messerschmitt 109.

There was an important difference of principle, however, between the old and new formations, since the number of machines in the former varied between three and six, according to aeroplane serviceability, while in Spain the Messerschmitt pilots found that owing to their increased speeds, greater turning radii and the restricted view from their enclosed cockpits, especially behind, it was essential to build their formations around the smallest fighting unit, the pair, for a lone pilot was more vulnerable than ever before. Flying in this fashion, a Messerschmitt squadron of 12 fighters stretched some mile and a half (2.5km) across the sky, and each Schwarm flew at varying heights, so that the starboard group, deployed down-sun from the leader, could search into the sun and guard the rest from surprise attack. These staggered heights gave cross-cover in all directions, and also made the fighters far less conspicuous in the sky.

The Messerschmitts carried radio telephones and, for the first time, fighter pilots could receive and transmit clear and distinct speech. When he manoeuvred before attacking, Mölders could keep his team fully in the picture — a tremendous improvement over the previous methods when a leader signalled his intentions by rocking his wings or firing coloured lights. So far air fighting had been inarticulate. In Spain it became articulate; this made for better teamwork in the air, and closer control from the ground. For the

Above: The Henschel Hs 123 was the last biplane to be used operationally by the Luftwaffe, and saw service in Poland and France. It is seen here flying the tight vic formation which was widely used during World War I. It has just one advantage; the pilots on the wings can easily see the leader's hand signals. It has several disadvantages, one of which is that the wingmen spend too much time watching the leader.

Right: The Messerschmitt Bf 109E was the standard single engined Luftwaffe fighter during the Battle. While it could be out-turned by the Spitfire and Hurricane, it outperformed them both at high altitude.

ROTTE FORMATION

Right: The basic Luftwaffe fighter formation was the Rotte of two aircraft.

ROTTENFLIEGER   ROTTENFUHRER
4   3

SCHWARM FORMATION

ROTTENFLIEGER   SCWARMFUHRER   ROTTENFUHRER   ROTTENFLIEGER
4   2   3   4

Above: A pair of Rotte made up a four aircraft Schwarm, with the second pair generally staggered in both height and position. Each pilot searched astern and inwards both high and low, to cover all blind spots.

Above: a pilot's eye view from a Heinkel He 111 as a formation storms in over England. This would not be a good height from which to attack; they are well within range of light AA and even small arms fire, and there is no spare altitude to trade for distance or speed on the long haul home with perhaps even damaged engines losing power.

STAFFEL FORMATION

ROTTENFLIEGER   SCWARMFUHRER
4   2

ROTTENFLIEGER   ROTTENFUHRER
4   3

ROTTENFLIEGER   STAFFELFUHRER
4   1

ROTTENFUHRER   ROTTENFLIEGER
3   4

SCWARMFUHRER   ROTTENFLIEGER
2   4

ROTTENFUHRER   ROTTENFLIEGER
3   4

Above: A Staffel consisted of three Schwarme formed up more or less abreast. The loose spacing allowed for a combination of flexibility and rapid manoeuvring with ease of command and control. If the formation became disrupted, the individual Rotte would still provide mutual defensive support.

Below: The Staffel would also be staggered in the vertical. The leader would take the low central position, and normally got the best shooting chances, which accounts for the high scores achieved by some Luftwaffe pilots. The Schwarm on the left shows a formation variant that was sometimes used.

ROTTENFLIEGER
4

ROTTENFUHRER
3
ROTTENFLIEGER
4

SCWARMFUHRER
2

STAFFEL FORMATION FROM BEHIND

ROTTENFLIEGER
4

STAFFELFUHRER
1

ROTTENFUHRER   ROTTENFLIEGER
3   4

SCWARMFUHRER   ROTTENFLIEGER
2   4

ROTTENFUHRER   ROTTENFLIEGER
3   4

air fighters it was a big step forward.

Victory for Franco ended the Spanish Civil War, and the Condor Legion returned to Germany, where the lessons of air warfare were carefully studied. The radius of action of the Messerschmitt 109 was considered insufficient, and drop tanks, which could be jettisoned before a fight, were ordered. The three light machine guns were found to be inadequate for modern air combat and the 20mm Oerlikon cannon was developed for the Messerschmitt. Experienced German fighter pilots thought the salient features of the ideal fighter to be (in order of precedence): a high speed and a good climb to engage, manoeuvrability to get out of trouble, fire power to knock down an opponent in a few seconds, and a good radius of action so that the fighter could be used offensively.

In Spain, for the first time in history, an army and an air force fought to a joint air-ground plan, where centralised control gave the Condor Legion such flexibility that it was able to concentrate its striking power and paralyse the opposing ground forces. General Wolfram von Richthofen, the driving force, had fashioned his command into a highly successful tactical air force and, once back in Berlin, he argued his case for more tactical air forces to fight not in air battles, but jointly with the ground forces in air-ground battles. He was opposed by those high ranking officers of the Luftwaffe who foresaw that more tactical air forces would inevitably mean less resources for the strategic bomber force, but Richthofen so won the day

STUKA DIVE ATTACK

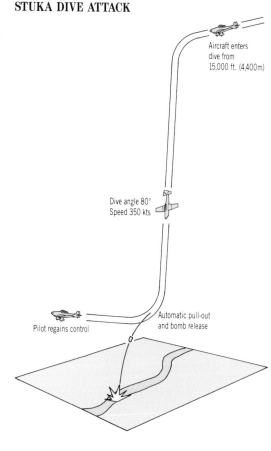

Aircraft enters
dive from
15,000 ft. (4,400m)

Dive angle 80°
Speed 350 kts

Automatic pull-out
and bomb release

Pilot regains control

that Luftflotten were formed, consisting of bomber, reconnaissance, fighter and ground-attack squadrons.

Strategic bombing came to be regarded as a short-term and often short-range affair. Influenced by success in Spain, the German concept of modern war was for bombers to attack enemy airfields and industrial centres as the immediate prelude to air-ground operations, which would consist of great masses of armour rolling deeply into enemy territory, supported by fighters to cope with the remants of an opposing air force, more fighters to scout ahead of and on the flanks of the armoured columns, dive bombers to reduce the ground opposition and attack all road and rail communications and to terrorize the civilian population, fighter-bombers to quarter and harass the surrounding countryside, taking out practically anything that dared move, paratroops to secure the flanks, and for all these violent, irresistible thrusts to be actively supported by Quislings and a Fifth Column. This was a new type of mechanised war, and it was known by a new and appropriate name — Blitzkreig: Lightning War.

On May 10, 1940, this combination of armour and aeroplane blasted through the Ardennes with such awesome power that Holland surrendered in five days, Belgium in a further ten days and France on June 17.

Now Hitler was master of Europe. German grand strategy depended on Operation "Sealion" with which Hitler aimed to conquer Britain within the following few months. There would be massive attacks against the Royal Air Force, the Channel would be a major river

Below: A Kette of Junkers Ju 87B Stukas on their way to a target in Poland. A neat touch was an air-driven siren fitted to their wheel housings, the noise from which during their attacking dive was demoralising to the troops on the ground.

Above: The Stuka commenced its attack with a bunt from medium altitude into an 80 deg dive with air brakes extended. The pull-out

height was preset at about 4,000ft (1,200m), with automatic bomb release soon after. Once level flight was regained, the pilot took over control.

Below: The nose of a captured Messerschmitt Bf 110C is opened to reveal a battery of four machine guns; two 20mm MGFF cannon were also mounted beneath the cockpit and projected beneath the nose. These weapons gave formidable hitting power.

FIGHTER SQUADRON FORMATIONS

Right: The standard British fighter formation was the three aircraft section or Vic. On it were built the Fighter Command Attacks which were designed to deal with unescorted bombers.

NO.1 SECTION

Sections echeloned to side most convenient

NO.2 SECTION

SEARCH AND CRUISE FORMATIONS

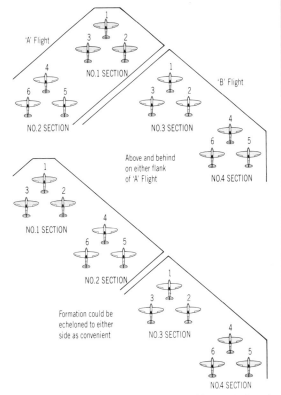

'A' Flight

NO.1 SECTION

NO.2 SECTION

NO.3 SECTION

'B' Flight

Above and behind on either flank of 'A' Flight

NO.4 SECTION

NO.1 SECTION

NO.2 SECTION

Formation could be echeloned to either side as convenient

NO.3 SECTION

NO.4 SECTION

Above: Twelve aircraft made up the standard British fighter squadron formation. This was split into two flights, each of two sections as shown. The two flights could formate on each other in one of two ways;

either the flights echeloned to opposite sides as shown in the top example, or both echeloned the same way, as in the lower one. Either way the formation was unwieldy, and rapid changes of direction were difficult.

crossing, and the German armies well supported by the Luftwaffe would, as before, carry all before them.

By the end of July the Luftwaffe forces that were deployed to conquer Britain comprised some 2,600 aeroplanes, of which there were 120 bombers, 280 Stukas and 980 fighters, and they were based on operational airfields stretching from Norway to Britanny so that attacks against England could be made from this wide geographical arc. This was a formidable force, manned by experienced aircrews whose morale, flushed by their recent victories, was high. But as we shall see, it had three flaws — lack of a sophisticated radar system on the Channel coast, the very limited range of the Bf 109s and Goering's appalling leadership.

What of its adversary — RAF Fighter Command?

Unfortunately, Fighter Command's tactical training was based on the theory that the air threat to Britain

''We learned tactics pretty quickly, but there wasn't much time during the Battle. We learned to spread the vics. One chap was put in as 'weaver' — arse-end Charlie — weaving about behind our formation, keeping look-out. They were often shot down, weaving behind and never seen again.

Sailor Malan was the best pilot of the war, a good tactician; above average pilot and an excellent shot. In the end it comes down to being able to shoot. I was an above average pilot, but not a good shot, so the only way I could succeed was to get closer than the next chap. This wasn't easy. Johnnie Johnson was a pretty good, average pilot, but an excellent shot.

The answer was that there were was no really successful shooting parameter above 5 degree deflection. Most kills were from behind, coming down on the enemy, or head-on, or in 5 degrees deflection.

The Spitfire's guns were harmonised to about 450 yards, but this was spread too far across. Sailor Malan trimmed his own guns down to 200-250 yards, and we all followed suit.

At the end of the day, you had to have luck, and I had my share. Once I had my watch shot off my wrist. It was my own watch, and the Air Ministry wouldn't pay me back for it! Another had a bullet hit his headphones. His ear was a bit of a mess, but at least he was alive.''

**Air Commodore Alan Deere
CBE. DSO. DFC.**

Above: Two Junkers Ju 87Bs swoop to the attack in this carefully posed picture attributed to the French campaign. In fact they never dived in pairs like this or in any other formation, but singly.

VIC AND CROSS-OVER TURN

Below: A fighter flying solo is very manoeuvrable, but when in formation much of this agility is lost, due to the need to maintain integrity in the turn. Formations are necessary in order to get as many aircraft as possible into the fight in a single mass. The Luftwaffe four-ship Schwarm proved superior to the British three-ship section.

Above: Turning a British section meant that the leader and the inside man had to throttle back while the outside man accelerated in order to keep position. The turn had therefore to be fairly gentle.

Above: The Jagdflieger had re-invented the cross-over turn, which called for no juggling of throttles and which permitted a tight turn to be made. Positions within the Schwarm were reversed.

would be hordes of German bombers flying in close formation, and not escorted by fighters, since the Messerschmitt 109 could not reach our shores from airfields in Germany. Apparently those who assessed the nature of the threat did not take into account either the possibility of more adjacent airfields becoming available to the Luftwaffe, or that Willi Messerschmitt might double the range of his angular-looking fighter by fitting long-range drop tanks under the fuselage and wings. Dog-fighting was considered a thing of the past, and rigid air fighting tactics were introduced which, by a series of complicated and time-wasting manoeuvres, aimed at bringing the greatest number of guns to bear against the bombers.

The RAF's tactical unit was the tight vic of three fighters and using this as a basis the Air Fighting Development Establishment worked out six types of

FIGHTER ATTACK No. 1 (FROM DEAD ASTERN)

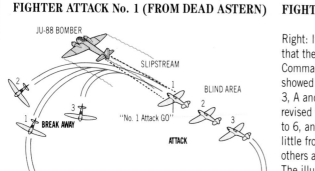

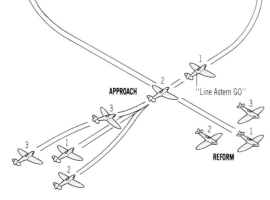

Above: Fighter Attack No.1 was formulated for a section of fighters to deal with a lone bomber. Moving into line astern, the leader gets to a position about 2,400ft (730m) astern and between 100 and 200ft 630-60m) below. Closing slowly, the leader opens fire, only breaking off when out of ammunition, after which the second and third fighters repeat the dose.

FIGHTER ATTACK No.1 (FROM ABOVE CLOUD)

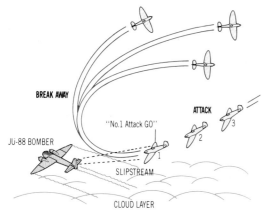

Above: If The bomber was flying just above a layer of cloud, or low above the sea, this would make the No.1 Attack impracticable as the fighters would be unable to attain a position below the target. In this event the No.1 Attack was to be made from slightly above either from dead astern or slightly to one side, but in any event, avoiding the slipstream of the bomber. The break after the attack would be made throttled back and to one side. The problems of this were avoiding losing sight of the target and building up excessive speed in the descent. The No.1 Attack had one advantage; there was little chance of friendly fighters colliding.

FIGHTER ATTACK No. 2 FROM (DIRECTLY BELOW)

Right: It should be noted that the original Fighter Command Attack document showed Attacks 1, 2, and 3, A and B. This was later revised to show Attacks 1 to 6, and while No.1 differs little from the original, others are very different. The illustrations and text are all from the later document.

Fighter Attack No.2 is a variation on a section of fighters attacking a solo bomber. On sighting the enemy, the section takes up line astern and closes in astern and about 2,000ft (600m) below. The leader then pulls into a steep climb, and opens fire at a deflection angle of about 40 degrees. He breaks away down and to one side just before reaching a position co-altitude and dead astern, at which point the next fighter commences its attack. It called for considerable deflection shooting ability.

formation attacks against unescorted bombers on which training was based. For example, Fighter Command Attack Number Six was the prescribed drill when a squadron of fighters attacked nine bombers.

Having sighted the bombers, the squadron commander ordered "Sections astern, GO" and closed to a position about 800 yards (730m) astern and slightly below the bombers. From here he ordered "Number Six attack, deploy, GO", whereupon Yellow and Green Leaders took their sections to port of their flight leaders. The squadron commander then ordered "Number Six attack, GO" and Red and Yellow Sections simultaneously attacked the starboard and port sections of the bomber formation. Care, said the manual, must be taken not to lose sight of adjacent fighters when firing. At the conclusion of the attack, the squadron commander ordered "Break away, GO" whereupon sections dived away outwards from the bombers. Meanwhile, B Flight, having waited patiently in the queue, attacked after A Flight.

Some of the other prescribed attacks were even more complicated and time-wasting than Number Six, and all were based on tight vic formations and opening fire together, so that a wingman found it impossible to keep a good lookout and to watch both his leader and his target.

The rigid, outmoded vic of three was flown by Fighter Command throughout the Battle of Britain. Luftwaffe ace Galland thought that RAF fighters were at a great disadvantage because of their rigid formations. Although some squadrons discarded the time-wasting fighter attacks, my log book records that in January of 1941, we of 616 Squadron were still practising those wretched attacks. Eventually in the spring of 1941, Fighter Command got back to a sensible style of air fighting, but the last words many a splendid fighter pilot heard were "Number . . . Attack, GO".

In the summer of 1940, Fighter Command had good aeroplanes, a sophisticated radar system, an excellent chain of command and a highly respected leader of impeccable integrity, but our main weakness was our abysmal fighter tactics.

Dowding saw clearly that during the July attacks against shipping, Goering was far less interested in

> "As young and inexperienced pilots, we were often too excited and fired our guns too early, from too far away. Fortunately, the armourers put tracer in toward the end of the ammo load, so that one would come up with a jolt and realise one didn't have much ammo left. It might have been better for us if they had put the tracer in first . . ."
>
> **Air Marshal Sir Denis Crowley-Milling**
> **KCB. CBE. DSO. DFC. AE.**

Left: A bomber's eye view of No.1 Attack. It was a typically sporting British tactic as it allowed the gunner to concentrate on just one target at a time instead of all three. Spitfires of No.610 County of Chester Sqn make a dry run against a Fairey Battle.

FIGHTER ATTACK No. 3 (FROM DEAD ASTERN) APPROACH PURSUIT

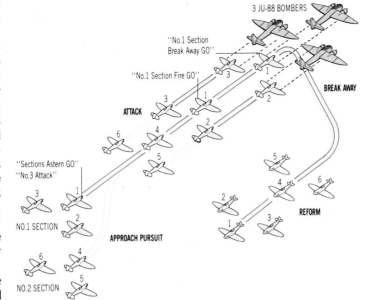

Left: The greater the number of fighters involved, the greater the potential for timewasting that the Fighter Command Attacks provided. This shows No. 3 Attack which is started when a section or flight sights an enemy formation within 45 deg of their nose. The section or flight leader then takes up a position about 2,400ft (730m) astern and slightly below his target. The leader then attacks the lead bomber while his Nos.2 and 3 attack their opposite numbers in the enemy formation. All fighters open fire together and break away together.

FIGHTER ATTACK No.3 (FROM DEAD ASTERN) APPROACH TURNING

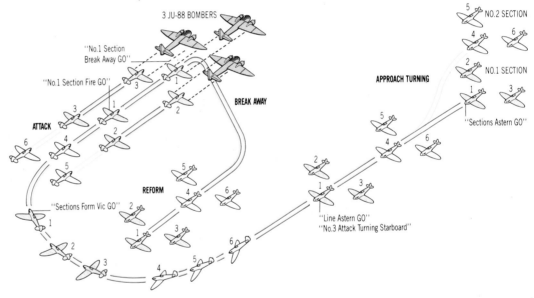

Above: The drill approach was carried out even further when the No.3 Attack commenced from a greater angle than 45 deg off the nose. First the sections moved into line astern; next the aircraft within the sections moved into line astern to aid reaching a position astern of the bombers. Having achieved this, the sections moved back into search formation, as the Vic was officially known, for the attack.

FIGHTER ATTACK No.3 (FROM ABOVE CLOUD)

Right: If the No.3 Attack was launched at a target flying just above a cloud layer, or just above the sea, it became much simpler. The attack was made from astern and slightly higher. Against a sea-skimming target this attack would have been unwise, due to the attention needed to fly accurate formation.

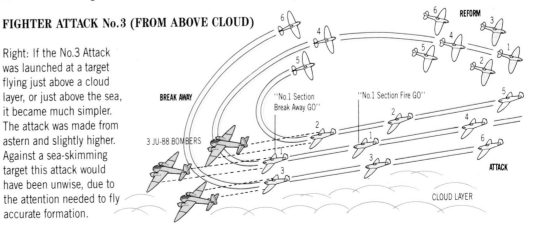

FIGHTER ATTACK No.4 (FROM DIRECTLY BELOW) TWO TYPES OF APPROACH

Right: The No.4 Attack was really a variation on the No.2 Attack, and pilots were enjoined to gain proficiency in this before attempting No.4. The fighter commander's orders were as follows: "Sections astern GO", and next "No.4 Attack", which was informative only, having no "Go" as an executive command. Then came "Sections line astern GO" followed by "Attack turning Port (or Starboard)" as the leader lined his force up. "Sections form Vic, GO" came next, followed by "No 4 Attack GO". The final command of the sequence was "No 1 section break away GO". When the leader of the second section heard this command, he commenced his attack immediately.

Official instructions covered the break, which was to be made by throttling back and diving gently away to one side, a rather suicidal ploy if an alert belly gunner was around.

Just one alternative was available to the leader. If he wished to repeat his attack, his command was "Repeat attack, GO!" and

carefully avoid the next section coming up.

The attack run was made in a steep formation climb with shooting at a high deflection angle. Like most of the Fighter Attacks, No.4 put a premium on accurate formation flying.

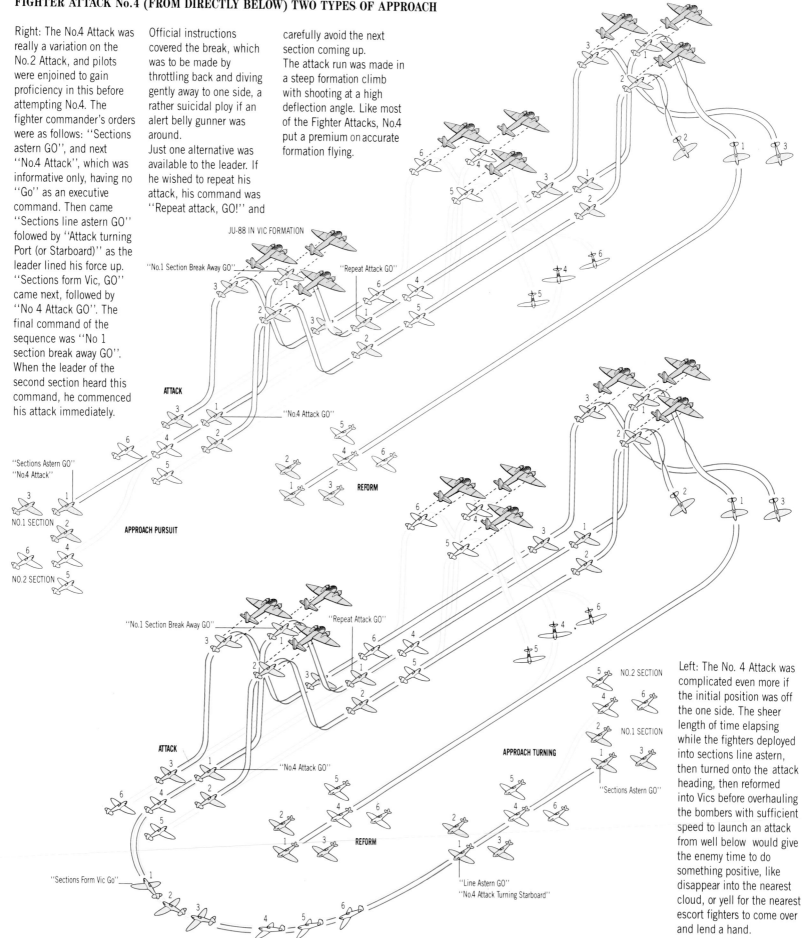

JU-88 IN VIC FORMATION

"No.1 Section Break Away GO"   "Repeat Attack GO"

ATTACK

"No.4 Attack GO"

REFORM

"Sections Astern GO"
"No.4 Attack"

NO.1 SECTION

APPROACH PURSUIT

NO.2 SECTION

"No.1 Section Break Away GO"   "Repeat Attack GO"

NO.2 SECTION

NO.1 SECTION

ATTACK

"No.4 Attack GO"

APPROACH TURNING

REFORM

"Sections Form Vic Go"

"Line Astern GO"
"No.4 Attack Turning Starboard"

Left: The No. 4 Attack was complicated even more if the initial position was off the one side. The sheer length of time elapsing while the fighters deployed into sections line astern, then turned onto the attack heading, then reformed into Vics before overhauling the bombers with sufficient speed to launch an attack from well below would give the enemy time to do something positive, like disappear into the nearest cloud, or yell for the nearest escort fighters to come over and lend a hand.

sinking ships than in bringing our fighters to battle and the hitherto invincible Stukas were the bait. But the Commander-in-Chief refused to be drawn by these attacks and only reinforced, when the need arose, our small convoy patrols of two or three fighters from his forward airfields. Indeed (Dolpho) Galland who had hoped for bigger battles over the convoys told me later how elusive our fighters seemed to be. Nevertheless because the sleek 109s, having no air brakes, could not stay alongside the steeply diving Stukas with their extended air brakes, the dive-bombers were very vulnerable when they pulled out of their dives and consequently received some harsh treatment from our fighters, who were always on the alert for a ''Stuka Party''.

Unhappy with their lot, the Stuka pilots called for more and closer fighter escorts and so, after a month on the Channel coast, both Galland and Mölders were summoned to Goering's estate at Karinhall where they were both decorated; but after this ceremony the Reichsmarschall let them know, in plain terms, that he was not satisfied with the performance of the Fighter Arm escorts and wanted to see a more aggressive spirit.

On August 12 Goering launched the type of attack Britain had most reason to fear when his bombers struck at five radar stations on the south coast. All suffered damage but only one was wrecked, and on the following day four radars were repaired and helped to identify German bombers at a range of 110 miles (177km).

August 13 saw heavy raids against our southern ports and airfields. The Luftwaffe ''beehive'' attack usually consisted of one bomber wing of between 50 and 80 aeroplanes, escorted by a fighter wing with other fighters free-lancing on the flanks of the bombers.

Below: Without a doubt the Junkers Ju 88 was the best of the German bombers used against England in the summer of 1940, although it was tricky to fly, especially on one engine.

FIGHTER ATTACK No.5 (FROM DEAD ASTERN) TWO TYPES OF APPROACH

Right: The No.5 Attack was intended to allow fighters to attack many bombers flying in a large Vic. As in previous attacks, fighters were to close to firing range in threes, thus not confusing the enemy gunners by giving them too many targets to deal with at any one time. Just three bombers out of the enemy formation were to be selected as targets, and these off to one flank. This must have been a great relief to the bomber formation leader. From their original ▼

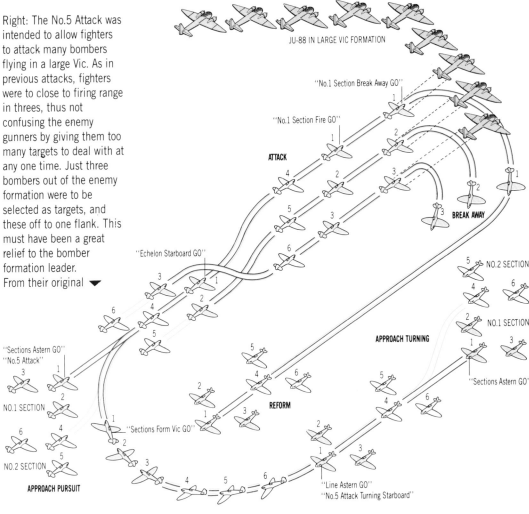

search formation, the fighter sections went into echelon to the side and angle matching the bomber

formation. In order to allow the fighter leader to lead, some complicated switching took place while

forming echelon as the leader moved to the required flank while Nos.2 and 3 took up their new

positions. This evolution had also to be reversed after the breakaway to reform the Vics.

FROM ABOVE CLOUD

Right: If the large enemy bomber Vic was flying very low, or just above an undercast, the No.5 Attack was also modified with the attack being made from slightly high. The same provisos as before applied; aiming guns while flying in close formation did nothing to make for marksmanship, neither did it reduce the risk of midair collisions. To give a good clear shot, the preferred closing speed was between 20 and 40mph (32 and 64km/hr), but it would have been difficult to stay inside these limits.

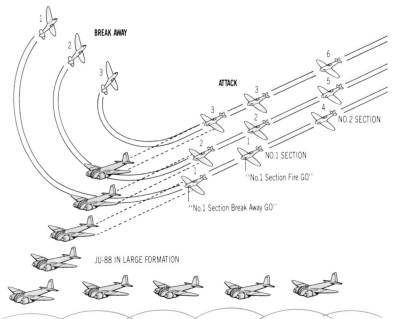

FIGHTER ATTACK No.6 (FROM DEAD ASTERN) TWO TYPES OF ATTACKS

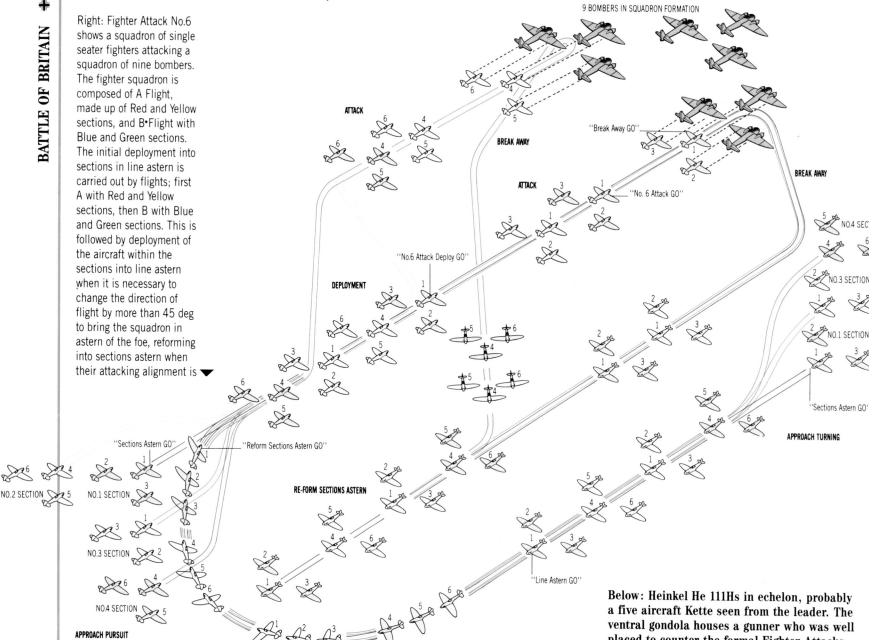

9 BOMBERS IN SQUADRON FORMATION

ATTACK

BREAK AWAY

"Break Away GO"

BREAK AWAY

ATTACK

"No. 6 Attack GO"

"No.6 Attack Deploy GO"

DEPLOYMENT

NO.4 SECTION

NO.3 SECTION

NO.1 SECTION

"Sections Astern GO"

APPROACH TURNING

"Sections Astern GO"

"Reform Sections Astern GO"

RE-FORM SECTIONS ASTERN

"Line Astern GO"

NO.2 SECTION

NO.1 SECTION

NO.3 SECTION

NO.4 SECTION

APPROACH PURSUIT

Right: Fighter Attack No.6 shows a squadron of single seater fighters attacking a squadron of nine bombers. The fighter squadron is composed of A Flight, made up of Red and Yellow sections, and B•Flight with Blue and Green sections. The initial deployment into sections in line astern is carried out by flights; first A with Red and Yellow sections, then B with Blue and Green sections. This is followed by deployment of the aircraft within the sections into line astern when it is necessary to change the direction of flight by more than 45 deg to bring the squadron in astern of the foe, reforming into sections astern when their attacking alignment is ▼

complete. At this point, the leader orders "No.6 Attack deploy, GO!". On the executive order being given, the leaders of Yellow and Green sections swing out to port and pull forward into positions abreast of Red and Blue Flights, which puts both flights into a sections abreast position, with B Flight immediately astern of A Flight. The order to carry out No.6 Attack being given, A Flight (Red and Yellow sections) move forward into firing

range, with Red section taking the right hand bomber Vic (or Kette as the Luftwaffe called it), and Yellow section attacking the left hand Kette. Meanwhile for the very first time in the Fighter Attacks, both optimism and some initiative appear. The document ponderously states "It is considered that, in war, a number of the bombers will be shot down during the first wave attack." As B Flight, following up behind A

Flight, are waiting their turn to go in, the flight leader has to deploy his six fighters into a formation suitable for an attack on their remaining bombers. He does this by selecting the extreme right hand surviving bomber as his own personal target while his No.2 takes the next one to its left, No.3 the third etc. The effect of this is to completey reshuffle the two sections of B Flight, a process which takes a certain amount of agility.

Below: Heinkel He 111Hs in echelon, probably a five aircraft Kette seen from the leader. The ventral gondola houses a gunner who was well placed to counter the formal Fighter Attacks launched from below.

Above: Three Dornier Do17Zs of 9/KG 76 pass Beachy Head heading for the fighter airfield at Kenley on August 18 (see text). Although below the radar cover, they were spotted by Observer Corps post K3 on top of the cliffs.

Right: Probably the best known of all Spitfire pictures is this early war study. For a short while, overwing roundels were outlined in yellow, but this was quickly amended to lower visibility red and blue.

Sometimes two or more bomber wings joined together and, later during the Battle, more than one thousand aeroplanes — the largest formation ever assembled in the history of air fighting — joined together over the French coast and set course for the London Docks. Crossing the English coast this great German legion of bombers, Stukas and fighters formed a phalanx in the sky some 20 miles long, 10 miles wide (32 x 16km) and was stacked-up in layers from 21,000 to 33,000 feet (6,400-10,060m). As Al Deere aptly remarked, ''It was like looking up the escalator at Piccadilly Circus''.

To try to shield the hard-pressed Stukas, it was decided that the proportion of escorting fighters to bombers should be doubled; in addition, a wing of 109s, called a reception escort, was to patrol in mid-Channel to protect the harrassed Stukas, and free-lance fighter sweeps would trail their coats off Dover.

The high summer began to fade: July passed, and during early August it was time for Goering to take stock. Four weeks, sufficient time to conquer half Europe, had gone since the beginning of the Channel fighting and, although his bombers ranged over England almost every night, causing protracted air-raid alarms, some loss of production and a few casualties, Goering must have known that the daytime struggle was not going according to plan. The much vaunted Messerschmitt ''Destroyer'' fighter, the 110, was proving a failure as an escort fighter, being vulnerable to the more maneouvrable Spitfire and Hurricane, and 109s frequently had to help the twin-engined fighters out of a tight spot.

Visiting the Channel coast the Reichmarschall could not understand how his all-conquering Luftwaffe, his hitherto shining sword, was losing its cutting edge, and vented his anger upon the Kommodoren; the great man wanted closer, and more rigid protection for the

One was often aware of being totally outnumbered. We thought, ''Oh God! However are we going to cope with this lot? The enemy bombers often poured a lot of firepower from the rear. But if you could get higher, or at same level, and attack head-on you could often split up the formation. They didn't have front guns, and the Me 109s had more difficulty protecting the bombers when they were split up.

The chap you wanted was the bomber, but you often got involved with the fighters. The 109s couldn't do a lot of damage other than to RAF fighters; our job was to stop the bombers.

**Air Commodore Peter Brothers
CBE. DSO. DFC.**

bombers and rejected his fighter leaders' thoughts about freedom of action for their fighters. There were more harsh words, but, as time ran short, he grew more amiable and asked the Kommodoren what they would like for their squadrons and, when Galland's turn came, he half-jestingly made his famous and oft-quoted remark: ''I should like an outfit of Spitfires for my group!''

During the following days, Luftflotte 2 attacked airfields in the south-east of England, Luftflotte 3 operated against the south, while Luftflotte 5 spread the RAF defences in the north-east. The majority of these attacks fell on targets within five miles (8km) of the coast, between the Solent and the Thames Estuary, where every airfield was attacked, regardless of whether or not it operated fighters, including heavy raids on the Coastal Command airfield at Gosport and

the Fleet Air Arm bases at Ford and Lee-on-Solent. The airfields at Croydon, Detling, Eastchurch, Hawkinge, Lympne, Manston, Martlesham, Thorney Island, and West Malling were attacked, sometimes frequently. Occasionally the Luftwaffe ranged well inland and bombed the flying training airfields at Brize Norton and Sealand, near Chester, the bomber airfield at Driffield in Yorkshire, the maintenance airfield at Colerne, and Fighter Command's vital sector stations at Middle Wallop, Tangmere and Biggin Hill.

Kenley was hit by a low-level raid of nine Dorniers, followed immediately by a bombing attack from 12,000 feet (3,660m). The high attack was intercepted, and some bombers were brought down. However, the low attackers, who flew just above the tree-tops, reached their target without loss and proceeded to carry out some extremely effective low bombing and strafing, during which a Dornier was brought down by the ground defenders. In all about one hundred bombs were dropped on this sector station, which cratered the runways and destroyed hangars, workshops and sick quarters, badly damaged many other buildings, wrecked several fighters, lorries, refuellers and transports, and killed some personnel.

Between August 13 and 18 some 34 airfields and five radar stations were attacked and some, such as Manston and Hawkinge, were bombed several times. Raids on the forward airfields were often made by Stukas, which approached at their usual height, flew once round the circuit for a quick survey, peeled-off, and made steep attacks from the sun. Dorniers and Junkers 88s, escorted by fighters, penetrated farther inland and released their bombs from medium altitudes.

In mid-August, owing to their heavy losses, the Stukas were temporarily withdrawn from the battle. Concentrating against the twin-engined bomber raids, which usually came in between 11,000 and 18,000 feet (3,350-5,490m) according to cloud cover, RAF fighters exploited the gap of a few thousand feet between the bombers and their escorting Messerschmitts, and sometimes trounced the bombers before the higher 109s could interfere.

RAF fighter tactics were slowly improving and 54 Squadron were flying in a wider formation — still a *vic* of three but no longer wing-tip to wing-tip with about fifty yards (45m) between fighters; and the admirable ''Sailor'' Malan, our greatest Battle of Britain pilot, was beginning to lead 74 Squadron in a more flexible line-astern formation.

As Fighter Command's tactics gradually improved, enemy bomber casualties increased, and the bomber crews were highly critical of their Fighter Arm because they wanted their escorting fighters to fly close to the bombers where they could be seen. The Kommodoren of course, were totally opposed to such suicidal tactics, and the dispute once again came to Goering's notice. He called Kesselring of Lufflotte 2 and Sperrle of Luftflotte 3 to Karinhall; thus on August 20 the Reichsmarschall issued more instructions about the conduct of the air battle.

A bomber wing had always to be supported by three fighter wings, he instructed, one of which would fly ahead and clear the target area, while the second and third carried out the duties of close escort and high escort respectively. But only part of the Fighter Arm was to be employed as escort to the bombers: the remainder were to fly free-lance operations so that they would engage British fighters on favourable terms and indirectly protect the bombers.

Whenever possible fighters were to attack RAF aircraft on the ground, and these low-level attacks were to be protected by other fighter formations. Attacks by single aircraft using cloud cover were to be flown

only by highly trained volunteers. Fighter pilots were to pay less attention to the shooting down of balloons. New pilots, led by veterans, were to gain experience over the Channel before flying over England.

Luftwaffe stocks of twin-engined fighters were low, and they were only to be used when the range of single-engined fighters was inadequate or to cover 109s during their withdrawal. There must never be more than one officer in any crew.

No radar site, the Reichsmarshall instructed, had yet been put out of action, and the attacks were to cease.

Because of their limited range the 109s sometimes had to leave the bombers escorted only by the vulnerable 110s until the ''beehive'' was met over the Channel by the reception escorts. Thus more bombers fell to the guns of RAF fighters, and their crews were far from happy: they foresaw heavier losses as the air battles moved farther inland, and their fears were justified when, on August 26, 19 bombers failed to return from raids against Folkestone, the sector stations at Hornchurch, Debden, and North Weald and, once more, Portsmouth town and dockyard. Further, many bombers returning to France were well shot-up and several contained badly injured crews. Thus the recent ugly dispute about escort tactics again flared up, the bomber commanders alleging that the fighter pilots were failing in their clear and first duty to protect the bombers.

Goering supported the bomber commanders and ruled that in future the bombers would have close, high, and top fighter escorts — three fighters for every bomber — and the fighter escorts were ordered to fly closer to the bombers. This increased the gulf between Goering and his Kommodoren who firmly believed in Manfred von Richthofen's doctrine . . .'' The fighter pilots have to be able to rove in the area alloted to them

PILOT EFFECTIVENESS

By the end of the Battle, the scores of the leading Luftwaffe fighter aces far surpassed those of the Royal Air Force. During the period of the Battle only, Adolf Galland led the field for the Germans with 37; Walter Oesau and Hans-Karl Mayer with 30+, and several others in the high 20s, including Werner Moelders who had succeeded in notching up 25 despite being wounded and being put out of action for a month. By contrast, the RAF leading scorer was Eric Lock with 18, followed by Josef Frantisek with 17, Archie McKellar, Brian Carbury and Bob Doe each credited with 15, and James Lacey, Colin Gray, P.C. Hughes and M.B. Czernin with 14 each. The leading scorers on both sides at the end of 1940, taking all campaigns into account, were Galland with 58, followed by Moelders and Wick with 55 each. Geoffrey Allard and James Lacey headed the RAF list with 23 apiece. What were the reasons for this disparity?

The dominant factor in air combat has always been surprise. In fighter versus fighter encounters, the historical record shows that four out of five victims never see their attacker until too late, if at all. There is no reason to think that the Battle of Britain differed in the least. What did differ was the tactical circumstances of the two fighter forces. As the aggressors, the Germans held the initiative, and the defending British fighters were forced to react to the situation at hand, with the result that the German fighters almost invariably held both positional and numerical advantages.

Of these, position was by far the most important, and the plunging attack from the direction of the sun accounted for many British fighters before they knew that they were under attack. A further factor was that the German bombers were the primary RAF targets. The escorting Bf 109s were invariably above the bombers, and any attempt to attack them brought down retribution in full measure. Many a young RAF fighter pilot was lost while trying to knock down a bomber before the 109s got him. A bomber was a bigger target, and was easier to hit than a 109, but it could absorb far more punishment and still fly. It could also shoot back. Often a token force was split from a British squadron to attempt to hold off the 109s while the remainder attacked the bombers, but this was usually numerically inadequate.

Mike Spick

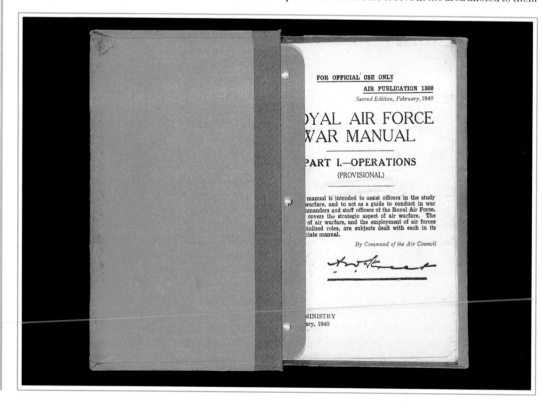

Left: The Royal Air Force War manual was issued in a second edition in February 1940. It was intended to be a guide to the study of strategic aspects of air warfare. Tactics and specialised missions were dealt with in separate documents.

in any way they like!'' The Kommodoren wanted freedom of action for their fighters — just as we had in the great daylight battles over Germany, later in the war. For the fighter must not wait until it is attacked — it must be used offensively where it can seek and destroy its opponents.

During the following days the bombers hammered at RAF sector airfields (Biggin, Hornchurch, Kenley, Northolt, North Weald and Tangmere) with their vital operations rooms and communications, and the Luftwaffe's strong fighter formations made life much more difficult for RAF fighters.

Park's squadrons usually fought singly because he did not have time to form his squadrons into wings. However, the genial Leigh-Mallory, with bases in Cambridgeshire, did have the time, and well-supported Douglas Bader's strong views about meeting strength with strength. And so it was that Douglas, aching to get at the ''Krauts'' (his words), often headed south from Duxford leading three, four and sometimes five fighter squadrons and inflicted much damage on the bombers.

This bombing of RAF sector airfields was the most critical phase of the battle. Between August 24 and September 7 there were 33 major bombing attacks, and 23 were concentrated against the RAF's vital nerve centres — the fighter airfields and sector stations of 11 Group whose job was to defend London and the south-east. By September 5 Park was reporting to Dowding that the damage by bombing was having a serious effect on the fighting efficiency of his group.

Thanks to their large fighter escorts the enemy bombers were getting through to RAF airfields and their casualties were reduced. During a four day period

Below: Spitfires of No.602 Squadron, B Flight, take off in their outmoded Vic formation. With 102 confirmed victories credited to them, 602 were the second highest scoring squadron. Their top scorer was Flt Lt R. F. Boyd with 11 confirmed.

NO II GROUP INSTRUCTIONS TO CONTROLLERS NO 4.

From Air Officer Commanding, No II Group, Royal Air Force.
To   Group Controllers and Sector Commanders, for Sector Controllers.
Date 19 August, 1940.

The German Air Force has begun a new phase in air attacks, which have been switched from coastal shipping and ports on to inland objectives. The bombing attacks have for several days been concentrated against aerodromes, and especially fighter aerodromes, on the coast and inland. The following instructions are issued to meet the changed conditions:

a) Despatch fighters to engage large enemy formations over land or within gliding distance of the coast. During the next two or three weeks, we cannot afford to lose pilots through forced landings in the sea;

b) Avoid sending fighters out over the sea to chase reconnaissance aircraft or small formations of enemy fighters;

c) Despatch a pair of fighters to intercept single reconnaissance aircraft that come inland. If clouds are favourable, put a patrol of one or two fighters over an aerodrome which enemy aircraft are approaching in clouds;

d) Against mass attacks coming inland, despatch a minimum number of squadrons to engage enemy fighters. Our main object is to engage enemy bombers, particularly those approaching under the lowest cloud layer;

e) If all our squadrons around London are off the ground engaging enemy mass attacks ask No 12 Group or Command Controller to provide squadrons to patrol aerodromes DEBDEN, NORTH WEALD, HORNCHURCH;

f) If heavy attacks have crossed the coast and are proceeding towards aerodromes, put a squadron or even the Sector Training Flight to patrol under clouds over each Sector aerodrome;

g) No 303 (Polish) Squadron can provide two sections for patrol of inland aerodromes especially while the older Squadrons are on the ground refuelling, when enemy formations are flying over land;

h) No I (Canadian) Squadron can be used in the same manner by day as other Fighter Squadrons.

Note: Protection of all convoys and shipping in the Thames Estuary are excluded from this instruction paragraph (a).

(Sgd) K. R. Park. Air Vice Marshal, Commanding, No II Group Royal Air Force.

---

of fighting the RAF shot down 106 enemy aeroplanes, including a small proportion of bombers, and lost 101 fighter pilots.

During the first three days of September the bombing attacks, with packs of escorting fighters, continued and 90 enemy aeroplanes were shot down with the loss of 85 pilots. The total wastage in RAF fighter pilots was about 120 pilots each week. The RAF's operational training units produced 65 inexperienced pilots each week and it was quite apparent to Dowding and Park that they were fighting a battle of diminishing returns. They realised that if the Luftwaffe kept up the pressure the control and reporting system would gradually disintegrate, and it would be only a question of time before the Germans dominated the air over southern England.

Fortunately at this time the conduct of the battle changed. On the night of August 24/25 the first bombs fell on central London. Winston Churchill ordered a retaliation raid against Berlin, and during the next week there were four more. Hitler demanded immediate reprisals and shouted in an hysterical broad-

Above: What does an air commander do? The above instruction gives just part of the story, with no hint of the endless analyses, or the constant visits to the squadrons to get the big picture at first hand.

cast: ''If they attack our cities, we will rub out their cities from the map. The hour will come when one of us two will break, and it will not be Nazi Germany.''

Goering eagerly responded and, late in the afternoon of Saturday September 7, sent over 372 bombers and 642 fighters to make two concentrated attacks against London in rapid succession. Dowding, however, anticipating daylight attacks against the capital, made more use of the big wings from 10 and 12 Groups, and Park instructed that whenever time permitted his squadrons were to be used in pairs.

The attacks on London and its suburbs continued with little respite from September 7 until October 5. It was the crux of the Battle and its turning point, for it gave Park the opportunity to repair his battered airfields and restore his communications.

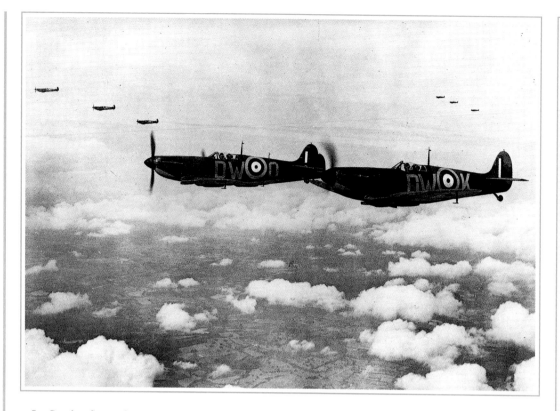

THE ACE FACTOR

The question of what makes an ace fighter pilot is a difficult one, and is still not fully understood. Flying ability, determination, and marksmanship are essential, yet many young men possessing these qualities have flown into battle but achieved little. Others consistently return with victories. The rule of thumb is that five per cent of pilots account for 40 per cent of all victories. The Battle of Britain was no exception. We have seen why the German aces notched up higher scores than their British counterparts, but these were a relative handful of the whole. For the RAF, Sqn Ldr McKellar and Pilot Officer Currant between them were credited with 25 victories and a further six shared, accounting for a full half of the score of No 605 Sqn. The little-known Don McDonell personally accounted for more than one quarter of No 64 Sqn's tally. In the better known No 74 Sqn, just three pilots, Malan, Freeborn and Stephen, notched up 38 per cent of the squadron's total of 86 victories. There were few units in which at least one victory in every eight could not be attributed to just one pilot.

The difference between the aces and the average pilots seems to lie in a quality called 'situational awareness'. This is the ability to keep track of a confused situation; a three dimensional dynamic space-time awareness; the ability to see, to assess, to weigh the risks, to judge very accurately what is going to happen and when. A fighter pilot first has to see the enemy. He then has to convert the sighting into a firing opportunity. The firing opportunity must then be converted into a kill. In three dimensions at high speed, all this calls for very fine judgement. But in addition, he must be able to judge how long he has to attempt the attack before another enemy aircraft can intervene. Situational awareness seems to be more of an instinct than a science, in the same way that some men are natural marksmen. In part it comes with experience, but with many pilots it seems innate. The difference between the aces and the others is that the aces stay alive long enough to build up a score.

Mike Spick

On Sunday September 15, Goering provided the strongest escort so far, five fighters for every bomber, to try and saturate Britain's defences. These big enemy formations took a long time to assemble; the RAF's radars gave ample warning, and Park had the precious time to form his squadrons into wings and to ask for reinforcements from the flanking groups.

The defensive arrangements, so carefully tended throughout the long weeks of fighting by Keith Park, worked so well that the Biggin Hill Wing fought escorting 109s south of Canterbury, the Kenley Wing made a head-on attack near Maidstone, and two squadrons were in action over Gravesend. Nevertheless, the three German formations forged on and were met, over south London, by the North Weald Wing, who sorted out the bombers with surprisingly little interference from enemy fighters.

The Duxford Wing, big even by Teutonic standards, were next in action, but Bader had to delay his attack until some friendly fighters had cleared away; then, as carefully rehearsed, the three Hurricane squadrons went for the bombers while the two Spitfire squadrons held off the 109s.

Some bombs were dropped, but they did only little damage to property, an electricity station, and a bridge or two; an unexploded bomb lodged near Buckingham Palace. Thirty Germans were brought down at a cost of seven RAF pilots. The arithmetic was improving.

After a two-hour break, which gave the defending squadrons ample time to rearm and refuel, the Luftwaffe put in its second big attack, again consisting of three heavily escorted bomber formations which crossed the coast on a 20-mile (32km) front between Dover and Dungeness, within five minutes of each other. This time the radar warning was shorter, but nine wings and several independent squadrons came into action over south London, where there was some stiff fighting.

Above: No.610 Squadron on patrol. While the three aircraft search and cruise formation is still in use, it is obvious that spacing between sections has been increased, which would improve manoeuvrability and lookout.

Once again, the defenders had the best of the exchange. There were fewer 109s than usual and these seemed less aggressive, so that some of the bombers were very roughly handled. Two formations were broken up near London — one retiring after a head-on attack by a lone Hurricane — and bombs were scattered over a wide area.

The Germans were harried by more Spitfires and Hurricanes as they withdrew. During this action RAF pilots claimed to have destroyed 59 bombers and 21 fighters at a cost of 11.

The fighting over London was at its height when about 20 Heinkels bombed Portland harbour. Only one squadron succeeded in intercepting, and that after the bombing. The final daylight operation was an attempt by 20 bombers to hit the Supermarine Works near Southampton, but the anti-aircraft gunners put up a heavy barrage and the factory was not damaged. At dark the bombers returned to London and continued their work throughout the night.

During this furious fighting the Luftwaffe lost 56 aeroplanes against 26 RAF pilots. More bombers struggled back to France, on one engine, badly shot-up, and with many crew members dead or injured. At the debriefings the bomber captains complained bitterly of incessant Hurricane and Spitfire attacks from Squadrons that had long ceased to exist — if they could believe their own Intelligence and the Berlin radio.

The fighting on this day, September 15, clinched the victory, for two days later, on Hitler's instructions, the Germany invasion fleet left the Channel ports for safer places, and Operation "Sealion" was called off, never to be repeated.

However, the offensive continued and again the bomber commanders complained bitterly about their fighter escorts which, because of the relatively slow speed of the bombers at 21,000 feet (6,400m), had to weave continuously to maintain the required close escort. This weaving sometimes took the fighters away from the bombers and once more Goering intervened with the absurd order that both Bf 109s and Bf 110s could not leave the bombers until they were attacked by RAF fighters!

''As little 'John Waynes', I am certain we had no idea how tricky things really were at that period. All the rubbish about the 'Big Wings', as defined by Douglas Bader, was a complete mystery to us and still is. To assemble three squadrons in the air, a total of thirty-six aircraft, form into a wing and then direct it towards the enemy, took far too long as the Huns were only just across the Channel, a mere twenty miles away. So what he was going on about I really don't know.''

Wing Commander Paddy Barthropp DFC. AFC.

Left: Heinkel He 111s in battle formation. Tight spacing enabled the gunners to put up an intense defensive crossfire against fighters, but a dense formation provided a good target for the British Ack-Ack.

As September drew to its close, there was another change of German tactics involving smaller bomber forces of about 30 Ju 88s escorted by between 200 and 300 fighters; but from the beginning of October enemy bombers operated only at night and the *Blitz*, in all its fury, was upon Britain. These raids, flown at great heights and taking every advantage of cloud cover, set Dowding new problems about high altitude interception, but they achieved little else, and Fighter Command continued along the path of recovery which had begun on September 7.

During his long tenure as Commander-in-Chief in the pre-war years, Dowding had recognised that radar would give him the ability to defend his island home and pressed hard to get the system completed before the inevitable war against Germany.

''Stuffy'' Dowding's pilots knew that behind that bleak and melancholy countenance was a man utterly devoted to his Command and his country. Few men in British history have shouldered such a burden of responsibility and he must be included in the great commanders of all time. His character and impeccable integrity flowed down the RAF's simple chain of command, through the groups to fighting men in the squadrons, and to all those airmen and airwomen who laboured on the ground to service the fighters, and who manned the essential control and radar system. Dowding's great qualities of leadership produced that priceless pearl, high morale, the most important single factor in the Battle of Britain.

Goering, unlike Dowding, had not done his homework. His Messerschmitt 109s should have had long-range tanks and he failed to realise the importance of radar. He cannot be blamed for Hitler's order to attack London, but he did not conduct himself well with his harsh words and his ever changing orders which baffled and dismayed his fighting airmen.

Goering had been a drug addict and his integrity was, therefore, suspect. He was, according to ''Dolpho'' Galland, and ''Macky'' Steinhoff, something of a bully and when some of his more intrepid fighter leaders complained about his foolish tactical instructions he

Above: German fighter pilots recorded their victories by means of these small bars painted on the fin, or in some cases the rudder. Seventeen victories are recorded for this Bf 109E of JG 53.

displayed the gangster-like methods which he and his evil cronies had used on their way to the top and threatened to have them shot — a habit not conducive to developing high morale. Indeed, the morale of the German Fighter Arm deteriorated as the battle progressed.

And so the great battle was fought and won over the Channel, over the fields of Kent and Sussex, over the wolds of Hampshire and Dorset, over the flat marshes of Essex and the sprawling mass of London. Unlike the previous battles of destiny — Waterloo, Trafalgar, the terrible roar and devastation of the Somme bombardments — there was little sound or fury. People on the ground went about their business with little ideas of what was taking place high in the sky. They saw a pattern of white vapour trails, slowly changing form and shape. Sometimes they saw the contestants as a number of tiny specks scintillating like diamonds in the splendid sunlight of those often cloudless days. The skillful parries of the defence continued throughout those long days of the late summer. Had they not done so London would have suffered the fate of Warsaw and Rotterdam.

THE OFFICIAL period known as the Battle of Britain lasted just 82 days, from July 10 to October 31, 1940. Like all battles, the events in it are confused, and tracing its course is not made easier by the apparent lack of a master plan by the Luftwaffe High Command. This notwithstanding, four distinct phases are discernible, although considerable overlap exists between them, and they are not clear cut.

The initial German aim was to gain air superiority over the English Channel and Southern England in order to give Operation Sealion, the proposed invasion of the British mainland, a chance of success. Later in the Battle, it seemed that the Germans hoped that England would capitulate to air power alone, thus rendering invasion unnecessary.

The first phase consisted of probing attacks designed to test and weaken the defences while the main body of the Luftwaffe deployed into position to mount an all-out assault. Mostly they consisted of attacks on British convoys around the south and east coasts, coupled with massive fighter sweeps over south eastern England. The convoys, which made up the bulk of the targets during this early period, were vital to the British economy of the period. Mainly they carried

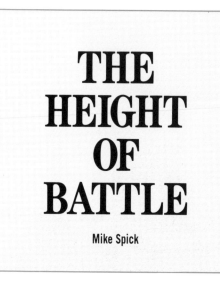

THE HEIGHT OF BATTLE

Mike Spick

coal and bulk raw materials. They could not be withdrawn without placing an unacceptably heavy load on the vulnerable rail network. The convoys had to be defended, but if the German fighter sweeps could be identified in time, they were not intercepted; the

attrition inevitably attendant upon such operations worked in favour of the British at no risk to themselves.

The second phase commenced during the second week in August, with heavy bombing attacks on airfields and radar stations in the south of England. These were intended to destroy RAF Fighter Command as an effective force.

The third phase came when the main weight of the German assault was switched to London on September 7, with the twofold intention of forcing the British fighters into the air, and of cowing the civilian population. Major daylight attacks on the metropolis continued until the end of the month. At the same time, heavy night raids on London commenced, adding to those already in progress against major industrial centres and ports, such as Liverpool, in the north west of England.

The fourth phase commenced after Operation Sealion had been cancelled late in September. The main weight of the assault was switched to the night bombing offensive, which continued long after the Battle was officially over. Daylight activity during this final period was, with a few exceptions, confined to fighter sweeps and fighter-bomber raids.

Left: With a groundcrewman guiding his feet, a Spitfire pilot enters his cockpit. A fighter pilot always mounts his machine from the left, like a cavalryman his horse.

Below: Heinkel He 111s over England on August 13, Adler Tag. A well flown close formation raised the morale of the bomber crews, who drew strength from each other.

Right: Bombs explode around a convoy off the south-east coast of England in the summer of 1940. Only by gathering ships together in convoys could fighter cover be provided.

FIGHTER COMMAND ORDER OF BATTLE, JULY 10, 1940

SECTOR	SQN	TYPE	BASE	COMMANDING OFFICER	SECTOR	SQN	TYPE	BASE	COMMANDING OFFICER
				11 GROUP					**12 GROUP**
Biggin Hill	32	Hurricane	Biggin Hill	S/L John Worral	Duxford	264	Defiant	Duxford	S/L Philip Hunter
	141	Defiant	Biggin Hill	S/L William Richardson		19	Spitfire	Fowlmere	S/L Philip Pinkham
	610	Spitfire	Gravesend	S/L A.T. Smith	Coltishall	66	Spitfire	Coltishall	S/L Rupert Leigh
	600	Blenheim	Manston	S/L David Clark		242	Hurricane	Coltishall	S/L Douglas Bader
North Weald	56	Hurricane	North Weald	S/L Minnie Manton	Kirton-in-Lindsey				
	151	Hurricane	North Weald	S/L Teddy Donaldson		222	Spitfire	Kirton	S/L Tubby Mermagen
	85	Hurricane	Martlesham	S/L Peter Townsend	Digby	46	Hurricane	Digby	F/L A.D. Murray
	25	Blenheim	Martlesham	S/L K.A.K. McEwan		611	Spitfire	Digby	S/L Jim McComb
Kenley	64	Spitfire	Kenley	S/L N.C. Odbert		29	Blenheim	Digby	F/L J.S. Adams
	615	Hurricane	Kenley	S/L Joseph Kayll	Wittering	229	Hurricane	Wittering	S/L H.J. Maguire
	111	Hurricane	Croydon	S/L John Thompson		266	Spitfire	Wittering	S/L Rodney Wilkinson
	501	Hurricane	Croydon	S/L Harry Hogan		23	Blenheim	Collyweston	S/L L.C. Bicknell
Hornchurch	65	Spitfire	Hornchurch	S/L Henry Sawyer	Church Fenton	73	Hurricane	Church Fenton	S/L J.W.C. More
	74	Spitfire	Hornchurch	S/L Francis White		616	Spitfire	Church Fenton	S/L Marcus Robinson
	54	Spitfire	Rochford	S/L James Leathart		249	Hurricane	Leconfield	S/L John Grandy
Tangmere	43	Hurricane	Tangmere	S/L John Badger					**13 GROUP**
	145	Hurricane	Tangmere	S/L John Peel	Catterick	41	Spitfire	Catterick	S/L H. West
	601	Hurricane	Tangmere	S/L Max Aitken		219	Blenheim	Catterick	S/L J.H. Little
	FIU	Blenheim	Shoreham	W/C George Chamberlain	Usworth	607	Hurricane	Usworth	S/L James Vick
Debden	17	Hurricane	Debden	S/L R.I.G. MacDougall		72	Spitfire	Acklington	S/L Ronald Lees
Northolt	1	Hurricane	Northolt	S/L David Pemberton		152	Spitfire	Acklington	S/L Peter Devitt
	604	Blenheim	Northolt	S/L Michael Anderson	Turnhouse	79	Hurricane	Turnhouse	S/L Hervey Heyworth (from12th)
	257	Hurricane	Hendon	S/L D.W. Bayne		253	Hurricane	Turnhouse	S/L Tom Gleave
		10 GROUP (Established 21 July 1940; until then part of 11 Group).				245	Hurricane	Turnhouse	S/L E.W. Whitley
Filton	92	Spitfire	Pembrey	S/L F.J. Sanders		603	Spitfire	Turnhouse	S/L George Denholm
	87	Hurricane	Exeter	S/L John Dewar		602	Spitfire	Drem	S/L Sandy Johnstone
	213	Hurricane	Exeter	S/L H.D. McGregor	(non-op)	605	Hurricane	Drem	S/L Walter Churchill
	234	Spitfire	St. Eval	S/L R.E. Barnett	Dyce	263	Hurricane	Grangemouth	S/L H. Eeles
Middle Wallop	609	Spitfire	Middle Wallop	S/L Horace Darley	Wick	3	Hurricane	Wick	S/L S.F. Godden
(non-op)	238	Hurricane	Middle Wallop	S/L Harold Fenton		504	Hurricane	Castletown	S/L John Sample

Phase 1

The Battle officially opened on July 10, 1940. The month had started with a few German probing attacks and reconnaissance sorties. Then, on July 4, the Germans started to get into their stride with major attacks on convoys, and the naval base at Portland, on the south coast. German fighter sweeps over southeastern England were also started on this day.

Operations during the first nine days of the month were hampered by poor weather, with heavy cloud and thunderstorms. This was a bad period for British squadron commanders; Sqn Ldrs Cooke of No 65 and Joslin of No 79 were both killed, while Sqn Ldr George Lott of No.43 was wounded.

The first major raid of the official Battle of Britain took place during the morning July 10, when the convoy codenamed ''Bread'' was detected by a reconnaissance Dornier Do 17P of 4(F) 121 when rounding the North Foreland in Kent. Six Spitfires of No 74 Sqn (Hornchurch) intercepted at about 1100hrs, but were outnumbered by the Luftwaffe escort, an entire Gruppe (20+ aircraft) of Bf 109s (I/JG 51). The Dornier crash landed at Boulogne heavily damaged. Two Spitfires were hit and force landed, one at Hornchurch, the other at Manston. A little later, Bf 109s in Staffel strength (between 8 and 12 aircraft) swept over the Dover area. Spitfires of No 610 Sqn intercepted, but scored no victories. Sqn Ldr Smith was hit in this encounter and force landed at Hawkinge.

Below: Trailing a thin layer of smoke, a Spitfire dives through a Heinkel formation. Often decried for lack of hitting power, the gunners of the German bombers managed to inflict a remarkable amount of damage.

Right: The opening action of the Battle of Britain took place on the morning of July 10. A convoy codenamed 'Bread' was sailing from the Thames Estuary towards the Straits of Dover when it was detected by a reconnaissance Dornier Do 17P of 4(F)121 while passing the North Foreland, escorted by a Gruppe of Bf 109s from I/JG 51. Six Spitfires of No.74 Sqn intercepted, but were heavily outnumbered by escorting fighters; 20 plus Bf 109s of I/JG 51. Despite this they managed to severely damage the Dornier, which crashed at Boulogne and was written off, two of its crew missing, one dead, and the fourth wounded. Two Spitfires force landed as a result of damage received in this action. Shortly after this clash, a Staffel of 109s carried out of a fighter sweep over the Dover area. Spitfires of 610 Sqn met them. A Spitfire was hit in the port wing and force landed at Hawkinge.

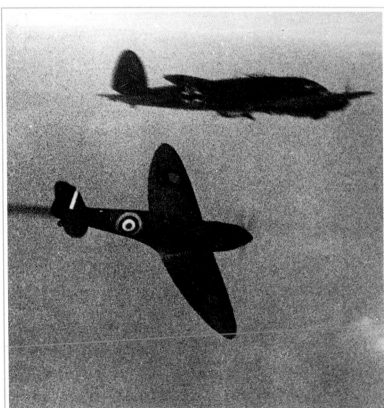

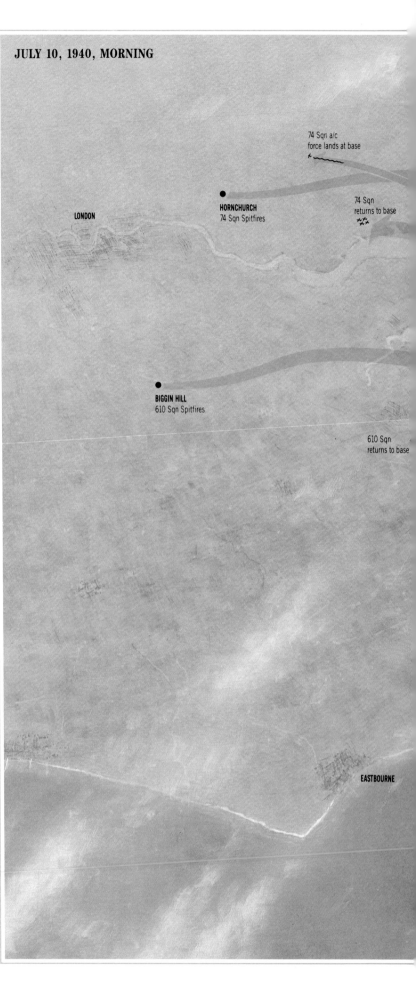

JULY 10, 1940, MORNING

74 Sqn a/c
force lands at base

LONDON

HORNCHURCH
74 Sqn Spitfires

74 Sqn
returns to base

BIGGIN HILL
610 Sqn Spitfires

610 Sqn
returns to base

EASTBOURNE

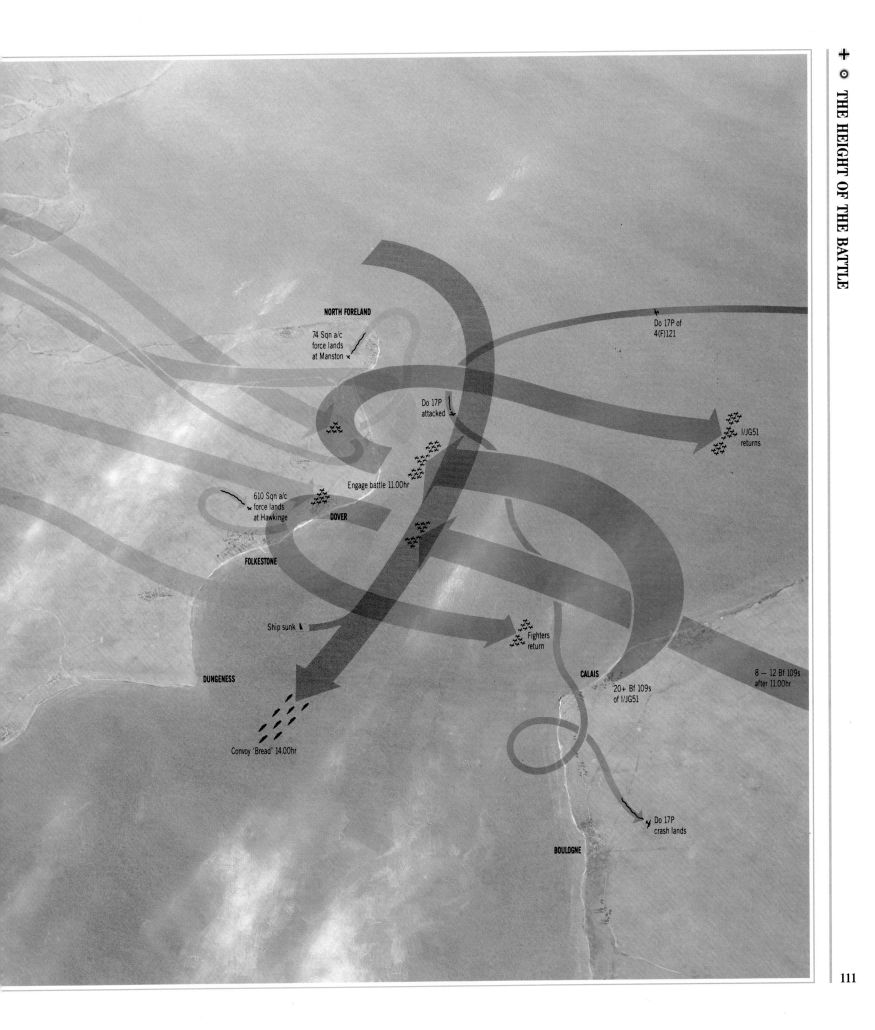

NORTH FORELAND

74 Sqn a/c
force lands
at Manston

Do 17P of
4(F)121

Do 17P
attacked

I/JG51
returns

Engage battle 11.00hr

610 Sqn a/c
force lands
at Hawkinge

DOVER

FOLKESTONE

Ship sunk

Fighters
return

CALAIS

20+ Bf 109s
of I/JG51

8 — 12 Bf 109s
after 11.00hr

DUNGENESS

Convoy 'Bread' 14.00hr

Do 17P
crash lands

BOULOGNE

Then, at 1350hrs, over 70 German aircraft were sighted approaching the convoy. This force was composed of about 24 Do 17Zs of I/KG 2, escorted by some 24 Bf 110s of ZG 26, and two dozen Bf 109s of I/JG 3 and JG 51. About 30 British fighters intercepted — Hurricanes of Nos 32 (Biggin Hill), 56 (North Weald operating from Manston) and 111 Sqns (Croydon), and Spitfires of No 74 Sqn. These were joined in the closing phase of the action by six Spitfires of No 64 Sqn (Kenley). While No 56 tackled the 109s, No 111 opened with what was to become its trademark during the Battle, a squadron strength head-on pass at the bombers.

A confused dogfight ensued. German losses were three Dorniers shot down or crash landed and one damaged; three 110s shot down and two damaged; and three 109s shot down or crash landed and one damaged. British losses during this action were one Spitfire which crash landed at Lympne, one Hurricane lost in a collision with a Dornier, two more crash landed, one of which was a writeoff, and two damaged. One British pilot was lost in this action. This rate of exchange was very acceptable to Fighter Command, but it would not always be maintained. More significant, although less spectacular, was the fact that only one ship in the entire convoy was sunk.

In the West, Luftflotte 3 had been active. At much the same time, Ju 88s of KG 51 raided both Swansea and Falmouth. The attacks were not intercepted, and a munitions factory at Swansea was hit. At this time No 10 Group of Fighter Command did not yet exist; it was inaugurated in late July.

Below: German bombs near miss a Royal Navy destroyer on convoy escort duty in the English Channel on July 14. Near misses could often do serious damage, although a moving ship was a difficult target.

Right: The early afternoon action around convoy "Bread" on July 10 saw even heavier fighting. At about 13.50, a large German raid of 70 plus was sighted approaching the convoy. It consisted of about two dozen Dornier Do 17Zs of I/KG 2, escorted by an equal number of Bf 110s from ZG 26, and the same amount again of Bf 109s from I/JG 3 and II and III JG 51. It was intercepted by elements of four British squadrons, totalling about 30 fighters, drawn from Nos.32, 56, and 111 Hurricane sqns, No.74 with Spitfires. 56 and 111 were first on the scene, and while 56 held off the 109s, 111 attacked the bombers head-on. A confused dogfight followed, with casualties to both sides. In the later stages British reinforcements arrived in the shape of a further six Spitfires of No.64 Sqn from Kenley. Only one ship from the convoy was sunk. In the air, German losses were nine aircraft. Far to the west, Ju 88s of KG 51 raided Swansea and Falmouth.

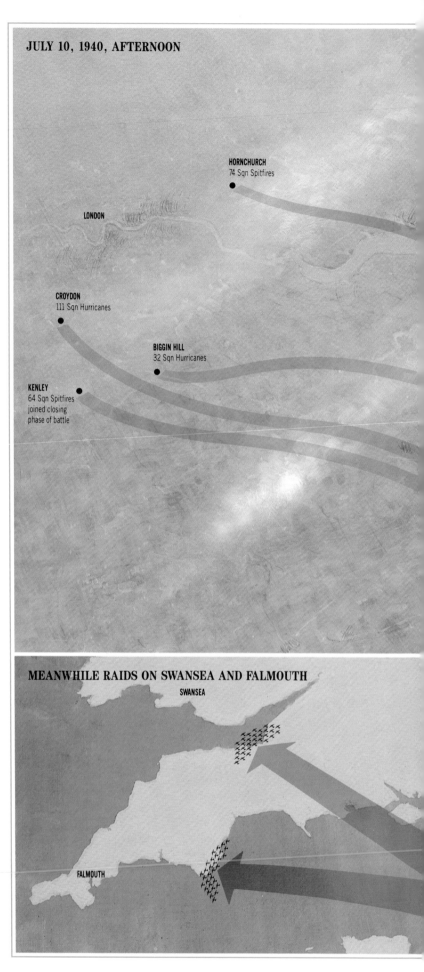

JULY 10, 1940, AFTERNOON

HORNCHURCH
74 Sqn Spitfires

LONDON

CROYDON
111 Sqn Hurricanes

BIGGIN HILL
32 Sqn Hurricanes

KENLEY
64 Sqn Spitfires
joined closing
phase of battle

MEANWHILE RAIDS ON SWANSEA AND FALMOUTH

SWANSEA

FALMOUTH

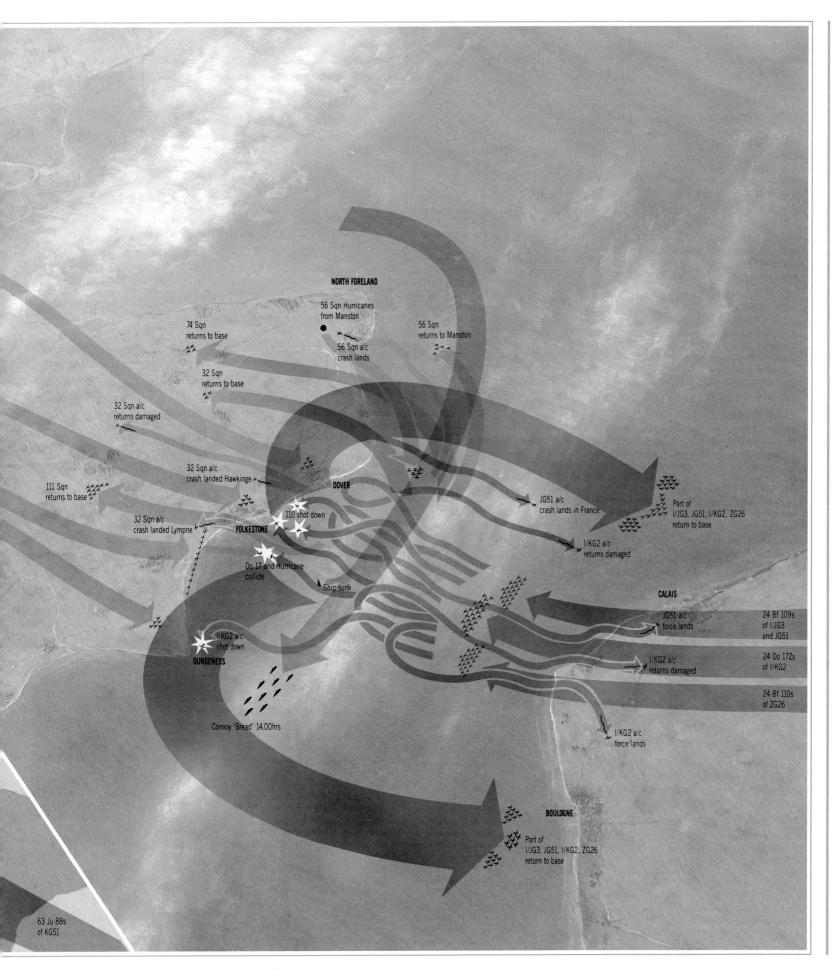

NORTH FORELAND

56 Sqn Hurricanes
from Manston

74 Sqn
returns to base

56 Sqn a/c
crash lands

56 Sqn
returns to Manston

32 Sqn
returns to base

32 Sqn a/c
returns damaged

111 Sqn
returns to base

32 Sqn a/c
crash landed Hawkinge

DOVER

JG51 a/c
crash lands in France

Part of
I/JG3, JG51, I/KG2, ZG26
return to base

32 Sqn a/c
crash landed Lympne

110 shot down

FOLKESTONE

I/KG2 a/c
returns damaged

Do 17 and Hurricane
collide

Ship sunk

CALAIS

JG51 a/c
force lands

24 Bf 109s
of I/JG3
and JG51

I/KG2 a/c
shot down

DUNGENESS

I/KG2 a/c
returns damaged

24 Do 17Zs
of I/KG2

24 Bf 110s
of ZG26

I/KG2 a/c
force lands

Convoy 'Bread' 14.00hrs

Part of
I/JG3, JG51, I/KG2, ZG26
return to base

BOULOGNE

63 Ju 88s
of KG51

Poor weather conditions restricted activity during the next week, although a few convoy attacks were mounted. It improved on July 19, by which time there were no fewer than nine convoys at sea. The day started with the usual Luftwaffe reconnaissance snoopers, one of which was shot down off the coast near Brighton. Just after 0800hrs, four Do 17s of an unidentified unit attacked the Rolls Royce aero engine works at Glasgow, causing heavy damage. They were not intercepted.

No 141 Defiant Squadron had moved south a few days earlier and, operating from Hawkinge, was patrolling in mid-Channel off Folkestone in the early afternoon when attacked by Bf 109s from III/JG 51. The unwieldy British turret fighters were outclassed and six were shot down, with the loss of 10 crewmen killed and two wounded. JG 51 lost just one aircraft and pilot. The disaster might have been complete had it not been for the arrival of No 111 Squadron, who fought an inconclusive engagement with the Messerschmitts.

Several other actions were fought on this day, and more casualties were suffered by Nos 1, 32, 43, 64, 145 and 603 Squadrons. Eleven British fighters were lost and four damaged against German air combat losses of two 109s shot down and two damaged, and a Heinkel He 111 and a Dornier 17P shot down. This was a black day for Fighter Command.

A quiet few days followed, thunderstorms all over southern England developing on July 20. Then three nights later a seemingly small but very significant event took place. Flying Officer Ashfield and his crew. Pilot Officer Morris and radar operator Sergeant Leyland, flying a radar-equipped Blenheim of the Fighter Interception Unit, shot down a Do 17Z of I/KG 3 at night. This was the first ever interception made using airborne radar.

Better weather on July 20 and 25 signalled the return of hard, if relatively small scale fighting. Dorniers attacked a convoy in the Straits of Dover during the morning of July 24. They were intercepted by six Spitfires of No 54 Sqn, who succeeded in spoiling the bomber's aim but little else. In return, three Spitfires were damaged, one of which force landed: the effectiveness of the German air gunners is often under-rated.

Later in the morning, 18 more Dorniers, this time escorted by about 40 Bf 109s of II and III/JG 26, approached another convoy in the Thames Estuary. Spitfires of Nos 54 and 65 Squadrons were scrambled to intercept; at the same time No 610 Sqn was ordered to patrol the Dover area to cut off the retreat. A sharp clash ensued, JG 26 losing three aircraft, including that of the II Gruppe Kommandeur, Hauptmann Noacke. No 54 Sqn lost one Spitfire shot down, with eight-victory ace Johnny Allen killed; another force landed but was later able to return to base, three damaged, and one written off after a forced landing out of fuel.

As JG 26 withdrew at low level, a sweep by III/JG 52 coming in to cover it was bounced by No 610 Sqn.

Right: A 111 Sqn Hurricane flown by T.P. Higgs was attacked by Walther Oesau of III/JG 51 over convoy 'Bread' on July 10. It collided with a Do 17 of 3/KG 2 and lost a wing. The pilot F/O Higgs, was killed.

In the fracas that followed, JG 26 lost four Bf 109s including those of the Kommandeur, Hptmn von Houwald, and Oblt Erlich, the Staffelkapitaen of 8 Staffel, who it is believed fell the the guns of Colin Gray of No.54 Sqn. This was a bad time for German fighter leaders, as just four days earlier Major Riegel, the Gruppe Kommandeur of I/JG 27 had been killed, while in the next four days casualties included Oblt Keidel, Staffelkapitaen of 8/JG 52, and the Luftwaffe leading scorer. Major Werner Moelders, the Geschwader Kommodore of JG 51, was shot down and severely wounded by Flt Lt John Webster of No 41 Sqn on July 28. He spent a month recovering from his injuries.

Meanwhile the weather worsened. Heavy thunderstorms on the afternoon of the 27th curtailed operations. So severe were they that the fighter air-

fields at Westhampnett and Martlesham Heath were flooded and put out of action for two or three days. The summer of 1940 was far from the endless sunshine of legend, but the storms cleared the air for the next few days and convoy attacks resumed.

Dover was raided during the early morning of July 29, the German force consisting of 48 Ju 87 divebombers from IV(Stuka)/LG 1, II/StG 1, and II/StG 4, escorted by the Bf 109s of JG 51, about 80 strong. Eleven Spitfires of No 41 Sqn were scrambled from Manston to intercept, and a dozen Hurricanes of No 501 Sqn from Hawkinge. Four of the Stukas were shot down; one crash landed and one was damaged, while JG 51 lost two fighters, plus another which crash landed in France. One Spitfire was shot down, while no fewer than four others crashed on landing back at

"We scrambled and the twelve aircraft formed up for a formation flight across the airfield in preparation for an intercept on a large German raid that was approaching the Thames estuary. As we passed south of Southend we saw the raiders. More than 50 He 111s plus the usual Me 109 escort. As we approached head-on the CO decided to use an attack which had previously stood us in good stead. The squadron closed up into tight formation and flew through the German bombers, head-on, with all our 96 Brownings firing. This had never failed to split them and after that it was a case of selecting individual targets.

This time, before the squadron had got into range, my aircraft began to be hit by machinegun fire. I held formation and opened fire but almost immediately was hit in the oil-cooler. Hot oil spurted into the cockpit and drenched me, also covering the inside of the windscreen, hood, and my goggles. Blindly I banked and pulled away from the formation, but the bullets from the He's front gunner continued to rip into my aircraft through the underside.

When the engine stopped pumping oil over me, I pushed up my goggles, slid the hood back without trouble and switched off the engine which was giving every indication that it intended to seize. Also just to prove that his previous shooting was not an accident, the German air gunner hit me again from directly behind. Hurriedly I prepared to bale out as there were too many Me 109s around for my liking. I jettisoned the emergency door on the right of the cockpit and undid my straps, but a glance over the side showed me I was over the water, and having no wish to fall into it I changed my mind and did my straps up again before I fell out as the air was very bumpy. I glided over the Isle of Sheppey with the intention of baling out over land, but when I realised that there was no real need to bale out and that I had a choice of various airfields on which to attempt a forced landing. I glided back to Gravesend, pumped the wheels and flaps down by hand and landed, rolling to a stop within inches of the spot where I had been parked previous to taking-off."

The late Squadron Leader J. H. (Ginger) Lacey DFM

Above: Defiants of No.264 Squadron. Intended as a bomber destroyer, the heavy and unhandy Defiant relied more than any other single engined fighter on flying a tight formation in order to achieve massed firepower.

Below: Operations board at Kampfgeschwader 54 shows the battle order for a raid on Portsmouth on July 13. This seems to be a staged propaganda photograph as the Heinkels of III/KG 54 were in Norway at this time.

Manston, fortunately without injury to the pilots. A 501 Sqn Hurricane suffered relatively minor damage, the others were unscathed, but No 56 Sqn, which joined the fray later, lost one Hurricane and a second was damaged. Two British pilots were killed in this action.

One of the two convoys in the area was attacked by a low level force of either Dorniers or Ju 88s, or it may have been a mix of both, from KG 76, while the other, which was off Harwich, was attacked by the fighter-bomber trials unit, Erprobungsgruppe 210, making its operational début. This unit, which was to carry out some of the most spectacular raids during the next few months, was not very successful on this occasion, claiming just two ships hit, and returning with one Bf 110 damaged by a Hurricane of No 151 Sqn. Its escort, Bf 110s of II/ZG 26, damaged two of No 151's Hurricanes, which force landed safely.

August commenced quietly, with adverse weather hampering operations. On the first day of the month, Air Chief Marshal Dowding increased the establishment of pilots by beefing-up the notional strength of each squadron, thus creating a paper deficiency of 134. Had he not done this, the pilot deficiency would have been just 40 on this date. With the benefit of hindsight, this was a very shrewd move, as it gave him leverage to demand the transfer of pilots from other Royal Air Force commands.

So quiet were these opening days of August that the only Fighter Command combat casualties during the first four days were a Hurricane of No 145 Sqn shot down by a Henschel Hs 126, and a Spitfire of No 616 Sqn damaged by return fire from a Ju 88, both on August 1. The Germans were not so lucky, losing four He 115s, one Hs 126, three Ju 88s, two Do 17Zs, one Do 17P and one He 111. Several others force landed after operational missions. A few skirmishes took place on August 5 but, in spite of good weather, no major attack developed. The Luftwaffe was conserving its strength for Adler Tag, or "Eagle Day", provisionally set for August 10. During this period, both sides lost more aircraft and crewmen in flying accidents than in combat.

The pot started coming to the boil on August 8. Fighter sweeps by elements of JGs 3, 26, 51, 53 and 54 during the late morning were engaged by Spitfires of Nos 41, 64, 65 and 610 Sqns. Honours were roughly even; four Spitfires being shot down and three pilots killed, a fifth force landed and a further two were damaged. A Blenheim of No 600 Sqn was also lost. German losses were a single Bf 109 shot down, four more that crash landed in France, and a sixth badly damaged.

Meanwhile, convoy "Peewit", consisting of 29 vessels including Royal Navy escorts, and protected by its own balloon barrage, was attacked by small units of Stukas during the morning as it sailed westward in the Channel. A heavy cloud base at 2,500 feet (760m) combined with the balloons to thwart the attackers, and patrolling British fighters held them at bay with no loss to either side.

Further down the Channel the weather was clearer. Luftflotte 3, which had already been in action against another convoy near Weymouth, launched a mass attack on "Peewit" as it neared the Isle of Wight. Fifty seven Ju 87s of StG 2, 3 and 77, escorted by 20 Bf 110s of V(Z)/LG 1 and about 30 Bf 109s from II and III/JG 27 were detected by Ventnor radar and intercepted before reaching the ships by 30 Spitfires and Hurricanes drawn from Nos 145, 257, and 609 Sqns. An intense dogfight took place, joined in its later stages by the Hurricanes of No 238 Sqn. They were unable to prevent the Stukas attacking the convoy, which scattered, thus reducing the balloon cover, and took heavy losses in consequence.

At about 1630hrs, Luftflotte 3 returned in force to where "Peewit" was reassembling off St. Catherine's Point. This time there were 82 Ju 87s escorted by 68 Bf 109s and 110s. No 10 Group had kept a constant fighter presence over the convoy, and Nos 43 and 145 Sqns were scrambled to intercept in sufficient time to gain both height and position, and launched a devastating attack, although this was not enough to save the shipping from further losses.

British losses in the day's convoy actions were heavy: 13 Hurricanes were lost, one force landed, and three more were damaged, while one Spitfire was lost and a further two damaged. No fewer than 12 pilots were killed, and three slightly hurt; all of them in Hurricanes. No 145 Sqn fared worst, losing five aircraft and pilots, two of them in the early morning action. Luftwaffe losses were also heavy. Eight Bf 109s, one 110, and seven Ju 87s were lost. Five more Ju 87s force landed, and two 109s, five 110s, and six 87s suffered various degrees of damage. Of these, one 109, two 110s, and three 87s were past repair. Bf 110 casualties were relatively light, because they had adopted their standard tactic of going into a defensive circle when attacked. (Later, Goering ordered this to be renamed the offensive circle; the change passed un-noticed by RAF Fighter Command!) Two Gruppe Kommandeurs ended in the water on this day; Hptm Werner Andres of III/JG 27 and Hptm Plewig of II/StG 77.

There was no major activity on August 9, although the Luftwaffe flew many reconnaissance sorties, and a few bombs were dropped by single aircraft and small formations. They were taking a breather before

Above: A Dornier Do 17Z unloads the first of its stick of bombs. Familiarly known as the Flying Pencil, in the summer of 1940 it was being replaced in many units by the faster and more capable Junkers Ju 88.

Below: Hurricanes of No.242 Squadron, the mainly Canadian outfit led by Douglas Bader. Credited with 68½ victories during the Battle, this squadron formed the spearhead of the Duxford-based "Big Wing".

Left: The armed minesweeper HMS Foylebank on fire and sinking off Portland harbour early in July 1940. Leading Seaman J. Mantle was awarded the posthumous V.C. for staying at his AA gun despite his wounds.

Adlerangriffe, the all-out assault planned for the next day. It was not realised in Britain that the "Peewit" battles of August 8 were not planned, but had been very much ad hoc ventures at a target of opportunity. But when August 10 dawned, thundery squalls combined with an adverse weather forecast caused a postponement. Numerous reconnaissance and minelaying sorties were flown, but surprisingly neither side suffered combat casualties, the last day for many weeks that this would happen.

Phase 2

Sunday, August 11, dawned fine, and the first attack came from the Jagdbomberflieger, or Jabos, of EprGr 210, which raided Dover harbour. This was followed

FIGHTER COMMAND ORDER OF BATTLE, AUGUST 1940

SECTOR	SQN	TYPE	BASE	COMMANDING OFFICER
11 GROUP				
Biggin Hill	32	Hurricane	Biggin Hill	S/L John Worral
	610	Spitfire	Biggin Hill	S/L John Ellis
	501	Hurricane	Gravesend	S/L Harry Hogan
	600	Blenheim	Manston	S/L David Clark
North Weald	56	Hurricane	North Weald	S/L Minnie Manton
	151	Hurricane	North Weald	S/L Teddy Donaldson
	85	Hurricane	Martlesham	S/L Peter Townsend
	25	Blenheim	Martlesham	S/L K.A.K.McEwan
Kenley	64	Spitfire	Kenley	S/L Don McDonell
	615	Hurricane	Kenley	S/L Joseph Kayll
	111	Hurricane	Croydon	S/L John Thompson
	1 Can.	Hurricane	Croydon	S/L Ernest McNab
		(operational 17th August from Northolt)		
Hornchurch	54	Spitfire	Hornchurch	S/L James Leathart
	65	Spitfire	Hornchurch	S/L A.L. Holland
	74	Spitfire	Hornchurch	S/L Francis White
	266	Spitfire	Eastchurch	S/L Rodney Wilkinson
Tangmere	43	Hurricane	Tangmere	S/L John Badger
	601	Hurricane	Tangmere	S/L Edward Ward
	FIU	Blenheim	Shoreham	W/C George Chamberlain
	145	Hurricane	Westhampnett	S/L John Peel
Debden	17	Hurricane	Debden	S/L Cedric Williams
	85	Hurricane	Debden	S/L Peter Townsend
Northolt	1	Hurricane	Northolt	S/L David Pemberton
	257	Hurricane	Northolt	S/L Hill Harkness
	303	Hurricane	Northolt	S/L Ronald Kellett/
				S/L Zdzislav Krasnodebski
10 GROUP				
Filton	87	Hurricane	Exeter	S/L T.G. Lovell-Gregg
	213	Hurricane	Exeter	S/L H.D. McGregor
Middle Wallop	238	Hurricane	Middle Wallop	S/L Harold Fenton
	609	Spitfire	Middle Wallop	S/L Horace Darley
	604	Blenheim	Middle Wallop	S/L Michael Anderson
	152	Spitfire	Warmwell	S/L Peter Devitt
St. Eval	234	Spitfire	St. Eval	S/L Joe O'Brien
	247	Gladiator	Roborough	F/L H.A. Chater
		(Single flight only)		
Pembrey	92	Spitfire	Pembrey	S/L P.J. Sanders

SECTOR	SQN	TYPE	BASE	COMMANDING OFFICER
12 GROUP				
Duxford	310	Hurricane	Duxford	S/L Douglas Blackwood/
				S/L Sasha Hess
		(operational from 18 August)		
	19	Spitfire	Fowlmere	S/L Philip Pinkham
Coltishall	66	Spitfire	Coltishall	S/L Rupert Leigh
	242	Hurricane	Coltishall	S/L Douglas Bader
Kirton-in-Lindsey	222	Spitfire	Kirton	S/L S/L John Hill
	264	Defiant	Kirton	S/L Philip Hunter
Digby	46	Hurricane	Digby	S/L J. R. McLachlan
	611	Spitfire	Digby	S/L Jim McComb
	29	Blenheim	Digby	S/L Stan Widdows
Wittering	229	Hurricane	Wittering	S/L H.J. Maguire
	23	Blenheim	Collyweston	S/L G.F.W. Heycock
Church Fenton	73	Hurricane	Church Fenton	S/L J.W.C. More
	249	Hurricane	Church Fenton	S/L John Grandy
	616	Spitfire	Leconfield	S/L Marcus Robinson
13 GROUP				
Catterick	41	Spitfire	Catterick	S/L Robin Hood
	219	Blenheim	Catterick	S/L J.H. Little
Usworth	607	Hurricane	Usworth	S/L James Vick
	72	Spitfire	Acklington	S/L A.R. Collins
	79	Hurricane	Acklington	S/L Hervey Heyworth
Turnhouse	253	Hurricane	Turnhouse	S/L Tom Gleave/
				S/L Harold Starr
	602	Spitfire	Drem	S/L Sandy Johnstone
	605	Hurricane	Drem	S/L Walter Churchill
	141	Defiant	Prestwick	S/L W.A. Richardson
Dyce	603	Spitfire	Montrose/Dyce	S/L George Denholm
	263	Hurricane	Grangemouth	S/L H. Eeles
		(converting to Whirlwinds)		
Wick	3	Hurricane	Wick	S/L S.F. Godden
	232	Hurricane	Sumburgh	F/L M.M. Stephens
	504	Hurricane	Castletown	S/L John Sample
Aldergrove	245	Hurricane	Aldergrove	S/L E.W. Whitley

Plus various Fighter Command aircraft for miscellaneous communications, transport liaison and general duties.

Right: Sharksmouth paint jobs have been a fairly common sight in many air forces over the past fifty years, but this Messerschmitt Bf 110C must have been one of the first to adopt such a scheme.

by three Luftwaffe fighter sweeps in quick succession, then a series of incursions by German fighters in Staffel strength over Kent and Sussex. Combat was generally refused by the British, but some inconclusive skirmishes took place.

At 0945hrs, Ventnor radar detected a large build-up near Cherbourg, France. This emerged as 54 Ju 88s of I and III/KG 54, and 20 He 111s of KG 27, escorted by 60-plus Bf 110s of II and III/ZG 2, and about 30 Bf 109s of III/JG 2. It was the biggest raid yet seen, and a total of 74 Hurricanes and Spitfires from eight squadrons were scrambled as the German formation moved inexorably towards Portland naval base. Many of the British fighters became entangled with the escorts, and fighter losses were high on both sides.

LUFTWAFFE ORDER OF BATTLE, *ADLER TAG*, AUGUST 13 1940

LUFTFLOTTE 2, based in France north of the Seine, Belgium and Holland		
Messerschmitt Bf 109 single engined fighter		
Jagdfliegerfuhrer (JAFU) 2, Oberst Theo Osterkamp, at Wissant		
Jagdgeschwader 3 commanded by Oberstleutnant Carl Viek, at Samer		
I/JG 3	Major Gunther Lutzow	Samer
II/JG 3	Hptmn Erich von Selle	Samer
III/JG 3	Hptmn Wilhelm Balthasar	Desvres
Jagdgeschwader 26 commanded by Major Gotthard Handrick, at Audembert		
I/JG 26	Hptmn Kurt Fischer	Audembert
II/JG 26	Hptmn Karl Ebbighausen	Marquise
III/JG 26	Major Adolf Galland	Caffiers
Jagdgeschwader 51 commanded by Major Werner Moelders, at Wissant		
I/JG 51	Hptmn Hans-Heinrich Brustellin	Wissant
II/JG 51	Hptmn Gunther Matthes	Wissant
III/JG 51	Major Hannes Trautloft	St. Omer
Jagdgeschwader 52 commanded by Major Hans Trubenbach, at Cocquelles		
I/JG 52	Hptmn Wolfgang Ewald	Cocquelles
II/JG 52	Hptmn von Kornatzki	Peuplingues
Jagdgeschwader 54 commanded by Major Martin Mettig, at Campagne		
I/JG 54	Hptmn Hubertus von Bonin	Guines
II/JG 53	Hptmn Winterer	Hermelinghen
III/JG 53	Hptmn Werner Ultsch	Guines
Lehrgeschwader 2		
I/LG 2	Hptmn Herbert Ihlefeld	Calais-Marck
Messerschmitt Bf 110 twin engined fighters		
Zerstorergeschwader 26 commanded by Oberstlt Joachim-Friedrich Huth, at Lille		
I/ZG 26	Hptmn Wilhelm Makrocki	St.Omer
II/ZG 26	Hptm Ralph von Rettburg	St.Omer
III/ZG 26	Hptm Johann Schalke	Arques
Zerstorergeschwader 76 commanded by Oberstlt Walter Grabmann, at Laval		
II/ZG 76	Hptmn Erich Groth	Abbeville
III/ZG 76	Hptmn Dickore	Laval
Fighter Bombers		
Erprobungsgruppe 210, one Staffel of Bf 109s and two Staffeln of Bf 110s, commanded by Hptmn Walter Rubensdorfer, based at Calais-Marck		

Lehrgeschwader 2		
II/LG 2	Hptmn Otto Weiss, Bf 109s	St. Omer
Junkers Ju 87 single engine dive bombers		
II/StG 1	Hptmn Anton Keil	Pas-de-Calais
IV(St)LG 1	Hptmn Bernd von Brauschitsch	Tramecourt
Bomber Units		
Kampfgeschwader 1, commanded by Obstlt Exss, at Rosieres-en-Santerre		
I/KG 1	He 111 Major Maier	Montdidier
II/KG 1	He 111 Obstlt Benno Kosch	Montdidier
III/KG 1	He 111 Major Willibald Fanelsa	Rosieres-en-Santerre
Kampfgeschwader 2, commanded by Oberst Johannes Fink, at Arras		
I/KG 2	Do 17 Major Gutzmann	Epinoy
II/KG 2	Do 17 Major Paul Weitkus	Arras
III/KG 2	Do 17 Major Adolf Fuchs	Cambrai
Kampfgeschwader 3, commanded by Oberst Wolfgang von Chamier-Glisczinski, at Le Culot		
I/KG 3	Do 17 Obst Frhr von Wechmar	Le Culot
II/KG 3	Do 17 Hptmn Pilger	Antwerp/Deurne
III/KG 3	Do 17 Hptmn Rathmann	St. Truiden
Kampfgeschwader 4, commanded by Oberstleutnant Hans-Joachim Rath, at Soesterberg		
I/KG 4	He 111 Hptmn Meissner	Soesterberg
II/KG 4	He 111 Major Dr. Gottlieb Wolf	Eindhoven
III/KG 4	Ju 88 Hptmn Erich Bloedorn	Amsterdam/Schipol
Kampfgeschwader 53, commanded by Oberst Stahl, at Lille		
I/KG 53	He 111 Major Kauffmann	Lille
II/KG 53	He 111 Major Reinhold Tamm(?)	Lille
III/KG 53	He 111 Major Ritzscherle	Lille
Kampfgeschwader 76, commanded by Oberstleutnant Stefan Froelich, at Cormeilles-en-Vexin		
I/KG 76	Do 17 Hptmn Lindeiner	Beauvais
II/KG 76	Ju 88 Major Moericke	Creil
III/KG 76	Do 17 Major Theodor Schweizer	Cormeilles-en-Vexin
Plus various specialist units; reconnaissance, coastal reconnaissance, weather reconnaissance, air-sea rescue, and night fighters.		

Things would have been worse for the Germans had it not been for the arrival of more Bf 109s from JG 27 to cover the withdrawal. The Zerstörer's defensive circle failed to save them on this occasion; they lost six aircraft, including that of Major Ott, the Gruppe Kommandeur of I/ZG 2, and five more were damaged.

Meanwhile, the Jabos of EprGr 210 were busy again, this time leading eight Dorniers of 9/KG 2 against convoy ''Booty'', off Harwich. They were met by elements of Nos 17, 74, and 85 Sqns, who handled them roughly, despite the efforts of their escorts, the Bf 110s of I/ZG 26.

As they withdrew, a further raid was building up. About 45 Dorniers of II and III/KG 2, accompanied by a handful of Stukas and escorted by 109s, headed for another convoy in the Thames Estuary. They were intercepted by Spitfires of No 74 Sqn. Nos 54 and 111 Sqns also attempted to engage, but rapidly deteriorating weather conditions rendered further action abortive.

German combat losses on the day were 15 Bf 109s, 10 Bf 110s, one Do 17Z, six Ju 88s, two Ju 87s, and two He 59s. In addition, one Bf 109, two 110s, and one Ju 88 force landed on return, while one Bf 109, five 110s and five Do 17s returned in various states of disrepair. British losses were also heavy; six Spit-

fires and 21 Hurricanes shot down; a further Spitfire and four Hurricanes force landed; two Spitfires and nine Hurricanes damaged. This was not an adequate exchange rate. Even worse, 26 RAF pilots were missing, a rate that could not long be sustained by Fighter Command.

German fighter sweeps started the ball rolling on the morning of August 12, followed by the most serious development yet; a co-ordinated attack on the British coastal radar chain. This was carried out by EprGr 210, commanded by Hptm Walter Rubensdorffer, who attacked Dover, Pevensey, Rye and Dunkirk in quick succession. They were difficult targets, and though the first three were temporarily put off the air, no lasting damage was done.

Minor convoy attacks followed, and a few aerial skirmishes took place. But at 1145hr Poling radar detected a 200-plus German force south of Brighton. It was the Ju 88s of KG 51, escorted by the Bf 110s of ZG 2 and

Right: It took a team of four armourers less than ten minutes to re-arm a Spitfire. The empty ammunition boxes had to be replaced by full ones, the belts fed through; the barrels swabbed out, and the guns cocked.

LUFTWAFFE ORDER OF BATTLE, *ADLER TAG*, AUGUST 13 1940

LUFTFLOTTE 3, based in France south of the Seine			Stukageschwader 3		
Messerschmitt Bf 109 single engined fighters			I/StG 3 Hptmn Walther Siegel		Caen
Jagdfliegerfuhrer (JAFU) 3, Oberst Werner Junck, at Cherbroug			Stukageschwader 77, commanded by Major Clemens Graf von Schonborn, at Caen		
Jagdgeschwader 3 commanded by Oberstleutnant Harry von Bulow-Bothkamp, at Evreaux			I/StG 77 Hptmn Herbert Meisel		Caen
			II/StG 77 Hptmn Alfons Orthofer		Caen
I/JG 2 Major Hennig Strumpell		Beaumont-le-Roger	III/StG 77 Hajor Helmut Bode		Caen
II/JG 2 Major Wolfgang Schellmann		Beaumont-le-Roger	**Bomber Units**		
III/JG 3 Hptmn Dr. Erich Mix		Le Havre	Lehrgeschwader 1, commanded by Oberst Alfred Bulowius, at Orleans/Bricy		
Jagdgeschwader 27 commanded by Major Max Ibel, at Cherbourg West			I/LG 1 Ju 88 Major Wilhelm Kern		Orleans/Bricy
I/JG 27 Major Eduard Neumann		Plumetot	II/LG 1 Ju 88 Major Debratz		Orleans/Bricy
II/JG 27 Hptmn Lippert		Crepon	III/LG 1 Ju 88 Major Ernst Bormann		Orleans/Bricy
III/JG 27 Major Joachim Schlichting		Carquebut	IV/LG 1 Ju 88 Hptmn Hans-Joachim Helbig		Orleans/Bricy
Jagdgeschwader 53 commanded by Major Hans-Jurgen von Cramon-Taubadel, at Cherbourg			Kampfgeschwader 27, commanded by Oberst Behrendt, at Tours		
			I/KG 27 He 111 Major Ulbrich		Tours
I/JG 53 Hptmn Hans-Karl Mayer		Rennes	II/KG 27 He 111 Maj. Schlicting PoW 12 Aug.		Dinard
II/JG 53 Major Gunther Frhr von Maltzahn		Dinan	III/KG 27 He 111 Major Frhr Speck von Sternberg		Rennes
III/JG 53 Maj. Hans-Joachim Harder KIA 12 Aug.		Brest	Kampfgeschwader 51, commanded by Oberst Dr. Fisser (KIA Aug 12), based at Orly		
Messerschmitt Bf 110 twin engined fighters			I/KG 51 Ju 88 Major Schulz-Hein		Melun Villaroche
Zerstorergeschwader 2 commanded by Oberstleutnant Friedrich Vollbracht, at Toussee-le-Noble			II/KG 51 Ju 88 Major Winkler		Orly
			III/KG 51 Ju 88 Major Walter Marienfeld		Etampes
I/ZG 2 Hptmn Heinlein		Amiens	Kampfgeschwader 54, commanded by Oberstleutnant Hoehne, at Evreaux		
II/ZG 2 Major Carl		Guyancourt	I/KG 54 Ju 88 Hptmn Heydebreck		Evreaux
Lehrgeschwader 1			II/KG 54 Ju 88 Obstlt Koestler		St. Andre
V(Z)/LG 1 Hptmn Otto Leinsberger		Caen	Kampfgeschwader 55, commanded by Oberst Alois Stoeckl (KIA next day), from Villacoublay; replaced by Major Korte of 1 Gruppe		
Junkers Ju 87 single engine dive bombers					
Stukageschwader 1, commanded by Major Walter Hagen, at Angers			I/KG 55 He 111 Maj. Korte/Maj. Friedrich Kless		Dreux
I/StG 1 Major Paul-Werner Hozzel		Angers	II/KG 55 He 111 Major von Lackemaier		Chartres
III/StG 1 Hptmn Helmuth Mahlke		Angers	III/KG 55 He 111 Major Schlemell		Villacoublay
Stukageschwader 2, commanded by Major Oskar Dinort, at St. Malo			Kampfgruppe 100, a precision night attack and pathfinder unit		
I/StG 2 Hptmn Hubertus Hitschold		St. Malo	KGr 100 He 111 Hauptmann Friedrich Aschenbrenner		Vannes
II/StG 2 Major Walter Ennercerus		Lannion	Plus various specialist units, reconnaissance, coastal reconnaissance, weather reconnaissance, and air-sea rescue.		

76, plus top cover of about two dozen Bf 109s from JG 53. As this armada steamrollered its way westwards, 58 fighters were scrambled to meet it. Somewhere off Selsey Bill, the German formation split into two groups. The larger of the two raided Portsmouth, causing heavy damage to both the town and naval installations, while the other struck at Ventnor radar, putting it out of action for many weeks. KG 51 paid heavily, with 10 Ju 88s shot down, two force landed in France, and a further two damaged. The Geschwader Kommodore, Oberst Dr. Fisser, paid for his success at Ventnor with his life.

In the afternoon came another serious development; fighter airfields in England were attacked for the first time. Manston was hit by EprGr 210 at about 13.00hrs; this was followed by a raid by Dorniers of KG 2, although these were identified as Heinkels in the station diary. In the late afternoon, Lympne and Hawkinge were damaged by Ju 88s of II/KG 76. On all three airfields, the damage was heavy but not critical. The day ended with heavy bombing raids on several Kent coastal towns.

Right: Navigation was difficult at low level and only specially trained crews were effective in this role. A fighter escort was ineffective down low, and these Dornier 17Zs relied on remaining unobserved for survival.

By contrast with the events of the previous two days, Adler Tag was an anticlimax. The initial raid was to have been by 74 Dorniers of Oberst Johannes Fink's KG 2, escorted by about 60 Bf 110s of ZG 26, which was commanded by the wooden legged veteran of WW I, Hans-Joachim Huth.

In the event, weather conditions forced a postponement, but Fink was not informed in time, and he pressed on through the cloud banks unescorted. His targets were the naval base at Sheerness and the Coastal Command airfield at Eastchurch. By a strange coincidence, Spitfires of No 266 Sqn and a flight from No 19 Sqn were based there, this being about the only time in the Battle that fighters were present on this airfield. KG 2 was intercepted by Nos 74, 111 and 151 (North Weald) Sqns, but now the clouds became the Dorniers' shield, and losses were light.

Meanwhile, other units had missed the postponement order. Fighter sweeps were mounted by I/JG 2, while Ju 88s of KG 54 crossed the coast to strike at Odiham and Farnborough airfields; neither of them operated by RAF Fighter Command. A combination of interception (by fighters from Tangmere and Northolt) and bad weather rendered this attack abortive. Yet another shambles was enacted further west when the Bf 110s of I/ZG 2 flew out to rendezvous with more Ju 88s of KG 54, which had by now learned of the postponement. The only rendezvous for the Zerstörers was with two squadrons of British fighters off Portland.

One of the most interesting points of this day's operations was that most of the radar stations were back on the air; only Ventnor was still out, and this fact was concealed by transmitting dummy signals, while the gap in the coverage was partly closed by a mobile radar set.

Below: Generalfeldmarschall Kesselring transferred to the Luftwaffe from the Artillery, but during the Battle and later in Italy he showed himself to be a competent commander of both air and ground forces.

Right: August 13 was Adler Tag, the start of the German attempt to wrest control of the skies over south-eastern and southern England away from fighter Command. Heavy attacks against British radar stations on the previous day had failed to blind the defensive system, and only Ventnor was still off the air. The weather during the morning was bad with low cloud and poor visibility causing the start of the attack to be postponed, a fact that was not communicated in time to several of the Luftwaffe units taking part. In the east, a large force of Dorniers of KG 2 attacked targets in northern Kent without their fighter escort. Three RAF fighter squadrons intercepted, but hampered by poor visibility, only shot down five bombers and damaged others. Further westwards a freijagd by JG 2 met with little success, while the Ju 88s of KG 54 not only failed to find their targets, but were intercepted by fighters, losing four aircraft. Near Portland, the Bf 110s of I/ZG 2 bumped two British squadrons but lost one aircraft.

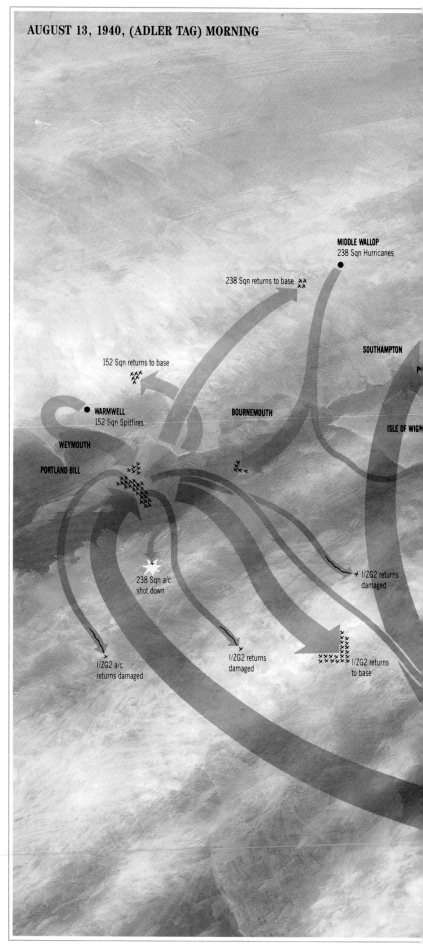

AUGUST 13, 1940, (ADLER TAG) MORNING

MIDDLE WALLOP
238 Sqn Hurricanes

238 Sqn returns to base

SOUTHAMPTON

152 Sqn returns to base

WARMWELL
152 Sqn Spitfires

BOURNEMOUTH

ISLE OF WIGHT

WEYMOUTH

PORTLAND BILL

238 Sqn a/c shot down

I/ZG2 returns damaged

I/ZG2 a/c returns damaged

I/ZG2 returns damaged

I/ZG2 returns to base

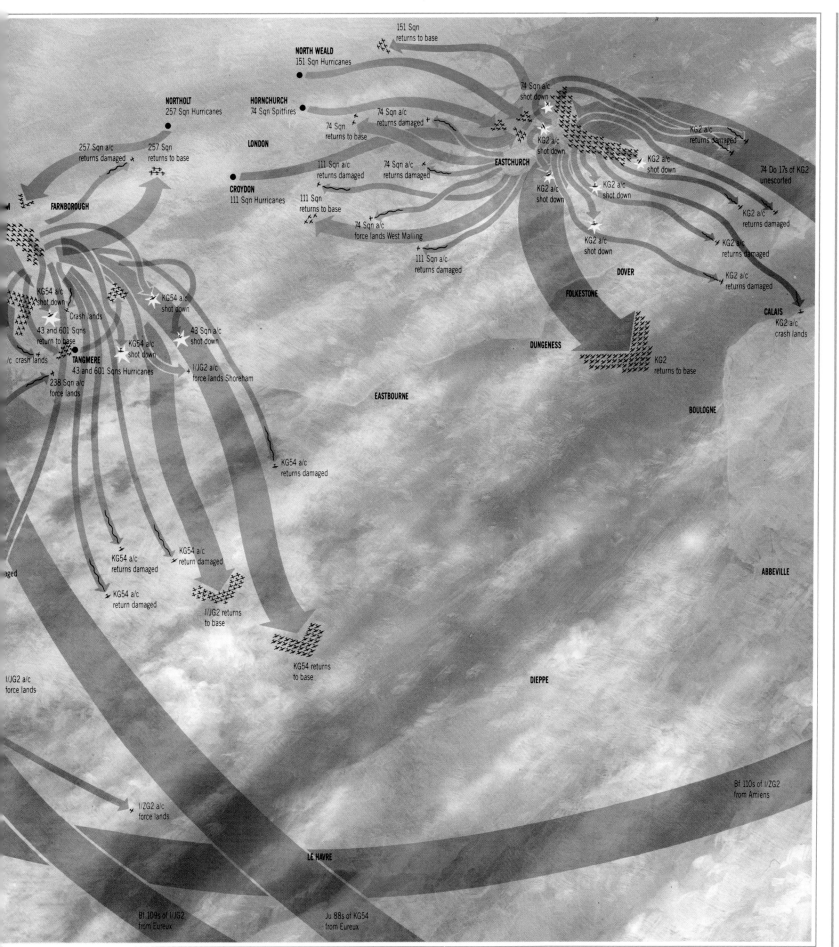

151 Sqn
returns to base

NORTH WEALD
151 Sqn Hurricanes

NORTHOLT
257 Sqn Hurricanes

74 Sqn a/c
shot down

74 Sqn a/c
returns damaged

KG2 a/c
returns damaged

HORNCHURCH
74 Sqn Spitfires

74 Sqn
returns to base

74 Sqn a/c
returns damaged

KG2 a/c
shot down

KG2 a/c
shot down

257 Sqn a/c
returns damaged

257 Sqn
returns to base

LONDON

111 Sqn a/c
returns damaged

74 Sqn a/c
returns damaged

EASTCHURCH

KG2 a/c
shot down

KG2 a/c
shot down

74 Do 17s of KG2
unescorted

CROYDON
111 Sqn Hurricanes

111 Sqn
returns to base

KG2 a/c
shot down

KG2 a/c
shot down

KG2 a/c
returns damaged

FARNBOROUGH

74 Sqn a/c
force lands West Malling

KG2 a/c
shot down

KG2 a/c
returns damaged

111 Sqn a/c
returns damaged

KG2 a/c
returns damaged

DOVER

KG54 a/c
shot down

KG54 a/c
shot down

FOLKESTONE

CALAIS
KG2 a/c
crash lands

Crash lands

43 and 601 Sqns
return to base

KG54 a/c
shot down

43 Sqn a/c
shot down

DUNGENESS

KG2
returns to base

/c crash lands

TANGMERE
43 and 601 Sqns Hurricanes

KG54 a/c
shot down

I/JG2 a/c
force lands Shoreham

238 Sqn a/c
force lands

EASTBOURNE

BOULOGNE

KG54 a/c
returns damaged

aged

ABBEVILLE

KG54 a/c
returns damaged

KG54 a/c
return damaged

KG54 a/c
return damaged

I/JG2 a/c
force lands

I/JG2 returns
to base

KG54 returns
to base

DIEPPE

I/ZG2 a/c
force lands

Bf 110s of I/ZG2
from Amiens

LE HAVRE

Bf 109s of I/JG2
from Eureux

Ju 88s of KG54
from Eureux

During the afternoon the weather improved, and radar detected raids on a wide front approaching the south coast. The various formations involved were 120 Ju 88s of KG 54 and LG 1, escorted by 30 Bf 110s of V/LG 1 to the west, and 77 Ju 87s drawn from II/StG 2 and StG 77 escorted by a mass of Bf 109s from JG 27 on the east side. Sweeping ahead of the bombers came 30 Bf 109s of II/JG 53. On reaching the Dorset coast they were intercepted by No 609 Sqn, losing three aircraft.

Most of LG 1 penetrated as far as Southampton by about 1600hrs, and caused heavy damage to both the docks and the city, although the Spitfire factory at Woolston emerged unscathed. Luftwaffe intelligence thought it made bombers! The remainder of LG 1s Ju 88s headed for the airfield at Andover. Meanwhile the Ju 88s of KG 54 attacked Portland, but were intercepted by Nos 152, 213 and 601 Sqns. At the same time, some of the Ju 87s made for Middle Wallop when they were intercepted by the Spitfires of No 609 Sqn, who were returning to base low on fuel and ammunition.

Shortly after 1700hrs, Ju 87s of II/StG 1 struck at Rochester, Kent, where Short Bros manufactured bombers, but failed to find the target. Intercepted by Hurricanes of No 56 Sqn, they turned back, jettisoning their bombs. Meanwhile, Ju 87s IV(St)/LG 1 badly damaged the Coastal Command airfield at Detling, near Maidstone, demolishing the Operations block and all the hangars. A fighter sweep in strength by JG 26 gave cover in the area at this time.

The scoreboard was in favour of the British on this day. Six Bf 109s, nine Bf 110s, five Ju 87s, seven Ju 88s, six Do 17s and one He 111 were shot down, while three 109s, nine 110s and three 88s force landed in France. Of these, three 110s and one 88 were written off. On the British side, 12 Hurricanes and one Spitfire were lost, two of each force landed; and eight Hurricanes and three Spitfires were damaged. A heartening feature was that only three RAF pilots were killed, and two wounded severely enough to take them off strength. This was in stark contrast to the events of August 11.

Below: Dornier Do 17Zs maintain tight formation over England. Some of the extra guns fitted to defend against fighters can be seen in this picture.

Right: The afternoon of Adler Tag saw clear skies return, bringing with them heavy fighting. The most intense action took place in the Portland/Southampton area where great balbos of German aircraft crossed the Channel on a wide frontage in the mid-afternoon. Nearly 200 Ju 87s and 88s escorted by well over 100 fighters swept in. The city and dock areas of Southampton were heavily bombed, although Luftwaffe intelligence had made a major blunder when the Spitfire factory beside the floating bridge at Woolston was not targetted. Other raids were aimed at the naval base at Portland, and the airfields of Andover and Middle Wallop. Several British fighter squadrons from both 11 and 10 Groups were scrambled to intercept and some vicious fighting took place. Meanwhile further east things were stirring again. The Stukas of II/StG 1 set out to raid the aircraft factory at Rochester, but jettisoned their bombs and turned back when intercepted by Hurricanes of No.56 Sqn. At the same time, the Stukas of IV(St) LG 1 attacked the Coastal Command airfield at Detling, causing heavy damage. Fighter protection was given by the Bf 109s of JG 26 who carried out a Freijagd in the area.

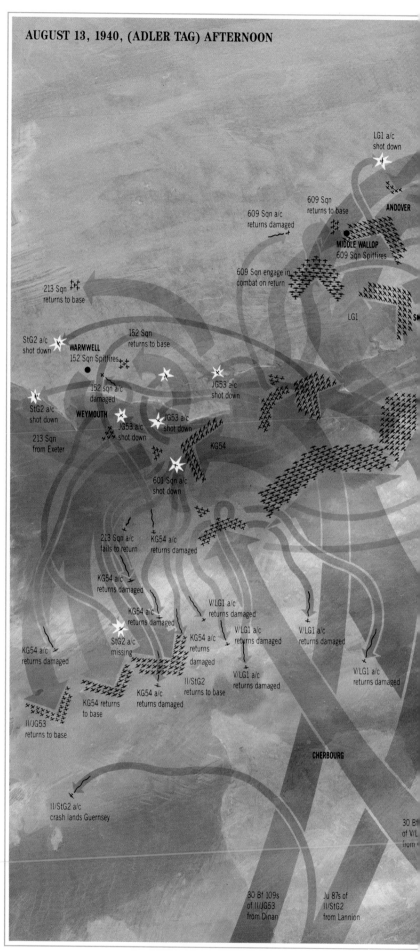

AUGUST 13, 1940, (ADLER TAG) AFTERNOON

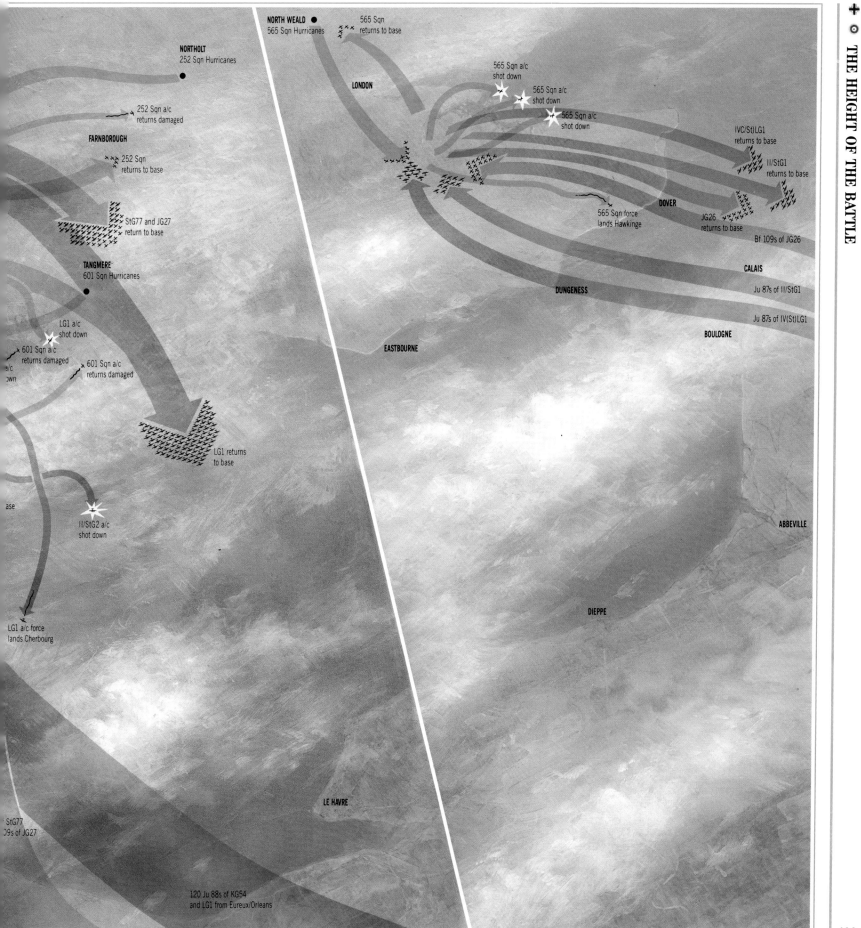

NORTH WEALD ●
565 Sqn Hurricanes

565 Sqn
returns to base

LONDON

565 Sqn a/c
shot down

565 Sqn a/c
shot down

565 Sqn a/c
shot down

IVC/St)LG1
returns to base

II/StG1
returns to base

NORTHOLT
252 Sqn Hurricanes

252 Sqn a/c
returns damaged

FARNBOROUGH

252 Sqn
returns to base

StG77 and JG27
return to base

565 Sqn force
lands Hawkinge

DOVER

JG26
returns to base

Bf 109s of JG26

TANGMERE
601 Sqn Hurricanes

CALAIS

DUNGENESS

Ju 87s of II/StG1

LG1 a/c
shot down

Ju 87s of IV(St)LG1

601 Sqn a/c
returns damaged

601 Sqn a/c
returns damaged

a/c
wn

BOULOGNE

EASTBOURNE

LG1 returns
to base

ase

ABBEVILLE

II/StG2 a/c
shot down

DIEPPE

LG1 a/c force
lands Cherbourg

LE HAVRE

StG77
O9s of JG27

120 Ju 88s of KG54
and LG1 from Eureux/Orleans

As darkness fell (after 2200hrs) on August 13, the night offensive started, with bombers roaming the length and breadth of the British Isles, bombing targets as far apart as Norwich, Aberdeen, Swansea, Liverpool, and Belfast, where Short Bros. bomber factory was hit. Otherwise there was little damage except to the rail network.

Daylight raids continued the next morning, although hampered by poor weather. Middle Wallop was hit by three Heinkels of KG 55 but they lost their Geschwaderkommodore Oberst Alois Stoeckl, a poor return for a damaged hangar.

The weather forecast for Thursday August 15 was not good, and major operations were postponed, while Reichsmarschall Goering summoned a conference of his senior commanders. A rapid improvement in conditions allowed the planned operations to proceed by late morning, the order for the attack being given by Oberst Paul Deichmann, Chief of Staff of II Fliegerkorps, in the absence of anyone more senior.

The raid traces on the British radar displays were so large that it became impossible to distinguish between individual formations. First into the fray were the Ju 87s of II/StG 1 and IV(St)/LG 1, attacking Hawkinge and Lympne. Heavy damage was caused at both airfields, and Lympne was put out of action for three days. Even more serious was the fact that power supplies to the radar stations at Dover, Rye, and Foreness were cut, putting them off the air for several hours. Nos 54 and 501 Sqns intervened, but were overrun by the escorting 109s. As the German aircraft withdrew, Manston was strafed by Bf 110s of II/ZG 76.

At this point, events shifted to the North East. In the early afternoon, the Newcastle/Sunderland area was raided by 65 He 111s of KG 26 escorted by 34 Bf 110s of I/ZG 76 from Norway, while airfields in Yorkshire were attacked by 50 unescorted Ju 88s of KG 30 from Denmark. Both raids were detected well out to sea, and fighters from 72, 605 and 609 Sqns intercepted them. German losses (eight He 111s, eight Ju 88s, eight 110s) were too heavy to be borne, and mass daylight attacks by Luftflotte 5 were never again tried.

Below: The first major attack on the British Isles by Heinkel He 111s was made on August 15, when 63 bombers of I and III/KG 26 flew from Norway against north eastern targets.

Right: The Luftwaffe plan of attack for August 15 1940 involved a series of raids over a wide frontage, with radar stations and fighter airfields as the main targets. The first attacks were on Hawkinge and Lympne on the Kent coast, by Stukas of II/StG 1 and IV/(St)LG 1. The latter was badly damaged and fortuitous hits on the electricity grid put the radar stations at Dover, Rye and Foreness off the air. Nos.54 and 501 Sqns were scrambled to meet this raid but were swamped by the Bf 109 escorts. Then as the raids withdrew, Bf 110s of II/ZG 76 strafed Manston. Meanwhile the action had switched to the north-east. Shortly after noon, radar detected a raid identified as 30 plus, approaching the Newcastle/Sunderland area. Elements of nine squadrons scrambled to intercept. It consisted of 65 He 111s of KG 26 and 34 Bf 110s of I/ZG 26, in two separate formations. Eight Heinkels and eight escorts were lost and others damaged; no British fighters were lost, and little damage was done by the raid. Shortly after, 50 Ju 88s of KG 30 were detected nearing the Yorkshire coast. These heavily damaged the bomber airfield at Driffield before being intercepted losing seven of their number plus one more to ground fire.

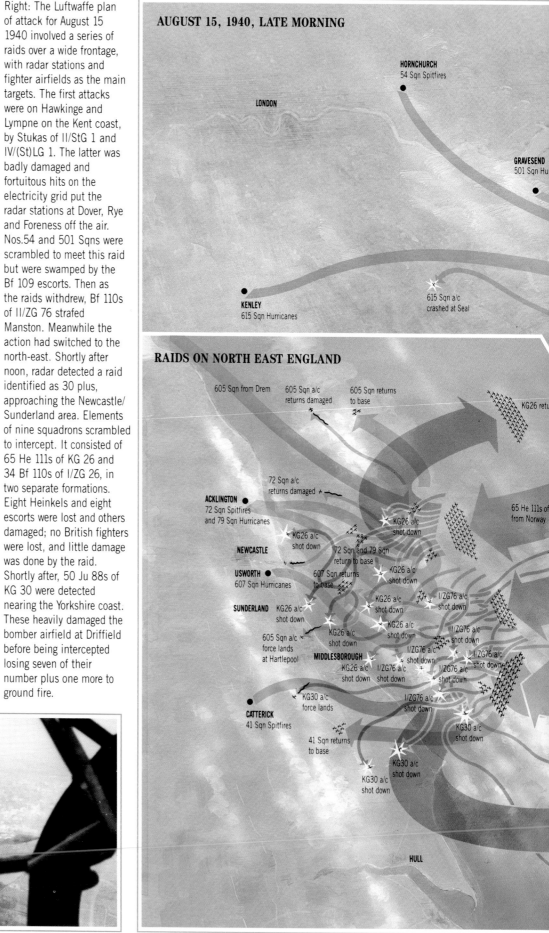

AUGUST 15, 1940, LATE MORNING

LONDON

HORNCHURCH
54 Sqn Spitfires

GRAVESEND
501 Sqn Hu

KENLEY
615 Sqn Hurricanes

615 Sqn a/c
crashed at Seal

RAIDS ON NORTH EAST ENGLAND

605 Sqn from Drem

605 Sqn a/c
returns damaged

605 Sqn returns
to base

KG26 retu

72 Sqn a/c
returns damaged

ACKLINGTON
72 Sqn Spitfires
and 79 Sqn Hurricanes

KG26 a/c
shot down

65 He 111s of
from Norway

NEWCASTLE

72 Sqn and 79 Sqn
return to base

KG26 a/c
shot down

USWORTH
607 Sqn Hurricanes

607 Sqn returns
to base

KG26 a/c
shot down

SUNDERLAND   KG26 a/c
shot down

KG26 a/c
shot down

I/ZG76 a/c
shot down

605 Sqn a/c
force lands
at Hartlepool

KG26 a/c
shot down

KG26 a/c
shot down

I/ZG76 a/c
shot down

I/ZG76 a/c
shot down

MIDDLESBOROUGH

KG26 a/c   I/ZG76 a/c
shot down   shot down

I/ZG76 a/c
shot down

KG30 a/c
force lands

I/ZG76 a/c
shot down

CATTERICK
41 Sqn Spitfires

41 Sqn returns
to base

KG30 a/c
shot down

KG30 a/c
shot down

KG30 a/c
shot down

HULL

54 Sqn returns
to base

MANSTON

501 Sqn a/c
returns damaged

II/ZG76
returns to base

Sqn a/c
ns damaged

501 Sqn a/c
crashes Hawkinge

615 Sqn returns
to base

501 Sqn a/c
shot down

54 Sqn a/c
shot down

DOVER

II/StG1 a/c
shot down

501 Sqn returns
to base

54 Sqn a/c
crash lands
Hawkinge

II/StG1
returns to base

54 Sqn a/c
shot down

IV(St)LG1
returns to base

109s return
to base

CALAIS

DUNGENESS

Ju 87s of II/StG1

10s of I/ZG76
rway

Escorting 109s

G76
urns to base

Ju 87s of
IV(St)LG1

BOULOGNE

50 Ju 88s of KG30
unescorted from Denmark

KG30 a/c
crash lands

KG30 returns
to base

KG30 a/c
crash lands
in Holland

Bf 110s of
II/ZG76

Back in the south east, further raids took place. EprGr 210 (mix of bomb-carrying 110s and 109s) hit the fighter airfield at Martlesham Heath, reducing its operational effectiveness for the next few days. Next, 88 Dornier 17s of KG 3 headed for Rochester and Eastchurch, joining with a strong fighter escort en route consisting of over 130 Bf 109s drawn from JG 51, 52 and 54. At the same time, 60 Bf 109s of JG 26 carried out a fighter sweep over Kent. No fewer than seven British squadrons were directed against this raid, but failed to penetrate the screen of escorts. Short Bros' aircraft factory, making Stirling bombers, was hard hit. Amid the confusion, small formations from KG 1 and KG 2 attacked Hawkinge and other targets, under cover of an Bf 109 fighter sweep by I/LG 2. Fighting was both heavy and confused.

Meanwhile, far to the West, two raids were plotted, one approaching Selsey Bill, the other approaching Portland. The first consisted of about 60 Ju 88s, escorted by 40 Bf 110s. Attacked by four British squadrons in turn, they penetrated the defences and attacked airfields at Middle Wallop, Odiham, and Worthy Down, causing little damage, although two hangars were hit at Wallop. Further westwards, Stukas strongly escorted by Bf 109s and 110s were attacking Portland again, opposed by one Spitfire and two Hurricane squadrons.

Below: The nose gunner's position in a Heinkel He 111. As can be deduced here, a right handed gunner can shoot slightly more easily at targets to his left. It took a marksman to get results with this weapon.

Right: The afternoon of August 15 saw the action switch once again to the south. Martlesham Heath was attacked by the fighter-bomber Bf 110s and 109s of the trials unit EprGr 210, while in Kent 88 Dorniers of KG 3 raided Rochester and Eastchurch with a huge Bf 109 escort. At the same time, two fighter sweeps over the area were made by JG 26 and LG 1, while small bomber formations attacked other targets in the region. Many British squadrons were scrambled but most became embroiled with the 109s. Meanwhile Luftflotte 3 joined in with attacks directed at Portland and airfields in the south, including Middle Wallop, Odiham, and Worthy Down. The Luftwaffe succeeded in its aim of forcing Fighter Command to rise and accept combat, and while the defenders were heavily outnumbered, the fighting was not decisive.

AUGUST 15, 1940, AFTERNOON

MIDDLE WALLOP
234 Sqn Spitfires

601 Sqn a/c
shot down

234
shot

ZG76 a/c
shot down

SOUTHAMPTON

87 Sqn Hurricanes
from Exeter

213 Sqn Hurricanes
from Exeter

WARMWELL
152 Sqn Spitfires

152 Sqn returns
to base

234 Sqn a/c
shot down

ISLE OF W

87 Sqn a/c
shot down

152 Sqn a/c
returns damaged

234 Sqn a/c
returns damaged

BOURNEMOUTH

StG2 a/c
shot down

WEYMOUTH

234 Sqn returns
to base

StG2 a/c
shot down

StG2 a/c
shot down

StG2 a/c
shot down

213 Sqn returns
to base

StG2 a/c
shot down

87 Sqn returns
to base

213 Sqn a/c
shot down

StG2 a/c
shot down

234 Sqn a/c
shot down

StG2 a/c
shot down

StG2 returns
to base

ZG76 returns
to base

StG2 a/c
returns damaged

ZG76 a/c
returns damaged

CHERBOURG

234 Sqn a/c
force lands

Ju 87s of StG2
escorted by Bf 109s
and Bf 110s

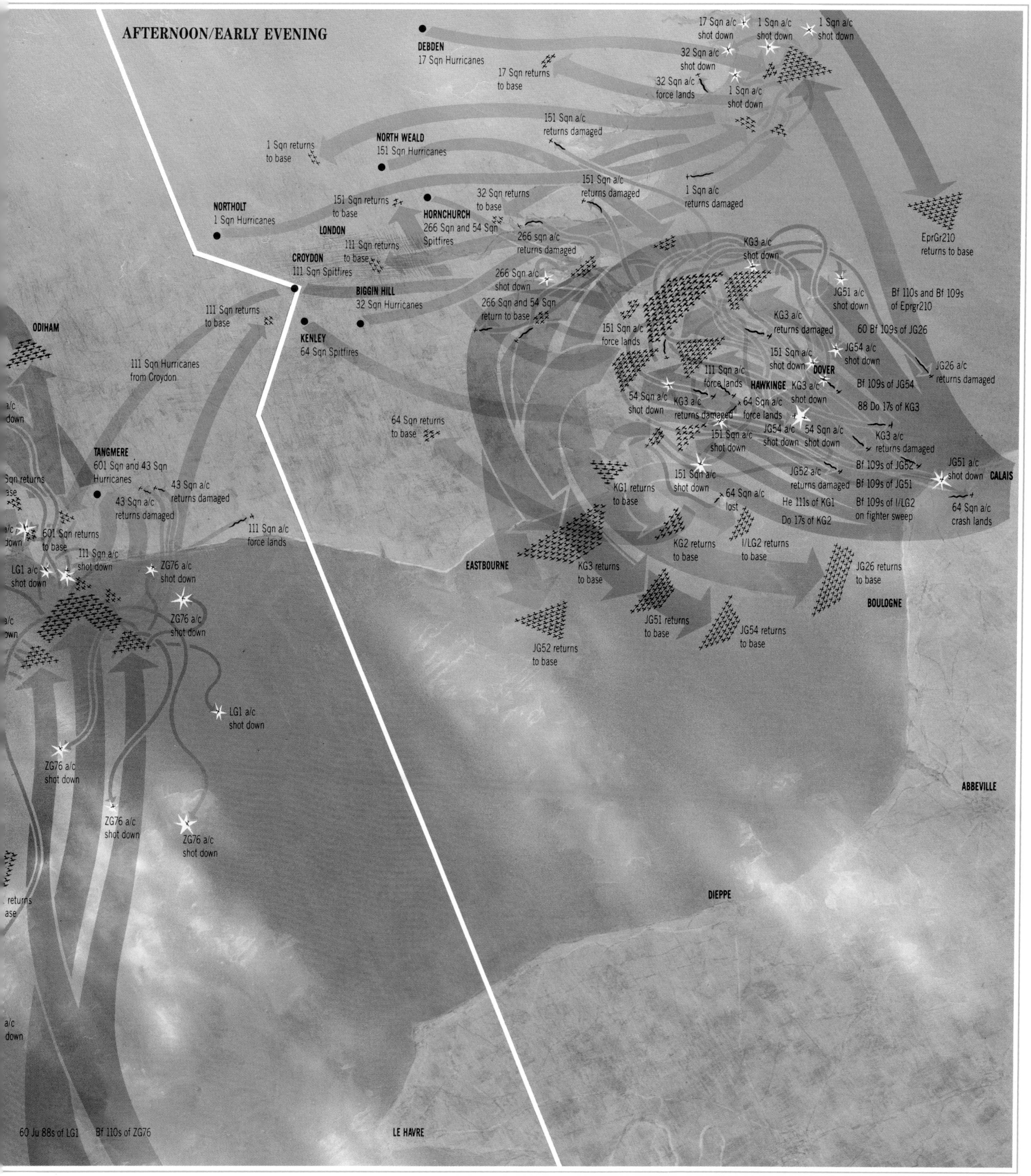

AFTERNOON/EARLY EVENING

DEBDEN
17 Sqn Hurricanes

17 Sqn returns
to base

17 Sqn a/c
shot down

1 Sqn a/c
shot down

1 Sqn a/c
shot down

32 Sqn a/c
shot down

32 Sqn a/c
force lands

1 Sqn a/c
shot down

151 Sqn a/c
returns damaged

1 Sqn returns
to base

NORTH WEALD
151 Sqn Hurricanes

151 Sqn a/c
returns damaged

1 Sqn a/c
returns damaged

NORTHOLT
1 Sqn Hurricanes

151 Sqn returns
to base

32 Sqn returns
to base

HORNCHURCH
266 Sqn and 54 Sqn
Spitfires

266 sqn a/c
returns damaged

EprGr210
returns to base

LONDON

111 Sqn returns
to base

CROYDON
111 Sqn Spitfires

266 Sqn a/c
shot down

266 Sqn and 54 Sqn
return to base

KG3 a/c
shot down

JG51 a/c
shot down

Bf 110s and Bf 109s
of Eprgr210

60 Bf 109s of JG26

111 Sqn returns
to base

BIGGIN HILL
32 Sqn Hurricanes

151 Sqn a/c
force lands

KG3 a/c
returns damaged

JG54 a/c
shot down

JG26 a/c
returns damaged

ODIHAM

151 Sqn a/c
shot down

DOVER

Bf 109s of JG54

KENLEY
64 Sqn Spitfires

111 Sqn Hurricanes
from Croydon

111 Sqn a/c
force lands

HAWKINGE

KG3 a/c
shot down

88 Do 17s of KG3

54 Sqn a/c
shot down

KG3 a/c
returns damaged

64 Sqn a/c
force lands

JG54 a/c
shot down

54 Sqn a/c
shot down

KG3 a/c
returns damaged

64 Sqn returns
to base

151 Sqn a/c
shot down

Bf 109s of JG52

a/c
down

JG52 a/c
returns damaged

JG51 a/c
shot down CALAIS

Bf 109s of JG51

TANGMERE
601 Sqn and 43 Sqn
Hurricanes

43 Sqn a/c
returns damaged

43 Sqn a/c
returns damaged

KG1 returns
to base

151 Sqn a/c
shot down

64 Sqn a/c
lost

He 111s of KG1

Do 17s of KG2

Bf 109s of I/LG2
on fighter sweep

64 Sqn a/c
crash lands

Sqn returns
ase

a/c
down

601 Sqn returns
to base

111 Sqn a/c
force lands

111 Sqn a/c
shot down

KG2 returns
to base

I/LG2 returns
to base

JG26 returns
to base

a/c
down

LG1 a/c
shot down

ZG76 a/c
shot down

EASTBOURNE

KG3 returns
to base

BOULOGNE

ZG76 a/c
shot down

JG51 returns
to base

JG54 returns
to base

returns
ase

LG1 a/c
shot down

JG52 returns
to base

ZG76 a/c
shot down

ABBEVILLE

ZG76 a/c
shot down

ZG76 a/c
shot down

a/c
down

DIEPPE

60 Ju 88s of LG1

Bf 110s of ZG76

LE HAVRE

The day was far from over. Back in Kent, various Dornier units were taking full advantage of the general confusion, while JG 26 Bf 109s mounted a fighter sweep in the area. One Dornier Gruppe was headed for the sector station at Biggin Hill, while the indefatigable EprGr 210 was to raid another sector station at Kenley. These were the first attacks launched at these vital targets.

Edging around to come in from the North, Rubensdorffer led his men into the attack, but the sun was low and visibility hazy. The airfield that he actually attacked was Croydon, a few miles from Kenley, and the Hurricanes of No 32 Sqn from Biggin Hill were waiting to greet him. One hangar was destroyed and two others damaged; many buildings were hit, and Croydon was rendered non-operational for two days. EprGr 210 paid a heavy price, however, losing five Bf 110s and a 109; Rubensdorffer himself went down in Sussex.

Meanwhile the Dorniers heading for Biggin Hill had also boobed, raiding West Malling instead, causing considerable damage. West Malling was a fighter airfield, but did not effectively become operational until the last day of the Battle, and so the effects of this raid were unimportant.

On August 15, usually described as the hardest fought day of the Battle, the Luftwaffe flew 2,199 sorties and was opposed by 974 Fighter Command sorties. The fighting was intense, and casualties were heavy. German losses totalled 75, including those that returned but were written off. They were seven Bf 109s; no fewer than 28 Bf 110s (six from ErpGr 210, eight from I/ZG 76 in the north east, and another 12 from II and III/ZG 76 in the south); six Ju 87s, 17 Ju 88s, including eight from I and II/LG 1 in the south and seven from KG 30 in the north east; 12 He 111s, eight of them from KG 26 in the north east; three Do 17s, and one each He 59 and Arado Ar 196.

Below: A Messerschmitt Bf 110C of II/ZG 26. Goering's vaunted Zerstorers had only one answer to the Spitfires and Hurricanes; the defensive circle. It was soon found that the heavy fighter needed a fighter escort.

Right: The air fighting of August 15 continued into the evening. A Gruppe of Dornier Do 17s targetted the sector station at Biggin Hill, but intercepted by two fighter squadrons, missed their objective and struck West Malling instead, causing considerable damage. This airfield, fortunately for Fighter Command, was non-operational. EprGr 210 were again in the fray, heading for Kenley. Coming in from the north, they were dazzled by the low sun and missed it in the haze. They attacked Croydon instead, but were met by the Hurricanes of Nos.32 and 111 Sqns, who shot down six Bf 110s and a Bf 109. This was the first recorded raid on the Greater London area. In terms of activity, August 15 was the hardest fought day of the Battle; the German total of 2,199 sorties was opposed by 974 from Fighter Command. 75 Luftwaffe aircraft were lost, against 30 British, including one own goal. 13 British pilots were killed, seven were wounded, and a further three were taken prisoner. The fighting, with the exception of that in the north was confused, and this made casualties comparatively light.

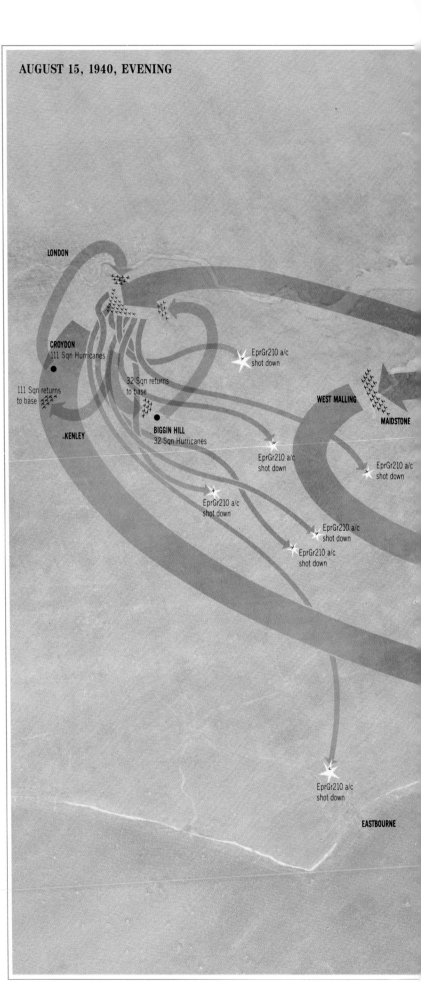

AUGUST 15, 1940, EVENING

LONDON

CROYDON
111 Sqn Hurricanes

111 Sqn returns
to base

KENLEY

32 Sqn returns
to base

BIGGIN HILL
32 Sqn Hurricanes

WEST MALLING

MAIDSTONE

EprGr210 a/c
shot down

EprGr210 a/c
shot down

EprGr210 a/c
shot down

EprGr210 a/c
shot down

EprGr210 a/c
shot down

EprGr210 a/c
shot down

EprGr210 a/c
shot down

EASTBOURNE

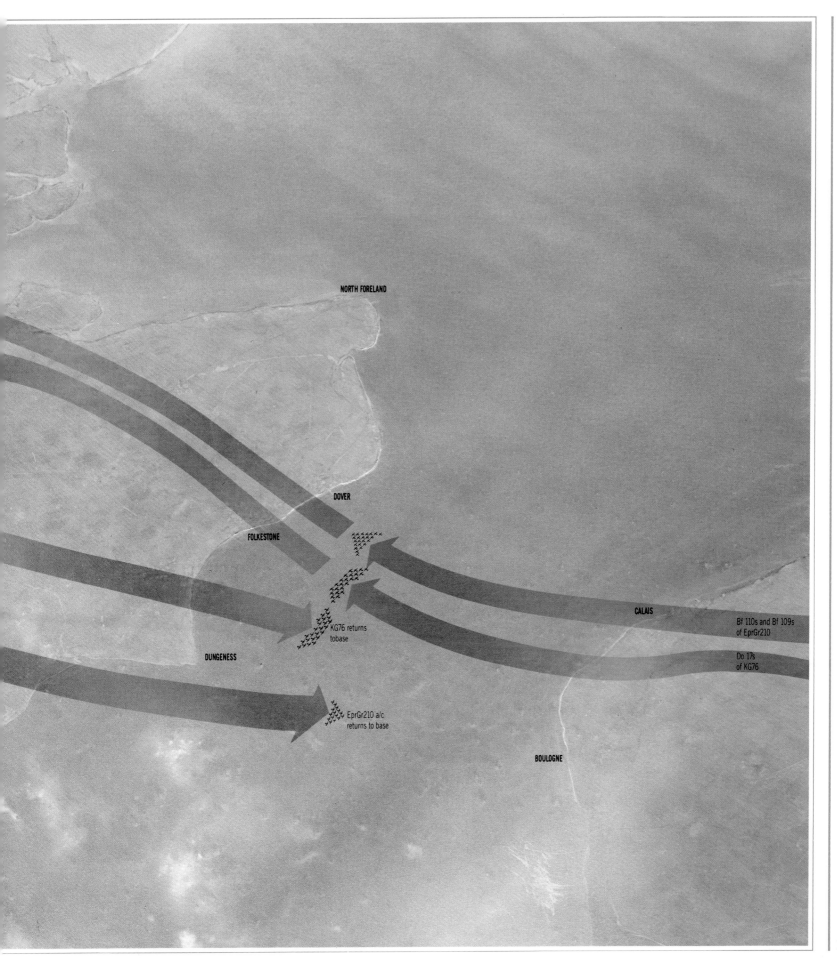

NORTH FORELAND

DOVER

FOLKESTONE

CALAIS

Bf 110s and Bf 109s
of EprGr210

KG76 returns
tobase

Do 17s
of KG76

DUNGENESS

EprGr210 a/c
returns to base

BOULOGNE

Above: A heavily doctored German photograph shows a Spitfire of No.64 Sqn in its blast pen at Kenley on August 18. Taken from a Dornier of 9/KG 76, the original shows very little dust and no destruction.

Below: German bombs burst on RAF Hemswell on August 27 1940. What was supposed to be a concentrated assault to break Fighter Command turned into a general attack against miscellaneous airfields.

It was also another bad day for Gruppen Kommandeurs. In addition to Hptm Rubensdorffer of ErprGr 210, Restemeyer of I/ZG 76 and Dickore of III/ZG 76 went down, while Brunstellin of I/JG 51 and von Wechmar of I/KG 3 were wounded.

British losses totalled 29, including those written off, or 30 if a Blenheim shot down by a friendly fighter is included. The split was 21 Hurricanes against eight Spitfires. Thirteen RAF pilots lost their lives; seven were wounded; while three ended up as prisoners of war. Eight Hurricanes and two Spitfires force landed, while 13 Hurricanes and three Spitfires were damaged.

The next day followed fairly much the same pattern but at a reduced intensity; only 1,715 Luftwaffe sorties were mounted. Many airfields were raided, but with the exception of Manston, and Tangmere, which was badly hit, they had little bearing on the Battle. A day of quiet then followed, as though both sides were gathering strength for a further effort.

Sunday, August 18 was another day of hard fighting, with about 800 Luftwaffe sorties in daylight matched by 886 Fighter Command sorties. This did not mean that the same numerical balance was achieved in the air. In the south, where the bulk of the action took place, the British fighters were still outnumbered in individual actions.

At lunchtime, Luftflotte 2 launched a heavy co-ordinated attack on the sector stations at Kenley and Biggin Hill. Kenley was badly hit; three of its four hangars were destroyed and its operations room was put out of action. The nine Dorniers of low flying specialist Staffel 9/KG 76 caused heavy damage during this raid, but was almost wiped out while doing so; only two aircraft, both damaged, returned to base.

The raid on Biggin Hill made a mess of the adjoining golf course but achieved little else. It was, however, the first in a series where Biggin Hill was raided daily and sometimes twice a day for an extended period, and was nearly put out of action. Croydon and Manston were also hit on this day.

Further down the coast another huge multiple raid was launched by Luftflotte 3, aimed at Thorney Island, Gosport and Ford airfields, and Poling radar station. Like the earlier incursion, this series of raids was strongly opposed by defending fighters, who took a heavy toll of the slow Stukas.

Later in the afternoon, Luftflotte 2 launched another major attack, this time against the sector stations of Hornchurch and North Weald. Defending fighters were up in force and action was joined, but then deteriorating weather obscured the target area and forced the bombers to turn back.

The loss ratio was not so far in the British favour on this day, but the Bf 109s had taken a beating with 18 lost. Most significant of all were the losses of the Bf 110s, Goering's famed Zerstörers, 17 of which were struck off charge, and the Stukas, of which 18 were lost. From this point on, Zerstörer operations were restricted, while the dive bombers were withdrawn from the battle altogether. British losses were 26 Hurricanes and five Spitfires written off, for 10 pilots killed.

The weather broke during the afternoon of August 18, and it remained poor, with heavy cloud and rain for the next few days. This gave the opposing commanders time to think. Goering issued instructions that the bombers must be escorted more closely. Air Vice Marshal Keith Park, commanding Fighter Command's No 11 Group, arranged for help to be given by the neighbouring No.10 and 12 Groups when requested.

Meanwhile, the occasional German incursion was made. A large fighter sweep over Kent on August 19 was recognized in time and ignored by the defenders. Cloud cover allowed small formations of bombers to penetrate over England on harassing raids, with airfields as the prime targets. The night offensive continued, with raids on centres including Liverpool, Sheffield, Derby, Coventry and Hull.

The weather improved on August 24, and heavy raids resumed, although apparently with a little more circumspection than had previously been shown. Airfields at Hornchurch, North Weald and Manston were again targets. Manston, with its proximity to France and Belgium, was the favourite alternative target for the Luftwaffe and, although well equipped with underground shelters, thanks to its Royal Navy origins, was rapidly becoming unusable. The Defiants of No 264 were operating from there, and on this day they were badly mauled. A heavy raid on Portsmouth took place in the late afternoon. That night over 100 aircraft were tracked heading in over London, and bombs were dropped in the City, Finsbury, Bethnal Green, Stepney and East Ham, among other places. This was a new and sinister turn of events.

RAF Bomber Command attacked Berlin on the night of August 25/26 as a reprisal for bombs that had fallen on London. This was the first in a series of events that was to provoke the Germans into switching their attack to London. But at this moment that could not be foreseen. During the day, the pattern persisted as before. Continued attacks on the British fighter airfields were beginning to tell as damage accumulated.

The pace began to slacken on August 27, when no

Above: A Ju 87B Stuka of I/StG 77 screams earthwards in its final dive with both crewmen still on board, near Chichester. August 18 saw the divebombers take such fearful casualties that they were finally withdrawn from the battle.

major raid was mounted, despite clear skies in the afternoon. Something else was afoot. The single seater fighter units of Luftflotte 3 had begun to move into the Pas de Calais, which meant that massive escorts for the bombers could be provided in the Luftflotte 2 area. Fighter Command's No 11 Group, concerned at certain plotting inadequacies that had become evident, introduced a scheme whereby formation leaders would radio a situation report on sighting the enemy and before engaging.

During the morning of August 29 all was quiet, then in mid-afternoon radar plots showed a build-up behind Calais. This proved to be a handful of bombers, covered by an estimated 650 fighters drawn from JG 3, 26, 51, 52 and 54; and ZG 26 and 76. No 11 Group put 13 fighter squadrons up; first into contact were the Hurricanes of No 85, who were told to disengage, and the other squadrons held back. There was literally no point in risking a massive fighter battle when realistically only bombers could cause serious harm.

The fine weather persisted, and the attacks on airfields continued, mingled with fighter sweeps and attacks on other targets. Rarely were the German intentions clear from the radar plot. A lucky hit on the electric grid supplying the radar stations put Beachy Head, Whitstable, Rye, Fairlight, Foreness, Pevensey and Dover off the air for a few hours on August 30. On this day, Fighter Command sorties reached 1,054 which was their peak during the Battle.

Activity was very high on the next day also, the Luftwaffe mounting 1,450 sorties opposed by 987 by Fighter Command. During the next few days, North Weald, Biggin Hill, Kenley, Hornchurch, Tangmere, Eastchurch, Croydon, Detling and Debden were all attacked, some many times. Biggin Hill in particular was badly damaged, and the third raid of the day on September 1 saw a direct hit scored on the Ops room. A temporary Ops room was set up in the village. For a few days, only one squadron could be based there. In an attempt to halt the incessant raids the Station Commander, Group Captain Grice, took the drastic step of having what remained of the hangars demolished, reasoning that from the air they still looked valid targets.

The cumulative effect of the damage on many airfields was rapidly becoming critical. Had it got much worse, the only solution would have been to pull the fighter bases back beyond the range of the escort fighters. This was to be avoided if at all possible, as in the event of an invasion the reaction time from airfields farther back would have been longer, while the endurance of the British fighters over the German bridgehead would have been much less.

Casualties among British squadron and flight commanders had been heavy. Aircraft reserves were still adequate, but the standard of replacement pilots was low. Extensive redeployment of squadrons was a feature of the first two weeks of the month. Attacks on factories producing fighters started now, a little late in the day. Brooklands was raided on September 2, but the Vickers works producing Wellington bombers was hit instead of the Hurricane factory.

Defence of the invaluable sector airfields was difficult. Often the RAF had little or no prior indication of the Luftwaffe target, and No.11 Group fighter squadrons scrambled only when it was clear that a raid include bombers was imminent and that the radar plot was not just a decoy. With large formations moving in before splitting into several individual raids, interception was a nightmare. Exhaustion was fast setting in among the pilots of Fighter Command, who were outnumbered and had often to cede height and position to the enemy.

Fairly typical of the problem was a midday raid on September 4, when 70-plus He 111s and Do 17s crossed the coast between Hastings and Dover, escorted by about 200 Bf 109s. They then split to attack five targets between Reigate and Canterbury, and nine British squadrons met them, with varying degrees of success. Meanwhile, a small force of Bf 110s, including some Jabos, was reported north of Guildford at low level, having penetrated thus far unnoticed. They were then intercepted by nine Hurricanes of No 253 Sqn and badly mauled, but the survivors reached their target at Brooklands, but again hit the Vickers factory rather than the Hawkers site.

As part of this general raid, which had the defenders running about in all directions, ErpGr 210 attacked the radar station at Poling, but were intercepted, losing their new Kommandeur, Hptm von Bolternstern. The entire series of attacks was co-ordinated to exploit the factor of confusion.

Losses this day were nearly equal, the Germans los-

ing six Bf 109s, 13 Bf 110s, most of them on the ill-fated Jabo sortie, and one He 111. British losses were six Hurricanes and nine Spitfires, with nine pilots killed. A further four Hurricanes and two Spitfires force landed.

The margin was closing. What the RAF desperately needed was some respite for the fighter airfields, and some pressure taken off the British pilots. Further heavy fighting took place on September 5 and 6, but on the very next day, from a most unlikely source the respite came.

Phase 3

The day (September 7) started much as any other, with German reconnaissance aircraft snooping about, and being harassed by defending fighters. But then activity died away until shortly before 1600hrs. Hermann Goering had taken personal command of his much-vaunted Luftwaffe and, throwing subtlety to the winds, launched the largest raid ever. No fewer than 348 bombers escorted by 617 fighters started across the intervening water. Twentyone British squadrons were scrambled to meet them, but their controllers were in a quandary. Guessing which were the targets was an impossible task. It looked like an all-out attack designed to smash No 11 Group. Expecting the assault on airfields to continue, most squadrons were ordered into positions to protect the vital sector stations and other likely targets such as the Thameshaven oil refinery.

The inevitable result was that comparatively few British fighters made contact before the first wave of bombers reached London, and these were swiftly embroiled with the escorting Bf 109s. Led by Oberst Fink's Dorniers of KG 2, the juggernaut rolled on, and bombs rained down on the docks from Rotherhithe to Tower Bridge. By the time that Fighter Command realised what was happening, and vectored the remaining

British squadrons towards it, the German Goliath had bombed and was on its way home, leaving behind roaring conflagrations and a pall of smoke darkening the sky.

Nor was the ordeal over. Shortly after 2000hrs, the second wave of bombers came up the Estuary, guided by raging fires on the ground. For the next eight hours they stoked them up, leaving the fire fighting services almost helpless due to the sheer scale of the devastation.

But that day, September 7, had seen the combat début of the No.12 Group ''Big Wing'' from Duxford. Consisting of Nos 242 and 302 Hurricane and No 19 Spitfire squadrons, and led by the indomitable Douglas Bader, its purpose was to meet force with force; numbers with numbers. Bader's idea was that his wing of 36 fighters should be scrambled early and meet the enemy forward in the Maidstone/Canterbury area. A mass assault would disrupt the enemy formation and leave it an easier target for the single squadrons of No No.11 Group. In practice it was never to be used in this manner. 11 Group asked for reinforcements only when the situation was getting desperate, and the Duxford Wing was inevitably scrambled late as a result.

The Wing was often criticised as taking too long to form up. In practice, Bader used to set course immediately after takeoff, without first orbiting base, and climb out on course throttled back just enough to allow the others to join up. From the scramble order to 20,000ft (6,100m) over the Thames Estuary took little longer for the Wing than for a single squadron. On

Below: The Tower of London and London Bridge are lit by a low sun against the pall of smoke from the burning dock area following the first major bombing raid on London on September 7.

September 7, they were scrambled late and were caught on the climb by the escorting 109s. They were thus denied the chance of making a mass attack on an unbroken Luftwaffe formation.

The fact that much of the combat had been between fighters was reflected in the relative casualties. Just 13 German bombers were shot down plus two more which force landed. At least four of these were not involved in the main daylight raid. By contrast, the Bf 109s lost 16; the Bf 110s eight, plus two more that force landed.

Above: A Heinkel prepares to take off at night for England. No navigation was needed to find London on the night of September 7; huge conflagrations raging in the East End and the docks lit the way.

Below: The Prime Minister tours a heavily damaged area of Battersea in September 1940. The Home Front was no idle expression. The aim of area bombardment was to break the will to resist of the civil population.

''From a fighter pilot's point of view, I hold that Bader's wing concept was wrong, and I consider that the German fighter tactics against the American daylight bombers prove my point. The Germans faced the same problem in 1943 as did Fighter Command in 1940, but with vastly more experience behind them, a more sophisticated radar control system, and a longer period of defensive operations in which to experiment and learn. Most important of all, they had adequate early warning of attacks on their homeland and time in which to concentrate their mass formations where and when they wanted them. In the end, having tried the mass formation technique, they resorted to small mobile formations of fighters concentrated in time and space, but operating independently. They found that too many fighters tied to a single leader sterilised flexibility of action and thought on the part of individual pilots, and usually resulted in only the leader getting a decent shot at the raiding bombers before the rest of the formation was set upon by the escorting fighters. Certainly, when on the offensive in the later stages of the war, and using the wing concept, I found that the maximum number of squadrons that could be efficiently handled in combat was two, not five as used in 1940/1941. I know that most wing leaders agree with me, and certainly those who had the benefit of later experience. Johnnie Johnson was one and in his book Wing Leader he supports this view. Douglas Bader, I know, did not agree.''

Air Commodore Al Deere
CBE, DSO, DFC

Six Spitfires and 17 Hurricanes were lost, but another 12 of the former and five of the latter force landed in varying states of disrepair. Eleven other fighters suffered damage. When one considers that many aircraft that force landed took many weeks, if not months, to repair, it can be seen that in material terms, Fighter Command had slightly the worst of things. Another 19 British pilots were out of the Battle, 14 of whom were killed.

Sunday September 8 was relatively quiet as the Luftwaffe rested from their exertions. For the first time, No 11 Group used paired squadrons for an interception, Nos 253 and 605 combining to attack one of the handful of small raids mounted. As dusk fell, the night assault on London resumed. It was to continue every night for the next seven weeks.

On the next day, the German invasion date was fixed as September 20, but the executive order had to be given as early as September 11. Time was running out for the Germans.

Daylight activity continued at a moderate level during September 9, with airfields and aircraft factories the main targets, then a break in the weather brought relief to the defenders.

A black day for Fighter Command was September 11, with combat losses exceeding those of the Luftwaffe. Two major co-ordinated attacks by the Luftwaffe were launched, both in the afternoon. The first, comprising He 111s of KG 1 and KG 26 headed up the Thames Estuary towards London, with a fighter escort 200 strong. The defending squadrons made little impression on the escorts at first and lost heavily; some of them had been scrambled too late and were caught on the climb. As on the 7th, the Bf 110s formed a holding pattern in the Croydon area, while the single-seaters ran themselves low on fuel. As a result, the Heinkels were quickly left without an escort and suffered in consequence, losing 10, plus four more which force landed in France, while a further 120 were damaged.

Meanwhile Luftflotte 3 mounted a raid on Portsmouth and Southampton, causing little damage. Luftwaffe combat losses for the day totalled 21, and another six force landed. Of these, only four were Bf 109s, although a fifth crashed as a result of a midair collision over France. Collisions were not that unusual; four Ju 87s were lost to this cause on a training mission also. Six Spitfires and nineteen Hurricanes were lost and a further six fighters crash landed. Twelve pilots were killed and four severely injured. This was an exchange rate that Fighter Command could not afford.

Activity during the next two days was minimal, due to adverse weather conditions, but picked up a little on September 14, when radar stations and some south coast towns were attacked. Once again, the decision to launch Sealion was deferred, this time until the 17th.

Battle of Britain Day

Then came the day now celebrated as ''Battle of Britain Day''; Sunday, September 15, 1940. Extensive redeployment had taken place in Fighter Command during the previous few days, with fresh units replacing tired and depleted ones. The lessening of attacks on their airfields, and the low rate of aerial activity over the past few days had allowed the British pilots to rest. Some squadrons in the battle area even managed to devote time to training their replacement pilots; a rare luxury during that hectic summer. When Sunday, September 15 dawned, a reconstituted and rested British fighter force awaited the day's events . . .

Below: A Dornier lies broken in an English field just outside Biggin Hill. This is the lead aircraft in the formation of 9/KG 76 Do 17s pictured on page 103, taken later that day after the Kenley low level attack.

Right: The death of a Bf 110 is captured by the camera gun of a Hurricane in September. Strikes can be observed, smoke streams back from the port engine, then the first flames appear, making its destruction certain.

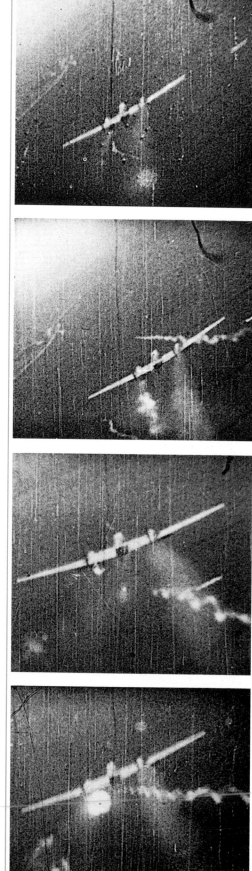

FIGHTER COMMAND ORDER OF BATTLE, SEPTEMBER 15, 1940

SECTOR	SQN	TYPE	BASE	COMMANDING OFFICER
11 GROUP				
Biggin Hill	72	Spitfire	Biggin Hill	S/L A.R. Collins
	92	Spitfire	Biggin Hill	S/L F.J. Sanders
	(half) 141	Defiant	Biggin Hill	S/L W.A. Richardson
	66	Spitfire	Gravesend	S/L Rupert Leigh
North Weald	249	Hurricane	North Weald	S/L John Grandy
	(half) 23	Blenheim/Beaufighter	North Weald	S/L G.F.W. Heycock
	46	Hurricane	Stapleford	S/L J.R. MacLachlan
Kenley	253	Hurricane	Kenley	S/L E.R. Bitmead
	501	Hurricane	Kenley	S/L Harry Hogan
	605	Hurricane	Croydon	S/L Walter Churchill
Hornchurch	603	Spitfire	Hornchurch	S/L George Denholm
	600	Blenheim/Beaufighter	Hornchurch	S/L H.L. Maxwell
	41	Spitfire	Hornchurch	S/L R.C. Lister
	222	Spitfire	Hornchurch	S/L John Hill
Tangmere	213	Hurricane	Tangmere	S/L D.S. Wilson-Macdonald
	607	Hurricane	Tangmere	S/L James Vick
	602	Spitfire	Westhampnett	S/L Sandy Jonstone
	(half) 23	Blenheim/Beaufighter	Ford	S/L G.F.W. Heycock
Debden	17	Hurricane	Debden	S/L A.G. Miller
	73	Hurricane	Debden	S/L Mike Beytagh
	257	Hurricane	Martlesham	S/L Robert Stanford Tuck
	(half) 25	Blenheim	Martlesham	S/L W.W. Loxton
Northolt	1 Can	Hurricane	Northolt	S/L Ernest McNab
	229	Hurricane	Northolt	S/L H.J. Maguire
	303	Hurricane	Northolt	S/L Ronald Kellett
	264	Defiant	Northolt	S/L Desmond Garvin
	504	Hurricane	Hendon	S/L John Sample
10 GROUP				
Middle Wallop	238	Hurricane	Middle Wallop	S/L Harold Fenton
	609	Spitfire	Warmwell	S/L Horace Darley
	604	Blenheim/Beaufighter	Middle Wallop	S/L Michael Anderson
	(half) 23	Blenheim	Middle Wallop	S/L G.F.W. Heycock
	152	Spitfire	Warmwell	S/L Peter Devitt
	56	Hurricane	Boscombe Down	S/L H.M. Pinfold
Filton	79	Hurricane	Pembrey	S/L Hervey Heyworth
Exeter	87	Hurricane	Exeter/Bibury	S/L R.S. Mills
	601	Hurricane	Filton	S/L Sir Archibald Hope
St. Eval	234	Spitfire	St. Eval	S/L Minden Blake
	236	Blenheim	St. Eval	S/L G.W. Montague
	247	Gladiator	Roborough	F/L H.A. Chater
12 GROUP				
Duxford	242	Hurricane	Duxford	S/L Douglas Bader
	302	Hurricane	Duxford	S/L Jack Satchell/ S/L M. Mumler
	310	Hurricane	Duxford	S/L Douglas Blackwood/ S/L Sasha Hess
	19	Spitfire	Fowlmere	S/L Bryan Lane
Coltishall	74	Spitfire	Wittering	S/L Sailor Malan
Kirton-in-Lindsey	616	Spitfire	Kirton	S/L Billy Burton
	(half) 264	Defiant	Kirton	S/L Desmond Garvin
Digby	151	Hurricane	Digby	S/L ??
	611	Spitfire	Digby	S/L Jim McComb
	29	Blenheim/Beaufighter	Digby	S/L Stan Widdows
Wittering	1	Hurricane	Wittering	S/L David Pemberton
	266	Spitfire	Wittering	Unfilled (S/L P.G. Jameson from September 17)
Church Fenton	85	Hurricane	Church Fenton	S/L Peter Townsend
	306	Hurricane	Church Fenton	S/L ?? (one Flight operational)
	64	Spitfire	Leconfield/Ringway	S/L Don McDonell
13 GROUP				
Catterick	54	Spitfire	Catterick	F/L F.P.L. Dunworth
	(half) 219	Blenheim/Beaufighter	Catterick	S/L J.H. Little
Usworth	43	Hurricane	Usworth	unfilled (S/L Tom Dalton-Morgan from 16th)
	32	Hurricane	Acklington	S/L Mike Crossley
	601	Spitfire	Acklington	S/L John Ellis
	(half) 219	Blenheim	Acklington	S/L J.H. Little
Turnhouse	3	Hurricane	Turnhouse	S/L S.F. Godden
	65	Spitfire	Turnhouse	S/L A.L. Holland
	141	Defiant	Turnhouse	S/L W.A. Richardson
	111	Hurricane	Drem	S/L John Thompson
	(non-op) 263	Hurricane/Whirlwind	Drem	F/L T.P. Pugh
Dyce	145	Hurricane	Dyce/Montrose	S/L John Peel
Wick	232	Hurricane	Sumburgh	S/L M.M. Stephens
Aldergrove	245	Hurricane	Aldergrove	S/L E.W. Whitley

Below: Smoke billows from Purfleet oil refinery in this German reconnaissance photograph after the strike of September 7.

As on many other days, the action was slow to develop. Not until nearly 1100hrs did a massive raid build up behind Calais, as the German bombers joined formation and awaited the arrival of their fighter escort. The first wave, consisting of Dorniers of KG 3 and III/KG 76 crossed the British coast near Dungeness at about 1130hrs, with a strong fighter escort.

Air Vice Marshal Park was to make extensive use of paired squadrons on this day; no fewer than 10 of his 21 squadrons operated in pairs against this first raid. The remainder of the No.11 Group squadrons were quickly airborne, and reinforcements were on the way from No.10 Group to the West, and No.12 Group to the North, this last consisting of the "Big Wing" from Duxford, now five squadrons strong, and led by the fire-eating Douglas Bader.

The first British units to engage were the two Spitfire squadrons from Biggin Hill; Nos 72 and 92, who intercepted near Maidstone. They were quickly joined by other units, and a large whirling battle commenced. As the German formation lumbered towards London, its escort fighters were peeled away from the bombers, and run low on fuel. So fierce was the opposition that by the time that the leading bomber formations reached the outskirts of London, their fighter escorts had vanished.

They were then confronted with the awesome sight of the Duxford Wing in perfect formation, three squadrons of Hurricanes covered by two squadrons of Spitfires 5,000 feet (1,525m) higher. At the same time, half a dozen other squadrons from No.11 Group approached from all sides, and a huge melée developed. Some German bombers jettisoned their loads at random; others were hunted all over the London suburbs, and their bombing runs spoiled.

Damage was widespread, although little of military value was hit. Spitfires and Hurricanes were elbowing each other out of the way in order to get a shot in. For once they had numbers on their side. Shortly after noon, the German armada was streaming back down the Thames Estuary and across the coast of Kent in extreme disarray.

Back on the other side of the Channel, the Luftwaffe prepared for the next stage. Two hours later they tried again, preceded by a fighter sweep. Again they met with fierce resistance, and huge dogfights developed. If anything, the level of confusion was even higher than in the earlier action. The Duxford Wing had come forward again, but this time had scrambled late. They were hit by 109s before they could get at the bombers and split up.

Faced with the unrelenting attacks by the British fighters, many bombers jettisoned their loads more or less at random and headed homewards. By 1600hrs, all that remained were smoking wrecks littering South Eastern England. Two further raids took place on the day. He 111s of III/KG 55 made an ineffective attack on Portland, while ErpGr 210, making its first appearance for several days, raided the Spitfire factory at Woolston.

The BBC announced that evening that 183 German aircraft had been shot down on the day. The actual combat loss was 56. Twelve more had force landed, and ten had limped home damaged, often with dead

Right: September 15 is the day chosen to celebrate the anniversary of the Battle of Britain. By now Luftflotte 3 was mainly assigned to night raiding, and many units had been transferred north to Luftflotte 2, including almost all the single seater fighter Gruppen. The major actions of the day were two huge raids on London; Goering eschewing tactical surprise in favour of concentration of force. The pot began to boil late in the morning, when British radar detected a huge build-up over the Pas de Calais. At this period, Keith Park of No.11 Group was making every effort to use paired squadrons to minimise the effect of being outnumbered. The vanguard of the raid, consisting of about 100 Dorniers drawn from III/KG 76 and KG 3, with a massive fighter escort, crossed the Kent coast at about 11.30 and headed inland. They were met over Maidstone by Spitfires of Nos.72 and 92 Sqns, who were reinforced by other units. Little impression was made on the bombers at first, although repeated attacks by the defenders gradually peeled away the escorting 109s. Then over the outskirts of London, the bombers encountered the 60 fighters of the Duxford Wing led by Douglas Bader, perfectly positioned to strike. Other squadrons approached from all sides and a huge dogfight took place. For once, the British fighters had the advantage of both numbers and height. Scattering their bombs at random over the capital and Kent, the German armada was hunted back to France. That afternoon they tried again, and again the defenders reacted in force. This was also beaten off with heavy losses.

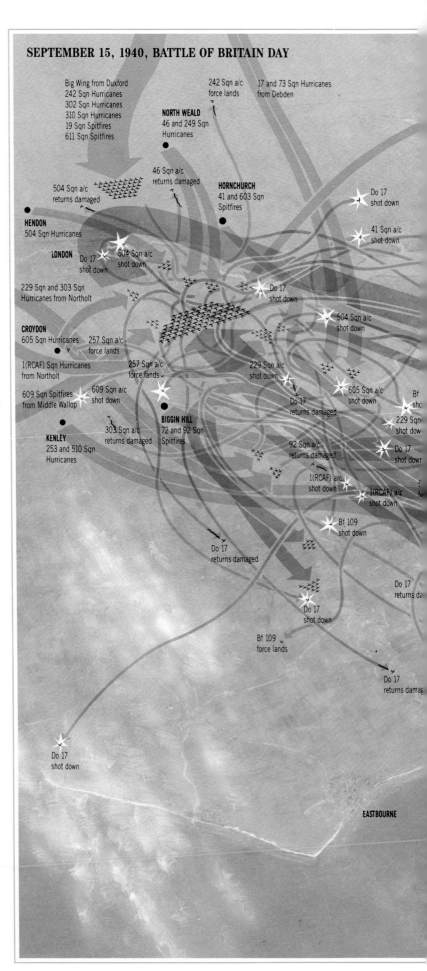

SEPTEMBER 15, 1940, BATTLE OF BRITAIN DAY

Big Wing from Duxford
242 Sqn Hurricanes
302 Sqn Hurricanes
310 Sqn Hurricanes
19 Sqn Spitfires
611 Sqn Spitfires

242 Sqn a/c force lands

17 and 73 Sqn Hurricanes from Debden

NORTH WEALD
46 and 249 Sqn Hurricanes

46 Sqn a/c returns damaged

HORNCHURCH
41 and 603 Sqn Spitfires

Do 17 shot down

504 Sqn a/c returns damaged

HENDON
504 Sqn Hurricanes

41 Sqn a/c shot down

LONDON
Do 17 shot down

504 Sqn a/c shot down

Do 17 shot down

229 Sqn and 303 Sqn Hurricanes from Northolt

504 Sqn a/c shot down

CROYDON
605 Sqn Hurricanes

257 Sqn a/c force lands

229 Sqn a/c shot down

1(RCAF) Sqn Hurricanes from Northolt

257 Sqn a/c force lands

605 Sqn a/c shot down

Bf

609 Sqn Spitfires from Middle Wallop

609 Sqn a/c shot down

Do 17 returns damaged

229 Sqn shot down

KENLEY
253 and 510 Sqn Hurricanes

303 Sqn a/c returns damaged

BIGGIN HILL
72 and 92 Sqn Spitfires

92 Sqn a/c returns damaged

Do 17 shot down

1(RCAF) a/c shot down

1(RCAF) a/c shot down

Bf 109 shot down

Do 17 returns damaged

Do 17 shot down

Bf 109 force lands

Do 17 returns da

Do 17 shot down

Do 17 returns damag

EASTBOURNE

257 Sqn Hurricanes
from Martlesham

NORTH FORELAND

Do 17
shot down

Do 17
shot down

73 Sqn a/c
shot down

Bf 109
shot down

501 Sqn a/c
shot down

Bf 109
shot down

Do 17
returns damaged

DOVER

III/KG76 and KG3
return to base

Do 17
crash lands
France

Bf 109
force lands
Dymchurch

Bf 109
lands in sea

Bf 109
force lands
France

Do 17
crash lands

CALAIS

Do 17s of III/KG76 and KG3
from Antwerp area

DUNGENESS

Bf 109
shot down

Bf 109
force lands
France

Do 17
crash lands

Bf 109
force lands
France

BOULOGNE

Bf 109
shot down

Bf 109 escorts

DESURES

SAMER

Do 17s of I/KG76
from Beauvais

137

or wounded crewmen on board. In detail, 22 Bf 109s, three Bf 110s, 19 Do 17s, nine He 111s, and three Ju 88s had been destroyed. The force landed figures were three 109s, three Do 17s, five He 111s and one Ju 88. British losses totalled 27: 20 Hurricanes and seven Spitfires, with five and two force-landed respectively. The ratio of damaged aircraft was high; 12 Hurricanes and four Spitfires. Pilot losses were 12 killed, one prisoner of war, and four severely injured.

In terms of the scoreboard, September 15 was not exceptional, although it was thought to be at the time. The reason for the overclaiming, which it must be said was equally rife in the Luftwaffe, lay in the high level of confusion, where several fighters would take a shot at a single aicraft in a very short space of time. In several individual actions, the British outnumbered the Germans, which increased the probability of this happening.

The true importance of September 15 lay in the morale of the two opposing air forces. For the first time, many of the British fighter squadrons had a positional advantage over the Germans; for the first time many of them fought with numbers on their side. By contrast, the Luftwaffe, and especially the fighter arm, were becoming disenchanted with their commanders. The refrain for many days past had been that the Royal Air Force was reduced to its last 50 Spitfires. On September 7, the defences had been fairly ineffective, and victory at last looked as though it might be in sight. Then on September 15, they had been met by a revitalised force. Not only were the British fighting harder than ever, but there seemed to be more of them than ever before. The Germans felt themselves outnumbered and beset on all sides. Suddenly victory looked farther away than ever. To the British, September 15 felt like a great victory. The mood had changed on both sides.

Adverse weather restricted operations during the next few days, although a small daylight raid on London was mounted on September 18. The night bombing campaign continued unabated. On September 19, the invasion was quietly cancelled, although the British had no way of knowing this at the time. The Reichsmarschall directed that airfields and aircraft factories were again to be the priority targets, and many German border units redeployed westwards from September 25. There were two days of intensive fighting before the month ended; on September 27 and 30.

September 27 started with the usual reconnaissance sorties, then a formation of Bf 110 Jabos escorted by 109s raided southern England in what appeared to be a fairly purposeless incursion. Intercepted, they lost eight of their number. This was followed by the Ju 88s of I and II/KG 77 heading for London who, due to an error in timing, came in unescorted. They were met by 10 squadrons of RAF fighters and very roughly handled, losing 12 aircraft before Bf 109s came to their rescue. Fierce fighter battles were fought as a result of both these actions. In the West, Luftflotte 3 launched a raid on the Bristol Aeroplane Company works at Filton with EprGr 210, which lost four Bf 110s, including that of their third Kommandeur in six weeks, Hptm Martin Lutz, and ZG 26, which lost seven aic-

raft. Total German casualties for the day were 54: 18 Bf 109s, 21 Bf 110s and 15 Ju 88s were written off. Two further Ju 88s crashed after a midair collision over France. British losses totalled 28: 15 Spitfires and 13 Hurricanes were written off and yet others forcelanded. More seriously, 20 RAF pilots were killed and a further five badly hurt.

September 30 started with fine weather, and two raids estimated as 200-plus headed for London. Intercepted, they turned back, and a ferocious fighter battle took place. Heinkels of I and II/KG 55 launched a raid on the Westland Aircraft factory at Yeovil in the afternoon, turning back after losing four of their number. Sixteen Spitfires and Hurricanes were lost on this day, but only four pilots were killed. Total German losses amounted to 44 aircraft written off, including 28 Bf 109s; a resounding success for the British fighters.

Phase 4

Early October saw a distinct shift in the emphasis of the Luftwaffe attacks. While the night offensive was to continue until May 1941, with London, Liverpool, Coventry and other industrial centres as the main targets, the mass daylight attacks virtually ceased, and were largely replaced with nuisance raids by Bf 109 Jabos. The rationale behind this was to keep the defenders extended and weaken them if possible, pending a resumption of the offensive in the spring of 1941. As had been found earlier in the Battle, the British fighters would not rise to oppose a sweep by Bf 109s alone, and it was no longer a viable proposition to use bombers as *Lockvogel*, or bait. Only bombs on England could get the defences to react, and bomb-laden Bf 109s could immediately revert to being fighters once they had dropped their load.

The month of October started cloudy with little activity, although fighter sweeps over southeastern England included a handful of Bf 109E-7 Jabos of LG 1. This was to set a new pattern. The Luftwaffe High

Above: A Junkers 88A of Stab III/KG 30 lies in shallow water off Pagham on September 9. Two crewman were killed, and the others, including Major Backbarth, the Gruppe Kommandeur, were captured.

Command had issued instructions that one Gruppe in every Jagdgeschwader was to be so equipped for Jabo operations. This did not do much for the morale of the Jagdflieger. It also posed RAF Fighter Command's No. 11 Group a different problem inasmuch as the Jabos would come in very fast and very high and, realistically, only the Spitfire squadrons could catch them. The Hurricane, good though it was lower down, simply did not have the performance at 25,000ft (7,620m).

Things remained fairly quiet until October 7, when a plethora of small raids and sweeps were mounted over the southeast and south coasts. Portsmouth and Yeovil were raided. The Yeovil raid was expensive for the Luftwaffe: their losses on this mission amounted to seven Bf 110s of II and III/ZG 26, and a Ju 88 of II/KG 51. Things would have gone even worse with them had it not been for the arrival of 109s to cover their withdrawal.

Much the same pattern continued, interspersed with bad weather breaks when daylight operations became minimal. Damage caused by the Jabos was light, the average 109 pilot being unable to obtain the same results as the highly trained specialists of EprGr 210. That the strain was beginning to tell on both sides there can be no doubt, as shown during this period by the spate of operational accidents, due to a combination of fatigue and bad weather.

Fighting flared up again on October 15, and some vicious little skirmishes developed over the Thames Estuary. The Jagdflieger had marginally the better of the action, losing 10 Bf 109s and a Ju 88, for four Spitfires and eight Hurricanes. Several British fighters force-landed. Two other German losses on this day were Bf 110 night fighters of NJG 1 and NJG 2, both shot down during the hours of darkness by British bombers. Also on this night, Greater London was badly hit, with 512 civilians killed, nearly 1,000 injured, and an estimated 11,000 made homeless. Most of the major rail termini, at Waterloo, Victoria, Liverpool Street and Paddington, were badly damaged in this raid, and rail services were severely disrupted.

Daylight activity during the rest of October slowly petered out. October 21 was a foul day with little activity. It was notable because for the first time in a very long while, Fighter Command suffered no combat casualties, an occurrence repeated on October 23 and 24. October 26 was notable only for the belated entry of the Italians into the battle, when 16 Fiat BR 20s of the Regia Aeronautica made a half-hearted raid on Harwich.

Some indication of the strain on Fighter Command at this late stage was the fact that no fewer than 1,007 sorties were flown on October 27, for very little result. The raids were by Jabos, plus small formations and even single bombers trying to penetrate the defences under cover of cloud. The targets were mainly airfields, both fighter and bomber, ranging from Hawkinge in

Kent to Driffield in Yorkshire. The scoreboard for this day was seven Bf 109s, two Ju 88s, two He 111s and one Do 17 lost, plus two 109s force-landed, set against four Spitfires and four Hurricanes written off. Poor weather conditions persisted until the last day of the month, when there were no combat casualties on either side, although two Dorniers of III/KG 76 were lost over France when they ran out of fuel after a mission.

* * *

The Battle of Britain has now been under the intense scrutiny of historians and others for half a century. Aided by hindsight, they have been able to raise various controversial issues. Criticism is all too easy for those who come after. To touch on but one issue, it is known that both sides overclaimed by a considerable amount. No-one who has not experienced air fighting can possibly imagine the confusion. Neither can they judge. Relative scores are an effect, not a cause. What is clear is that the Battle of Britain was won by Fighter Command because it defeated the Luftwaffe in the battle to control the air over southern England.

Below: A Dornier Do 17Z, separated from its formation, flies over London on September 7. A straggler like this would be easy meat for any marauding fighter. This was the day when the Blitzkreig on London started.

Right: For you the war is over! Young German bomber crewmen are escorted to a captivity that few thought would last long. But they stood a better chance of surviving the war than their comrades left behind.

THE life of an RAF fighter pilot during the Battle of Britain and the Battle of France, which immediately preceded it, was as varied as the fragments that form a pattern in a kaleidoscope. By examining the diverse range of individual experiences, however, a picture emerges of the dangers and problems faced by hard-pressed aircrew and the thoughts and feelings of a typical RAF pilot.

Who were the Few? A look at some of the Hurricane pilots of 1 Squadron during the Battle for France in May 1940 shows the typical variety of backgrounds from which the RAF recruited aircrew before the war, Squadron Leader P.J.H. ''Bull'' Halahan had joined via a public school and the RAF College at Cranwell. All the other officers had five-year short service commissions and came mostly from public or grammar schools. Flying Officer Paul Richey had been to Downside — ''the Catholic Eton'' — and Flight Lieutenants ''Johnny'' Walker and Prosser Hanks were also public school products. The Canadian ''Hilly'' Brown had the customary State education of his country. S.J. Soper, similarly educated in England, had joined the RAF as a sergeant. Flying Officer ''Boy'' Mould had started in the same way but entered the apprentice school at Halton when he was fifteen and showed such outstanding qualities that he was awarded a Cranwell cadetship at eighteen. Flying Officer Leslie Clisby, some of whose exploits are mentioned in other chapters, was an Australian, and ''Cobber'' Kain, of 73 Sqdn, whose record is also detailed elsewhere, was a New Zealander, each of them imbued with the characteristics of his native country and its schooling. Pilot Officer Albert Gerald Lewis, who was posted to 85 Sqdn while it was in France, and shot down nine enemy aircraft there, came from South Africa. Traditionally in this Service nobody cared from what economic or social level, or from which Allied country, a man came; it didn't matter who you were; all that counted was what manner of fighting material you showed yourself to be.

This pungent assortment of human types was further enriched when the war began and additional varieties of aircrew were embodied full-time. There was the Auxiliary Air Force, with its complete fighter squadrons, in which all the pilots had commissions and came from a wide range of middle- and upper-class occupations. There was the Volunteer Reserve, which was not organised in squadrons but provided a pool embracing all manner of middle- and working-class employment, from which the Regular and Auxiliary squadrons were supplemented. All its pilots were Sergeants. There were the Reserve, which consisted of officers who had left the RAF after various periods of service, and the Special Reserve, which comprised officers who had trained with the Service but not as Regulars. And there were the three University Air Squadrons at Oxford, Cambridge and London.

In this respect the RAF differed greatly from the stereotyped l'Armée de l'Air and Luftwaffe. In both France and Germany the great majority of pilots had received the same academic education at state schools, whatever their financial or social situation. If he wanted to join the air force, a Frenchman had a choice only between the Regular and the Reserve. For a Ger-

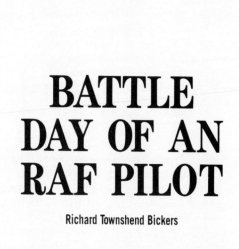

BATTLE DAY OF AN RAF PILOT

Richard Townshend Bickers

man there was no choice other than making the Service a full-time career.

Whether RAF pilots were high or low in the victory ratings, there was little disparity of professional opinion about the tools of their trade. The Hurricane was held in affection and respect for its ruggedness and manoeuvrability. The Mk I was not as fast as a Bf 109E but could turn inside it, which was the prime consideration in a dogfight. The Spitfire was greatly loved and a source of immense pride. It fought the Bf 109 on level terms and, in the hands of a good pilot, could also turnn inside it. The Hurricane was held to be the better gun platform because its wing was less flexible than the Spitfire's and the latter's outer gun on each

Below: The Unknown Warrior of Fighter Command. Fifty years on, this young pilot symbolises all those who fought in the Battle of Britain to protect the free world against totalitarian tyranny.

side was closer to the wingtip than the Hurricane's. In consequence, the Spitfire's bullets did not converge on so small an area as the Hurricane's. Against the Bf 110 both the Hurricane and Spitfire at once established themselves as tactically superior in a fight, despite the 110's rear-firing armament. The argument about the rival merits of machineguns and cannon did not develop until after the Battle of Britain. Most RAF aircrew respected their opponents as highly trained and determined fighters but none would concede any superiority in skill and motivation. It is a necessary characteristic of fighter pilots everywhere to believe in their own abilities, and deep down, every successful pilot secretly believes he at least as good as the opposition. The RAF in 1940 were no exception.

In general the radio equipment was deplored. High frequency (HF) sets were obsolescent and slowly being replaced by very high frequency (VHF) equipment. Pilots' dissatisfaction lay not so much in the range of HF as in the poor quality of reception, for it was susceptible to all manner of distorting interference. A further handicap was that an aircraft transmitter-receiver carried only one channel, so there was no communication between squadrons, whereas with the later VHF equipment there were four channels. Also, the system for fixing the position of an aircraft or formation imposed 14 seconds of radio silence on it HF every minute, which could mean missing vital messages and causing an aborted interception.

The name radar had not been coined and the term radio direction finding (RDF) was used. The equipment was secret but it was common knowledge that the tall ''radio'' masts on the south and east coasts supplied information to the Operations Rooms that controlled fighter interceptions. The deductive powers of a genius were not necessary to conclude that the positioning of defending fighters in the right place to intercept German raids was not mere chance. The existence of this still mysterious facility was a further boost for the already high confidence and morale of Fighter Command. So much for the men and the equipment. The question remains, however; what was it actually like to fly and fight in the Battle of Britain? The experience of individual pilots can be used to illustrate the problem and pressures of trying to hold back the most powerful aerial onslaught the world had seen.

A good example is that of New Zealand's most successful fighter pilot, Group Captain Colin Falkland Gray, DSO, DFC and two bars, who destroyed 27½ enemy aircraft, 15½ of them between early June and early September 1940. He joined the RAF before the war and was posted to No 54 Squadron.

About his participation in these air battles he says modestly, ''The whole thing was quite fortuitous and therefore those of us who happened to be concerned deserve no particular credit. Anyone in a fighter squadron in England at the time was automatically to be involved whether he liked it or not — it wasn't a matter of choice.''

He had hoped to be posted to fighters and says, ''I knew that if there was a war I was certainly likely to be in action and I accepted this. It was merely a case of being in the right place at the right time. Even the volunteers who joined after the outbreak didn't have much choice in the matter either. They had to go where they were sent.'' As for the rights and wrongs of the war: ''I figured that 'the mother country', as we New Zealanders called it, was not likely to be involved inn unjustified hostilities and this was probably the extent of our thoughts on the matter.''

As many other RAF fighter pilots have, he deplored their lack of realistic training in air-to-air firing and fighter-to-fighter combat. ''The first time I encountered any enemy aircraft was over France on May 24, 1940. By that time I had been in in the RAF for 16 months, and 6 months in a fighter squadron. I had flown a total of 140 hours on Spitfires so was reasonably experienced. I'd fired my guns a few times against ground targets but had no experience of air-to-air gunnery against high-speed targets and therefore no idea of the amount of deflection (angle off) required. The only experience I'd had against aerial targets was during training when we fired at a drogue towed at not much more than 100 mph, and this wasn't much help.''

He illustrates some of the problems. ''The muzzle velocity of a .303 bullet (our armament at that time), was 2,660ft per second (810m/sec). This would take the bullets 0.28 of a second to travel 250 yards (228m), the range at which our guns were harmonised. During that time a target travelling at 300mph (483km/h) would travel 41 yards (37m), which is a hell of a lot of deflection, especially for a 90 degree crossing shot. To add to this difficulty, the target would be lost to sight under the nose of a fighter pulling through in a normal curve of pursuit and one would be left shooting at a spot in space where the target should eventually arrive! Fortunately it seldom came to this,

Below: The British symbol of the Battle; the Supermarine Spitfire in factory fresh condition. The gun ports are open; normally they would have covers pasted over them to protect the barrels against mud and dust.

Above: RAF helmets and goggles, including three 'B' type helmets with various masks. Bottom Centre are commercial 'Luxor' goggles bought by many pilots in preferrence to issue items.

as our angles off were not normally as great as 90 degrees, but the deflection could range from 0 degrees for dead astern of the target to about 20 yards (18m) or more for a 45 degree crossing shot.

''The whole question of deflection was brought home to me in a very salutary way on July 24. We had been sent down to Rochford the previous day and on the 24th had already been in action against Dorniers attacking a convoy off Deal. Although we chased them back to France and I fired all my rounds at one of them, it didn't seem to have any effect. We returned to Rochford to refuel and rearm and were scrambled again just after

midday. This time we ran into 18 Dorniers, escorted by about 20 Mc 109s, attacking a convoy in the Thames estuary off Margate, and a terrific dogfight developed. In the general mêlée that ensued I had a good crack at a 109 but was unable to observe any positive results. The dogfight seemed to end as suddenly as it started and as I couldn't see anyone else around I set off for home.

''I hadn't been going for long before I heard one of our aircraft calling for a homing and thought I could see him in the distance but heading in the wrong direction, so I set off in hot pursuit to see if I could lead him home. He was going like the clappers and it took some time to catch him up, but when I finally did so I realised it wasn't a Spitfire at all but an Me 109. He obviously spotted me at the same time and started to turn hard to starboard. As I was close behind I pulled round and gave him a quick squirt, but in my excitement I allowed twice the deflection I had intended. To my astonishment my first burst caught him smack amidships and the pilot immediately baled out into the sea. From then on I always allowed twice the deflection I thought necessary and maybe a bit more for good luck.''

For the front-line squadrons, the daily routine from May to October 1940 varied little. Dowding tried to allow each squadron one day's rest a week, but this was not always possible. A normal battle day on a day fighter squadron began at about 3.30 am and carried on until stand-down at around 8 pm. Some flights or entire squadrons would be at readiness to take off

within five minutes which, in actual practice, meant two or three minutes. Sometimes there would be a section on standby, with the pilots in their cockpits and able to be off the ground in a minute or so. Breakfast and a sandwich lunch would probably be brought to the dispersal points around the airfield.

In the intervals between flights, pilots dozed on beds or chairs in the crew huts — or tents, at a satellite airfield — or on the grass. Some read, some played cards, draughts or chess. Tiredness inhibited conversation. When released, the favourite recreation was a couple of hours in a local pub. Some squadrons stationed close to London had a taste for night-clubbing, which often meant virtually no sleep apart from what could be snatched between sorties. The resilience of youth and the natural high spirits of most aircrew kept them alert

Right: The knights of the air wore a new armour. The leather B type helmet contained the radio earphones, and the D type mask the microphone. The 1936 pattern fur-lined boots gave a little protection against the cold, while the parachute was insurance against a long drop. The 1932 pattern Mae West would keep you afloat in the sea, although not warm, while the gauntlets protected against sharp edges as much as against the cold.

''Flying the Hurricane, there was a great feeling of power and thrust on takeoff. It made a wonderful noise. I always had the canopy open on takeoff and landings in case there was trouble. Didn't feel the draught. I understand that Peter Townsend used to fly with the canopy open because he could see better. This would have been noisier, and draughty, and couldn't have helped speed.

At height cold was a constant problem. The canopy would mist up, and ice used to form inside and out on the front, bullet-proofed windshield. I often had to scrape ice off the glass at front, but could see out of each side which was made of Perspex. Goggles also used to mist up and were a nuisance, uncomfortable. But they were useful if you had to bale out, and helped prevent burning of the eyes if you were hit.

I reckon that about 10,000ft was the maximum you could fly any time without oxygen. I did fly sometimes at 28,000ft without, but you could easily pass out. I once had to shoot down a barrage balloon which had become a hazard at about 28,000ft, but I was unable to turn on the oxygen. I managed to shoot it down, but didn't see where it landed. I found out later that it came down over Caterham, in Surrey, and that the cables shorted out the electricity and cut train services!''

Air Commodore Peter Brothers
CBE, DSO, DFC

in the air, no matter how hard they drove themselves when off duty.

Group Captain Bobby Oxspring DFC, AFC, describes how the peace and quiet of the dispersal could be transformed into frantic action in a few seconds.

"The hectic actions filled the long days and we slipped into a routine. An hour before dawn we crawled out of bed, forced down some breakfast and got shaken into wakefulness as we were transported to dispersal in a hard-arsed lorry. We arrived to the cacophony of Merlin engines being warmed up and tested all round the airfield by the reliable fitters. Having chalked up the allocations of pilots to aircraft and formation compositions we donned our Mae West life jackets, collected our parachutes and helmets and trudged out to our aircraft. Detailed walk round inspections such as are the mode today would have been an insult to our conscientious ground crews, many of whom had been up all night rectifying faults and repairing battle damage. A quick kick on the tyres followed by a nervous pee on the rudder was quite sufficient.

"The next move was to carefully arrange the safety harness and parachute straps, plug in the helmet leads to radio and oxygen so that on a scramble the least possible time would be lost in getting strapped in and away. Quick checks to see that the oxygen was flowing through the mask, that the gunsight was working with spare bulb in place and we were ready to go. As we fidgeted about with these essential tasks we exchanged facetious banter with our faithful ground crews. Very often in those autumn days there was a murky pre-dawn mist soaking the aircraft in heavy condensation which ran off the windscreen and cockpit canopy. We'd grab a rag from the rigger and help him polish the transparent areas as clear as we could get them. We had learned the hard way that unrestricted visibility was vital to fighter pilots whose aggression and indeed survival depended so much on clarity of vision.

"We lounged around the dispersal talking, playing cards or just sitting. Periodically the telephone rang jerking us all into boggle-eyed alertness. More often than not the telephone orderly would call one of us to some innocuous administrative call and the tension of another anticipated order to combat receded. That telephone played hell with our nerves. I don't think any of us pilots ever again appreciated the virtues of Mr Bell's invention. Sooner or later though, the action charged instruction came through. The orderly would pause, listen and then bawl:

'Squadron scramble, Maidstone, Angels two zero.'

"Before he'd relayed the message we were away sprinting to our Spitfires. As we ran, the fitters fired the starter cartridges and the propellers turned with engines roaring into life. From strapping in to chocks away was a matter of seconds. Taxiing to the take-off point on the broad grass airfield took even less time. Pausing to let the last aircraft get roughly in position, the squadron commander's upraised hand signal then came down and twelve pilots gunned their throttles speeding away on the take-off in a wide vic formationn of flights.

"As the squadron got airborne canopies snapped shut and wheels sucked into the wells. The leader's voice

crackled in the earphones: 'Rastus, Fibus airborne.'

The controller's response was immediate: 'OK, Fibus Leader, one hundred plus bandits south of Ashford heading north west angels fifteen. Vector 130, Buster.'

"Buster meant the fastest speed attainable. The squadron commander held the maximum power setting he could afford to ensure that the rest of the squadron had a slight margin of speed to keep up with him. Cutting the corners on every variation of the leader's heading the flight gradually slid into the climb formation of sections line astern.

"Struggling to gain every inch of height in the shortest possible time we gradually emerged out of the filthy brown haze which perpetually hung like a blanket over London. Suddenly, around 12,000 feet we broke through the smog layer and a different world emerged, starling in its sun-drenched clarity.

"Long, streaming contrails snaked way above us from the Channel coast as the Messerschmitt high-flying fighters weaved protectively over their menacing bomber formations. Our radios became almost unintelligible as pilots in our numerous intercepting squadrons called out sightings, attack orders, warnings and frustrated oaths. Green 2 and 3, our two weavers who criss-crossed above the squadron formation, took up their stations to guard against attacks from the vulnerable blind area behind. Somehow a familiar voice of any one of our pilots would break through the radio chatter with an urgent, 'Fibus Leader, bandits eleven o'clock level.'

"Interception of the enemy almost always developed this way, but the ensuing action depended on variable circumstances of the time: the position of the bombers, the proximity of enemy fighters, the manoeuvrings of our fellow squadrons, our height advantage or otherwise over our targets and a host of factors which dictated our immediate tactics.

Above: A miscellaneous collection includes Johnnie Johnson's medal ribbons and scarf, the armour backplate from a Hurricane; a reflector gunsight, an aircraft compass and a wanderlight for the cockpit.

"The Group Commander's basic strategy was to direct his more numerous Hurricane squadrons on to the enemy bomber formations at the same time hopefully providing protective cover for them from his faster Spitfire squadrons. Often this plan fell down because for various reasons our interceptors engaged at slightly different times and which, if only a minute apart, could spoil any intended coordination. At the same time the primary objective of the RAF defences was the destruction of enemy bombers. The Messerschmitts were unable to inflict any primary damage except to our defending fighters. Frequently our squadron would plummet into an attack on the bomber formations, but the fast reacting German fighter cover headed in to cut us off. This usually resulted in our leading flight getting in amongst the bombers whilst we in B flight had to turn into the attacking 109's coming at us from the rear.

"From that moment our squadron cohesion broke up. Flights split into sections, battle with the enemy was joined, and in the following violent manoeuvres the sections broke down into pairs and often single aircraft. Multiple and single combats rippled out across the sky as opposing fighters locked into deadly conflict. Squadrons which had managed to get among the bombers closed in their attack to point blank range. Breaking away they used their superior speed to climb out on the flanks and seek opportunities to set up renewed passes. Again our formations whittled down to sections and these in turn became vulnerable to the greatly superior number of the German fighter Staffels who peeled down from above.

''Flak shells from our anti-aircraft batteries below winked in and around the enemy armadas. The lingering smoke from the bursts tracked the invaders' course and made it easy for those pilots breaking off dog fights to pick up the centre of the action again. At all heights the combats milled, the sun glinting on wings over which staccato bursts of grey gunsmoke reamed back into the slipstream as opposing fighter pilots strove to nail each other.

''Stricken aircraft littered the sky and depleted bomber formations heralded the carnage inflicted by our fighters. Spiralling plumes of dirty smoke marked the death dives of savagely hit Heinkels and Dorniers. Battle-damaged bombers stroke to keep up with their formations or struggled to the flanks to be set upon by vengeful Hurries and Spits. Here and there the horizon was dissected by black trails of flaming fighters as victims on both sides fell out of the sky. British and German parachutes floated down in all directions as the battle reached its climax.

''Ammunition dominated every fighter pilot's life. With it he was lethal; without it he was useless. Sooner or later he would expend his fifteen seconds worth and

Below: Pat Wells of No. 249 Squadron stands on the wing of his Hurricane surrounded by his ground crew; four armourers, a fitter, rigger, radio mechanic etc. All these were needed to turn the aircraft around quickly.

Right: The tunic worn by Pat Wells in the picture below. Flying Hurricane P3594, GN-O, he was shot down while attacking a Heinkel over Faversham on September 7 and baled out wounded. His aircraft was lost.

then was the time to retire from the battle.

"Back at base the aircraft returned in ones and twos — most of them, that is. Sometimes one or more Spits were missing. Our loyal ground crews kept tally of the planes as they swept into the circuit, ready as always with oxygen, fuel, and ammunition to 'turn the kites round quick'. Rarely did they exceed twelve minutes for a whole squadron. Watching 'their' pilots touch down, grins spread across faces as they heard the whine of exposed gun ports singing the message that bullets had fired in anger. Those whose pilots did not return hung around their vacant dispersals and gazed dejectedly at an empty sky.

"The mission completed, pilots ambled back to the crew room, completed the debrief, in some cases stopped a rocket from the CO or flight commanders for some piece of poor airmanship, and then grabbed something to eat. One by one the aircraft were reported back as turned round. Spare Spitfires and pilots, if any, were chalked up on the operations board and the squadron reported back to readiness.

"The high tension and excitement generated throughout the squadron gradually receded. Pilots' sweat-ridden shirts dried out, and stomachs returned to normal. If this had been a morning show, we all knew that there could be at least two more formidable raids to contest before the day was through. Occasionally the activity called for five scrambles in the hours of daylight, but some were false alarms and not all resulted in combat. A quick visit to our aircraft for the usual cockpit check and we'd settle down with some apprehension to await the next call to action."

As Oxpring's account makes clear, the constant waiting followed by a made rush into the air and the almost inevitable combat would wear away at the

Below: Hurricanes of B Flight, No.85 Sqn at Castle Camps having just re-equipped after returning from France in June 1940. During the Battle of Britain, the white hexagon was carried beneath the cockpit.

morale and the nerves of the pilots and an almost overwhelming fatigue would eventually set in. Out of all the RAF pilots who are officially recognised as having taken part in the Battle, 451 served throughout. The average life expectancy of a pilot during those 114 days was 87 flying hours.

Every flyer had to come to terms with his fears and the constant grinding tension in his own way, and force himself to keep going even when constantly outnumbered and often in an inferior tactical position. Another New Zealander, Air Commodore Al Deere, CBE, DSO, DFC, comments: "The question 'when does a man lack the moral courage for battle' poses a tricky problem and one that has never been satisfactorily solved. There are so many intangibles; if he funks it once, will he the next time? How many men in similar circumstances would react in exactly the ame way? And so on. There can be no definite yardstick, each case must be judged on its merits as each set of circumstances will differ.

"In the case of day fighter pilots, in particular, it presented squadron and flight commanders with a really difficult problem and one with which they were being continually faced. Up till the moment the air battle is joined, each pilot is a member of a team and should he be inclined to cowardice the presence of other aircraft serves as an antidote to his feelings, the more so when he knows that for the initial attack he is under the censorious eyes of the other pilots in the formation. It is immediately subsequent to this first attack that the opportunity occurs for the less courageous to make their get-away without seeming to avoid the issue. Against unescorted bombers, or perhaps small enemy formations, the opportunity doesn't normally occur, and in such cases there exists a natural feeling of superiority sufficient to convince the waverer that he is in a position to impose his terms. It is against overwhelming odds, as faced in the convoy battles of July, that the urge to run is uppermost in one's mind, and it is on these occasions that fear normally gets the upper hand. But, under just such circumstances is it

Above: A young Flying Officer at readiness in Mae West and boots, and with helmet at the ready, tries to relax. At the height of the Battle, front line squadrons spent most of their spare time just loafing about.

most difficult to prove that a particular pilot has not pulled his weight. After the initial attack it is almost impossible to observe the actions of any one pilot, and unless a watch has been set on a suspect — it has been done — there can be no positive proof of cowardice. Lack of proof, however, doesn't rule out suspicion and, in some cases, a conviction that a suspect member of the team is 'yellow'.

"I know only too well the almost overpowering urge to either break off an engagement, or participate in such a way as to ensure one's safety, when surrounded and outnumbered. On many an occasion in July I had to grit my teeth and overcome fear with determination in just such circumstances or, alternatively, when I became temporarily isolated from the main battle, to talk myself into going back. I refuse to believe that there are those among us who know no fear. Admittedly, there are those who show no fear and again others who are demonstratively more brave than their comrades in arms; but everyone in his innermost heart is afraid at some time.

"The dangerous state is reached in battle when one is so tired mentally and physically that the ever present urge of self-preservation overrules the more normal urge to do one's duty."

The public understood well the threats to the life of a Hurricane, Spitfire or Defiant pilot. The Blenheim night fighter crews, however, received little publicity. Pilot Officer Paul Le Rougetel (now Wing Commander, DFC) of 600 Sqdn was on patrol in a Blenheim at 15,000ft (4,570m) on the night of August 9, 1940, when he had to bale out. His account of this event is so impassive that, in the RAF tradition, it invests a potentially fatal accident with the appearance of a trivial misadventure. ''I fell into the middle of Pegwell Bay, off Ramsgate, between half and three-quarters of a mile from the shsore. My radar operator, Smith, landed in shallow water, on the beach. His immediate expectation was death by drowning, as he was a non-swimmer. However, he discoverd in his pre-death throes that he was within his depth and was able to walk ashore!''

The radar operator had leaped out at 6,000ft (1,830m). For the pilot, escaping from a Blenheim might have taxed the ingenuity of Houdini; and Paul Le Rougetel wasn't one of the taller members of the Service. The floor escape hatch, to the right and forward of the pilot's seat, was rectangular and about 24 inches by 18 inches (60 by 45cm). What he had to do was unlock two fasteners, pull the hatch into the aircraft, then turn and throw it as far towards the tail as possible. It didn't quite work like that.

''To extend the powered glide I had trimmed the Blenheim into a gentle turning descent with port power on. I moved to the hatch, leaned forward and groped for the latches. On pulling the hatch into the cockpit an unexpectedly strong rush of air forced my arms, holding the hatch, upwards and sideways. Twisting to get rid of the hatch to the rear, I tripped and fell heavily backwards in a sitting position, ending up with my parachute pack jammed into the opening, while my legs and arms were inside the cabin. Eventually I discovered I could reach halfway up the back of the control column. By leaning forward and pushing on it I was able to reduce speed and overcome the suction effect. I could then wriggle back into the cabin, put

Below: The wing of a Hurricane or Spitfire was the best place to leave a parachute. If left in the cockpit, the straps could get entangled with the Sutton harness, with fatal results in an emergency.

my legs through the escape hatch and fall through.

''I probably could have swum ashore by discarding my Mae West life jacket, but decided not to risk it as my back was a bit painful; so I lined up the direction of land by the Milky Way and swam encumbered towards it. The calm sea became a bit choppy and I must have passed out! I had no idea of time as my watch had stopped. I came to and saw what I thought was a car headlight. I called for help and passed out again.''

The light was from the Ramsgate lifeboat that was searching for him. The crew heard his calls and turned towards him but could not find him and after a considerable time were about to give up, when; ''The coxswain saw what appeared to be a shoal of small fish, steered towards it and found me.'' It was the luminous dial of his watch that the lifeboatman had mistaken for the phosphorescence of fish.

The mutability of daily life for the sort of pilot who forms the indestructible hard core of any air force is well illustrated in the career and character of Wing Commander E.A. Shipman, AFC, who enlisted in 1930 and joined No 41 Squadron as a sergeant pilot straight from Service Flying Training School in 1936. Ted Shipman had his first taste of action soon after the squadron had converted from the biplane Hawker Fury to the Spitfire, and long before most of the fighter pilots whose names were blazoned in newspaper headlines during the ensuing six years. On October 17, 1939, operating from Catterick, Yorkshire, he was flying No 2 in a section when he spotted an He 111. As the section leader could not discern the target, Flight Sergeant Shipman took over from him and was therefore the first to overtake it and attack. The upper gunner returned fire but did not damage the Spitfire. The Heinkel landed on the sea and two survivors of the four crew paddled ashore in a dinghy, Shipman recalls: ''This first sighting of an enemy aircraft and shooting it down caused mixed feelings. First, one of regret then the immediate realisation of the inevitability of the situation. On the whole I cannot say I was elated.''

On May 25, 1940, the squadron moved to Hornchurch to take part in covering the Dunkirk evacuation. The element of chance in meeting the enemy is clear in what Shipman reports about the ten sorties they flew from there. ''For me Dunkirk seemed a frustrating period. The weather was difficult and the lack of good communications with other squadrons on patrol made matters worse. The length of the patrols stretched the economical engine handling to the limit, the fuel capacity being only 85 gallons (386 litres)''.

Because there were more pilots than aircraft, he did not fly on all the 10 patrols that the squadron carried out. Of the seven sorties he did fly, only one gave him a glimpse of the enemy, ''. . . popping in and out of cloud some distance away''. To aggravate his frustration, ''the other three patrols the squadron made were full of activity''.

His reference to other squadrons on patrol is of particular interest in view of the ''Big Wing'' controversy that provoked so much disagreement between Air Vice Marshals Park and Leigh-Mallory later that summer. It is not widely known that at this period three or four squadrons were sent, on occasion, from different stations to patrol the same section of the French

coast simultaneously. Because they were equipped with TR9D HF radio, which had only one channel, they each had to use a different frequency and could not intercommunicate: a powerful argument in favour of Park.

No 41 returned to Catterick, flew a lot of convoy patrols, spent some time at Hornchurch once more, on the same duties, and then went back to Catterick as the Battle of Britain was reaching its height. By this time Shipman had been commissioned. August 15 was a heavy day for the whole of Fighter Command and at 1238 13 Spitfires of 41 Squadron, P/O Shipman's among them, were scrambled to help meet a big raid on the north-east. ''We were ordered to attack Me 110 fighters escorting He 111s at 18,000ft (5,485m) in the Durham area. Leading Green Section, I attacked the section of Me 110s on the left of the formation, but before getting into range my target turned about and offered a brief opportunity to fire a two-second burst, without result. I then picked another target and managed to get in a series of deflection shots while the enemy aircraft was evading quite violently. Finally at 200 yards (180m) range I put the starboard engine out of action. The 110 made an erratic turn to port, emitting clouds of smoke, and disappeared into cloud below, apparently out of control. This was the only occasion when my camera gun worked and the film clearly showed all that had happened, confirming my claim.''

P/Os Bennions and Lovell and Sgt Usman each also shot down a Bf 110 in the same action.

Throughout the battle, one of the advantages held by the British was that if a pilot was shot down and survived, he could be in the air with a new aircraft the next day. German aircrew shot down over the British Isles were lost to the Luftwaffe whether they survived or not, although a skilled and courageous rescue service recovered many pilots from the English Channel. Al Deere typifies the RAF pilot who kept fighting after being shot down on numerous occasions; and in fact survived the wreck of his aircraft nine times in his combat career. He tells of one of these battles: ''Fastening on to the tail of a yellow nosed Messerschmitt I fought to bring my guns to bear as the range rapidly decreased, and when the wingspan of the enemy aircraft fitted snugly into the range scale bars of my reflector sight, I pressed the firing button. There was an immediate response from my eight Brownings which, to the accompaniment of a slight bucketing from my aircraft, spat a stream of lethal lead targetwards. 'Got you,' I muttered to myself as the small dancing yellow flames of exploding 'De Wilde' bullets

Right: British fighter pilot gear varied, although judging by the photographic record of the period, few of them bothered with flying overalls, and rarely this Sidcot 1930 pattern flying suit, which was more the province of the ''bomber baron''. Points of interest are: commercial ''Luxor'' goggles, and an Enfield .38 No.2 Mk 1 service revolver stuck in the top of the left boot, which was more convenient than a holster.

''As I have said, our own pilots were fighting with the utmost gallantry and determination, but the mass raids on London, which were the main feature of the third phase of the Battle, involved a tremendous strain on units which could no longer be relieved as such. Some Squadrons were flying 50 and 60 hours per diem.

Many of the pilots were getting very tired. An order was in existence that all pilots should have 24 hours' leave every week, during which they should be encouraged to leave their station and get some exercise and change of atmosphere: this was issued as an order so that the pilots should be compelled to avail themselves of the opportunity to get the necessary rest and relaxation. I think it was generally obeyed, but I fear that the instinct of duty sometimes over-rode the sense of discipline. Other measures were also taken to provide rest and relaxation at stations, and sometimes to find billets for pilots where they could sleep away from their aerodromes.''

Air Chief Marshall Lord Dowding
GCB, GCVO, CMG

spattered along the Messerschmitt's fuselage. My exultation was short-lived. Before I could fire another burst two 109s wheeled in behind me. I broke hard into the attack pulling my Spitfire into a climbing, spiralling turn as I did so; a manoeuvre I had discovered in previous combats with 109s to be particularly effective. And it was no less effective now; the Messerschmitts literally ''fell out of the sky'' as they stalled in an attempt to follow me.

''I soon found another target. About 3,000 yards directly ahead of me, and at the same level, a Hun was just completing a turn preparatory to re-entering the fray. He saw me almost immediately and rolled out of his turn towards me so that a head-on attack became inevitable. Using both hands on the control column to steady the aircraft and thus keep my aim steady, I peered through the reflector sight at the rapidly closing enemy aircraft. We opened fire together, and immediately a hail of lead thudded into my Spitfire. One moment the Messerschmitt was a clearly defined shape, its wingspan nicely enclosed within the circle of my reflector sight, and the next it was on top of me, a terrifying blur which blotted out the sky ahead. Then we hit.

''The force of the impact pitched me violently forward on to my cockpit harness, the straps of which bit viciously into my shoulders. At the same moment, the control column was snatched abruptly from my gripping fingers by a momentary, but powerful, reversal of elevator load. In a flash it was over; there was clear sky ahead of me, and I was still alive. But smoke and flame were pouring from the engine which began to vibrate, slowly at first but with increasing momentum causing the now regained control column to jump back and forwards in my hand. Hastily I closed the throttle and reached forward to flick off the ignition switches, but before I could do so the engine seized

Above: Pilots and gunners of the ill-fated No.264 Defiant Squadron play draughts between sorties. Posted to 11 Group at the height of the Battle, casualties were so high that they had to be quickly withdrawn.

Below: The Spitfire was the glamour aircraft of Fighter Command, and has overshadowed the Hurricane in the public mind. Spitfires made up one third of the force and accounted for one third of the victories scored.

and the airscrew stopped abruptly. I saw with amazement that the blades had been bent almost double with the impact of the collision; the Messerschmitt must have been just that fraction above me as we hit.

''With smoke now pouring into the cockpit I reached blindly forward for the hood release toggle and tugged at it violently. There was no welcoming and expected rush of air to denote that the hood had been jettisoned. Again and again I pulled at the toggle but there was no response. In desperation I turned to the normal release catch and exerting my full strength endeavoured to slide back the hood. It refused to budge; I was trapped. There was only one thing to do; try to keep the aircraft under control and head for the nearby coast. The speed had by now dropped off considerably, and with full backward pressure on the stick I was just able to keep a reasonable gliding altitude. If only I could be lucky enough to hit in open country where there was a small chance that I might get away with it.

''Frantically I peered through the smoke and flame

''Towards the end of the Battle I had taken just about as much as I could bear. My nerves were in ribbons and I was scared stiff that one day I would pull out and avoid combat. That frightened me more than the Germans and I pleaded with my CO for a rest. He was sympathetic but quite adamant that until he got replacements I would have to carry on. I am glad now that he was unable to let me go. If I had been allowed to leave the squadron, feeling as I did, I am sure that I would never have flown again.''

The late Squadron Leader J. H. (Ginger) Lacey DFM

enveloping the engine, seeking with streaming eyes for what lay ahead. There could be no question of turning; I had no idea what damage had been done to the fuselage and tail of my aircraft, although the mainplanes appeared to be undamaged, and I daren't risk even a small turn at low level, even if I dould have seen to turn.

''Through a miasmatic cloud of flame and smoke the ground suddenly appeared ahead of me. The next moment a post flashed by my wingtip and then the aircraft struck the ground and ricocheted into the air again finally returning to earth with a jarring impact, and once again I was jerked forward on to my harness. Fortunately the straps held fast and continued to do so as the aircraft ploughed its way through a succession of splintering posts before finally coming to a halt on the edge of a cornfield. Half blinded by smoke and frantic with fear I tore at my harness release pin. And then with my bare hands wielding the strength of desperation, I battered at the perspex hood which entombed me. With a splintering crash it finally cracked open, thus enabling me to scramble from the cockpit to the safety of the surrounding field.''

Two other pilots who have never received national acclaim, but whose dedication and selflessness were also typical of all the RAF pilots, are Wing Commander Roddick Lee Smith, OBE, and Squadron Leader L.A. Throgood, DFC. Dick Smith joined the RAF with a short service commission in 1935 and, after being assessed ''Above Average'' on his training course, was posted to No 19 Squadron. He was later assessed

Below: Items from a 1940 fighter station include a field telephone, microphone, mess clock and gramophone. The small device with the triangular aperture is used to judge the distance of approaching aircraft.

Above: Keeping the fighters serviceable often took all night as well as all day. Ground crewmen of No.264 Defiant Squadron catch up on some well earned rest while their fighters are in the air.

''Exceptional'' and was also a brilliant shot. At Malvern College he had been in the shooting eight, and in 19 Squadron was in the team of three led by Sqdn Ldr (now Air Chief Marshal) Sir Harry Broadhurst, GCB, KBE, DSO, DFC, AFC, that won the RAF air firing competition. In 1936 he was seconded to the Fleet Air Arm, with which he served for three years, during which he did 68 deck landings, three of them at night. In June 1940 he arrived at North Weald as a flight lieutenant to command B Flight of 151 Squadron, under Sqdn Ldr E.M. Donaldson (now Air Commodore, CB, CBE, DSO, AFC) and fly Hurricanes. As he had no combat experience and the squadron had seen much action over France, he put in many hours practising dogfighting before his first operational sortie.

On June 12 the squadron did two sweeps over France, on which two pilots, both flying No 3 in their sections, were shot down without any of the others being aware of it. On June 17 he did air-to-ground firing for the first time with eight guns. All his 1,000 flying hours had been in biplanes, ''I had only 12 hours on Hurricanes and I was a flight commander!''

Early in July Dick Smith noticed a Hurricane in the hangar ''with tubes sticking out of each wing'' and asked the squadron engineering officer what they were. They were 20mm cannon, which at that time were still secret. ''As I had always been keen on guns, I asked why it was not being flown and was told that the other pilots considered it was a much less safe aircraft than the other Hurricanes, which had eight .303 Brownings, because it was much slower, less manoeuvrable and had guns that were highly unreliable, prone to inconvenient misfeeds and stoppages.''

As he was leading B Flight and often the whole squadron, and having a leader with a slow aircraft helped the rest to keep up, he voluntarily flew this aircraft on all his sorties. He made 133 operational flights with this and another Hurricane that had four cannon and was therefore even heavier and slower. He was surprised that higher authority did not take more interest in the development of this weapon: he can recall no urgency for detailed reports.

On July 12 when he and ''Buzz'' Allen, a New Zealander, intercepted two Dorniers off the east coast, and he tried to fire his cannon, ''there was just a hiss — the compressor had broken down''. Allen pressed on and was seen to fly into the sea. Another day, the squadron was bounced by Bf 109s and, ''I found myself in my heavy and slow four-cannon aircraft when I noticed two 109s about a mile to my right and climbing much faster than I was. My only hope of survival was to attack. I immediately turned into the lower one, which dived away. I followed, firing vertically downwards at extreme range. As I knew the first 109 must be on my tail, I hauled the aircraft into a maximum-rate turn and climb in which I blacked out through positive g. Tracer shot past me and I hauled back again. The aircraft flicked into a spin. When I recovered I was alone in the sky.''

The thought occurred to him that he would not have liked to be below, in Kent, on the receiving end of his cannon volley. Some time later he was introduced at a party to a man with a limp, who complained that

Above: The tailplane was also a handy place to leave a parachute while awaiting a scramble. This No.85 Squadron Hurricane has been adapted for night operations, as evidenced by the exhaust flame shield.

a cannon shell had passed through his foot while he was gardening . . . in Kent. Handicapped by his ponderous aircraft, Dick Smith's score at the end of the Battle was one destroyed, three probables and two damaged.

Laurence ''Rubber'' Thorogood had joined the RAFVR in December, 1938, and went to 89 Squadron as a sergeant pilot straight from flying school, assessed ''Above Average'' but without any combat training, an experience common to most novice fighter pilots at that hard-pressed period. On the squadron he was given tactical training but no air firing, and had only 28 hours on Hurricanes before his first combat. His description of the spirit in Fighter Command could be extended to the whole nation in that time of crisis. ''We never thought we would not win. We were fighting over our home ground and this had a great bearing on our morale. The Luftwaffe certainly had the numbers but this only seemed to spur us on. We certainly got tired but we were fit and young. On 87 Squadron we were a fairly abstemious bunch of chaps. Nobody went round the bend, as far as I know.'' He flew 59 sorties during the Battle, which yielded him one Ju 88 destroyed and one Ju 87 damaged.

Ted Shipman, Dick Smith and Laurence Thorogood are typical of the pilots who were the backbone of the defence of Britain during the great air battles. From first to last light day after day they were subjected to the stress of waiting to meet the enemy and of being in action, yet personal fame never touched them. They showed the same bravery, determination and mastery of their aircraft as those who emerged from the air fighting that summer with a record of victories in double figures and decorations to go with them.

The most successful pilots were epitomised by the late Sgt J.H. ''Ginger'' Lacey, DFM and bar, later a squadron leader, and the late Squadron Leader (later

Gp Capt) DRS Bader, DSO, DFC and bar. Ginger Lacey had joined the RAFVR when it was formed, in 1936. Within two years he had become an instructor at the Yorkshire Aeroplane Club. By January 1939 he had completed 250 Service flying hours and was spending three weeks with No 1 Squadron at Tangmere, where he flew a Hurricane for the first time. When war came Sgt Lacey was posted to 501 Squadron at Filton, Bristol and took part in the battles in France. On returning to England he added a Bf 109 to his list of victories

Above: The erk on the telephone was the link between command and the squadrons. The words ''squadron scramble'' would send the pilots on their way. On this occasion, the message is apparently not urgent. On the right is a readiness board giving the state of each section, indicated by a coloured counter.

on July 20. On August 12 he destroyed two Ju 87s in the same combat. On September 15, the day when the RAF achieved its greatest number of successes and set the seal on the Luftwaffe's defeat, he brought down three more enemy aircraft and severely damaged a fourth in two combats.

On the squadrons second sortie of the day, they intercepted the enemy at 2 pm over Heathfield, Sussex. Lacey found himself flying head-on at 12 yellow-nosed 109s. He dipped his nose as though about to dive under them, then pulled back the stick and swept up and over in a loop to attack the last one, which was lagging. Still inverted, he fired and sent it down in flames, then rolled off the top and followed the enemy formation. Closing to 250 yards (230m) he fired on No 3 in the rear section and it pulled out with a stream of glycol leaking from its radiator. It was about 8 pm when, weary and on his fourth scramble of the day, he shot down a 109 and an He 111, making his score to date 19 destroyed, three probables and four damaged.

Douglas Bader's best score in one day was two, and he achieved it three times. The first occasion was on August 30 when the squadron he commanded, No 242, encountered more than 70 bombers approaching six abreast with more than 30 110s above to cover them. Bader led his squadron in a dive at the fighters, which instantly broke formation. One, ahead of him, was too slow and he set it alight with a couple of bursts. Two more bursts sent another down in flames.

On September 7, when the Luftwaffe first attacked London, he destroyed a Bf 110 that went down with smoke pouring from it and another that crashed near a railway line and exploded. In the process, his own Hurricane's port aileron was torn to shreds and the cockpit was holed. On September 10, leading, for the first time, the Big Wing for which he had been pleading, he took his own and four other squadrons into action. Levelling off at 23,000ft (7,000m), he could see some 40 enemy aeroplanes over the Thames estuary at 16,000ft (4,875m). He led his formation down and in the ensuing whirligig of twisting, climbing, diving aircraft and a network of tracer bullets and shells, amid the smoke and flames of burning aeroplanes, in a sky

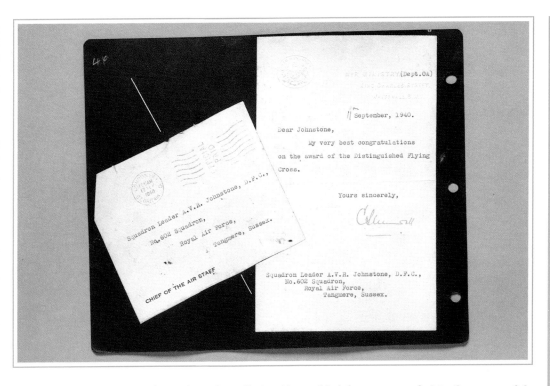

dotted with descending parachutes, he took out first a Ju 87 and then a Do 17. These made his score 11½ confirmed.

There is one name to add and one more event, which appropriately happened on the last night of the Battle of Britain, to tell about those who fought in it without finding themselves in the limelight. Perhaps in narrow terms of definition Wg Cdr W.S. Gregory, DSO, DFC, DFM, doesn't strictly qualify for inclusion in an account of pilots' battle days, but he belongs by every possible right in any narrative about distinguished fighter aircrew. He is known as ''Sticks'', because

Below: The power operated four gun turret was the sole armament of the Defiant. To enter it, it had to be turned as seen here. Leaving it in flight was close to impossible as many unfortunate gunners discovered.

Above: Medals were awarded to the successful few. This brief note from Cyril Newall, the Chief of Air Staff, congratulates Sandy Johnstone, commanding No.602 Squadron, on the award of the Distinguished Flying Cross.

before the war he played the drums in a well-known dance band. He was also flying in his spare time as an air gunner in the VR and was posted to 29 (Blenheim) Squadron when war was declared. In 1941, as a radar navigator, he was crewed up with Wg. Cdr. J.R.D. Braham, whose prowess as a night fighter pilot won him a DSO with two bars and a DFC with two bars. But on October 31, 1940, he was flying with a P/O Rhodes when the controller told them they were very close to a hostile. They couldn't see it, but, Sticks Gregory remembers, ''We came out of cloud and there, following us, was an He 111 with its cockpit lights on, crew map-reading! I don't know who was the more frightened, the German gunner or me. Anyway, I fired my single Vickers into the cockpit without stopping. The range was no more than 200ft. The Heinkel went into a dive under us and Rhodes finished it off with his four Brownings.''

An agreeable note on which to conclude. But that wasn't quite the end of it. ''We were happy, Sector were happy and so was Squadron Leader Widdows, our CO. He was congratulating us when the Flight Sergeant armourer came into the Ops Room and asked who was the gunner on Blenheim L6741. I said, 'I was, Chiefy.' 'You're on a charge,' he announced, 'for shooting off a full pan of ammunition without a pause.' And he produced a bent and ruined gun barrel!''

Obviously the hazards an RAF pilot or air gunner faced in the course of his battle day — or night — did not all lie in the guns of the enemy. And if life was a compendium of inconsistencies, the unifying factors that were common to all participants were high morale, total determination to win and inexhaustible courage.

BECAUSE the British traditionally do not dramatise a situation, the average RAF fighter pilot felt no personal hatred for his enemies in the air. Animosity was directed at the machines they flew, whose intrusion over Britain was resented as an intolerable insolence. Similarly, German pilots regarded the RAF as opponents in a lethal sport, not as detested foes; but the differentiating truth remains that they were in the wrong and Britain and her allies, defending their countries, were in the right.

Life for both sides ran on much the same lines. Whether operating from bases in Germany or, after the conquest of the Low Countries and France, from airfields in the Pas de Calais, the daily routine was basically the same for German fighter pilots as it was for British. They rose at first light, they were released at dusk and in the intervals they waited at dispersals to be sent into action. On small French aerodromes the crew room was a tent, the aircraft were dispersed under camouflage netting, among trees where possible, and meals were eaten out of doors. Men passed the time by reading, playing cards or board games, sleeping and leg-pulling. As the British squadrons in France had done, the Germans either lived under canvas or in billets with local families; they set up their messes in huts on the airfield or hotels.

At the end of a hard day a German fighter pilot sought relaxation in the nearest town's restaurants, dance halls and cinemas. Female company was not hard to find. Politically, France was divided and lethargic. In general, the Nazis were not unpopular. The French Army and Air Force had been soundly defeated and earned contempt. Success and the power it bestowed exerted a strong attraction. Healthy, uninhibited, dashing young German airmen, under orders to be on their best behaviour towards the race they had beaten, and with money to burn, had the magnetism of any conqueror, to which Frenchwomen were not immune. The German bomber crews shared this existence from the beginning of the Blitzkrieg on France until the end of the Battle of Britain, because they were carrying out the assault and the fighters were present only to defend them.

Leutnant Kurt Ebersberger, of II/JG26, who later commanded a Staffel, 4/JG26, has provided an excellent description of the life of a fighter pilot during the early days of the assault on France. He refers to a comrade, Leutnant Otto-Heinrich Hilleke, who was killed in action on June 26; ''We miss his humour and harmonica playing''. (In this form of musical diversion there was a sharp difference between what was acceptable in a German officers' mess and a British; in the latter a mouth-organ was definitely not considered an officer-like instrument). Ebersberger recalls, ''Often when we were at Chicore, our second base in Belgium, after dinner in our handsome Château, with a bottle of good burgundy at hand, Hilleke used to play for us. We would discuss the events of the day and air fighting as well as many matters that were not connected with the Service. Anything unpleasant was dismissed with a joke, so that we were always in a happy and confident mood. We were at ease and out of sight of higher authority. When we felt like it we went out roaming the district.''

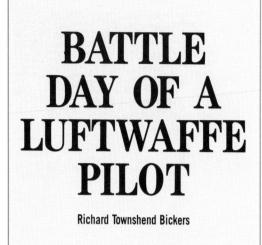

BATTLE DAY OF A LUFTWAFFE PILOT

Richard Townshend Bickers

Next morning they were out at dispersals at first light once again to escort bombing raids on Boulogne, Calais and Dunkirk. ''Going back and forth we saw below us the widespread fighting in Flanders, burning towns and villages, flames at the mouths of heavy guns, which were often a signpost for us when returning with our last drop of petrol. Until Dunkirk fell we flew almost every days with our bombers as they attacked ports, fuel tanks and ammunition dumps along the coast. The British began to embark their troops and ship them back to their island.''

On most days they made contact with Spitfires and Hurricanes. ''It didn't suit the British that we interfered with their withdrawal plan.'' That must be the prize platitude of the campaign. ''We were often

Below: German fighter pilots passing the time at an airfield in northern France. Apart from the uniforms this scene could have been repeated at any RAF fighter airfield.

outnumbered, which didn't bother us in the slightest.'' And that must be the most unconvincing boast; the Luftwaffe consistently outnumbered the RAF. ''The Gruppe commander flew in the lead with 'Hinnak' (Hilleke's nickname) near him. They were the first to engage the enemy and had a stack of victories. Hinnak was our most successful pilot and hasn't yet been overtaken.'' His score was 21 when he was shot down. ''We often heard him say something jocular on the radio, to make everyone feel relaxed.

''The most memorable experience we had was the first time we took off from Chicore to rendezvous with a bomber formation. The weather was atrocious and we hadn't the slightest idea of our whereabouts. The bombers were above cloud and couldn't see us. We were flying so slowly that it seemed we were almost at a standstill. Presently we saw water below. We were over the Channel. Hinnak called, 'We're flying against England!' and burst into the *England Song*.'' This was the popular song whose first line was ''Wir fliegen gegen En-ge-land''. They had to keep a close watch on their petrol consumption and on the radio somebody asked, ''Can everyone swim?'' It was the sort of quip that would equally have amused their opponents. Then they saw Dover and ''. . . great was the delight at being over England for the first time''.

Hilleke's sense of humour was also typical of fighter pilots the world over. On another sortie across the Channel when the formation had momentarily scattered under attack, a voice on the radio was heard saying plaintively, ''Wait for me to catch up, I'm all alone.''

''You're not alone,'' Hilleke retorted immediately. ''There's a Spitfire on your tail.''

On June 3 there was a big raid on Paris. In the morning they flew to an aerodrome half way to the target and refuelled. At about 1400hrs they were ordered off and, ''glowing with ardour, we started our engines''. Luftwaffe formations came from all directions. ''It was an impressive sight.'' Hilleke's aircraft developed trouble and he had to turn back, as did Ebesberger shortly before reaching Paris. The latter says that when they discussed the mission that evening they were all astonished by the paucity of defending fighters and anti-aircraft guns.

A few days later they moved to Le Touquet. ''It was an incomparable moment when we were all sitting together on the terrace of our hotel, to see the sun sink into the sea. Hardly had we settled down than we were off inland again; the next day we found ourselves on a big clover field at Bois Jean, south of Montreuil. At Le Touquet we had installed ourselves in big tents captured from the British. A pleasant camp life soon established itself. Our quarters lay a good distance from the airfield. In the evenings after dark the British flew regularly over the aerodrome on their way south to the Front. We tried a couple of times to take them by surprise, but never succeeded because of the thick haze.

''Our most enjoyable flights were along the steep coast from Dieppe to Le Havre with British or French warships going to and fro beneath us. On the way back we would fly low over the beaches all the way from Le Touquet and French people peacefully swimming would point at us. How fast we went and what a row we made. Unfortunately we went swimming only once, on our second free day since May 10. All the essential servicing of the aircraft was done in the morning, then we all crammed into vehicles and went off to lie on the beach. During such hours one forgot the war.''

From Le Touqet and Bois Jean they moved to Morgny, 43 miles (70km) north of Paris. The airfield, says Ebersberger, was the usual sort of place, but with a little contrivance soon became most comfortable. They lived in a château belonging to the Comte de Fabymasnille, a grand place set in a huge estate. The German Army had crossed the Seine but there wasn't much employment for the Staffel. Soon after, the French capitulated and it returned to Germany. ''We would rather have attacked England immediately, but orders are orders.''

Oberst Josef Priller, known as ''Pips'', who in turn commanded No 1 Staffel and No III Gruppe of JG26 before commanding the Geschwader itself, and was credited with 101 victories, described life on the Channel coast as ''readiness and sorties''. Fighter pilots existed in a state of uncertainty greater than any experienced by ground troops. A soldier in the front line could foretell by numerous signs if and when an enemy attack were imminent. When he was to make an attack, he was told in advance the exact time that he would do so. A fighter pilot had to be ready to take off at once with virtually no warning before the order came. In the summer months, these conditions prevailed for three quarters of the 24 hours in every day. The weeks and months passed in this manner with seldom a short break on a rare quiet day. Even during the Battle of Britain, when most of his time in the air was spent escorting bombers, the pilot had to be prepared to fend off an enemy air raid at any moment.

The Gruppe to which at that time Priller's Staffel belonged moved to the Calais area on July 22, 1940. He says that after the turbulent air operations in France an even harder period began for the Luftwaffe pilots on airfields along the Channel. It was the height of summer, which meant 16 to 18 hours of daylight and for fighter pilots as many hours of alertness, and hasty take-offs to repel expected attacks or to cover their own bombers. Moving such a large formation with all its technical equipment was arduous, but by the 25th it was fully operational and flying over England. It lost two of its number near Margate and three near Dover that day. It was noteworthy, he points out in apparent complaint, that the Luftwaffe fighters were not only under extreme pressure, severely stretched and fighting over hostile territory, but also were faced by the entire British Empire plus a large number of Czechs, Poles and Frenchmen.

Right: Fighter pilots the world over liked to wear leather jackets and boots with coloured silk scarves, and the Luftwaffe Jagdflieger were no exception. The white leather flying jacket was popular summer wear together with the uniform riding breeches and peaked cap. Note the pistol and holster and the canvas flying helmet with headphones, intercom lead and oxygen mask tucked into the belt.

When escorting bombers over England, he alleges, the Messerschmitts were constantly meeting large formations of Spitfires and Hurricanes numbering 20, 40 and even 60, coming at them from all directions. Dowding and Park would have been gratified to know that this was the impression given by the small numbers of defending fighters they were eking out.

After taking part in a few sorties, Staffel and Gruppe commanders quickly formed a clear picture of the enemy, Priller recounts. Squadrons, flights and sections were led by experienced pilots who were highly competent and keen, while the rest were novices who still had a lot to learn. The Luftwaffe fighters' tactic, like the RAF's, was to split up the opposing formation as quickly as possible. The south of England was strongly defending, Priller records, especially around London, and repeats that the Germans were on most occasions assailed from all sides by large numbers of fighters.

His memory does not seem to be entirely accurate, for his statements do not conform exactly with British records, which include diagrams made at the time showing the tracks of enemy incursions and of the fighters that went up to intercept them. However, from the cockpit of a Bf 109 the impressions of a pilot who was of necessity highly apprehensive of the Spitfire, which he had learned in the most unpleasant way was more than a match for his own aircraft, were understandably different from those of anyone studying archives many decades later. From the cockpit of any aircraft in contact with the enemy there always seemed to be a frightening number of them around and a lot more flak sites than had been mentioned at briefing. The problem, as Priller says, was to take evasive action without being scattered far and wide.

''When a Staffel broke and the foursomes and pairs separated in violent twisting and turning, the

Below: Clockwise from left to right; an aircrew lifejacket with gas bottle, a back parachute, a pilot's seat parachute, a canvas helmet with throat microphone, oxygen mask and goggles.

character, pluck and training of the German fighter pilots was revealed,'' Priller writes and later admits: ''In such confused fighting, the claims for aircraft shot down and the loss ratios on both sides are misleading.

''It was no easy task over England in August 1940. Sometimes the youngsters were the victims of their inexperience and over-enthusiasm. There were times when we heard a plea from someone who was confused and disoriented, and nothing could be done about it. I remember one occasion when a lad who hadn't, as we used to say, tasted much English air, lost sight of our formation after some frenzied twisting and turning about the sky. But we could see him: he had dived steeply and was over the outskirts of London. He should have stayed with the Staffel instead of chasing off on his own. When he grasped the situation he called for help: 'Come quickly! I'm on my own over London.'

''He hadn't called in vain. By return post, as it were, his Schwarm leader, whom he couldn't see but who could see him clearly and had followed astern and above him, gave the comforting message; 'Hang on a second and you'll have a couple of Spitfires behind, then you won't be alone any longer.' Therewith the Schwarm leader, who had indeed seen the enemy and for that very reason had remained higher, successfully attacked one of the Spitfires. The other half-rolled and dived away.''' One has to conclude that the second Spitfire had run out of ammunition.

Priller laments that it was not only the enemy with which the German fighter pilots had to reckon when far from base. ''It often happened, particularly over the Channel, that the unpredictable weather cooked up some nasty surprise. Fighter aircraft had a relatively short range and sometimes had barely enough fuel left to get them home. In settled weather, one could calculate with reasonable accuracy how much to keep in hand for the return leg, but those conditions seldom prevailed in the operational zone.'' Even in neighbouring areas the weather could differ considerably. When it was fine over an airfield near Boulogne, it might have changed by the time the fighter reached Calais, 18 miles (30km) away, and made landing impossible.

Above: A Heinkel He 111 of Kampfgeschwader 53 stands ready to take off from Marquise airfield near Calais in August. The glazed noses of the German bombers made their crews feel very vulnerable to a head-on attack.

''A Gruppe in our Geschwader experienced an example of this one day when tricky weather during the morning enforced an urgent change in the planned operations. In the afternoon the sun came out and this Gruppe was ordered to take off. It penetrated about 30 or 40 miles (50 or 60km) deep into England, 'free hunting', which meant looking for enemy aircraft, and low-level attack. On the way back they found that suddenly the whole French coast had become covered with cloud and fog. No fewer than 11 machines were reported missing. During the course of the evening 10 others turned up one at a time. They had had to go separately far inland to look for somewhere to put down. Most of them had eventually found an airfield but one had had to make a belly landing.

Pilots on a fighter Staffel lived on their nerves to the same extent as those on an RAF fighter squadron. Both were subject to the sudden harsh blare of loudspeakers ordering them to scramble, but on a German airfield at the Channel coast these seemed to be even more intrusive than on the British aerodromes. The immediate effect was the same: a racing pulse, fear that had to be stifled instantly, and, for some, an irresistible urge to retch or vomit before sprinting to their aeroplanes.

One German pilot's recollection of the call to arms on a typical summer's day describes the ubiquitous means by which the summons came. ''They were everywhere, the loudspeakers: in the mess, naturally, in the crew room, in the sleeping quarters, on the trees around the airfield. Even in the lavatories. No-one

within the precincts of the aerodrome could escape their din. They didn't say anything welcome but they said it loudly and made the buildings shake."

For the most part, the first sounds were the rasping of the officer on duty in the Operations Room testing his microphone, which brought the ground crews to their feet. In the mess, cards were flung down on the table, spoons were let fall into soup plates, chairs were overturned. But sometimes the message was an anticlimax: "Loudspeaker test. Report back if understood." With customary Teutonic thoroughness this was repeated several times a day, to check that no corner of the establishment failed to hear every broadcast. Mostly the words that echoed about the camp were the equally familiar, "Attention! Attention! Action alarm!"

This anonymous pilot reminisces; "One fine summer day in particular remains firmly in my memory; not only because it was one of my first days after joining a Gruppe that lived in waiting for just such a summons, but also because it was in all respects typical. We were having lunch in the Gruppe staff mess when the loudspeakers barked at us. 'Damn!' the Gruppe Kommandeur grumbled, dropping the fork that was half way to his mouth. His chair clattered against the wooden wall of the hut and a moment later he was outside and rushing to his aircraft with giant strides."

He followed the Kommandeur towards the sandbagged blast pens where the aeroplanes were kept hidden and from which they could taxi straight out onto the field. By the time a pilot reached his machine the mechanics were already standing by ready to help him to put on his helmet and plug in the radio lead, fasten the safety harness, start the engine and close the cockpit canopy. The order to start up had not been given yet and everybody wondered if it was another false alarm. But the loudspeaker bellowed, "Attention! Attention! Targets at 3,000 metres near Dunkirk. No take-off yet."

This pilot, though not detailed for the mission, was as highly charged with vicarious emotions as the others were with the reality. He knew the feelings of those who were sitting in their cockpits with all their thoughts and expectations concentrated on the imminence of combat. Foremost in their minds was the hope that the take-off would not be cancelled. The moments of uncertainty ended abruptly; "Attention! Attention! Numbers One and Three Staffeln led by Hauptmann Pingel take off immediately. Instructions; barrier patrol in the area." Even before the message ended the starter motors began to whirr.

The first of the Bf 109s rolled out of concealment in the woods and presently from all around the half-

Right: There were many individual variations in flying equipment, and this is a 1st Lieutenant with a lightweight blue-grey tunic over later pattern flying overalls. His helmet has the standard throat microphone units which can just be seen at his collar, although the straps are not in place. A leather helmet and high-altitude oxygen assembly lies at his feet together with the regulator valve.

circle of pens the rest converged on the down-wind end of the grass runway. They reminded the onlooker of a swarm of angry hornets lusting for the fray. "An overpowering impression," he remembers.

The weather was ideal for an enemy attack. Visibility was clear for 5 to 6 miles (8-10km) and great clumps of cloud, among which the stalking aeroplanes could hide, were scattered all over the sky. While the Messerchmitts circled their base, making height and getting into formation before setting course, the noise of heavy flak reached the airfield from the nearby coast.

Those who had to stay behind gathered in the Operations Room, where they could not only follow the track of their own two Staffeln but also listen through headphones to the exchange of radio messages. In this way they formed a clear idea of how accurately the Central Operations Room was directing the fighters towards the incoming raid. They enjoyed the casual humour in the comments that crackled briefly between aircraft, the cryptic wit of fighter pilots of any nation. The distance between the adversaries narrowed until a warning "Red Indians" came as unemotionally as the most prosaic comment; as unemphatically as someone waiting at a bus stop might say, "Here's one coming now"; as unhurriedly as at that same moment some RAF fighter pilot must have been reporting, "Bandits". Then followed what one of the listeners in the Gruppe Operations Room described as, "a lively brawl punctuated by brief radio flashes that told little except that hectic things were happening".

Presently the drone of returning 109s reached the airfield. The first one already had its undercarriage down when it came in sight and made a neat landing. Next came Hauptmann Pingel, his bullet-holed machine wobbling with damaged control surfaces. The last to land arrived with a swoop, to soar into a loop and a roll over the centre of the field. A few minutes later the hornets were back in their nests. The petrol bowsers came trundling along, the mechanics gathered around their pilot to hear what he had to say about the way his machine had performed and what in particular needed attention, before they set to work on the engine, the airframe, the electrics and the armament. They hadn't had lunch yet. Food would have to wait until the servicing had been done.

The Kommandeur went out to meet Pingel, who was coming towards the Operations Room, and congratulate him on the two aircraft the 109s had shot down. "But Feldwebel Hoffman is missing," he added.

"What? That's impossible." Pingel looked incredulous. "How could it have happened that he let himself get shot down? What was I doing?"

He was obviously concerned and blaming himself. He strove always to place his formation in the most advantageous position before engaging the enemy. He listened to his pilots' account of the fight, as always and, reconstructing it in his mind, wondered aloud if he had made some mistake. He had not seen the two British machines go down. He wandered off on his own, his face pale and his brow furrowed, listening for the sound of a Bf 109 coming in to land. Nobody intruded on his thoughts. Then a messenger came running from the Operations Room, panted up to him, saluted and said "Sir . . . Feldwebel Hoffman is all right . . .

Above the end of the final mission for this Messerschmitt Bf 110 as it lands in the sea. The force of the impact can be gauged by the fact that in the lower picture it can be seen that the propeller blades are bent.

Left: Ask a fighter pilot to sit on his hands and he goes dumb! Luftwaffe ace Helmut Wick of Jadgeschwader 2, the third German pilot to attain fifty victories, demonstrates his methods in the time-honoured manner to a pair of enthusiastic young Bf 109 pilots.

his fuel supply packed up . . . blocked feedpipe, he thinks . . . and he had to make a force landing."

"Well, now, isn't that exactly what I said must have happened?" And Pingel returned to the mess to resume his interrupted lunch. Everything looked better on a full stomach. The Staffel had two more victories to add to its record. The day was turning out quite well.

The hours passed quietly until it was almost time for coffee break, when an attack alarm violated the torpor of the warm afternoon. The pilots and mechanics pelted towards their aircraft while the voice that had roused them chuntered on with instructions on the height to make, where to form up and the course to steer. Once again the hunt was on. The wild rush began. Parachute on . . . snatch helmet from the hand that offered it . . . hoist yourself into the cockpit . . .

plug in radio and oxygen . . . the starter whines . . . smoke and a lick of flame belch from the exhausts . . . the aircraft vibrates, the engine roars, the propeller becomes a blur . . .

"Attention! Attention! Alarm cancelled."

Men look at their watches and at the sky. Rain clouds are spreading. With a little luck they'll get off early and be able to spend the sort of evening they look forward to but don't often have the chance to enjoy. Coffee cups are refilled. The Kommandeur turns to his adjutant. "Go and ask Geschwader Headquarters if they can justify keeping us at readiness with the weather closing in like this." The adjutant mentally composes a more tactful request. The door has scarcely closed behind him when "Attack alarm!" disrupts the pleasant mood of expectation that release for the day is imminent.

"This time it is a British bomber formation that has crossed the coast somewhere in another sector and looks to be coming our way. At midday that would have been wonderful news. But since the weather had changed meanwhile, it will be sheer luck if we find the raid, which is still a long way off."

While the fighters were probing around between cloud layers, looking for the enemy, two Blenheim bombers flew over the airfield low enough to identify without field glasses. Sweat formed on the duty officer's brow as he telephoned the information to

Below: The Luftwaffe fighter pilot's life vest and one man dinghy are shown here. In the early days of the Battle, the German air/sea rescue facilities were superior to those of RAF Fighter Command.

Geschwader HQ. "Where were our own fighters? Were we going to be bombed? Then we heard someone say he'd spotted the bombers at the coast, but the weather was deteriorating there. Before our chaps could attack, the flak opened fire. A Blenheim was hit and crashed near the beach in shallow water." The fighters were recalled.

The penultimate message that the loudspeakers broadcast was, "Staff Flight and Numbers One and Two Staffeln released. Number Three remain at readiness."

Above: Exuberantly, German pilots gather round their leader after a successful mission. The yellow nose, adopted for instant identification in the confusion of a dogfight, is clearly seen here.

It wasn't long before the next good news came. "The whole Gruppe may stand down."

Now for dinner and then into the nearest town to beat it up a bit.

Anyone on a fighter station in southern England at that period would have felt at home in this atmosphere. For RAF pilots the most evident difference would have been the lack of early warning by radar of the enemy's approach and of an efficient control and reporting system. Luftwaffe fighter pilots were subject to many more false alarms than RAF pilots were and kept in greater suspense from uncertainty during the long periods of waiting between scrambles because of it.

August 18, 1940, is often described as Fighter Command's hardest day in the Battle of Britain. The general impression of such a day's fighting is of the almost ceaseless embroilment throughout the day of every pilot on the Battle Order and a huge number of individual claims of victories. The diary kept by Hauptmann Kramer, Technical Officer of No III Gruppe of JG26 for six days ending on that date, puts the effort of a typical Gruppe, which corresponded with an RAF wing, in perspective.

"**13th.** Two patrols in the Dover area and along the coast. Escort for air-sea rescue aircraft and S-boats (*schnell*, or fast boats, known to the British, for some reason, as E-boats).

"**14th.** One operation over Dover harbour, escorting three Gruppen of Ju 87s. Shot down six enemy aircraft; Major Galland, Oberleutnant Münchberg, Oblt Beyer, Oblt Schöpfel, Leutnant Bürschgens, Lt Mülle-Dühe, one each.

"**15th.** Four escort missions for KG1 and 2. Attacks on Hawkinge and Maidstone. Combat with Spitfires over Boulogne. Gruppe shot down 18. No 7 Staffel got

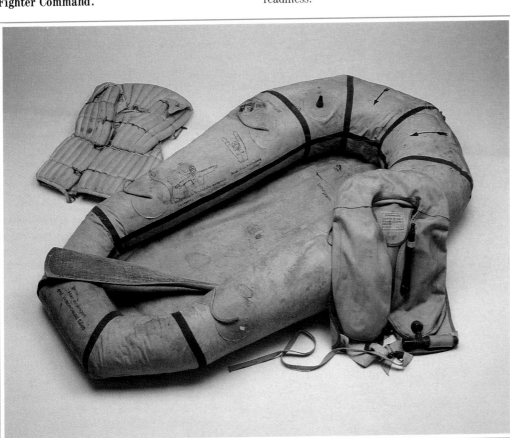

six: Oblt Beyer and Lt Bürschgens two each; one each for Lt Blume and Lt Müller-Düche.

"**16th.** At one hour's readiness. One scramble for Spitfires over Calais. One shot down by Lt Müller-Dühe.

"**17th.** At 30 minutes readiness. Aircraft serviced. III/JG26's total victories to August 15, 119.

"**18th.** Two operations north of London. Ten victories: Oblt Schöpfel four; Oblt Sprick one; Lt Bürschgens two; Lt Ebeling one; two by No 8 Staffel. The Gruppe flew an offensive patrol over North Weald and Hornchurch. Lt Müller-Dühe was shot down. Lt Blume is missing.''

On the 18th, Major Galland was absent, summoned by Goering to an interview. His second-in-command, Oberleutnant Schöpfel, accordingly led III Gruppe that day, and gave the following report of an engagement in the Folkestone-Canterbury area.

"Suddenly I found a squadron of Hurricanes below me in the usual British formation of tight three, which were climbing in a spiral. I circled about 3,300ft (1,000m) above them. Then I saw a pair of Hurricanes weaving behind the formation, on guard against attack from astern. I waited until they were curving north-westwards from Folkestone, then attacked out of sun and below.'' According to his Combat Report he shot down both the weavers without the others being aware of it. "Now I was beneath a third machine. I fired a short burst. This aircraft likewise fell apart. The British flew on, having noticed nothing. I positioned myself under a fourth machine. This time I had to get closer. When I pressed the firing button the Hurricane was so close to me that fragments from it hit

Below: This collection of miscellaneous and navigation equipment includes various manual disc computers and an early 'moving map display' using rolled map sheets. A fighter reflector sight is top left.

my aircraft. Oil covered my cockpit so thickly that I couldn't see, and after two minutes of action had to break off.''

At that time the Bf 109E had two cannon, each with 60 rounds, of which he still had 15 left.

"After I had broken off,'' Schöpfel continues, "Oberleutnant Sprick led No 8 Staffel in an attack on the British, who were now aware that Germans were right behind them and dived. However, Sprick managed to shoot down two more. I think this was the first time in this war that a pilot shot down four British aircraft

Above: The end of the road for another Zerstoerer as a Bf 110C of I/ZG 2 force lands in a French field. ZG 2 was the most unsuccessful of the Bf 110 units, producing not a single experte.

on the same sortie. Looking back at those anxious moments, it was not very difficult. My shots must have hit the right place, so that there was no time for the others to be warned. These four brought my score to a total of 12.''

No II Gruppe habitually flew at a maximum of 26,000 to 30,000ft (8,000-9,000m), where lone Spitfires were sure to be found. On August 13, II JG 26 were at 26,000ft (8,000m) with I JG26 below them. They were approaching the coast with the cliffs of Dover in sight, but to the west spread an unbroken bank of cloud 6,500ft (2,000m) high. The Kommandeur, Hauptmann Ebbinghausen, flew through it.

In his diary, Leutnant Borris wrote: "Low on our left a formation appeared, apparently enemy fighters, by the suspicious look of their flying in threes. Low on our right someone reported another formation, towards which our Kommandeur turned. I was flying in the Staff Flight with März and Leibing. Ahead and beneath us flew three machines that I recognised as Hurricanes. Apparently the Kommandeur hadn't seen these, as he was watching the two big formations which were still some five kilometres in front of us. I dived . . . 400 metres . . . 300 . . . 200. I had the Tommy on the left in my sights. Would the other two turn on me? My concentration was stretched to breaking point. One hundred metres . . . 70 metres, the Hurricane grew big. Now! It swerved aside. I stopped shooting. It was on fire. I hauled my machine round in a climbing turn to rejoin my flight. In front of me a Bf 109 was firing at a Hurricane, but couldn't turn as tightly as it. I side-

slipped down on the Hurricane . . . 70 metres . . . 50. My four machineguns hurled bullets at it. Thick black smoke and flames belched from it. I broke upwards. A little lower a Hurricane had spotted me. Climb! The Tommy couldn't keep up with me. He gave up and swung away. Where were my friends? I couldn't see anything. From above and behind an aeroplane was hurtling towards me. In an instant I rolled onto my back and disappeared.''

Borris flew home alone, striving to stay in cloud until he reached the mouth of the Somme, and arrived cheerfully over the airfield. On his landing approach the 109 dived to the right. He quickly raised the undercarriage, climbed to about 3,300ft (1,000m) and tried again. Once more the aileron stuck and he found himself about to hit the ground. He would have to land without flaps. März and Leibing landed after him. Unteroffizier Wemhöner had reported during the combat that he had been shot down (he was taken prisoner). The whole of No 6 Staffel was missing and four pilots of No 5 Staffel. They had lost their way in thick cloud and landed in the Reims and Verdun areas.

On May 19 II Gruppe had lost their Kommandeur, Hauptmann Herwig Knüppel, and on the July 24 his successor, the dashing Hauptmann Erich Noack. On August 16 Borris recorded that 20 aircraft of the Gruppe were half way across the Channel on their way to carry out an offensive patrol in the area of Dover and Folkestone, under the leadership of Hauptmann Karl Ebbighausen, when 20 Spitfires jumped them. He was at 23,000ft (7,000m), line abreast with the Gruppe Kommandeur and Eckart Roch while Leibing and März

Below: Various flying helmets (from left to right); leather winter helmet, canvas helmet and lightweight net helmet with oxygen mask and shatterproof sun glasses. Standard issue goggles are below.

flew behind. To their left ahead and above were the Spitfires. During the dogfight seven Spitfires engaged the five Bf 109s of the staff flight. In the confusion Borris saw a 109 some distance astern being attacked by a Spitfire. The 109 reacted swiftly with a diving turn. The pilot was Waldi März, whom he had been unable to warn, because his radio was faulty. März landed with 20 bullet holes and an overheated engine. Borris was able to confirm a victory for Eckart Roch.

Above: A Heinkel crew stroll away from their aircraft after completing a night mission. British night defences were not regarded as particularly hazardous during 1940, although they later became very effective.

He says that how Ebbinghausen was shot down when the flight was attacked by ''only seven Spitfires'' remained a mystery. Ebbinghausen, he points out, had fought in Spain and was highly experienced.

There is no mystery about it: the Germans had met more than their match. The pilots on each side respected their opponents' courage and skill and acknowledged the quality of their respective aircraft. No RAF pilot conceded that the Bf 109 was superior to the Spitfire, although many regarded it as equal. Among the Luftwaffe, on the contrary, there was a host of Spitfire admirers, among whom was Galland. This infuriated Goering when the Commander-in-Chief visited his fighter Geschwader on the Channel coast in the first week of September. Goering first asked Mölders what he most wanted and nodded approvingly at the reply: ''A new series of Me 109s with more powerful engines.'' He then put the same question to Galland, whose reply, ''A Geschwader of Spitfires'', threw him into such a fury that he walked away without comment.

The only advantage that the Bf 109 had over the Spitfire at that time was petrol injection instead of a carburettor. This meant that when a German pilot rolled his fighter onto its back and dived vertically his petrol supply did not falter. When a British pilot did the same manoeuvre, there was an interval of a couple of seconds during which his petrol flow was interrupted: sufficient time for the enemy to put enough distance

between them to ensure his escape. Later, when petrol injection was introduced to the Rolls Royce Merlin engine, the Bf 109 pilots suffered some unpleasant shocks.

"My most successful day," says Oberleutnant Heinz Ebeling, who was shot down and taken prisoner on November 5, 1940, "was August 31." After a long duel with a Hurricane he managed to shoot it down, but discovered that his radiator was leaking. "From well to the north of London I got as far as 10 kilometres out over the Channel beyond Dover, accompanied by my Number Two, before I had to bale out. I had transmitted on the radio for my position to be fixed and an hour and a half later a Do 18 flying boat fished me out. At the sea rescue centre in Boulogne where I was given a beer glass full of cognac and some pea soup, a car came to fetch me back to the airfield. It was then about 1400hrs. I flew on the Gruppe's next mission and bagged two more Hurricanes. That evening I met our Geschwader Kommodore, Major Galland, who told me that Generalfeldmarschall Kesselring had awarded me a goblet of honour." In the Great War, German pilots were awarded a goblet for each victory and the custom of awarding such a trophy for special feats survived. "Shortly thereafter Goering presented me with it personally. The victory I had scored that morning was my thirteenth, but it had brought me good luck!"

Equal with Galland in the respect and admiration with which he was regarded and in which his memory is held, was Werner Mölders. He was the first fighter pilot in the world to surpass Manfred von Richthofen's Great War record of 80 victories and the first to reach a score of 100 enemy aircraft destroyed. Both these figures, however, included the 14 he shot down in Spain, where he was the Luftwaffe's highest scorer, which were a lot easier to achieve than sending down a French or British fighter.

At the age of 27, when he took command of JG53, Mölders was already a man of considerable maturity of character and high principles. An ardent Catholic, he was of a serious nature and became known at once to the members of his Geschwader as "Vati", "Daddy". He fought his first combat of the war on September 20, 1939, when he shot down a French Air Force Curtiss, a week before being appointed to lead No III Gruppe of JG53. On June 5, 1941, by which time he

Below: Oberst Werner Mölders, as depicted on the cover of "Signal". One of the great fighter leaders of all time, he once remarked that if Adolf Galland wished to be the Luftwaffe's Richthofen, he was content to be its Boelcke.

had increased his score to 25 (11 in the current war), he was shot down by a French pilot, as has been described in the chapter on the prelude to the Battle of Britain, and taken prisoner. His incarceration was short. Two weeks later France capitulated and he was given command of JG51, to become the youngest Geschwaderkommodore in the Luftwaffe.

He became at once involved in the fighting over England and is regarded as the Luftwaffe's outstanding figure in the Battle of Britain. By October 29 he had flown 208 operational sorties and added 54 kills to the 14 he had made in Spain. His logbook shows the intensity of his activities during the second half of the Battle of Britain.

Perhaps more typical of his character, than the days when he was out hunting the RAF, was the occasion at the end of the Battle of Britain when his friend Oberleutnant Claus was shot down in the Thames estuary. Mölders personally gave orders to the air-sea rescue service to begin searching for him without delay, before going up himself to look for some sign of his friend. No-one on the Geschwader HQ staff could reason with him. Accompanied by Leutnant Eberle he dashed back over the Channel and made a fruitless search all over the Thames estuary, where the 109 must have sunk long ago. During this dangerous search he was totally distraught and took no heed of where he went: a wonderful target for the RAF. But he lived to return to base.

In May 1941 Werner Mölders, at the age of 28, was promoted to General of Fighters. By then he had 101 victories, not counting the 14 in Spain. On November 22, 1941, he was killed when an He 111 in which he was a passenger crashed. The 29-year-old Adolf

Below: An anonymous (and no wonder) German bomber pilot complete with oxygen mask held very firmly in place. Compare his mask, helmet and goggles with those shown on page 159.

WERNER MÖLDERS' LOGBOOK

SORTIE NUMBER	DATE	TIME	AIRCRAFT TYPE	VICTORY NUMBER	PLACE
161	6.9.40	1440	1 Spit	33	Folkestone
165	7.9.40	1830	1 Spit	34	London
166	9.9.40	1845	1 Spit	35	London
167	1.9.40	1705	1 Hurri	36	S.E. of London
169	4.9.40	1740	1 Spit	37	S.W. of London
173	16.9.40	0850	1 Hurri	38	London
179	20.9.40	1234	2 Spits	39,40	Dungeness
180	27.9.40	1700	1 Spit	41	Maidstone
181	28.9.40	1500	1 Spit	42	Littlestone
193	11.10.40	1230	1 Spit	43	Folkestone
195	12.10.40	1040	1 Hurri	44	Liquizue
		1045	1 Hurri	45	Cauberberg
196		1412	1 Hurri	46	Dungeness
197	15.10.40	0915	1 Hurri	47	Kneilig
201	17.10.40	1625	1 Spit	48	London
204	22.10.40	1510	3 Hurris	49,50,51	Maidstone
205	25.10.40	1045	1 Spit	52	N.W. of Dover
206		1310	1 Spit	53	Margate
208	29.10.40	1355	1 Hurri	54	Dungeness

Above: Major Adolf Galland pictured shortly after being appointed as Kommodore of JG 26. Having 13 victories at the end of June, he passed the fifty mark late in October, just behind Werner Mölders.

Below: Jadgeschwader 27, at first based near Cherbourg, was among the first units to sport the new oversea camouflage. The airborne Bf 109 also bears the white scissors insignia behind the cockpit.

Galland succeeded him in Command of the Luftwaffe fighter arm.

Galland, who became Germany's most famous fighter pilot, had qualified for his wings in 1934. In April 1935 he was posted to JG132 (later JG2), the ''Richthofen'' Geschwader, first fighter Geschwader of the new Luftwaffe. In 1937 he went to Spain as a member of the Legion Kondor that was fighting on the Fascist side in the civil war. His unit, Jagdstaffel 3, flew the obselete He 51 biplane while the Republicans were equipped with the greatly superior American Curtiss and the Russian Polikarpov. Hence the Staffel that Galland commanded was compelled to limit its activity to strafing in support of the ground troops, which denied him the chance to shoot down any enemy aircraft. In May 1939 Werner Mölders took over the Staffel.

While Galland was in Spain he compiled a report on close support based on his 300 operational sorties. The Air Staff, whose thinking had turned to a new use of aircraft, dive bombing, to which ground attack was closely related, was much impressed and posted him to the Air Ministry. This was not what he had expected and he strove incessantly to return to flying.

In 1939 he was given command of a Staffel in a close support Gruppe equipped with the biplane Hs 123 dive bomber. This unit was the first to put into effect the technique of dive bombing as an important element of Blitzkrieg. Its effect was devastating. The lessons learned in the Spanish Civil War paid off. Galland was heavily engaged in the onslaught. In 27 days he flew up to four sorties a day and was awarded the Iron Cross Second Class. As a recognised expert in this form of aerial warfare, it seemed most probable that he would spend his whole career practising it. He had become too valuable and his reputation now stood in the way of his unwavering desire to be a fighter pilot. It was always in his mind that two months after Mölders took over command of his Staffel in Spain it converted to Bf 109s: and Mölders had scored 14 victories there.

It was obvious to him that henceforth he would fly only second- and third-class aircraft and never do what he considered to be real air fighting, unless he took drastic action. He resorted to a ruse and reported sick with alleged rheumatism. The Gruppe medical officer referred him to higher authority. The next doctor to examine him was a friend and understood the mentality of young pilots. He reported that Galland must not fly in an open cockpit; which meant automatic transfer to modern aeroplanes. Shortly afterwards Galland joined JG27, commanded by Oberstleutnant Max Ibel; but, to his disappointment, he was made adjutant, which would involve trayfuls of paperwork and leave little time for flying.

It was not until May 12, 1940 that, he made his first kill: a Belgian Air Force Hurricane. On the same sortie he shot down a second and, later in the day, a third. He says, ''I took all this quite naturally, as a matter of course. There was nothing special about it. I had not felt any excitment and I was certainly not elated by my success. I had something approaching a twinge of conscience. An excellent weapon and luck had been on my side.'' These sentiments were often expressed by British pilots, too.

THE BATTLE of Britain, which was to prove so decisive and far-reaching in its outcome, was one which neither side wanted to fight. Even Hitler, on whose personal orders, embodied in a Directive dated July 16, 1940, the Battle was launched, had hoped to avoid it. And how, in retrospect, he must have wished that he had succeeded in doing so; for the Battle of Britain was his first failure and it turned out to be the precursor of a long run of declining fortune leading eventually to calamitous defeat.

After the Blitzkreig which, in the course of a few springtime weeks, brought about the defeat and occupation of Denmark, Norway, Holland, Belgium and France, Hitler not only hoped but also believed that Britain would sue for peace on the best terms she could get. The Führer, in fact, would probably have made those terms superficially attractive. For about a month he was, so to speak, sitting by the telephone waiting for Britain to call. He waited in vain. And so, early in July, he issued his Directive:

"As England, in spite of her hopeless military position, has so far shown herself unwilling to come to any compromise, I have decided to begin preparations for and, if necessary, to carry out the invasion of England.

"This operation is dictated by the necessity to eliminate Great Britain as a base from which the war against Germany can be fought. If necessary the island will be occupied . . . I therefore issue the following orders:

1. The landing operation must be a surprise crossing on a broad front extending approximately from Ramsgate to a point west of the Isle of Wight . . . The preparations . . . must be concluded by the middle of August.
2. The following preparations must be undertaken to make a landing in England possible:
   (a) The English air force must be eliminated to such an extent that it will be incapable of putting up any substantial opposition to the invading troops . . ."

Note that the first priority was the elimination of the RAF. In issuing that invasion order — code-named "Operation Sealion" — Hitler was backed and supported by the assurance of Reichsmarshall Goering that the Luftwaffe could bring about the required defeat and elimination of Fighter Command. There is no doubt that if Goering's two operational commanders — Generalfeldmarshall Albert Kesselring, commanding Luftflotte 2, and Generalfeldmarshall Hugo Sperrle, commanding Luftflotte 3 — had been given a choice they would have opted for delay. Although the German air force had carried all before it in the spring campaign, it had not done so without suffering heavy losses. Different authorities give different figures, but the total would have been at least 2,000, including those lost during the campaign, but not due to enemy action. Certainly the number of bombers available at the beginning of July was still some 15 per cent less than at the beginning of March.

Across the channel the two main operational commanders, Dowding and Park were also at the head of a force which had by no means recovered from the part it had been compelled to play in the Battle of France

BATTLE SUMMARY

Group Captain Sir Hugh Dundas
CBE. DSO. DFC. DL.

"Victory in the Battle of Britain was achieved by a narrow margin; how narrow, very few people realize. Its achievement should have brought just reward to the two commanders who had been the architects, but for Dowding there was the dubious appointment to serve on a mission to the United States, and for Park, command of a training Group. Dowding and Park won the Battle of Britain, but they lost the battle of words that followed with the result that they, like Winston Churchill at the post-war polls, were cast aside in their finest hour."

Air Commodore Al *Deere*
CBE. DSO. OBE. DFC.

Below: The Führer and his Reichmarschall acknowledge the cheering crowds from the balcony of the Reichschancelry in Berlin on July 6, 1940. In the event, the celebrations proved to be rather premature.

and its aftermath. Dowding's determined efforts in resisting pressures upon him to commit more and more of his Command's precious fighters to the Battle of France are part of popular history. It may therefore come as a surprise to many to learn that every one of his squadrons, with the exception only of three based in Scotland, became engaged, to a greater or lesser extent, in that spring campaign. The few weeks of respite following the completion of the Dunkirk evacuation were used to good advantage to rebuild the Command's strength in terms of both men and aircraft. But Dowding and Park must both have prayed for the longest possible postponement of the onslaught.

Dowding and Park — they were the key men from start to finish. It is impossible to over-emphasise the dominating as well as the crucial role which those officers played in the Battle. It was fortunate indeed for Britain that two such remarkable men stood in the breach at the time. It is no less fortunate that, by and large, they were allowed to get on with it, to do it their way, without interference either from the Air Council or from Government. It was also perhaps no less fortunate for our country that Kesselring and Sperrle were by contrast subject to the constant intervention of their Commander-in-Chief, Goering, and also, at a critical time and in a critical way, of Hitler himself.

An earlier chapter of this book describes Fighter Command's infrastructure and organisation, built up in the two or three years leading to 1940, and its astonishingly complete and effective communications system, involving a vast and exclusive telephone and teleprinter network — rightly described by John Terraine as "a magnificently quick and secret achievement of the Post Office" — which enabled the Dowding system to function effectively. And, of course, it *was* the Dowding system, very much and very personally the Commander-in-Chief's own creation.

Future generations of British people should never forget what they owe to the perspicacity and skill of this retiring, unglamorous, outwardly rather grumpy man. All too often history teaches us the sorry lessons to be learned from the experience of having the wrong

men in the wrong place at the critical time. In the case of Dowding, exactly the reverse is true. And he had been in the right places for an astonishingly long time; for his appointment as Commander-in-Chief of Fighter Command, in 1936, had been preceded by a four-year stint as a Member of the Air Council with a role which enabled him to exercise decisive influence in defining the specification and development of the planes with which in due course the Battle was to be fought.

In Keith Park, the 48-year-old New Zealander, who had first fought for Britain as an artillery soldier at Gallipoli and on the Somme, before gaining a Com-

Left: Air Chief Marshal Dowding, to whom much of the credit for the British victory in the summer of 1940 must go. The strength of purpose of this austere man has been underrated by many post-war commentators.

Below: A Spitfire passes below a Dornier Do 17Z. The position of the wing roundels on the latter indicate that this German archive picture is probably faked. The only archive information given is ''Sommer 1940''.

mission and transferring to the Royal Flying Corps, Dowding had a subordinate who was totally committed to the implementation of his Commander-in-Chief's plans and *modus operandi*. To quote Terraine once more: ''Dowding controlled the Battle from day to day; Park controlled it from hour to hour.'' It would, I believe, be impossible to over-emphasise the skill, perception and sensitivity with which that hour-to-hour control — so often, as the drama developed, hours involving tremendous stress and momentous decisions based on incomplete information — was exercised by a superb commander whose name is virtually unknown to the British public today.

The detailed tactics of the Battle of Britain have been excellently and expertly described by my old friend and comrade, Johnnie Johnson. I will not go over that ground again, but will try to pick out and illustrate the main moves and factors which, in the end, proved decisive.

The Battle is deemed, for the purposes of history, to have begun on July 10. Its first phase, as has already been described, was fought out mainly over the Channel and along the south east coast of England. For the Germans it was a kind of probing operation, combined with a genuine attempt to disrupt the passage of Channel convoys and to damage the harbours along their routes. But that limitation in the nature of this phase of the attack was probably not evident at all to most observers at the time. The ferocity of the engagements between Royal Air Force and Luftwaffe was clear for all to see. To the watching world, as well as to the people of Britain, it was obvious that the first moves in the intended subjugation of our islands had been set in hand.

What, then, were the reactions of Dowding and Park? They were cautious and limited. both men believed deeply that their primary role was to defend the country against the attack of the main German bomber force, when it came. Those bombers had to destroy certain key targets if Hitler's purpose was to be achieved. Enemy activity in this opening phase did not, for the most part, fall within that category and so Dowding and Park, determined to avoid to the greatest possible extent losses in fighter-versus-fighter combat, kept their response to a minimum. Above all, Dowding stolidly refused to transfer squadrons from Nos. 12 and 13 Groups to reinforce No. 11 Group, although he did press forward with all possible despatch the establishment of No. 10 Group on Park's right flank, a move which was to pay priceless dividends in the next and critical phase of the Battle.

That phase was initiated in the beginning of August, though its full force and fury were not apparent until the middle of that month. Once again Hitler gave the order, personally, in his Directive Number 17, issued on August 1, which stated that the Luftwaffe should ''use all forces at its disposal to destroy the British Air Force as quickly as possible''. Seven days later Goer-

Left: Although titular head of the Luftwaffe, Goering was more interested in personal aggrandisement than in solid military achievement, a trend reflected in his spectacular uniforms and accoutrements.

ing followed this up with his own personal order to his squadrons. This stated that "within a short period you will wipe the British Air Force from the sky".

The day chosen for the true initiation of that process, after some delays caused partly by adverse weather, was August 13. But the first truly major assault came two days later, when the Luftwaffe flew nearly 1,800 sorties, aimed very specifically at Fighter Command — its airfields, its ground installations, its radar stations and, of course, its aircraft and pilots as they were scrambled to intercept the invading air fleets. For the first and last time in the Battle a large-scale attack was also launched against the north east of England. It was carried out by bombers of Luftflotte 5, which crossed the North Sea from their bases in Scandinavia escorted by twin-engined Bf 110s. They were met and destroyed in large numbers by squadrons from Nos. 12 and 13 Groups which Goering, perhaps, had imagined would by now have been diverted to the Battle in the south east.

Seventy six German planes were destroyed that day, according to figures assembled from records which became available after the war, for the loss of 35 of our own fighters. But our own most serious and dangerous losses were in the form of damage on the ground. Further onslaughts against Fighter Command followed daily, reaching a peak of ferocity on August 18. That was the day when Kenley, a key fighter base just a few miles south of London, received 100 enemy bombs, including direct hits on its operations room, where the controlling staff, including a large number of WAAFs, displayed a degree of heroism and fortitude which fully matched that of the airmen they were directing into battle.

But if Kenley suffered most, nearly all Park's major bases, as well as others outside No. 11 Group, came under attack that day and his pilots were stretched to the limit in the air. Losses were severe; more than 70 fighters were put out of action, about half of them damaged beyond repair; a substantial number of other RAF planes of various types were also destroyed or damaged on the ground; and the communications network which enabled Dowding's system of defence to operate so effectively, beginning at the radar stations standing exposed around the coastline, was also put under great strain. In my book "Flying Start", I summarise this phase of the Battle, as follows:

"By the end of the first week in September the policy was beginning to pay off. Day after sunlit day an average of one thousand German airplanes came over. Dawn after chilly dawn the weary British pilots assembled at their dispersal points and waited quietly for the telephone call which would send some of them to death, even before breakfast. Night after weary night the reckoning was made and though the advantage was constantly in Britain's favour and though no doubt the German pilots were almost as bone-weary as our own and the Luftwaffe's morale must have been severely affected by the daily loss of dozens of crews and the grisly spectacle of many more aircraft returning riddled by bullets and soaked in blood — yet the steamroller technique was beginning to tell against Dowding and England.

"The supply of pilots began to dry up. Some were

"On the other hand, the pilot position was critical. The position in which 54 Squadron found itself towards the end of August, particularly in relation to shortage of leaders, illustrates the point, which is confirmed by the History of the Royal Air Force in these words: 'By the opening week of September Dowding's squadrons had, on the average, only sixteen operational pilots out of their full complement of twenty-six.' When we consider quality as well as numbers, the gravity of the pilot position becomes even more apparent. The newcomers, though magnificent material, did not match their predecessors in flying experience nor in their knowledge of the technicalities of air fighting."

Air Commodore Al Deere
CBE. DSO. OBE. DFC.

Above: A Heinkel He 111 unloads "somewhere over England". In this aircraft the bombs are carried nose upwards and released tail first. In this picture they can be seen toppling to come right side up.

shot down two or three times, but, escaping injury, returned to the battle. Others were killed before they had fired a shot. Most survived a few days before falling in the fury of the fight, either to their death or to a period of convalescence from their wounds. Dowding could not rotate his squadrons fast enough to keep pace with the losses. Squadrons in the south became depleted before others, taken out of the line to re-form, could build up their strength again. Dowding had to take experienced pilots from the squadrons which were resting and re-forming, in order to plug the gaps in other squadrons, which should really have been taken out of the line. It was a policy of desperation and it could not last for long. In the darkness of that crisis it may well have seemed to our fifty-eight-year old commander that it was a problem without a solution.

"It might have been so, but for the intervention of Hitler himself, who now had one of those flashes of intuition which, from time to time, brought such dire

Below: The Spitfire Mk II entered squadron service during August, too late to have any real effect on the Battle. It incorporated various improvements including the Merlin Mk XII and constant speed propeller.

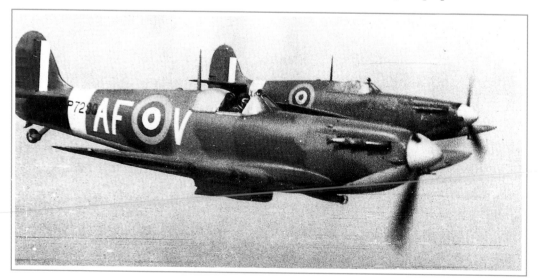

consequences to his country. At the moment when the battle was in the balance, when the weight of Goering's strategy was coming close to success, when Fighter Command was near to breaking point — at that precise moment of crisis something else broke. It was Hitler's patience. The Führer spoke and Goering obeyed. The point and purpose of the German attack was diverted from the destruction of the RAF to the cowing and subjugation of London.

''It was the turning point. London burned; but Britain was saved.''

For those who want them, the statistics are all available now, honed down by careful historical research to fine limits of accuracy. Indeed, they are here between the covers of this book. They do no more or less, I believe, than support and illustrate my simplified account. They show that during the second half of August and the beginning of September the Royal Air Force was bleeding very severely. It was bleeding to the extent that its ability to prevent the Luftwaffe from achieving air superiority over south east England was slipping away. In other words, we were coming close to losing the Battle. And that was happening because the Germans continued relentlessly to focus their attack against Fighter Command, against its planes, its pilots, its airfields, its entire apparatus. For a time the flow of new pilots and new planes into Dowding's command fell short of the losses. And, in the squadrons, the survivors were suffering intense fatigue.

It is all too easy to over-simplify. But it really does seem obvious to me that if Hitler had not at that moment diverted the attack from the air defence system to London and other cities the outcome would most probably have been different. The move, however, did nothing to lessen the strain on Dowding, Park and their pilots. There was much hard air fighting still to come, including the day, September 15, which has long been marked and celebrated as ''Battle of Britain Day'';

Above: The two architects of victory. Air Chief Marshals Sir Keith Park (left), who commanded No.11 Group, and Fighter Command C-in-C Lord Dowding are seen at an anniversary celebration in 1946.

the day when Goering, obedient to his Fürher's command, threw every available bomber and fighter against London; the day when Churchill, watching the build-up of this huge enemy force and the response of our fighters as plotted on the table of the operations room at No.11 Group, turned to Park and asked: ''How many fighters have you left?'' and Park replied ''None, sir.''

And so it is only with hindsight that one can see clearly where the turning point came, for certainly it was not clear at the time, any more to those directly involved in the Battle than to the millions on the ground

who suffered from the daily and nightly bombings. But, although Operation Sealion was not officially postponed until early October, the real opportunity to invade, to activate the huge fleet of assorted vessels assembled across the Channel, had passed by mid-September. And from then on, Fighter Command's strength, instead of ebbing away, began to pick up again. The all-out assault of September 15 was repeated, twice, albeit on a reducing scale — on September 17 and 28. But, by then, although we did not know it at the time, the Battle had been won and lost. There was more fierce fighting to come in October, but it is significant that, after September 28, the German twin-engine bombers were withdrawn from daylight operations. A number of Bf 109s and 110s were converted to the fighter-bomber role. Their attacks were more than merely irritating and meant that the squadrons of No.11 Group were kept hard at it all through October; but they were not capable of completing the job which Goering had undertaken so confidently three months before.

In reviewing the course of this decisive battle it is impossible to avoid the one aspect of the RAF's conduct of it which gave rise to serious discordance. I refer to what came to be known as ''the Big Wing controversy''. The ''Big Wing'' in question was assembled by the Air Officer Commanding No.12 Group. Air Vice

> *''The Battle of Britain was a great period to have lived through, but I often wonder what would have happened if the German fighter ace Adolf Galland and his merry men had long range jettison tanks fitted to their aircraft to allow them rather more than fifteen minutes combat time over London. Together with their superior numbers, this would certainly have given them an even greater advantage, and the outcome of the Battle of Britain might have been very different.*
>
> *The momentous aerial combat fought in the Summer of 1940 was won by the inspiring leadership of Commander-in-Chief Fighter Command, Lord Dowding. His foresight in refusing to send further fighter squadrons to France against the wishes of Winston Churchill and his military advisers gave Britain the resources and breathing space to continue the war until victory was achieved.*
>
> *Although statues have been erected to Churchill, Mountbatten, Eisenhower and Montgomery in prominent places, it is ironic that nothing has been erected in honour of 'Stuffy' Dowding who was shamefully dismissed in October, 1940.''*
>
> **Wing Commander Paddy Barthropp**
> **DFC. AFC.**

Left: Although just after the Battle proper, the massive night raid on Coventry left an indelible mark on the British public. This view shows some of the terrible damage caused in the cathedral area of the city.

Above: Air Vice Marshal Trafford Leigh-Mallory commanded No.12 Group. An advocate of numbers, his "Big Wing" based on Duxford and led by Douglas Bader, became the cause of controversy both then and since.

Marshal Trafford Leigh-Mallory. The boundary between him and No.11 Group was only a few minutes flying time, by Spitfire or Hurricane, north of London, the Group's southernmost sector being at Duxford, a few miles south west of Cambridge. There, in late August, Leigh-Mallory assembled a force of three squadrons to operate as a single wing formation under the leadership of one of the RAF's most brilliant and courageous officers, Squadron Leader Douglas Bader. Early in September the strength was increased to five squadrons, three of Hurricanes and two of Spitfires. Day after day, as the Battle raged in the south over No.11 Group's area, this formidable force stood ready

at Duxford. It could only enter the Battle to the south, over No.11 Group's area, as and when so directed by Fighter Command and requested by No.11 Group. Frequently the request was made and there were several occasions when the Duxford Wing was in action.

The controversy arose because Leigh-Mallory insisted, in a rather vociferous and public manner, that his squadrons could have been used by Park to much greater and better effect. In short, he felt that he and his squadrons were deliberately excluded from the centre stage of the action. At the time it seemed to me, from the worm's eye view of a junior pilot officer, that Leigh-Mallory's attitude was justified. My own squadron frequently formed part of the Duxford Wing during September, having been withdrawn from No.11 Group to reform following very severe losses when flying from Kenley during the second half of August. And, indeed, quite often we did find ourselves sitting there on the ground while large-scale actions were taking place to the south of us.

I have thought about this question a great deal and studied it in some detail. My own interest in it is the greater because of my unbounded admiration of and affection for Douglas Bader, with whom I flew throughout the summer of 1941 when Fighter Command had turned from defence to attack. The broad conclusion I have come to is that the squadrons assembled at Duxford could have been used more effectively, but that the reason why they were not is to be found more in Leigh-Mallory's attitude than in Park's. It was essential that full control of the battle over London and the south east should rest with Park and that the squadrons made available to him from Nos.10 and 12 Groups should be fitted into his tactics, as they developed hour by hour and minute by minute.

There was a marked difference between the attitudes of Leigh-Mallory and Brand, his No.10 Group opposite number, in this regard. The latter unhesitatingly and unfailingly put his squadrons at Park's disposal and did so without reservation. Leigh-Mallory, on the other hand, having developed his theory about the usefulness of operating at Wing strength, sought to influence the

Below: Hurricanes of No.85 Squadron, led by Peter Townsend in the third aircraft from the left. 85 were in the thick of the fighting until the late stages of the Battle when they became a C category squadron.

way in which his squadrons should be used by No.11 Group, an attitude exemplified by his decision, already mentioned, to increase the strength and size of his Wing from three squadrons to five. That decision was undoubtedly made in the knowledge that Park was, to say the least, lacking in enthusiasm about the usefulness of a Big Wing in the circumstances in which he was fighting the Battle. And undoubtedly it reduced the Wing's flexibility and increased the time it took to get off the ground, assemble and reach the area where Park needed it. There was certainly no doubt about Bader's desire and determination to get to grips with the enemy. His leadership, given the inherent limitation of the Big Wing's usefulness in the circumstances of the Battle at the time, was, as always, inspirational. And there were occasions when Bader's "balbo" came together with the enemy with great effect. There were also occasions when No.12 Group's help was desperately needed and called for but failed to materialise as Park and his controllers required and this led to much bitterness and recrimination.

All of this resulted, I believe, more from a clash of strong and unbending personalities than anything else. And its bitterness was exacerbated when, the Battle of Britain having been won, and that great victory having been achieved essentially by Park's brilliant handling of Dowding's superb creation, the former was, in November, replaced by Leigh-Mallory as Commander of No.11 Group and the latter was put out to grass. And so those in No.12 Group, who had sometimes felt that they were being kept out of the Battle, perhaps because Park and No.11 Group wanted to "hog" it all, were inclined to crow; and those in No.11 Group, who had borne the main burden of Battle, felt let down. It was the one unhappy and unworthy aspect of an

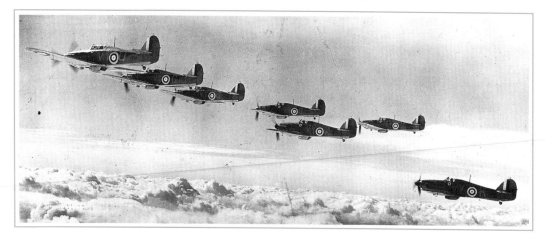

otherwise glorious triumph for the Royal Air Force and Fighter Command.

And triumphant it certainly was. There can be no doubt that the Battle of Britain was one of the truly decisive battles of history. In reaching that conclusion it is necessary to ask oneself two questions. First, — what would have been the consequence, for Britain and for the world, if, as so nearly happened, Fighter Command had been brought to breaking point in September 1940? And what was the impact on the subsequent course of the war of the fact that, by the narrowest of margins, near-defeat was tipped over to victory?

The short answer to the first question is that the Germans would have made a determined effort to invade and would probably have succeeded. It is true that the British Home Fleet would have remained intact and no doubt the Royal Navy would have moved that fleet down into the unsheltered south eastern approaches in an effort to destroy the invasion fleet. But with the Luftwaffe in control of the skies it is doubtful whether sea power alone could have prevailed. Indeed, the Royal Navy would undoubtedly have suffered terrible losses. We were to see, a few months later, how naval superiority counted for nothing against air superiority, when the Royal Navy lost ship after ship at the hands of the Luftwaffe while attempting to disrupt the German occupation of Crete, which was successfully carried out by air power alone. Even if, for some reason, the Germans had found it necessary to postpone the actual invasion, Britain's plight would have been dire. The Luftwaffe would have been in command of our skies, able to disrupt the production of aircraft, fighters and bombers alike, and of weapons desperately needed by the Army, to sink the convoys as they approached our harbours and to do great damage to internal communications, including the railway network.

Although the spirit of the nation, buoyed up by Churchill's leadership and exhortation, was utterly defiant, it is hard to see how we could have survived as a fighting force, still less how the anti-invasion ground forces, under the command of General Sir Alan Brooke, could have been built up and strengthened to a condition in which they might have prevailed against an invasion launched in the spring of 1941. When Brooke took over, after Dunkirk, he found himself with one Corps Headquarters, one Regular Division and two Territorial Divisions — all desperately short of equipment — with

Above: Much of the fighting took place at altitudes too high for the observer on the ground to see, and often contrails and the faint noise of engines at full throttle were the only indications that battle had joined.

which to defend the coast from Kent to Wales. And although, under Fighter Command's umbrella, he had succeeded in building up the strength of his force by September, it remained terribly inadequate in relation to what Hitler could have sent over against it.

Without doubt, therefore, the frustration of the orders issued by Hitler and Goering to the effect that

Below: The short endurance of the Bf 109E often made the return trip a very ''iffy'' affair, and a significant number were forced to seek the sanctuary of the wide firm sands of the coast near Cap Blanc Nez.

the RAF was to be destroyed averted a disaster of catastrophic proportions. What, then, were the positive effects?

I think that one which is not often identified or mentioned, probably because it is intangible, is the far-reaching effect which the RAF victory — perhaps, even more so, the Luftwaffe's defeat and the consequent failure to invade — had on the hearts and minds not only of the protagonist nations but of the watching world at large, and most particularly the people of North America. Following the subjugation of all northern and western Europe in a few weeks of devastating Blitzkreig, most people probably thought that the German war machine was unbeatable. And, although the memory of it has conveniently been allowed to die, there is no doubt that quite a lot of people, most particularly in North America, still saw Hitler and Hitler's Germany as a quite desirable bulwark against Bolshevism. To them the prospect of a patched up peace between Germany and Britain was therefore, in June and July 1940, not altogether unwelcome.

The Battle of Britain did much to change both attitudes and expectations. It was fought in full daylight and in full view of millions of spectators. It was fought to the encouraging and incomparable commentary of Winston Churchill, whose words affected attitudes far beyond Britain. And it was fought also to the commentary of some outstandingly brilliant reporters, notably the Columbia Broadcasting Company's great Ed Murrow whose daily broadcasts — ''This is London . . .'' — carried the mood and the sound and the drama of the Battle into millions of American homes. The David and Goliath nature of the conflict, as it was projected, the reports and photographs of the bombing of London and other British cities, the undoubted heroism not only of British airmen but of millions of men and women on the ground, tilted sympathy our way.

All of that added up to a factor of enormous importance in the development of the war against Germany. It was a factor which cannot be precisely measured, but it must certainly have contributed as significantly to ultimate victory as did others of a more tangible and measurable nature.

The first and most obvious of these was that the British were able to institute the process of turning their own war machine from one which was primarily focused on the anti-invasion role to one more concerned with offence. It is true that Sealion was not finally abandoned altogether as part of the German war plan until February 1942. Hitler had reluctantly accepted its postponement on October 12, 1940, but it had been,

Left: The strain of constant fighting told even on the toughest, and this poignant picture of exhaustion shows Sgt G. Booth of No.85 Sqn, who was shot down on September 1 and died of wounds in February 1941.

quite specifically, only a postponement. And so in the spring and summer of 1941 the British Army in southern Britain still assumed a defensive stance. Even when the Germans invaded Russia, in July of that year, the idea that England itself might be invaded was not altogether or formally set aside either in the German or the British High Commands. There were those in the latter as well as the former who believed that Russian resistance would last only a few weeks. And so the switch from a defensive to an offensive attitude was a gradual one. But the mental move towards it had already begun as the last daylight raids of the Battle of Britain took place in October 1940.

By the spring of 1941 the Army was already thinking in terms of offensive operations, against Fortress Europe, manifested in the first place by ''Commando'' raids and eventually to culminate in full-scale invasions, first through Sicily and Italy and later through Normandy. Bomber Command of the Royal Air Force was carrying the war to Germany's heartland night after night. Fighter Command was embarking on a campaign which was to reproduce over north east France the daily pattern of high altitude dog fights which only a few months previously had been seen over south east England. The aircraft factories, which for a few desperate weeks in September 1940 had been unable to maintain a rate of production equal to the rate of fighter Command's losses, were now building up output in comparative safety, for although they were still vulnerable to night bombing, this was infinitely less effective than the daylight attacks of 1940.

And so Fighter Command's victory had been crucial in opening the way for our own bomber offensive and, perhaps even more important, for the expansion of Coastal Command, which now had to play a role over the Atlantic no less vital than that which Fighter Command had played over south east Britain and the Channel. The Battle of the Atlantic was about to begin, in earnest. It does not have the historical glamour of the Battle of Britain. But it was every bit as vital to victory. And it could not have been won if the Battle of Britain had not been won first, because air power as well as sea power was an essential factor in its prosecution.

The frustration of Hitler's plan to crush Britain was also, of course, a factor of enormous importance in his

Above left: Veterans of the Battle meet again two years on. From left to right; Max Aitken, Sailor Malan, Alan Deere, Lord Dowding, Elspeth Henderson, Richard Hillary, Johnny Kent and Brian Kingcombe.

Left: A Spitfire of No.19 Squadron at Duxford. No.19 was the first unit to fly the cannon-armed version, but persistent lack of serviceability led to them being re-equipped with the old machinegun Spitfires.

most far-reaching plan of all — the invasion and defeat of Russia. As the eastward advance developed in the late summer and autumn of 1941 it seemed to many that Russian resistance must inevitably collapse. Of course, Russia's capacity for absorbing punishment, for surviving and continuing the fight, for producing infantry division after division after division to replace those steam-rollered out of existence by the Germans in defeat after defeat after defeat, was a war-winning factor all on its own. But whether it could have done the trick if Germany had been able to concentrate its entire war effort on the eastern front, on Russia and Russia alone, must be doubtful. And so the outcome of the Battle of Britain most certainly was a factor of major importance on the outcome of the Battle for Russia.

There is really no end to the chain of consequences which flows from an event as decisive as the Battle of Britain. But I believe I have listed those which are most significant:

Firstly, the German invasion plan, Operation Sealion, had to be called off. If it had gone forward, in conditions where the Germans exercised control of the air, it would most probably have succeeded.

Secondly, the Battle of Britain was the first major military set-back for Germany and for Hitler himself; the effect on the morale of the protagonists and on the attitudes of the world at large was, though intangible and therefore not precisely calculable, a major factor in the further prosecution of the war.

Thirdly, the British Army gradually changed its stance and role from that of an anti-invasion force to one of attack and invasion.

Fourthly, Britain's aircraft factories were able to build up production of planes for Bomber and Coastal Commands so that the assault against Germany itself could be carried forward by the RAF, long before the 1944 landings, and the battle for the maintenance of our supply lines could be successfully fought out over the hostile Atlantic Ocean.

Fifthly, the German invasion of Russia had to be carried out with an enemy at her back — and an enemy of ever increasing strength.

As the British people — and some, no doubt, in the nations of the old Empire whose pilots played so bold a part in the Battle — celebrate the fiftieth anniversary of the Battle of Britain, their thoughts will probably be focused on the image as it has been projected over the years — the image of vapour trails in the blue summer sky above Kent and Sussex; of the rattle of machinegun and light cannon fire as small formations of Spitfires and Hurricanes dived into great wedges of Swastika-marked German bombers; of young men with silk scarves and yellow ''Mae West'' life-jackets scrambling from bomb-pocked airfields; of pretty but

Right: The Hurricane was the most numerically important of the British fighters, and although lacking the performance of the Spitfire, was a rather more rugged machine and a steadier gun platform.

business-like WAAFs moving the plots around like roulette chips on the ops room boards; and of the death and destruction in a thousand city streets across the face of south east England, but most particularly in London and its outer suburbs.

Those are the stereotype images and they are accurate enough. But behind them and above them you should look for the image of Lord Dowding, who conceived and built the system of air defence which was capable of saving Britain from German invasion and who then, most brilliantly supported by Keith Park, directed its use when the test came. And you should consider the dire consequences if that unique and effective system had not been in place — dire consequences not only for Britain but also, as we have seen, for the whole of the civilised world.

Below: The most evocative picture of the blitz as St. Pauls rises above the smoke. The area around it was largely flattened, but, by some miracle, the cathedral itself escaped largely unscathed.

''Although they are called the Few in fact nearly 3,000 aircrew (Blenheim and Defiant fighters carried aircrew as well as the pilot) fought in the Battle, although less than half were in the front-line at any one time. Of these 3,000 one in three were killed or wounded; and, as the Battle ground remorselessly on, some became so exhausted that they had to be withdrawn for rest. But the aircrew formed only a small minority of those who played essential parts in the Battle. For every pilot in air operations there are dozens of backers-up, not only the obvious ones like those who directly service the aircraft but also the fighter and air-traffic controllers, the radar operators, the intelligence and planning staffs and the commanders. And behind these again are the suppliers, the drivers, cooks and clerks, men and women, all cogs of varying importance in a great machine but none insignificant.

Nor was the Battle fought by Fighter Command; every operational RAF Command played its specialist part, as well as the guns and the balloons. Not every one remembers that Churchill's famous words 'Never was so much owed by so many to so few' constituted only one sentence in a paragraph paying tribute to the RAF as a whole.

But perhaps above all the victory was a people's victory. Other governments and peoples had cracked under the Blitzkrieg. To the surprise and discomfiture of the enemy the British not only suffered it but sustained it, and never failed to maintain the fight or their determination to see it through. In underestimating them the Germans made their most critical mistake.''

Air Chief Marshal Sir Christopher Foxley-Norris GCB, DSO, OBE, MA, FBIM, FRSA

THE BATTLE of Britain is deemed by British historians to have begun on July 10 and ended on October 31, 1940. A clasp on the ribbon of the 1939-45 Star — indicated by a rosette when medal ribbons only are worn — was awarded to aircrew who served under the operational control of Fighter Command between those dates. But the four phases into which the battle is officially divided did not begin until August 8. This first phase continued until August 18. The second phase was August 19 to September 5, the third September 6 to October 5, and the fourth October 6 to 31.

German historians see it differently. In the eyes of the Luftwaffe, the Battle opened on August 8, 1940 and did not close until May 11, 1941, with the 500-bomber raid on London on the night of the 10th/11th. Moreover, they consider that it was waged in five phases. But the period from February 9 to May 11, 1941 is regarded as an appendix to the main battle; a sixth phase. Thus the five phases proper, as seen by German historians, are defined as: August 8 to August 18 — Beginning Of The All-Out Onslaught; August 19 to September 6 — Severest Fighter Combats; September 7 to October 5 — The Air Battle At Its Height; October 6 to October 31 — Fighters As Bombers; November 1, 1940 to February 8, 1941 — The End Of the Air Battle.

That the battle had to be fought at all was a consequence of Hitler's swift conquest of the Low Countries and France. On May 10, 1940, Germany had invaded Belgium and Holland and entered France on the 13th. On May 26 the British Expeditionary Force began to retreat from France. The bulk of the evacuation was completed by June 4, but the last British troops did not leave until the 17th. On that day the French Government asked Germany for surrender terms and on June 22 the armistice was signed. The last RAF squadrons based in France withdrew on June 18.

Before the battle came a brief breathing space for those already hard-pressed RAF fighter squadrons that had been fighting in French air space against heavy odds. Had Hitler launched an immediate invasion, treading on the heels of the departing British Expeditionary Force (BEF) and the 112,000 officers and men of the French Army who accompanied them, he might have established a foothold on the south coast of England, even if it were only temporary. But he would have had to put an immense naval force at risk to protect his invasion fleet and to pound the Kent or Sussex shore. He would have had to cross at or near the Straits of Dover, to make the passage as short as possible. He would have had to concentrate the whole weight of his assault on only one or two points for it to be effective.

Hitler did not, for many reasons which are given elsewhere. Two of them were that he believed Britain, under a pusillanimous and appeasing Prime Minister, was too weak in both military strength and morale to fight, so would sue for peace. Another was that he could not resist showing off his victory ostentatiously to the world: hence the several days' delay while he staged a vulgar, tawdry armistice ritual at Compiègne, when he should have been on a clifftop near Calais, watching his army, navy and air force trying to hammer Britain into surrender. In any event, the Royal Navy would have sunk a great part of an invasion fleet in those narrow waters, while the RAF's Bomber and Coastal Command aircraft, however exiguous the protection that the grossly outnumbered Fighter Command could afford them, would have accounted for as many again.

The air battle did not suddenly burst upon Britain on July 10, 1940, without any preliminaries. The Luftwaffe was not entirely inactive during this lull. It had made its first large-scale raids on the night of June 18, when 100 bombers attacked targets between Yorkshire and Kent. A South African Flight Lieutenant, A.G. Malan of No.74 Squadron, considered by his fellows to be the outstanding personality in the Battle, an exceptional pilot and gifted leader, was flying a Spitfire that night and shot down two bombers that were caught by searchlights. The next night, 100 bombers raided targets in southern, eastern and northern England, and south Wales. On seven more nights that month mainland Britain felt the impact of German bombs on the eastern counties, the Midlands, the south-west and west of England, south Wales and

BATTLE DIARY

Richard Townshend Bickers

Scotland. On two successive nights, June 25 and 26, the defending pilots, groping their way about in the dark, flying aeroplanes designed for day fighting, and relying on their eyesight and searchlights to pick up a target, shot down three raiders. On June 28 the Channel Islands were bombed.

The Luftwaffe made its first daylight raid on July 1, on Hull, in Yorkshire and Wick, in Scotland; and repeated this performance on the next two days. On July 3 the RAF brought down six bombers. On July 4 Portland was the target, again in daylight. Some small ships were sunk or damaged, buildings battered and civilians killed. On July 5, 6, 7, 8 and 9 many parts of Britain suffered day and night raids during which slight damage was done to ports and factories and more people were blown apart. Aircraft on both sides were destroyed; not always a mere few — on July 8 the RAF shot down eight for the loss of three.

Now the most intensive aggression against Britain was about to be unleashed. Its objectives were:

1. The blockade of the British Isles in co-operation with the German Navy: attacks on ports and shipping, and the mining of harbour entrances and sea lanes.

2. The achievement of air supremacy as a preliminary to the invasion.

3. Annihilation of Britain by total air warfare.

It is salutary at this point to consider what would have been the consequences if this final objective had been attained. Among all the admiration and respect that has been expressed by former enemy airmen for each other, the much vaunted chivalry shared by the opposing air forces, and the general forgiveness and friendliness that have burgeoned in the half-century that has passed since the Battle, it should never be forgotten that victory for Germany in the Battle of Britain would have meant victory in the war.

RAF Fighter Command, Anti-Aircraft Command, the Observer Corps (later Royal), the Fire Service, the Civil Defence, were all fighting for the lives of their compatriots, men, women and children, and the freedom of future generations: generations of Britons who would never have been born if the Luftwaffe had had its way.

The following is a day-to-day diary of the immense struggle Britain underwent against tremendous odds during those summer months of 1940.

Below: Junkers Ju 88s of I/KG 30 miss a British cruiser lying at anchor near the Forth Bridge. Two were later shot down and one damaged by Spitfires of No.603 Squadron.

JULY 1940

Wednesday, July 10: Rain over most of Britain. Showers south-east England and Channel.
Day: RAF No.11 Group began detaching whole squadrons instead of flights to forward airfields at first light. Enemy dawn weather reconnaissance, and tactical reconnaissance during morning. A few inconclusive interceptions. Enemy activity heavier than usual. By 1330hrs some 20 Do 17s, 20 Bf 109s and 30 Bf 110s forming up in Calais area seen on radar. These attacked convoy escorted by six Hurricanes off Dover. Four more squadrons sent reinforcing Hurricanes. One ship sunk, three Hurricanes and four Bf 109s shot down. Near Newhaven, train attacked, driver killed. Seventy-bomber raid on Falmouth and Swansea killed 30, damaged ships, railways, power station and ordnance factory. RAF station Martlesham Heath in Suffolk slightly damaged.
Night: Scotland, south-east and east coast raided.
Aircraft losses: RAF 6, Luftwaffe 13.

Thursday, July 11: Overcast in south, bright intervals and thunder elsewhere.
Day: Early morning, radar reported three formations approaching convoy off Dorset. Six Hurricanes ordered to intercept while six Spitfires covered ships. None sunk. Late morning, Douglas Bader scored his second victory, his first in the Battle of Britain. Taking off in rain and poor visibility to investigate an unidentified aircraft, he found it, recognised it as a Dornier 17, opened fire and last saw it disappear into cloud. Five minutes after he landed, the Observer Corps reported having seen the Do 17 crash into the sea. Early afternoon, six Hurricanes arrived at Portland while 15 Ju 87s, escorted by 30-plus Bf 110s, were bombing. Two Bf 110s destroyed. Afternoon, six Spitfires intercepted 12 Bf 109s off Deal, escorting Heinkel 59 seaplane, with Red Cross marking, on air-sea rescue, and shot down the He 59, which beached near Deal. Two Bf 109s and two Spitfires shot down. Afternoon, six Hurricanes attacked 12 He 111s and 12 Bf 110s over Isle of Wight.
Night: Bombs on Portsmouth, eastern and north-western England.
Aircraft losses: RAF 4, Luftwaffe 11.

Friday, July 12: Cloudy, some thunderstorms.
Day: Bombers over convoys off Orfordness, Suffolk, and North Foreland,

Kent. Three Defiants and nine Hurricanes protected convoy off Suffolk while 12 Hurricanes went for attackers. Spitfires shot down a He 111 near Aberdeen. Small raids intercepted over wide area. 11 Group reinforced by moving 152 (Spitfire) Squadron from Acklington, Northumberland to Middle Wallop, Hampshire.
Night: South Wales and Bristol attacked.
Aircraft losses: RAF 6, Luftwaffe 8.

Saturday, July 13: Poor after early fog cleared.
Day: Weather kept down scale of enemy effort. Two raids on Dover thwarted but two convoys off Harwich and ships at Portland bombed.
Night: Thames Estuary mined.
Aircraft losses: RAF 1, Luftwaffe 7.

Sunday, July 14: Fair.
Day: Germans evidently using Red Cross seaplanes on convoy reconnaissance. British Government therefore announced that these were no longer immune from attack. Start of six days of reduced enemy activity. Morning, bomber's attempt to hit a destroyer off Swanage failed. Convoy near Dover damaged.
Night: Bombers over west, south, south-east and east England.
Aircraft losses: RAF 4, Luftwaffe 2.

Monday, July 15: Low cloud and heavy rain.
Day: Small raid damaged Westland Aircraft factory and runway at Yeovil in Somerset. Light force of Do 17s prevented by Hurricanes from hitting Channel

convoy. At RAF station St Athan, south Wales, airfield cratered. Railway lines near Avonmouth, Somerset, hit.
Night: No bombing, some mines laid.
Aircraft losses: RAF 1, Luftwaffe 3.

Tuesday, July 16: Foggy in Channel, south-eastern England and northern France.
Day: Convoys off southern and eastern English and north-eastern Scottish coasts, and Westland Aircraft harassed when weather lifted a trifle.

Above: The Spitfire became a legend during the summer of 1940; its sleek lines coupled with its fighting record gave it an unequalled mass appeal.

Below: With a typically theatrical use of a banner, Reichmarschall Goering addresses Luftwaffe aircrews at the height of the Battle, September 1940.

Night: Minelaying in north-east England.
Aircraft losses: RAF 2, Luftwaffe 5.

Major Josef Schmid, chief of Abteilung (Department) V, the Intelligence Service, submitted to Hitler a document entitled, ''A Comparative Appreciation of the Striking Power of the RAF and the Luftwaffe''. In this he stated that the British had 900 first-line fighters, of which 675 could be considered fully serviceable. Not a bad estimate: the actual number available on an ideal day was 587. Schmid was less accurate when he wrote, ''Taking into account both their combat performance and the fact that they are not yet equipped with cannon, the Hurricane and the Spitfire are both inferior to the Messerschmitt 109.'' But right in adding, ''The Messerschmitt 110, however, is inferior to the Spitfire . . .'', although his proviso, ''if the latter is well piloted'' was nonsense. He concluded that the odds favoured the Luftwaffe ''so long as the large-scale operations are begun early enough to permit the exploitation of the relatively favourable meteorological conditions of July to early October.''

Hitler issued an order, Directive No 16, that a landing operation against England must be prepared. This was code-named Operation Sealion.

Wednesday, July 17: Rainy and dull.
Day: Bad flying conditions hindered even the daily weather and tactical reconnaissance sorties. In the afternoon

bombers molested shipping off eastern England and Scotland.

Night: Mines sown off the Welsh coast at Swansea and Cardiff and in the Thames. A few bombers over south-west England.

Aircraft losses: RAF 1, Luftwaffe 2.

Thursday, July 18: Cloud over eastern Channel, showers in southern England. The Goodwin lightship was sunk and bombs fell on the St Margaret's Bay (Kent) coastguard station. Uncoordinated incursions against shipping in the Channel and harbours on its coast led to one major engagement when 28 Bf 109s were intercepted by 15 Spitfires.

Friday, July 19: Fair in the Channel. Bright intervals between showers elsewhere.

Day: 20 Bf 109s bounced 9 Defiants (two-seater with four-gun turret) of No.141 Sqn and shot 5 down into the Channel, and one at Dover before 12 Hurricanes drove them off. In the afternoon some 70 enemy bombers with fighter escort attacked Dover and were intercepted by 35 Hurricanes and Spitfires.

Night: Sporadic raids on Harwich, Thames estuary and Plymouth — Isle of Wight area.

Aircraft losses: RAF 11, Luftwaffe 2.

Hitler made a speech in the Reichstag appealing to Britain to surrender and threatening that continued resistance would mean her complete destruction.

Goering held a conference with the Commanders of Luftflotten 2 and 3, and their Air Corps commanders. He told them, "Fighting alone all these weeks on the Channel Front, Jagdgeschwader 51 has already shot

Below: Hitler's "final appeal to reason" supplied Londoners with toilet paper.

From the Führer's Speech

down 150 of the enemy's aircraft: quite enough to have weakened him seriously. Think now of all the bombers we can parade in the English sky. The few RAF fighters will not be able to cope."

Saturday, July 20: Clouds at first over Straits of Dover, followed by bright intervals and sunny afternoon in the south. Some thunderstorms elsewhere.

Day: In the afternoon, Sergeant J.H. "Ginger" Lacey, who had scored five victories in France and was destined to be the top-scoring RAF pilot in the Battle of Britain, made his first kill of the Battle and was awarded the Distinguished Flying Medal. His squadron, No 501, was scrambled from Middle Wallop, in Hampshire, to intercept Ju 87s, escorted by Bf 109s, attacking a convoy which the sector controller said was near Jersey. They found it halfway between there and Portland Bill. Lacey picked on a 109 that was heading towards him, turned inside it, gave it three bursts while following it through its desperate attempts at evasion and recalls: "I can clearly remember watching him slanting down the sky at a hell of a steep angle. A beautiful little blue and grey mottled aircraft with white and black crosses standing out startlingly clear, getting smaller and smaller; and thinking what a terribly small splash he made when he went straight into the Channel." Lacey spotted another 109 and thought, "Well, he's making a fool of himself. He's going due north. He'll have to turn any moment now, and then I've got him." "Then," he says, "as his turn continued, I thought for one awful moment that he was going to crash into me. Then I suddenly saw the aeroplane almost stagger as my bullets hit it. Its propeller started to slow down. We flashed past each other a few feet apart. By the time I had whipped round, "Pan" Cox latched onto it. He didn't fire until he was in to about 20 yards (20in). It went in almost beside the oily patch where my first had gone in. I put no claim in for the half-share, because it was Pan Cox's first success."

Night: Mines laid along the east coast. In the west, from the Isle of Wight to Cornwall and the Bristol Channel.

Aircraft Losses: RAF 3, Luftwaffe 9.

Sunday, July 21: Fine at first, becoming cloudy, then fine in the evening.

Day: Raids on convoys in the Channel, during one of which three squadrons drove off 20 Ju 87s and Bf 109s.

Night: Merseyside bombed.

Aircraft losses: RAF 6, Luftwaffe 7.

Above: The Anderson air raid shelter was widely used by civilians in many areas.

Hitler summoned his Commanders-in-Chief to consider plans for an invasion. The Army would not guarantee success unless the Navy transported 40 Divisions across the Channel. The Navy accepted responsibility for only 10. Generalfeldmarschal Halder, Chief of the Army General Staff, condemned this as suicidal. Goering declared that, given five days of good weather, he could do such damage to the RAF that 10 Divisions would suffice. On this assumption, the meeting settled details about logistics; and the administration of a subjugated Britain, down to the value of currency (£1 to equal 9.60 Marke). And it was now that the decision was taken to remove forcibly all British males between 17 and 45 to exile. But Hitler still seemed to have doubts. "The invasion of England is a specially audacious venture. Although the crossing will be short, we are not contending with a river, but the open sea controlled by a well-prepared enemy," he warned.

Goering sent for newly-promoted Field Marshals Kesselring and Sperrle, commanding Air Fleets II and III and ordered them to make plans. They in turn similarly charged the commanders of their Air Corps. There was general agreement that first must come the demolition of the RAF.

Monday, July 22: Fair in the Dover Straits, cloudy down-Channel. In eastern England, showery with bright intervals.

Day: Light attacks against ships in the Channel.

Night: Mines sewn between Kent and north-east Scotland.

Aircraft losses: RAF 1, Luftwaffe 1.

Tuesday, July 23: Dover Straits hazy, cloud and intermittent rain elsewhere.

Day: Little activity. Ships off east coast attacked.

Night: A few bombers inland. Minelaying, eastern England and Scotland.

Aircraft losses: RAF 0, Luftwaffe 3.

That night "Ginger" Lacey flew a night patrol. "After being vectored all over the sky by the controller, I unexpectedly saw a Heinkel 111 caught in the searchlights some two miles (3km) ahead and slightly above, so started to climb after it. Immediately some of the searchlights switched to my Hurricane." (Pilots identified themselves by flashing the Letters of the Day, if they were fighters, and bombers fired Verey light Colours of the Day.) Lacey flashed the letters he had memorised on his downward light. The Heinkel fired a red light followed by a green. "To my surprise, the rest of the searchlights holding the hostile aircraft also switched over to me." Ten seconds later the anti-aircraft guns opened up at him. Blinded by searchlights, in danger of being shot down, he lost the He 111. On landing, he says, "I found that the time was past midnight, when the Colours and Letters of the Day had changed. I had flashed the wrong identification and the Germans had fired the right one: whether because enemy intelligence was superbly accurate, or by sheer fluke, who knows?" Night patrols flown by single-seat fighters with no radar were extremely lucky to find enemy aircraft.

Below: A London civil defence volunteer extinguishes an incendiary with sand.

The expected attempt at invasion, and the increased danger to shipping in the Western Approaches since enemy occupation of France, meant the bulk of Britain's sea traffic would have to travel up and down the east coast. Convoy movements in the Channel by daylight were restricted. The increased provision of convoy patrols imposed a demand on Fighter Command that could be met only by forming more squadrons. Until the necessary strength was attained, an adequate number of fighters must be kept for the defence of London, while others were moved about the coast as required.

Wednesday, July 24: Fog spreading across the country from the west. Clouds over the Channel.
Day: An unexpected interval of fair weather gave Adolf Galland — promoted to Major on July 18 — the opportunity to lead his Geschwader in action over England for the first time when they escorted bombers on a raid against a convoy in the Thames estuary. Flight Lieutenant Alan Deere led a section when No 54 Sqn was scrambled to intercept. At 20,000ft (6,700m) they saw that a second mass of enemy aircraft was attacking another convoy, near Dover. On instructions from the ground, the squadron split and sent one flight (two sections) to tackle each enemy formation, while reinforcing fighters were ordered off. Galland reports, "We made a surprise attack with height advantage. I glued myself to the tail of a Spitfire and during a right turn managed to get in a long burst. It went down almost vertically." He saw the pilot bale out and crash to his death in the water when his parachute failed to open. His comment in retrospect was, "On landing, we were no longer in doubt that the RAF would prove a most formidable opponent."

At Brooklands, where the first flight in Britain was made, in 1909, and which became the cradle of British aviation, there was a small aircraft factory. A solitary Ju 88 joined the circuit with several aeroplanes that were landing there, and bombed the buildings but did little harm.
Night: No activity.
Aircraft losses: RAF 3, Luftwaffe 8.

Thursday, July 25: Mist in Straits of Dover, elsewhere fine.
Day: The Germans now had some radar on the Channel coast. This morning it picked up 21 merchant ships with two armed trawlers as escort, off Southend.

The mist cleared as they entered the Straits. Sixty Ju 87s, escorted by Bf 109s led by Galland, attacked. They sank five and damaged five. Two destroyers that went out from Dover were also bombed and both hit. Two New Zealanders, Flight Lieutenant Alan Deere and Pilot Officer Colin Gray (who ended the war as New Zealand's most highly decorated pilot and top scorer with 27½ kills) were among five Spitfire pilots scrambled to intercept. A squadron of Hurricanes arrived later. Galland reported, "In the space of about fifteen minutes I saw four fighters hit the sea and one pilot parachuting." Other Channel shipping was attacked during the day.
Night: Reconnaissance west of England and Channel, mines layed Thames and Firth of Forth.
Aircraft losses: RAF 7, Luftwaffe 16.

Friday, July 26: Rain and thick cloud.
Day: Ships off Isle of Wight and in Channel bombed, some sunk.
Night: Mines laid Severn, east coast and Thames.
Aircraft losses: RAF 2, Luftwaffe 2.

Saturday, July 27: Fair in Dover area, Channel cloudy, eastern England and Midlands rainy.
Day: Dover harbour bombed twice. Bf 109s used for the first time as fighter-bombers. Ships in Channel attacked. Air Ministry directed Fighter Command to send fighters in greater strength than the enemy's to intercept raids on Dover. This necessitated increasing the number of fighter squadrons to 28. Plymouth, Wick (Scotland) and Belfast bombed.

Below: Hurricanes of No.32 Sqn in unprotected dispersal at Hawkinge, taken on 31 July 1940 at the height of the Battle of Britain.

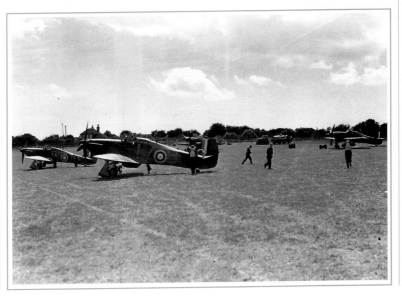

Night: South-west England raided.
Aircraft losses: RAF 1, Luftwaffe 4.

Sunday, July 28: Fine at first, deteriorating to fair and then cloudy.
Day: Two abortive raids on Dover. One turned back in mid-Channel; the other, comprising 50 bombers and 50 fighters, was intercepted and driven off by two Hurricane and two Spitfire squadrons. Ports on south coast and Dover raided.
Night: Bombers over western and northern England, Midlands, Scotland and Wales, mines laid along east coast.
Aircraft losses: RAF 5, Luftwaffe 15.

Monday, July 29: Misty in Straits of Dover, otherwise fair.
Day: Raid on Dover and convoy by 30 Ju 87s and 50 Bf 109s intercepted and foiled. Attack on Harwich intercepted.
Night: Light raids.
Aircraft losses: RAF 3, Luftwaffe 6.

Tuesday, July 30: Low cloud and light rain.
Day: Weather precluded much enemy activity. Convoys off Essex and Suffolk coasts raided.
Night: Bombers over Midlands and south Wales.
Aircraft losses: RAF none, Luftwaffe 5.

Hitler ordered Goering to be ready to start main assault at 12 hours' notice, but he asked for more time.

Britain initiated a respite in the scale of fighting over the Channel by sending no convoys through there for the next few days. The Luftwaffe's priority was to destroy the RAF's fighter force as a preliminary to wiping out aerodromes and the bomber force, which was essential

before an invasion could be attempted. But with no convoys to protect, RAF fighters were not aloft to be drawn into combat by the Luftwaffe. Galland and his comrades constantly trailed their coats over England but Fighter Command would not respond. The Germans resorted to sending out a weak bomber force as a decoy for a strong fighter formation waiting at high altitude under Galland's command, but failed to lure Dowding. Galland expressed considerable frustration over this period.

Wednesday, July 31: Generally fair, but mist in Channel.
Day: Convoys off south-west, south and south-east England, and Dover balloon barrage, raided.
Night: Mines laid. Bombs on Thames Estuary and south Wales.
Aircraft losses: RAF 3, Luftwaffe 5.

Hitler informed Generalfeldmarschal von Brauchitsch, the Army C-in-C, and Generalfeldmarschal Halder, the Chief of the General Staff, Goering and General Jeschonnek, Chief of Air Staff, that he intended to attack Russia that year. "With Russia defeated," he said, "Britain's last hope will be gone."

Meanwhile the German Navy and Army had been arguing acrimoniously about Operation Sealion. Hitler had decreed that "The landing operation must be a surprise crossing on a broad front from Ramsgate to a point west of the Isle of Wight."

In what manner he supposed that a surprise could be sprung on the British is obscure. The few hours of darkness on a summer night would not have been enough to conceal the approach of a fleet of over 2,000 tugs towing barges at a speed of some four knots. Nor would the other vessels have gone undetected. The shortest crossing would have taken perhaps five hours, the longer ones up to three times as much. Add to that the propensity for soldiers to succumb to seasickness, amply demonstrated during many landings later in the war; a quarter of those who got ashore would not have been fit for combat.

Plans, he demanded, must be complete by the end of August and the invasion carried out by September 15. The Army had compromised by making such a massive reduction in the estimated size of the necessary force that the grasp of reality displayed by its Generals must have caused the Admirals and Air Generals some dismay. But in an autocracy, where seasoned professionals had to bend to the whims of an

Above: An ominous sign that Hitler meant business came when air reconnaissance revealed a build-up of barges in the Channel ports, ready for the invasion.

unqualified dictator or lose their livelihoods at the least and their lives at the worst, these shifts of attitude were an obligation. The Army had reduced its requirement to 13 Divisions; but insisted on a broad front of 200 miles (320km) from Ramsgate to Weymouth. The Navy would not agree to more than a 50-mile (80km) front, from Dover to Eastbourne. The Army wished to land 90,000 men and 650 tanks on the first day. The Navy agreed but said that carrying the remaining 170,000 men and 34,000 vehicles would take two or three days. The Army demanded swifter transportation. The Navy claimed that assembling 155 ships, 470 tugs, 1,700 barges and 1,000 motorboats must delay the invasion until some time between September 19 and October 15. The autumn weather made this unacceptable to the Army and the Luftwaffe. The wrangling dragged on . . .

AUGUST 1940

Thursday, August 1: Channel and Dover Straits overcast, improving later, low cloud over east coast, fair generally.
Day: Two bombers off east coast intercepted. Two raids intercepted off Sussex coast; Norwich bombed, goods yard hit.

Night: Minelaying north-east Scotland and Thames. Bombers over widely separated parts of England, Scotland and south Wales, many of them dropping leaflets headlined ''The Last Appeal To Reason'', a translation of Hitler's speech to the Reichstag on July 19 when he had appealed to Great Britain to sue for peace.
Aircraft losses: RAF 1, Luftwaffe 5.

Hitler issued Directive No 17, in which he said: ''I have decided that war against Great Britain will be pursued and intensified by sea and by air with the object of bringing about the country's final defeat.

''1. The Luftwaffe must deploy its full strength in order to destroy the British air force as soon as possible.

''2. When command of the air has been achieved, even on a local or temporary basis, the air attack will be directed against the ports and special attention will be given to food depots, particularly those that serve London.

''3. Attacks on shipping, whether naval or merchant, will be accorded a priority second only to the efforts directed against the destruction of the enemy's power in the air.''

The order went on to define how the objective was to be achieved . . .

First the aircraft, then their ground support organisation and fuel supplies would be destroyed. Afterwards the aircraft industry, including the factories producing anti-aircraft weapons would be attacked.

The intensification of the war in the air should begin on August 5, but the Luftwaffe General Staff would determine the exact date nearer the time, and bearing in mind the state of combat preparedness of men and aircraft and the vital long range weather forecasts.

Friday, August 2: Cloud and drizzle in Channel, elsewhere fine.
Day: East coast and Channel convoys attacked.
Night: Bombers over RAF School of Technical Training, Halton (Buckinghamshire), Catterick (Yorkshire), Farnborough (Hampshire) and Romford (Essex) airfields, and Forth Bridge, in Scotland. Mines laid.
Aircraft losses: RAF 0, Luftwaffe 3.

Goering issued orders for *Adlertag*, Eagle Day, the day on which both Luftflotten 2 and 3 would begin the all out — and, it was intended, final — air assault on Britain. The first objective was to destroy the whole Fighter Command organisation: aircraft in the air and on the ground, airfield buildings and landing areas, and radar stations. This was expected to take three days, so 72 consecutive hours of fine weather were essential. The meteorological experts predicted that these would occur at the beginning of August. But the air fleets needed six days' preparation, so August 10 was the chosen date.

Saturday, August 3: Dull with bright intervals.
Day: No ships in the Channel, so no dive bombers to try to lure RAF fighters into battle.
Night: Raids on Bradford (Yorkshire), Crewe (Cheshire), Liverpool (Lancashire), south Wales, Orkneys, Firth of Forth.
Aircraft losses: RAF 0, Luftwaffe 4.

RAF Fighter Command strength at this point was 708 aircraft serviceable, 1,434 pilots.

GERMAN ORDER OF BATTLE — FIGHTERS AND DESTROYERS BEFORE THE START OF THE AIR ASSAULT AUGUST 3, 1940

Fighter Units
10 Fighter Geschwader Headquarters and 28 Fighter Groups

Locations:
For Home Defence
2 Geschwader HQ (JG1 and JG77)
3 Fighter Groups (II and III/JG77 and III/JG52)

In Air Fleet 2
5 Geschwader HQ with 16 Fighter Groups
JG3 with HQ, I, II, III/JG3
JG26 with HQ, I, II, III/JG26
JG51 with HQ, I, II, III, IV/JG51
JG52 with HQ, I, II/JG52 and I/LG2
JG54 with HQ and I, II, III/JG54

In Air Fleet 3
3 Geschwader HQ with 9 Fighter Groups
JG2 with HQ, I, II, III/JG2
JG27 with HQ, I, II, III/JG27
JG53 with HQ, I, II, III/JG53

Fighter Aircraft

Establishment 1171. Actual 1065.
Available 878
Crews
Establishment 1171. Actual 1118.
Available 869

Destroyer Units
On August 3, 1940, the following units existed:
3 Destroyer Geschwader HQ and 8 Destroyer Groups
These were allocated as follows:

In Air Fleet 2
2 Geschwader HQ with 5 Destroyer Groups
ZG2 with HQ, I, II/ZG2
ZG26 with HQ, I, II, III/JG26

In Air Fleet 3
1 Geschwader HQ with 3 Destroyer Groups

Destroyer Aircraft
Establishment 448. Actual 414.
Available 320
Crews
Establishment 448. Actual 381.
Available 268

Note: Of the Destroyer Units, the following were detailed for night fighter duties.
I/ZG1 (IV/ZG26)
II/ZG1 as I/NJG2
I/ZG76 as II/NJG 1
V/LG 1 as I/NJG3
I/ZG2 as 4/NJG2

Sunday, August 4: Fair to fine, becoming cloudy. Bright intervals.
Day: Bristol Channel and south coast reconnoitred.
Night: No raids.
Aircraft losses: RAF 0, Luftwaffe 0.

Monday, August 5: Channel misty, otherwise fine.
Day: Enemy patrolling Channel in strength to seek shipping.
Night: Mines laid east coasts England and Scotland.
Aircraft losses: RAF 1, Luftwaffe 6.

Tuesday, August 6: Cloudy.
Day: Reconnaissance over Channel.
Night: Mines on east and south-east coasts.
Aircraft losses: RAF 1, Luftwaffe 1.

Wednesday, August 7: Fair, some thunder and cloud.
Day: East coast convoy attacked, shipping reconnaissance over Channel.
Night: Bombers over many areas of England and Scotland.
Aircraft losses: RAF 0, Luftwaffe 4.

Thursday, August 8: Clouds over Channel. Generally showery with bright intervals.
Day: At 0900hrs, Ju 87s and Bf 109s attempted an attack on convoy of 20 ships in Channel met by six Hurricane and Spitfire squadrons. Second raid by 60 Ju 87s at 1245hrs approaching Isle of Wight in battle with 4½ RAF squadrons. At 1700hrs, over 80 Ju 87s and Bf 109s made third attack. Seven RAF squadrons in position to intercept them. Photographic reconnaissance of southern harbours and airfields.
Night: Minelaying and small bomber raids.
Aircraft losses: RAF 19, Luftwaffe 31.
RAF Order of the Day promulgated: "The Battle of Britain is about to begin. Members of the Royal Air Force, the fate of generations lies in your hands."
Goering confirmed August 10 as *Adlertag*

Friday, August 9: Cloudy in Channel, rain between bright intervals.
Day: East coast convoys attacked, sporadic raids inland, Sunderland shipyard hit.
Night: Minelaying and attacks on east coast shipping.
Aircraft losses: RAF 3, Luftwaffe 5.

Saturday, August 10: Channel cloudy, thunderstorms, windy, bright patches.
Day: Norwich bombed. Reconnaissance

inland and over coastal waters.
Night: Minelaying.
Aircraft losses: RAF 0, Luftwaffe 0.
Weather forced postponement of *Adlertag* by 24 hours.

Sunday, August 11: Cloudy, but fair morning.
Day: By 0700hrs, No.74 Squadron was on patrol, led by Squadron Leader Malan. They met two formations of 15-plus Bf 110s and Bf 109s attacking Dover balloon barrage. A second attack on the same target was a diversion while 150 Ju 88s, He 111s, Bf 110s and Bf 109s raided Portland naval base. Five Hurricane and two Spitfire squadrons scrambled to engage them. Channel and east coast ships bombed.
Night: Minelaying. Raids on Mersey area. Mines in Bristol Channel.
Aircraft losses: RAF 27, Luftwaffe 36.
Adlertag was again postponed.

Goering announced that 0530hrs on August 13 was Zero Hour for *Adlertag*. Meteorological forecast favourable.

Monday, August 12: Fine with patchy mist.
Day: Raids on radar stations, and Thames Estuary convoys and ships in the Channel. Ventnor radar put out of action but Germans not aware of it. Dunkirk (Kent) radar station damaged. Some damage to Dover aerial towers. Buildings in Rye demolished but technical installations undamaged. Pevensey hit and electricity supply partly affected. Heavy attacks on Manston, Hawkinge and Lympne airfields. Fires in Portsmouth docks and town. Dover and Hastings bombed.
Night: Minelaying, and indiscriminate bombing of villages and towns.
Aircraft losses: RAF 22, Luftwaffe 31.
Weather was deteriorating, instead of expected improvement, during the night.

Tuesday, August 13: Overcast at dawn. Foggy at French airfields, Channel under thick cloud. Mist and scattered drizzle, some cloud, otherwise fair.
Goering postponed *Adlertag* Zero Hour to afternoon.
Day: Some formations had already taken off before the order reached their units. One of these was led by Oberst Johannes Fink, Commander of KG2. He kept his rendez-vous with the fighter escort at 0530hrs, but there were no 109s in sight, only a few Bf 110s. They kept closing on him, then diving away. He could not understand their message, nor did he share a radio frequency with them. Puzzled, he set course for his

target with Nos II and III Gruppen following. They crossed the English coast at 1640ft (500m). The RAF radar had misread the strength of the 55-strong formation as "only a few", so only No.74 (Spitfire) Squadron had been scrambled. Meanwhile the Do 17s had found RAF Station, Eastchurch. Their bombs cratered the airfield, damaged hangars and other buildings and destroyed five Blenheims. The Spitfires, joined by Nos.111 and 151 Sqns' Hurricanes, caught them on their homeward journey. Before the bombers could hide in cloud, four were shot down and four damaged.

Goering's new Zero Hour was 1400hrs. By then the weather had worsened further. Hauptmann Liensberger took off with 23 Bf 110s of V/LG1. His orders were to make landfall at Portland, then decide what to do next. Immediately his formation was over the English coast they saw Spitfires astern. British accounts state that this operation misfired because no bombers arrived to meet the 110s. In fact, the 110s were not intended as an escort, but as a decoy to draw fighters away from the bombers who would follow. The ruse was successful: two Spitfire squadrons were scrambled (the German version claims that there were 55 aircraft). The Messerschmitts sent three down, but lost five and many of the rest were badly damaged. The Germans failed to take advantage of having drawn the Spitfires: the first wave of follow-up bombers, Ju 87s, did not arrive until three hours later, by when the Spitfires had refuelled and rearmed. There was thick cloud down to 3,000ft (914m), so

dive-bombing was impossible. The Stukas returned to base with their bombs. General von Richthofen's diary entry reads, "The attack was a failure. The weather forecast had been wrong and the attack ordered from 'on high'. Thank goodness the English fighters came too late."

Raids on Odiham and Farnborough airfields were driven off. Southampton docks and Detling airfield were severely damaged. Six bombers reported that they had hit tents and sheds around the landing field at RAF Middle Wallop. Twelve bombers damaged nearby RAF Andover, but this was not a fighter station. A raid bound for RAF Rochford (not Rochester as alleged in some British accounts) failed to find the target and jettisoned over Canterbury.
Night: Norwich, Midlands, West Country and Scotland raided.
Aircraft losses: RAF 13, Luftwaffe 34.

Wednesday, August 14: Cloud with bright intervals.
Day: The weather limited Luftwaffe operations to less than Gruppe strength. The designated targets were fighter airfields, radar stations and aircraft factories. Single bombers made many nuisance raids. Sixteen Bf 110s dived on Manston from cloud and destroyed four hangars, while a spoof raid on Dover was diverting the defence. Barrage balloons at Dover and Folkestone were shot down and the Goodwin lightship was sunk. Hawkinge, Colerne (Somerset), Sealand (Cheshire) and Lympne airfields were bombed. At Southampton and elsewhere

Below: This slightly premature headline refers to the fighting of the day before Adler Tag. Victory and loss totals stated here vary widely from the actual figures.

Above: Irish traitor William Joyce was usually known as Lord Haw Haw.

railway lines were attacked. Maintaining civilian morale was as important as shooting down the enemy and increasing the output of aircraft and munitions factories. The town and harbour of Dover, the Straits and RAF Manston were prime targets for the Luftwaffe and all had been considerably bombed and strafed. Only No.60 Squadron, flying Blenheims, was stationed at Manston, but Spitfire and Hurricane squadrons used it as a forward base during daylight. If anxiety was felt most acutely in and around the extreme south-east corner of England, Kent as a whole was expectant of an attempted German landing at any moment. Not only for the benefit of this population, but also of the entire country, the world's news reporters congregated at Dover, an appearance of confidence had to be kept up. To forbid the Channel to shipping by day would have been taken as a sign not of prudence but of timidity: so ships — albeit lightly laden — continued to traverse it. To ensure that Fighter Command's meagre force was seen to be present, aircraft taking off from, or landing at, Manston were required to fly low over its neighbouring towns, Ramsgate and Dover, to reassure the inhabitants that enemy claims about RAF's allegedly crippling losses, broadcast daily by the traitor Lord Haw-Haw from Berlin, were false.

Night: Scattered weak nuisance raids.
Aircraft losses: RAF 8, Luftwaffe 19.

Thursday, August 15: Fine over Britain. Began with cloud over France and the Channel, but this cleared by early afternoon.

This, one of the three days that most influenced the outcome of the whole Battle, became known to the Luftwaffe as "Black Thursday".

For the first time, Generaloberst Stumpff's Luftflotte 5, based in Norway and Denmark, was to take part in operations against Britain. Its targets were in north-east England. Air Fleet 2's were in the south-east and No 3's in the south. Their aerodromes stretched from Stavanger to Cherbourg and they were dispersed as follows:

Bf 109 and Bf 110: Guernsey, Caen, Le Havre, Dieppe, Abbeville, Wissant, St. Omer, Calais, Rotterdam, Stavanger.

Ju 87: Flers, Falaise, Pas de Calais.

Ju 88, He 111 and Do 17: Tours, Orléans-Bricy, Chartres, Evreux, Villacoublay, Montdidier, Laon, Cambrai, Lille, Brussels, Amsterdam, Iborg (Denmark), Stavanger (Norway).

The Luftwaffe Intelligence Section had wrongly assessed the RAF fighter strength as 300: approximately half the actual figure.

Day: At 1130hrs 60 Ju 87s and about 40 Bf 109s attacked Lympne, which was out of use for the next two days, and also Hawkinge and Manston. Damage to mains electricity put radar stations at Dover, Rye and Foreness off the air. Nos 54 and 501 squadrons intercepted this raid.

At 1245hrs, 63 He 111s from Stavanger escorted by 21 Bf 110s (with drop tanks) were 25 miles (40 km) north-east of their target, Newcastle-on-Tyne, when No.72 Sqn jumped them, thanks to radar detecting activity soon after noon, apparently heading for the Firth of Forth. This was a feint, made by 20 German seaplanes. Coincidentally, when the real raid approached, it made a vast navigational error and also appeared off the Firth of Forth before turning south. This was No 13 Group's first daylight raid. Nos 14, 65, 79 and 607 were also sent up. The attackers were driven off with the loss of 8 Heinkels and 7 Messerschmitts. No bombs hit the target airfields. For a second raid of some 50 unescorted Ju 88s from Årlborg, Nos.73, 264, 616 and 219 Sqns were ordered off. No 616 and a flight of No.73 intercepted these. Bombs fell on houses and an ammunition dump at Bridlington (Yorkshire). The bomber station at Driffield (Yorks) was damaged and 10 aeroplanes were destroyed on the ground. Six of the enemy were brought down.

Luftflotte 5 did not attack by day again.

In the afternoon Ju 87s, Bf 109s and 110s bombed and strafed the fighter station at Martlesham Heath (Suffolk). Raids of 150 and 100 were engaged by Nos.1, 17, 32, 64, 151 and 601 Sqns, but damaged the aircraft factory at Rochester. Some attacked Dover, Rye, Foreness and Bawdsey radars but without doing much harm. Late that afternoon more heavy raids were mounted. Even fighter squadrons took off to deal with them. Biggin Hill, Worthy Down and Odiham aerodromes, and Portland, were damaged. Bombs intended for Kenley hit Croydon airfield. This was in Greater London and therefore proscribed by Hitler. Both he and Goering were enraged: not for humanitarian reasons, but because they feared a reprisal on Berlin. RAF flew 974 sorties. Abteilung 8, the Research Section, calculated that the Luftwaffe flew 1,786 sorties: 801 by bombers and dive bombers, 1,149 by fighters, of Air Fleets 2 and 3; and 169 of both by Air Fleet 5.

Night: Bristol, Birmingham, Boston, Southampton, Crewe, Harwich, Swansea and the Yorkshire non-industrial town of Beverley were bombed.

Aircraft losses: RAF 30 fighters and 17 pilots, 16 pilots wounded. Luftwaffe: 75. Because the weather had looked unpromising that morning, Goering had summoned Sperrle and Kesselring to his home, Karinhall. His main theme was that the Stukas were too vulnerable to fighter attack. The decisions he took that day were:

1. That "Operations are to be directed exclusively against the enemy air force, including the aircraft industry. Shipping should be attacked only when circumstances are exceptionally favourable. Other targets are to be ignored."

2. That three fighter formations must accompany each Stuka formation. The first would go ahead to take on the defending fighters. The second would

Below: Headlines such as this were wonderful for the morale of the civil population but the inaccuracy of the score really reflects the intensity of the air fighting.

Above: This Heinkel He 111H of I/KG 27 fell at night to the guns of Pilot Officer Alan Wright of No.92 Sqn. It came down near Fordingbridge on August 29.

dive with the Stukas. The third would give high cover.

3. That there must be only one officer in any crew flying over Britain.

4. That he doubted the value of raiding radar sites "as not one of those so far attacked has been put out of action."

The first two decisions betrayed either his obstinacy or his obtuseness: it was not possible for fighters to fly as slowly as any bombers without wasting time and fuel on weaving; and, having no air brakes, they would out-dive the Stukas and leave them unprotected when they were at their most vulnerable. And he could, or would, not see that the RAF fighters were breaking up his raids: hence bombs falling elsewhere than on airfields and aircraft factories were either being jettisoned or aimed at secondary targets chosen by the pilots. The third decision acknowledged his sudden fear of Fighter Command. The fourth was a delusion for which faulty German intelligence was to blame.

Friday, August 16: Fair, but Channel hazy. Despite the inaccuracy of their Intelligence, the Luftwaffe opened the day with justified optimism. Germany calculated that Fighter Command's strength was down to 430, of which 300

were operationally serviceable; and assessed monthly aircraft production as a maximum of 300. The facts were that Dowding had 570 Spitfires and Hurricanes and 102 Defiants, Gladiators and Blenheims at his disposal, with a reserve of 235 Spitfires and Hurricanes. Aircraft production had risen to 440 a month. (Bf 109 production was 164 in June, 220 in July, 173 in August, 218 in September.) Britain's lack lay in fighter pilots, and that day there were only 1,379 against an establishment of 1,558.

But the enemy did have the advantage in numbers, because Fighter Command's squadrons were spread throughout the British Isles, whereas the preponderance of the Luftwaffe's strength was thrown against one, two or three small areas at a time. Also, the enemy bombers, which outnumbered even their escorting fighters, had a formdable aggregate of fire power. Every raid that the RAF met, therefore, out-gunned it massively. The obvious comparison is with David and Goliath, and it is a good one.

Day: Raids began by noon. West Malling was rendered unserviceable for four days. This, Tangmere, and its satellite Westhampnet, and Manston were the only fighter stations attacked. Other airfields hit were Farnborough, Harwell,

Brize Norton, Gosport, Lee-on-Solent (Fleet Air Arm). Many aircraft were destroyed on the ground, but only three fighters. London docks and suburbs attacked, civilians killed, railway lines hit. Ventnor (Isle of Wight) radar put out of action, despite Goering's edict. Flight Lieutenant James Nicolson of No.249 Squadron won Fighter Command's first Victoria Cross. His aircraft set on fire by a Bf 110, he stayed with it until he had shot his enemy down.

Night: Light attacks on Bristol, Chester, Newport, Swansea, Portland, Tavistock (Devon non-industrial town), Worcester (cathedral city).

Aircraft losses: RAF 22, Luftwaffe 45.

Saturday, August 17: Fine.
Day: Frustrated, weary Luftwaffe flew only reconnaissance.
Night: Small raids on Wales, north-west England and Midlands.
Aircraft losses: RAF 0, Luftwaffe 3.

Sunday, August 18: Fine, becoming cloudy.

This was the day on which Germany expected to smash Fighter Command once and for all. Goering had available 276 Ju 87; 768 Ju 88, He 111 and Do 17; 194 Bf 110; 745 Bf 109; and, for reconnaissance, 52 Bf 110, Ju 88, He 111 and Do 17.

Fighter Command's serviceability state was 419 Hurricanes and 211 Spitfires. There were also 25 Blenheims, 21 Defiants, 1 Gladiator.

Day: Midday saw attacks by huge formations on West Malling, Biggin Hill, Kenley — grievously damaged by 100 bombs — and Croydon. In early afternoon, heavy raids struck three

Coastal Command and Naval airfields at Gosport, Thorney Island and Ford, and Poling radar station. No.152 Sqn Spitfires and No.43 Sqn Hurricanes did such terrible execution among the Stukas — I/St 77 alone lost 12 out of 28, and six barely limped back to France — that these were withdrawn from the battle. Galland was absent, on his way to see Goering. His second-in-command, Oberleutnant Schöpfel, leading III/JG26, shot down four Hurricanes in two minutes in the Folkestone-Canterbury area. On the subject of the Luftwaffe's losses during the past 10 days, Galland said, comparing the Hurricanes' and Spitfires' 8 machineguns with the Bf 109s' one cannon and two machineguns, that the latter armament was "A good idea for a very good shot, but the average pilot is not so good: he needs a shotgun. The Spitfire is a real shotgun, so is better armed than the 109 when shooting while turning."

Night: :Bombs fell on Bristol, eastern England and south Wales. Minelaying in Bristol Channel.

Aircraft losses: RAF 31, Luftwaffe 53.

This day's fighting forced a radical change of policy on Hitler and Goering. The Luftwaffe's morale was greatly lowered by the disparity between their leaders' assurances of easy victory and the reality of Fighter Command's performance. The invasion date was postponed to September 17.

Monday, August 19: Cloudy, eastern England showery.
Day: Weather limited activity. The Luftwaffe flew many photographic reconnaissance sorties. Raids occurred at Dover, Portsmouth, Southampton and

Below: An amusing juxtaposition has the "More Please!" slogan for Brown and Polson's custard powder next to the headline "115 RAIDERS OUT OF 600 DESTROYED".

Above: London's dockland area made an unmissable target for the Luftwaffe when Hitler finally unleashed his bombers against the capital during September 1940.

Pembroke Dock, in south Wales, where oil storage tanks were set alight. German records state: "In the second phase of the Battle of Britain from August 19 to September 6, 1940, airfields in inland England were attacked. These attacks were made by small bomber forces under strong fighter escort while other fighters flew 'free chase'. That was a continuation of the action that had started on 21 July." (The term "free chase" refers to fighter sweeps clearing the way and challenging RAF fighters to engage them.)

Night: Nuisance raiders bombed Bristol, Southampton, Sheffield, Wolverhampton, Derby, Hull, Nottingham, Leicester, Liverpool.

Aircraft losses: RAF 3, Luftwaffe 6.
Goering held a conference at Karinhall, attended by his Air Corps and Geschwader commanders. He told them that the decisive period of the air war against Britain had been reached, and reiterated, "Our first priority is the destruction of the enemy's fighters. If they do not take the air, we shall attack them on the ground. Surprise attacks on the aircraft industry must be made by day and night." The secondary targets were bomber stations. "There will no longer be any restriction on the choice of targets, but I reserve the right to order the bombing of London and Liverpool."

After this meeting, decorating Galland and Mölders, his two most successful Gruppen-Kommandeure, with the gold pilot's badge with jewels, he told them that he was not satisfied with the general performance of the fighters. He wanted young men with a high tally of victories to lead his Geschwader. Accordingly, he appointed Galland Kommandeur of JG26 with effect from August 22, 1940, in place of Major Gotthardt Handrick, winner of the gold medal for the modern pentathlon in the 1936 Olympic Games; and Mölders was appointed to command JG51 in place of Major General Osterkamp. Further, he replaced the Kommandeure of JG3, JG52 and JG54.

Air Vice Marshal Keith Park took fresh measures to counter the enemy's air strategy, by instructing sector controllers:

1. To avoid forced landings on the sea by positioning fighters to intercept over land or within gliding distance of it.

2. Not to let fighters chase reconnaissance aeroplanes or small fighter formations out to sea.

3. To intercept single reconnaissance aircraft overland with a pair of fighters.

4. When the enemy approaches in cloud, to patrol one or two fighters over any airfield under threat.

5. To use the minimum number of fighters to intercept enemy fighters: bombers being the more important targets.

6. To request fighters from No.12 Group to patrol certain No.11 Group airfields, if all No.11 Group squadrons based near London are airborne.

Tuesday, August 20: Mainly fine over Channel. Elsewhere, rain and cloud.
Day: Pembroke Dock bombed. West Malling, Manston, Eastchurch airfields and Dover balloon barrage hit. Ships off Welsh and East Anglian coasts attacked.
Night: Bombers over south-west.
Aircraft losses: RAF 2, Luftwaffe 6.

Winston Churchill made his famous speech in the House of Commons that ended with, "Never in the field of human conflict was so much owed by so many to so few."

Wednesday, August 21: Rain and cloud.
Day: In the morning Bf 109s shot down some 50 barrage balloons at Dover. Formations of one bomber Gruppe escorted by a Geschwader of fighters attacked Debden, Eastchurch and Detling. In the afternoon Hornchurch and Biggin Hill were severely hit. But the raiders were badly mauled each time and Oberleutnant Hahn of I/JG3 spoke for them all when he said, "Only a few of us have not yet had to ditch in the Channel with a badly damaged aeroplane or dead engine." Weariness and discouragement were sapping the Germans. According to Lieutenant Ostermann of III/JG54, "Utter exhaustion had set in. For the first time, pilots discussed the prospects of posting to a quieter sector."

Bombers over airfields: Bircham Newton, Coltishall, Stradishall, Horsham, St Faith, St Eval, Exeter, Watton. Towns attacked: Southampton, Grimsby, Norwich, Canterbury, Bournemouth, Newmarket.
Night: Small raids on Harwich, Firth of Forth and Hull.
Aircraft losses: RAF 1, Luftwaffe 12.

Thursday, August 22: Clouds and rain squalls.
Goering put Luftflotte III's fighters under Luftflotte II's command and ordered them to move from Cherbourg area to Pas de Calais.
Day: Channel shipping attacked. Manston airfield and Dover bombed.
Night: Convoy attacked at Wick; airfields North Coates, Manston, St Eval, Wick, Filton and aircraft factory at Filton bombed.
Aircraft losses: RAF 5, Luftwaffe 2.

Friday, August 23: Cloudy, showers, bright patches.
Day: Light raids on airfields at Abingdon, Biggin Hill, Tangmere. Bombs jettisoned over London residential suburbs. Bombers attacked Portsmouth, Maidstone, St Albans, Cromer and convoys off Essex and Norfolk coasts.
Night: Pembroke Dock, Midlands factories, and a convoy attacked.
Aircraft losses: RAF 0, Luftwaffe 5.

Saturday, August 24: Fine south, showers north.
Climactic days resumed and Britain entered a period of greatest jeopardy.
Day: Heavy raid on Manston, destroying buildings and telephone lines, leaving unexploded bombs on landing area, compelling evacuation. Raids on Hornchurch, North Weald, Dover, Ramsgate and Portsmouth.
Night: 170 raiders over northern and south-eastern England. Bombs intended for Thames Haven and Rochester fell on central London.
Aircraft losses: RAF 22, Luftwaffe 38.

Sunday, August 25: Fair, turning cloudy.
All German bomber units received a telegram from Goering demanding the

Below: The facade of a blazing building collapses outwards, and tons of masonry cascade into the street below, just missing a fire engine.

names of aircraft captains whose crews dropped bombs within the London perimeter. Luftwaffe High Command would punish them by posting to infantry regiments.
Day: Quiet until mid-afternoon. Warmwell airfield badly damaged, and targets in west of England, Scilly Isles RAF wireless station, and Pembroke Dock bombed. Heavy raid on Dover and Thames estuary.
Night: Minelaying west and south. Midlands heavily raided, also south Wales, south of England, and airfield at Montrose, Scotland.
Aircraft losses: RAF 16, Luftwaffe 20.
The night RAF Bomber Command put up 81 Hampdens to attack the Siemens-Halske factory and other targets in Berlin. Crews unable positively to identify objectives through cloud jettisoned bombs over the city. This first damage to the enemy capital brought ridicule on Goering, who had boasted that it would never happen.

Monday, August 26: Channel cloudy. Britain generally cloudy; south better than the rest.
Day: At 1100hrs 150-plus hostiles attacked Biggin Hill and Kenley, bombed Folkestone and set fire to balloon barrage at Dover. Six RAF squadrons and three flights intercepted and scattered them. In the afternoon 100-plus hostiles made for Hornchurch and North Weald but were met and disrupted, managing only to attack Debden quite severely. A third 150-plus raid was intercepted. Portsmouth, Warmwell, Debden, Biggin

Hill, Kenley under attack.
Night: Bombs on Plymouth, Coventry, Bournemouth and St Eval.
Aircraft losses: RAF 31, Luftwaffe 41.

Tuesday, August 27: Straits hazy, clouds over Channel clearing, rain Midlands and east.
Day: Luftwaffe reconnaissance flights spotted.
Night: Bombers over south and south-east.
Aircraft losses: RAF 0, Luftwaffe 3.

Wednesday, August 28: Straits cloudy, generally fair to fine.
Day: Eastchurch, Rochford bombed. Enemy fighter sweeps over Kent and Thames estuary provoked engagement by RAF.
Night: 150 raiders on Liverpool, London, Birmingham, Coventry, Sheffield, Manchester, Derby.
Aircraft losses: RAF 28, Luftwaffe 30; one mail-carrying Gortha 154 lost its way and forced-landed.

Thursday, August 29: Bright intervals between rain.
Day: Light raids on south-east and south.
Night: Liverpool hit by 130 bombers. Diversionary singletons over Midlands and London.
Aircraft losses: RAF 9, Luftwaffe 17.

Friday, August 30: Channel fine, elsewhere fair.
Day: Shipping in Thames estuary attacked. This was to distract attention from main targets; at 1030, 1100 and

Above: The expression "Minor Damage" often concealed individual disaster. A raid on coastal towns in Kent on August 26 left these two ladies homeless.

1130hrs raids, each 30-plus, over French coast setting course for England. Sixteen defending squadrons airborne. Biggin Hill damaged. At 1330hrs three raids totalling more than 40 on Kenley, Biggin Hill, Tangmere, Shoreham; eight squadrons sent up to turn them back. Radar stations at Rye, Pevensey, Foreness, Dover, Fairlight, Beachy Head, Whitstable rendered unserviceable; electricity mains damaged. Another raid at 1600hrs targeted Kenley, Biggin Hill, North Weald and a convoy; Oxford, Luton and Detling were badly damaged. At about 1800hrs approximately 10 hostiles attacked Biggin Hill and caused widespread severe damage.
Night: Raids began at 2030hrs on London, Liverpool and south Wales. Singletons aimed at North Weald, Debden, Biggin Hill, Hornchurch, Detling, Eastchurch, Thorney Island, Calshot, Rochford, Broxbourne, Derby, Norwich and Peterborough.
Aircraft losses: RAF 25, Luftwaffe 36.

Saturday, August 31: Fair, Straits of Dover hazy.
Day: Action opened at 0800hrs. Dover balloon barrage destroyed. Debden hit by 100 bombs. North Weald, Croydon, Hornchurch, Biggin Hill, Detling all bombed or strafed during the day's attacks. Radar stations at Pevensey, Rye, Beachy Head, Whitstable, Foreness damaged.
Night: Liverpool badly damaged, Portsmouth, Manchester, Bristol, Rotherhithe, Durham, Stockport, Gloucester, Worcester bombed.
Aircraft losses: RAF 39, Luftwaffe 41.

Fighter Command was feeling the increasing wear and tear of two months' dawn readiness and unrelenting action. Pilots were weary. Some, even among the bravest and the most successful, were showing signs of excessive nervous tension. Dowding, his Group and Sector Commanders and the Operations Controllers were concerned about the high losses among squadron and flight commanders and the problem of finding replacements. They were no less worried by the curtailed training of the new pilots being hurried through the Operational Training Units and committed to meeting the enemy with only five to ten hours on Hurricanes or Spitfires, and without any practice at air-to-air firing. But that unquantifiable essential for victory, high morale, remained as buoyant as ever.

The Luftwaffe, both fighter pilots and bomber crews, were equally tired and worn. Although their fighting spirit remained unabated, they were disillusioned. Their leaders had promised them swift conquest, yet they had been unable to accomplish it. Instead of recognising his own defects, Goering heaped blamed on his fighter units. However courageous the fighter pilots, they were nagged by the ever-present anxiety that their aircraft endurance allowed only ten minutes' fighting time over England, and the Channel waited to swallow them up if empty fuel tanks forced them down. They had grown to hate the Channel and had many abusive names for it, the least scabrous being, "The Sewer". Under-achievement and Goering's incessant recriminations had sapped their morale.

Below: The first RAF bombing raid on Berlin took place on August 25. It is recorded in the logbook of Flying Officer Chesters DFM, a Hampden crewman.

Date	Hour	Aircraft Type and No.	Pilot	Duty	Remarks	Flying Times Day	Night
					Times brought forward —	22410	94·15.
August 3rd	21·30	HAMPDEN P1393.	F/S CLAYTON	GARDENING AT KIEL	BOMBED CARGO BOATS LANDEDHI. HATFIELD WOODHOUSE. U/S MACHINE		7·00
7TH	2·48.	P1339.	F/S CLAYTON	BOMBING	SHIPS OR DOCKS AT KIEL L.2000. LB S		7·00
11TH	20·50.	P4371.	F/S CLAYTON.	GARDENING KIEL FJORD	2 (250#) BOMBS ON SONDERBURG PORT		7·10
14TH	22·00	P4371	F/S CLAYTON	BOMBING AT COLOGNE	6, 250#		4·45
16TH	21·00	P1338	W/C REID	TO MERSEBURG (LEUNA WORKS)	41.500# U/S		7·55
19TH	16·40	P2136	F/S CLAYTON	TEST.		3·05	
19TH	20·55.	P2136.	F/S CLAYTON.	GARDENING BALTIC.			7·15.
22nd	20·45	P2136	F/S CLAYTON	FRANKFURT.	6,250# & INCENDIARY.		7·00
25th	21·40	P4371.	F/S CLAYTON	BOMBED	HANGARS & BUILDINGS JOHANNISTHAL BERLIN.		8·10.
28th	20·20.	P4240.	F/S CLAYTON.	BOMBED.	BEMOLROITE BERLIN. SEIMENS. WORKS BERLIN.		8·05
					Total Time	23215	158·35

SEPTEMBER 1940

Sunday, September 1: Fine.
Goering ordered operations to concentrate on 30 factories making aircraft or aircraft parts.
Day: Heavy attacks on airfields at Eastchurch, Detling, Biggin Hill, Hawkinge, Lympne, and also on Dover and Tilbury.
Night: Bombs on Sheffield, Stafford, Liverpool area, Hull, Grimsby, Burton, Kent, south Wales.
Aircraft losses: RAF 15, Luftwaffe 14.

Monday, September 2: Fine, Straits hazy.
Day: Attacks on Rochford, Biggin Hill, North Weald, Eastchurch, Debden, Kenley, Digby, Hornchurch, Detling; and on airfield and aircraft factory at Brooklands. Random bombing of Kent.
Night: Minelaying and bombing south Wales, Liverpool, Birmingham and small towns.
Aircraft losses: RAF 31, Luftwaffe 35.

Tuesday, September 3: Mostly fine.
Day: Debden, Hornchurch, North Weald severely hit.
Night: South Wales, Liverpool and south-east England bombed.
Aircraft losses: RAF 16, Luftwaffe 16.

Wednesday, September 4: Fine.
Day: Action on Goering's directive about attacking the aircraft industry was initiated. Dover balloon barrage, Lympne, Eastchurch, Brooklands (and aircraft factory) hit. Also aircraft factory at Rochester.
Night: Bristol, south Wales, Liverpool, Manchester, Newcastle, Tilbury, Gravesend airfield, Nottingham, all bombed.
Aircraft losses: RAf 15, Luftwaffe 20.

Thursday, September 5: Mostly fine.
Day: North Weald, Croydon, Lympne, Biggin Hill, Eastchurch airfields attacks.
Night: Liverpool, London, Manchester and more than 40 other places bombed.
Aircraft losses: RAF 20, Luftwaffe 23.

Friday, September 6: Fine.
Day: Inaccurate bombing of Biggin Hill airfield and aircraft factory at Brooklands.
Night: Scattered light raids.
Aircraft losses: RAF 23, Luftwaffe 35.

Saturday, September 7: Fair.
Armageddon was the name of the biblical last great struggle between Good and Evil. It could appropriately be applied to the period of plenary raids on

Above: Bombs rain down on the airfield at Rochester on September 4.

London that began on this day.
The Operations Order issued on the previous day by Grauert, the General Officer Commanding I Air Corps, is a statement of intention and method that summarises and illustrates the many further high-intensity attacks that followed.

"1. In the evening of 7.9 Luftflotte 2 will conduct a major strike against target Loge (the code word for London).

"To this end the following units will operate in succession: for the Initial Attack: at 1800 one KG of II Air Corps; for the Main Attack: at 1840 II Air Corps at 1845 I Air Corps, reinforced by KG30.

"2. Disposition of I Air Corps Units: KG 30 (plus IIKG/76) on the right; KG1 central. KG76 (less II/KG76) on the left. For target see General Appendix.

"3. Fighter Cover. (a) Purpose of Initial Attack is to force English fighters into the air so that they will have reached end of endurance at time of Main Attack. (b) fighter escort will be provided by Jafu 2 in the proportion of one fighter Geschwader for each bomber Geschwader. (c) ZG76 (for this operation under I Air Corps command) will, from 1840, clear the air of enemy fighters over I Air Corps targets, thereby covering attack and retreat of bomber formations. (d) Jafu 2 guarantees two fighter Geschwader to cover I and II Air Corps.

"4. Execution. (a) Rendezvous: To be made with fighter escort before crossing coast. Bombers will fly direct. (b) Courses: KG30, St Omer — just south of Cap Griz Nez — railway fork north of 'Seveneae' — to the target. KG1, St Pol — mouth of 1a Slack — Riverhead — to

the target. KH76, Hesdin — north perimeter boulogne — Westerham — target. (c) Fighter escort: JG26 for KG30, JG54 for KG1, JG27 for KG76. In view of the fact that the fighters will be operating at the limit of their endurance, it is essential that direct courses be flown and the attack completed in minimum time. (d) Flying altitudes after RV with fighters: KG30: 5,000-5,500 metres (16,400-18,000ft). KG1: 6,000-6,500m (19,700-21,300ft). KG76: 5,000-5,500m (16,400-18,000ft). To stagger heights as above will provide maximum concentration of attacking force. On return flight some loss of altitude is permissible, in order to cross the English coast at approximately 4,000m (13,000ft).
(e) The intention is to complete the operation by a single attack. In the events of units failing to arrive directly over target, other suitable objectives in Loge may be bombed from altitude of approach. (It is chilling to pause here and reflect that the "other suitable objectives" permitted in 4(e) were the men, women and children of London.) (f) Return flight: After releasing bombs formations will turn to starboard. KG27 will do so with care after first establishing that starboard units have already attacked. Return course will then be Maidstone — Dymchurch — escort fighter bases. (g) Bomb-loads: He 111 and Ju 88, no 50kg bombs, 20 per cent incendiaries, 30 per cent delayed-action 2-4 hours and 10-14 hours (the latter without concussion fuses); Do17, 25 per cent disintegrating containers with BI, EL and no SD 50; Load only to be limited by security of aircraft against enemy Flak.

Fuel sufficient for completion of operation and marginal safety to be carried only.

"5. To achieve the necessary maximum effect it is essential that units fly as highly concentrated forces during approach, attack and especially on return. The main objective of the operation is to prove that the Luftwaffe can achieve this."
Day: London heavily bombed; widespread carnage and fires. Valiant and unremitting defence by RAF.
Night: Ruthless savage bombing of London.
Aircraft losses: RAF 25 aircraft (19 pilots). Luftwaffe 37.

Sunday, September 8: Fair, turning cloudy.
Day: Light attacks on Detling, Hornchurch, West Malling, Gravesend, Dover and Sevenoaks.
Night: 207 bombers on London kill 412 and grievously injure 747.
Aircraft losses: RAF 2, Luftwaffe 15.

Monday, September 9: Rain and thunder.
Day: Ineffectual raids on Brooklands factory and London. Bombs jettisoned on residential areas in London and suburbs. Purley, Norbiton, Surbiton, Canterbury, Kingston, West Malling all bombed: Tangmere strafed.
Night: London badly hit.
Aircraft losses: RAF 19, Luftwaffe 28.

Tuesday, September 10: Cloud and rain.
Day: Tangmere strafed; West Malling slightly bombed.
Night: London, south Wales, Liverpool area raided.
Aircraft losses: RAF 0, Luftwaffe 3.

Below: The early days of the blitz caused considerable damage to the City of London; here the Prime Minister inspects a bomb crater on September 9.

Above: The headline that lifted British morale as never before. Much has since been made of this overclaim, but the fact remains that a great victory was won.

Wednesday, September 11: Mainly fine.
Day: Germans deferred intended invasion of England to 14th after RAF mauled attacks on London. Bombs on London Hornchurch, Biggin Hill, Kenley, Brooklands, Eastchurch, Detling and Colerne.
Night: London pounded. Merseyside, west and east England attacked. Mines off east and south coasts.
Aircraft losses: RAF 25, Luftwaffe 21.

Thursday, September 12: Poor.
Day: Fairlight radar station slightly bombed.
Night: London, Midlands, north-east, east, south-east England attacked lightly.
Aircraft losses: RAF 0, Luftwaffe 4.

Friday, September 13: Poor.
Day: Bombs on London.
Night: London again bombed.
Aircraft losses: RAF 1, Luftwaffe 4.

Saturday, September 14: Rain, clouds, thunder.
Day: London attacked. Invasion, delayed again to 17th.
Night: London, Cardiff, Ipswich, Maidstone attacked.
Aircraft losses: RAF 14, Luftwaffe 14.

Sunday, September 15: Fair, becoming fine.
This date is observed annually as Battle of Britain Day. It was the third of the most critical days of the Battle, and the ultimately decisive one. The Luftwaffe was determined finally to break Fighter Command and the spirit of the civil population by the scale of its attacks that were intended to engage the RAF's

dwindling numbers of defending aircraft and pilots, while raining an annihilating weight of bombs on London. The outcome was not the overwhelming of Great Britain, but the further frustration and final disillusionment of the Luftwaffe, which suffered its heaviest losses of the Battle.
Day: Tremendous bombing of London rendered inaccurate by the fervour and passion with which the RAF's fighter squadrons waded into one huge enemy formation after another and dispersed it. The bombs struck, nonetheless, scattered widely over inner and outer London, bringing ruin to homes and death to their occupants. The capital was not the only target: Portland and Southampton were also attacked.
Night: London badly hit. Lesser raids on Liverpool, Manchester, Bristol, Cardiff.
Aircraft losses: RAF 27 aircraft (13 pilots), Luftwaffe 56.

Monday, September 16: Cloudy, rain.
Day: Little activity. London raided.
Night: London strongly attacked; Bristol and Merseyside bombed.
Aircraft losses: RAF 1, Luftwaffe 9.

Tuesday, September 17: Poor.
Day: Invasion postponed indefinitely. German fighter sweeps foiled.
Night: London gravely hit; lighter raids on Glasgow and Liverpool.
Aircraft losses: RAF 5, Luftwaffe 8.

Wednesday, September 18: Squalls and bright intervals.
Day: Thames Estuary bombed.
Night: London and Liverpool area raided.
Aircraft losses: RAF 12, Luftwaffe 19.

Thursday, September 19: Wet.
Day: Bombers over London and Thames Estuary.
Night: Central London, Heston airfield and Merseyside attacked.
Aircraft losses: RAF 0, Luftwaffe 8.

Friday, September 20: Fair.
Day: Luftwaffe fighter sweep over Kent.
Night: London hit.
Aircraft losses: RAF 7, Luftwaffe 8.

Saturday, September 21: Fine.
Day: Brooklands slightly damaged. London, Kenley, Hornchurch and Biggin Hill attacked.
Night: London and Liverpool area raided.
Aircraft losses: RAF 0, Luftwaffe 9.

Sunday, September 22: Bad, becoming good.
Day: A few enemy intrusions.
Night: Heavy bombing of London.
Aircraft losses: RAF 0, Luftwaffe 5.

Monday, September 23: Fine.
Day: Fighter sweeps over Kent.
Night: London bombed.
Aircraft losses: RAF 11, Luftwaffe 16.

Tuesday, September 24: Hazy and foggy.
Day: Attacks on Southampton and Tilbury. Galland scored his 40th victory — over the Thames estuary — and was awarded the oak leaves to the Knight's Cross, the third German to be thus honoured. The predecessors were General Dietl (Army) and Galland's friend

and fellow Geschwader Commander, Werner Mölders, who had scored his 40th kill three days earlier. Hitler accorded Galland a private audience when he decorated him.
Night: Merseyside and London bombed.
Aircraft losses: RAF 4, Luftwaffe 11.

Wednesday, September 25: Haze over Channel, followed by cloud and bright intervals.
Day: Raids on Plymouth and Bristol. Bristol aircraft factory badly damaged and production set back for many weeks. Heavy casualties among personnel.
Night: London, north-west England and north Wales bombed.
Aircraft losses: RAF 4, Luftwaffe 13.

Thursday, September 26: Fair.
Day: Aircraft factory at Southampton devastated.
Night: Raids on London and Merseyside.
Aircraft losses: RAF 9, Luftwaffe 9.

Friday, September 27: Fair.
Day: Raids on London and Bristol thwarted.
Night: London, Midlands and Liverpool area raided.
Aircraft losses: RAF 28, Luftwaffe 54.

Saturday, September 28: Fair to fine, but Straits cloudy.
Day: Raids on London and Portsmouth largely foiled.
Night: London savaged again.
Aircraft losses: RAF 16, Luftwaffe 10.

Below: Feldwebel Heinz Friedrich and his crew are marched into captivity at Burmarsh on September 11, as smoke rises from their burning Heinkel He 111H.

Sunday, September 29: Mostly fair.
Day: Nuisance attacks on convoys and also east and south-east.
Night:
Aircraft losses: RAF 5, Luftwaffe 10.

Monday, September 30: Fair.
Day: Fighter sweeps over south-east, some raiders reached London. Non-industrial town of Sherborne bombed when Luftwaffe tried to hit aircraft factory at Yeovil (error of 7 miles/11km) through cloud.
Night: London, Bristol, Liverpool, eastern England battered.
Aircraft losses: RAF 16, Luftwaffe 44.

OCTOBER

The bombs the Luftwaffe was dropping on London had increased in size since the first deliberate raid on September 7, when the heaviest used had weighed 110lb (50kg). Now 1,100, 1,650 or 2,200lb (500, 750 or 1,000kg) high-explosive bombs burst among the inhabitants, combined with incendiaries, as before.

The RAF had no operational purpose-designed night fighters yet. The Defiants had suffered such appalling casualties that they had been withdrawn from front-line service by day in August. They were now beginning to equip night fighter squadrons, but still lacked airborne radar. For the time being the eyes of a single-seater pilot or a Defiant pilot and air gunner had to suffice, to spot a hostile bomber's exhaust flames or discern its silhouette against the clouds. Night fighter squadrons flying Blenheims were experimenting with the first — erratic, temperamental — radar sets to be fitted in aeroplanes. Searchlights were the best help available to those who hunted in the dark, until they had mistakenly illuminated friend in mistake for foe and invited a burst from a raider's guns. But their limit was 12,000ft (3,660m) and most hostiles flew higher. Close control from ground radar stations was operating by this time, but it was rough and ready and a reliable radar set in the aircraft was essential for the last stage of an interception; but only the Blenheims had one, and dependable it was not.

The RAF made unrewarding attempts to use a new weapon effectively. This consisted of a bomb suspended beneath a parachute by 2,000ft (610m) of piano wire. A special flight of obsolete Harrow bombers converted for the purpose

released these in the path of incoming raids, but lack of success soon led to the abandonment of this bizarre practice.

Tuesday, October 1: Cloudy but fair.
The first raid, at 0700hrs, heralded a change of enemy policy. Goering had decided to use his bombers mainly by night and to send out Bf 109s each carrying a 550lb (250kg) bomb and Bf 110s carrying up to four of these by day. They came in formations of 50 to 100, flying high. Throughout the Battle, the RAF's severest tactical handicap had been lack of time to make altitude. When radar reported an approaching raid over the French coast and fighters scrambled to deal with it, they would have to climb away from it while gaining height, or they would have flown under it and been shot down themselves. This disadvantage became greater when German fighter-bombers climbed quickly over their own territory and arrived over England at a greater height than the day bombers used to.
Day: Raids on London, Portsmouth,

Southampton, mostly by fighter-bombers, frustrated. Intruders over Scotland.
Night: Bombs on London, Manchester, Liverpool areas.
Aircraft losses: RAF 4, Luftwaffe 6.

Wednesday, October 2: Fine.
Day: Fighter-bombers between 20,000 and 30,000ft (6,100-9,145m) attacked Biggin Hill and London continuously from 0930 to 1300hrs.
Night: Starting at 1915hrs, 180 bombers, of which 100 concentrated on London, crossed the English and Scottish coasts. Manchester, Aberdeen and the vicinities of airfields at Northolt, Hornchurch, Kenley, Hendon, Brooklands, Eastchurch, Redhill, Usworth and Duxford were hit.
Aircraft losses: RAF 1, Luftwaffe 17.

Thursday, October 3: Rain. Visibility over England down to 500 yards (460m).
Day: Previous night's raids continued until 0615hrs. Fighter-bombers, singly and in pairs, attack RAF stations at Cosford, Tangmere and Cardington, and also Thames Haven, Cambridge,

Leamington, Bedford, Worcester, Reading, and the de Havilland aircraft factory at Hatfield.
Night: London bombed.
Aircraft losses: RAF 0, Luftwaffe 9.

Friday, October 4: Mist and rain by day, fog at night.
Day: A succession of some 70 German fighter-bombers singly and in pairs attacked London, Canterbury and other Kent towns and two convoys off Kent.
Night: London and Liverpool attacked.
Aircraft losses: RAF 3, Luftwaffe 12
Hitler still deluded himself that Operation Sealion, the invasion of England, was practicable. His Navy wanted him to call it off and the Luftwaffe admitted that, with the deteriorating British weather, they had abandoned all hope of destroying the RAF in the air or on the ground. Their bomber crews were having to find their way through thick cloud. In recent months so many crews experienced in blind flying had been killed over Britain or been taken prisoner that there was an urgent need for replacements. But many of the Ju 52s used by the blind-flying training schools that had been borrowed to transport troops for the invasion of Holland and Norway had been lost, which delayed and reduced the output of new crews.

German fighter pilots' morale was affected by the compulsion to operate as fighter-bombers with a load that made their Bf 109s sluggish. Also, as Goering never admitted any responsibility for failure, but always blamed his pilots and crews, it was now their turn to incur his venom. They complained to one another that they were reduced to being what General Galland described as "stopgaps and scapegoats".

"We fighter pilots looked on this violation of our aircraft with great bitterness," he says. "The fighter-bombers were put into action in a great hurry. There was hardly time to give the pilots bombing training. The Bf 109 carried a 500lb (227kg) bomb. The Bf 110 carried two of them plus four 100-pounders (45kg). No great effect could be achieved with that. Even less so because the fighter pilots were annoyed at carrying cargo and were glad to get rid of the bombs anywhere."

Throughout the Battle of Britain, Dowding, Park, Leigh-Mallory, Saul and Brand understood the psychology of their pilots and treated them accordingly, whereas Goering had no understanding at all of how to handle his.

Below: Oberleutnant Fischer of 7/JG 27 survived this forced landing in Windsor Great Park on September 30 after a combat with RAF fighters.

Park issued a directive to counter the enemy's new tactic, from which the following excerpts are most relevant. "With the prevailing cloudy skies and inaccurate heights given by RDF the group controllers' most difficult problem is to know the height of incoming enemy raids. Occasionally reconnaissance Spitires and Hurricanes from Hornchurch or Biggin Hill are able to sight and report the height and particulars of enemy formations. Moreover the special fighter reconnaissance flight is now being formed at Gravesend (attached to No.66 Squadron) for the purpose of getting information about approaching enemy raids."

Because of lack of height reports and the delays in receipt RDF and Observer Corps information at Group, and the longer time recently taken by squadrons to take off, pairs and wings of squadrons were meeting enemy formations above them, before reaching the height ordered by Group.

Park: "Tip-and-run raids across Kent by Bf 110s carrying bombs or small formations of long-range bombers escorted by fighters give such short notice that the Group controller is sometimes compelled to detail even single fighter squadrons that happen to be in the air to intercept the enemy bombers before they attack aircraft factories, sector aerodromes, or other such vital points as docks, Woolwich, etc. Normally, however, Group controller has

sufficient time to detail from one to three pairs (two to six squadrons) to intercept raids heading for London.

"Whenever time permits I wish Group controllers to get the readiness squadrons in company over sector aerodromes, Spitfires 25,000feet (7,602m), Hurricanes 20,000 (6,100m), and wait until they report they are in good position before sending them to patrol lines or to intercept raids having a good track in fairly clear weather."

Saturday, October 5: Rain with bright periods.
Day: Southampton, Folkestone and Detling all hit. Fighter-bombers on London.
Night: London and eastern airfields raided.
Aircraft losses: RAF 9, Luftwaffe 9.

Sunday, October 6: Wet.
Day: London and east England under light attacks. Low-flying fighter-bombers demolished three barrack blocks at Biggin Hill.
Night: Slight enemy activity over London and environs.
Aircraft losses: RAF 1, Luftwaffe 6.

Monday, October 7: Poor.
Day: Yeovil aircraft factory raided.
Night: London, Merseyside, Firth of Forth under attack. Airfields at Hatfield, Ford, Tangmere, Eastleigh, Lee-on-Solent hit.
Aircraft losses: RAF 17, Luftwaffe 21.

Above: The abiding memory of the blitz is St. Pauls rising above the smoke, but the cathedral was hit on the night of 10/11 October and the high altar destroyed.

Below: Fighter pilots called bits of enemy aircraft trophies, but for small boys (and their fathers), the collection of souvenirs was actively discouraged.

Goering announced a new plan for the demoralisation of London and the provinces. Its objectives were : 1, Absolute control of the Channel and the English coastal area. 2, Progressive and complete annihilation of London, with all its military objectives and industrial production. 3, A steady paralysing of Britain's technical, commercial and civil life. 4, Demoralisation of the civil population of London and its provinces. 5, Progressive weakening of Britain's forces.

Instead of weakening, the RAF was reacting with growing strength. On that very day, it flew 825 sorties and, as shown above, destroyed 25 per cent more enemy aeroplanes than it lost. And the civilian population remained defiant, its morale high. Instead of fear, its attitude towards Hitler and Goering was of ridicule: the former on account of his ranting and insane rages, the other for

his obesity and flashy uniforms that were more appropriate to musical comedy than to the dignity of a Field Marshal.

Tuesday, October 8: Fair.
Day: London persistently bombed.
Night: London bombed again.
Aircraft losses: RAF 4, Luftwaffe 14.

Wednesday, October 9: Poor.
Day: Raids on south-eastern airfields and London.
Night: London caught it badly.
Aircraft losses: RAF 1, Luftwaffe 9.

Thursday, October 10: Patchy.
Day: Incessant raids by small numbers of fighter-bombers and bombers on south-east airfields, outer London and Weymouth.
Night: London, Merseyside, Manchester and airfields attacked.
Aircraft losses: RAF 5, Luftwaffe 4.

Friday, October 11: Showers, fair intervals, early mist, night fog.
Day: Raids on Weymouth, Folkestone, Canterbury, Deal, and on airfields at Southend, Kenley, Biggin Hill.
Night: Bombs on London, Tyneside, Teesside, Merseyside, Manchester.
Aircraft losses: RAF 9, Luftwaffe 7.

Saturday, October 12: Mist and fog dispersed by light wind.
Day: London attacked.
Night: London bombed again.
Aircraft losses: RAF 19, Luftwaffe 11.

Hitler at last conceded that he must admit that he could not invade Britain that year. His decision was announced by Generalfeldmarschall Wilhelm Keitel, head of the unified Defence Staff, which had replaced the War Ministry and the Army Command in 1938. Hitler had chosen him for the post because of his lack of personality or intellect. Known as ''Lakaitel'' — Lakai means lackey — he carried out orders without question. His announcement read: ''The Führer has decided that from now until the spring, preparations for Sealion shall be continued solely for the purpose of maintaining political and military pressure on England. Should the invasion be reconsidered in the spring or early summer of 1941, orders for renewal of operational readiness will be issued later. In the meantime military conditions for a later invasion are to be improved.''

Sunday, October 13: Early fog clearing to fine, deteriorating afternoon to cloud.
Day: Fighter-bomber raid on London.
Night: Bombers attacked London, Wales, Merseyside, Bristol and Dundee.
Aircraft losses: RAF 2, Luftwaffe 5.

Monday, October 14: Rain.
Day: Scattered light raids over Midlands and south-east.
Night: London gravely damaged by Bf 110s taking advantage of the full moon. Waterloo railway station was left with only two lines open. Services had to stop at all five main termini. Underground tracks were damaged. Roads, gasworks and power stations were hit, while 900 fires spread devastation with the usual heavy loss of civilian lives.
Aircraft losses: RAF 0, Luftwaffe 3.

Tuesday, October 15: Fair, Straits cloudy.
Day: Fighter-bombers on London and Kent.
Night: Ferocious bombing of London and Birmingham.
Aircraft losses: RAF 12, Luftwaffe 13.

Wednesday, October 16: Foggy in France and Germany; Britain mist and rain at night.
Day: Weather prevented all but sporadic single sorties over west and south-east England.
Night: London lightly assaulted.
Aircraft losses: RAF 1, Luftwaffe 13.

Thursday, October 17: Rain with bright spells.
Day: Fighter-bombers on Central London, Stanmore, site of HQ Fighter Command, seaside resorts of Margate and Broadstairs.
Night: South-east raided.
Aircraft losses: RAF 3, Luftwaffe 15.

Friday, October 18: Fog in south-east.
Day: Widespread small-scale raids.
Night: The same.
Aircraft losses: RAF 4, Luftwaffe 15.

Saturday, October 19: Cloud.
Day: Little activity.
Night: Feeble incursions over Bristol, London, Merseyside.
Aircraft losses: RAF 5, Luftwaffe 5.

Sunday, October 20: Cloud.
Day: London and Kent hit fighter-bomber raids.

Above: Soldiers remove unit insignia from a shot-down German aircraft off Sandwich in September. Indiscriminate souvenir hunting such as this hampered crash investigation work. But like many other things at the time, it was good for morale.

Below: During the blitz, the safest place was underground, and thousands of Londoners spent their nights on the platform, despite still running trains.

Above: The force expended against Coventry was no more than London had endured on several occasions, but damage was concentrated into a much smaller area.

Above: Temporarily unopposed, a Heinkel He 111 sweeps in over the English coast during September. The German splinter camouflage scheme can clearly be seen.

Night: London and Coventry grievously damaged.
Aircraft losses: RAF 4, Luftwaffe 14.

Monday, October 21: Rain, cloud, fog.
Day: London, west England, Merseyside raided.
Night: London, Coventry, Liverpool, Birmingham, Wolverhampton, south coast radar stations all bombed.
Aircraft losses: RAF 0, Luftwaffe 6.

Tuesday, October 22: Rain and fog.
Day: Convoy in Thames estuary and two off Dover fruitlessly attacked.
Night: London, Coventry, Merseyside bombed.
Aircraft losses: RAF 6, Luftwaffe 11.

Wednesday, October 23: Cloudy, rain.
Day: London and airfields at Tangmere, Biggin Hill, plus ports at Southampton, Cromer and Harwich all suffered nuisance raids.
Night: London and Glasgow bombed.
Aircraft losses: RAF 6, Luftwaffe 4.

Thursday, October 24: Low cloud.
Day: Sporadic intrusions over eastern and central England.
Night: London and Birmingham lightly hit.
Aircraft losses: RAF 0, Luftwaffe 8.

Friday, October 25: Fair with low cloud.
Day: London and south-east hit by both aimed and jettisoned bombs.
Night: Harwich raided by Italian Air Force (Regia Aeronautica Italiana).
Aircraft losses: RAF 10, Luftwaffe 20, RAI 2.

Saturday, October 26: Cloudy, improving to fair.
Day: Frequent fighter-bomber attacks on London, south-east and a Channel convoy.
Night: London, Manchester, Merseyside bombed.
Aircraft losses: RAF 2, Luftwaffe 10.

Sunday, October 27: Cloud.
Day: Mostly sweeps by fighters and fighter-bombers in formations up to 50 strong, which began at 0745hrs with attacks on convoys in the Thames Estuary and on London. The docks and south-eastern suburbs were damaged. At 1630hrs London, Southampton and Martlesham Heath airfield were attacked.
Night: London, Bristol, Liverpool, bombed, RAF fighter stations at Kirton-in-Lindsey, Driffield, Coltishall, Leconfield, Hawkinge, Feltwell and Honington strafed.
Aircraft losses: RAF 8, Luftwaffe 12.

Monday, October 28: Cloud, some fog.
Day: London bombed, also convoys in Thames and Dover.
Night: Raids on London, Midlands and Merseyside.
Aircraft losses: RAF 2, Luftwaffe 11.

Tuesday, October 29: Haze and low cloud.
Day: The enemy made their last great effort of the Battle. The first raid, aimed at London, was engaged at 1100hrs. When the second raid came in, No 602 Squadron, flying in pairs instead of threes, shot down eight fighter-bombers in 10 minutes, and another four when chasing the attackers back over the Channel. Three formations of fighter-bombers, numbering 112, attacked Portsmouth. The Italian Air Force, making its second appearance, with 73 Fiat CR42 Falco fighters escorting 15 Fiat BR20 Cigogna bombers, bombed Ramsgate.
Night: London and central England badly hit.
Aircraft losses: RAF 7, Luftwaffe 19.

Wednesday, October 30: Rain and overcast.
Day: At noon 80 German bombers and fighter-bombers appeared over the Thames Estuary and a quarter of an hour later two formations, together numbering over 100, crossed the coast at Dymchurch. Six RAF fighter squadrons on patrol intercepted them. In the late afternoon 130 enemy aircraft were over the south coast and a few managed to reach London. Poor visibility and general bad weather hampered both attackers and defenders.
Night: Scattered small raids.
Aircraft losses: RAF 5, Luftwaffe 8.

Thursday, October 31: Hazy and wet.
Day: Limp effort by fighter-bombers against London and Kent.
Night: Weak bomber effort.
Aircraft losses: None on either side.

The Battle of Britain was over. With regard to total losses contemporary claims were over-estimated by both sides. The speed and confusion of air fighting made this unavoidable. The British claimed that they had destroyed 2,698 aircraft. The Germans alleged that they had shot down 3,058.

Post-war investigation proved that the true figures were: RAF losses 915; Luftwaffe losses 1,733.

GEOFFREY ALLARD, known as "Sammy", joined the RAF as an apprentice in 1929 and was a sergeant pilot on 85 Sqn when war broke out. The squadron was posted to France with the Air Component of the British Expeditionary Force. On May 10, 1940, Allard shot down an He 111. He made more kills before the squadron returned home later that month and was awarded the DFM. He destroyed an He 111 on July 8 and shared a Bf 110 with another member of the squadron on July 30. During the next month be brought down five Bf 110s, three Do 17s and two He 111s. He also shared a Do 17 with two other pilots and was credited with two probables. For these he received a bar to the DFM, his commission and a DFC. He shot down a Do 17 and an Bf 109 on September 1, which made his total 17 plus his shared victories. On March 13, 1941, Flt Lt Allard was killed in a flying accident.

HAROLD DERRICK ATKINSON was on 213 Sqn at the outbreak of war. He shot down two Bf 109s, a Bf 110 and a fourth aircraft, with a share of four more, in France during May 1940, for which he was given a DFC. In August he destroyed an He 111, a Bf 109 and two Bf 110s, and in September a Bf 109 to bring his score to 11. He was killed soon after.

DOUGLAS ROBERT STEWARD BADER went from St Edward's School, Oxford, to the RAF College, Cranwell, in 1928, graduated two years later and was posted to 23 Sqn. In 1931 he lost both legs when he crashed doing aerobatics and was invalided out of the Service in 1933. He was readmitted for flying duties in 1939 and on February 7, 1940 joined 19 Sqn, which was equipped with Spitfires. He was soon promoted to flight lieutenant and transferred to 222 Sqn as a flight commander. On June 1 he shot down a Bf 109. He was promoted again in July and given 242 Sqn to command. On July 11 he destroyed a Do 17 and another on August 21. He sent down two Bf 110s nine days later, a 110 and a Bf 109 on September 7 and a Do 17 on the 9th. (On December 13 his DSO was gazetted.) On September 15 he got a Do 17, a Ju 88 and a Do 17 on the 18th. On September 27 he was credited with one confirmed and one probable Bf 109.

Early in 1941 he was awarded a DFC, promoted to wing commander and made leader of the Tangmere Wing of three Spitfire squadrons. In the course of several sweeps over France he shot down three 109s and shared another, in June,

RAF HEROES

Richard Townshend Bickers

Selection of those airmen whose RAF service careers are summarised in the following pages is based on their achievements during the Battle of Britain and its immediate prelude in May and June. With a few exceptions, the following pilots shot down at least ten enemy aircraft during the Battle of France and the Battle of Britain. Thus many pilots who by the end of the war had shot down more enemy aircraft than these have been omitted. The exceptions are five men who merit special mention: Air Marshal Sir Dennis Crowley-Milling, DSO, DFC and bar; Air Vice Marshal J.E. Johnson, CB, CBE, DSO and two bars, DFC and bar, DL, who had a total of 38 victories and destroyed more German aircraft in combat than any other pilot, all of them fighters; Air Commodore P.M. Brothers, CBE, DSO, DFC and bar; Group Captain Sir Hugh Dundas, KBE, DSO and bar, DFC; and Wing Commander M.H. Brown, DFC and bar.

Below: Momentoes of Sir Douglas Bader. The rear view mirror and dashboard clock of his Spitfire, a cigarette case presented to his surgeon, and his many honours.

and six more with a half share in a seventh during July. On August 9, after bringing down two 109s, he collided with a third, baled out and was taken prisoner. His total score was 23.

JAMES MICHAEL BAZIN went to France with 607 Sqn in 1939. He shot down an He 111 in May 1940 and 9 more enemy aircraft in the Battle of Britain, to end with 10 and a DFC. Later he transferred to bombers, became a wing commander and got a DSO.

GEORGE HARMAN BENNIONS joined the RAF before the war. In July 1940 he shot down a Bf 109 and in August a 110. By the end of September he had a score of 11 and a DFC. By this time he had also lost an eye. His final rank was squadron leader.

RONALD BERRY nicknamed "Razz", joined the RAFVR in 1937, was posted as a sergeant to 603 Sqn in September 1939 and commissioned in June 1940. By the end of the Battle of Britain he was credited with seven Bf 109s and enough whole or shared bombers to bring his total to 10, which earned him a DFC. He added six more and a DSO during the rest of the war.

Below: Squadron Leader Bader at Duxford as CO of No.242 Hurricane Squadron.

ADRIAN HOPE BOYD was commissioned in the RAF in 1936 and in October 1939 was a flight lieutenant on 145 Sqn. In May 1940 he shot down two Ju 87s and two Bf 110s, and two 110s in June. With a DFC to his name he went on to destroy two He 111s, two Bf 110s, three 109s and a Ju 87 during the Battle of Britain. The end of the war found him a group captain with a bar to the DFC and a score of 18.

ROBERT FINLAY BOYD was on 602 Sqn at the outbreak of war. He brought down two Ju 87s and three Bf 109s in August 1940. In September he got three 109s and a Do 17. By the end of October he had scored at least 12 and won a DFC. Later in the war he was given a DSO and had scored at least 20.

PETER MALAM BROTHERS joined 32 Sqn in 1936. In 1938 the squadron converted from Gauntlets to Hurricanes. He shot down a Bf 109 over Dunkirk on May 19, a Bf 110 on the 23rd, a 109 on July 19 and another the next day. He devised an original and most intelligent way of spoiling the aim of German fighter pilots who fired at him. The essence of accurate shooting was to calculate the right degree of deflection to allow. He reasoned that evading enemy bullets lay in making his track unpredictable. Accordingly, he trimmed his rudder so that instead of flying straight ahead he was always crabbing slightly to one side. This ruse he imparted to the members of his flight when he was given one to command. On August 16 he added a Bf 110 to his tally and on the 18th a Do 17 and a Bf 109. Soon after destroying yet one more 109 on the 24, he was awarded a DFC. In September he was posted to 257 "Burma" Sqn as a flight lieutenant. His last scores in the Battle were a Do 17 and another shared, on September 15. His final score was 15 destroyed and his decorations DSO, DFC and bar. His post-war service in the RAF earned him a CBE and culminated with reaching the eventual rank of air commodore.

MARK HENRY BROWN joined the RAF in 1936. Known as "Hilly", in 1939 he went to France with No 1 Sqn and by May 14, 1940, had destroyed five enemy aircraft, which made him the war's first Canadian ace. He was killed in November 1941, when a wing commander with a DFC and bar and a score of at least 18 confirmed enemy aircraft destroyed.

RAF FIGHTER COMMAND AIRCREW DURING BATTLE OF BRITAIN

Nationalities of Pilots and aircrew	Number of each nationality who took part in the Battle	Number of each nationality killed in the Battle
United Kingdom, including Commonwealth pilots and aircrew serving in the Royal Air Force who cannot be identified separately	2,365	397
United Kingdom, serving in the Fleet Air Arm but also including FAA personnel seconded to RAF squadrons	56	9
Australian	21	14
New Zealander	103	14
Canadian	90	20
South African	21	9
Southern Rhodesian	2	—
Jamaican	1	—
Irish	9	—
American	7	1
Polish	141	29
Czech	86	8
Belgian	29	6
Free French	13	—
Palestinian	1	—
Total	2,945	507
Approximate number of wounded — all nationalities		500
Approximate total casualties killed and wounded — all nationalities		1,007
Source: Battle of Britain Fighter Association.		

BRIAN JOHN GEORGE CARBURY, a New Zealander, was on 603 Sqn in 1939. He destroyed seven Bf 109s in August 1940, five of them in one day. He shot down seven more during the next two months, which gained him a DFC and bar. He was shot down and taken prisoner in August 1941.

FRANK REGINALD CAREY joined the RAF in 1927 as an apprentice before being sent to 43 Sqn. In 1935 he got his wings as a sergeant pilot and returned to the sqn. On January 3, 1940 he shared in downing an He 111 during a convoy patrol, and again on March 28. He was commissioned, joined 3 Sqn in France during May and scored the squadron's first kill by shooting down an He 111. By the end of that month he was credited with 11 confirmed and several probables. In July he rejoined 43 squadron to command a flight. His further victories during the Battle of Britain were: July 9 a Bf 110; 19th a 109; August 12 a Ju 88; 13th a Ju 88; 16th two Ju 87s; 18th a Ju 87. During the months since he got his commission he was decorated with the DFC and bar. He survived the war as a group captain with a second bar to his DFC. Loss of records makes his total

score uncertain but it is estimated as at least 28, four of them Japanese.

LESLIE REDFORD CLISBY was born in Australia in 1914, joined the RAF and by the time war was declared he was a flying officer on No 1 Sqn, which immediately went to France. On march 31, 1940, he opened his score with a Bf 110 to which he added a Bf 109 on April 1. Showing a reckless disregard for danger that was conspicuous even in the brave and dashing company of the other fighter pilots who flew in the Battle for France, he shot down a Do 17 on May 10 before being hit by a French anti-aircraft battery. On May 11 he destroyed three 109s and an He 111. The last of these crashed in a field, so he landed alongside. One of the crew bolted but Clisby chased him and brought him down with a flying tackle. On the 12th he claimed two Hs 126s and a 109, and was awarded a DFC. On the 13th he probably sent down a 110 and an He 111. On the 15th he shot down two 109s, before being killed. His victories totalled at least 10 enemy aircraft.

WILFRED GREVILLE CLOUSTON was a New Zealander. He joined the RAF in 1936

and by 1940 was a flight lieutenant on 19 Sqn. In the last eight days of May 1940 he shot down an He 111, a Bf 109, a Do 17 and two Ju 87s. In June he added another 109 and got a DFC. Flying a Spitfire experimentally fitted with two 20mm cannon, he destroyed a 109, a 110, a Do 17 and a Ju 88 during August and September. In 1942, when a wing commander, he was captured by the Japanese. His total score then was 12.

ARTHUR VICTOR CLOWES, a sergeant, went to France with No 1 Sqn immediately the war began. He made his first kill, an He 111, on November 23, 1939. In March 1940 he bagged two Bf 110s. In May he got a 109 and a Ju 87, and a 109 in June. He was given a DFM. In August he shot down two Ju 88s and an He 111. In September he got a 110, and a 109 in October. He had been commissioned and now was gazetted a DFC. He later commanded two squadrons, eventually reached the rank of wing commander and won the DSO.

MICHAEL NICHOLSON CROSSLEY, who was educated at Eton and the College of Aeronautical Engineering, joined the RAF in 1936, was posted to 32 Sqn and by September 3, 1939, was a flight commander. He opened his account on May 19, 1940, with a Bf 109 destroyed, followed by a second the next day, with two more claims on the 23rd and a Ju 88 on the 26th. He was given a DFC, before shooting down two He 111s on June 8. In July he claimed a 109 and shared in a 110. In August, by when he was commanding the squadron, he got two 109s on the 12th, and on the 16th a 109, a 110 and a Ju 88. On the 14th he sent a 109 and a Ju 88 down, damaged at Do 17, claimed a probable 110, but was himself shot down and had to bale out. His DSO was awarded at this time. On August 25 he added a Do 17 and a Bf 109 to his tally, making it at least 18. He became a wing commander in 1941, enjoyed no further successes but survived the war.

STANLEY DUDLEY PEARCE CONNORS was a pre-war officer who, by 1940, was commanding a flight of 111 Sqn. He won the DFC on May 26 for shooting down three He 111s, two Ju 87s and a Bf 109. June brought him another 109 and July saw him destroy one more and a Ju 88. His August kills were a 109, a Ju 88 and a Do 17. These earned a bar to his decoration. He was killed by British anti-aircraft fire in September.

NICHOLAS GRESHAM COOKE, having joined the pre-war RAF, was a flight lieutenant on 264 (Defiant) Sqn by 1939. His air gunner was Corporal Albert Lippett. On May 10 they joined three Spitfires of 66 Sqn in shooting down an He 111. Two days later they destroyed an He 111 on their own and again shared one, with two Defiants, on the 27th. On May 29 they brought down a Bf 110 and two 109s on their first patrol; and, on their second, five Ju 87s, after which they shared two Ju 88s with two other Defiants. Cooke was given a DFC and Lippet a DFM, but they were killed in action on May 30, with 10 victories.

DENNIS CROWLEY-MILLING, known to his comrades as "Crow", joined the RAFVR in 1937 when he left Malvern College. In 1940 he went to 607 Sqn as a pilot officer when it was part of the Air Component of the British Expeditionary Force and saw action in France. On his return to England he was posted to 242 Sqn, under Douglas Bader's command. He shot down his first enemy aircraft, an He 111, on August 30. His Hurricane was hit on September 6 and he had to make a forced landing. On the 7th he shot down a Bf 110 and a Do 17, and a Bf

Below: McKnight, Ball, Bader, Campbell and Crowley-Milling of 242 Squadron.

109 on the 15th.

On February 8, 1941, he shared a Do 17. In April his DFC was gazetted and he was posted to command a flight in 610 Sqn. He shared a Bf 109 on June 21 and was credited with a probable 109 on the 25th. He took over command of the squadron, was shot down, evaded capture and returned to England in 1942 after a long sojourn in a Spanish concentration camp. He returned to his squadron, now commanded by Sqn Ldr J.E. Johnson, as B Flight's commander and took part in the air operations covering the Commando raid on Dieppe on August 19, during which he probably destroyed a 109. In September he was awarded a bar to his DFC. He went on to command a Typhoon squadron, No 181, and to lead No 124 Typhoon Wing. In December 1943 he received a DSO and finished the war with eight confirmed victories. He continued his career to attain the rank of Air Marshal and was given knighthood.

CHRISTOPHER FREDERICK CURRANT, known as "Bunny", was a sergeant on 46 Sqn from 1937 until he joined 151 in 1939. When commissioned in March 1940 he was posted to 605. He shot down an He

Right: Flt Lt W. D. David flew with both 87 and 213 Sqns during the Battle.

111 in August, two Bf 109s, a 110, an He 111 and a Do 17 in September, and was given a DFC. In October he got a 109. Having shared in destroying several others he was reckoned to have a score of 13 and was awarded a bar to his medal. He went on to command a squadron and then a wing, win the DSO and attain 15 kills.

MANFRED BECKETT CZERNIN was a Polish count by birth but a naturalised Briton. Having joined the RAF before the war, he went to France with 504 Sqn in 1940 and transferred there to 85. In May he brought down an He 111, two Do 17s and an Hs 126. He was posted to 17 Sqn in June and bagged an He 111 on the 12th. In July he shot down a Do 17. By the end of October he had added five Bf 110s and two 109s as well as several shared. By then he had a DFC. He later won a DSO and an MC.

WILLIAM DENNIS DAVID was serving with 87 Sqn when the war started and went at once to France. He destroyed a Do 17 and shared an He 111 on May 10, but records were lost and there are no details of his accredited 11 victories before the squadron returned to England, for which he was awarded a DFC. In August he bagged two Ju 88s, two Bf 109s, a Ju 87 and a Bf 110. In September he got an He 111. In October moved to 213 Sqn and destroyed a Ju 88. He ended the war as a group captain.

ALAN CHRISTOPHER DEERE, born in New Zealand, underwent probably the most hectic experiences and the narrowest escapes from death or injury of all the pilots who fought in the air battles of May to October 1940. Having joined the RAF in 1937 and qualified for his wings, he was posted to 74 Sqn and later to No 54, which re-equipped with Spitfires in 1939. He made his first sortie over France on May 15, 1940.

On May 23 when both 54 and 74 (Tiger) Sqns, based at Hornchurch, were covering the withdrawal of the BEF from Dunkirk, Flt Lt James Anthony "Prof" Leathart of 54 Sqn, saw Sqn Ldr Drogo White, who commanded 74, forced-land at Calais Marck aerodrome. No 54 Sqn had a new Miles Master advanced trainer, which could attain 226mph (364km/h), so Leathart obtained the Station Commander's permission to fly it over the Channel, covered by two of his flight, Alan Deere and Johnny Allen, and try to fetch White home. On landing in France Leathart could not see White, so took off.

Above: Flt Lt Alan Deere of No.54 Sqn became a byword for indestructibility.

At about 1,000ft (300m) he saw tracer flitting past the Master and landed again. Allen had seen the enemy — "about a dozen" — and warned Deere on the radio while he himself engaged them. He shot one down and probably two more. The Master was not on the Spitfires' frequency, so the only warning Deere had been able to give his squadron commander was to dive on him. Allen called to say he was surrounded. Deere shot down the 109 that had attacked Leathart, climbed to join Allen and bagged another 109. He probably destroyed a third. Leathart, meanwhile, had jumped into a ditch, where he found Drogo White, who had not seen him land. Allen's aircraft had been holed and both he and Deere had used all their ammunition, so they went back to base. With German troops on the road near the airfield, Leathart and White started the Master by cranking it manually and also got home unscathed.

Al Deere was shot down over Dunkirk, baled out and returned to the squadron. During the Battle of Britain he made forced landings, collided with a 109, baled out more than once and was taking off from Hornchurch on August 31 when a bomb burst near his aircraft and hurled it upside down. His score at the end of the Battle was 17 and he had a DFC and bar. He later earned a DSO and ended the war as a wing commander with 22 victories. He retired as an air commodore and had an OBE to add to his decorations.

ROBERT FRANCIS THOMAS DOE of 234 Sqn destroyed his first enemy machine, a Bf 110, on August 14, 1940. He shot down his eleventh on September 7, including three 110s in one day. With a DFC to his name, he was posted to 238

Sqn, with whom he made two more kills and got a bar to his DFC before being wounded and shot down. At the end of the war he was a squadron leader with 15 confirmed victories and a DSO at the head of his medals.

EDWARD MORTLOCK DONALDSON, known in the Service as "Teddy", was a Cranwell graduate. He first served on No 1 Sqn and was in its aerobatic team. In 1937 he went to 72 as a flight commander, and in November 1939 took command of 151. Dick Smith, who joined 151 to command a flight in June 1940, says of

Below: HM King George VI decorates Al Deere at Hornchurch, June 27 1940.

Below: Left to right: Cocky Dundas, Buck Casson and Ken Holden of No.616 Sqn.

him, "He was an altogether exceptional pilot: he could fly lower, do better aerobatics and shoot better than anyone I had met up to then." His first success came in May 1940 over France when he shot down two Ju 87s. By the beginning of August he had 10½ confirmed, then went on rest. He had no more victories, survived the war and retired as an air commodore, CB, CBE, DSO, AFC.

JOHN CHARLES DUNDAS joined 609 Sqn of the Auxiliary Air Force before the war. Between May 31, 1940, when he shot down an He 111 and a Do 17 over Dunkirk, and October 15, when he got a Bf 110 and had won a DFC, he destroyed at least 12½. On November 27, by which time he was a flight lieutenant, he shot down a Bf 109 flown by a leading German ace, Helmut Wick (56 victories), but the latter's wing man shot him down and he was killed.

HUGH SPENCER LISLE DUNDAS, known as "Cocky", and John's younger brother, also served in the AAF, on 616 Sqn, whose Gauntlets were replaced by Spitfires soon after the outbreak of war. Based at Leconfield, on July 3, 1940, he damaged a Do 17 and on August 15 shot

down a Ju 88 and shared another. On the 19th the squadron moved to Kenley and three days later a Bf 109 shot him down. He went to hospital and his injuries kept him grounded for ten days. The squadron suffered such heavy casualties that on September 4 it was sent to Coltishall to reform.

On February 26, 1941, 616 Sqn, on which Johnnie Johnson was also serving, joined Douglas Bader's Tangmere Wing. F/O Dundas's victories began to mount and on July 19 his DFC was gazetted. By then, still not 21 years of age, he was commanding a flight. Further promotions followed, until at 23 he was the youngest group captain in the RAF. He finished the war with 11 confirmed victories, and a DSO and bar to add to his DFC.

ROY GILBERT DUTTON joined 111 Sqn in 1937. He destroyed an He 111 in March 1940. In May and June he shot down two He 111s, two Bf 109s and a Bf 110. In July he got two Do 17s and an He 111 and was given a DFC. In the next three months he claimed six more of various types and won a bar to his DFC. He rose to wing commander by the end of the war.

WILLIAM LAWRENCE DYMOND began his operational career as a sergeant on 111 Sqn in 1940. He shot down two Do 17s and two He 111s in May, a Bf 109 in June, and three Do 17s, and an He 111 in August. He shared in destroying several other enemy machines and was awarded a DFM. His total came to 11 enemy aircraft. He was killed in action on September 2, 1940.

JOHN ELLISS was commanding a flight of 610 Sqn in 1940 when he shot down a Bf 109 over Dunkirk on May 29 and a Do 17 on the 31st. In June he brought down a 109 and in July five more of these, which earned him a DFC. He took command of the squadron and destroyed five 109s and an He 111 in August. In 1941 a bar to his DFC was gazetted. Later he led a wing in Malta and survived the war.

HENRY MICHAEL FERRISS, an officer on 111 Sqn, shot down three Bf 110s and a 109 over France in May 1940. He got a 109 on June 2, and his DFC came through. He downed another 109 on the 10th. On July 10 he added one more 109 to his tally. In August he shot down a Do 17, and shared in destroying several enemy aeroplanes. Later that month he crashed into one and was killed.

Top: Figaro was carried on Ian Gleed's Hurricanes as his personal insignia.

Above: Pictured in 1942 are Wg Cdrs Sheen, Widge Gleed and Max Aitkin.

Below: R. Plenderleith and Jim Hallowes, both with No. 43 Squadron early in 1940.

WILLIAM HENRY FRANKLIN was an RAF apprentice who rose to the rank of sergeant pilot, on 65 Sqn, before the war. His first combat was over Dunkirk on May 22 when he shared in damaging a Ju 88. He had a share in damaging three more hostiles before shooting down a Bf 110 and a 109 on the 26th. He was promoted to flight sergeant and awarded the DFM, claimed several more victories and by the end of October, when he was commissioned, was believed to have a score of 14½. He was killed on operations in 1942.

JOSEPH FRANTISEK was in the Czech Air Force when Germany invaded his country. He escaped and joined the Polish Air Force. When Poland fell he went to France and flew with the French Air Force. By the time France fell he had destroyed 11 German machines. He next arrived in England and was posted to 303 Sqn. Between September 2 and 30 he shot down nine Bf 109s, three 110s,

four He 111s and a Ju 88. On October 8 he was killed in a crash landing. He was the most successful Czech fighter pilot of the war.

JOHN CONNELL FREEBORN joined 74 Sqn in 1938. Between May 21 and September 11, 1940 he destroyed five Bf 109s, two Bf 110s, two Do 17s and two Ju 88s, for which he was given a DFC. He later commanded 118 Sqn, increased his score to 13½ and survived the war.

JOHN ALBERT AXEL GIBSON, a New Zealander, joined the RAF in 1938. In May 1940 he went to 501 Sqn in France, where he shot down an He 111. During July, August and September he brought down five Ju 87s, three Bf 109s, a Do 17 and a Ju 88, before being wounded. He won a DFC.

IAN RICHARD GLEED, nicknamed "Widge", was in 46 Sqn at the outbreak of war and was posted to command a flight in

266 later in 1939. In May 1940 he was transferred to 87 Sqn in France, where he destroyed two Bf 110s, a 109, an He 111 and a Do 17. After returning to England he got five more 110s, won a DFC and took command of the squadron. He later operated in North Africa as a Wing Leader and increased his score to 15. He was killed in 1943.

COLIN FALKLAND GRAY, who was on 54 Sqn when the war started, became New Zealand's top-scoring fighter pilot. He shared in bringing down several enemy aircraft. His individual successes began with two Bf 109s in July. In August he got six Bf 109s, two of them on one sortie, and three 110s, again two on the same operation. In September he destroyed two Bf 109s, a 110 and an He 111. By then he had a DFC and bar. He became a wing commander, survived the war with a score of 27½, a DSO and a second bar to his DFC, and retired as a group captain.

HERBERT JAMES LAMPRIERE HALLOWES joined the RAF as an apprentice, qualified for his wings and promotion to sergeant, and joined 43 Sqn in 1940. His first action was on February 3, 1940 when he shared an He 111 with two others. On April 8 he shot an He 111 down. Over the French coast on June 1 he claimed three Bf 109s. Six days later

in a fight with a 109 his engine was hit and as he was about to bale out his adversary fired at him again. He regained his seat and shot it down. On August 8, with a DFM to his name by now, he sent down two Bf 109s. He had several more successes until, by the end of the Battle of Britain, he was credited with 19 victories, which earned him a bar to the DFM and commission. He went on to command 122 Sqn, was promoted to wing commander in 1944 and finished the war with a total of 21-plus.

FREDERICK WILLIAM HIGGINSON, always known as "Taffy", joined the RAF as a Halton apprentice at the age of 15. He was posted to 7 (Bomber) Sqn three years later as a fitter and volunteered to be an air gunner, which was then a part-time occupation in conjunction with an airman's basic skilled trade. He next qualified as a sergeant pilot and went to 56 Sqn, by which time he had made a name for himself at boxing and rugger. On the declaration of war the Air Minister, Kingsley Wood, visited North Weald, where 56 was stationed. He informed the pilots that when the fighting started their life expectancy would be three weeks! The response to this was laughter and a loud request from one of them that, in view of this, they should be allowed to put Service petrol in their cars.

On May 16, 1940, by which time Taffy Higginson was a flight sergeant, he was one of six pilots from his squadron detached to France to form a composite squadron with a flight of No 43. The following day he destroyed a Do 17 and an He 111. The next day he shot down a Bf 110. Only he and one other member of his flight survived to return to England on the 20th. On July 15 he was awarded a DFM. During the Battle of Britain he shot down four Do 17s and two Bf 109s, and damaged or shared in destroying 109s and 110s. One of the Do 17s crashed on Romney Marsh and he repeatedly flew over it taking photographs with his camera gun. But his engine had been damaged and seized up. He landed forcibly and in his anxiety to quit the resulting conflagration he tripped and fell into a cowpat, thereby revealing an unsuspected hazard of the fighter pilot's trade.

Shot down in France in 1941, when his score stood at 12½, he made an outstanding evasion of capture, was caught on the Spanish frontier, escaped and eventually got home, to increase his score to 15, rise to wing commander, acquire a DFC and eventually survive the war.

HAROLD NORMAN HOWES, a sergeant on 85 Sqn, which went to France in September 1939, shot down four Do 17s in one sortie on May 29, 1940. On returning to England he shot down two Bf 110s and a Do 17 in August, which brought him a DFM. In September he destroyed a Do 17 before being posted to 605 Sqn, then got a 109 in October. With shares in others, his total came to 12. He was killed in November 1940.

PATERSON CLARENCE HUGHES was an Australian. He joined the RAF before the war, served on 64 and 247 Sqns, then joined 234 in November 1939. After sharing two Ju 88s in July, he shot down a Bf 110 and shared another on August 14. On the 16th he got two Bf 109s, two again on the 18th and one on the 26th. He was awarded a DFC, then destroyed three 110s on September 4, two 109s on the 5th and a 109 on the 6th. On the 7th he blew up a Do 17, but was so close that fragments damaged his own aircraft and he crashed to his death, credited with 15½ kills.

PHILIP ALGERNON HUNTER of 264 (Defiant) Squadron was one of the most admired, respected and loved squadron commanders of the war. He and his air gunner, Leading Aircraftman Frederick Harry King, shared a record reading: shot down a Ju 88 on May 12; a Bf 109 and a shared He 111 over Dunkirk on the 27th; destroyed a Bf 109, a Me 110 and a Ju 87, shared a Ju 88 on the 29th. Hunter now had a DSO and King a DFM. On May 31 they got a Bf 109 and an He 111 and shared a He 111. They were shot down and killed in August, with a total of 10½.

JAMES EDGAR JOHNSON always known as "Johnnie", became the RAF's top-scoring ace by the end of the war. He learned to fly in the RAFVR and joined 19 Sqn in late August 1940. The squadron was too busy to break in new pilots, so three days later he was posted to 616 Sqn, which had just been taken out of the front line for a rest and would have time to train novices. The consequences of an old injury to his shoulder necessitated an operation and by the time he was fully fit the Battle of Britain was over. He therefore was not in a position to shoot down his first enemy aircraft until 1941. All his victims were single-engine fighters, the most difficult

of targets, except for one Bf 110 that he shared with three other pilots. His own aircraft was hit only once, by a single cannon shell. He ended the war as a group captain, commanding a Spitfire Wing in France and Germany.

EDGAR JAMES KAIN, a New Zealander nicknamed "Cobber", was the first RAF ace of the war. Having joined 73 Sqn before the war he found himself in France in September 1939. His successes were meteoric. He shot down his first enemy aircraft, a Do 17, on November 8, 1939. On the 23rd he destroyed another at the great height of

Above: Top scoring fighter pilot Johnnie Johnson pictured later in the war.

27,000ft (8,300m). His third kill came in March 1940, a Bf 109 that damaged his Hurricane in return so badly that he had to bale out. On March 26 he scored over a Bf 109 that set his aircraft on fire, but he did not bale out until he had also shot down its companion 109. These successes won him a DFC. He amassed 17 confirmed victories before being killed in a flying accident in June 1940.

JAMES ROBERT KAYLL joined 604 Sqn, Auxiliary Air Force, in 1934 and accompanied it to France in September 1939, but was transferred to command 615 Sqn in March 1940. In May that year

Below: Cobber Kain was the first RAF fighter pilot known to the public.

Below: Johnnie Johnson's Commission, honours, and other memorabilia.

he shot down two Bf 110s, and an He 111. He claimed six additional kills and before returning to Britain at the end of May had been given a DSO and a DFC. In addition to sharing sundry victories he individually shot down two He 111s and a Do 17 in the Battle of Britain. In July 1941, when leading the Hornchurch Wing, he was shot down and captured.

JOHN IGNATIUS KILMARTIN joined the RAF before the war and went to France with No 1 Sqn on the outbreak. As early as November 23, 1939, he shot down a Do 17 and bagged a Bf 109, a Ju 88 and an He 111 in April 1940. In May and June he destroyed seven Bf 110s and two 109s. After a spell on instructing he became a flight commander on 43 Sqn and shot down a Bf 110 in September 1940. His DFC was awarded the following month. He went on to become a wing commander and survive the war.

HARRY JAMES LACEY joined the RAFVR in 1937 and by the outbreak of war was an instructor at the Yorkshire Aeroplane Club. He was posted to 501 Sqn, which went to France on May 10, 1940. On the 13th he shot down a Bf 109 and an He 111 on the same sortie, and a Bf 110 on his next, for which he was awarded the *Croix de Guerre*. On May 27 in one combat he destroyed two He 111s and was mentioned in despatches.

The squadron left France on June 18. On July 20 he shot down a Bf 109 and was given a DFM. During August he was credited with a Ju 87 confirmed and one probable (same combat), a Do 17 damaged, a Ju 88 destroyed, a Do 215 damaged, two Bf 109s destroyed and one damaged, and a probable Bf 110. On September 2 he shot down a Bf 109 on one sortie and another 109 and a Do 215 on his next. On the 5th he got two more 109s in the same fight. On the 7th he went on leave.

When he rejoined the squadron on the 13th it was at Kenley and the weather was cloudy. The Operations Room telephoned 501's dispersal hut to ask for a volunteer to intercept a Heinkel that was scudding about in the London area. The message warned that, as the whole of the south-east was cloud-covered, the volunteer would probably not be able to land and he would have to bale out. Ginger Lacey took the job on. At 14,000ft (4,270m) over solid cloud he was steering courses given on the radio by the Ops Room controller until, after a long stalk, he says, "I saw it, slipping through the cloud tops, making for the coast. I didn't know where I was, because I hadn't seen the ground since taking off. I dived on him and got in one quick burst which killed his rear gunner.'' The Heinkel dropped into cloud, so Lacey throttled back and followed. The bomber broke cloud and Lacey saw the dead gunner being pulled away. Someone else manned the gun and fired at him. A gaping hole appeared in the bottom of Lacey's cockpit. His entire radiator had been shot away and his Hurricane was burning. He fired all his ammunition at the Heinkel before baling out. He came out of cloud in time to see it crash. When he returned to Kenley he learned that this aircraft had bombed Buckingham Palace.

By the end of October he had 18 victories, which made him the highest-scoring pilot in the Battle of Britain, to add to his five in France. He won a bar to the DFM, was commissioned, then went on to command a squadron and achieve a total score of 28 confirmed. He continued serving after the war.

ALBERT GERALD LEWIS was a South African who joined the RAF before the war and went to France with 504 Sqn on May 10, 1940. He is credited with nine enemy aircraft before returning to England and shooting down another nine in the Battle, to win a DFC and bar.

REGINALD THOMAS LLEWELLYN, a pre-war member of the RAF, opened his score as a sergeant on 213 Sqn, with two Bf 109s, and an He 111 on May 29, 1940. He shot down four Ju 88s, three Bf 110s and a Bf 109 in August, and two 110s in September. He was given a DFM and a commission, and survived the war.

ERIC STANLEY LOCK was in the RAFVR. In May 1940 he joined 41 Sqn. On August 15 he destroyed a Bf 110 and a Ju 88. During the rest of the Battle of Britain he claimed two He 111s, two Ju 88s, nine Bf 109s and a Bf 110, and was decorated with the DFC and bar. He was killed in action in 1941.

AENEAS RANALD DONALD MACDONELL was commanding 64 Sqn when he shot down two Ju 87s and a Bf 109 in July 1940. He ended the Battle of Britain with a DFC and a score of 10½, which included a Do 17 and several Bf 109s, as well as sundry shares in various types.

ADOLF GYSBERT MALAN, a South African, acquired his nickname, ''Sailor'', because after leaving school he became

a cadet on the training ship *General Botha*. Instead of the merchant marine, he joined the RAF in 1935 and became a flight commander on 74 ''Tiger'' Sqn in 1938. He rapidly became the most notorious pilot in Fighter Command by shooting down 2 Ju 88s, 2 He 111s, a Do 17 and a Bf 109 between May 21 and 27, earning a DFC, then shooting down two He 111s at night on June 19, for which a bar was added to his decoration. He claimed seven more during the Battle of Britain. By the end of 1941 he was credited with 32 kills and remained for some time the RAF's top scorer, until overtaken by Johnnie Johnson, earning a DSO and bar and becoming a group captain.

ANDREW McDOWALL belonged to 602 Sqn, Auxiliary Air Force, before the war. On July 24, 1940, flying a Spitfire at night, he shot down an He 111. In August he destroyed a Bf 109 and an He 111. In September he claimed two Ju 88s, four Bf 109s and a Bf 110, which brought him a DFM. His score rose to 14 in 1941 and eventually to 18, by which time he was a wing commander.

ARCHIE ASHMORE McKELLAR was a pilot officer on 602 Sqn, AAF when the war began. Before the Battle of Britain he shot down an He 111 and shared another. In August 1940 he was a flight lieutenant

on 605 Sqn and claimed three He 111s on the 15th. On September 9 he fired at an He 111 that exploded and destroyed the bomber on each side of it. On the same sortie he shot down a Bf 109. Another feat attributed to him was the shooting down of five Bf 109s on October 7, four of them in ten minutes. When he was killed on November 1, 1940 in a presumed fight with a Bf 109, he was considered to have 20 victories to justify his DFC and bar.

WILLIAM LIDSTONE MCKNIGHT was a Canadian who joined the RAF in 1939 and 615 Sqn, in France, in May 1940. He shot down a Bf 109 before the squadron returned to England and he was posted to 242 Sqn. Between May 28 and October 18 his score read: five Bf 109s, five Bf 110s, two Do 17s, two Ju 87s. He had a DFC and bar, but was killed in action in January 1941.

DESMOND ANNESLEY PETER MCMULLEN of 64 Sqn shot down a Bf 110 in May 1940, over Dunkirk. In July he bagged a Bf 109. In August he got three 109s. In September he claimed a Bf 110 before being posted to 222 Sqn, with whom he destroyed two 109s that month. In October he got three more 109s. He also shared in numerous kills. Later in the war he commanded 65 Sqn and ended with 19 victories and a DFC and bar.

JAMES WINTER CARMICHAEL MORE, known as ''Hank'' a pre-war member of the RAF, went to France in April 1940 to take command of 73 Sqn. During that month and May he destroyed a mixed bag of 11 Bf 109s, 110s, Ju 87s and He 111s. He was given a DFC and after a short rest returned to the squadron but had no victories in the Battle of Britain and was killed later in the war.

GARETH LEOFRIC NOWELL, a sergeant on 87 Sqn in France, personally shot down or shared in destroying 12 of the enemy in one week of May 1940. These included Bf 109s, Hs 126s and Do 17s. He shot down one more 109 and a Bf 110, was rewarded with a DFM and bar, and was severely wounded on May 23. He lived to see the end of the war, by which time he had shot down two more enemy aircraft.

NEWELL ORTON, nicknamed ''Fanny'', a flying officer on 73 Sqn, was one of the three most successful pilots in the Battle of France, with 15 confirmed victories and several probables, which brought him a DFC and bar. He was instructing during the Battle of Britain but shot down two Bf 109s when commanding 54 Sqn in 1941. In a fight in which he probably destroyed another Bf 109 on September 17, 1941, he was shot down and killed.

IAN BEDFORD NESBITT RUSSELL was an Australian who joined 609 Sqn in November 1939. In May 1940 he went to 609 and later to 607. He is credited with 11 victories in May. Details are confused by loss of records and his death in action on May 31, by when he had a DFC.

JOHN EVELYN SCOULAR joined the RAF pre-war and by the outbreak was a flight lieutenant on 73 Sqn, which at once went to France. He was credited with 12 victories during May 1940 and by the end of that month was one of the only two original pilots still with the squadron. He was awarded a DFC.

HARBOURNE MACKAY STEPHEN, who joined the RAFVR in 1937, was one of the most prominent performers in the air fighting of May to October 1940. He first joined 605 Sqn but was posted to 74 in May 1940. After sharing in the destruction of two Hs 126s, two Do 17s and a Ju 88, he shot down a Do 17 on the 26th. He claimed six more kills before the Battle of Britain, in which he was credited with shooting down three Bf 109s and two 110s, damaging a 109 and a 110 and probably sending down a 109, all in the course of three sorties. By the end of the year he was credited with 22½ and had a DSO, DFC and bar. He later became a wing commander in India.

JAMES ERIC STORRAR of 145 Sqn opened his score with a Bf 110 on May 23, 1940, and a Do 17 next day, followed by a Bf 110 on the 27th and an He 111 on June 11. On July 21 he shot down an He 111, a Bf 109 on the 27th, a Ju 88 on the 29th and a Bf 109 on the 30th, which gained him a DFC. In August he got a Ju 87. He also had shares in several kills. He survived the war to attain wing commander rank and a bar to his DFC.

EDWARD ROWLAND THORN was a sergeant pilot on 264 (Defiant) Sqn with Leading Aircraftman Barker as his air gunner. On May 28 they destroyed three Bf 109s, and on 30th, two Ju 87s and a Bf 110. For these feats they both got the DFM. On May 31 they shot down an He 111. Both were promoted to flight sergeant. On August 24 they got a Ju 88, on the 26th two Do 17s, and a Bf 109 that was shooting them down. They made a crash landing. They had one more success before being given bars to their decorations. Thorn went on to win a DSO and a DFC and bar and command 169 Sqn before being killed. Barker survived the war.

ROBERT ROLAND STANFORD TUCK joined the RAF in 1935. After serving with 65 Sqn he joined 92 as a flight lieutenant on May 1, 1940. On the 23rd he shot down a Bf 109 and two Bf 110s over Dunkirk, and an He 111 and a Bf 109 on June 2, which brought him a DFC. He destroyed a Ju 88 one night and another by day on August 13. On the 14th he got two more of the same. With a bar to his DFC, he was promoted to command 257 Sqn and opened his score with them by shooting down a 110 on September 15. He had four more victories during the Battle. In December he was awarded a DSO and in March 1941 a second bar to the DFC. In 1942 he was shot down over France and captured and escaped in 1945. He was credited with a total of 29.

PERCIVAL STANLEY TURNER joined the RAF before the war and in 1940 went to 242 Sqn. In May he got four Bf 109s in the Dunkirk area. In June the squadron moved to France and he took out two more 109s before returning to England. His Battle of Britain record was two Do 17s and a Bf 109. With shares, this made his total 10, and he was given a DFC. A group captain by the end of the war, he had a DSO and a bar to his DFC.

GEORGE CECIL UNWIN was a sergeant on 19 Sqn when war was declared. By May 1940 he was a flight sergeant. he shot down an Hs 126 and a Bf 109 that month. In June he destroyed a Bf 110. In August and September he shot down six Bf 110s and a Bf 109. His decorations were DFM and bar.

WITOLD URBANOWICZ was in the pre-war Polish Air Force. When Germany seized Poland he made his way to England, joined the RAF and was posted to 145 Sqn. In August he destroyed a Bf 109 and a Ju 88, before being moved the following month to 253 Sqn, with whom he scored two more kills. Next he was posted to 303 Sqn. On September 6 he shot down a Bf 109, on the 7th a Do 17, on the 15th two Do 17s, an He 111 on the 26th, and two Ju 88s, a Do 17 and a Bf 109 on the 27th. In October he had victories over Bf 109s and a Do 17. This gave him the highest score by a Polish

Above: Robert Stanford Tuck at the controls of his 257 Sqn Hurricane.

Below: Wing Commander Tuck's medals include bars to both the DSO and DFC.

pilot flying with the RAF and earned a DFC. In April he became Leader of the Polish Wing. In 1944, when, at the age of 38 he was unable to continue on operations with the RAF he transferred to the USAAF and shot down three Japanese Zero fighters.

JOHN WOLFERSTAN VILLA, known as ''Pancho'' joined the RAF before the war and in 1940 was on 72 Sqn. He shot down a Bf 109 on September 1, 1940, a Bf 110 on the 2nd, and on the 15th two 109s and a Do 17. He got an He 111 on the 27th, was awarded a DFC, and added a 109 on the 28th and a Do 17 on October 11. Joining 92 Sqn to command a flight, he destroyed a 109 and a 110 before the Battle of Britain ended. He took command of 65 Sqn in August 1941 but was grounded in 1943 with sinus trouble, by which time his victories numbered 15.

JOHN TERENCE WEBSTER, having joined the RAF in 1938, was a flight commander on 41 Sqn by the time war broke out. On May 1 he shot down two Do 17s and on the 31st a Bf 109. In June he shot down three Bf 109s over France and received a DFC. In July he got two Bf 109s. On August 8 he shot down three 109s. He was credited with at least four more victories, before being killed in action on September 5, 1940.

RONALD DEREK GORDON WIGHT, who was on 213 Sqn at the outset of war, was a flight lieutenant when the squadron went to France in May 1940. He shot down four enemy aeroplanes and shared in others before returning to England later that month. On the 27th he sent down two Bf 109s over Dunkirk, another two the following day and two more on the 31st. He was decorated with a DFC and his score was rated as 10½. In August he was killed when leading three Hurricanes against 60 Bf 110s.

PATRICK PHILIP WOODS-SCAWEN entered the RAF before the war, joined 85 Sqn and went to France in September 1939. On May 19, 1940 he got three Bf 109s. When he returned to England — with a DFC — his score stood at 6½. He bagged a Do 17 in July. In August he shot down a Bf 110 and, again in one day, three Bf 109s. In addition he had shared in many victories. On September 1 he was shot down and killed, without knowing that his younger brother Charles, a regular officer on 43 Sqn, had been killed in action the previous day.

Aircrew who fought under Fighter Command operational control in the Battle of Britain, July 10-October 31, 1940.

The number following the nationality is the squadron in which the aircrewman served.
*Personnel killed during the Battle of Britain

ADAIR, Sgt. H. H. British. 213-151. Killed
ADAMS, P/O D. A. British. 611-41
ADAMS, P/O H. C. British. 501. Killed*
ADAMS, F/Lt. J. S. British. 29
ADAMS, Sgt. R. T. British. 264. Killed
ADAMS, Sgt. E. H. British. 236
ADDISON, Sgt. W. N. British. 23
AEBERHARDT, P/O R. A. C. British. 19. Killed*
AGAZARIAN, P/O N. le C. British. 609. Killed
AINDOW, Sgt. C. R. British. 23
AINGE, Sgt. E. D. British. 23
AINSWORTH, Sgt. S. British. 23
AITKEN, Sgt. A. British. 219
AITKEN, Sgt. H. A. British. 54
AITKEN, Wg/Cdr. M. British. 601
AKROYD, P/O H. J. British. 152. Killed*
ALBERTINI, Sgt. A. V. 600
ALDOUS, P/O E. S. British. 610-41. Killed
ALDRIDGE, P/O F. J. British. 610-41
ALDRIDGE, P/O K. R. British. 32-501
ALDWINGLE, P/O A. J.M. British. 601
ALEXANDER, P/O J. N. E. British. 151
ALEXANDER, Sgt. E. A. British. 236. Killed
ALLAN, F/O H. L. N/Zealander. 151. Killed*
ALLARD, P/O G. British. 85. Killed
ALLCOCK, P/O P. O. D. British. 229. Died
ALLEN, F/O J. L. British. 54. Killed*
ALLEN, P/O H. R. British. 66
ALLEN, Sgt. J. W. British. 266
ALLEN, Sgt. L. H. British. 141
ALLEN, Sgt. K. M. British. 43-257-253
ALLGOOD, Sgt. H. H. British. 85-253. Killed*
ALLISON, Sgt. J. W. British. 611-41. Killed
ALLSOP, S/Ldr. H. G. L. British. 66
ALLTON, Sgt. L. C. British. 92. Killed*
AMBROSE, P/O C. F. British. 46
AMBROSE, P/O R. British. 25. Killed
AMBRUS, P/O J. K. Czech. 312
ANDERSON, P/O D. J. British. 29
ANDERSON, Sgt. J. D. British. 604
ANDERSON, S/Ldr. M. F. British. 604
ANDERSON, Sgt. J. A. British. 253
ANDREAE, P/O C. J. D. British. 64. Killed*
ANDREW, Sgt. S. British. 46. Killed*
ANDREWS, Sgt. M. R. N/Zealander. 264
ANDREWS, P/O S. E. British. 32-207. Killed
ANDREWS, P/O S. E. British. 257. Killed
ANDRUSZKOW, Sgt. T. Polish. 303. Killed*
ANGUS, Sgt. R. A. British. 611-41. Killed*
ANGUS, Sgt. J. G. C. British. 23
APPLEBY, P/O M. J. British. 609
APPLEFORD, P/O A. N. R. L. British. 66
ARBER, Sgt. I. K. British. 602. Died
ARBON, P/O P. W. British. 85
ARBUTHNOT, Sgt. J. British. 1-229. Killed
ARCHER, Sgt. H. T. British. 23. Killed
ARCHER, Sgt. S. British. 236
ARIES, P/O E. W. British. 602
ARMITAGE, F/Lt. D. L. British. 266
ARMITAGE, Sgt. J. F. British. 242. Killed
ARMSTRONG, P/O W. British. 54. Died
ARNFIELD, Sgt. S. J. N/Zealander. 610. Died
ARTHUR, P/O I. R. British. 141
ARTHUR, P/O C. J. British. 248. Killed*
ASH, F/Lt. R. C. V. British. 264. Killed
ASHCROFT, Sgt. A. E. British. 141. Killed
ASHFIELD, F/O G. British. F.I.U. Killed

ASHTON, F/O D. G. British. 266. Killed*
ASHTON, Sgt. D. K. British. 32. Killed
ASHWORTH, Sgt. J. British. 29
ASLETT, Sgt. A. T. R. British. 235
ASLIN, Sgt. D. J. British. 257-32
ASSHETON, P/O W. R. British. 222
ATKINS, Sgt. F. P. J. British. 141. Killed*
ATKINSON, P/O R. British. 242. Killed*
ATKINSON, F/Lt. M. R. British. 43. Killed
ATKINSON, Sgt. G. British. 151. Killed
ATKINSON, P/O H. D. British. 213. Killed*
ATKINSON, P/O G. B. British. 248
ATKINSON, P/O R. British. 111-213. Killed*
ATKINSON, P/O A. A. British. 23. Killed
AUSTIN, P/O. British. 151
AUSTIN, Sgt. A. T. British. 29
AUSTIN, Sgt. A. L. British. 604. Killed*
AUSTIN, F/O F. British. 46. Killed
AUSTIN, Sgt. S. British. 219. Killed
AYERS, Sgt. D. H. British. 600-74. Killed*
AYLING, Sgt. C. A. H. British. 43-66-421 Flt. Killed*

BABBAGE, Sgt. C. F. British. 602
BACHMANN, P/O J. H. British. 145. Killed
BACON, P/O C. H. British. 610. Killed*
BADDELEY, Sgt. D. H. British. 25. Killed
BADER, S/Ldr. D. R. S. British. 242
BADGER, F/Sgt. I. J. British. 87
BADGER, S/Ldr. J. V. C. British. 43. Killed*
BAILEY, P/O C. G. British. 152
BAILEY, Sgt. G. J. British. 234-603
BAILEY, P/O J. C. L. D. British. 46. Killed*
BAILEY, P/O J. R. A. British. 264-85
BAILEY, P/O G. G. British. 56. Killed
BAILEY, P/O H. N. D. British. 54
BAILEY, Sgt. C. British. 23
BAILLON, P/O P. A. British. 609. Killed
BAIN, P/O G. S. P. British. 111
BAINES, S/Ldr. C. E. J. British. 238
BAIRD, P/O G. H. British. 248
BAKER, P/O. British. 600
BAKER, P/O H. C. British. 421 Flt.
BAKER, Sgt. A. C. British. 610
BAKER, P/O H. C. British. 41
BAKER, Sgt. R. D. British. 56. Killed*
BAKER, P/O S. British. 54-66. Killed
BAKER, Sgt. B. British. 264. Killed*
BAKER, Sgt. E. D. British. 145. Killed*

BAKER, P/O C. C. M. British. 23
BAKER, Sgt. L. V. British. 236
BALL, F/Lt. G. E. British. 242. Killed
BAMBERGER, Sgt. C. S. British. 610-41
BANDINEL, P/O J. J. F. H. British. 3. Killed
BANHAM, F/Lt. A. J. British. 264-229
BANISTER, Sgt. T. H. British. 219
BANKS, Sgt. W. H. British. 245-32-504
BANN, Sgt. E. S. British. 238. Killed*
BARALDI, P/O F. H. R. British. 609
BARANSKI, F/Lt. W. Polish. 607
BARBER, P/O R. H. British. 46
BARCLAY, P/O R. G. A. British. 249. Killed
BARKER, Sgt. J. K. British. 152. Killed*
BARKER, P/O G. L. British. 600. Killed
BARKER, Sgt. F. J. British. 264
BARNARD, Sgt. E. C. British. 600
BARNES, P/O W. British. 405
BARNES, Sgt. L. D. British. 257-615-607
BARNES, F/O J. G. C. British. 600
BARNETT, S/Ldr. R. E. British. 234
BARON, P/O R. V. British. 219. Killed*
BARRACLOUGH, Sgt. S. M. British. 92
BARRACLOUGH, Sgt. R. G. V. British. 266
BARRAN, F/Lt. P. H. British. 609. Killed*
BARRETT, Sgt. W. R. British. 25
BARRON, Sgt. N. P. G. British. 236
BARROW, Sgt. H. I. R. British. 607-43-213. Killed
BARRY, F/O N. J. M. S/African. 3-501. Killed*
BARTHROPP, F/O P. P. C. British. 602
BARTLETT, Sgt. L. H. British. 17
BARTLEY, P/O A. C. British. 92
BARTON, P/O A. R. H. British. 32-253. Killed
BARTON, F/Lt. R. A. British. 249
BARTOS, P/O J. Czech. 312. Killed
BARWELL, P/O E. G. British. 264-242
BARY, P/O R. E. British. 229. Killed
BASHFORD, Sgt. H. British. 248
BASSETT, F/O F. B. British. 222. Killed
BATCHELOE, P/O G. H. British. 54. Killed
BATT, Sgt. L. G. British. 238
BAXTER, Sgt. S. British. 222. Killed*
BAYLES, F/O I. N. British. 152
BAYLEY, Sgt. E. A. British. 32-249. Killed*
BAYLISS, P/O D. British. 604
BAYLISS, Sgt. E. J. British. 248. Killed
BAYLY, Sgt. J. N/Zealander. 111
BAYNE, F/Lt. A. W. A. British. 17

BAYNE, S/Ldr. D. W. British. 257
BAYNHAM, P/O G. T. British. 234-152
BAZIN, F/Lt. J. M. British. 607
BAZLEY, F/Lt. S. H. British. 206. Killed
BEAKE, P/O P. H. Canadian. 64
BEAMISH, Wg/Cdr. F. V. Irish. 151-249-56. Killed
BEAMISH, Sgt. R. British. 601
BEAMONT, F/O R. P. British. 87
BEARD, Sgt. J. M. B. British. 249
BEARDMORE, P/O E. W. B. Canadian. 1 (Can.) (401)
BEARDSLEY, P/O R. A. British. 610-41
BEATTY, Sgt. M. A. British. 266
BEAUMONT, P/O W. British. 152. Killed*
BEAUMONT, F/Lt. S. G. British. 609
BEAZLEY, P/O H. J. S. British. 249
BEDA, Sgt. A. Polish. 302
BEE, Sgt. E. H. British. 29
BEECHEY, Sgt. A. F. British. 141
BEER, Sgt. C. S. F. British. 235. Killed*
BEGG (F.A.A.), Sub/Lt. H. W. British. 151. Killed
BELC, Sgt. M. Polish. 303. Killed
BELCHEM, S/Ldr. L. G. British. 264. Killed
BELEY, P/O W. G. Canadian. 151. Killed*
BELL, F/O C. A. British. 29
BELL, Sgt. C. H. British. 234. Killed
BELL, F/O J. S. British. 616. Killed*
BELL, Sgt. D. British. 23. Killed
BELL, Sgt. R. British. 219
BELL-SLATER, F/O D. B. British. 253
BELL-WALKER, Sgt. H. J. British. 72
BENN, Sgt. G. W. British. 219
BENNETT, P/O C.C. Australian. 248. Killed*
BENNETT, Sgt. H. E. British. 43. Killed
BENNETTE, F/O G. R. British. 17. Killed
BENNIONS, P/O G. H. British. 41
BENNISON, Sgt. A. A. N/Zealander. 25
BENSON, P/O N. J. V. British. 603. Killed*
BENSON, P/O J. G. British. 141
BENT, Sgt. B. British. 25
BENZIE, P/O J. Canadian. 242. Killed*
BERESFORD, F/Lt. H. R. A. British. 257. Killed*
BERGMAN, P/O V. Czech. 310
BERKLEY, Sgt. T. C. E. British. 85. Killed
BERNARD, Sgt. F. A. Czech. 238-601
BERNAS, P/O B. Polish. 302
BERRIDGE, Sgt. H. W. British. 219. Died
BERRY, F/Sgt. F. G. British. 1. Killed*

BERRY, P/O R. British. 603
BERRY, Sgt. A. British. 264. Killed*
BERWICK, Sgt. R. C. British. 25. Killed
BEVERIDGE, Sgt. C. British. 219
BEYTAGH, S/Ldr. M. L. British. 73. Died
BICKERDYKE, P/O J. L. N/Zealander. 85. Killed*
BICKNELL, Sgt. British. 23
BICKNELL, S/Ldr. L. C. British. 23
BIDGOOD, P/O E. G. British. 253. Killed
BIDGOOD, Sgt. I. K. British. 213. Killed
BIGGAR, S/Ldr. A. J. British. 111
BIGNALL, Sgt. J. British. 25. Killed
BINHAM, Sgt. A. E. British. 64
BIRCH (F.A.A.), Lt. R. A. British. 804. Killed
BIRD-WILSON, P/O H. A. C. British. 17
BIRKETT, P/O T. British. 219. Killed
BIRRELL (F.A.A.), Mid/Ship. M. A. British. 804-79
BISDEE, P/O J. D. British. 609
BISGOOD, P/O D. L. British. 3. Killed
BITMEAD, S/Ldr. E. R. British. 266-310-253. Died
BLACK, Sgt. A. British. 54. Killed
BLACK, Sgt. H. E. British. 46-257-32. Killed*
BLACKADDER, F/Lt. W. F. British. 607
BLACKWOOD, S/Ldr. G. D. M. British. 310-213
BLAIR, P/O C. E. British. 600. Killed
BLAIR, P/O K. H. British. 151. Died
BLAIZE, W/O P. Free French. 111
BLAKE (F.A.A.), Sub/Lt. A. G. British. 19. Killed*
BLAKE, S/Ldr. M. V. N/Zealander. 238-234
BLAND, P/O J. W. British. 601-501. Killed*
BLANE, Sgt. W. H. British. 604
BLATCHFORD, F/O H. P. Canadian. 17-257. Killed
BLAYNEY, P/O A. J. British. 609
BLENKHARN, Sgt. F. British. 25
BLOOMELEY, P/O D. H. British. 151
BLOOR, Sgt. E. British. 46. Killed
BLOW, Sgt. K. L. O. British. 235. Killed
BODDINGTON, Sgt. M. C. B. British. 234
BODIE, P/O C. A. W. British. 66. Killed
BOITEL-GILL, F/Lt. B. P. A. British. 152. Killed
BOLTON, Sgt. H. A. British. 79. Killed*
BOMFORD, Sgt. British. 601
BON-SEIGNEUR, P/O C. A. Canadian. 257. Killed*
BOOT, P/O P. V. British. 1
BOOTH, Sgt. J. J. British. 23-600
BOOTH, Sgt. G. B. British. 85. Killed*
BORET, P/O R. J. British. 41. Killed

Above: Flt Lt Eric Ball was a flight commander with No.242 Squadron.

Above: Paddy Barthropp (right) flew Spitfires with No.602, the second highest scoring RAF fighter squadron, with 102 confirmed victories.

Above: Wing Cdr F. V. Beamish commanded the North Weald Wing.

BOROWSKI, F/O J. Polish. 302. Killed*
BOSWELL, Sgt. R. A. British. 19
BOULDING, F/O R. J. E. British. 74
BOULTER, F/O J. C. British. 603. Killed
BOULTON, F/O J. F. British. 603-310. Killed*
BOUQUILLARD, Adj. H. Free French. 615-249. Killed
BOWEN, P/O F. D. British. 264. Killed
BOWEN, P/O N. G. British. 266. Killed*
BOWEN, F/Lt. C. E. British. 607. Killed*
BOWEN-MORRIS, Sgt. H. British. 92
BOWERMAN, Sgt. O. R. British. 222
BOWMAN, Sgt. L. D. British. 141
BOWRING, F/O B. H. British. 111-600
BOYD, F/Lt. R. F. British. 602
BOYD, F/Lt. A. H. McN. British. 145-600
BOWYER, F/O W. S. British. 257. Killed
BOYLE, Sgt. C. British. 236
BOYLE, F/O J. G. Canadian. 41. Killed*
BRACTON, Sgt. British. 602
BRAHAM, S/Ldr. J. R. D. British. 29
BRAMAH (F.A.A.), Sub/Lt. H. G. K. British. 213
BRANCH, F/O G. R. British. 145. Killed*
BRASH, Sgt. G. B. British. 248. Killed*
BREEZE, Sgt. R. A. British. 222
BREJCHA, Sgt. V Czech. 43. Killed
BRENNAN, Sgt. J. S. N/Zealander. 23
BRETT, F/O P. N. British. 17
BREWSTER, P/O J. British. 615-616. Killed
BRIERE, P/O Y. J. Free French. 257. Killed
BRIESE, F/O. Canadian. 1 (Can.) (401)
BRIGGS, P/O M.F. British. 234. Killed
BRIGGS, Sgt. D. R. British. 236. Killed
BRIGHT, F/O V. M. British. 229. Killed
BRIMBLE, Sgt. G. W. British. 242. Killed
BRIMBLE, Sgt. J. J. British. 73. Killed*
BRINSDEN, F/Lt. F. N. N/Zealander. 19
BRITTON, P/O H. W. A. British. 17. Killed
BRITTON, F/O A. W. N. British. 263. Killed*
BROADHURST, S/Ldr. H. British. 1
BROADHURST, P/O J. W. British. 222. Killed*
BROOKER, F/O R. E. P. British. 56. Killed
BROOKMAN, Sgt. R. W. A. N/Zealander. 253
BROOM, Sgt. P. W. British. 25
BROTHERS, F/Lt. P. M. British. 32-257
BROWN, Sgt. C. B. British. 245
BROWN, F/Lt. G. A. British. 253
BROWN, F/Sgt. F. S. British. 79. Died
BROWN, F/O D. P. Canadian. 1. (Can.) (401)
BROWN, P/O M. K. Canadian. 242. Killed
BROWN, F/Lt. M. H. Canadian. 1. Killed
BROWN, P/O B. W. British. 610-72
BROWN, P/O M. P. British. 611-41
BROWN, P/O R. C. British. 229
BROWN, P/O R. J. W. British. 111
BROWN, P/O A. W. British. 25
BROWN, Sgt. J. W. British. 600. Killed
BROWN, Sgt. C. W. D. British. 236. Killed

BROWN, Sgt. R. S. British. 604
BROWN, Sgt. P. G. F. British. 234. Killed
BROWN, F/O D. M. British. 1
BROWNE, Sgt. C. British. 219
BROWNE, P/O D. O. M. British. 1. Killed*
BRUCE, F/Lt. D. C. British. 111. Killed*
BRUMBY, Sgt. N. British. 615-607. Killed*
BRUNNER, P/O G. C. British. 43
BRYANT-FENN, P/O L. T. British. 79
BRYNE, Sgt. E. L. British. F.I.U.
BRYSON, P/O J. Canadian. 92. Killed*
BRZEZINA, F/Lt. S. Polish. 74. Killed
BRZOZOWSKI, Sgt. M. Polish. 303. Killed*
BUCHANAN, P/O J. British. 29. Killed
BUCHANAN, P/O J. R. British. 609. Killed*
BUCHIN, P/O M. S. H. C. Belgian. 213. Killed*
BUCK, Sgt. J. A. British. 43. Killed*
BUCKNOLE, Sgt. J. S. British. 54. Killed
BUDD, F/Lt. G. O. British. 604
BUDZINSKI, Sgt. J. Polish. 605-145
BULL, P/O J. C. British. 600
BULL, F/Lt. C. H. British. 25. Killed
BULMER (F.A.A.), Sub/Lt. G. G. R. British. 32. Killed*
BUMSTEAD, Sgt. R. F. British. 111
BUNCH, Sgt. D. C. British. 219
BUNCH (F.A.A.), Sub/Lt. S. H. British. 804. Killed
BUNGEY, F/O R. W. Australian. 145
BURDA, P/O F. Czech. 310
BURDEKIN, Sgt. A. G. British. 600
BURGESS, Sgt. J. H. H. British. 222
BURGOYNE, P/O E. British. 19. Killed*
BURLEY, Sgt. P. S. British. 600
BURNARD, F/Sgt. F. P. British. 74-616
BURNELL-PHILLIPS, Sgt. P. A. British. 607. Killed
BURNETT, F/O N. W. British. 266-46. Killed
BURNS, Sgt. W. R. N/Zealander. 236
BURNS, Sgt. O. V. British. 235
BURT, Sgt. A. D. British. 611-603
BURTENSHAW, Sgt. A. A. British. 54. Killed
BURTON, F/Sgt. C. G. British. 23
BURTON, S/Ldr. H. F. British. 66
BURTON, F/Lt. H. British. 242
BURTON, F/O P. R. F. S/African. 249. Killed*
BURTON, P/O L. G. N/Zealander. 236. Killed
BURTON, Sgt. L. British. 248
BUSH, P/O C. R. N/Zealander. 242
BUSH, Sgt. B. M. British. 504
BUSHELL, Sgt. G. D. British. 213. Killed
BUTTERFIELD, Sgt. S. L. British. 213. Killed*
BUTTERICK, Sgt. A. F. British. 3-232. Killed
BUTTERWORTH, Sgt. K. British. 23
BYNG-HALL, P/O P. British. 29. Died

CAIN, Sgt. A. R. British. 235. Killed
CAISTER, P/O J. R. British. 603
CALDERHEAD, P/O G. D. British. 54. Killed
CALDERWOOD, Sgt. T. M. British. 85

CALE, P/O F. W. Australian. 266. Killed*
CALTHORPE, Sgt. British. 25
CAMBELL, Sgt. D. C. O. British. 66
CAMBRIDGE, F/Lt. W. P. British. 253. Killed*
CAMERON, Sgt. N. British. 1-17
CAMERON, F/Sgt. M. British. 66
CAMERON, Sgt. J. D. British. 604. Killed
CAMPBELL, P/O A. R. McL. Canadian. 54
CAMPBELL, Sgt. A. N/Zealander. 264
CAMPBELL, F/Lt. A. M. British. 29
CAMPBELL, Sgt. D. B. N/Zealander. 23
CAMPBELL, P/O G. L. British. 236. Killed
CAMPBELL, P/O N. N. Canadian. 242. Killed*
CAMPBELL-COLQUHOUN, F/Lt. E. W. British. 264-66
CANDY, P/O R. J. British. 25
CANHAM, Sgt. A. W. British. 600
CANNON, Sgt. B. British. 604
CAPEL, Sgt. B. British. 23
CAPON, P/O C. F. A. British. 257. Killed
CAPSTICK, P/O H. Jamaican. 236. Died
CARBURY, F/O B. J. G. N/Zealander. 603
CARDELL, P/O P. M. British. 603. Killed*
CARDNELL, P/O C. F. British. 23. Killed
CAREY, F/Lt. F. R. British. 43
CARLIN, P/O S. British. 264. Killed
CARNABY, F/O W. F. British. 264-85. Killed
CARNALL, Sgt. R. British. 111
CARPENTER (F.A.A.), Sub/Lt. J. C. British. 229-46. Killed*
CARPENTER, P/O J. M. V. British. 222
CARR, F/O W. J. British. 235. Killed
CARR-LEWTY, Sgt. R. A. British. 41
CARRIER, P/O J. C. Canadian. 219
CARSWELL, F/O M. K. N/Zealander. 43
CARTER, P/O V. A. British. 607
CARTER, Sgt. L. R. British. 610-41. Killed
CARTER, P/O C. A. W. British. 611
CARTER, P/O P. E. G. British. 73-302. Killed*
CARTHEW, P/O G. C. T. Canadian. 253-145
CARVER (F.A.A.), Lt. R. H. P. British. 804
CARVER, P/O K. M. British. 229
CARVER, F/O J. C. British. 87. Killed
CASE, P/O H. R. British. 64-72. Killed*
CASSIDY, F/O E. British. 25
CASSON, P/O L. H. British. 616-615
CASTLE, Sgt. C. E. P. British. 219. Killed
CAWSE, P/O F. N. British. 238. Killed*
CAVE, P/O J. G. British. 600
CEBRZYNSKI, F/O A. Polish. 303. Killed*
CHABEPA, Sgt. F. Czech. 312
CHADWICK, Sgt. D. F. British. 64
CHAFFE, P/O R. I. British. 245-43. Killed*
CHALDER, P/O H. H. British. 266-41. Killed*
CHALUPA, P/O S. J. Polish. 302
CHAMBERLAIN, P/O J. T. R. British. 235
CHAMBERLAIN, Wg/Cdr. G. P. British. F.I.U.
CHANDLER, Sgt. H. H. British. 610

CHAPMAN, Sgt. V. R. British. 246
CHAPPELL, P/O A. K. British. 236
CHAPPELL, P/O C. G. British. 65
CHAPPLE, Sgt. D. W. E. British. 236. Killed
CHARD, Sgt. W. T. British. 141
CHARLES, F/O E. F. J. Canadian. 54
CHARNOCK, Sgt. G. British. 25
CHARNOCK, Sgt. H. W. British. 64-19
CHATER, F/Lt. G. F. S/African. 3
CHEETHAM, Sgt. J. C. British. 23. Killed
CHELMECKI, P/O M. Polish. 257-17-6
CHESTERS, P/O P. British. 74. Killed
CHETHAM, P/O C. A. G. British. 1. Killed
CHEVRIER, P/O J. A. Canadian. 1
CHEW, Sgt. C. A. British. 17. Killed
CHIGNELL, S/Ldr. R. A. British. 145. Killed
CHILTON (F.A.A.), Sub/Lt. P. S. C. British. 804
CHIPPING, Sgt. D. J. British. 222
CHISHOLM, P/O R. E. British. 604
CHLOPIK, F/Lt. T. P. Polish. 302 Killed*
CHOMLEY, P/O J. A. G. British. 257. Killed*
CHORAN, F/Sgt. French. 64
CHRISTIE, Sgt. J. McBean. British. 152. Killed*
CHRISTIE, F/Lt. G. P. British. 66-242. Killed
CHRISTMAS, P/O B. E. British. 1 (Can.) (401)
CHRYSTALL, Sgt. C. British. 235
CHURCHES, P/O E. W. G. British. 74. Killed
CHURCHILL, S/Ldr. W. M. British. 605. Killed
CIZEK, P/O E. Czech. 1. Killed
CLACKSON, F/Lt. D. L. British. 600
CLANDILLON, F/O J. A. British. 219. Killed
CLARK, P/O H. D. British. 213
CLARK, Sgt. W. T. M. British. 219
CLARK, P/O C. A. G. S/African. F.I.U. Killed
CLARK, Sgt. G. P. British. 604
CLARKE, S/Ldr. D. de B. British. 600
CLARKE, Sgt. H. R. British. 610
CLARKE, S/Ldr. R. N. British. 235. Killed
CLARKE, P/O A. W. British. 504. Killed*
CLARKE, Sgt. G. S. British. 248. Killed*
CLARKE, P/O R. W. British. 79. Killed
CLARKE, Sgt. G. T. British. 151. Killed
CLEAVER, F/O G. N. S. British. 601
CLENSHAW, Sgt. I. C. C. British. 253. Killed*
CLERKE, F/Lt. R. F. H. British. 79
CLIFT, F/O D. G. British. 79
CLIFTON, P/O J. K. G. British. 253. Killed*
CLOUSTON, S/Ldr. A. E. N/Zealander. 219
CLOUSTON, F/Lt. W. G. N/Zealander. 19
CLOWES, P/O A. V. British. 1. Died
CLYDE, F/O W. C. British. 601
COATES (F.A.A.), Lt. J. P. British. 804. Killed
COBDEN, P/O D. G. N/Zealander. 74. Killed*
COCHRANE, P/O A. C. Canadian. 257. Killed
COCK, P/O J. R. Australian. 87
COCKBURN (F.A.A.), Lt Cdr. J. C. British. 804
COCKBURN (F.A.A.), Sub Lt. R. C. British. 808
COGGINS, P/O J. British. 235. Killed

COGHLAN, F/O J. H. British. 56. Killed
COKE, F/O The Hon. D. A. British. 257. Killed
COLE, Sgt. C. F. J. British. 236
COLEMAN, P/O E. J. British. 54. Killed
COLEBROOK, P/O British. 54
COLLARD, F/O P. British. 615. Killed*
COLLETT, Sgt. G. R. British. 54. Killed*
COLLINGBRIDGE, P/O L. W. British. 66
COLLINS, S/Ldr. A. R. British. 72
COLLYNS, P/O B. G. N/Zealander. 238. Killed
COMELY, P/O P. W. British. 87. Killed*
COMERFORD, F/Lt. H. A. G. British. 312
COMPTON, Sgt. J. W. British. 25
CONNELL, P/O W. C. British. 32
CONNOR, F/O F. H. P. British. 234
CONNORS, F/Lt. S. D. P. British. 111. Killed*
CONSIDINE, P/O B. B. Irish. 238
CONSTANTINE, P/O A. N. Australian. 141. Killed
COOK, Sgt. A. W. British. 604
COOK, Sgt. H. British. 66-266
COOK, Sgt. R. V. British. 219
COOKE, P/O C. A. British. 66
COOKE, Sgt. H. R. British. 23
COOMBES, Sgt. E. British. 219. Killed
COOMBS, Sgt. R. J. British. 600
COONEY, F/Sgt. C. J. British. 56. Killed*
COOPE, S/Ldr. W. E. British. 17. Killed
COOPER, Sgt. C. F. British. 600. Killed*
COOPER, Sgt. T. A. British. 266
COOPER, Sgt. S. F. British. 253
COOPER, Sgt. D. C. British. 235
COOPER, P/O J. E. British. 610. Killed
COOPER, Sgt. R. N. British. 610. Killed
COOPER-KEY, P/O A. M. British. 46. Killed*
COOPER-SLIPPER, P/O T. P. M. British. 605
COOTE, Sgt. L. E. M. British. 600. Killed
COPCUTT, Sgt. R. British. 248. Killed*
COPELAND, Sgt. P. British. 616-66. Killed
COPELAND, Sgt. N. D. British. 235
COPEMAN, P/O J. H. H. British. 111. Killed*
CORBETT, F/Lt. V. B. Canadian. 1 (Can) (401)
CORBETT, P/O G. H. Canadian. 66. Killed*
CORBIN, Sgt. W. J. British. 610-66
CORCORAN, P/O J. British. 236. Killed*
CORDELL, Sgt. H. A. British. 64
CORFE, Sgt. D. F. British. 73-66-610. Killed
CORK (F.A.A.), Sub Lt. R. J. British. 242. Killed
CORKETT, P/O A. H. British. 253
CORNER, P/O M. C. British. 264. Died
CORY, P/O G. W. British. 41
CORY, P/O. British. 25
COSBY, Sgt. E. T. British. 3-615
COSBY, F/Lt. I. H. British. 610-72
COTES-PREEDY, P/O D. V. C. British. 236
COTTAM, Sgt. G. British. 25
COTTAM, P/O H. W. British. 213. Killed
COURTIS, Sgt. J. B. N/Zealander. 111
COURTNEY, F/O R. N. H. British. 151
COUSSENS, Sgt. H. W. British. 601
COUZENS, P/O G. W. British. 54
COVERLEY, F/O W. H. British. 602. Killed*
COVINGTON, P/O A. R. British. 238
COWARD, F/Lt. J. B. British. 19
COWEN, Sgt. W. British. 25
COWLEY, Sgt. J. British. 87
COWSILL, Sgt. J. R. British. 56. Killed*
COX, Sgt. D. G. S. R. British. 19
COX, P/O G. J. British. 152
COX, P/O K. H. British. 610. Killed*
COX, F/O P. A. N. British. 501. Killed*
COX, P/O R. C. R. British. 248. Killed*
COX, Sgt. British. 421 Flt.
COX, Sgt. G. P. British. 236
COX, Sgt. W. E. British. 264. Killed
COXON, Sgt. J. H. British. 141. Killed
CRABTREE, Sgt. D. B. British. 501. Killed

Above: The medals of Bob Braham, who flew Blenheim bombers modified as night fighters during the Battle of Britain.

Above: Percy Burton of 249 Sqn collided with a 110 in September.

Above: Sgt J. Cowley of No.87 Squadron flew Hurricanes.

CRAIG, Sgt. J. T. British. 111. Killed
CRAIG, F/O G. D. British. 607
CRANWELL, Sgt. E. W. British. 610
CRAWFORD, P/O H. H. N/Zealander. 235. Killed
CRESTY, Sgt. K. G. British. 219. Killed
CRESWELL, Sgt. D. G. British. 141. Killed
CREW, P/O E. D. British. 604
CRISE, Sgt. J. L. British. 43. Killed
CROCKETT, P/O R. F. British. 236. Killed
CROFTS, F/O P. G. British. 615-605. Killed*
CROKER, Sgt. E. E. N/Zealander. 111
CROMBIE, Sgt. R. British. 141. Killed*
CROOK, P/O D. M. British. 609. Killed
CROOK, Sgt. V. W. J. N/Zealander. 264
CROOK, Sgt. H. K. British. 219
CROSKELL, Sgt. M. E. British. 213
CROSSEY, P/O J. T. British. 249
CROSSLEY, F/Lt. M. N. British. 32
CROSSMAN, Sgt. R. G. British. 25. Killed
CROSSMAN, P/O J. D. Australian. 46. Killed*
CROWLEY, P/O H. R. British. 219-600
CROWLEY-MILLING, P/O D. W. British. 242
CRUICKSHANKS, P/O I. J. A. British. 66. Killed*
CRUTTENDEN, P/O J. British. 43. Killed*
CRYDERMAN, P/O L. E. Canadian. 242
CRYSTALL, Sgt. C. British. 235
CUDDIE, P/O W. A. British. 141. Killed
CUKE, Sgt. V. Czech. 253
CULLEN, Sgt. R. W. British. 23
CULMER, Sgt. J. D. British. 25
CULVERWELL, Sgt. J. H. British. 87. Killed*
CUMBERS, Sgt. A. B. British. 141
CUNNINGHAM, F/Lt. J. L. G. British. 603. Killed*
CUNNINGHAM, F/Lt. W. British. 19
CUNNINGHAM, F/Lt. J. British. 604
CUNNINGHAM, Sgt. J. British. 29
CUNNINGTON, Sgt. W. G. British. 607. Killed
CUPITT, Sgt. T. British. 29
CURCHIN, P/O J. British. 609. Killed
CURLEY, Sgt. A. G. British. 141. Killed*
CURRANT, P/O C. F. British. 605
CURTIS, Sgt. F. W. British. 25
CUTTS, F/O J. W. British. 222. Killed*
CZAJKOWSKI, P/O F. Polish. 151. Killed
CZERNIAK, P/O J. M. Polish. 302. Killed
CZERNIN, F/O Count M. B. British. 17. Died.
CZERNY, F/Lt. H. Polish. 302
CZERWINSKI, F/O T. Polish. 302. Killed
CZTERNASTEK, P/O. Polish. 32

DAFFORN, F/O R. C. British. 501. Killed
DALTON, Sgt. R. W. British. 604
DALTON-MORGAN, F/Lt. T. F. British. 43
DALY, Sgt. J. J. British. 141
DANN, Sgt. J. E. British. 23
DANNATT, Sgt. A. G. British. 29
D'ARCH-IRVINE, F/O B. W. J. British. 257. Killed*
DARGIE, Sgt. A. M. S. British. 23. Killed
DARLEY, S/Ldr. H. S. British. 609
DARLING, Sgt. A. S. British. 611-603. Killed
DARLING, Sgt. E. V. British. 41. Killed
DARWIN, P/O C. W. W. British. 87. Killed
DASZEWSKI, P/O J. Polish. 303
DAVEY, P/O B. British. 257-32. Killed
DAVEY, P/O J. A. J. British. 1. Killed*
DAVID, P/O W. D. British. 87-213
DAVIDSON, Sgt. H. J. British. 249. Killed
DAVIES, P/O R. B. British. 29
DAVIES, P/O A. E. British. 222. Killed*
DAVIES, P/O C. G. A. British. 222
DAVIES, Sgt. M. P. British. 1-213. Killed
DAVIES, F/Lt. J. A. British. 604. Killed
DAVIES, F/O P. F. M. British. 56
DAVIES, Sgt. L. British. 151
DAVIES-COOKE, P/O P. J. British. 72-610. Killed*
DAVIS, Sgt. British. 222. Killed

DAVIS, F/Lt. C. R. S/African. 601. Killed*
DAVIS, F/O C. T. British. 238. Killed
DAVIS, Sgt. W. L. British. 249
DAVIS, Sgt. J. N. British. 600
DAVIS, Sgt. J. British. 54
DAVIS, Sgt. P. E. British. 236
DAVIS, Sgt. A. S. British. 235
DAVISON, P/O. British. 235
DAVY, P/O T. D. H. British. 72-266. Killed
DAW, P/O V. G. British. 32. Killed
DAWBARN, P/O P. L. British. 17
DAWICK, Sgt. K. N/Zealander. 111
DAWSON, Sgt. T. British. 235
DAWSON-PAUL (F.A.A.), Sub Lt. F. British. 64. Killed*
DAY, P/O R. L. F. British. 141. Killed
DAY, Sgt. F. S. British. 248. Killed
DEACON, Sgt. A. H. British. 85-111
DEACON-ELLIOTT, P/O R. British. 72
DEANSLEY, F/Lt. E. C. British. 152
DEBENHAM, P/O K. B. L. British. 151. Killed
DEBREE, P/O. British. 264
DEE, Sgt. O. J. British. 235. Killed
DEERE, F/Lt. A. L. N/Zealander. 54
DE GRUNNE, P/O R. C. C. Belgian. 32. Killed
DE JACE, P/O L. J. Belgian. 236. Killed
DE LA BOUCHER, W/O F. H. Free French. 85. Killed
DE LA PERRELE, P/O V. B. N/Zealander. 245
DELLER, Sgt. A. L. M. British. 43
DE MANCHA, P/O R. A. British. 43. Killed*
DEMETRIADI, P/O R. S. British. 601. Killed*
DEMOULIN, Sgt. R. J. G. Belgian. 235. Killed
DE MOZAY, 2nd Lt. J. E. French. 1
DENBY, P/O G. A. British. 600. Killed
DENCHFIELD, Sgt. H. D. British. 610
DENHOLM, S/Ldr. G. L. British. 603
DENISON, F/Lt. R. W. British. 236. Killed
DENTON, Sgt. D. A. British. 236. Killed
DERBYSHIRE, P/O J. M. British. 236
DERMOTT, P/O. British. 600
DE SCITIVAUX, Capt. C. J. M. P. French. 245
DESLOGES, F/O. Canadian. 1 (Can) (401)
DE SPIRLET, P/O F. X. E. Belgian. 87. Killed
DEUNTZER, Sgt. D. C. British. 247
DEVITT, S/Ldr. P. K. British. 152
DEWAR, Wg Cdr J. S. British. 87-213. Killed*
DEWAR, P/O J. M. F. British. 229. Killed
DEWEY, P/O R. B. British. 611-603. Killed*
DEWHURST, F/O K. S. British. 234
DEXTER, P/O P. G. British. 603-54. Killed
DIBNAH, P/O R. H. 1-242
DICKIE, P/O W. G. British. 601. Killed*
DICKINSON, Sgt. J. H. British. 253. Killed
DIEU, P/O G. E. F. Belgian. 236
DIFFORD, F/O I. B. S/African. 607. Killed*
DIGBY-WORSLEY, Sgt. M. P. British. 248. Killed*
DITZEL, Sgt. J. W. British. 25

DIXON, Sgt. F. J. P. British. 501. Killed*
DIXON, P/O J. A. British. 1
DIXON, Sgt. C. A. W. British. 601
DIXON, Sgt. G. British. F.I.U.
DIXON, Sgt. L. British. 600
DODD, P/O J. D. British. 248. Killed
DODGE, Sgt. C. W. British. 219
DOE, P/O R. F. T. British. 234-238
DOLEZAL, P/O F. Czech. 19
DOMAGALA, Sgt. M. Polish. 238
DON, P/O R. S. British. 501. Killed
DONAHUE, P/O A. G. American. 64. Killed
DONALD, F/Lt. I. D. G. British. 141. Killed*
DONALDSON, S/Ldr. E. M. British. 151
DOSSETT, Sgt. W. S. British. 29
DOUGHTY, P/O N. A. R. British. 247
DOUGLAS, P/O W. A. British. 610
DOULTON, P/O M. D. British. 601. Killed*
DOUTHWAITE, P/O B. British. 72
DOUTREPONT, P/O G. L. J. Belgian. 229. Killed*
DOWDING, P/O The Hon. D. H. T. British. 74
DOWN, P/O P. D. M. British. 56
DRABY, Sgt. British. 25
DRAKE, P/O G. J. S/African. 607. Killed*
DRAKE, F/O B. British. 213-1
DRAPER, P/O B. V. British. 74. Killed
DRAPER, F/O G. G. F. British. 41-610
DRAPER, Sgt. R. A. British. 232
DREDGE, Sgt. A. S. British. 253. Killed
DREVER, F/O N. G. British. 610
DREW, S/Ldr. P. E. British. 236. Killed*
DROBINSKI, P/O B. H. Polish. 65
DRUMMOND, F/O J. F. British. 46-92. Killed*
DUART, P/O J. H. British. 219
DUBBER (F.A.A.), P/O R. E. British. 808. Died
DUCKENFIELD, P/O B. L. British. 501
DUDA, P/O J. Czech. 312
DUFF, P/O S. S. British. 23
DUKE-WOOLLEY, F/Lt. R. M. B. D. British. 253-23
DULWICH, Sgt. W. H. British. 235. Killed
DUNCAN, Sgt. British. 29
DUNDAS, P/O J. C. BRitish. 609. Killed
DUNDAS, F/O H. S. L. British. 616
DUNLOP-URIE, F/Lt. J. British. 602
DUNMORE, Sgt. J. T. British. 22. Killed
DUNN, Sgt. I. L. British. 235
DUNNING-WHITE, F/O P. W. British. 145
DUNSCOMBE, Sgt. R. D. British. 213-312. Killed
DUNWORTH, S/Ldr. T. P. R. British. 66-54
DUPEE, Sgt. O. A. British. 219
DURRANT, Sgt. C. R. N/Zealander. 23. Killed
DURYASZ, F/Lt. M. Polish. 213
DUSZYNSKI, Sgt. S. Polish. 238. Killed*
DUTTON, S/Ldr. R. G. British. 145
DUTTON, Sgt. G. W. British. 604
DU VIVIER, P/O R. A. L. Belgian. 229. Killed
DVORAK, Sgt. A. Czech. 310. Killed
DYE, Sgt. B. E. British. 219. Killed

DYER, Sgt. N/Zealander. 600
DYGRYN, Sgt. J. Czech. 1
DYKE, Sgt. L. A. British. 64. Killed*
DYMOND, Sgt. W. L. British. 111. Killed*

EADE, Sgt. A. W. British. 266-602
EARP, Sgt. R. L. British. 46
EASTON, Sgt. D. A. British. 248
ECKFORD, F/Lt. 4. F. British. 23-253-242
EDGE, F/Lt. G. R. British. 253-605
EDGE, F/O A. R. British. 609
EDGLEY, Sgt. A. British. 601-253
EDGWORTHY, Sgt. G. H. British. 46. Killed*
EDMISTON, P/O G. A. F. British. 151
EDM OND, P/O N. D. Canadian. 615. Killed*
EDMUNDS, P/O E. R. N/Zealander. 245-615
EDRIDGE, P/O H. P. M. British. 222. Killed*
EDSALL, P/O E. F. British. 54-222. Died
EDWARDS, F/O R. L. Canadian. 1 (Can) (401). Killed*
EDWARDS, P/O H. D. Canadian. 92. Killed*
EDWARDS, Sgt. F. British. 29
EDWARDS, Sgt. British. 604
EDWARDS, P/O K. C. British. 600
EDWARDS, Sgt. H. H. British. 248
EDWARDS, P/O I. N. British. 234
EDWARDS, F/Lt. R. S. J. Irish. 56
EDWARDS, Sgt. British. 247
EDY, P/O A. L. British. 602. Killed
EGAN, Sgt. E. J. British. 600-501. Killed*
EIBY, P/O W. T. N/Zealander. 245
EKINS, Sgt. V. H. British. 111-501
ELCOMBE, Sgt. D. W. British. 602. Killed*
ELEY, Sgt. F. W. British. 74. Killed*
ELGER, P/O F. R. C. Canadian. 248
ELIOT, P/O H. W. British. 73. Killed
ELKINGTON, P/O J. F. D. British. 1
ELLACOMBE, P/O J. L. W. British. 151
ELLERY, P/O C. C. British. 264
ELLIOTT, F/O G. J. Canadian. 607
ELLIS, Sgt. R. V. British. 73
ELLIS, F/Lt. J. British. 610
ELLIS, Sgt. J. H. M. British. 85. Killed*
ELLIS, Sgt. W. T. British. 92
ELLIS, F/O G. E. British. 64
ELSDON, F/O T. A. F. British. 72
ELSDON, Sgt. H. D. B. British. 236. Killed*
ELSE, Sgt. P. British. 610
EMENY, Sgt. C. N/Zealander. 264
EMMETT, F/O W. A. C. British. 25. Killed
EMMETT, Sgt. G. British. 236
ENGLISH, P/O C. E. British. 85-605. Killed*
ENSOR, F/O P. S. B. British. 23. Killed
ETHERINGTON, Sgt. W. J. British. 17
EVANS, P/O H. A. C. British. 236
EVANS, Sgt. W. R. British. 85-249
EVANS, P/O D. British. 607-615. Killed
EVANS, Sgt. C. R. British. 235. Killed

EVANS, Sgt. G. J. British. 604
EVERITT, Sgt. G. C. British. 29. Killed
EVERITT, Sgt. A. D. British. 235
EYLES, Sgt. P. R. British. 92. Killed*
EYRE, F/O A. British. 615. Killed

FAJTL, F/Lt. F. Czech. 17-17
FALKOWSKI, F/O J. P. Polish. 32
FARLEY, F/Lt. British. 151-46
FARMER, F/Lt. J. N. W. British. 302
FARNES, Sgt. P. C. P. British. 501
FARNES, P/O E. British. 141
FARQUHAR, Wg/Cdr. A. D. British. 257
FARROW, Sgt. J. R. British. 1-229. Killed*
FARTHING, Sgt. J. British. 235
FAWCETT, Sgt. D. R. British. 29. Killed
FAYOLLE, W/O F. E. Free French. 85. Killed
FEARY, Sgt. A. N. British. 609. Killed*
FEATHER, Sgt. J. L. British. 235. Killed0
FECHTNER, P/O E. Czech. 310. Killed*
FEJFAR, F/O S. Czech. 310. Killed
FENMORE, Sgt. S. A. British. 245-501. Killed
FENN, Sgt. C. F. British. 248
FENTON, S/Ldr. H. A. British. 238
FENTON, Sgt. British. 604
FENTON, P/O J. O. British. 235. Killed
FENWICK, P/O C. R. British. 610
FENWICK, F/O British. 601
FERDINAND, P/O R. F. British. 263. Killed
FERGUSON, Sgt. E. H. British. 141. Killed
FERGUSON, F/O P. J. British. 602
FERIC, P/O M. Polish. 303
FERRIS, F/Lt. H. M. British. 111. Killed*
FILDES, Sgt. F. British. 25
FINCH, F/O T. R. H. British. 151
FINLAY, S/Ldr. D. O. British. 41-54
FINNIE, P/O A. British. 54. Killed*
FINNIS, F/Lt. J. F. F. British. 1-229
FINUCANE, P/O B. E. Irish. 65. Killed
FISHER, P/O A. G. A. British. 111
FISHER, P/O G. British. 602
FISHER, P/O B. M. British. 111. Killed*
FISKE, P/O W. M. L. American. 601. Killed*
FITZGERALD, F/Lt. T. B. N/Zealander. 141
FIZELL, Sgt. J. F. British. 29
FLEMING, P/O J. British. 605
FLEMING, P/O R. D. S. British. 249. Killed*
FLETCHER, Sgt. J. G. B. British. 604. Killed*
FLETCHER, F/Lt. A. W. Canadian. 235
FLETCHER, Sgt. British. 3
FLETCHER, Sgt. W. T. N/Zealander. 23
FLINDERS, P/O J. L. British. 32
FLOOD, F/Lt. F. W. Australian. 235. Killed*
FLOWER, Sgt. H. L. British. 248
FOGLAR, Sgt. V. Czech. 245
FOTT, P/O E. A. Czech. 310
FOKES, Sgt. R. H. British. 92. Killed
FOLLIARD, Sgt. J. H. British. 604

Above: Paul Davies-Cooke was killed on Sept 27.

Above: Sgt J. Ellis of 85 Sqn failed to return on September 1.

Above: Don Finlay, the 1936 Olympics hurdler.

Above: The DSO and DFC awarded to Paddy Finucane.

FOPP, Sgt. D. British. 17
FORBES, S/Ldr. A. S. British. 303-66
FORD, Sgt. R. C. British. 41
FORD, Sgt. E. G. British. 3-232. Killed
FORDE, F/O D. N. British. 145-605
FORREST, Sgt. D. H. British. 66
FORRESTER, P/O G. M. British. 605. Killed*
FORSHAW, F/O T. H. T. British. 609
FORSTER, F/O A. D. British. 151-607
FORSYTH, Sgt. C. L. M. N/Zealander. 23. Killed
FORWARD, Sgt. R. V. British. 257
FOSTER, P/O R. W. British. 605
FOTHERINGHAM, Sgt. British. 3
FOWLER, Sgt. R. J. British. 247
FOWLER, F/O A. L. British. 248. Killed
FOX, Sgt. P. H. British. 56
FOX, Sgt. L. British. 29
FOXLEY-NORRIS, F/O C. N. British. 3
FOX-MALE, P/O D. H. British. 152
FRANCIS, P/O C. D. British. 253. Killed*
FRANCIS, Sgt. D. N. British. 257
FRANCIS, Sgt. C. W. British. 74
FRANCIS, Sgt. J. British. 23
FRANCIS, Sgt. British. 3
FRANCIS, P/O N. I. C. British. 247. Killed
FRANKLIN, F/O W. D. K. British. 74
FRANKLIN, P/O W. H. British. 65. Killed
FRANTISEK, Sgt. J. Czech. 303. Killed*
FRASER, Sgt. R. H. B. British. 257. Killed*
FREEBORN, F/Lt. J. C. British. 74
FREEMAN, Sgt. R. R. British. 29
FREER, Sgt. P. F. British. 29. Killed
FREESE, Sgt. L. E. British. 611-74. Killed
FRENCH, Sgt. T. L. British. 29. Killed
FREY, F/Lt. J. A. Polish. 607
FRIEND, Sgt. J. R. British. 25. Killed
FRIENDSHIP, P/O A. H. B. British. 3
FRIPP, Sgt. J. H. British. 248
FRISBY, P/O E. M. British. 504. Killed
FRITH, Sgt. E. T. G. British. 611-92. Killed*
FRIZELL, P/O C. G. Canadian. 257
FROST, P/O J. L. British. 600
FULFORD, Sgt. D. British. 64. Killed
FULFORD, Sgt. British. 19
FUMERTON, P/O R. C. Canadian. 32
FURNEAUX, Sgt. R. H. British. 3-73
FURST, Sgt. B. Czech. 310-605

GABSZEWICZ, F/O A. Polish. 607
GADD, Sgt. Pilot J. British. 611
GAGE, P/O D. H. British. 602. Killed
GALLUS, Sgt. British. 3
GAMBLEN, F/O D. R. British. 41. Killed*
GANE, P/O S. R. British. 248. Killed*
GANT, Sgt. E. British. 236
GARDINER, F/O F. T. British. 610. Killed
GARDINER, Sgt. G. C. British. 219. Killed*
GARDINER, Sgt. W. M. British. 3

GARDNER, Sgt. B. G. D. British. 610. Killed
GARDNER, P/O P. M. British. 32
GARDNER (F.A.A.), Sub Lt. R. E. British. 242
GARDNER, P/O J. R. British. 141
GARFIELD, Sgt. W. J. British. 248. Killed*
GARRARD, P/O A. H. H. British. 248. Killed
GARSIDE, Sgt. G. British. 236
GARTON, Sgt. G. W. British. 73
GARVEY, Sgt. L. A. British. 41. Killed*
GARVIN, S/Ldr. G. D. British. 264
GASH, Sgt. F. British. 264
GASKELL, P/O R. S. British. 264
GAUNCE, F/Lt. L. M. Canadian. 615. Killed
GAUNT, P/O G. N. British. 609. Killed*
GAUNT, Sgt. W. D. British. 23
GAVAN, Sgt. A. British. 54
GAWITH, P/O A. A. N/Zealander. 23
GAYNER, F/O J. R. H. British. 615
GEAR, Sgt. A. W. British. 32
GEDDES, P/O K. I. British. 604
GEE, Sgt. V. D. British. 219. Killed
GENNEY, P/O T. British. 604. Killed
GENT, Sgt. R. J. K. British. 501-32. Killed
GIBBINS, Sgt. D. G. British. 54-222
GIBBONS, Sgt. C. M. British. 236
GIBSON, F/Lt. J. A. A. British. 501
GIDDINGS, F/Lt. H. S. British. 615-111. Killed
GIL, P/O J. Polish. 229-43
GILBERT, P/O E. G. British. 64
GILBERT (F.A.A.), Mid/Ship. P. R. J. British. 111
GILBERT, P/O H. T. British. 601. Killed
GILDERS, Sgt. J. S. British. 72. Killed
GILL, Sgt. J. V. British. 23. Killed
GILLAM, F/Lt. D. E. British. 312-616
GILLAM, Sgt. E. British. 248. Killed
GILLAN, P/O J. British. 601. Killed*
GILLEN, F/O T. W. British. 247
GILLESPIE, P/O J. L. British. 23. Killed
GILLIES, Sgt. British. 421 Flt.
GILLIES, F/Sgt. J. British. 602. Killed
GILLIES, Fl/Lt. K. M. British. 66. Killed*
GILLMAN, P/O K. R. British. 32. Killed*
GILROY, P/O G. K. British. 603
GILYEAT, Sgt. H. R. British. 29
GIRDWOOD, Sgt. A. G. British. 257. Killed*
GLASER, P/O E. D. British. 65
GLEAVE, S/Ldr. T. P. British. 253
GLEDHILL, Sgt. G. British. 238. Killed*
GLEED, F/Lt. I. R. British. 87. Killed
GLEGG, P/O A. J. British. 600
GLENDENNING, Sgt. J. N. British. 54-74. Killed
GLEW, Sgt. N. British. 72. Killed
GLOWACKI, Sgt. W. J. Polish. 605-145. Killed*
GLOWACKI, Sgt. A. Polish. 501
GLYDE, F/O R. L. Australian. 87. Killed*
GMUR, Sgt. F. Polish. 151. Killed*
GNYS, P/O W. Polish. 302
GODDARD, F/Lt. H. G. British. 219

GODDARD, P/O W. B. British. 235. Killed
GODDEN, S/Ldr. S. F. British. 3
GOLDSMITH, F/O C. W. S/African. 54-603. Killed*
GOLDSMITH, Sgt. J. E. British. 236. Killed
GONAY, P/O H. A. C. Belgian. 235. Killed
GOODALL, P/O H. I. British. 264. Killed*
GOODERHAM, Sgt. A. T. British. 46
GOODERHAM, Sgt. A. J. British. 25. Killed
GOODMAN, Sgt. G. British. 85
GOODMAN, P/O G. E. Palestinian. 1. Killed
GOODMAN, Sgt. M. V. British. 604
GOODWIN, P/O H. McD. British. 609. Killed*
GOODWIN, Sgt. C. British. 219. Killed*
GOODWIN, Sgt. S. A. British. 266
GOODWIN, Sgt. R. D. British. 64
GORDON, S/Ldr. J. A. G. Canadian. 151. Killed
GORDON, P/O W. H. G. British. 234. Killed*
GORDON, Sgt. S. British. 235. Killed
GORE, F/Lt. W. E. British. 607. Killed*
GORRIE, P/O D. G. British. 43. Killed
GORZULA, P/O M. Polish. 607
GOSLING, P/O R. C. British. 266
GOTH, P/O V. Czech. 501-310. Killed*
GOTHORPE, Sgt. 25
GOULD, P/O D. L. British. 601-607
GOULD, F/O C. L. British. 607-32. Killed
GOULD, Sgt. G. L. British. 235
GOULDSTONE, Sgt. R. J. British. 29. Killed*
GOUT, P/O G. K. British. 234. Killed*
GOWERS, P/O A. V. British. 85. Killed
GRACIE, F/Lt. E. J. British. 56. Killed
GRAHAM, F/Lt. E. British. 72
GRAHAM, P/O L. W. S/African. 56
GRAHAM, Sgt. J. British. 236. Killed
GRAHAM, P/O K. A. G. British. 600. Killed
GRANDY, S/Ldr. J. British. 249
GRANT, Sgt. E. J. F. British. 600. Killed
GRANT, P/O S. B. British. 65
GRANT, Sgt. N/Zealander. 151
GRANT (F.A.A.), Sub Lt. M. D. British. 804
GRASSICK, P/O R. D. Canadian. 242
GRAVES, Sgt. British. 235
GRAVES, P/O R. C. British. 253
GRAY, F/O A. P. British. 615
GRAY, P/O C. F. British. 54
GRAY, P/O C. K. British. 43
GRAY, P/O D. McT. British. 610. Killed
GRAY, Sgt. M. British. 72. Killed*
GRAY, Sgt. K. W. British. 85. Killed
GRAY, P/O T. British. 64
GRAYSON, F/Sgt. C. British. 213. Killed
GREEN, F/Lt. C. P. British. 421 Flt.
GREEN, Sgt. W. J. British. 501
GREEN, P/O M. D. British. 248. Killed*
GREEN, P/O W. V. British. 235. Killed*
GREEN, Sgt. H. E. British. 141
GREEN, Sgt. G. G. British. 236
GREEN, Sgt. F. W. W. British. 600

GREENWOOD, P/O J. D. B. British. 253
GREENSHIELDS (F.A.A.), Sub Lt. H. la Fore. British. 266. Killed*
GREGORY, P/O F. S. British. 65. Killed*
GREGORY, Sgt. A. E. British. 219
GREGORY, Sgt. A. H. British. 111. Killed
GREGORY, Sgt. W. J. British. 29
GRELLIS, P/O H. E. British. 23 Died
GRETTON, Sgt. R. H. British. 266-222
GRIBBLE, P/O D. G. British. 54. Killed*
GRICE, P/O D. H. British. 32
GRICE, P/O D. H. British. 600. Killed*
GRIDLEY, Sgt. R. V. British. 235. Killed
GRIER, P/O T. British. 601. Killed
GRIFFEN, Sgt. J. J. British. 73 Killed
GRIFFITHS, Sgt. G. British. 17-601
GRIFFITHS, Sgt. British. 32
GROGAN, P/O G. J. Irish. 23
GROSZEWSKI, F/O. Polish. 43
GROVE, Sgt. H. C. British. 501-213. Killed
GRUBB, Sgt. E. G. British. 219
GRUBB, Sgt. H. F. British. 219
GRUSZKA, F/O F. Polish. 65. Killed*
GRZESZEZAK, F/O B. Polish. 303
GUERIN, Adj. C. Free French. 232. Killed
GUEST, P/O T. F. British. 56
GUNDRY, P/O K. C. British. 257. Killed
GUNN, P/O H. R. British. 74. Killed*
GUNNING, P/O P. S. British. 46. Killed*
GUNTER, P/O E. M. British. 43-501. Killed*
GURTEEN, P/O J. V. British. 504. Killed*
GUTHRIE (F.A.A.), Sub Lt. G. C. M. British. 808
GUTHRIE, Sgt. N. H. British. 604
GUY (F.A.A.), Mid/Ship. P. British. 808. Killed
GUY, Sgt. L. N. British. 601. Killed
GUYMER, Sgt. E. N. L. British. 238

HACKWOOD, P/O G. H. British. 264. Killed
HAIG, P/O J. G. E. British. 603
HAIGH, Sgt. C. British. 604. Killed*
HAINE, P/O R. C. British. 600
HAINES, F/O L.A. British. 19. Killed
HAIRE, Sgt. J. K. British. 145. Killed
HAIRS, P/O P. R. British. 501
HALL, P/O R. M. D. British. 152
HALL, F/Lt. N. M. British. 257. Killed*
HALL, P/O R. C. British. 219
HALL, Sgt. British. 235
HALL, Sgt. British. 29
HALL, P/O W. C. British. 248. Killed
HALLAM, F/O I. L. McG. British. 222. Killed
HALLIWELL, P/O A. B. British. 141
HALLOWES, Sgt. H. J. L. British. 43
HALTON, Sgt. D. W. British. 615. Killed*
HAMALE, Sgt. R. E. de J'a Belgian. 46. Killed
HAMAR, P/O J. R. British. 151. Killed*
HAMBLIN, Wg/Cdr. British. 17
HAMER, Sgt. British. 141

HAMILL, P/O J. W. N/Zealander. 299. Killed
HAMILTON, F/Lt. H. R. Canadian. 85. Killed
HAMILTON, Sgt. J. S. British. 248. Killed
HAMILTON, Sgt. C. B. British. 219. Killed
HAMILTON, P/O A. L. Australian. 248
HAMILTON, P/O A. C. British. 141. Killed*
HAMILTON, P/O C. E. British. 234. Killed*
HAMLYN, Sgt. R. F. British. 610
HAMMERTON, Sgt. J. British. 615. Killed
HAMMERTON, Sgt. J. British. 3. Killed
HAMMOND, P/O D. J. British. 253-245
HAMPSHIRE, Sgt. C. W. British. 85-111-249
HANBURY, P/O B. A. British. 1
HANBURY, P/O O. V. British. 602. Killed
HANCOCK, P/O N. P. W. British. 1
HANCOCK, P/O N. E. British. 152-65
HANCOCK, P/O E. L. British. 609
HANNON, P/O G. H. British. 236
HANSON, F/O D. H. W. British. 17. Killed*
HANUS, P/O J. Czech. 310
HANZLICEK, Sgt. O. Czech. 312. Killed*
HARDACRE, F/O J. R. British. 504. Killed*
HARDCASTLE, Sgt. J. British. 219. Killed
HARDIE, Sgt. British. 232
HARDING, Sgt. N. D. British. 29
HARDING, F/O N. M. British. 23. Killed
HARDMAN, P/O H. G. British. 111
HARDWICK, Sgt. W. R. H. British. 600
HARDY, P/O R. British. 234
HARDY, Sgt. O. A. British. 264
HARE, Sgt. M. British. 245
HARGREAVES, P/O F. N. British. 92. Killed*
HARKER, Sgt. A. S. British. 234
HARKNESS, S/Ldr. H. Irish. 257
HARNETT, F/O T. P. Canadian. 219
HARPER, F/Lt. W. J. British. 17
HARRIS, P/O P. A. British. 3. Killed
HARRISON, Sgt. A. R. J. British. 219
HARRISON, P/O J. H. British. 145. Killed*
HARRISON, P/O D. S. British. 238. Killed*
HARROLD, F/O F. C. British. 151-501. Killed*
HART, F/O J. S. Canadian. 602-54
HART, P/O K. G. British. 65. Killed
HART, P/O N. Canadian. 242. Killed
HARTAS, P/O P. McD. British. 603-421 Flt. Killed
HARVEY, Sgt. L. W. British. 54
HASTINGS, P/O D. British. 74. Killed*
HATTON, Sgt. British. 604
HAVERCROFT, Sgt. R. E. British. 92
HAVILAND, P/O J. K. American. 151
HAVILAND, P/O R. H. S/African. 248. Killed
HAW, Sgt. C. British. 504
HAWKE, Sgt. P. S. British. 64
HAWKE, Sgt. S. N. British. 604. Killed
HAWKINGS, Sgt. R. P. British. 601. Killed*
HAWLEY, Sgt. F. B. British. 266. Killed*
HAWORTH, F/O F. F. J. British. 43. Killed*
HAY, F/O I. B. D. E. S/African. 611
HAY (F.A.A.), Lt. R. C. British. 808
HAYDEN, Sgt. L. H. British. 264
HAYES, S/Ldr. British. 242
HAYES, F/O T. N. British. 600
HAYLOCK, Sgt. R. A. British. 236
HAYSON, F/Lt. G. D. L. British. 79
HAYTER, F/O J. C. F. N/Zealander. 605-615
HAYWOOD, Sgt. D. British. 504
HAYWOOD, Sgt. D. British. 151
HEAD, Sgt. F. A. P. British. 236. Killed*
HEAD, Sgt. G. M. British. 219. Killed
HEAL, P/O P. W. D. British. 604
HEALY, Sgt. T. W. R. British. 41-611. Killed
HEATH, F/O B. British. 611
HEBRON, P/O G. S. British. 235
HEDGES, P/O A. L. British. 245-257
HEIMES, Sgt. L. British. 235

Above: Douglas Gage survived the Battle but not the war.

Above: Peter Hairs flew with No.501 Squadrons.

Above: Canadian pilot O. V. Hanbury of No.602 Squadron.

Above: Nobby Hargreaves of No.92 Sqn disappeared on September 11.

HELCKE, Sgt. D. A. British. 504. Killed*
HELLYER, F/Lt. R. O. British. 616
HEMINGWAY, P/O J. A. Irish. 85
HEMPTINNE, P/O B. M. de. Belgian. 145. Killed
HENDERSON, P/O J. A. Mc.D. British. 257
HENDRY, Sgt. D. O. British. 219
HENN, Sgt. W. B. British. 501
HENNEBERG, F/O Z. Polish. 303
HENSON, Sgt. B. British. 32-257. Killed
HENSTOCK, F/Lt. L. F. British. 64
HERON, P/O H. M. T. British. 266-66
HERRICK, P/O M. J. British. 25. Killed*
HERRICK, P/O B. H. N/Zealander. 236. Killed
HESLOP, Sgt. V. W. British. 56
HESS, P/O A. Czech. 310
HETHERINGTON, Sgt. E. L. British. 601. Killed
HEWETT, Sgt. G. A. British. 607
HEWITT, P/O D. A. Canadian. 501. Killed*
HEWLETT, Sgt. C. R. British. 65
HEYCOCK, S/Ldr. G. F. W. British. 23
HEYWOOD, P/O N. B. British. 32-607-257. Killed*
HEYWORTH, S/Ldr. J. H. British. 79
HICK, Sgt. D. T. British. 32
HIGGINS, Sgt. W. B. British. 253-32. Killed*
HIGGINSON, F/Sgt. F. W. British. 56
HIGGS, F/O T. P. K. British. 111. Killed*
HIGHT, P/O C. H. N/ZEALANDER. 234. Killed*
HILES, P/O A. H. British. 236. Killed
HILKEN, Sgt. C. G. British. 74
HILL, P/O H. P. British. 92. Killed*
HILL, S/Ldr. J. H. British. 222
HILL, P/O S. J. British. 609. Killed
HILL, P/O M. R. S/African. 266 Killed
HILL, Sgt. C. R. N/Zealander. 141
HILL, P/O A. E. British. 248. Killed
HILL, Sgt. A. M. British. 25
HILL, Sgt. G. British. 65
HILL, P/O G. E. British. 245. Killed
HILLARY, P/O R. H. British. 603. Killed
HILLCOAT, F/Lt. H. B. L. British. 1. Killed*
HILLOCK, P/O F. W. 1 (Can) (401)
HILLMAN, Sgt. R. W. British. 235. Killed
HILLWOOD, Sgt. P. British. 56
HIMR, P/O J. J. Czech. 56. Killed
HINDRUP, Sgt. F. G. N/Zealander. 600
HINE, Sgt. British. 65
HIRD, Sgt. L. British. 604. Killed
HITHERSAY, Sgt. A. J. B. British. 141
HLAVAC, Sgt. J. Czech. 56. Killed*
HLOBIL, P/O A. Czech. 312
HOARE-SCOTT, P/O J. H. British. 601. Killed
HOBBIS, P/O D. O. British. 219. Killed
HOBBS, Sgt. S. J. British. 235. Killed
HOBBS, P/O J. B. British. 3. Killed
HOBBS, Sgt. W. H. British. 25
HOBSON, P/O C. A. British. 600. Killed*
HOBSON, S/Ldr. W. F. C. British. 601
HOBSON, F/LT. D. B. British. 64
HODDS, Sgt. W. H. British. 25
HODGE, Sgt. J. S. A. British. 141. Killed
HODGKINSON, P/O A. J. British. 219. Killed
HODGSON, P/O W. T. N/Zealander. 85. Killed
HODSON, Sgt. C. G. British. 229-1
HOGAN, S/Ldr. H. A. V. British. 501
HOGG, F/O E. S. British. 152
HOGG, Sgt. R. D. British. 17-257-56. Killed
HOGG, P/O R. M. British. 152. Killed*
HOGG, P/O D. W. British. 25. Killed*
HOGG, Sgt. J. H. British. 141. Killed
HOGG, Sgt. R. V. British. 616. Killed
HOLDEN, F/Lt. E. British. 501
HOLDEN, P/O K. British. 616
HOLDER, Sgt. R. N/Zealander. 151. Killed
HOLDER, P/O G. A. British. 236
HOLDERNESS, F/Lt. J. B. S/Rhodesian. 1-229
HOLLAND, S/Ldr. A. L. British. 501-65

HOLLAND, P/O D. F. British. 72. Killed*
HOLLAND, Sgt. K. C. Australian. 152. Killed*
HOLLAND, P/O R. H. British. 92. Killed
HOLLAND, Sgt. R. M. British. 600
HOLLIS, Sgt. E. J. British. 25
HOLLOWAY, Sgt. S. V. British. 25
HOLLOWELL, Sgt. K. B. British. 25
HOLMES, P/O F. H. British. 152. Killed
HOLMES, Sgt. R. T. British. 504
HOLMES, P/O G. H. British. 600. Killed
HOLMES, Sgt. G. British. 25
HOLMES, Sgt. E. L. British. 248. Killed
HOLROYD, Sgt. W. B. British. 501-151
HOLTON, Sgt. A. G. V. British. 141
HOMER, F/O M. G. British. 242-1. Killed*
HONE, P/O D. H. British. 615
HONOR, F/O D. S. G. British. 145
HOOD, S/Ldr. H. R. L. British. 41. Killed*
HOOK, Sgt. A. British. 248. Killed
HOOKWAY, F/O B. British. 234
HOOPER, P/O B. G. British. 25
HOPE, F/O R. British. 605. Killed*
HOPE, F/Lt. Sir A. P. British. 601
HOPEWELL, Sgt. J. British. 616-66. Killed
HOPGOOD, Sgt. British. 64
HOPKIN, P/O W. P. British. 54-602
HOPTON, Sgt. B. W. British. 73. Killed
HORNBY, Sgt. W. H. British. 234
HORNER, Sgt. F. G. British. 610
HORROX, F/O J. M. British. 151. Killed
HORSKY, Sgt. V. Czech. 238. Killed*
HORTON, F/O P. W. N/Zealander. 234. Killed
HOUGH, P/O H. B. A. British. 600. Killed
HOUGHTON, P/O C. G. British. 141
HOUGHTON, Sgt. O. V. British. 501. Killed*
HOWARD, P/O J. British. 74-54. Killed
HOWARD, Sgt. British. 235
HOWARD-WILLIAMS, P/O P. I. British. 19
HOWARTH, Sgt. E. F. British. 501. Killed
HOWE, P/O B. British. 25. Killed
HOWE, P/O D. C. British. 235
HOWELL, F/Lt. F. J. British. 609. Killed
HOWELL, Sgt. F. British. 87
HOWES, P/O P. British. 54-603. Killed*
HOWES, Sgt. H. N. British. 85-605. Killed
HOWITT, P/O G. L. British. 615-245
HOWITT, Sgt. I. E. British. 41
HOWLEY, P/O R. A. Canadian. 141. Killed*
HOYLE, Sgt. H. N. British. 257
HOYLE, Sgt. G. V. British. 232. Killed
HRADIL, P/O F. Czech. 19-310. Killed
HRUBY, P/O O. Czech. 111
HUBACEK, Sgt. J. Czech. 310
HUBBARD, F/O T. E. British. 601
HUBBARD, Sgt. B. F. R. British. 235. Killed
HUCKIN, Sgt. P. E. British. 600
HUGHES, F/Lt. J. McM. British. 25. Killed
HUGHES, F/Lt. D. P. British. 238. Killed*

HUGHES, P/O F. D. British. 264
HUGHES, F/Lt. P. C. Australian. 234. Killed*
HUGHES, Sgt. D. E. N/Zealander. 600. Killed*
HUGHES, F/Sgt. W. R. British. 23
HUGHES, P/O D. L. British. 141
HUGHES, Sgt. A. J. British. 245
HUGHES-REES, Sgt. J. British. 609. Killed
HUGO, P/O P. H. S/African. 615
HULBERT, Sgt. F. H. R. British. 601
HULBERT, Sgt. D. J. British. 257-501
HULL, S/Ldr. C. B. S/African. 263-43. Killed*
HUMPHERSON, F/O J. B. W. British. 32-607. Killed
HUMPHREY, P/O A. H. British. 266
HUMPHREYS, P/O J.S. N/Zealander. 605
HUMPHREYS, P/O P. C. British. 32
HUMPHREYS, F/O J. D. British. 29. Killed
HUMPHREYS, F/O P. H. British. 152. Killed
HUNT, Sgt. D. A. C. British. 66
HUNT, P/O D. W. British. 257
HUNT, P/O H. N. British. 504. Killed
HUNTER, F/Lt. British. 600
HUNTER, S/Ldr. P. A. British. 264. Killed*
HUNTER, Sgt. British. 604. Killed
HUNTER, Sgt. D. J. British. 29
HUNTER, P/O A. S. British. 604. Killed
HUNTER-TOD, F/Lt. British. 23
HURRY, Sgt. C. A. L. British. 43-46
HURST, P/O P. R. S. British. 600. Killed
HUTCHINSON, Sgt. I. British. 222
HUTCHINSON (F.A.A.), Sub Lt. D. A. British. 804. Killed
HUTLEY, P/O R. R. British. 32-213. Killed*
HUTTON, Sgt. R. S. British. 85. Killed
HYBLER, P/O J. Czech. 310
HYDE, Sgt. R. J. British. 66
HYDE, P/O J. W. British. 229
HYDE, F/O Canadian. 1 (Can) (401)

IEVERS, F/Lt. N. L. Irish. 312
IGGLESDEN, F/O C. P. British. 234
IMRAY, Sgt. H. S. British. 600
INGLE, F/O A. British. 605
INGLE-FINCH, P/O M. R. British. 607-151-56
INNES, Sgt. R. A. British. 253
INNESS, P/O R. F. British. 152
INNISS, F/O A. R. de H. British. 236
IRVING, F/Lt. M. M. British. 607. Killed*
ISHERWOOD, Sgt. D. W. British. 29
ISAAC, Sgt. L. R. British. 64. Killed*
IVESON, Sgt. T. C. British. 616
IVEY, Sgt. R. British. 248

JACK, F/O D. M. British. 602
JACKSON, Sgt. P. F. British. 604. Killed
JACKSON, Sgt. A. British. 29. Killed*
JACKSON, P/O P. A. C. British. 236
JACOBS, P/O H. 219-600

JACOBSON, Sgt. N. British. 29. Killed*
JAMES, Sgt. R. H. British. 29
JAMES, F/Lt. R. S. S. British. 248. Killed
JAMESON, S/Ldr. P. G. British. 266
JANICKI, P/O Z. Polish. 32
JANKIEWICZ, F/O J. S. Polish. 601. Killed
JANOUGH, P/O S. Czech. 310
JANUSZEWICZ, P/O W. Polish. 303. Killed
JARRETT, Sgt. G. W. British. 501-245. Killed
JASKE, P/O J. A. Czech. 312
JASTRZEVSKI, F/Lt. F. Polish. 302. Killed*
JAVAUX, P/O L. L. G. Belgian. 235. Killed
JAY, P/O D. T. British. 87. Killed*
JEBB, F/O M. British. 504. Killed*
JEFF, F/Lt. R. V. British. 87. Killed*
JEFFCOAT, P/O H. J. British. 236. Killed
JEFFERIES, P/O C. G. St. D. British. 3-232
JEFFERIES, F/Lt. J. (ex. J. LATMER). British. 310
JEFFERSON, Sgt. G. British. 43
JEFFERSON, P/O S. F. British. 248
JEFFERY, F/O A. J. O. British. 64. Killed*
JEFFERY-CRIDGE, Sgt. H. R. British. 236
JEFFERYS, Sgt. G. W. British. 46-43. Killed*
JEKA, Sgt. J. Polish. 238
JENKINS, P/O D. N. O. British. 253. Killed*
JENNINGS, Sgt. B. J. British. 19
JERAM (F.A.A.), Sub Lt. D. M. British. 213
JERECZEK, P/O E. W. Polish. 229-43
JESSOP, Sgt. E. R. British. 253-111-43-257. Killed
JICHA, P/O V. Czech. 1. Killed
JIROUDEX, F/Sgt. M. Czech. 310
JOHNS, Sgt. G. B. British. 229
JOHNSON, P/O A. E. British. 46. Killed
JOHNSON, P/O J. E. British. 616
JOHNSON, Sgt. J. I. British. 222. Killed*
JOHNSON, P/O C. E. British. 264. Killed*
JOHNSON, Sgt. W. J. British. 145
JOHNSON, Sgt. R. B. British. 222
JOHNSON, Sgt. G. B. N/Zealander. 23
JOHNSON, P/O S. F. British. 600. Killed
JOHNSON, Sgt. R. A. British. 43
JOHNSON, Sgt. C. A. British. 25
JOHNSON, Sgt. A. E. British. 23. Killed
JOHNSON, Sgt. R. K. H. British. 235. Killed
JOHNSTON, P/O J. T. Canadian. 151. Killed*
JOHNSTONE, S/Ldr. A. V. R. British. 602
JOLL, P/O I. K. S. British. 604
JONES, P/O W. R. British. 266
JONES, F/O D. A. E. British. 3-501
JONES, Sgt. H. D. B. British. 504. Killed
JONES, P/O C. A. T. British. 611
JONES, P/O J. S. B. British. 152. Killed
JONES, P/O R. E. British. 605
JONES, P/O R. L. British. 64-19
JONES, Sgt. E. British. 29. Killed
JONES, P/O J. T. British. 264. Killed*
JONES, F/O. British. 616

JOTTARD, P/O A. R. I. Belgian. 145. Killed*
JOUBERT, P/O C. C. O. British. 56
JOWITT, Sgt. L. British. 85. Killed*
JULEFF, P/O J. R. British. 600

KAHN, P/O A. H. E. British. 248. Killed
KANE, P/O T. M. British. 234
KANIA, F/Sgt. J. Polish. 303
KARASEK, Sgt. L. R. British. 23. Killed*
KARUBIN, Sgt. S. Polish. 303. Killed
KARWOSKI, P/O W. E. Polish. 302
KAUCKY, Sgt. J. Czech. 310
KAWALECKI, P/O T. W. Polish. 151
KAY, P/O D. H. S. British. 264. Killed
KAY, P/O J. K. British. 111-257
KAY, Sgt. A. British. 248. Killed*
KAYLL, S/Ldr. J. R. British. 615
KEARD, P/O J. A. British. 235. Killed
KEARSEY, P/O P. J. British. 607-213. Killed
KEARSEY, Sgt. A. W. British. 152
KEAST, Sgt. F. J. British. 600. Killed*
KEATINGS, Sgt. J. British. 219
KEE, Sgt. E. H. C. British. 253. Killed
KEEL, Sgt. G. E. British. 235. Killed*
KEELER, Sgt. R. R. G. British. 236
KEIGHLEY, P/O G. British. 610
KELLETT, S/Ldr. R. G. British. 303-249
KELLETT, F/O M. British. 111
KELLIT, Sgt. W. H. British. 236
KELLOW, F/O R. W. British. 213
KELLS, P/O L. G. H. British. 29. Died
KELLY, F/Lt. D. P. D. G. British. 74
KELSEY, Sgt. E. N. British. 611. Killed
KEMP, P/O J. R. N/Zealander. 141. Killed*
KEMP, P/O N. L. D. British. 242
KEMP, P/O J. L. British. 54
KENDAL, P/O J. B. British. 66. Killed
KENNARD, P/O H. C. British. 66
KENNARD-DAVIS, P/O P. F. British. 64. Killed*
KENNEDY, Sgt. R. W. British. 604. Killed
KENNEDY, F/Lt. J. C. Australian. 238. Killed*
KENNER, P/O P. L. British. 264. Killed*
KENNETT, P/O P. British. 3. Killed
KENSALL, Sgt. G. British. 25. Killed
KENT, F/Lt. J. A. Canadian. 303
KENT, P/O R. D. British. 235
KEOUGH, P/O V. C. American. 609. Killed
KEPRT, Sgt. J. Czech. 312
KER-RAMSAY, F/Lt. R. G. British. 25. F.I.U.
KERSHAW, P/O A. British. 1. Killed
KERWIN, F/O B. V. Canadian. 1 (Can) (401). Died
KESTIN (F.A.A.), Sub Lt. I. H. British. 145. Killed*
KESTLER, Sgt. O. Czech. 111. Killed
KEYMER, Sgt. M. British. 65. Killed*
KEYNES, Sgt. J. D. British. 236. Killed
KIDSUN, P/O R. N/Zealander. 141. Killed*
KILLICK, Sgt. P. British. 245

Above: W. T. "Ace" Hodgson flew Hurricanes with No.85 Squadron and was one of the many who gave rather more than they received.

Above: The medals of Canadian pilot John Alexander Kent, a flight commander with the top scoring No.303 Polish Squadron.

Above: Denis Crowley-Milling flew Hurricanes with No.242 Squadron.

Above: Wing Cdr Brian Kingcombe seen after the Battle.

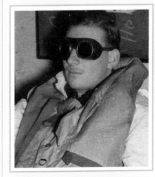

Above: J. A. F. MacLachlan with goggles to preserve night vision.

Above: Henry Matthews of No.603 Sqn fell to the Bf 109s of II/JG 26.

McCANN, Sgt. T. A. British. 601. Died
McCARTHY, Sgt. T. F. British. 235. Killed
McCARTHY, Sgt. J. P. British. 235
McCAUL, Sgt. J. P. British. 219. Killed*
McCHESNEY, Sgt. R. I. N/Zealander. 236. Killed
McCLINTOCK, P/O J. A. P. British. 615. Killed
McCOMB, S/Ldr. J. E. British. 611
McCONNELL, Sgt. J. British. 145
McCONNELL, P/O W. W. Irish. 607-245-249
McCORMACK, Sgt. J. B. British. 25. Killed
McDERMOTT, Sgt. J. N/Zealander. 23
McDONOUGH, P/O B. M. Australian. 236. Killed*
McDOUGALL, P/O R. British. 3-232
McDOWALL, Sgt. A British. 602
McFADDEN, P/O A. British. 73
McGAW, P/O C. A. British. 73-66. Killed
McGIBBON, P/O J. British. 615. Killed
McGLASHAN, P/O K. B. British. 245
McGOWAN, F/O R. A. British. 46
McGOWAN, P/O H. W. British. 92
McGRATH, P/O J. K. British. 601
McGREGOR, F/Lt. G. R. Canadian. 1 (Can) (401)
McGREGOR, P/O P. R. British. 46
McGREGOR, S/Ldr. H. D. British. 213
McGREGOR, P/O A. J. British. 504
McGUGAN, Sgt. R. British. 141
McHARDY, P/O E. H. N/Zealander. 248
McHARDY, P/O D. B. H. British. 229
McINNES, P/O A. British. 601-238
McINTOSH, Sgt. P. R. C. British. 151-605. Killed
McINTYRE, P/O A. G. British. 111
McKAY, Sgt. D. A. S. British. 501-421 Flt.
McKELLAR, F/Lt. A. A. British. 605. Killed
McKENZIE, P/O J. W. British. 111. Killed*
McKIE, Sgt. E. J. British. 248
McKNIGHT, P/O W. L. Canadian. 242. Killed
McLAUGHLIN, Sgt. J. W. British. 238
McLURE, P/O A. C. R. British. 87. Killed
McMAHON, Sgt. British. 235
McMULLEN, F/O D. A. P. British. 222-54
McNAB, S/Ldr. E. A. Canadian. 1 (Can) (401)-111
McNAIR, Sgt. R. J. British. 249-3
McNAY, Sgt. A. British. 73. Killed*
McPHEE, Sgt. J. British. 249-151
McPHERSON, F/Sgt. R. R. British. 65. Killed
MEAKER, P/O J. R. B. British. 249. Killed*
MEARES, S/Ldr. British. 54
MEASURES, F/Lt. W. E. G. British. 74-238
MEDWORTH, Sgt. J. British. 25
MEESON, Sgt. C. V. British. 56. Killed
MELVILLE, P/O J. C. British. 264
MELVILLE-JACKSON, P/O G. H. British. 236
MERCER, Sgt. British. 609
MERCHANT, Sgt. H. J. British. 1
MEREDITH, Sgt. A. D. British. 242-141
MERMAGEN, S/Ldr. H. W. British. 266-222
MERRETT, Sgt. J. C. British. 235
MERRICK, P/O C. British. 610
MERRYWEATHER, Sgt. S. W. British. 229. Killed
MESNER, Sgt. B. W. British. 248. Killed*
METCALFE, Sgt. A. C. British. 604
METHAM, Sgt. J. British. 253. Killed
MEYER, Sgt. R. H. R. British. 236. Killed
MICHAIL, Sgt. British. 501
MICHIELS, Sgt. A. C. A. Belgian. 235. Died
MIDDLEMISS, Sgt. W. British. 235
MIDDLETON, P/O. British. 266
MIERZWA, P/O B. Polish. 303
MILBURN, Sgt. R. A. British. 601
MILDREN, P/O P.R. British. 54-66. Killed
MILEHAM, P/O D. E. British. 41. Killed
MILES, Sgt. E. E. British. 236
MILES, Sgt. S. F. British. 23
MILEY, P/O M. J. British. 25. Killed*
MILLAR, F/O W. B. N. Canadian. 1 (Can) (401)
MILLARD, P/O J. G. P. British. 1

MILLER, F/Lt. A. G. British. 17-F.I.U.
MILLER, P/O R. F. G. Australian. 609. Killed*
MILLER, Sgt. A. J. British. 23
MILLER, Sgt. A. C. British. 604
MILLER, Sgt. T. H. British. 25. Killed
MILLER, F/Lt. R. R. British. 3. Killed
MILLINGTON, P/O W. H. Australian. 79-249.
   Killed*
MILLIST, P/O K. M. British. 73-615. Killed
MILLS, S/Ldr. R. S. British. 87
MILLS, Sgt. J. P. British. 43-249
MILLS, Sgt. J. B. British. 23
MILNE, P/O J. A. Canadian. 605
MILNE, F/O R. M. British. 151
MILNES, Sgt. A. H. British. 32
MITCHELL, P/O H. T. Canadian. 87
MITCHELL, F/O R. G. British. 257. Killed*
MITCHELL, F/O P. H. G. British. 266
MITCHELL, S/Ldr. H. M. British. 25
MITCHELL, Sgt. G. British. 23
MITCHELL, P/O G. T. M. British. 609. Killed
MITCHELL, Sgt. R. R. British. 229
MITCHELL, Sgt. H. R. N/Zealander. 3
MITCHELL, Sgt. British. 65
MOBERLEY, F/O G. E. British. 616. Killed*
MOLSON, F/O H. de M. Canadian. 1 (Can) (401)
MONK, P/O E. W. J. British. 25. Killed
MONK, Sgt. D. A. British. 236
MONTAGU, S/Ldr. G. W. British. 236. Killed
MONTAGUE-SMITH, F/Lt. A. M. British. 264
MONTBON, Sgt. Xavier de. Free French. 64
MONTGOMERY, Sgt.H. F. British. 43. Killed*
MONTGOMERY, P/O C. R. British. 614. Killed*
MOODY, P/O H. W. British. 602. Killed*
MOODY, Sgt. D. G. British. 604
MOORE, Sgt. A. R. British. 245-615-3
MOORE, P/O W. R. British. 264
MOORE, Sgt. P. J. British. 253. Killed
MOORE, F/O W. S. British. 236. Killed
MORE, S/Ldr. J. W. C. British. 73. Killed
MOREWOOD, F/Lt. R. E. G. British. 248
MORFILL, F/Sgt. P. F. British. 501
MORGAN, P/O P. J. British. 238
MORGAN-GRAY, P/O H. British. 46. Killed
MORRIS, P/O E. J. S/African. 79
MORRIS, P/O J. R. B. British. F.I.U.
MORRIS, P/O J. British. 248
MORRISON, Sgt. N. British. 54-74-72. Killed
MORRISON, Sgt. J. P. British. 46-43. Killed*
MORROUGH-RYAN, P/O O. B. British. 41. Killed
MORTIMER, P/O P. A. British. 257. Died
MORTON, P/O J. S. British. 603
MOSS /F.A.A.), Sub/Lt. W. J.M. British. 213.
   Killed*
MOSS, Sgt. R. C. British. 29
MOTT, Sgt. W. H. British. 141
MOTTRAM, P/O R. British. 92. Killed
MOUCHOTTE, Adj. R. Free French. 615. Killed

MOULD, Sgt. E. A. British. 74. Killed
MOULTON, Sgt. E. W. British. 600
MOUNSDON, P/O M. H. British. 56
MOUNT, F/O C. J. British. 602
MOWAT, F/Lt. N.J. N/Zealander. 245
MOWAT, Sgt. R. I. British. 248
MOYNHAM, Sgt. H. F. J. British. 248. Killed
MRAZEK, P/O K. Czech. 46
MUDIE, P/O M. R. British. 615. Killed*
MUDRY, Sgt. M. Polish. 79
MUIRHEAD, F/Lt. I. J. British. 605. Killed*
MUMLER, W/Cdr. M. Polish. 302
MUNGO-PARK, F/O J. C. British. 79-74. Killed
MUNN, F/Sgt. W. S. British. 29
MURCH, F/O L. C. British. 253. Died
MURLAND, Sgt. W. J. British. 264
MURRAY, Sgt J. British. 610
MURRAY, P/O T. B. British. 616
MURRAY, S/Ldr. A. D. British. 73-501
MURRAY, Sgt. P. H. British. 23. Killed

NAISH, Sgt. K E. British. 235
NARUCKI, P/O A. R. Polish. 607
NAUGHTIN, Sgt. H. T. British. 235. Killed
NEER, Sgt.British. 29
NEIL, P/O T. F. British. 249
NELSON, F/O W. H. Canadian. 74
NELSON, F/Sgt. D. British. 235
NELSON-EDWARDS, P/O G. H. British. 79
NENAGE, Sgt. T. N. British. 29. Killed
NESBITT, F/O A. D. Canadian. 1 (Can) (401)
NEVILLE, Sgt. W. J. British. 610. Killed*
NEWBURY, P/O J. C. British. 609
NEWBURY, P/O M. A. British. 145. Killed
NEWHAM, Sgt. E. A. British. 235
NEWLING, P/O M. A. British. 145. Died
NEWPORT, Sgt. D. V. British. 235
NEWTON, Sgt.H. S. British. 111
NEWTON, Sgt. E. F. British. 29
NICHOLAS, F/O J. B. H. British. 65
NICHOLLS, Sgt. T. G. F. British. 23. Killed
NICHOLLS, Sgt. D. B. F. British. 151
NICHOLS, Sgt. D. H. British. 56
NICOLSON, F/Lt. J. B. British. 249. Killed
NICOLSON, Sgt. P. B. British. 232. Killed
NIEMIEC, F/O P. Polish.17
NIGHTINGALE, P/O F. G. British. 219. Killed
NIVEN, P/O H. G. British. British. 601-602
NIXEN, Sgt. W. British. 23. Killed
NOBLE, Sgt. W. J. British. 54
NOBLE, P/O B. R. British. 79
NOBLE, Sgt.D. British. 43. Killed*
NOKES-COOPER, F/O B. British. 236. Killed*
NORFOLK, P/O N. R. British. 72
NORRIS, P/O R. W. Canadian. 1 (Can) (401)
NORRIS, F/Lt. S. C. British. 610
NORRIS, Sgt. P. P. British. 213. Killed*
NORTH, P/O G. British. 257. Killed

NORTH, P/O H. R.British. 43
NORTH-BOMFORD, Sgt. D. J. British. 17
NORWELL, Sgt. J. K. British. 54-41
NORWOOD, P/O R. K. C. British. 65
NOSOWICZ, P/O Z. Polish. 56
NOWAK, P/O T. Polish. 253
NOWAKIEWICZ, Sgt. E. J. A. Polish. 302
NOWELL (F.A.A.), Sub/Lt. W. R. British. 804
NOWIERSKI, P/O T. Polish. 609
NUNN, P/O S. G. British. British. 236
NUTE, Sgt. R. R. J. British. 23. Killed
NUTTER, Sgt. R. C. British. 257

OAKS, Sgt. T. W. N/Zealander. 235
O'BRIAN, F/O P. G. St.G. Canadian. 247-152
O'BRIEN, S/Ldr. J. S. British. 92-234. Killed*
O'BRIEN, F/Lt. 247
O'BRYNE, Sgt. P. British. 73-501
O'CONNELL, F/O A British. 264
OBELOFSE, P/O J. R S. S/African. 43. Killed*
ODBERT, S/Ldr. N. C. British. 64
OFFENBERG, P/O J. H. M. Belgian. 145. Killed
OGILVIE, P/O D. B. British. 601
OGILVIE, F/O A. K. Canadian. 609
OLDFIELD, Sgt. T. G. British. 64-92. Killed*
O'LEARY, Sgt.A. A. British. 604
OLENSEN, P/O W. P. British. 607. Killed
OLENSKI, F/O Z. Polish. 234-609
OLEWINSKI, Sgt. B. Polish. 111. Killed
OLIVE, F/Lt. C. G. C. Australian. 65
OLIVER, P/O P. British. 611
OLIVER, Sgt. G. D. British. 23. Killed
OLVER, P/O. British. 603
O'MALLEY, F/O D. H. C. British. 264. Killed*
O'MANNEY, Sgt. R. J. British. 229. Killed
O'MEARA, P/O J. J. British. 421 Flt-64-72
O'NEILL F/O D. H. British. 611-41. Killed
O'NEILL, F/Lt. J. A. British. 601-238
ORCHARD, Sgt. H. C. British. 65. Killed
ORGIAS, P/O E. N/Zealander. 23. Killed*
ORTMANS, P/O V. M. M. Belgian. 229. Killed
ORZECHOWSKI, P/O J. Polish. 607
OSMAND, P/O A. I. British. 3-213
OSTOWICZ, F/O A. Polish. 145. Killed*
OTTEWILL, Sgt. P. G. British. 43
OVERTON, P/O C. N. British. 43
OWEN, Sgt. A. E. British. 600
OWEN, Sgt. H. British. 219
OWEN, Sgt. W. G. British. 235
OXSPRING, F/Lt. R. W. British. 66

PAGE, P/O A. G. British. 56
PAGE, Sgt. W. T. British. 1. Killed
PAGE, Sgt. V. D. British. 610-601
PAGE, Sgt. A. J. British. 257. Killed
PAGE, F/Lt. C. L. British. 234
PAGE, Sgt. A. D. British. 111. Killed
PAIN, P/O J. F. British. 32. Killed

PAISEY, Sgt. F. G. British. 235
PALAK, Sgt. J. Polish. 303-302
PALLISER, Sgt. G. C. C. British. 249-43
PALMER, Sgt.N. N. British. 248. Killed
PALUSINSKI, P/O J. H. Polish. 303
PANKRATZ, F/Lt. W. Polish. 145. Killed*
PANNELL, Sgt. G. C. N/Zeland. 3
PARKE (F.A.A.), Sub Lt. T. R. V. British. 804.
   Killed
PARKER, Sgt. K. B. British. 64-92. Killed*
PARKER, P/O T. C. British. 79
PARKER, Sgt. D. K. British. 66
PARKER, P/O V. British. 234. Killed
PARKER, Wg/Cdr. L. R. British. 611
PARKES, Sgt. British. 501
PARKIN, P/O E. G. British. 501
PARKINSON, Sgt. C. British. 238.
   Killed*
PARNALL, P/O S. B. British. 607. Killed*
PARNALL, F/Lt. D. G. British. 249. Killed*
PARR, Sgt. L. A. British. 79
PARR, Sgt. D. J. British. 29. Killed
PARROTT, F/O D. T. British. 19. Killed
PARROTT, F/O P. L. British. 145-605
PARROTT, Sgt. R. J. British. 32. Killed
PARRY, Sgt. M. E. British. 604
PARRY, Sgt. E. British. 23. Killed
PARSONS, Sgt. E. E. N/Zeland. 23
PARSONS, Sgt. C. A. British. 66-610. Killed
PARSONS, F/O P. T. British. 504. Killed
PARSONS, P/O J. G. British. 235
PASSY, F/O C. W. British. 605
PASZIEWICZ, F/O L. W. Polish. 303. Killed*
PATEREK, Sgt. E. Polish. 302-303. Killed
PATERSON (F.A.A.), Lt. B.British. 804
PATERSON, F/Lt.J. A. N/Zealander. 92. Killed*
PATRICK, Sgt.L. F. British. 222
PATSON, Sgt. A. G. British. 604
PATTEN, F/O H. P. F. British. 64
PATTERSON (F.A.A.), Mid/Ship. P. J. British. 242.
   Killed
PATTERSON, P/O R. L. British. 235. Killed*
PATTERSON, (F.A.A.), Sub Lt. N. H. British. 804.
   Killed
PATTERSON, Sgt. L. J. British. 501. Killed
PATTISON, F/O A. J. S. British. 616-23-92.
   Killed*
PATTISON, Sgt. K. C. British. 611. Killed*
PATTISON, F/O. Canadian. 1 (Can) (401)
PATTISON, F/O J. G. British. 266
PATTULLO, P/O W. B. 151-249-46. Killed*
PAVITT, Sgt. British. 235
PAVLU, Sgt. O. Czech. 1. Killed
PAYNE, Sgt. A. D. British. British. 610
PAYNE, Sgt. R. I. British. 23. Killed*
PAYNE, P/O R. A. British. 602. Killed
PEACHMENT, P/O C. B. G. British. 236
PEACOCK, Sgt. W. A. British. 46. Killed*

Above: Hurricane pilot A. C. R. McLure flew with No.87 Sqn.

Above: Brian Meaker was with No.249 Squadron.

Above: Miles Miley of No.25 Sqn died in a crash in September.

Above: Sgt P. Mitchell, a Spitfire pilot with No.65 Squadron.

PEACOCK, F/O R. J. British. 235. Killed
PEACOCK, Sgt. D. C. 605
PEACOCK-EDWARDS, P/O S. R. British. 253-615
PEARCE, Sgt. L. H.B. British. 32-249. Killed
PEARCE, Sgt. P. G. British. 600. Killed
PEARCE, Sgt. W. J. British. 236-23. Killed
PEARCE, Sgt. R. British. 29
PEARCY, Sgt. D. J. British. 219. Killed
PEARMAN, P/O S. J. British. 141
PEARSE, Sgt. L. L. British. 236
PEARSON, Sgt. D. E British. 236
PEARSON, Sgt. G. W. British. 501. Killed*
PEARSON, Sgt. P. British. 238. Killed
PEASE, P/O A. P. British. 74-603. Killed*
PECHA, Sgt. J. Czech. 310
PEEBLES, Sgt. W. British. 235. Killed
PEEL, S/Ldr. J.R. A. British. 145
PEEL, F/O C. D. British. 603. Killed*
PEGGE, P/O C. O. J. British. 610. Killed
PEMBERTON, S/Ldr. D. A. British. 1. Killed
PENFOLD, P/O P. E. British. 29
PENFOLD, Sgt. W. D. British. 236
PENFOLD, F/Sgt. V. W. R. British. 23
PENNINGTON, P/O D. A. British. 253-245
PENNINGTON-LEIGH, F/Lt. A. W. British. 232-248. Killed
PENNYCUICK, Sgt. B. British. 236
PERCY, P/O H. H. British. 264. Killed
PERKIN, Sgt. F. S. British. 73-421 Flt.
PERRIN, Adj. G. Free French. 615-249.
PERRY, Sgt. H. T. British. 23. Killed*
PETERS, F/O G. C. B. British. 79. Killed*
PETERSON, F/O O. J. Canadian. 1 (Can) (401). Killed*
PETTET, P/O A. H.British. 248. Killed
PETTIT, Sgt. H. W. British. 605-1. Killed
PEXTON, F/O R. D. British. 615
PFEIFFER, P/O J. Polish.257-32
PHILLIPART, P/O J. A. L. Belgian. 213. Killed*
PHILLIPS, Sgt. A British. 604
PHILLIPS, F/Sgt. N. T. British. 65. Killed*
PHILLIPS, Sgt. R. F. P. British. 602
PHILLIPS, P/O E. R. British. 25. Killed
PHILLIPS, Sgt. J. British. 25. Killed
PHILLIPSON, Sgt. J. R. British. 604. Killed
PHILO, P/O R. F. British. 151
PIATKOWSKI, P/O S. Polish. 79. Killed*
PICKERING, Sgt. T. G. British. 501-32
PICKERING, Sgt. J. British. 64
PICKERING, P/O J. H. British. 66. Killed
PICKFORD, Sgt. J. T. British. 604
PIDD, Sgt. L. British. 238. Killed*
PIGG, F/O O. St.J. British. 72. Killed*
PILKINGTON, Sgt. A. British. 23
PILKINGTON-MIKSA, P/O W. J. Polish. 303
PILCH, P/O E. Polish. 302. Killed
PINCKNEY, F/O D. J. C. British. 603. Killed
PINFOLD, F/Lt. M.H. British. 56

PINKHAM, S/Ldr. P. C. British. 19. Killed*
PIPA, Sgt. J. British. 43
PIPER, Sgt. A.H. British. 236
PIPPARD, P/O H. A. British. 29
PIPPETT, F/O J. G. British. 64. Killed
PISAREK, F/O M. Polish. 303
PITCHER, F/O P. B. Canadian. 1 (Can) (401)
PITTMAN, P/O G. E. British. 17
PLANT, Sgt. R. E. British. 611-72. Killed
PLEDGER, P/O G. F. C. British. 141. Killed
PLINDERLEITH, Sgt. R. British. 73
PLUMMER, F/O R. P. British. 46. Killed*
PLZAK, Sgt. S. Czech. 310-19. Killed
POCOCK, Sgt. M. H. British. 72
POLLARD, P/O P. S. C. British. 611. Killed
POLLARD, Sgt. J. K. British. 232. Killed
POND, F/Sgt. A. H. D. British. 601
PONTING, P/O W. A. British. 264. Killed*
POOL, P/O P. D. British. 266-72
POOLE, Sgt. E. R. L. British. 604
POPLAWSKI, P/O J. Polish. 111-229
PORTER, Sgt. J. A. British. 615-19-242
PORTER, Sgt. E. F. British. 141. Killed
PORTER, Sgt. O. W. British. 111. Killed
POSENER, P/O F. H. S/African. 152. Killed*
POULTON, P/O H. R. C. British. 64
POUND, Sgt. R. R. C. British. 25
POWELL, F/Lt. R. P. R. British. 111
POWELL, Sgt. S. W. M. British. 141
POWELL, P/O R. J. British. 248. Killed
POWELL, Sgt. E. British. 25. Killed
POWELL, Sgt. S. W. M. British. 141
POWELL-SHEDDEN, F/Lt. G. British. 242
POWER, F/Lt. R. M. Australian. 236
PRCHAL, Sgt. E. M.Czech. 310
PREATER, Sgt. S. G. British. 235
PREVOT, P/O L. O. J. Belgain. 235
PRIAK, P/O K. 32-257. Killed
PRICE, P/O A. O. British. 236
PRICE, Sgt. N. A. J. British. 236
PRICE, Sgt. R. B. British. 245-222-73. Killed
PRICE, Sgt. J. British. 29
PRIESTLEY, F/O British. 235
PRITCHARD, F/Lt. C. A. British. 600
PROCTOR, Sgt. J. British. 602. Killed
PROCTOR, P/O J. E. N/Zealander. 32
PROSSER, Sgt. P. R. British. 235. Killed
PROUDMAN, Sgt. D. H. British. 248. Died
PROWSE, P/O H. A. R. British. 266-603
PTACEK, Sgt. R. Czech. 43 Killed
PUDA, Sgt. R. Czech. 310-605
PUDNEY (F.A.A.), Sub Lt. G. B. British. 64. Killed
PUGH, Sgt. J. S. British. 25
PUGH, F/Lt. T. P. British. 263. Killed
PUSHMAN, P/O G. R. Canadian. 23
PUTT, F/Lt. A. R. British. 501
PUXLEY, Sgt. W. G. V. British. 236
PYE, Sgt. J. W. British. 25

PYMAN, P/O L. L. British. 65. Killed*
PYNE, Sgt. C. C. N/Zealander. 219

QUELCH, Sgt. B. H. British. 235
QUILL, F/O J. K. British. 65
QUINN, Sgt. J. British. 236

RABAGLIATI, F/Lt. A. C. British. 46. Killed
RABONE, P/O P. W. British. 145. Killed
RABONE, F/O J. H. M. British. 604
RADOMSKI, P/O J. Polish. 303
RADWANSKI, P/O G. Polish. 151-56-607
RAFTER, P/O R.F. British. 603
RAINE, Sgt. W. British. 610. Killed
RAINS, Sgt. D. N. British. 248. Killed
RALLS, Sgt. L. F. British. 605
RAMSAY, Sgt. N. H. D. British. 610-222
RAMSAY, P/O J. B. British. 151. Killed*
RAMSAY, Sgt. J. S. British. 235. Killed
RAMSHAW, Sgt. J. W. British. 222. Killed*
RASMUSSEN, Sgt. L. A. W. N/Zealander. 264. Killed*
RAVENHILL, P/O M. British. 229. Killed*
RAWLENCE, P/O A. J. British. 600
RAWNSLEY, Sgt. C. F. British. 604
RAY, Sgt. British. 56
RAYMOND, F/O P. British. 609
RAYNER, P/O R. M. S. British. 87
READ, F/O W. A. A. British. 603
REAM, Sgt. C. A. British. 235
REARDON-PARKER (F.A.A.), Sub Lt J. British. 804
REDDINGTON, Sgt. L. A. E. British. 152. Killed*
REDFERN, Sgt. E. A. British. 232. Killed
REDMAN, P/O J. British. 257-245-43. Killed
REECE, Sgt. L. H. M. British. 235. Killed*
REED, Sgt. H. British. 600
REES, P/O B. V. British. 610
REID, P/O R. British. 46. Killed
REILLEY, P/O H. W. Canadian. 64-66. Killed*
REILLY, Sgt. C. C. N/Zealander. 23. Killed
RENVOIZE, Sgt. J. V. British. 247
REYNELL, F/Lt. R. C. Australian. 43. Killed*
REYNO, F/Lt. E. M. Canadian. 1 (Can) (401)
RHODES, P/O R. A. British. 29. Killed
RHODES-MOORHOUSE, F/O W. H. British. 601. Killed*
RICALTON, P/O A. L. British. 74. Killed*
RICH, Sgt. P. G. British. 25
RICHARDS (F.A.A.), Sub Lt. D. H. British. 111. Died
RICHARDS, Sgt. W. C. British. 235. Killed
RICHARDSON, Sgt. E. British. 242
RICHARDSON, S/Ldr. W. A. British. 141
RICHARDSON, Sgt. R. W. British. 610
RICHARDSON, Sgt. British. 141
RICKETTS, Sgt. H. W. British. 235. Killed
RICKETTS, P/O V. A. British. 248. Killed
RICKS, Sgt. L. P. V. J. Canadian. 235

RIDDELL-HANNAM, Sgt. J. D. British. 236
RIDDLE, F/O C. J. British. 601
RIDDLE, F/O H. J. British. 601
RIDLEY, Sgt. M. British. 616. Killed*
RIGBY, P/O R. H. British. 236. Killed*
RILEY, F/Lt. W. British. 302. Killed
RILEY, P/O F. British. 236. Killed
RIMMER, F/Lt. R. F. British. 229. Killed*
RINGWOOD, Sgt. E. A. British. 248. Killed*
RIPLEY, Sgt. W. G. British. 604. Died
RIPPON, P/O A. J. British. 601. Killed
RISELEY, Sgt. A. H. British. 600
RITCHER, P/O G. L. British. 234
RITCHIE, Sgt. R. D. British. 605. Killed
RITCHIE, P/O I. S. British. 603
RITCHIE, P/O J. R. British. 111
RITCHIE, P/O T. G. F. British. 602. Killed
RITCHIE, P/O J. H. British. 141
RITCHIE, P/O J. H. British. 600
ROACH, P/O R. J. B. British. 266
ROBB, P/O R. A. L. British. 236
ROBBINS, P/O R. H. British. 54-66
ROBERTS, Wg/Cdr. D. N. British. 609-238
ROBERTS, Sgt. A. J. A. British. 29
ROBERTS, P/O R. British. 615-64
ROBERTS, Sgt. D. F. British. 25. Killed
ROBERTS, Sgt. E. C. British. 23
ROBERTS (F.A.A.), Mid/Ship. G. W. British. 808. Killed
ROBERTSON, Sgt. F. N. British. 66. Killed
ROBERTSON, Sgt. British. 56
ROBERTSON, Sgt. B. L. British. 54. Killed
ROBINSON, F/Lt. A. I. British. 222. Died
ROBINSON, Sgt. D. N. British. 152
ROBINSON, Sgt. J. British. 111. Died
ROBINSON, P/O J. C. E. British. 1. Killed
ROBINSON, F/Lt. M. L. British. 610-619-238-66. Killed
ROBINSON, P/O G. British. 264
ROBINSON, S/Ldr. M. W. S. British. 73
ROBINSON, F/Lt. P. B. British. 601
ROBINSON, Sgt. P. E. M. British. 56. Killed
ROBINSON, Sgt. P. T. British. 257
ROBINSON, S/Ldr. M. British. 616
ROBSHAW, P/O F. A. British. 229
ROBSON, P/O N. C. H. British. 72. Killed
RODEN, Sgt. H. A. C. British. 19. Died
ROFF, P/O B. J. British. 25. Killed
ROGERS, P/O B. A. British. 242. Killed
ROGERS, Sgt. G. W. British. 234. Killed
ROGERS, P/O E. B. British. 501-615
ROGOWSKI, Sgt. J. Polish. 303-74
ROHACEK, P/O R. B. Czech. 238-601. Killed
ROLLS, Sgt. W. T. E. British. 72
ROMAN, P/O C. L. Belgian. 236
ROMANIS, Sgt. A. L. British. 25. Killed
ROOK, F/Lt. A. H. British. 504
ROOK, P/O M. British. 504. Killed

ROSCOE, F/O G. L. British. 87. Killed
ROSE, F/O J. British. 32-3
ROSE, P/O S. N. British. 602
ROSE, Sgt. J. S. British. 23. Killed
ROSE, P/O E. B. M. British. 234. Killed
ROSE-PRICE, P/O A. T. British. 501. Killed*
ROSIER, S/Ldr. F. E. British. 229
ROSS, P/O J. K. British. 17. Killed
ROSS, P/O A. R. British. 25-610. Killed
ROTHWELL, P/O J. H. British. 601-605-32. Killed
ROUND, Sgt. J. H. British. 248. Killed*
ROURKE, Sgt. J. British. 248
ROUSE, Sgt. G. W. British. 236
ROWDEN, P/O J. H. British. 64-616. Killed
ROWELL, Sgt. P. A. British. 249
ROWLEY, P/O R. M. B. British. 145. Killed
ROYCE, F/O M. E. A. British. 504
ROYCE, F/O W. B. British. 504
ROZWADWSKI, P/O M. Polish. 151. Killed*
ROZYCKI, P/O W. Polish. 238
RUDDOCK, Sgt. W. S. British. 23
RUDLAND, Sgt. C. P. British. 263
RUSHMER, F/Lt. F. W. British. 603. Killed
RUSSELL, F/Lt. H. a'b. British. 32
RUSSELL, F/O B. D. Canadian. 1(Can) (401)
RUSSELL, Sgt. N/Zealander. 264
RUSSELL, P/O G. H. British. 236
RUSSELL, Sgt. A. G. British. 43
RUSSELL, P/O. British. 141
RUSSELL (F.A.A.), Lt. G. F. British. 804. Killed
RUST, Sgt. C. A. British. 85-249
RUSTON, F/Lt. P. British. 604. Died
RUTTER, P/O R. D. British. 73
RYALLS, P/O D. L. British. 29-F.I.U. Killed
RYDER, F/Lt. E. N. British. 41
RYPL, P/O F. Czech. 310

SADLER, P/O N. A. British. 235. Killed
SADLER, F/Sgt H. S. British. 611. Killed
ST. AUBIN, F/O. E. F. British. 616. Killed
ST. JOHN, P/O P. C. B. British. 74. Killed*
SALMON, F/O H. N. E. British. 1-229
SALWAY, Sgt. E. British. 141. Killed
SAMOLINSKI, P/O W. M. C. Polish. 253. Killed*
SAMPLE, S/Ldr. J. British. 504. Killed
SAMPSON, Sgt. A. British. 23
SANDERS, S/Ldr. F. J. British. 92
SANDERS, F/Lt. J. G. British. 615
SANDIFER, Sgt. A. K. British. 604
SARGENT, Sgt. R. E. B. British. 219
SARRE, Sgt. A. R. British. 603
SASAK, Sgt. W. British. 32. Killed
SATCHELL, S/Ldr. W. A. J. British. 302
SAUNDERS, P/O C. H. British. 92
SAUNDERS, F/Lt. G. A. W. British. 65
SAVAGE, Sgt. T. W. British. 64. Killed
SAVILL, Sgt. J. E. British. 242-151
SAVILLE, Sgt. British. 501. Killed
SAWARD, Sgt. C. J. British. 615-501
SAWICE, F/O T. Polish. 303
SAWYER, S/Ldr. H. C. British. 65. Killed*
SAYERS, F/Sgt. J. E. British. 41
SCHOLLAR, P/O E. C. British. 248
SCHUMER, P/O F. H. British. 600. Killed
SCHWIND, F/Lt. L. H. British. 257-213. Killed*
SCLANDERS, P/O K. M. Canadian. 242. Killed*
SCOTT, Sgt. A. E. British. 73. Killed
SCOTT, Sgt. G. W. British. 64-19
SCOTT, Sgt. N/Zealander. 246
SCOTT, Sgt. E. British. 222. Killed*
SCOTT, Sgt. J. A. British. 611-74. Killed*
SCOTT, F/Lt. D. R. British. 605
SCOTT, Sgt. H. J. British. 3-607. Killed
SCOTT, P/O D. S. British. 73
SCOTT, F/O W. J. M. British. 41. Killed*
SCOTT, F/O R. H. British. 604

Above: Sgt J. Morrison fell in combat on October 22.

Above: J. B. Nicolson's VC, the only fighter VC of the war.

Above: Flt Lt T. P. Pugh flew the twin-engined and highly secret Whirlwind fighters with No.263 Squadron.

SCOTT, Sgt. British. 422 Flt.
SCOTT-MALDEN, P/O F. D. S. British. 611-603
SCRASE, F/O G. E. T. British. 600. Killed
SEABOURNE, Sgt. E. W. British. 238
SEARS, P/O L. A. British. 145. Killed*
SECRETAN, P/O D. British. 72-54
SEDA, Sgt. K. Czech. 310
SEDDON, P/O J. W. British. 601. Killed
SEGHERS, P/O E. G. A. Belgian. 46-32. Killed
SELLERS, Sgt. R. F. British. 46-111
SELWAY, F/O J. B. British. 604
SENIOR, Sgt. J. N. British. 23. Killed
SENIOR, Sgt. B. British. 600
SEREDYN, Sgt. A. Polish. 32
SERVICE, Sgt. A. British. 29. Killed
SEWELL, Sgt. D. A. British. 17. Killed
SHANAHAN, Sgt. M. M. British. 1. Killed*
SHAND, P/O British. 54
SHARMAN, P/O H. R. British. 248
SHARP, P/O L. M. British. 111. Killed
SHARP, Sgt. B. R. British. 235. Killed*
SHARP, Sgt. R. J. British. 236
SHARPLEY, Sgt. H. British. 234. Killed
SHARRATT, Sgt. W. G. British. 248. Killed
SHAW, P/O R. H. British. 1. Killed*
SHAW, F/O I. G. British. 264. Killed*
SHAW (F.A.A.), Petty/Off. F. J. British. 804. Killed
SHEAD, Sgt. H. F. W. British. 257-32
SHEARD, Sgt. H. British. 236. Killed
SHEEN, F/O D. F. B. Australian. 72
SHEPHERD, Sgt. F. W. British. 264. Killed
SHEPLEY, P/O D. C. British. 152. Killed*
SHEPPARD, Sgt. British. 236
SHEPHERD, Sgt. J. B. British. 234. Killed
SHEPPERD, Sgt. G. E. British. 219. Killed*
SHEPPHERD, Sgt. E. E. British. 152. Killed*
SHEPHERD, Sgt. F. E. R. British. 611. Killed
SHERIDAN, Sgt. S. British. 236
SHERRINGTON, P/O T. B. A. British. 92
SHEWEL, Sgt. British. 236
SHIPMAN, P/O E. A. British. 41
SHIRLEY, Sgt. S. H. J. British. 604. Killed
SHORROCKS, P/O N. B. British. 235. Killed*
SHUTTLEWORTH, P/O Lord R. U. P. KAY-. British. 145. Killed*
SIBLEY, Sgt. F. A. British. 238. Killed*
SIKA, Sgt. J. Czech. 43
SILK, Sgt. F. H. British. 111
SILVER, Sgt. W. G. British. 152. Killed*
SILVESTOR, Sgt. G. F. British. 229
SIM, Sgt. R. B. British. 111. Killed*
SIMMONDS, P/O V. C. British. 238
SIMPSON, F/O G. M. N/Zealander. 229. Killed*
SIMPSON, F/Lt. J. W. C. British. 43. Died
SIMPSON, P/O P. J. British. 111-64
SIMPSON, P/O L. W. British. 141-264
SIMS, Sgt. I. R. British. 248. Killed
SIMS, P/O J. A. British. 3-232
SINCLAIR, F/O G. L. British. 310
SINCLAIR, P/O J. British. 219
SING, F/Lt. J. E. J. British. 213
SIZER, P/O W. M. British. 213
SKALSKI, P/O S. Polish. 501-615
SKILLEN, Sgt. V. H. British. 29. Killed
SKINNER, Sgt. W. M. British. 74
SKINNER, F/O C. D. E. British. 604
SKINNER, F/Lt. S. H. British. 604. Killed
SKOWRON, Sgt. H. Polish. 303. Killed
SLADE, Sgt. J. W. British. 64.Killed
SLATTER, P/O D. M. British. 141. Killed*
SLEIGH (F.A.A.), Lt.J. W. British.804
SLOUF, Sgt. V. Czech. 312
SLY, Sgt. O. K. British. 29. Killed
SMALLMAN, Sgt. J. British. 23
SMART, P/O T. British 65. Killed
SMITH, Sgt. A. D. British. 66. Killed*

SMITH, P/O D. N. E. British. 74. Killed
SMITH, P/O E. British. 229
SMITH, F/O D. S. British. 616. Killed*
SMITH, S/Ldr. A. T. British. 610. Killed*
SMITH, P/O E. B. B. British. 610
SMITH, F/Lt. F. M. British. 72
SMITH, P/O I. S. N/Zealander. 151
SMITH, P/O J. D. Canadian. 73. Killed
SMITH, F/Lt. R. L. British. 151
SMITH, Sgt. K. B. British. 257. Killed*
SMITH, P/O R. R. Canadian. 229
SMITH, F/Lt. W. A. British. 229
SMITH, P/O P. R. British. 25. Killed
SMITH, F/Lt. C. D. S. British. 25. Killed
SMITH, P/O A. W. British. 141. Killed
SMITH (F.A.A.), Sub Lt. F. A. British. 145. Killed*
SMITH, P/O A. J. British. 74
SMITH, Sgt. R. C. British. 236. Killed
SMITH, P/O E. L. British. 604
SMITH, Sgt. W. B. British. 602
SMITH, F/O E. S. British. 600
SMITH, Sgt. L. E. British. 234-602
SMITH, Sgt. St. James. British. 600. Killed
SMITH, Sgt. F. British. 604. Killed
SMITH, Sgt. G. E. British. 264
SMITH, Sgt. A. British. 600. Killed
SMITH, Sgt. L. British. 219
SMITH, Sgt. P. R. British. 236. Killed
SMITH, Sgt. N. H. J. British. 235
SMITH, Sgt. E. C. British. 600
SMITH, F/Lt. W. O. L. British. 263. Killed
SMITHERS, P/O J. L. British. 601. Killed*
SMITHERS, F/O R. Canadian. 1 (Can) (401). Killed*
SMITHSON, Sgt. R. British. 249. Killed
SMYTH, Sgt. R. H. British. 111
SMYTHE, Sgt. G. British. 56
SMYTHE, P/O R. F. British. 32
SMYTHE, F/O D. M. A. British. 264
SNAPE, Sgt. W. G. British. 25. Killed
SNELL, P/O V. R. British. 501-151
SNOWDEN, Sgt. E. G. British. 213. Killed
SOARS, Sgt. H. J. British. 74
SOBBEY, Sgt. E. A. British. 235. Killed
SODEN, P/O J. F. British. 266-603. Killed
SOLAK, P/O J. J. Polish. 151-249
SOLOMAN, P/O N. D. British. 17. Killed*
SONES, Sgt. L. C. British. 605
SOUTHALL, Sgt. G. British. 23. Killed
SOUTHORN, Sgt. G. A. British. 235
SOUTHWELL, P/O J. S. British. 245. Killed
SPEARS, Sgt. British. 421 Flt.
SPEARS, Sgt. A. W. P. British. 222
SPEKE, P/O H. British. 604. Killed
SPENCE, P/O D. J. N/Zealander. 245. Killed
SPENCER, S/Ldr. D. G. H. British. 266
SPENCER, Sgt. G. H. British. 504
SPIERS, Sgt. A. H. British. 236

SPIRES, Sgt. J. H. British. 235
SPRAGUE, Sgt. M. H. British. 602. Killed*
SPRAGUE, P/O H. A. Canadian. 3
SPRENGER, F/O Canadian. 1 (Can) (401)
SPURDLE, P/O R. L. N/Zealander. 74
SPYER, Sgt. R. A. British. 607. Killed
SQUIER, Sgt. J. W. C. British. 64
STANGER, Sgt. N. M. N/Zealander. 235
STANLEY, P/O D. A. British. 64. Killed
STANLEY, Sgt. D. O. N/Zealander. 151. Killed
STANSFELD, F/O W. K. British. 242-229
STAPLES, Sgt. R. C. J. British. 72
STAPLES, P/O L. British. 151
STAPLES, P/O M. E. British. 609. Killed
STAPLETON, P/O B. G. British. 603
STARLL, Sgt. British. 601
STARR, S/Ldr. H. M. British. 245-253. Killed*
STAVERT, P/O C. M. British. 1-504
STEADMAN, Sgt. D. J. British. 245
STEBOROWSKI, F/O M. J. Polish. 238. Killed*
STEELE, Sgt. R. M. British. 235
STEERE, F/Sgt. H. British. 19. Killed
STEERE, F/Sgt. J. British. 72
STEFAN, Sgt. J. Czech. 1
STEGMAN, P/O S. Polish. 111-229
STEHLIK, Sgt. J. Czech. 312
STEIN, P/O D. British. 263. Killed
STENHOUSE, F/O J. British. 43
STEPHEN, P/O H. M. British. 74
STEPHENS, P/O M. M. British. 232-3
STEPHENS, Sgt. C. British. 23. Killed*
STEPHENSON, F/Lt. P. J. T. British. 607
STEPHENSON, F/O I. R. British. 264. Killed
STEPHENSON, P/O S. P. British. 85
STERBACEK, P/O J. Czech. 310. Killed
STEVENS, Sgt. G. British. 213
STEVENS, P/O L. W. British. 17. Killed
STEVENS, P/O R. P. British. 151. Killed
STEVENS, P/O E. J. British. 141
STEVENS, P/O W. R. British. 23
STEVENS, Sgt. R. E. British. 29. Killed*
STEVENSON, P/O P. C. F. British. 74. Killed
STEWARD, Sgt. G. A. British. 17. Killed
STEWART, Sgt. C. N. D. British. 604. Killed
STEWART, P/O C. N/Zealander. 222-54. Killed
STEWART, P/O D. G. A. British. 615. Killed
STEWART, Sgt. H. G. British. 236
STEWART-CLARKE, P/O D. British. 603. Killed
STICKNEY, F/Lt. P. A. M. British. 235
STILLWELL, Sgt. R. L. British. 65
STOCK, Sgt. E. British. 604
STOCKS, Sgt. N. J. British. 248. Killed*
STOCKWELL (F.A.A.), Petty/Off. W. E. J. British. 804
STODDART, F/Lt. K. M. British. 611
STOKES, P/O R. W. British. 264. Killed
STOKOE, Sgt. J. British. 603
STOKOE, Sgt. S. British. 29. Killed

STONE, F/Lt. C. A. C. British. 249-254
STONE, Sgt. T. F. E. British. 72
STONES, P/O D. W. A. British. 79
STONEY, F/Lt. G. E. B. British. 501. Killed*
STOODLEY, Sgt. D. R. British. 43. Killed*
STORIE, P/O J. M. British. 607-615
STORRAR, Sgt. British. 421 Flt.
STORRAR, P/O J. E. British. 145-73
STORRAY, S/Ldr. British. 501
STORRIE, P/O A. J. British. 264. Killed
STRAIGHT, P/O W. W. British. 601
STRANGE, P/O J. T. N/Zealander. 253
STREATFEIND, S/Ldr. V. C. F. British. 248
STRETCH, Sgt. R. R. British. 235
STRICKLAND, P/O C. D. British. 615. Killed
STRICKLAND, P/O J. M. British. 213. Died
STRIHAUKA, F/Sgt. J. Czech. 310
STROUD, Sgt. G. A. British. 249
STUART, Sgt. M. British. 23
STUCKEY, Sgt. S. G. British. 213. Killed*
STUDD, P/O J. A. P. British. 66. Killed*
SUIDAK, Sgt. A. Polish. 302-303. Killed*
SULMAN, J. E. British. 607. Killed
SUMMERS, Sgt. R. B. G. British. 219
SUMNER, Sgt. F. British. 23. Killed
SUMPTER, Sgt. C. H. S. British. 604
SURMA, P/O F. Polish. 151-607-257. Killed
SUTCLIFFE, Sgt. W. A. British. 610. Killed
SUTHERLAND, P/O I. W. British. 19. Killed*
SUTTON, P/O F. C. British. 264
SUTTON, P/O F. B. British. 56
SUTTON, P/O J. R. G. British. 611. Killed
SUTTON, P/O N. British. 72. Killed*
SUTTON, Sgt. H. R. British. 235
SUTTON, F/O K. R. N/Zealander. 264
SUTTON, P/O N. British. 611
SWANWICK, Sgt. G. W. British. 54
SWANWICK, Sgt. British. 141
SWITCH, Sgt. L. Polish. 54
SWORD-DANIELS, P/O A. T. British. 25
SYDNEY, F/Sgt. C. British. 266-92. Killed*
SYKES (F.A.A.), Sub Lt. J. H. C. British. 64
SYKES, Sgt. D. B. British. 145
SYLVESTER, P/O E. J. H. British. 501. Killed*
SYLVESTER, Sgt. British. 245
SYMONDS, Sgt. J. E. British. 236
SZAFRANCIEC, Sgt. W. Polish. 151-56-607. Killed
SZAPOSZNIKOW, F/O E. Polish. 30,3
SZCZESNY, P/O H. Polish. 74
SZLAGOWSKI, Sgt. J. Polish. 234-152
SZULKOWSKI, P/O W. Polish. 65.

TABOR, Sgt. British. 152
TABOR, Sgt. G. British. 65
TAIT, F/O K. W. British. 87
TALMAN, P/O J. M. British. 213-145. Killed
TALMAN, P/O. British. 151

TAMBLYN, P/O H. N. Canadian. 242-141. Killed
TANNER, F/Sgt. J. H. British. 610. Killed*
TATE, Sgt. British. 604
TATNELL, Sgt. R. F. British. 235. Killed
TAYLOR (F.A.A.), Petty/Off. D. E. British. 808
TAYLOR, F/O D. M. British. 64
TAYLOR, P/O R. British. 235. Died
TAYLOR, Sgt. K. British. 29
TAYLOR, Sgt. R. N. British. 601. Killed
TAYLOR, Sgt. R. H. W. British. 604. Killed
TAYLOR, Sgt. G. N. British. 236
TAYLOR, Sgt. G. S. N/Zealander. 3
TAYLOR, Sgt. E. F. British. 29-600. Killed
TAYLOUR (F.A.A.), Lt. E. W. T. British. 808. Killed
TEARLE, Sgt. F. J. British. 600
TEMLETT, P/O C. B. British. 3. Killed
TERRY, Sgt. P. A. R. R. A. British. 72-603
TEW, F/Sgt. P. H. British. 54
THATCHER, P/O. British. 32
THEASBY, Sgt. A. J. British. 25. Killed
THEILMANN, F/Sgt. J. G. British. 234
THOMAS, Sgt. British. 247. Killed
THOMAS, Sgt. British. 236
THOMAS, Sgt. G. S. British. 604
THOMAS, F/O E. H. British. 222-266
THOMAS, F/Lt. F. M. British. 152
THOMAS, Sgt. S. R. British. 264
THOMAS, F/O C. R. D. British. 236. Killed*
THOMAS, P/O R. C. British. 235. Killed*
THOMPSON, F/O A. R. F. British. 249
THOMPSON, F/Lt. J. A. British. 302
THOMPSON, F/O R. A. British. 72
THOMPSON, S/Ldr. J. M. British. 111
THOMPSON, P/O P. D. British. 605-32
THOMPSON, F/O T. R. British. 213
THOMPSON, P/O F. N. British. 248
THOMPSON, Sgt. W. W. British. 234
THOMPSON, Sgt. J. B. British. 25. Killed
THOMPSON, Sgt. J. R. British. 236. Killed
THORN, Sgt. E. R. British. 264. Killed
THOROGOOD, Sgt. L. A. British. 87
THORPE, Sgt. British. 145
TIDMAN, P/O A. R. British. 64. Killed
TILL, Sgt. J. British. 248. Killed
TILLARD (F.A.A.), Lt. R. C. British. 808. Killed
TILLETT, P/O J. British. 238. Killed
TITLEY, P/O E. G. British. 609. Killed
TOBIN, P/O E. Q. American. 609. Killed
TOMLINSON, P/O P. A. British. 29
TONGUE, P/O R. E. British. 3-504
TOOGOOD, Sgt. British. 43. Killed
TOOMBS, Sgt. J. R. British. 236-264
TOPHAM, P/O J. G. British. 219
TOPOLNICKI, F/O J. Polish. 601. Killed
TOUCH, Sgt. D. F. British. 235. Killed
TOWER-PERKINS, P/O W. British. 238
TOWNSEND, S/Ldr. P. W. British. 85
TOWNSEND, Sgt. T. W. British. 600

Above: Sgt E. E. Shepperd was killed on October 18.

Above: Hurricane pilot K. W. Tait flew with No.87 Sqn.

Above: Another 87 Sqn pilot was Sgt L. A. Thorogood.

Above: Sqn Ldr Peter Townsend commanded No.85 Squadron.

TRACEY, P/O O. V. British. 79. Killed
TREVANA, F/O. Canadian. 1 (Can) (401)
TROUSDALE, P/O R. M. N/Zealander. 266. Killed
TRUEMAN, F/O A. A. G. Canadian. 253. Killed*
TRUHLAR, Sgt. F. Czech. 312
TRUMBLE, F/Lt. A. J. British. 264
TRURAN, P/O A. J. J. British. 615
TUCK, F/Lt. R. R. S. British. 92-257
TUCKER, F/O A. B. British. 151
TUCKER, P/O B. E. British. 266-66
TUCKER, Sgt. R. Y. British. 235. Killed*
TUCKER, Sgt. F. D. British. 236
TURLEY-GEORGE, P/O D. R. British. 54
TURNBULL, Sgt. R. N. British. 25
TURNER, F/O R. S. Canadian. 242
TURNER, F/Sgt. G. British. 32
TURNER, F/Lt. D. E. British. 238. Killed*
TURNER, Sgt. R. C. British. 264. Killed*
TWEED, Sgt. L. J. British. 111
TWITCHETT, Sgt. F. J. British. 229-43
TYRER, Sgt. E. British. 46
TYSON, S/Ldr. F. H. British. 213-3

UNETT, Sgt. J. W. British. 235. Killed
UNWIN, F/Sgt. G. C. British. 19
UPTON, P/O H. C. British. 43-607
URBANOWICZ, F/O W. Polish. 145-303-601
URWIN-MANN, P/O J. R. British. 238
USMAR, Sgt. F. British. 41

VAN-DEN HOVE, P/O. Belgian. 501-43. Killed
VAN-LIERDE, P/O W. E. Belgian. 87
VAN-MENTZ, P/O B. Belgian. 222. Killed
VAN-WAYEN BERGHE, P/O A. A. L. Belgian. 236. Killed*
VARLEY, P/O G. W. British. 247-79
VASATKO, P/O A. Czech. 312. Killed
VELEBRNOVSKI, P/O A. Czech. 1. Killed
VENESOEN, Sgt. F. A. Belgian. 235. Killed
VENN, P/O J. A. British. 236
VERITY, P/O V. B. S. N/Zealander. 229
VESELY, P/O V. Czech. 312
VICK, S/Ldr. J. A. British. 607
VIGORS, P/O T. A. British. 222
VILES, Sgt. L. W. British. 236
VILLA, F/Lt. British. 72-92
VINCENT, G/Capt. S. F. British. 229
VINDIS, Sgt. F. Czech. 310
VINYARD, Sgt. F. F. British. 64. Killed*
VLAD, P/O. Czech. 501
VOKES, P/O A. F. British. 19. Killed
VOPALECKY, W/O. Czech. 310
VRANA, F/O. Czech. 312
VYBIRAL, P/O T. Czech. 312
VYKOURAL, P/O K. J. Czech. 111-73. Killed

WADDINGHAM, P/O J. British. 141. Died
WADE, P/O T. S. British. 92. Killed

WADHAM, Sgt. J. V. British. 145. Killed*
WAGHORN, Sgt. British. 249-111
WAGNER, Sgt. A. D. British. 151. Killed
WAINWRIGHT, P/O A. G. British. 151. Killed
WAINWRIGHT, P/O M. T. British. 64
WAKE, Sgt. British. 264
WAKEFIELD, P/O H. K. British. 235
WAKEHAM, P/O E. C. J. British. 145. Killed*
WAKELING, Sgt. S. R. E. British. 87. Killed*
WALCH, F/Lt. S. C. Australian. 238. Killed*
WALKER, Sgt. S. British. 236. Killed
WALKER, Sgt. A. N/Zealander. 600
WALKER, F/O J. H. G. British. 25. Killed
WALKER, Sgt. N. McD. British. 615. Killed
WALKER, P/O W. L. B. British. 616
WALKER, P/O J. A. Canadian. 111
WALKER, P/O J. R. Canadian. 611-41. Killed
WALKER, P/O British. 616
WALKER, Sgt. G. A. British. 232
WALKER, P/O R. J. British. 72
WALKER-SMITH, Sgt. F. R. British. 85. Killed
WALLACE, P/O C. A. B. Canadian. 3. Killed
WALLACE, Sgt. T. Y. British. 111. Killed
WALLEN, F/Lt. D. S. British. 604
WALLENS, P/O R. W. British. 41
WALLER, Sgt. G. A. British. 29
WALLEY, Sgt. P. K. British. 615. Killed*
WALLIS, Sgt. D. S. British. 235. Killed
WALSH, Sgt. E. British. 141
WALSH, P/O J. J. Canadian. 615. Died
WALSH (F.A.A.), Sub Lt. R. W. M. British. 111
WALTON, Sgt. British. 152
WALTON, Sgt. H. British. 87
WANT, Sgt. W. H. British. 248. Killed*
WAPNIAREK, P/O S. Polish. 302. Killed*
WARD, Sgt. R. A. British. 66. Killed*
WARD, Sgt. W. B. British. 604
WARD, F/O D. H. N/Zealander. 87. Killed
WARD, P/O J. L. British. 32. Killed
WARD, S/Ldr. E. F. British. 601
WARDEN, Sgt. N. P. British. 610. Killed
WARD-SMITH, Sgt. P. British. 610
WARE, Sgt. R. T. British. 3
WAREHAM, P/O M. P. British. 1. Killed
WAREING, Sgt. P. T. British. 616
WARING, Sgt. W. British. 23
WARMSLEY, Sgt. H. W. British. 248. Killed
WARNER, F/Lt. W. H. C. British. 610. Killed*
WARREN, Sgt. S. British. 1
WARREN, Sgt. T. A. British. 236
WARREN, Sgt. J. B. W. British. 600. Killed
WARREN, P/O C. British. 152
WARREN, P/O D. A. P. British. 248. Killed
WATERSTON, F/O R. McG. British. 603. Killed*
WATKINS, F/O D. H. British. 611
WATKINSON, P/O A. B. S/African. 66
WATLING, P/O W. C. British. 92. Killed

WATSON, Sgt. J. G. British. 604
WATSON, P/O A. R. British. 152. Killed
WATSON, P/O E. J. British. 605. Killed
WATSON, P/O L. G. British. 29
WATSON, F/O R. F. British. 87
WATSON, P/O. British. 64
WATSON, P/O F. S. Canadian. 3. Killed
WATTERS, P/O J. N/Zealander. 236
WATTS, P/O R. F. British. 253
WATTS, Sgt. E. L. British. 248. Killed
WATTS, Sgt. R. D. H. British. 235. Killed*
WAY, P/O L. B. R. British. 229
WAY, F/Lt. B. H. British. 54. Killed*
WCZELIK, F/O. Polish. 302. Killed
WEAVER, F/Lt. P. S. British. 56. Killed*
WEBB, F/O P. C. British. 602
WEBBER, P/O W. F. P. British. 141
WEBBER, Sgt. J. British. 1
WEBER, P/O F. Czech. 145
WEBSTER, F/Lt. J. T. British. 41. Killed*
WEBSTER, P/O F. K. British. 610. Killed*
WEBSTER, Sgt. H. G. British. 73. Killed
WEBSTER, Sgt. E. R. British. 85
WEDGEWOOD, F/Lt. J. H. British. 253. Killed
WEDLOCK, Sgt. G. V. British. 235
WEDZIK, Sgt. M. Polish. 302
WEIR, P/O A. N. C. British. 145. Killed
WELCH, Sgt. E. British. 604. Killed
WELFORD, P/O G. H. E. British. 607
WELLAM, P/O G. H. A. British. 92
WELLS, P/O E. P. N/Zealander. 41-266
WELLS, F/O P. H. V. British. 249
WELLS, P/O M. L. British. 248
WELSH, P/O T. D. British. 264
WENDEL, P/O K. V. N/Zealander. 504. Killed*
WEST, S/Ldr. H. British. 151-41
WEST, P/O D. R. British. 141
WESTCOTT, Sgt. W. H. J. British. 235
WESTLAKE, Sgt. G. H. British. 43-213
WESTLAKE, P/O R. D. British. 235
WESTMACOTT, F/O I. B. British. 56
WESTMORELAND, Sgt. T. E. British. 616. Killed*
WHALL, Sgt. B. E. P. British. 602. Killed*
WHEATCROFT, P/O N. R. British. 604. Killed
WHEELER, P/O N. J. British. 615
WHELAN, Sgt. J. British. 64-19
WHINNEY, P/O M. T. British. 3
WHIPPS, Sgt. G. A. British. 602. Killed
WHITBREAD, P/O H. L. British. 222. Killed*
WHITBY, Sgt. A. W. British. 79
WHITE, P/O B. E. British. 504. Killed
WHITE, Sgt. J. W. British. 32-3-F.I.U.
WHITE, S/Ldr. F. L. British. 74
WHITE, Sgt. J. British. 72. Killed
WHITE, Sgt. British. 604
WHITE, Sgt. R. British. 235
WHITE, Sgt. J. British. 248. Died
WHITEHEAD, Sgt. C. British. 56. Killed

WHITEHEAD, Sgt. R. O. British. 253-151
WHITEHOUSE, P/O British. 32
WHITEHOUSE, Sgt. S. A. H. British. 501
WHITFOELD, Sgt. J. J. British. 56. Killed*
WHITLEY, S/Ldr. E. W. N/Zealander. 245
WHITLEY, P/O D. British. 264. Killed*
WHITNEY, P/O D. M. N/Zealander. 245
WHITSUN, Sgt. A. D. British. 236. Killed
WHITTICK, Sgt. H. G. British. 604
WHITTINGHAM, F/O C. D. British. 151
WHITTY, F/O W. H. R. British. 607
WHITWELL, Sgt. P. N/Zealander. 600. Killed
WICKINGS-SMITH, P/O P. C. British. 235. Killed*
WICKINS, Sgt. A. S. British. 141
WICKS, P/O B. J. British. 56. Killed
WIDDOWS, S/Ldr. S. C. British. 29
WIGG, P/O R. G. N/Zealander. 65
WIGGLESWORTH, P/O J. S. British. 238. Killed
WIGHT, F/Lt. R. D. G. British. 213. Killed*
WIGHTMAN (F.A.A.), Mid/Ship. O. M. British. 151. Killed
WILCOCK, Sgt. C. British. 248. Died
WILCOX, P/O E. J. British. 72. Killed*
WILDBLOOD, P/O T. S. British. 152. Killed*
WILDE, P/O D. C. British. 236
WILKES, Sgt. G. N. British. 213. Killed*
WILKINSON, S/Ldr. R. L. British. 266. Killed*
WILKINSON, Sgt. W. A. British. 501
WILKINSON, Sgt. K. A. British. 616
WILKINSON, F/Lt. R. C. British. 3
WILLANS, P/O A. J. British. 23. Killed
WILLCOCKS, Sgt. P. H. British. 610-66. Killed
WILLCOCKS, Sgt. C. P. L. British. 610
WILLIAMS, S/Ldr. C. W. British. 17. Killed*
WILLIAMS, P/O D. G. British. 92. Killed*
WILLIAMS, F/Sgt. E. E. British. 46. Killed*
WILLIAMS, F/O T. D. British. 611
WILLIAMS, P/O W. D. British. 152
WILLIAMS, P/O W. S. N/Zealander. 266. Killed
WILLIAMS, Sgt. G. T. British. 219
WILLIAMS, P/O D. C. British. 141. Killed
WILLIAMS, P/O A. British. 604
WILLIS, Sgt. N/Zealander. 600
WILLIS, Sgt. R. F. British. 219. Killed
WILLIS, Sgt. W. C. British. 73-3. Killed
WILSCH, P/O. British. 141
WILSDON, Sgt. A. A. British. 29. Killed
WILSON, F/O D. S. British. 610
WILSON, P/O R. R. Canadian. 111. Killed*
WILSON, P/O D. F. British. 141
WILSON, Sgt. W. C. British. 29
WILSON, Sgt. W. British. 235
WILSON-MACDONALD, S/Ldr. D. S. British. 213
WINGFIELD, Sgt. V. British. 29. Killed
WINN, P/O C. V. British. 29
WINSKILL, P/O A. L. British. 603-54-72
WINSTANLEY, Sgt. J. British. 151
WINTER, P/O D. C. British. 72. Killed*

WINTER, P/O R. A. British. 247
WISE, Sgt. J. F. Britain. 141. Killed*
WISEMAN, P/O W. D. British. 600
WISSLER, P/O D. H. British. 17. Killed
WITHALL, F/Lt. L. C. Australian. 152. Killed*
WITORZENC, F/O S. Polish. 501
WLASNOWOLSKI, P/O B. Polish. 607-32-213. Killed
WOJCICKI, Sgt. A. Polish. 213. Killed*
WOJCIECHOWSKI, Sgt. M. Polish. 303. Killed
WOJTOWICZ, Sgt. S. Polish. 303. Killed*
WOLFE, S/Ldr. E. C. British. 141-219
WOLTON, Sgt. R. British. 152
WOOD, Sgt. S. V. British. 248
WOOD, Sgt. K. R. British. 23. Killed
WOODGATE, Sgt. J. E. British. 141. Killed
WOODGER, P/O D. N. British. 235. Killed*
WOODLAND, Sgt. N. N. British. 236
WOODS-SCAWEN, P/O C. A. British. 43. Killed*
WOODS-SCAWEN, F/O P. P. British. 85. Killed*
WOODWARD, F/O H. J. British. 64-23. Killed
WOODWARD, P/O R. S. British. 600. Killed
WOOLLEY, Sgt. A. W. British. 601. Killed
WOOTTEN, P/O E. W. British. 234
WORDSWORTH, P/O D. K. A. British. 235. Killed
WORRALL, S/Ldr. J. British. 32
WORRALL (F.A.A.), Sub Lt. T. V. British. 111. Killed
WORALL, P/O P. A. British. 85-249. Killed
WORSDELL, P/O K. W. British. 219. Killed*
WORTHINGTON, F/O A. S. British. 219
WOTTON, Sgt. H. J. British. 234. Killed
WRIGHT (F.A.A.), Lt. A. J. British. 804
WRIGHT, Sgt. B. British. 92
WRIGHT, F/Lt. A. R. British. 92
WRIGHT, Sgt. E. W. British. 605
WRIGHT, Sgt. J. British. 79. Killed
WRIGHT, Sgt. D. L. British. 235. Killed
WRIGHT, P/O W. British. 604. Killed
WRIGHT, Sgt. R. R. British. 248
WROBLEWSKI, P/O Z. T. A. Polish. 302
WUNSCHE, F/Sgt. K. Polish. 303
WYATE, Sgt. J. P. British. 25. Killed*
WYATT-SMITH, P/O P. British. 263. Killed
WYDROWSKI, P/O. Polish. 607
WYNN, P/O R. E. N. E. British. 249. Killed

YAPP, D. S. British. 253-245
YATES, Sgt. T. M. British. 64
YATES, Sgt. G. British. 248
YATES, Sgt. W. British. 604
YORK, Sgt. R. L. British. 610. Killed
YOUNG, P/O C. R. British. 615-607-46. Killed
YOUNG, P/O M. H. British. 264
YOUNG, Sgt. R. B. M. N/Zealander. 264. Killed*
YOUNG, Sgt. R. British. 23
YOUNG, F/O J. R. C. British. 249
YOUNG, P/O J. H. R. British. 74. Killed*
YOUNG, P/O J. S. British. 234
YUILE, F/O A. Canadian. 1 (Can) (401)
YULE, P/O R. D. British. 145. Killed

ZAK, P/O W. Polish. 303
ZALUSKI, Sgt. J. Polish. 302. Killed*
ZAORAL, P/O V. Czech. 310. Killed
ZAVORAL, Sgt. A. Czech. 1. Killed
ZENKER, P/O P. Polish. 501. Killed*
ZIMA, Sgt. R. Czech. 310
ZIMPRICH, P/O S. Czech. 310. Killed
ZUKOWSKI, P/O A. Polish. 302. Killed*
ZUMBACH, P/O J. Polish. 303
ZURAKOWSKI, P/O J. Polish. 234-609

Source: This list was compiled for the Battle of Britain Fighter Association by Flight Lt. J. H. Holloway, MBE.

Above: R. F. "Watty" Watson was with No.87 Squadron.

Above: Sgt G. A. Whipps of No.602 Squadron perches on the cowling of his Spitfire. On September 6, he baled out unhurt over Sussex.

Above: E. E. Williams of No.46 Sqn went missing October 15.

INDEX

Unless they are mentioned elsewhere in the book, this Index does not include names from the alphabetical
Aircrew List on pages 194-203.

Page numbers in *italic* type indicate the inclusion of subjects of illustrations mentioned in captions.

PICTURE CREDITS

Page 1: (Top) Mark Holt Collection, (Bottom) RAF Museum, Hendon. **2-3:** (Top) Ernie and Tony Gilberts 39/45 Warbirds Club, (Bottom) RAF Museum. **4-5:** (Top) RAF Museum, (Bottom) Andy Saunders. **6-7:** (Bottom Left) AM Sir Denis Crowley-Milling, (Bottom Centre) IWM, (Top Right) Messerschmitt AG, (Bottom Right) AM Sir Denis Crowley-Milling. **8-9:** (Bottom Left) RAF Museum, (Bottom Centre) IWM, (Top Right) RAF Museum. **10-11:** (Left) Imperial War Museum, (Bottom Centre) Military Archive Research Services, (Top Right) Salamander, (Bottom Right) MARS. **12-13:** (Left) IWM (Right) RAF Museum. **14-15:** (Top Left) Paul Smith Collection, (Bottom Left and Right) RAF Museum, (Top Right) IWM. **16-17:** (Bottom Right) RAF Museum, (Rest) IWM. **18-19:** (Top Left) IWM/MARS, (Bottom Left) Andy Saunders, (Top and Bottom Right) RAF Museum. **20-21:** (Top Left) IWM, (Bottom Left) Bundesarchiv, (Right) Ullstein Bilderdienst. **22-23:** (Top Left) Wg Cmdr P.P.C. Barthropp, (Bottom Left) IWM, (Right) RAF Museum. **24-25:** (Left) IWM, (Top Right) Hulton-Deutsch, (Bottom Right) Bundesarchiv/MARS. **26-27:** (Bottom Left) RAF Museum, (Bottom Centre) IWM, (Top Right) Popperfoto, (Bottom Right) Ernie and Tony Gilberts, 39/45 Warbirds Club. **28-29:** (Top Centre) AVM A.V.R. Johnstone, (Bottom Left) Hulton-Deutsch, (Rest) RAF Museum. **30-31:** (Top Left) IWM, (Top Left Centre) IWM, (Centre Left) AVM J.E. Johnson, (Top Right Centre) Science Museum, (Top Right) RAF Museum. **32-33:** (Bottom Right) Hulton- Deutsch. **34-35:** (Top and Bottom Left) IWM, (Rest) RAF Museum. **36-37:** (Bottom Left) Ernie and Tony Gilberts, 39/45 Warbirds Club, (Top Right) Popperfoto, (Rest) IWM. **39-39:** (Left) RAF Museum, (Top Centre) Hulton-Deutsch, (Top Right) IWM, (Centre Right) Andy Saunders. **40-41:** (Top Left) Ernie and Tony Gilberts, 39/45 Warbirds Club, (Top Right) Popperfoto, (Rest) IWM. **43-43:** (Left) Salamander, (Top Right) Hawker Siddeley/MARS, (Bottom Right) Hawker Siddeley. **44-45:** (Top Right) Hulton-Deutsch, (Centre Right) Andy Saunders. **46-47:** (Top Right) Hulton-Deutsch, (Top and Bottom Right) Vickers/MARS. **48-49:** (Top Right) RAF Museum, (Bottom Right) Popperfoto. **50-51:** (Both) RAF Museum. **52-53:** RAF Museum. **54-55:** (Top Left) IWM, (Top Right) MARS, (Bottom Right) Salamander. **56-57:** (Bottom Left and Centre) Ernie and Tony Gilberts, 39/45 Warbirds Club, (Right Centre) IWM, (Rest) Luftwaffenmuseum. **58-59:** (Top Left and Centre Right) Luftwaffenmuseum, (Top Right) Andy Saunders, (Rest) RAF Museum. **60-61:** (Top Left) Salamander, (Bottom Left) Ernie and Tony Gilberts, 39/45 Warbirds Club, (Top Right) Andy Saunders, (Centre Right) Luftwaffenmuseum. **62-63:** (Top Left) Ernie and Tony Gilberts, 39/45 Warbirds Club, (Bottom Left) RAF Museum, (Centre Right) Luftwaffenmuseum, (Top Left) MARS. **64-65:** (Top Left) MARS, (Bottom Left) Ernie and Tony Gilberts, 39/45 Warbirds Club, (Top Right) Bundesarchiv/MARS. **66-67:** (Bottom Left and Centre) RAF Museum, (Top Right) Suddeutscher Verlag, (Bottom Right) Ullstein. **68-69:** (Top Right) RAF Museum, **70-71:** (Bottom Left) RAF Museum, (Top Right) Salamander, (Centre Right) MARS. **72-73:** (Centre Left) RAF Museum, (Bottom Right) MARS. **74-75:** (Bottom Left) Suddeutscher Verlag. **76-77:** (Top Right) Suddeutscher Verlag, (Rest) MARS. **78-79:** (Top Right) BAPTY & Co. **80-81:** (Bottom Right) Ullstein, (Rest) RAF Museum. **84-85:** (Both) IWM. **86-87:** (Bottom Right) IWM, (Rest) RAF Museum. **88-89:** (Top Left and Top Right) Hulton-Deutsch, (Rest) RAF Museum. **90-91:** (Bottom Left) IWM, (Bottom Right) Hulton-Deutsch/MARS (Rest) RAF Museum. **92-93:** (Top Left) Hulton-Deutsch, (Centre Left) MARS, (Bottom Left) Bildarchiv Preussischer Kulturbesitz, (Right) Luftwaffenmuseum. **94-95:** (Bottom Left) IWM, (Top Right) Ullstein, (Bottom Right) Air Cdre Alan Deere. **96-97:** (Bottom Left) MARS, (Centre Left) Hulton-Deutsch, (Bottom Right) Ullstein. **98-99:** (Bottom Right) RAF Museum. **100-101:** (Bottom Centre) Ullstein. **102-103:** (Bottom Centre) Salamander, (Top Centre) Ullstein, (Top Right) MARS. **104-105:** (Bottom Left) Paul Smith Collection, (Bottom Right) Wg Cdr P.P.C. Barthropp. **106-107:** (Top Left) IWM, (Top Centre) Salamander, (Centre Right) Bildarchiv Preussischer Kulturbesitz. **108-109:** (Bottom Left) Hulton-Deutsch, (Bottom Centre) Suddeutscher Verlag, (Top Right) Ullstein. **110-111:** (Bottom Left) Bundesarchiv/MARS. **112-113:** (Bottom Left) Ullstein. **114-115:** (Left) Ullstein, (Rest) RAF Museum. **116-117:** (Top Left) RAF Museum, (Centre Left) IWM, (Bottom Left) Borough of Weymouth and Portland Museums Services, (Bottom Right) Ullstein. **118-119:** (Bottom Left) IWM, (Bottom Right) RAF Museum. **120-121:** (Bottom Left) RAF Museum. **122-123:** (Bottom Left) RAF Museum. **124-125:** (Bottom Left) RAF Museum. **126-127:** (Bottom Left) Bildarchiv Preussischer Kulturbesitz. **128-129:** (Bottom Left) RAF Museum. **130-131:** (Top Left) Ullstein, (Bottom Left) IWM, (Top Right) Topix/MARS. **132-133:** (Bottom Left) IWM/MARS, (Top Right) RAF Museum, (Bottom Right) Hulton-Deutsch. **134-135:** (Bottom Left) IWM, (Centre) IWM/MARS, (Bottom Right) RAF Museum, (Rest) IWM. **138-139:** (Bottom Right) RAF Museum, (Rest) IWM. **140-141:** (Top Right) Ernie and Tony Gilberts, 39/45 Warbirds Club and Paul Smith Collection, (Rest) Hulton-Deutsch. **142-143:** (Left) Paul Smith Collection, (Right) Ernie and Tony Gilberts, 39/45 Warbirds Club and Paul Smith Collection. **144-145:** (Top Left) Ernie and Tony Gilberts, 39/45 Warbirds Club, (Top Right) Popperfoto, (Rest) IWM. **146-147:** (Left) IWM, (Right) Paul Smith Collection. **148-149:** (Bottom Right) Ernie and Tony Gilberts, 39/45 Warbirds Club, (Rest) RAF Museum. **150-151:** (Top Left) Andy Saunders, (Bottom Left) Hulton-Deutsch, (Top Right) AVM A.V.R. Johnstone, (Bottom Right) IWM. **152-153:** (Left) MARS, (Right) Luftwaffenmuseum. **154-155:** (Top Left) Bildarchiv Preussischer Kulturbesitz, (Bottom Left) RAF Museum, (Right) Luftwaffenmuseum. **156-157:** (Bottom Left) Bundesarchiv/MARS, (Top Right) RAF Museum, (Bottom Right) Luftwaffenmuseum, (Rest) BAPTY & Co. **158-159:** (Top Left and Right) RAF Museum, (Rest) Luftwaffenmuseum. **160-161:** (Top Left) MARS, (Bottom Left) Andy Saunders. (Rest) RAF Museum. **162-163:** (Bottom Left) MARS, (Centre Right) RAF Museum, (Top Right) Ullstein, (Bottom Right) Personality Pics/MARS. **164-165:** (Top Left) RAF Museum, (Top Right) Wg Cmdr P.P.C. Barthropp, (Rest) IWM/MARS. **166-167:** (Bottom Left) IWM/MARS, (Bottom Right) RAF Museum, (Rest) IWM. **168-169:** (Top Left) South-Eastern Newspapers/MARS, (Centre Left) Hulton-Deutsch, (Bottom Left) IWM/MARS, (Centre Right) Popperfoto, (Bottom Right) IWM. **170-171:** (Bottom Left) Associated Press, (Top Right) IWM/MARS, (Bottom Right) IWM. **172-173:** (Bottom Left) Paul Smith Collection, (Bottom Right) Hulton-Deutsch, (Rest) MARS. **174-175:** (Left) IWM, (Right) John Frost. **176-177:** (Top Left) IWM, (Top Right) Southern Newspapers, (Rest) John Frost. **178-179:** (Top Left) MARS, (Bottom Left) IWM, (Top Right) Hulton-Deutsch, (Bottom Right) Paul Smith Collection. **180-181:** (Top Left) Ullstein, (Top Right) John Frost, (Rest) Hulton-Deutsch. **182-183:** (Top Right) IWM, (Rest) Hulton-Deutsch. **184-185:** (Bottom Left) IWM, (Bottom Right) Ullstein, (Rest) Hulton-Deutsch. **186-187:** (Left) RAF Museum, (Right) IWM. **188-189:** (Top Left) RAF Museum, (Bottom Left) AM Sir Denis Crowley-Milling, (Top Right) IWM, (Centre Right) RAF Museum, (Bottom Right) AVM J.E. Johnson. **190-191:** (Centre Left) Popperfoto, (Centre Top) IWM, (Bottom Right) AVM J.E. Johnson, (Rest) RAF Museum. **192-193:** (Top Left) Hulton-Deutsch, (Top Right) IWM, (Rest) RAF Museum. **194-195:** (Second from Left) Wg Cdr P.P.C. Barthropp, (Far and Second from Right) Andy Saunders, (Rest) RAF Museum. **196-197:** (Third and Fourth from Left) RAF Museum, (Fourth from Right) AVM J.E. Johnson, (Rest) Andy Saunders. **198-199:** (From Left to Right) Andy Saunders, RAF Museum, Hulton-Deutsch, AM Sir Denis Crowley-Milling, IWM/Andy Saunders, Andy Saunders. **200-201:** (Second from Right) RAF Museum, (Rest) Andy Saunders. **202-203:** (Third from Left) IWM, (Rest) Andy Saunders.

ACKNOWLEDGEMENTS

A book like this would be impossible to produce without the help of many individuals and organisations, and the publishers are grateful to everyone who helped by supplying photographs, mementoes and collectors' items and by granting interviews and giving permission to use personal memoirs and quotes. Special thanks are due to: David Bickers and the Douglas Bader Foundation; Air Chief Marshal Sir Christopher Foxley-Norris, GCB. DSO. OBE. and Wing Commander N.P.W. Hancock, DFC. of the Battle of Britain Fighter Association; Air Vice Marshal A.V.R. (Sandy) Johnstone, CB. DFC. AE. DL; Andrew Cormack and the staff of the RAF Museum at Hendon; Lt. Col. Dr. Dieter Rogge, Oberleutnant Peter-Jorg Wiesener, Regierungsoberinspektor Hartmann and the staff at the Luftwaffenmuseum in Hamburg; Andy Saunders and the Tangmere Military Aviation Museum Trust; Tony Gilberts and the 39/45 Warbirds Club; the late Paul Smith; The RAF Air Historical Branch. Picture research was carried out by Military Archive Research Services (MARS).